Michel Foucault, acknowledged as the preeminent philosopher of France in the seventies and eighties, continues to have enormous impact throughout the world in many disciplines.

Arnold I. Davidson is the Robert O. Anderson Distinguished Service Professor at the University of Chicago and Professor of the History of Political Philosophy at the University of Pisa. He is coeditor of the volume *Michel Foucault: Philosophie*.

Translator Graham Burchell has written essays on Michel Foucault and was an editor of *The Foucault Effect*.

Security, Territory, Population

Also in this series

SOCIETY MUST BE DEFENDED
ABNORMAL
HERMENEUTICS OF THE SUBJECT
PSYCHIATRIC POWER

Forthcoming in this series

THE BIRTH OF BIOPOLITICS
THE WILL TO KNOW
PENAL THEORIES AND INSTITUTIONS
THE PUNITIVE SOCIETY
ON THE GOVERNMENT OF THE LIVING
SUBJECTIVITY AND TRUTH
THE GOVERNMENT OF SELF AND OTHERS
THE COURAGE OF TRUTH

MICHEL FOUCAULT

Security, Territory, Population

LECTURES AT THE COLLÈGE DE FRANCE,

1977–1978

Edited by Michel Senellart
General Editors: François Ewald and Alessandro Fontana

English Series Editor: Arnold I. Davidson

Translated by Graham Burchell

PICADOR

palgrave
macmillan
NEW YORK

www.picadorusa.com

Picador ® is a U.S. registered trademark and is used by Palgrave Macmillan under license from Pan Books Limited.

For information on Picador Reading Group Guides, please contact Picador.
E-mail: readinggroupguides@picadorusa.com

ISBN-13: 978-0-312-20360-3
ISBN-10: 0-312-20360-8

First published in the United States by Palgrave Macmillan

20 19 18 17 16 15 14 13

CONTENTS

Foreword: François Ewald and Alessandro Fontana   xiii
Introduction: Arnold I. Davidson   xviii

one   11 JANUARY 1978   1

*General perspective of the lectures: the study of
bio-power.* ∽ *Five proposals on the analysis of mechanisms
of power.* ∽ *Legal system, disciplinary mechanisms, and
security apparatuses* (dispositifs). *Two examples: (a) the
punishment of theft; (b) the treatment of leprosy, plague, and
smallpox.* ∽ *General features of security apparatuses (1): the
spaces of security.* ∽ *The example of the town.* ∽ *Three
examples of planning urban space in the sixteenth and
seventeenth centuries: (a) Alexandre Le Maître's La*
Métropolitée (1682); (b) Richelieu; (c) Nantes.

two   18 JANUARY 1978   29

*General features of the apparatuses of security (II): relationship
to the event: the art of governing and treatment of the uncertain*
(l'aléatoire). ∽ *The problem of scarcity* (la disette) *in the
seventeenth and eighteenth centuries.* ∽ *From the mercantilists to the
physiocrats.* ∽ *Differences between apparatuses of security and
disciplinary mechanisms in ways of dealing with the event.* ∽ *The new
governmental rationality and the emergence of "population."* ∽
Conclusion on liberalism: liberty as ideology and technique of government.

three 25 JANUARY 1978   55

General features of apparatuses of security (III). ~ Normation (normation) and normalization. ~ The example of the epidemic (smallpox) and inoculation campaigns in the eighteenth century. ~ The emergence of new notions: case, risk, danger, and crisis. ~ The forms of normalization in discipline and in mechanisms of security. ~ Deployment of a new political technology: the government of populations. ~ The problem of population in the mercantilists and the physiocrats. ~ The population as operator (operateur) of transformations in domains of knowledge: from the analysis of wealth to political economy, from natural history to biology, from general grammar to historical philology.

four 1 FEBRUARY 1978   87

The problem of "government" in the sixteenth century. ~ Multiplicity of practices of government (government of self, government of souls, government of children, etcetera). ~ The specific problem of the government of the state. ~ The point of repulsion of the literature on government: Machiavelli's The Prince. *~ Brief history of the reception of* The Prince *until the nineteenth century. ~ The art of government distinct from the Prince's simple artfulness. ~ Example of this new art of government: Guillaume de la Perrière* Le Miroir politique *(1555). ~ A government that finds its end in the "things" to be directed. ~ Decline of law to the advantage of a variety of tactics. ~ The historical and institutional obstacles to the implementation of this art of government until the eighteenth century. ~ The problem of population an essential factor in unblocking the art of government. ~ The triangle formed by government, population, and political economy. ~ Questions of method: the project of a history of "governmentality." Overvaluation of the problem of the state.*

five 8 FEBRUARY 1978   115

Why study governmentality? ~ The problem of the state and population. ~ Reminder of the general project: triple displacement

*of the analysis in relation to (a) the institution, (b) the function,
and (c) the object. ∼ The stake of this year's lectures. ∼ Elements
for a history of "government." Its semantic field from the thirteenth
to the sixteenth century. ∼ The idea of the government of men. Its
sources: (A) The organization of a pastoral power in the
pre-Christian and Christian East. (B) Spiritual direction
(direction de conscience). ∼ First outline of the pastorate. Its
specific features: (a) it is exercised over a multiplicity on the move;
(b) it is a fundamentally beneficent power with salvation of the
flock as its objective; (c) it is a power which individualizes.*
Omnes et singulatim. *The paradox of the shepherd*
(berger). ∼ *The institutionalization of the pastorate by the
Christian Church.*

six   15 FEBRUARY 1978   135

*Analysis of the pastorate (continuation). ∼ The problem of the
shepherd-flock relationship in Greek literature and thought: Homer,
the Pythagorean tradition. Rareness of the shepherd metaphor in
classical political literature (Isocrates, Demosthenes). ∼ A major
exception: Plato's* The Statesman. *The use of the metaphor
in other Plato texts (Critias, Laws, The Republic). The critique of
the idea of a magistrate-shepherd in* The Statesman. *The pastoral
metaphor applied to the doctor, farmer, gymnast, and teacher. ∼ The
history of the pastorate in the West, as a model of the government of
men, is inseparable from Christianity. Its transformations and crises up
to the eighteenth century. Need for a history of the pastorate. ∼
Characteristics of the "government of souls": encompassing power
coextensive with the organization of the Church and distinct from
political power. ∼ The problem of the relationships between political
power and pastoral power in the West. Comparison with the
Russian tradition.*

seven   22 FEBRUARY 1978   163

*Analysis of the pastorate (end). ∼ Specificity of the
Christian pastorate in comparison with Eastern and Hebraic
traditions. ∼ An art of governing men. Its role in the history of*

governmentality. ∼ *Main features of the Christian pastorate from
the third to the sixth century (Saint John Chrysostom. Saint
Cyprian, Saint Ambrose, Gregory the Great, Cassian, Saint
Benedict): (1) the relationship to salvation. An economy of merits
and faults: (a) the principle of analytical responsibility; (b) the
principle of exhaustive and instantaneous transfer; (c) the principle
of sacrificial reversal; (d) the principle of alternate correspondence.
(2) The relationship to the law: institution of a relationship of
complete subordination of the sheep to the person who directs them.
An individual and non-finalized relationship. Difference between
Greek and Christian* apatheia. *(3) The relationship to the truth:
the production of hidden truths. Pastoral teaching and spiritual
direction.* ∼ *Conclusion: an absolutely new form of power that
marks the appearance of specific modes of individualization. Its
decisive importance for the history of the subject.*

eight   1 MARCH 1978   191
The notion of "conduct." ∼ *The crisis of the pastorate.* ∼ *Revolts
of conduct in the field of the pastorate.* ∼ *The shift of forms of
resistance to the borders of political institutions in the modern age:
examples of the army, secret societies, and medicine.* ∼ *Problem of
vocabulary: "Revolts of conduct," "insubordination* (insoumission*),"
"dissidence," and "counter-conduct." Pastoral counter-conducts.
Historical reminder: (a) asceticism; (b) communities; (c) mysticism;
(d) Scripture; (e) eschatological beliefs.* ∼ *Conclusion: what is at
stake in the reference to the notion of "pastoral power" for an
analysis of the modes of exercise of power in general.*

nine   8 MARCH 1978   227
*From the pastoral of souls to the political government of
men.* ∼ *General context of this transformation: the crisis of the
pastorate and the insurrections of conduct in the sixteenth century. The
Protestant Reformation and the Counter Reformation. Other factors.*
∼ *Two notable phenomena: the intensification of the religious
pastorate and the increasing question of conduct, on
both private and public levels.* ∼ *Governmental reason specific*

to the exercise of sovereignty. ∼ *Comparison with Saint Thomas.* ∼
Break-up of the cosmological-theological continuum. ∼ *The question
of the art of governing.* ∼ *Comment on the problem of intelligibility
in history.* ∼ Raison d'État *(1): newness and object of scandal.* ∼
Three focal points of the polemical debate around raison d'État*:
Machiavelli, "politics" (*la *"politique"), and the "state."*

ten   15 MARCH 1978   255

Raison d'État *(II): its definition and principal characteristics
in the seventeenth century.* ∼ *The new model of historical
temporality entailed by* raison d'État. ∼ *Specific features of*
raison d'État *with regard to pastoral government: (1) The
problem of salvation: the theory of* coup d'État *(Naudé).
Necessity, violence, theatricality.* ∼ *(2) The problem of obedience.
Bacon: the question of sedition. Differences between Bacon and
Machiavelli.* ∼ *(3) The problem of truth: from the wisdom of the
prince to knowledge of the state. Birth of statistics. The problem of
the secret.* ∼ *The reflexive prism in which the problem of the state
appeared.* ∼ *Presence-absence of "population" in this new
problematic.*

eleven   22 MARCH 1978   285

Raison d'État *(III).* ∼ *The state as principle of
intelligibility and as objective.* ∼ *The functioning of this
governmental reason: (A) In theoretical texts. The theory
of the preservation of the state. (B) In political practice.
Competition between states.* ∼ *The Treaty of Westphalia
and the end of the Roman Empire.* ∼ *Force, a new element of
political reason.* ∼ *Politics and the dynamic of forces.* ∼ *The
first technological ensemble typical of this new art of
government: the diplomatic-military system.* ∼ *Its objective: the
search for a European balance. What is Europe? The idea
of "balance."* ∼ *Its instruments: (1) war; (2) diplomacy;
(3) the installation of a permanent military apparatus
(*dispositif*).*

twelve   29 MARCH 1978   311

*The second technological assemblage characteristic of the
new art of government according to* raison d'État: *police.
Traditional meanings of the word up to the sixteenth century.
Its new sense in the seventeenth and eighteenth centuries:
calculation and technique making possible the good use of the
state's forces.* ∼ *The triple relationship between the system of
European balance and police.* ∼ *Diversity of Italian,
German, and French situations.* ∼ *Turquet de Mayerne,* La
Monarchie aristodémocratique. ∼ *The control of
human activity as constitutive element of the force of the state.* ∼
*Objects of police: (1) the number of citizens; (2) the
necessities of life; (3) health; (4) occupations; (5) the
coexistence and circulation of men.* ∼ *Police as the art of
managing life and the well-being of populations.*

thirteen   5 APRIL 1978   333

Police (continuation). ∼ *Delamare.* ∼ *The town as
site for the development of police. Police and urban regulation.
Urbanization of the territory. Relationship between police
and the mercantilist problematic.* ∼ *Emergence of the market
town.* ∼ *Methods of police. Difference between police and
justice. An essentially regulatory type of power. Regulation
and discipline.* ∼ *Return to the problem of grain.* ∼ *Criticism
of the police state on the basis of the problem of scarcity.
The theses of the* économistes *concerning the price of grain,
population, and the role of the state.* ∼ *Birth of a new
governmentality. Governmentality of the* politiques *and
governmentality of the* économistes. ∼ *The transformations
of* raison d'État: *(1) the naturalness of society; (2) new
relationships between power and knowledge; (3) taking
charge of the population (public hygiene, demography, etc.);
(4) new forms of state intervention; (5) the status of
liberty.* ∼ *Elements of the new art of government: economic
practice, management of the population, law and respect*

for liberties, police with a repressive function. ~ *Different forms of counter-conduct relative to this governmentality.* ~ *General conclusion.*

Course Summary   363

Course Context   369

Name Index   403

Subject Index   409

FOREWORD

MICHEL FOUCAULT TAUGHT AT the Collège de France from January 1971 until his death in June 1984 (with the exception of 1977 when he took a sabbatical year). The title of his chair was "The History of Systems of Thought."

On the proposal of Jules Vuillemin, the chair was created on 30 November 1969 by the general assembly of the professors of the Collège de France and replaced that of "The History of Philosophical Thought" held by Jean Hyppolite until his death. The same assembly elected Michel Foucault to the new chair on 12 April 1970.[1] He was 43 years old.

Michel Foucault's inaugural lecture was delivered on 2 December 1970.[2] Teaching at the Collège de France is governed by particular rules. Professors must provide 26 hours of teaching a year (with the possibility of a maximum of half this total being given in the form of seminars[3]). Each year they must present their original research and this obliges them to change the content of their teaching for each course. Courses and seminars are completely open; no enrolment or qualification is required and the professors do not award any qualifications.[4] In the terminology of the Collège de France, the professors do not have students but only auditors.

Michel Foucault's courses were held every Wednesday from January to March. The huge audience made up of students, teachers, researchers and the curious, including many who came from outside France, required two amphitheaters of the Collège de France. Foucault often complained about the distance between himself and his "public" and of how few exchanges the course made possible.[5] He would have liked a seminar in which real collective work could take place and made a number of attempts to bring this about. In the final years he devoted a long period to answering his auditors' questions at the end of each course.

This is how Gérard Petitjean, a journalist from *Le Nouvel Observateur*, described the atmosphere at Foucault's lectures in 1975:

> When Foucault enters the amphitheater, brisk and dynamic like someone who plunges into the water, he steps over bodies to reach his chair, pushes away the cassette recorders so he can put down his papers, removes his jacket, lights a lamp and sets off at full speed. His voice is strong and effective, amplified by loudspeakers that are the only concession to modernism in a hall that is barely lit by light spread from stucco bowls. The hall has three hundred places and there are five hundred people packed together, filling the smallest free space . . . There is no oratorical effect. It is clear and terribly effective. There is absolutely no concession to improvisation. Foucault has twelve hours each year to explain in a public course the direction taken by his research in the year just ended. So everything is concentrated and he fills the margins like correspondents who have too much to say for the space available to them. At 19.15 Foucault stops. The students rush towards his desk; not to speak to him, but to stop their cassette recorders. There are no questions. In the pushing and shoving Foucault is alone. Foucault remarks: "It should be possible to discuss what I have put forward. Sometimes, when it has not been a good lecture, it would need very little, just one question, to put everything straight. However, this question never comes. The group effect in France makes any genuine discussion impossible. And as there is no feedback, the course is theatricalized. My relationship with the people there is like that of an actor or an acrobat. And when I have finished speaking, a sensation of total solitude . . ."[6]

Foucault approached his teaching as a researcher: explorations for a future book as well as the opening up of fields of problematization were formulated as an invitation to possible future researchers. This is why the courses at the Collège de France do not duplicate the published books. They are not sketches for the books even though both books and courses share certain themes. They have their own status. They arise from a specific discursive regime within the set of Foucault's "philosophical activities." In particular they set out the program for a genealogy of knowledge/power relations, which are the terms in which he thinks of his work from the beginning of the 1970s, as opposed to the program of an archeology of discursive formations that previously orientated his work.[7]

The courses also performed a role in contemporary reality. Those who followed his courses were not only held in thrall by the narrative that unfolded week by week and seduced by the rigorous exposition, they also found a perspective on contemporary reality. Michel Foucault's art consisted in using history to cut diagonally through contemporary reality. He could speak of Nietzsche or Aristotle, of expert psychiatric opinion or the Christian pastoral, but those who attended his lectures always took from what he said a perspective on the present and contemporary events. Foucault's specific strength in his courses was the subtle interplay between learned erudition, personal commitment, and work on the event.

✤

With their development and refinement in the 1970s, Foucault's desk was quickly invaded by cassette recorders. The courses—and some seminars—have thus been preserved.

This edition is based on the words delivered in public by Foucault. It gives a transcription of these words that is as literal as possible.[8] We would have liked to present it as such. However, the transition from an oral to a written presentation calls for editorial intervention: at the very least it requires the introduction of punctuation and division into paragraphs. Our principle has been always to remain as close as possible to the course actually delivered.

Summaries and repetitions have been removed whenever it seemed to be absolutely necessary. Interrupted sentences have been restored and faulty constructions corrected. Suspension points indicate that the recording is inaudible. When a sentence is obscure there is a conjectural integration or an addition between square brackets. An asterisk directing the reader to the bottom of the page indicates a significant divergence between the notes used by Foucault and the words actually uttered. Quotations have been checked and references to the texts used are indicated. The critical apparatus is limited to the elucidation of obscure points, the explanation of some allusions, and the clarification of critical points. To make the lectures easier to read, each lecture is preceded by a brief summary that indicates its principal articulations.

The text of the course is followed by the summary published by the *Annuaire du Collège de France*. Foucault usually wrote these in June, some time after the end of the course. It was an opportunity for him to pick out retrospectively the intention and objectives of the course. It constitutes the best introduction to the course.

Each volume ends with a "context" for which the course editors are responsible. It seeks to provide the reader with elements of the biographical, ideological, and political context, situating the course within the published work and providing indications concerning its place within the corpus used in order to facilitate understanding and to avoid misinterpretations that might arise from a neglect of the circumstances in which each course was developed and delivered.

Security, Territory, Population, the course delivered in 1978, is edited by Michel Senellart.

✤

A new aspect of Michel Foucault's "œuvre" is published with this edition of the Collège de France courses.

Strictly speaking it is not a matter of unpublished work, since this edition reproduces words uttered publicly by Foucault, excluding the often highly developed written material he used to support his lectures. Daniel Defert possesses Michel Foucault's notes and he is to be warmly thanked for allowing the editors to consult them.

This edition of the Collège de France courses was authorized by Michel Foucault's heirs who wanted to be able to satisfy the strong demand for their publication, in France as elsewhere, and to do this under indisputably responsible conditions. The editors have tried to be equal to the degree of confidence placed in them.

FRANÇOIS EWALD AND ALESSANDRO FONTANA

1. Michel Foucault concluded a short document drawn up in support of his candidacy with these words: "We should undertake the history of systems of thought." "Titres et travaux" in *Dits et Écrits, 1954-1988*, four volumes, eds. Daniel Defert and François Ewald (Paris: Gallimard, 1994) vol. 1, p. 846; English translation by Robert Hurley, "Candidacy Presentation: Collège de France" in *The Essential Works of Michel Foucault, 1954-1984, vol. 1: Ethics: Subjectivity and Truth*, ed. Paul Rabinow (New York: The New Press, 1997) p. 9.

2. It was published by Gallimard in May 1971 with the title *L'Ordre du discours* (Paris). English translation by Rupert Swyer, "The Order of Discourse," appendix to M. Foucault, *The Archeology of Knowledge* (New York: Pantheon, 1972).

3. This was Foucault's practice until the start of the 1980s.

4. Within the framework of the Collège de France.

5. In 1976, in the vain hope of reducing the size of the audience, Michel Foucault changed the time of his course from 17.45 to 9.00. See the beginning of the first lecture (7 January 1976) of *"Il faut défendre la société." Cours au Collège de France, 1976* (Paris: Gallimard/Seuil, 1997); English translation by David Macey, *"Society Must be Defended." Lectures at the Collège de France 1975-1976* (New York: Picador, 2003).

6. Gérard Petitjean, "Les Grands Prêtres de l'université française," *Le Nouvel Observateur*, 7 April 1975.

7. See especially, "Nietzsche, la généalogie, l'histoire" in *Dits et Écrits*, vol. 2, p. 137. English translation by Donald F. Brouchard and Sherry Simon, "Nietzsche, Genealogy, History" in *The Essential Works of Michel Foucault 1954-1984, vol. 2: Aesthetics, Method, and Epistemology*, ed. James Faubion (New York: The New Press, 1998) pp. 369-392.

8. We have made use of the recordings made by Gilbert Burlet and Jacques Lagrange in particular. These are deposited in the Collège de France and the Institut Mémoires de l'Édition Contemporaine.

INTRODUCTION*

IN THE YEARS BETWEEN December, 1976 and May, 1984 Michel Foucault published no new books. Yet far from being a period of silence, Foucault concentrated an extraordinary amount of intellectual activity in essays, lectures, interviews, and especially in his courses at the Collège de France. Without access to these courses, it was extremely difficult to understand Foucault's reorientation from an analysis of the strategies and tactics of power immanent in the modern discourse on sexuality (1976) to an analysis of the ancient forms and modalities of relation to oneself by which one constituted oneself as a moral subject of sexual conduct (1984). In short, Foucault's passage from the political to the ethical dimension of sexuality seemed sudden and inexplicable. Moreover, it was clear from his published essays and interviews that this displacement of focus had consequences far beyond the specific domain of the history of sexuality.

Security, Territory, Population contains a conceptual hinge, a key concept, that allows us to link together the political and ethical axes of Foucault's thought. But this essential moment has been rather undervalued due to the fact that the main legacy of this course has been to give rise to so-called "governmentality studies." There is absolutely no doubt that the practices of governmentality and the historically precedent practices of pastoral power studied by Foucault in this course open up a new and significant field of inquiry, both within Foucault's own work and more generally. Yet one should not overlook the fact that pastoral

---

* This introduction is dedicated to my students at the University of Pisa who read *Security, Territory, Population* with me in Spring, 2007.

power and governmentality are historically and philosophically contiguous in that they take as the object of their techniques and practices the *conduct* of human beings. If the "government of men" is understood as an activity that undertakes to conduct individuals, "pastoral power" concentrates this activity in the regime of religious institutions, while governmentality locates it in the direction of political institutions. As Foucault remarks,

> ... from the end of the seventeenth and the beginning of the eighteenth century, generally speaking I think that inasmuch as many pastoral functions were taken up in the exercise of governmentality, and inasmuch as government also begins to want to take responsibility for people's conduct, to conduct people, then from then on we see revolts of conduct arising less from the religious institution and much more from political institutions.[1]

Indeed, it is Foucault's analysis of the notions of conduct and counter-conduct in his lecture of 1 March 1978 that seems to me to constitute one of the richest and most brilliant moments in the entire course. Beginning from the Greek expression *oikonomia psuchōn* and the Latin expression *regimen animarum*, Foucault proposes the concept of *conduct* as the most adequate translation of these expressions, taking philosophical advantage of the way in which "conduct" can refer to two things:

> Conduct is the activity of conducting (*conduire*), of conduction (*la conduction*) if you like, but it is equally the way in which one conducts oneself (*se conduit*), lets oneself be conducted (*se laisse conduire*), and finally, in which one behaves (*se comporter*) under the influence of a conduct as the action of conducting or of conduction (*conduction*).[2]

One already sees here the double dimension of conduct, namely the activity of conducting an individual, conduction as a relation between individuals, and the way in which an individual conducts himself or is conducted, his conduct or behavior in the narrower sense of the term. Yet Foucault moves quickly from the quite specific form of power that takes as its object the conduct of individuals to the correlative counter-movements that he initially designates as specific revolts of conduct.

> Just as there have been forms of resistance to power as the exercise of political sovereignty and just as there have been other equally intentional [*voulues*, that is "willed"] forms of resistance or refusal that were directed at power in the form of economic exploitation, have there not been forms of resistance to power as conducting?[3]

These forms of resistance also have a double dimension. They are movements characterized by wanting to be conducted differently, whose objective is a different type of conduction, and that also attempt to indicate an area in which each individual can conduct himself, the domain of one's own conduct or behavior.[4]

In the first volume of his history of sexuality *La Volonté de savoir* (*The Will to Know*), writing from a directly political point of view, Foucault had already insisted that resistance is not in a position of exteriority with respect to power, and that points of resistance do not answer to a set of principles heterogenous to relations of power.[5] Resistance is "coextensive and absolutely contemporaneous" to power; resistances exist within the strategic field of relations of power and relations of power themselves only exist relative to a multiplicity of points of resistance.[6] In *Security, Territory, Population*, Foucault also emphasizes the non-exteriority, the immanent relation, of conduct and counter-conduct. The fundamental elements of the counter-conduct analyzed by Foucault are not absolutely external to the conduct imposed by Christian pastoral power. Conduct and counter-conduct share a series of elements that can be utilized and re-utilized, re-implanted, re-inserted, taken up in the direction of reinforcing a certain mode of conduct or of creating and re-creating a type of counter-conduct:

> ... the struggle was not conducted in the form of absolute exteriority, but rather in the form of the permanent use of tactical elements that are pertinent in the anti-pastoral struggle to the very extent that they are part, even in a marginal way, of the general horizon of Christianity.[7]

Moreover, it is noteworthy that in the case of power/resistance and in that of conduct/counter-conduct, Foucault stresses that the tactical immanence of both resistance and counter-conduct to their respective fields of action should not lead one to conclude that they are simply a passive underside, a merely negative or reactive phenomenon, a kind of disappointing after-effect.[8] In each case Foucault employs the same kind of almost technical expression: resistance is not "*la marque en creux*" of power, counter-conducts are not "*les phénomènes en creux*" of the pastorate.[9] As he says in the interview "Non au sexe roi", if resistance were nothing more than the reverse image of power, it would not resist; in order to resist one must activate something "as inventive, as mobile, as productive" as power itself.[10] Foucault similarly underlines the productivity of counter-conduct which goes beyond the purely negative act of disobedience.[11] Finally, as a counterpart to the celebrated motto "where there is power, there is resistance," one could invoke Foucault's remark about the "immediate and founding correlation between conduct and counter-conduct," a correlation that is not only historical but also conceptual.[12]

In light of all of these parallels between resistance and counter-conduct, what does the creation of the couple conduct/counter-conduct in 1978 add to Foucault's previous conceptualization? On the one hand, the notion of counter-conduct adds an explicitly ethical component to the notion of resistance; on the other hand, this notion allows one to move easily between the ethical and the political, letting us see their many points of contact and intersection. Foucault's three initial examples—the appearance of desertion-insubordination, the development of secret societies, and the rise of medical dissent—bring to light both of these aspects of the notion of conduct/counter-conduct. Furthermore, Foucault's problem of vocabulary, his attempt to find a specific word to designate the resistances, refusals, revolts against being conducted in a certain way, show how careful he was in wanting to find a concept that neglected neither the ethical nor the political dimensions and that made it possible to recognize their nexus. After rejecting the notions of "revolt," "disobedience," "insubordination," "dissidence," and "misconduct," for reasons ranging from their being notions that are either too strong, too weak, too localized, too passive, or too substance-like,

Foucault proposes the expression "counter-conduct"—"counter-conduct in the sense of struggle against the procedures implemented for conducting others"—and notes that anti-pastoral counter-conduct can be found at a doctrinal level, in the form of individual behavior, and in strongly organized groups.[13]

When Foucault returns to the notion of conduct in his essay "Le sujet et le pouvoir," he emphasizes that this notion is perhaps "one of those that best allows us to grasp what is specific to relations of power," immediately placing "conduct" in a political field.[14] As in 1978, he observes that "conduct is both the act of 'directing' ['*mener*'] others (according to more or less strict mechanisms of coercion) and the way of behaving [*se comporter*] in a more or less open field of possibilities", and then adds that the exercise of power consists in " 'conducting conduct' ['*conduire des conduites*']."[15] Next, Foucault draws a direct connection between power and government, again distinguishing government from political and economic subjection, and highlighting the fact that to govern an individual or a group is "to act on the possibilities of action of other individuals," is a "mode of action on the actions of others."[16] Thus, according to Foucault, "to govern, in this sense, is to structure the possible field of actions of others."[17] Although much less conceptually detailed in *La Volonté de savoir*, Foucault's fundamental idea of studying power as a multiplicity of force relations has many of the same consequences as his later articulation of the notion of conduct. These force relations, unequal but also local and unstable, give rise to states of power, and modifications of these same relations transform those situations of power.[18] A force is not a metaphysical substance or abstraction, but is always given in a particular relation; a force can be identified as any factor in a relation that affects the elements of the relation; *anything* that influences the actions of individuals in a relation, that has an effect on their actions, is in this sense a force. And thus force relations structure the possible field of actions of individuals. Resistance and counter-conduct modify these force relations, counter the locally stabilized organizations of power, and thereby affect, in a new way, the possibilities of action of others. A force relation can be immanent in a physical environment, in a social configuration, in a pattern of behavior, in a bodily gesture, in a certain attitude, in a way of life. All of these features can structure the field of action of individuals, and thus power and resistance "come from everywhere."[19]

Foucault's analysis of the different forms of counter-conduct found in a number of anti-pastoral communities in the Middle Ages brings clearly to the forefront the political dimension of counter-conduct. As he says in concluding his discussion, "in some of these communities there was a counter-society aspect, a carnival aspect, overturning social relations and hierarchy."[20] But even apparently personal or individual forms of counter-conduct such as the return to Scripture or the adherence to a certain set of eschatological beliefs have a political dimension, that is, modify force relations between individuals, acting on the possibilities of action. Reading Scripture as "a spiritual act that puts the faithful in the presence of God's word and which consequently finds its law and guarantee in this inner illumination" is a counter-conduct that is "used against and to short-circuit, as it were, the pastorate."[21] And eschatological beliefs that imply that the faithful "will no longer need a shepherd" are also a way of "disqualifying the pastor's role," a counter-conduct with profound political effects.[22]

The ethical dimension of counter-conduct is clearly present when Foucault mentions the *devotio moderna*, an anti-pastoral struggle expressed and manifested in "a whole new attitude, religious comportment, way of doing things and being, and a whole new way of relating to God, obligations, morality, as well as to civil life."[23] Foucault's detailed discussion of asceticism as a form of counter-conduct—beginning from the idea that "ascesis is an exercise of self on self; it is a sort of close combat of the individual with himself in which the authority, presence, and gaze of someone else is, if not impossible, at least unnecessary"—cannot help but bring to mind his late idea of ethics as a relation to oneself, the constitution of oneself as a moral subject, and the related notions of "modes of subjectivation" and "practices of the self."[24] When Foucault introduces the idea of ethics as the self's relation to itself, as distinct from a moral code and the actual behavior of individuals with respect to this code, he does so by claiming that there are "different ways of 'conducting oneself' ['*se conduire*'] morally," emphasizing this other aspect of morality, namely "the way in which one should 'conduct oneself' ['*se conduire*']."[25] What then follows is a much more precise and unambiguous description, from the ethical point of view, of the second sense of "conduct" mentioned in *Security, Territory, Population*. And Foucault's conclusion links together the aspects of conduct as moral action and as moral self-constitution:

> There is no specific moral action that does not refer to the unity of a moral conduct; no moral conduct that does not call for the constitution of oneself as a moral subject; and no constitution of the moral subject without "modes of subjectivation" and without an "ascetics" or "practices of the self" that support them [the modes of subjectivation].[26]

In the first lecture of *The Hermeneutics of the Subject*, when Foucault takes up the notion of the "care of the self" (*epimeleia heauton*), he identifies three components of this care: a general attitude with respect to oneself, to others, and to the world; a form of attention turned towards oneself; a series of practices or techniques of the self.[27] Attitude, attention, and practices of the self are all features of the ethical sense of conduct.

In "Le sujet et le pouvoir" Foucault stresses that power, understood as the government of men, includes the element of freedom:

> Power is only exercised on "free subjects" and only insofar as they are "free"—understanding by this claim individual or collective subjects faced with a field of possibility in which several conducts, several reactions, and various modes of behavior can take place.[28]

This quotation underscores Foucault's assertion that power never exhaustively determines a subject's possibilities, and it specifies the relevant field of possibility as that of conduct or behavior, taking the latter in the widest sense of the term. If we recall Foucault's remark that "ethics is the deliberative form that freedom takes," the "deliberative practice of freedom," we can also see that for Foucault ethics is in effect a kind of freedom of conduct.[29] In a series of remarkable formulas concerning freedom, Foucault speaks of the "insubordination of freedom," the "rebelliousness of the will and the intransitivity of freedom," the "art of voluntary inservitude" and of "deliberative indocility."[30] All of these phrases belong to the semantic field of counter-conduct and make evident the double ethical and political scope of this counter-conduct.

The discussion of asceticism in *Security, Territory, Population* is a perfect example of the art of voluntary intractability, the exercise of freedom as a form of counter-conduct. According to Foucault's analysis, Christianity is not an ascetic religion, since the organization of pastoral power with its requirement of permanent obedience and renunciation of one's individual will is incompatible with the structure and practice of asceticism:

> ... whenever and wherever pastoral counter-conducts develop in the Middle Ages, asceticism was one of their points of support and instruments against the pastorate ... Insofar as the pastorate characterizes its structures of power, Christianity is fundamentally anti-ascetic, and asceticism is rather a sort of tactical element, an element of reversal by which certain themes of Christian theology or religious experience are utilized against these structures of power.[31]

The challenge represented by the ascetic exercise of the self on the self, which becomes a kind of egoistic self-mastery, provokes a counter-conduct to pastoral obedience, and gives rise to a type of *apatheia* that is much closer to the Greek *apatheia* which guarantees the mastery of oneself than to the Christian *apatheia*, part of pastoral power, which requires the continual renunciation of a will that is turned towards oneself.[32] Finally, mysticism is a form of counter-conduct that has the distinction of being an experience that "by definition escapes pastoral power."[33] Eluding pastoral examination, confession, and teaching, mystical experience short-circuits the pastoral hierarchy:

> In the pastorate, the pastor's direction of the individual's soul was necessary, and no communication between the soul and God could take place that was not either ruled out or controlled by the pastor.[34]

The direct, immediate communication between the soul and God in mysticism thus marks the distance separating mysticism from the pastorate.

When in the discussion following his lecture "Qu'est-ce que la critique? [Critique et Aukflärung]," given less than two months after the conclusion of *Security, Territory, Population*, Foucault designates mysticism as one of the first major revolts of conduct in the West, he underlines the conjunction of the ethical and the political in the history of mysticism: "mysticism as individual experience and institutional and political struggle are absolutely united, and in any case constantly referred to one another."[35] Spiritual movements intertwined with popular struggle are one historically prominent source of counter-conduct.

It is astonishing, and of profound significance, that the autonomous sphere of conduct has been more or less invisible in the history of modern (as opposed to ancient) moral and political philosophy. The "juridification" of moral and political experience has meant that the role of conduct has typically been subordinated to that of the law, thus losing its specificity and its particular force.[36] Perhaps the major exception to this absence of attention to the sphere of conduct can be found in the third chapter of John Stuart Mill's *On Liberty*, where the political and moral importance of conduct is central.[37] As Mill says,

> No one's idea of excellence in conduct is that people should do absolutely nothing but copy one another. No one would assert that people ought not to put into their mode of life, and into the conduct of their concerns, any impress whatever of their own judgment, or of their own individual character.[38]

But as Mill goes on to observe, we are governed by custom, "the traditions or customs of other people are the rule of conduct," and we do not choose our plan of life or determine our own conduct.[39]

> I do not mean that they [individuals] chose what is customary, in preference to what suits their own inclination. It does not occur to them to have any inclination, except for what is customary. Thus the mind itself is bowed to the yoke: even in what people do for pleasure, conformity is the first thing thought of; they like in crowds; they exercise choice only among things commonly done: peculiarity of taste, eccentricity of conduct, are shunned equally with crimes . . .[40]

"Eccentricity of conduct" is Mill's name for counter-conduct, and he strikingly opposes "originality in thought and action" to the "despotism of custom."[41] Indeed, *On Liberty* contains moments of lyrical encomium to counter-conduct:

> In this age the mere example of non-conformity, the mere refusal to bend the knee to custom, is itself a service. Precisely because the tyranny of opinion is such as to make eccentricity a reproach, it is desirable, in order to break through that tyranny, that people should be eccentric . . . That so few now dare to be eccentric, marks the chief danger of the time.[42]

And Mill recognizes that uniformity of conduct weakens the possibility of resistance:

> The demand that all other people shall resemble ourselves, grows by what it feeds on. If resistance waits till life is reduced *nearly* to one uniform type, all deviations from that type will come to be considered impious, immoral, even monstrous and contrary to nature. Mankind speedily become unable to conceive diversity, when they have been for some time unaccustomed to see it.[43]

The counter-conduct required by putting into practice one's "own mode of laying out his existence" is the only domain of force consonant with the political principle of liberty and the politics of individual differences.[44] However much Mill's conclusions may differ from Foucault's, *On Liberty* has the merit of both isolating the conceptual specificity of conduct and of identifying its singular ethical-political value.

Foucault's appreciation of the feminist and gay movements can best be understood from the point of view of the notion of conduct/counter-conduct. Already in *Security, Territory, Population*, Foucault connects one historically important form of counter-conduct to the status of women: "these revolts of conduct are often linked up with the problem of women and their status in society, in civil society or in religious society."[45] And he gives as examples the movement of Rhenish *Nonnenmystik*, the groups formed around women prophets in the Middle Ages, and various Spanish and French groups of spiritual direction in the sixteenth and seventeenth centuries. Foucault's interest in the modern history of relations among women revolves around the question of female friendship, how it develops, what kind of conduct it involves, how women were bound to one another through a certain type of affect, of affection. He was especially attentive to the "response [of women], often innovative and creative, to a status that was imposed upon them."[46] And he was well aware that the creative counter-conduct of women was often the target of the harshest criticism against them, as if the civil debate around juridical issues could not but degenerate when the topic turned to the behavior of women. He would certainly have shared the acute perception of Mill: ". . . the man, and still more the woman, who can be accused either of doing 'what nobody does', or of not doing 'what everybody does', is the subject of as much depreciatory remark as if he or she had committed some grave moral delinquency."[47]

Foucault's famous remark that what makes homosexuality "disturbing" is the "homosexual mode of life much more than the sexual act itself" is directly related to the way in which this mode of life is a center of counter-conduct.[48] Foucault attaches great significance to that aspect of the gay movement which puts into play "relations in the absence of codes or established lines of conduct," "affective intensities," "forms that change."[49] Foucault describes these relations with the same expression, *court-circuit*, that he had used to describe religious counter-conduct: "these relations create a short-circuit, and introduce love where there should be law, rule, habit."[50] Gay counter-conduct, a new mode of life, gay culture in the widest sense of the term, is what fascinated Foucault:

> . . . a culture that invents modalities of relations, modes of existence, types of values, forms of exchange between individuals that are really new, that are not homogenous to nor superimposable on general cultural forms. If this is possible, then gay culture will not be simply a choice of homosexuals for homosexuals. It will create relations that are, up to a certain point, transposable to heterosexuals. One has to overturn things a bit, and rather than say what one said at a certain moment—"Let us try to reintroduce

homosexuality into the general normality of social relations"—let us say the opposite: "No. Let it [homosexuality] escape as far as possible from the type of relations that are proposed to us in our society, and let us try to create in the empty space in which we find ourselves new relational possibilities."[51]

This new space of, so to speak, gay counter-conduct will create the possibility for others to "enrich their life by modifying their own scheme of relations," with the effect that "unforeseen lines of force will be formed."[52]

This space of counter-conduct cannot be reduced to the juridical sphere, and that is why Foucault maintained that one should consider "the battle for gay rights as an episode that cannot represent the final stage" of the struggle.[53] The real effects (*effets réels*) of the battle for rights should be looked for much more in "attitudes, [in] schemes of behavior, than [in] legal formulations," and thus the attempt to create a new mode of life is much more pertinent than the question of individual rights.[54] The rights that derive from marital and family relations are a way of stabilizing, rendering stationary, certain forms of conduct; as Foucault says, extending these rights to other persons is but a first step, since "if one asks people to reproduce marriage bonds in order for their personal relation to be recognized, the progress realized is slight."[55] Our legal, social, institutional world is one in which the only relations possible are "extremely few, extremely schematized, extremely poor."[56] Given that "a rich relational world would be extremely complicated to manage," the institutional framework of our society has attempted to narrow the possibility of relations, and, following Foucault's diagnosis, we have "to fight against the impoverishment of the relational fabric" of our social world.[57] We have all heard the "progressive" sentiments of those liberals who announce that they are not opposed to gay marriage as long "as they behave like married couples." It is precisely the threat of counter-conduct, and not the legal status, that is most disruptive and unsettling.

This is certainly one reason why Foucault announced that after studying the history of sexuality, he wanted to understand the history of friendships—friendships that for centuries allowed one to live "very intense affective relations" and that also had "economic and social implications."[58] The kinds of counter-conduct made possible by these friendships both changed the force relations between individuals and modified one's relation to oneself. One conducts oneself in another way with friends, fabricating new ethical and political possibilities. Beginning in the sixteenth century, as we find texts that criticize (especially male) friendships as "something dangerous," this type of friendship begins to disappear.[59] And Foucault's suggestion was that this space of dangerous friendship came to be occupied by the problem of homosexuality, of sexual relationships between men: "the disappearance of friendship as a social relation and the fact that homosexuality was declared a social, political, and medical problem are part of the same process."[60] The constitution of homosexuality as a separate medical and psychiatric problem was much more effective as a technique of control than the attempt to regulate friendship. Even today, behind every intense friendship lurks the shadow of sex, so that we no longer see the striking perturbations of friendship. The counter-conduct of friendship has become pathologized—the unruliness of friendship is but a form of abnormality.

What Foucault once named the "struggles against subjection" and "for a new subjectivity" could also be described as a struggle against a certain type of conduction and for another form of conduct.[61] The Kantian question of "who we are at this precise moment of history" is inseparable from this question of our conduct.[62] To become other than what we are requires an ethics and politics of counter-conduct. Foucault arrived at the conclusion that,

> Probably the principal objective today is not to discover but to refuse what we are . . . We have to promote new forms of subjectivity while refusing the type of individuality that has been imposed on us for several centuries.[63]

This double refusal and promotion is the domain of counter-conduct, a sphere of revolt that incites a process of productivity.[64] Moreover, Foucault explicitly links this domain to his definition of the "critical attitude," a political and moral attitude, a manner of thinking, that is a critique of the way in which our conduct is governed, a "partner and adversary" of the arts of governing.[65] This critical attitude is part of a philosophical *ēthos*, and no such *ēthos* is effective without a permanent exercise of counter-conduct.[66]

One of Foucault's most disquieting acclamations of counter-conduct is his discussion in favor of suicide, against "the humiliations, the hypocrisies, the dubious procedures" to which one constrains the conduct of suicide.[67] Should not we instead "prepare ourselves with all the care, the intensity, and the ardor that we desire," a "patient preparation, without respite, without inevitability either" that will shed light on all one's life:[68]

> I'm in favor of a true cultural combat in order to teach people again that there is no conduct that is more beautiful, that, consequently, deserves to be considered with as much attention as suicide. One should work on one's suicide all one's life.[69]

The government of conduct with respect to death, which extends to the "appalling banality" of the behavior of funeral homes, compellingly diminishes the force of any critical attitude, "as if death must extinguish every effort of imagination."[70] And here Foucault's imagination is itself a form of counter-conduct, a vision of

> the possibility of places without geography or schedule where one would enter in order to try to find, in the midst of the most ridiculous scenery, with nameless partners, opportunities to die free of all identity: one would have an indeterminate time there, seconds, weeks, perhaps months, until, with an imperious self-evidence, the opportunity presented itself that one would immediately recognize one could not miss: it would have the form without form of pleasure, absolutely simple.[71]

The ethical and political impact of counter-conduct is also at the heart of Foucault's last courses, concerned with the practice of *parrhesia*, and is especially prominent in his discussion of the apex of philosophical counter-conduct, namely Cynic *parrhesia* and the Cynic way of life. The

Cynic discourse that challenged all of the dependencies on social institutions, the Cynic recourse to scandalous behavior that called into question collective habits and standards of decency, Cynic courage in the face of danger—all of this parrhesiastic conduct could not but result in the association of this behavior with "dog-like" conduct: "the noble philosophers of Greece, who usually comprised an elite group, almost always disregarded the Cynics."[72] Cynic provocation stands as an emblem of the risks and the intensities of counter-conduct. Politically and ethically, *counter-conduct* is the invention of a new philosophical concept.

If counter-conduct at the end of life can be decisively shocking, we should not underestimate its more everyday occasions throughout the course of one's early life. Notwithstanding the cultural diversity of conduct, one of the most universal and dispiriting memories of every child's life is the constant exclamation of adults: behave yourself. Let's hope that it is an admonition that we can still learn to combat.

ARNOLD I. DAVIDSON
University of Chicago / Università di Pisa

---

1. This volume, pp. 197-198.
2. This volume, p. 193. I have very slightly modified Graham Burchell's more elegant translation of the end of this phrase in order to make it as literal as possible.
3. This volume, p. 195.
4. This volume, pp. 194-195.
5. Michel Foucault, *Histoire de la sexualité, vol. 1: La Volonté de savoir* (Paris: Galllimard, 1976), pp. 125-127.
6. Michel Foucault, "Non au sexe roi" in *Dits et écrits II*, 1976-88 (Paris: Gallimard, 2001), p. 267 and *La Volonté de savoir*, p. 126.
7. This volume, p. 125. Translation slightly modified.
8. *La Volonté de savoir*, pp. 126-127 and this volume, p. 195.
9. *La Volonté de savoir*, p. 126; the second quoted phrase appears on p. 198 of the French edition of *Security, Territory, Population*.
10. "Non au sexe roi", p. 267.
11. This volume, p. 200. See also p. 201.
12. *La Volonté de savoir*, p. 125 and this volume, p. 196.
13. This volume, pp. 201, 204.
14. Michel Foucault, "Le sujet et le pouvoir" in *Dits et écrits II*, p. 1056. Although this essay was published in 1982, there is compelling internal evidence that parts of it were written several years earlier.
15. Ibid. p. 1056.
16. Ibid.
17. Ibid.

18. *La Volonté de savoir*, pp. 121-123.

19. Ibid. p. 122.

20. This volume, pp. 211-212.

21. This volume, p. 213.

22. This volume, p. 214.

23. This volume, p. 204.

24. This volume, p. 205; *Histore de la sexualité, vol. 2: L'Usage des plaisirs* (Paris, Gallimard, 1984), pp. 36-45; "À propos de la généalogie de l'éthique: un aperçu du travail en cours" in *Dit et écrits II*, pp. 1437-1441.

25. *L'Usage des plaisirs*, p. 37.

26. Ibid. p. 40.

27. Michel Foucault, *The Hermeneutics of the Subject* (New York: Palgrave Macmillan, 2005), pp. 10-11.

28. "Le sujet et le pouvoir", p. 1056.

29. "L'éthique du souci de soi comme pratique de la liberté" in *Dits et écrits II*, pp. 1530-1531.

30. "Le sujet et le pouvoir", p. 1056 and "Qu'est-ce que la critique? [Critique et Aufklärung]" in *Bulletin de la société française de philosophie*, avril-juin 1990, p. 39.

31. This volume, p. 207.

32. This volume, pp. 178-179, 206-208.

33. This volume, p. 212.

34. This volume, p. 213.

35. "Qu'est-ce que la critique? [Critique et Aufklärung]", p. 59.

36. *L'Usage des plaisirs*, pp. 41-42.

37. See the chapter on Mill in Stanley Cavell, *Cities of Words* (Cambridge: Harvard University Press, 2004) as well as Piergiorgio Donatelli, *Introduzione a Mill* (Roma-Bari: Laterza, 2007).

38. John Stuart Mill, *On Liberty* in *The Collected Works of John Stuart Mill*, vol. XVIII, ed. by J. M. Robson (Toronto-London: University of Toronto Press, 1977), p. 262.

39. Ibid. pp. 261, 262-263.

40. Ibid. pp. 264-265.

41. Ibid. pp. 268, 272.

42. Ibid. p. 269.

43. Ibid. p. 275.

44. Ibid. 270, 272-275.

45. This volume, pp. 196-197.

46. "Entretien avec M. Foucault" in *Dits et écrits II*, p. 1108.

47. Mill, *On Liberty*, p. 270.

48. "De l'amitié comme mode de vie" in *Dits et écrits II*, p. 983.

49. "Choix sexuel, acte sexuel" in ibid. p. 1152 and "De l'amitié comme mode de vie", pp. 982-983.

50. "De l'amitié comme mode de vie", p. 983.

51. "Le triomphe social du plaisir sexuel: une conversation avec Michel Foucault" in *Dits et écrits II*, p. 1130.

52. Ibid. and "De l'amitié comme mode de vie", p. 983.

53. "Le triomphe social du plaisir sexuel: une conversation avec Michel Foucault", p. 1127.

54. Ibid. pp. 1127-1128.

55. Ibid. 1128.

56. Ibid.

57. Ibid. pp. 1128-1129.

58. "Michel Foucault, une interview: sexe, pouvoir et la politique de l'identité" in *Dits et écrits II*, p. 1563.

59. Ibid.

60. Ibid. 1564.

61. "Le sujet et le pouvoir", pp. 1046-1047.

62. Ibid. pp. 1050-1051.

63. Ibid. p. 1051.

64. This volume, p. 200.
65. "Qu'est-ce que la critique? [Critique et Aufklärung], p. 38.
66. "Qu'est-ce que les Lumières?" in *Dits et écrits II*, pp. 1387, 1390, 1396.
67. "Un plaisir si simple" in ibid. p. 777.
68. Ibid. pp. 778-789.
69. "Conversation avec Werner Schroeter" in ibid, p. 1076.
70. "Un plaisir si simple", p. 779.
71. Ibid.
72. Michel Foucault, *Fearless Speech* (Los Angeles: Semiotext(e), 2001), p. 122. For Foucault's detailed discussion of the Cynics, see ibid. pp. 115-133 and his still unpublished final course at the Collège de France, *Le Gouvernement de soi et des autres: le courage de la vérité*.

one

11 JANUARY 1978

General perspective of the lectures: the study of bio-power. ∼ Five proposals on the analysis of mechanisms of power. ∼ Legal system, disciplinary mechanisms, and security apparatuses (dispositifs). Two examples: (a) the punishment of theft; (b) the treatment of leprosy, plague, and smallpox. ∼ General features of security apparatuses (1): the spaces of security. ∼ The example of the town. ∼ Three examples of planning urban space in the sixteenth and seventeenth centuries: (a) Alexandre Le Maître's La Métropolitée (1682); (b) Richelieu; (c) Nantes.

THIS YEAR I WOULD like to begin studying something that I have called, somewhat vaguely, bio-power.[1] By this I mean a number of phenomena that seem to me to be quite significant, namely, the set of mechanisms through which the basic biological features of the human species became the object of a political strategy, of a general strategy of power, or, in other words, how, starting from the eighteenth century, modern Western societies took on board the fundamental biological fact that human beings are a species. This is roughly what I have called bio-power. So, to begin with, I'd like to put forward a few proposals that should be understood as indications of choice or statements of intent, not as principles, rules, or theorems.

First, the analysis of these mechanisms of power that we began some years ago, and are continuing with now, is not in any way a general theory of what power is. It is not a part or even the start of such a theory.

This analysis simply involves investigating where and how, between whom, between what points, according to what processes, and with what effects, power is applied. If we accept that power is not a substance, fluid, or something that derives from a particular source, then this analysis could and would only be at most a beginning of a theory, not of a theory of what power is, but simply of power in terms of the set of mechanisms and procedures that have the role or function and theme, even when they are unsuccessful, of securing power. It is a set of procedures, and it is as such, and only as such, that the analysis of mechanisms of power could be understood as the beginnings of something like a theory of power.

Second indication of choice: the relations, the set of relations, or rather, the set of procedures whose role is to establish, maintain, and transform mechanisms of power, are not "self-generating"* or "self-subsistent"†; they are not founded on themselves. Power is not founded on itself or generated by itself. Or we could say, more simply, that there are not first of all relations of production and then, in addition, alongside or on top of these relations, mechanisms of power that modify or disturb them, or make them more consistent, coherent, or stable. There are not family type relationships and then, over and above them, mechanisms of power; there are not sexual relationships with, in addition, mechanisms of power alongside or above them. Mechanisms of power are an intrinsic part of all these relations and, in a circular way, are both their effect and cause. What's more, in the different mechanisms of power intrinsic to relations of production, family relations, and sexual relations, it is possible, of course, to find lateral co-ordinations, hierarchical subordinations, isomorphic correspondences, technical identities or analogies, and chain effects. This allows us to undertake a logical, coherent, and valid investigation of the set of these mechanisms of power and to identify what is specific about them at a given moment, for a given period, in a given field.

Third, the analysis of these power relations may, of course, open out onto or initiate something like the overall analysis of a society. The analysis of mechanisms of power may also join up with the history of economic transformations, for example. But what I am doing—I don't

---

* autogénétiques: in inverted commas in the manuscript.
† autosubsistantes: in inverted commas in the manuscript.

say what I am cut out to do, because I know nothing about that—is not history, sociology, or economics. However, in one way or another, and for simple factual reasons, what I am doing is something that concerns philosophy, that is to say, the politics of truth, for I do not see many other definitions of the word "philosophy" apart from this. So, insofar as what is involved in this analysis of mechanisms of power is the politics of truth, and not sociology, history, or economics, I see its role as that of showing the knowledge effects produced by the struggles, confrontations, and battles that take place within our society, and by the tactics of power that are the elements of this struggle.

Fourth indication: I do not think there is any theoretical or analytical discourse which is not permeated or underpinned in one way or another by something like an imperative discourse. However, in the theoretical domain, the imperative discourse that consists in saying "love this, hate that, this is good, that is bad, be for this, beware of that," seems to me, at present at any rate, to be no more than an aesthetic discourse that can only be based on choices of an aesthetic order. And the imperative discourse that consists in saying "strike against this and do so in this way," seems to me to be very flimsy when delivered from a teaching institution or even just on a piece of paper. In any case, it seems to me that the dimension of what is to be done can only appear within a field of real forces, that is to say within a field of forces that cannot be created by a speaking subject alone and on the basis of his words, because it is a field of forces that cannot in any way be controlled or asserted within this kind of imperative discourse. So, since there has to be an imperative, I would like the one underpinning the theoretical analysis we are attempting to be quite simply a conditional imperative of the kind: If you want to struggle, here are some key points, here are some lines of force, here are some constrictions and blockages. In other words, I would like these imperatives to be no more than tactical pointers. Of course, it's up to me, and those who are working in the same direction, to know on what fields of real forces we need to get our bearings in order to make a tactically effective analysis. But this is, after all, the circle of struggle and truth, that is to say, precisely, of philosophical practice.

Finally, a fifth and final point: I think this serious and fundamental relation between struggle and truth, the dimension in which philosophy has developed for centuries and centuries, only dramatizes itself, becomes emaciated, and loses its meaning and effectiveness in polemics within theoretical discourse. So in all of this I will therefore propose only one imperative, but it will be categorical and unconditional: Never engage in polemics.[2]

Now I would like to begin the lectures. Their title is "security, territory, population."[3]

The first question is obviously: What are we to understand by "security"? I would like to devote today and maybe next week to this question, depending on how quickly or slowly I go. I will take an example, or rather a series of examples, or rather one example modulated in three stages. It is a very simple, very childish example, but we will start from there and I think it will enable me to say certain things. Take a completely simple penal law in the form of a prohibition like, say, "you must not kill, you must not steal," along with its punishment, hanging, or banishment, or a fine. In the second modulation it is still the same penal law, "you must not steal," and it is still accompanied by certain punishments if one breaks this law, but now everything is framed by, on the one hand, a series of supervisions, checks, inspections, and varied controls that, even before the thief has stolen, make it possible to identify whether or not he is going to steal, and so on. And then, on the other hand, at the other end, punishment will not just be the spectacular, definitive moment of the hanging, fine, or banishment, but a practice like incarceration with a series of exercises and a work of transformation on the guilty person in the form of what we call penitentiary techniques: obligatory work, moralization, correction, and so forth. The third modulation is based on the same matrix, with the same penal law, the same punishments, and the same type of framework of surveillance on one side and correction on the other, but now, the application of this penal law, the development of preventive measures, and the organization of corrective punishment will be governed by the following kind of questions. For example: What is the average rate of criminality for this [type]*? How can we can predict statistically the number of thefts at a given moment, in a given society, in a given town, in the town or in the

---

* M.F.: kind (*genre*)

country, in a given social stratum, and so on? Second, are there times, regions, and penal systems that will increase or reduce this average rate? Will crises, famines, or wars, severe or mild punishment, modify something in these proportions? There are other questions: Be it theft or a particular type of theft, how much does this criminality cost society, what damage does it cause, or loss of earnings, and so on? Further questions: What is the cost of repressing these thefts? Does severe and strict repression cost more than one that is more permissive; does exemplary and discontinuous repression cost more than continuous repression? What, therefore, is the comparative cost of the theft and of its repression, and what is more worthwhile: to tolerate a bit more theft or to tolerate a bit more repression? There are further questions: When one has caught the culprit, is it worth punishing him? What will it cost to punish him? What should be done in order to punish him and, by punishing him, reeducate him? Can he really be reeducated? Independently of the act he has committed, is he a permanent danger such that he will do it again whether or not he has been reeducated? The general question basically will be how to keep a type of criminality, theft for instance, within socially and economically acceptable limits and around an average that will be considered as optimal for a given social functioning. These three modalities seem to me to be typical of different things that we have studied, [and of] those that I would now like to study.

You are familiar with the first form, which consists in laying down a law and fixing a punishment for the person who breaks it, which is the system of the legal code with a binary division between the permitted and the prohibited, and a coupling, comprising the code, between a type of prohibited action and a type of punishment. This, then, is the legal or juridical mechanism. I will not return to the second mechanism, the law framed by mechanisms of surveillance and correction, which is, of course, the disciplinary mechanism.[4] The disciplinary mechanism is characterized by the fact that a third personage, the culprit, appears within the binary system of the code, and at the same time, outside the code, and outside the legislative act that establishes the law and the judicial act that punishes the culprit, a series of adjacent, detective, medical, and psychological techniques appear which fall within the domain of surveillance, diagnosis, and the possible transformation of individuals. We have looked

at all this. The third form is not typical of the legal code or the disciplinary mechanism, but of the apparatus (*dispositif*) of security,[5] that is to
say, of the set of those phenomena that I now want to study. Putting it in
a still absolutely general way, the apparatus of security inserts the
phenomenon in question, namely theft, within a series of probable
events. Second, the reactions of power to this phenomenon are inserted in
a calculation of cost. Finally, third, instead of a binary division between
the permitted and the prohibited, one establishes an average considered
as optimal on the one hand, and, on the other, a bandwidth of the acceptable that must not be exceeded. In this way a completely different
distribution of things and mechanisms takes shape.

I have taken this simple example in order to stress straightaway two
or three things that I would like to be quite clear, for all of you, and first
of all, of course, for myself. I have apparently given you the bare bones,
if you like, of a kind of historical schema. The legal system is the archaic
form of the penal order, the system we are familiar with from the
Middle Ages until the seventeenth or eighteenth century. The second
we could call the modern system, which was established from the
eighteenth century, and then the third is the, let's say, contemporary
system, the problematic of which began to appear fairly early on, but
which is currently being organized around new penal forms and the
calculation of the cost of penalties; these are the American,[6] but also
European techniques that we are now seeing. Actually, to describe
things in this way, as the archaic, ancient, modern, and contemporary,
misses the most important thing. The main thing is missing, in the first
place, because, of course, the ancient modalities I spoke about involve
those that appear as newer. It is absolutely clear that in the juridico-
legal system, which functioned, or at any rate was dominant, until the
eighteenth century, the disciplinary side was far from being absent
since, after all, when a so-called exemplary punishment was imposed on
an action, even and above all when the action was apparently of little
importance or consequence, it was in fact precisely with the aim of
having a corrective effect, if not on the culprit himself—because he was
hardly corrected if he was hung—[then at least on the]* rest of the

---

* Foucault says: on the other hand, the correction, the corrective effect was clearly addressed to the

population. To that extent, the practice of public torture and execution as an example was a corrective and disciplinary technique. Just as, in the same system, when one severely punished domestic theft—with the death penalty for a theft of very, very minor importance if it was committed in a house by someone who was received there or who was employed as a servant—it was clear that what was targeted was basically a crime that was only important due to its probability, and we can say that here too something like a mechanism of security was deployed. We could [say]* the same with regard to the disciplinary system, which includes a whole series of dimensions that absolutely belong to the domain of security. Basically, when one undertakes to correct a prisoner, someone who has been sentenced, one tries to correct the person according to the risk of relapse, of recidivism, that is to say according to what will very soon be called dangerousness—that is to say, again, a mechanism of security. So, disciplinary mechanisms do not appear just from the eighteenth century; they are already present within the juridico-legal code. Mechanisms of security are also very old as mechanisms. Conversely, I could also say that if we take the mechanisms of security that some people are currently trying to develop, it is quite clear that this does not constitute any bracketing off or cancellation of juridico-legal structures or disciplinary mechanisms. On the contrary, still in the penal domain, look at what is currently taking place in the domain of security for example. There is an increasingly huge set of legislative measures, decrees, regulations, and circulars that permit the deployment of these mechanisms of security. In comparison, in the tradition of the Middle Ages and the Classical age, the legal code concerning theft was very simple. If you consider the body of legislation concerning not only theft, but theft by children, the penal status of children, mental responsibility, and the whole body of legislation regarding what are called, precisely, security measures, the supervision of individuals after they leave a penal institution, you can see that getting these systems of security to work involves a real inflation of the juridico-legal code. In the same way, with the establishment of these mechanisms of security there is a considerable activation and propagation of the disciplinary corpus.

* M.F.: take (*prendre*)

For in order actually to guarantee this security one has to appeal, to take just one example, to a whole series of techniques for the surveillance of individuals, the diagnosis of what they are, the classification of their mental structure, of their specific pathology, and so on; in short one has to appeal to a whole disciplinary series that proliferates under mechanisms of security and is necessary to make them work.

So, there is not a series of successive elements, the appearance of the new causing the earlier ones to disappear. There is not the legal age, the disciplinary age, and then the age of security. Mechanisms of security do not replace disciplinary mechanisms, which would have replaced juridico-legal mechanisms. In reality you have a series of complex edifices in which, of course, the techniques themselves change and are perfected, or anyway become more complicated, but in which what above all changes is the dominant characteristic, or more exactly, the system of correlation between juridico-legal mechanisms, disciplinary mechanisms, and mechanisms of security. In other words, there is a history of the actual techniques themselves. For example, you could perfectly well study the history of the disciplinary technique of putting someone in a cell, which goes back a long way. It was already frequently employed in the juridico-legal age; you find it used for debtors and above all you find it in the religious domain. So, you could study the history of this cell technique (that is to say, [of] its shifts, [of] its utilization), and you would see at what point the cell technique, cellular discipline, is employed in the common penal system, what conflicts it gives rise to, and how it recedes. You could also analyze the security technique of criminal statistics. Crime statistics do not date from the present, but neither are they very old. In France, crime statistics were made possible by the famous Accounts of the Minister of Justice from 1826.[7] So, you could study the history of these techniques. But there is another history, which would be the history of technologies, that is to say the much more general, but of course much more fuzzy history of the correlations and systems of the dominant feature which determine that, in a given society and for a given sector—for things do not necessarily develop in step in different sectors, at a given moment, in a given society, in a given country—a technology of security, for example, will be set up,

taking up again and sometimes even multiplying juridical and disciplinary elements and redeploying them within its specific tactic. Still with
regard to the penal domain, there is a very clear example of this at the
moment. For some time now, for a good dozen years at least, it has been
clear that the essential question in the development of the problematic
of the penal domain, in the way in which it is reflected as well as in the
way it is practiced, is one of security. Basically, the fundamental question
is economics and the economic relation between the cost of repression
and the cost of delinquency. Now what we see is that this problematic
has led to such an inflation in disciplinary techniques, which were set up
long ago however, that this increase of the disciplinary has been the
point at which, if not scandal, at least friction has broken out—and the
wound has been sufficiently sensitive to have provoked some real and
even violent reactions. In other words, in a period of the deployment of
mechanisms of security, it is the disciplinary that sparked off, not the
explosion, for there has not been an explosion, but at least the most evident and visible conflicts. So, in this year's lectures I would like to show
you in what this technology consists, in what some of these technologies
[of security]* consist, it being understood that each of them consists to
a great extent in the reactivation and transformation of the juridico-legal
techniques and the disciplinary techniques I have talked about in
previous years.

I will just outline another example in order to introduce another set
of problems or to emphasize and generalize the problem (and again,
these are examples that I have talked about a hundred times[†]). Take the
exclusion of lepers in the Middle Ages, until the end of the Middle
Ages.[8] Although there were also many other aspects, exclusion essentially took place through a juridical combination of laws and regulations, as well as a set of religious rituals, which anyway brought about a
division, and a binary type of division, between those who were lepers
and those who were not. A second example is that of the plague (which
again I have talked about,[9] so I will return to it very briefly). The plague

---

* M.F.: disciplinary
[†] Foucault adds: and which are (*followed by a word that is inaudible*)

regulations formulated at the end of the Middle Ages, in the sixteenth and still in the seventeenth century, give a completely different impression, act in a completely differently way, have a completely different end, and above all use completely different instruments. These plague regulations involve literally imposing a partitioning grid on the regions and town struck by plague, with regulations indicating when people can go out, how, at what times, what they must do at home, what type of food they must have, prohibiting certain types of contact, requiring them to present themselves to inspectors, and to open their homes to inspectors. We can say that this is a disciplinary type of system. The third example, which we are currently studying in the seminar, is smallpox or inoculation practices from the eighteenth century.[10] The problem is posed quite differently. The fundamental problem will not be the imposition of discipline, although discipline may be called on to help, so much as the problem of knowing how many people are infected with smallpox, at what age, with what effects, with what mortality rate, lesions or after-effects, the risks of inoculation, the probability of an individual dying or being infected by smallpox despite inoculation, and the statistical effects on the population in general. In short, it will no longer be the problem of exclusion, as with leprosy, or of quarantine, as with the plague, but of epidemics and the medical campaigns that try to halt epidemic or endemic phenomena.

Here again, moreover, we need only look at the body of laws and the disciplinary obligations of modern mechanisms of security to see that there is not a succession of law, then discipline, then security, but that security is a way of making the old armatures of law and discipline function in addition to the specific mechanisms of security. So, in Western societies, in the domain of law, in the domain of medicine, and in other domains also, which is why I have given this other example, you can see a somewhat similar evolution and more or less the same type of transformations. What is involved is the emergence of technologies of security within mechanisms that are either specifically mechanisms of social control, as in the case of the penal system, or mechanisms with the function of modifying something in the biological destiny of the species. Can we say then—and this is what is at stake in what I want to analyze—that the general economy of power in our societies is becoming a domain of security? So, in these lectures I would like to undertake a sort of history of technologies of security and try to identify whether we can really speak of a society of security. At any rate, under this name of a society of security, I would like simply to investigate whether there really is a general economy of power which has the form [of], or which is at any rate dominated by, the technology of security.

So, some general features of these apparatuses (*dispositifs*) of security. I would like to identify four, I don't know how many . . . anyway I will start by analyzing some of them. First of all I would like to study a little, just in an overview, what could be called spaces of security. Second, I would like to study the problem of the treatment of the uncertain, the aleatory. Third, I will study the form of normalization specific to security, which seems to me to be different from the disciplinary type of normalization. And finally, I will come to what will be the precise problem of this year, which is the correlation between the technique of security and population as both the object and subject of these mechanisms of security, that is to say, the emergence not only of the notion, but also of the reality of population. Population is undoubtedly an idea and a reality that is absolutely modern in relation to the functioning of political power, but also in relation to knowledge and political theory, prior to the eighteenth century.

So, first, questions of space, broadly speaking. Baldly, at first sight and somewhat schematically, we could say that sovereignty is exercised within the borders of a territory, discipline is exercised on the bodies of individuals, and security is exercised over a whole population. Territorial borders, individual bodies, and a whole population, yes . . . but this is not the point and I don't think it holds together. In the first place it does not hold together because we already come across the problem of multiplicities in relation to sovereignty and discipline. If it is true that sovereignty is basically inscribed and functions within a territory, and that the idea of sovereignty over an unpopulated territory is not only a juridically and politically acceptable idea, but one that is absolutely accepted and primary, nevertheless the effective, real, daily operations of the actual exercise of sovereignty point to a certain multiplicity, but one which is treated as the multiplicity of subjects, or [as] the multiplicity of a people.

Discipline is of course also exercised on the bodies of individuals, but I have tried to show you how the individual is not the primary datum on which discipline is exercised. Discipline only exists insofar as there is a multiplicity and an end, or an objective or result to be obtained on the basis of this multiplicity. School and military discipline, as well as penal discipline, workshop discipline, worker discipline, are all particular ways of managing and organizing a multiplicity, of fixing its points of implantation, its lateral or horizontal, vertical and pyramidal trajectories, its hierarchy, and so on. The individual is much more a particular way of dividing up the multiplicity for a discipline than the raw material from which it is constructed. Discipline is a mode of individualization of multiplicities rather than something that constructs an edifice of multiple elements on the basis of individuals who are worked on as, first of all, individuals. So sovereignty and discipline, as well as security, can only be concerned with multiplicities.

On the other hand, problems of space are equally common to all three. It goes without saying for sovereignty, since sovereignty is first of all exercised within the territory. But discipline involves a spatial division, and I think security does too, and the different treatment of space by sovereignty, discipline, and security, is precisely what I want to talk about.

We will take again a series of examples. Obviously, I will look at the case of towns. In the seventeenth century, and at the beginning of the eighteenth century, the town still had a particular legal and administrative definition that isolated it and marked it out quite specifically in comparison with other areas and spaces of the territory. Second, the town was typically confined within a tight, walled space, which had much more than just a military function. Finally, it was much more economically and socially mixed than the countryside.

Now, in the seventeenth and eighteenth centuries this gave rise to a number of problems linked to the development of administrative states, for which the juridical specificity of the town posed a difficult problem. Second, the growth of trade, and then, in the eighteenth century, urban demography, raised the problem of the town's compression and enclosure within its walls. The development of military techniques raised the same problem. Finally, the need for permanent economic exchanges between the town and its immediately surrounding countryside, for means of subsistence, and with more distant areas, for its commercial relations, [ensured that] the enclosure and hemming in of the town [also] posed a problem. Broadly speaking, what was at issue in the eighteenth century was the question of the spatial, juridical, administrative, and economic opening up of the town: resituating the town in a space of circulation. On this point I refer you to a study that, since it was made by an historian, is extraordinarily complete and perfect: it is Jean-Claude Perrot's study of Caen in the eighteenth century, in which he shows that the problem of the town was essentially and fundamentally a problem of circulation.[11]

Take a text from the middle of the seventeenth century, *La Métropolitée*, written by someone called Alexandre Le Maître.[12] Alexandre Le Maître was a protestant who left France before the Edict of Nantes and who became, and the term is significant, general engineer of the Elector of Brandenburg. He dedicated *La Métropolitée* to the king of Sweden, the book being published in Amsterdam. All of this—protestant, Prussia, Sweden, Amsterdam—is not entirely without significance. The problem of *La Métropolitée* is: Must a country have a capital city, and in what should it consist? Le Maître's analysis is the following: The state, he says, actually comprises three elements, three orders, three estates even; the peasants, the artisans, and what he calls the third order, or the third estate, which is, oddly, the sovereign and the officers in his service.[13] The state must be like an edifice in relation to these three elements. The peasants, of course, are the foundations of the edifice, in the ground, under the ground, unseen but ensuring the solidity of the whole. The common parts, the service quarters of the edifice, are, of course, the artisans. As for the noble quarters, the living and reception areas, these are the sovereign's officers and the sovereign himself.[14] On the basis of this architectural metaphor, the territory must also comprise foundations, common parts, and noble parts. The foundations will be the countryside, and it goes without saying that all the peasants, and only peasants, must live in the countryside. Second, all the artisans, and only artisans, must live in the small towns. Finally, the sovereign, his officers, and those artisans and tradesmen who are indispensable to the functioning of the court and the sovereign's entourage, must live in the capital.[15] Le Maître sees the relationship between the capital and the rest of the territory in different ways. It must be a geometrical relationship in the sense that a good country is one that, in short, must have the form of a circle, and the capital must be right at the center of the circle.[16] A capital at the end of an elongated and irregular territory would not be able to exercise all its necessary functions. In fact, this is where the second, aesthetic and symbolic, relationship between the capital and the territory appears. The capital must be the ornament of the territory.[17] But this must also be a political relationship in that the decrees and laws must be implanted in the territory [in such a way] that no tiny corner of the realm escapes this general network of the sovereign's orders and laws.[18] The capital must also have a moral role, and diffuse throughout the territory all that is necessary to command people with regard to their conduct and ways of doing things.[19] The capital must give the example of good morals.[20] The capital must be the place where the holy orators are the best and are best heard,[21] and it must also be the site of academies, since they must give birth to the sciences and truth that is to be disseminated in the rest of the country.[22] Finally, there is an economic role: the capital must be the site of luxury so that it is a point of attraction for products coming from other countries,[23] and at the same time, through trade, it must be the distribution point of manufactured articles and products, etcetera.[24]

We can leave aside the strictly utopian aspect of this project. All the same, I think it is interesting because it seems to me that this is essentially a definition of the town, a reflection on the town, in terms of sovereignty. That is to say, the primary relationship is essentially that of sovereignty to the territory, and this serves as the schema, the grid, for arriving at an understanding of what a capital city should be and how it can and should function. Moreover, it is interesting how, through this grid of sovereignty, a number of specifically urban functions appear as the fundamental problem: economic, moral, and administrative functions, etcetera. In short, the interesting thing is that Le Maître dreams of connecting the political effectiveness of sovereignty to a spatial distribution. A good sovereign, be it a collective or individual sovereign, is someone well placed within a territory, and a territory that is well policed in terms of its obedience to the sovereign is a territory that has a good spatial layout. All of this, this idea of the political effectiveness of sovereignty, is linked to the idea of an intensity of circulations: circulation of ideas, of wills, and of orders, and also commercial circulation. Ultimately, what is involved for Le Maître—and this is both an old idea, since it is a matter of sovereignty, and a modern idea, since it involves circulation—is the superimposition of the state of sovereignty, the territorial state, and the commercial state. It involves fastening them together and mutually reinforcing them. I don't need to tell you that in this period, and in this region of Europe, we are right in the middle of mercantilism, or rather of cameralism,[25] that is to say, of the problem of how to ensure maximum economic development through commerce within a rigid system of sovereignty. In short, Le Maître's problem is how to ensure a well "capitalized" state, that is to say, a state well organized around a capital as the seat of sovereignty and the central point of political and commercial circulation. Since Le Maître was the general engineer of the Elector of Brandenburg, we could see here a filiation between the idea of a well "capitalized"* state or province, and Fichte's famous closed commercial state,[26] that is to say the evolution from cameralist mercantilism to the German national economy of the beginning of the nineteenth century. In any case, in this text the town-capital is thought in terms of relations of sovereignty exercised over a territory.

I will now take another example. I could just as well have taken it from the same part of the world, that is to say, from the region of Northern Europe extending from Holland to Sweden, around the North Sea and the Baltic Sea, which was so important in the thought and political theory of the seventeenth century. Kristiania,[27] and Gothenburg[28] in Sweden would be examples. I will take an example from France. A whole series of artificial towns were built, some in Northern Europe and some here in France, in the time of Louis XIII and Louis XIV. Take a little town called Richelieu, which was built from scratch on the borders of Touraine and Poitou.[29] A town is built where previously there was nothing. How is it built? The famous form of the Roman camp is used, which, along with the military institution, was being reutilized at this time as a fundamental instrument of discipline. The form of the Roman camp was revived at the end of the

---

* The inverted commas appear in the manuscript for the lectures, p. 8.

sixteenth and the beginning of the seventeenth century, precisely in protestant countries—and hence the importance of all this in Northern Europe—along with the exercises, the subdivision of troops, and collective and individual controls in the major undertaking of the disciplinarization of the army.[30] Now, whether it is Kristiania, Gothenburg, or Richelieu, the form of the camp is used. The form is interesting. Actually, in the previous case, Le Maître's *La Métropolitée*, the layout of the town was basically thought of in terms of the most general, overall category of the territory. One tried to think about the town through a macrocosm, since the state itself was thought of as an edifice. In short, the interplay of macrocosm and microcosm ran through the problematic of the relationship between town, sovereignty, and territory. In the case of towns constructed in the form of the camp, we can say that the town is not thought of on the basis of the larger territory, but on the basis of a smaller, geometrical figure, which is a kind of architectural module, namely the square or rectangle, which is in turn subdivided into other squares or rectangles.

It should be stressed straightaway that, in the case of Richelieu at least, as in well-planned camps and good architecture, this figure, this module, is not merely the application of a principle of symmetry. Certainly, there is an axis of symmetry, but it is framed by and functions thanks to well-calculated dissymetries. In a town like Richelieu, for example, there is a central street that divides the rectangle of the town into two rectangles, and then there are other streets, some parallel to and others at right angles to the central street, but at different distances from each other, some closer, others further apart, such that the town is subdivided into rectangles of different sizes, going from the larger to the smaller. The biggest rectangles, that is to say, where the streets are furthest apart, are at one end of the town, and the smallest, with the tighter grid, are at the other. People must live on the side of the biggest rectangles, where the grid is widest and the roads are broad. Conversely, trades, artisans, and shops, as well as markets, must be situated where the grid is much tighter. And this commercial area—we can see how the problem of circulation [. . .*], more trade means more circulation and

---

* Incomplete sentence.

the greater need for streets and the possibility of cutting across them, etcetera—is flanked by the church on one side, and by the market on the other. There will be two categories of houses in the residential area where the rectangles are bigger. On the one hand, there are those over-looking the main thoroughfare, or the streets parallel to it, which will be houses with a number of floors, two I think, and attics. On the other hand, the smaller houses with only one floor will be in the streets perpendicular to the main street: difference of social status, of wealth, etcetera. In this simple schema I think we find again the disciplinary treatment of multiplicities in space, that is to say, [the] constitution of an empty, closed space within which artificial multiplicities are to be constructed and organized according to the triple principle of hierarchy, precise communication of relations of power, and functional effects specific to this distribution, for example, ensuring trade, housing, and so on. For Le Maître and his *Métropolitée* what was involved was "capitalizing" a territory. Here, it is a case of structuring a space. Discipline belongs to the order of construction (in the broad sense of construction).

And now, the third example. This will be the real development of towns that actually existed in the eighteenth century. There are a whole series of them. I will take the example of Nantes, which was studied in 1932, I think, by someone called Pierre Lelièvre, who provided different construction and development plans for Nantes.[31] It is an important town because, on the one hand, it is undergoing commercial development, and, on the other, its relations with England meant that the English model was employed. The problem of Nantes is, of course, getting rid of overcrowding, making room for new economic and administrative functions, dealing with relationships with the surrounding countryside, and finally allowing for growth. I will skip the nonetheless delightful project of an architect called Rousseau who had the idea of reconstructing Nantes around a sort of boulevard-promenade in the form of a heart.[32] It's true that he is dreaming, but the project is nonetheless significant. We can see that the problem was circulation, that is to say, for the town to be a perfect agent of circulation it had to have the form of a heart that ensures the circulation of blood. It's laughable, but after all, at the end of the eighteenth century, with Boullée,[33]

Ledoux,[34] and others, architecture still often functions according to such principles, the good form having to be the support of the exact exercise of the function. In actual fact, the projects realized at Nantes did not have the form of the heart. They were projects, and one project in particular put forward by someone called Vigné de Vigny,[35] in which there was no question of reconstructing everything, or of imposing a symbolic form that could ensure the function, but projects in which something precise and concrete was at stake.

It involved cutting routes through the town, and streets wide enough to ensure four functions. First, hygiene, ventilation, opening up all kinds of pockets where morbid miasmas accumulated in crowded quarters, where dwellings were too densely packed. So, there was a hygienic function. Second, ensuring trade within the town. Third, connecting up this network of streets to external roads in such a way that goods from outside can arrive or be dispatched, but without giving up the requirements of customs control. And finally, an important problem for towns in the eighteenth century was allowing for surveillance, since the suppression of city walls made necessary by economic development meant that one could no longer close towns in the evening or closely supervise daily comings and goings, so that the insecurity of the towns was increased by the influx of the floating population of beggars, vagrants, delinquents, criminals, thieves, murderers, and so on, who might come, as everyone knows, from the country [...*]. In other words, it was a matter of organizing circulation, eliminating its dangerous elements, making a division between good and bad circulation, and maximizing the good circulation by diminishing the bad. It was therefore also a matter of planning access to the outside, mainly for the town's consumption and for its trade with the outside. An axis of circulation with Paris was organized, the Erdre was developed along which wood for heating was bought from Brittany. Finally, Vigny's redevelopment plan involved responding to what is, paradoxically, a fairly new and fundamental question of how to integrate possible future developments within a present plan. This was the problem of the commerce of the

---

* Some inaudible words.

quays and what was not yet called the docks. The town is seen as developing: a number of things, events and elements, will arrive or occur. What must be done to meet something that is not exactly known in advance? The idea is quite simply to use the banks of the Loire to build the longest, largest possible quays. But the more the town is elongated, the more one loses the benefit of that kind of clear, coherent grid of subdivisions. Will it be possible to administer a town of such considerable extent, and will circulation be able to take place if the town is indefinitely elongated? Vigny's project was to construct quays along one side of the Loire, allow a quarter to develop, and then to construct bridges over the Loire, resting on islands, and to enable another quarter to develop starting from these bridges, a quarter opposite the first, so that the balance between the two banks of the Loire would avoid the indefinite elongation of one of its sides.

The details of the planned development are not important. I think the plan is quite important, or anyway significant, for a number of reasons. First, there is no longer any question of construction within an empty or emptied space, as in the case of those, let's say, disciplinary towns such as Richelieu, Kristiania, and suchlike. Discipline works in an empty, artificial space that is to be completely constructed. Security will rely on a number of material givens. It will, of course, work on site with the flows of water, islands, air, and so forth. Thus it works on a given. [Second], this given will not be reconstructed to arrive at a point of perfection, as in a disciplinary town. It is simply a matter of maximizing the positive elements, for which one provides the best possible circulation, and of minimizing what is risky and inconvenient, like theft and disease, while knowing that they will never be completely suppressed. One will therefore work not only on natural givens, but also on quantities that can be relatively, but never wholly reduced, and, since they can never be nullified, one works on probabilities. Third, these town developments try to organize elements that are justified by their poly-functionality. What is a good street? A good street is one in which there is, of course, a circulation of what are called miasmas, and so diseases, and the street will have to be managed according to this necessary, although hardly desirable role. Merchandise will be taken down the street, in which there will also be shops. Thieves and possibly rioters will also be able to move down the street. Therefore all these different functions of the town, some positive and others negative, will have to be built into the plan. Finally, the fourth important point, is that one works on the future, that is to say, the town will not be conceived or planned according to a static perception that would ensure the perfection of the function there and then, but will open onto a future that is not exactly controllable, not precisely measured or measurable, and a good town plan takes into account precisely what might happen. In short, I think we can speak here of a technique that is basically organized by reference to the problem of security, that is to say, at bottom, to the problem of the series. An indefinite series of mobile elements: circulation, x number of carts, x number of passers-by, x number of thieves, x number of miasmas, and so on.* An indefinite series of events that will occur: so many boats will berth, so many carts will arrive, and so on. And equally an indefinite series of accumulating units: how many inhabitants, how many houses, and so on. I think the management of these series that, because they are open series can only be controlled by an estimate of probabilities, is pretty much the essential characteristic of the mechanism of security.

To summarize all this, let's say then that sovereignty capitalizes a territory, raising the major problem of the seat of government, whereas discipline structures a space and addresses the essential problem of a hierarchical and functional distribution of elements, and security will try to plan a milieu in terms of events or series of events or possible elements, of series that will have to be regulated within a multivalent and transformable framework. The specific space of security refers then to a series of possible events; it refers to the temporal and the uncertain, which have to be inserted within a given space. The space in which a series of uncertain elements unfold is, I think, roughly what one can call the milieu. As you well know, the milieu is a notion that only appears in biology with Lamarck.[36] However, it is a notion that already existed in physics and was employed by Newton and the Newtonians.[37] What is the milieu? It is what is needed to account for action at a distance of one

---

* Foucault repeats: An indefinite series of mobile elements.

body on another. It is therefore the medium of an action and the element in which it circulates.[38] It is therefore the problem of circulation and causality that is at stake in this notion of milieu. So, I think the architects, the town planners, the first town planners of the eighteenth century, did not actually employ the notion of milieu, since, as far as I have been able to see, it is never employed to designate towns or planned spaces. On the other hand, if the notion does not exist, I would say that the technical schema of this notion of milieu, the kind of—how to put it?—pragmatic structure which marks it out in advance is present in the way in which the town planners try to reflect and modify urban space. The apparatuses of security work, fabricate, organize, and plan a milieu even before the notion was formed and isolated. The milieu, then, will be that in which circulation is carried out. The milieu is a set of natural givens—rivers, marshes, hills—and a set of artificial givens—an agglomeration of individuals, of houses, etcetera. The milieu is a certain number of combined, overall effects bearing on all who live in it. It is an element in which a circular link is produced between effects and causes, since an effect from one point of view will be a cause from another. For example, more overcrowding will mean more miasmas, and so more disease. More disease will obviously mean more deaths. More deaths will mean more cadavers, and consequently more miasmas, and so on. So it is this phenomenon of circulation of causes and effects that is targeted through the milieu. Finally, the milieu appears as a field of intervention in which, instead of affecting individuals as a set of legal subjects capable of voluntary actions—which would be the case of sovereignty—and instead of affecting them as a multiplicity of organisms, of bodies capable of performances, and of required performances—as in discipline—one tries to affect, precisely, a population. I mean a multiplicity of individuals who are and fundamentally and essentially only exist biologically bound to the materiality within which they live. What one tries to reach through this milieu, is precisely the conjunction of a series of events produced by these individuals, populations, and groups, and quasi natural events which occur around them.

It seems to me that with this technical problem posed by the town—but this is only one example, there are many others and we will come back to this—we see the sudden emergence of the problem of the "naturalness"* of the human species within an artificial milieu. It seems to me that this sudden emergence of the naturalness of the species within the political artifice of a power relation is something fundamental, and to finish I will just refer to a text from someone who was no doubt the first great theorist of what we could call biopolitics, biopower. He speaks of it in connection with something different, the birth rate, which was of course one of the major issues, but very quickly we see the notion of milieu appear here as the target of intervention for power, and which appears to me completely different from the juridical notion of sovereignty and the territory, as well as from disciplinary space. [With regard to] this idea of an artificial and natural milieu, in which artifice functions as a nature in relation to a population that, while being woven from social and political relations, also functions as a species, we find in Moheau's *Recherches sur la population*[39] a statement of this kind: "It is up to the government to change the air temperature and to improve the climate; a direction given to stagnant water, forests planted or burnt down, mountains destroyed by time or by the continual cultivation of their surface, create a new soil and a new climate. The effect of time, of occupation of the land, and of vicissitudes in the physical domain, is such that the most healthy districts become morbific."[40] He refers to a verse in Virgil concerning wine freezing in barrels, and says: Will we ever see wine freeze in barrels today in Italy?[41] Well, if there has been so much change, it is not the climate that has changed; the political and economic interventions of government have altered the course of things to the point that nature itself has constituted for man, I was going to say another milieu, except that the word "milieu" does not appear in Moheau. In conclusion he says: "If the unknown principle that forms the character and the mind is the outcome of the climate, the regime, the customs, and the habit of certain actions, we can say that sovereigns, by wise laws, by useful establishments, through the

---

* In inverted commas in the manuscript, p. 16. Foucault writes: "To say that this is the sudden emergence of the 'naturalness' of the human species in the field of techniques of power would be excessive. But what [before] then appeared above all in the form of need, insufficiency, or weakness, illness, now appears as the intersection between a multiplicity of living individuals working and coexisting with each other in a set of material elements that act on them and on which they act in turn."

inconvenience of taxes, and the freedom resulting from their suppression, in short by their example, govern the physical and moral existence of their subjects. Perhaps one day we will be able to call on these means to give whatever hue we wish to morality and the national spirit."[42] You can see that we again encounter the problem of the sovereign here, but the sovereign is no longer someone who exercises his power over a territory on the basis of a geographical localization of his political sovereignty. The sovereign deals with a nature, or rather with the perpetual conjunction, the perpetual intrication of a geographical, climatic, and physical milieu with the human species insofar as it has a body and a soul, a physical and a moral existence; and the sovereign will be someone who will have to exercise power at that point of connection where nature, in the sense of physical elements, interferes with nature in the sense of the nature of the human species, at that point of articulation where the milieu becomes the determining factor of nature. This is where the sovereign will have to intervene, and if he wants to change the human species, Moheau says, it will be by acting on the milieu. I think we have here one of the axes, one of the fundamental elements in this deployment of mechanisms of security, that is to say, not yet the appearance of a notion of milieu, but the appearance of a project, a political technique that will be addressed to the milieu.

1. See, *"Il faut défendre la société." Cours au Collège de France, 1975-1976*, eds. M. Bertani and A. Fontana (Paris: Gallimard-Le Seuil, 1997) p. 216; English translation by David Macey, *"Society Must Be Defended." Lectures at the Collège de France, 1975-1976*, eds. M. Bertani and A. Fontana, English series ed. Arnold Davidson (New York: Picador, 2003) p. 243: "What does this new technology of power, this biopolitics, this bio-power that is beginning to establish itself, involve?"; *La Volonté de savoir* (Paris: Gallimard, 1976) p. 184; English translation by Robert Hurley, *The History of Sexuality, vol. 1: An Introduction* (New York: Pantheon, 1978) p. 140.

2. These phrases should be brought together with those made by Foucault at the end of the same year in his long interview with D. Trombadori, on his disappointment, returning from Tunisia, with the theoretical polemics of the movements of the extreme left following May 1968: "We have spoken of the hyper-Marxism in France, of the explosion of theories, of anathemas, and the fragmentation into little groups. This was precisely the exact opposite, the reverse, the contrary of what had fascinated me in Tunisia [with the student riots of March 1968]. Perhaps this explains the way in which I tried to approach things from that time, standing back from those infinite discussions, that hyper-Marxization [...] I tried to do things that involved a personal commitment that was physical and real, and which would pose problems in concrete, precise, and definite terms in a given situation." "Entretien avec Michel Foucault" in Michel Foucault, *Dits et Écrits, 1954-1988*, in 4 volumes, eds. D. Defert and F. Ewald, with the assistance of Jacques Lagrange (Paris: Gallimard, 1994). vol. 4, p. 80; English translation (of Italian version) by R. James Goldstein and James Cascaito, as *Remarks on Marx. Conversations with Duccio Trombadori* (New York: Semiotext(e), 1991) p. 139. On the link between this conception of commitment and Foucault's observations on the events in Iran in October and November 1978, see the "Course Context" below, pp. 375-376.

3. See the lecture of 1 February 1978 (below p. 108) in which Foucault notes that a more accurate title for the course would have been "a history of 'governmentality.'" The lecture has appeared separately as: "La 'gouvernementalité'," *Dits et Écrits*, vol. 3, p. 655; English translation (from Italian) by Rosi Braidotti, revised by Colin Gordon, "Governmentality" in Michel Foucault, *Essential Works of Foucault, 1954-1984, vol. 3: Power*, ed. James D. Faubion, trans. Robert Hurley and others (New York: The New Press, 2000) p. 219.

4. See, Michel Foucault, *Surveiller et Punir. Naissance de la prison* (Paris: Gallimard, 1975); English translation by A. Sheridan, *Discipline and Punish. Birth of the Prison* (London: Allen Lane and New York: Pantheon, 1977).

5. Foucault distinguishes security mechanisms from disciplinary mechanisms for the first time in the final lecture (17 March 1976) of the 1975-1976 course *"Il faut défendre la société"* p. 219; *"Society Must Be Defended"* p. 246. However, the concept of "security" is not taken up in *La Volonté de savoir* where, in opposition to the disciplines, which are exercised on the bodies of individuals, Foucault prefers to speak of "regulatory controls" that take charge of the health and life of populations (p. 183; *History of Sexuality, vol. 1*, p. 145).

6. On these new penal forms in American neo-liberal discourse, see *Naissance de la biopolitique. Cours au Collège de France, 1978-1979*, ed. M. Senellart (Paris: Gallimard-Le Seuil, 2004), lecture of 21 March 1979, p. 245 *sq.*

7. These are the judicial statistics published every year, since 1825, by the Minister of Justice. See, A.-M. Guerry, *Essai sur la statistique morale de la France* (Paris: Crochard, 1833) p. 5: "The first authentic documents published on the administration of criminal justice in France only go back to 1825. (...) Today, every quarter the public prosecutors send to the Minister of Justice accounts of the criminal or correctional matters brought before the courts of their jurisdiction. These reports drafted according to uniform models, so that they present only positive and comparable results, are carefully examined at the Ministry, checked against each other in their various parts, and the analysis of them at the end of the year forms the *General account of the administration of criminal justice.*"

8. See, *Histoire de la folie à l'âge classique* (Paris: Gallimard, 1972) pp. 13-16; (abridged) English translation by R. Howard, *Madness and Civilization* (New York: Random House, 1965 and London: Tavistock, 1967) pp. 3-7; *Les Anormaux. Cours au Collège de France,*

1974-1975, eds. V. Marchetti and A. Salomoni (Paris: Gallimard-Le Seuil, 1999) lecture of 15 January 1975, pp. 40-41; English translation by Graham Burchell, *Abnormal*. *Lectures at the Collège de France 1974-1975*, English series ed. Arnold I. Davidson (New York: Picador, 2003) pp. 43-44; *Surveillir et Punir*, pp. 197-200; *Discipline and Punish*, pp. 198-200.

9. *Les Anormaux*, pp. 41-45; *Abnormal*, pp. 44-48; *Surveillir et Punir*, pp. 197-200; *Discipline and Punish*, pp. 198-200.

10. Foucault returns to this theme in the lecture of 25 January, p. 57 *sq*. On the paper given by A.-M. Moulin in the seminar, see below, lecture of 25 January, note 2.

11. Jean-Claude Perrot, *Genèse d'une ville moderne. Caen au XVIII siècle*, University of Lille thesis, 1974, 2 volumes (Paris-The Hague: Mouton, 1975). Michèle Perrot refers to this book in her postface to Jeremy Bentham, *La Panoptique* (Paris: Belfond, 1977): "L'inspecteur Bentham" p. 189 and p. 208. Foucault contributed to this work in his interview with J.-P. Barrou and M. Perrot, "L'œil du pouvoir"; English translation by Colin Gordon, "The eye of power" in Michel Foucault, *Power/Knowledge*. *Selected Interviews and Other Writings 1972-1977*, ed. Colin Gordon (Brighton: The Harvester Press, 1980).

12. Alexandre Le Maître (Quartermaster and General Engineer for S.A.E. Brandenburg), *La Métropolitée, ou De l'établissement des villes Capitales, de leur Utilité passive & active, de l'Union de leurs parties & de leur anatomie, de leur commerce, etc.* (Amsterdam: B. Bockholt, 1682, reprinted, Éditions d'histoire sociale, 1973).

13. *La Métropolitée*, ch. X, pp. 22-24: "Of the three Estates that should be distinguished in a Province; their function and their qualities."

14. Ibid.

15. Ibid. ch. XI, pp. 25-27: "As in the Countryside or villages there are only peasants, the Artisans must be distributed in the small towns, having only in the big Towns, or the Capital cities, the leading people and those Artisans who are absolutely necessary."

16. Ibid. ch. XVIII, pp. 51-54: "The size that the country, the Province, must have; or the district in which one will situate the Capital city."

17. Ibid. ch. IV, pp. 11-12: "The Capital city does not only possess the useful, but also the honor, not only of wealth, but also of rank and glory."

18. Ibid. ch. XVIII, p. 52: "[The Capital] will be the political heart giving life and movement to the entire body of the Province, through the fundamental principle of the ruling science, which forms a whole of several parts, without destroying them."

19. Ibid. ch. XXIII, p. 69: "It is (...) necessary that the Prince's Eye casts its rays over the movements of his people, that he observes their conduct, can note them closely, and that his presence alone keeps vice, disorder, and injustice in check. This can best be achieved only through the union of the parts in the *Métropolitaine*."

20. Ibid. pp. 67-72: "The Sovereign's presence is necessary in his Estates where the greatest commerce takes place, to be witness of the actions and trade of his Subjects, to keep them in equity and fear, to be seen by the people, and be like their Sun, which illuminates them by his presence."

21. Ibid. ch. XXVIII, pp. 79-87: "In the *Métropolitaine* the professors and preachers must be famous orators."

22. Ibid. ch. XVIII, pp. 76-79: "There are powerful reasons for the foundation of Academies in the Capital cities, or *Métropolitaines*."

23. Ibid. ch. XXVII, pp. 72-73: "The Capital, having the greatest consumption, must also be the site of commerce."

24. Ibid. ch. V, pp. 12-13: "The essential and final cause of the Capital city can only be public Utility, and to this end it must be the most opulent."

25. Cameralistics, or cameral science (*Cameralwissenschaft*), designates the science of finance and administration that developed from the seventeenth century in the "chambers" of princes, the organs of planning and bureaucratic control that will gradually replace traditional councils. In 1727 the discipline obtained the right to enter the universities of Halle and Frankfurt an der Oder, becoming an object of teaching for future state functionaries. See, M. Stolleis, *Geschichte des öffenntlichen Rechts in Deutschland, 1600-1800* (Munich: C.H. Beck, 1988) vol. 1; French translation by M. Senellart, *Histoire du droit public en Allemagne, 1600-1800* (Paris: PUF, 1998) pp. 556-558. The creation of chairs in *Oeconomie-Policey und Cammersachen* was the result of the desire of Frederick

William I of Prussia to modernize the administration of his realm and to add the study of economics to that of law in the training of future functionaries. A.W. Small summarizes the thought of the cameralists in the following way: "To the cameralists the central problem of science was the problem of the state. To them the object of all social theory was to show how the welfare of the state might be secured. They see in the welfare of the state the source of all other welfare. Their key to the welfare of the state was revenue to supply the needs of the state. Their whole social theory radiated from the central task of furnishing the state with ready means." A.W. Small, *The Cameralists: The pioneers of German social polity* (Chicago: The University of Chicago Press, and London: T. Fisher Unwin, 1909) p. viii. On mercantilism, see below lecture of 5 April, p. 337.

26. Johann Gottlieb Fichte (1762-1814), *Der geschlossene Handelsstaat* (Tübingen: Gotta); French translation by J. Gibelin, *L'État commercial fermé* (Paris: Librairie générale de droit et de jurisprudence, 1930; new edition with introduction and notes by D. Schulthess, Lausanne: L'Âge d'homme, 1980). In this work dedicated to the Minister of Finance, the economist Struensee, Fichte protests against both liberalism and mercantilism, that he accuses of impoverishing the majority of the population, and opposes to them the model of a contractually founded "State of reason" controlling production and planning the allocation of resources.

27. Kristiania, or Christiania: old name for the capital of Norway (today Oslo, since 1925), rebaptized by the king Christian IV in 1624 after the fire that destroyed the town. Foucault always says "Kristiania."

28. Founded by Gustave II Adolphe in 1619, the town was constructed on the model of Dutch cities because of marshy terrain.

29. Situated south east of Chinon (Indre-et-Loire), on the side of the Mable, the town was built by Cardinal Richelieu, who demolished the old hovels, on the site of the patrimonial domain, in order to reconstruct it, starting in 1631, on a regular plan outlined by Jacques Lemercier (1585-1654). The work was directed by the latter's brother, Pierre Lemercier, who provided the plans of the chateau and the town in its entirety.

30. The Roman camp (*castra*) was a square or a rectangle subdivided into different squares and rectangles. On the Roman *castramétation* (or art of establishing armies in the camps), see the very detailed note in the *Nouvelle Larousse illustré*, vol. 2, 1899, p. 431. On the revival of this model, at the beginning of the seventeenth century, as a condition of military discipline and ideal form for "'observatories' of human multiplicities"—"The camp is the diagram of a power that acts by means of general visibility"—see *Surveillir et Punir*, pp. 173-174, and fig. 7; *Discipline and Punish*, pp. 170-172. The bibliography cited by Foucault is mainly French, with the exception of the treatise of J.J. von Wallhausen, *L'Art militaire pour l'infanterie* (Francker: Uldrick Balck, 1615) translation by J.Th. de Bry of *Kriegskunst zu Fusz* (cited p. 172, n. 1; trans. p. 171, n. 1, p. 316). Wallhausen was the first director of the *Schola militaris* founded at Siegen in Holland by Jean de Nassau in 1616. On the characteristics of the Dutch "military revolution" and its spread in Germany and Sweden, see the rich bibliography given by G. Parker in *The Thirty Years' War* (London: Routledge and Kegan Paul, 1984); French translation, *La Guerre de Trente Ans*, trans. A. Charpentier (Paris: Aubier, 1987).

31. P. Lelièvre, *L'Urbanisme et l'Architecture à Nantes au XVIII*, doctoral thesis (Nantes: Librairie Durance, 1942).

32. *Plan de la ville de Nantes et des projets d'embellissement; présentés par M. Rousseau, architecte,* 1760, with this dedication: "Illustrissimo atque ornatissimo D.D. Armando Duplessis de Richelieu, duci Aiguillon, pari Franciae." See P. Lelièvre, *L'Urbanisme*, pp. 89-90. "The only interest of such an utterly arbitrary imagination is its disconcerting fantasy." The plan of Nantes, with its heart form, is reproduced on the verso of p. 87. See also p. 205: "Is it absurd to suppose that the idea of 'circulation' could have inspired this anatomical figure criss-crossed with arteries? We go no further with this analogy confined to the schematic and stylized contour of the organ of circulation."

33. Étienne-Louis Boullée (1728-1799), French architect and designer. He preached the adoption of geometrical forms inspired by nature (see his projects for a Museum, a National Library, and a capital Palace for a great empire, or a tomb in honor of Newton, in J. Starobinski, *1789, Les Emblèmes de la raison* (Paris: Flammarion, 1973) pp. 62-67; English translation by Barbara Bray, *1789, The Emblems of Reason* (Charlottesville: University Press of Virginia, 1982) pp. 77-81.

34. Claude-Nicolas Ledoux (1736-1806), French architect and designer, author of *L'Architecture considérée sous le rapport de l'art, des mœurs et de la législation* (Paris: published by the author, 1804).

35. *Plan de la ville de Nantes, avec les changements et les accroissements par le sieur de Vigny, architecte du Roy et da la Société de Londres, intendant des bâtiments de Mgr le duc d'Orleans.–Fait par nous, architecte du Roy, à Paris, le 8 avril 1755*. See, P. Lelièvre, *L'Urbanisme*, pp. 84-89; see also the study devoted to him by L. Delattre, in *Bulletin de la Société archéologique et historique de Nantes* (1911) vol. LII, pp. 75-108.

36. Jean-Baptiste Monet de Lamarck (1744-1829), author of *Philosophie zoologique* (1809); see, George Canguilhem, "Le vivant et son milieu" in his *La Connaissance de la vie* (Paris: Vrin, 1965, p. 131): "Lamarck always speaks of milieus, in the plural, and by this expression he understands fluids like water, air, and light. When Larmarck wants to designate the set of actions exerted on a living being from outside, that is to say what we today call the milieu, he never says the milieu, but always, 'influential circumstances (*circonstances influentes*).' Consequently, for Lamarck, circumstances is a genus of which climate, location and milieu are the species."

37. See G. Canguilhem, ibid. pp. 129-130: "Considered historically, the notion and word milieu were imported into biology from mechanics in the second half of the eighteenth century. The mechanical notion, but not the word, appears with Isaac Newton, and the word, with its mechanical meaning, is present in D'Alembert's and Diderot's *Encyclopedia*. (...) The French mechanists called milieu what Newton understood by fluid, the type, if not the archetype, of which in Newton's physics is the ether." Canguilhem explains that it is through the intermediary of Buffon that Lamarck borrows from Newton the explanatory model of an organic reaction through the action of a milieu. On the emergence of the idea of milieu in the second half of the eighteenth century, through the notion of "penetrating forces (*forces pénétrantes*)" (Buffon), see Foucault, *Histoire de la folie*, pp. 385-392; *Madness and Civilization*, pp. 212-220. ("A negative notion (...) which appeared in the eighteenth century to explain variations and diseases rather than adaptations and convergences. As if these 'penetrating forces' formed the other, negative side of what will subsequently become the positive notion of milieu" p. 385 [this passage is omitted from the English translation].)

38. G. Canguilhem, *Connaisance de la vie*, p. 130: "The problem to be solved for mechanics in Newton's time was that of the action at a distance of distinct physical individuals."

39. Moheau, *Recherches et Considérations sur la population de la France* (Paris: Moutard, 1778; republished with an introduction and analytical table by R. Gonnard, Paris: P. Geuthner, "Collection des économistes et des réformateurs sociaux de la France," 1912; republished, annotated by E. Vilquin, Paris: INED/PUF, 1994). According to J.-Cl. Perrot, *Une histoire intellectuelle de l'économie politique, XVIIᵉ-XVIIIᵉ siècle* (Paris: Éd. de l'EHESS, "Civilisations et Sociétés," 1992) pp. 175-176 this book constitutes "the true 'spirit of the laws' of demography of the eighteenth century." The identity of the author ("Moheau," with no forename) has been the subject of controversy since the book was published. Behind the pseudonym, some have identified the baron Auget de Montyon, successively the *intendant* of Riom, Aix, and La Rochelle. It now appears to have been established that it was written by Jean-Baptiste Moheau, who was his secretary until 1775, and who died on the guillotine in 1794. See R. Le Mée, "Jean-Baptiste Moheau (1745-1794) et les *Recherches*... Un auteur énigmatique ou mythique?" in Moheau, *Recherches et Conidérations*, 1994 edition, pp. 313-365.

40. *Recherches et Considérations*, Book II, part 2, ch. XVII: "The influence of Government on all the causes that can determine the progress or the loss of population," 1778 edition, pp. 154-155; 1912 edition, pp. 291-292; and 1994 edition, p. 307. The sentence is completed with "(...) and no relationship at all is found between the degrees of cold and warmth in the same countries in different epochs."

41. Ibid.: "Virgil astonishes us when he speaks of wine freezing in barrels in Italy; certainly the Roman countryside was not what it is today, of the time of the Romans who improve the habitation of all the places that they submit to their domination" (1778, p. 155; 1912, p. 292; 1994, p. 307).

42. Ibid. p. 157; p. 293; pp. 307-308.

two

18 JANUARY 1978

*General features of the apparatuses of security (II): relationship to the event: the art of governing and treatment of the uncertain (*l'aléatoire*).* ∼ *The problem of scarcity (*la disette*) in the seventeenth and eighteenth centuries.* ∼ *From the mercantilists to the physiocrats.* ∼ *Differences between apparatuses of security and disciplinary mechanisms in ways of dealing with the event.* ∼ *The new governmental rationality and the emergence of "population."* ∼ *Conclusion on liberalism: liberty as ideology and technique of government.*

WE HAVE BEGUN TO study a part of what could be called the form, simply the form, of some of the important apparatuses of security. Last week I said a few words about the relations between the territory and the milieu. Through some texts, but also through some projects and real town plans in the eighteenth century, I tried to show you how the territorial sovereign became an architect of the disciplined space, but also, and almost at the same time, the regulator of a milieu, which involved not so much establishing limits and frontiers, or fixing locations, as, above all and essentially, making possible, guaranteeing, and ensuring circulations: the circulation of people, merchandise, and air, etcetera. To tell the truth, this structuring function of space and territory is not something new to the eighteenth century. After all, what sovereign has not wanted to build a bridge over the Bosphorus or move mountains?*

---

* In place of this phrase there are three names: Nimrod, Xerxes, Yu Kong.

Again, we need to know the general economy of power within which this project and structuring of space and territory is situated. Does it involve marking out a territory or conquering it? Is it a question of disciplining subjects, making them produce wealth, or is it a question of constituting something like a milieu of life, existence, and work for a population?

I would now like to resume this analysis of apparatuses of security with another example in order to pick out something that is no longer the relationship to space and the milieu, but the relationship of government to the event.* I will take straightaway the example of scarcity. As defined by an economist of the second half of the eighteenth century, about whom we shall have to speak shortly, dearth or scarcity (*la disette*), which is not exactly famine, is "the *present* insufficiency of the amount of grain necessary for a nation's subsistence."[1] That is to say, scarcity is a state of food shortage that has the property of engendering a process that renews it and, in the absence of another mechanism halting it, tends to extend it and make it more acute. It is a state of scarcity, in fact, that raises prices. And, of course, the more prices rise, the more those possessing scarce objects are inclined to hoard them and monopolize them so that prices rise even more, and this occurs precisely when the most basic needs of the population are not being met. For government, for the French government in the seventeenth and eighteenth centuries at any rate, scarcity is exactly the type of event to be avoided for a number of obvious reasons. I recall only what is clearest and, for the government, most dramatic. The immediate and most perceptible consequences of scarcity appear first of all, of course, in the urban milieu, since it is always relatively less difficult to withstand food shortage—relatively—in a rural milieu. Anyway, it appears in the urban milieu and, with great probability, almost immediately leads to revolt. Now after the experiences of the seventeenth century, urban revolt is, for sure, the major thing for government to avoid. So it is the scourge of the population on one side, and, on the other, catastrophe, crisis if you like, for government.

---

* Foucault breaks off here to make a comment about the tape recorders: "I am not against any apparatuses, but I don't know—forgive me for saying so—I'm just a bit allergic . . ."

Generally speaking, if we simply want to situate the kind of philosophical-political horizon that is the background against which scarcity appears, I would say that, like all scourges, [it] is taken up in the two categories by which political thought tried to think about inevitable misfortune. [First], the old Greco-Latin concept of fortune, of bad fortune. After all, food shortage is misfortune in the pure state, since its most immediate, most apparent factor is bad weather, drought, ice, excessive humidity, or anyway everything outside of one's control. And you know that bad fortune is not just the recognition of impotence. It is also a political, moral, and cosmological concept that, from Antiquity to Machiavelli, and ultimately to Napoleon, was not just a way of thinking about political misfortune philosophically, but also a schema of behavior in the political field. The politician in Greco-Roman antiquity, in the Middle Ages, and up to Napoleon, and perhaps even beyond, operates with bad fortune, and Machiavelli showed that there is a series of rules of the game in relation to bad fortune.[2] So, scarcity appears as one of the fundamental forms of bad fortune for a people and for a sovereign.

Second, the other philosophical and moral framework for thinking about scarcity is man's evil nature. This is linked to phenomena of scarcity insofar as scarcity is seen as a punishment.[3] However, in a more concrete and precise way, man's evil nature will have an influence on scarcity by figuring as one of its sources, inasmuch as men's greed—their need to earn, their desire to earn even more, their egoism—causes the phenomena of hoarding, monopolization, and withholding merchandise, which intensify the phenomena of scarcity.[4] The juridical-moral concept of evil human nature, of fallen nature, and the cosmological-political concept of fortune are the two general frameworks for thinking about scarcity.

In a much more precise and institutional sense, what action will be taken against scarcity in the techniques of government for the political and economic management of a society like that of seventeenth and eighteenth century France? For a long time scarcity was countered by a system that I would say was both juridical and political, a system of legality and a system of regulations, which was basically intended to prevent food shortage, that is to say, not just to halt it or eradicate it when it occurs, but literally to prevent it and ensure that it cannot take place at all. This is a juridical and disciplinary system that, concretely, takes the classical forms you are familiar with: price control, and especially control of the right to store; the prohibition of hoarding with the consequent necessity of immediate sale; limits on export,* the prohibition of sending grain abroad with, as the simple restriction on this, the limitation of the extent of land under cultivation, because if the cultivation of grains is too extensive, the surplus from this abundance will result in a collapse of prices, so that the peasants will not break even. So, there are a series of controls on prices, storing, export, and cultivation. This is also a system of constraints, since people will be compelled to sow at least a minimal amount, or the cultivation of this or that crop will be prohibited. For example, people will be required to pull up vines so as to force them to sow grain. Merchants will be forced to sell before waiting for prices to rise and a system of supervision established after the first harvests will enable stocks to be checked and prevent circulation between different countries and provinces. The maritime transport of grain will be prohibited. What is the aim of the organization of this juridical and disciplinary system of controls, constraint, and permanent supervision? The objective is of course for grain to be sold at the lowest possible price so that peasants make the smallest possible profit and townspeople can thus be fed at the lowest possible cost and are consequently paid the lowest possible wages. As you know, regulation by lowering the selling price of grain, peasant profit, the purchase cost for the people, and wages, is the great political principle that was developed, organized, and systematized throughout what we can call the mercantilist period, if by mercantilism we understand those techniques of government and management of the economy that practically dominated Europe from the start of the seventeenth until the start of the eighteenth century. This system is basically an anti-scarcity system, since what are these prohibitions and obstacles intended to achieve? On the one hand, all the grain will be put on the market as quickly as possible. [With grain] put on the market as quickly as possible, the phenomenon of scarcity will be

---

* M.F.: import

relatively limited, and what is more the prohibition of export,* hoarding, and price rises will prevent the thing that is most feared: prices racing out of control in the towns and the people in revolt.

This anti-scarcity system is basically focused on a possible event, an event that could take place, and which one tries to prevent before it becomes reality. We don't need to insist on the well-known failures of this system that have been noted a thousand times. These failures consist, in the first place, in that the first effect of keeping the price of grain as low as possible is ruin for the peasants, even where grain is abundant, or rather especially when grain is abundant, since plenty of grain means a tendency for prices to fall, and finally the price† of wheat for the peasants will be lower than the investment they have made to produce it; so, profit tends towards zero, and peasant earnings may even fall below the cost of production. The second consequence will be that the peasants will inevitably be forced to sow little because they have drawn insufficient profit from their harvest, even in years when there is plenty of wheat. Obviously, the less profit they make, the less they will be able to sow. The immediate consequence of this poor sowing is that the smallest climatic irregularity, the least climatic fluctuation—a bit too dry, a bit too cold, a bit too humid—and the quantity of wheat will fall below the norms of what is required to feed the population and shortages will appear in the following year. So, the politics of the lowest possible price exposes one to the risk of shortages at every moment, and so to precisely the scourge it sought to avoid.

[Please excuse] the highly schematic and somewhat dry character of all this. What happens in the eighteenth century, when there is the attempt to unblock this system? Everyone knows, and it is undeniably correct, that it is within a new conception of the economy, and maybe even within the founding act of economic thought and economic analysis represented by physiocratic doctrine, that freedom of commerce and of the circulation of grain began to be laid down as the fundamental principle of economic government.[5] This is the theoretical consequence, or rather the practical consequence of a fundamental theoretical principle of the physiocrats, namely that the only, or just about the only net profit

---

* M.F.: import
† M.F.: cost price

(*produit net*) that can be obtained in a nation is the peasant profit (*produit*).[6] In truth, it is undeniable that the free circulation of grain really was one of the logical theoretical consequences of the physiocratic system. That physiocratic thought itself, the influence of the physiocrats, imposed this on the French government in the years 1754 to 1764 is also true in part, although it is of course not sufficient. But I think it would be wrong in fact to consider this form of political choice, this program of economic regulation as no more than the practical consequence of an economic theory. It seems to me that it would be fairly easy to show that what happened, and what led to the great edicts or "declarations" of the years 1754-1764, maybe through and thanks to the relay, the support of the physiocrats and their theory, was in reality a complete change, or rather a phase in a major change in the techniques of government and an element in the deployment of what I will call apparatuses of security. In other words, you could read the principle of the free circulation of grain as the consequence of a theoretical field and also as an episode in the mutation of technologies of power and an episode in the installment of this technique of apparatuses of security that seems to me to be one of the typical features of modern societies.

One thing is true at any rate, which is that some governments thought, well before the physiocrats, that the free circulation of grain was not only a better source of profit, but also a much better mechanism of security against the scourge of scarcity. This, anyway, was the idea that English politicians had very early, from the end of the seventeenth century, since in 1689 they developed, and got Parliament to adopt, a legislative package that imposed or accepted the free circulation and commerce of grain, with, however, a support and a corrective. The first was freedom of export, which, in prosperous periods, and so in periods of plenty and good harvests, should make it possible to support the price of wheat, of grain in general, that was in danger of collapse due to this very abundance. Not only would export be permitted to support the price, but it would be helped by a system of subsidies, establishing a stimulant to this freedom.[7] Second, to avoid an excessive import of wheat into England in favorable periods, import taxes were established so that the surplus of abundance coming from imported products did not cause prices to fall.[8] So, the good price was obtained by these two series of measures.

This English model of 1689 will be the great hobby-horse of theorists of the economy, but also of those who, in one way or another, had an administrative, political, or economic responsibility in eighteenth century France.[9] And then, this was the thirty years during which the problem of the freedom of grain was one of the major political and theoretical problems in eighteenth century France. There were three phases: first, a phase of polemics, before 1754 when the old juridical-disciplinary system was in full operation with its negative consequences; second, 1754, and the adoption of a regime in France more or less modeled on that of England, and so a relative freedom, but corrected and supported as it were[10]; then from 1754 to 1764, with the arrival of the physiocrats on the theoretical and political scene,[11] but only at this point, there is a series of polemics in favor of the freedom of grain, and finally the edicts of May 1763[12] and August 1764[13] that, apart from a few restrictions, establish almost complete freedom of grain. A victory then for the physiocrats,[14] but also for all those who had supported the cause, like Gournay's disciples for example,[15] without being physiocrats directly. So in 1764 there is freedom of grain. Unfortunately, the edict is made in August 1764. In September of the same year, some weeks later, bad harvests in Guyenne cause prices to rise at an astronomical rate, and already there is a question of whether one should not go back on this freedom of grain. The result of this is a third campaign of discussions, this time defensive, in which the physiocrats, and those who support the same principles without being physiocrats, will have to defend the freedom for which they had obtained almost complete recognition in 1764.[16]

So, there is a whole package of texts, projects, programs, and explanations. I will refer to just one of these, which is both the most schematic and clearest and was, moreover, very important. It is a text dating from 1763 called *Lettre d'un négociant sur la nature du commerce des grains*. It was written by someone called Louis-Paul Abeille,[17] who is important both for the influence his text exerted and by the fact that, as a disciple of Gournay, he actually combined most of the physiocratic positions. He represents, then, a [sort] of pivotal position in the economic thought of that time. So, [if we take] this text as a reference—but it simply exemplifies a whole series of other texts in which I think we could find the same principles, with some modifications, as those that Abeille puts to work in his *Lettre d'un négociant*—basically, what does it do? Once again, we could consider Abeille's text within an analysis of a theoretical field by trying to discover its guiding principles, the rules of formation of its concepts, its theoretical elements, and so on, and we would no doubt have to go back over the theory of the net profit.[18] But I do not want to look at it in this way, and instead of considering it in terms of an archeology of knowledge, I would like to consider it from the perspective of a genealogy of technologies of power. I think we could reconstruct the function of the text, not according to the rules of formation of its concepts, but according to its objectives, the strategies that govern it, and the program of political action it proposes.

I think the first thing to appear would be that, for Abeille, the physiocrats, and for those who thought in the same way, the very thing that in the juridical-disciplinary system was to be avoided at any cost, even before it occurs, namely scarcity and high prices, was basically not an evil at all. And it should not be thought of as an evil, that is to say, it should be considered as a phenomenon that, in the first place, is natural, and so consequently, secondly, neither good nor evil. It is what it is. This rejection of analysis in terms of morality, or simply in terms of good and evil, of things to avoid or not to avoid, implies that the main target will not be the market, that is to say the selling price of the product according to supply and demand. Analysis will move back a notch, as it were, or no doubt several notches, and take as its object, not so much the phenomenon of scarcity-dearness, but what I will call the history of grain from the moment it is put in the ground, with what this implies in terms of work, time passed, and fields sown—of cost, consequently. What happens to grain between seeding and the time when it will have finally produced all the profits that it can? The unit of analysis will no longer be the market therefore, with its effects of scarcity-dearness, but grain with everything that may happen to it and will happen to it naturally, as it were, according to a mechanism and laws in which the quality of the land, the care with which it is cultivated, the climatic conditions of dryness, heat, and humidity, and finally the abundance or scarcity, of course, and its marketing and so forth, will also play a part. The event on which one tries to get a hold will be the reality of grain, much more than the obsessive fear of scarcity. On this reality of grain, on its entire history, and with all the fluctuations and events that may, as it were, change its history or divert it from an ideal line, one will try to graft an apparatus so that fluctuations of abundance and cheapness, of scarcity and dearness, are not prevented in advance or prohibited by a juridical and disciplinary system that, by preventing from this and constraining to that, seek to avoid them. Abeille, the physiocrats, and the economic theorists of the eighteenth century, tried to arrive at an apparatus (*dispositif*) for arranging things so that, by connecting up with the very reality of these fluctuations, and by establishing a series of connections with other elements of reality, the phenomenon is gradually compensated for, checked, finally limited, and, in the final degree, canceled out, without it being prevented or losing any of its reality. In other words, by working within the reality of fluctuations between abundance/scarcity, dearness/cheapness, and not by trying to prevent it in advance, an apparatus is installed, which is, I think, precisely an apparatus of security and no longer a juridical-disciplinary system.

What will this apparatus consist of that is connected up to a reality that is, as it were, acknowledged and accepted, neither valued nor depreciated, but simply recognized as nature? What is the apparatus that, connecting up to the reality of fluctuation, will permit its regulation? We know what it is and I will just summarize. First, authorizing and even favoring a rise in the price of grain, instead of aiming for the lowest possible price. A rise in the price of grain may be ensured by employing slightly artificial means, like the English method of subsidizing exports or putting pressure on imports by taxing them. But there is also the liberal solution around which the physiocrats rally—I will come back to this word "liberal" in a moment—which consists in [suppressing] the prohibition of hoarding so that people are able to store their grain and hold it back, as and when they wish, and as much as they want, thereby relieving the market when there is abundance. The prohibition of export will also be suppressed, so that people will have the right to send their grain abroad when they want, or when external prices are favorable to them. Here again there is a new relief, a new clearing of the market, with the result that, when there is abundance, the possibility of storing on the one hand, and the permission to export on the other, will maintain prices. In this way we will get a result that is paradoxical with regard to the previous system, which was impossible and not looked for, namely abundance and relatively high prices at the same time. It so happened that Abeille, for example, and others at the same time, were writing when a series of good harvests between 1762 and 1764 made it possible to use this good example.

So, prices rise even in periods of abundance. What will this rise in prices give us? First, we will get an extension of cultivation. Having been well remunerated by the previous harvest, the peasants will be able to have more grain for sowing and to pay the costs necessary for extensive sowing and good cultivation. As a result, after this well-paid first harvest, there will be a much greater chance of the following harvest being good. And even if the climatic conditions have not been very favorable, more fields sown and better cultivation will compensate for these poor conditions and there will be a much greater chance of avoiding shortages. But anyway, what will happen as a result of extending cultivation in this way? The first increase in prices will not be followed by a similar increase and of the same proportion the following year, because it is obvious that the greater the abundance, the more prices will tend to fall, so that a necessary consequence of a first price rise will be a reduced risk of shortages and a falling off in prices or a slowing down of their increase. The probability of scarcity and the probability of price increases will [therefore] be diminished proportionally.

On the basis of this schema in which two consecutive years have been in fact favorable, the first very favorable with price increase, the second sufficiently favorable—with, in these cases, the consequent slowing down of the increase in prices—let us now assume that the second year is one of pure and unequivocal scarcity. This is how Abeille reasons. At bottom, he says, what is scarcity? It is never the pure and simple total absence of the means of subsistence necessary for a population, because if that were the case the population would quite simply die. It would die in days or weeks, he says, and we have never seen a population disappear due to the absence of food. Scarcity, he says, is "a chimera."[19] This means that, however small the harvest, there is always enough to feed the population for ten, eight, or six months, that is to say, the population will be able to live for a certain time at least. Of course, the scarcity will become apparent very early. The phenomena to be dealt with will not occur only at the end of the sixth month when the people no longer have anything to eat. From the start, as soon as one sees that there is going to be a poor harvest, a number of phenomena and fluctuations will occur.

And, straightaway, prices will rise, which the sellers have immediately calculated, saying to themselves: Last year, with such a quantity of wheat, for every sack of wheat, every *setier** of wheat, I got such a sum; this year I have half as much wheat, so I will sell every *setier* at double the old price. And prices rise on the market. But, says Abeille, allow this increase to take place. This is not what is important. As soon as people know that commerce is free—free within the country and free also between one country and another—they know full well that at the end of six months imports will relieve the country's lack. Now those who have wheat and can sell it, and who would be tempted to hold it back until the famous sixth month when prices should race out of control, do not know how much wheat will be able to come from the exporting countries and so how much will arrive in the country. In short, they do not know whether there will be so much wheat in the sixth month that the price will collapse. So, not knowing if prices will fall, instead of waiting for the sixth month they will prefer to profit from the start, from the first notice of a bad harvest, from the small sudden rise in prices that occurs. They will throw their grain onto the market and there will not be the phenomena seen in periods of regulatory controls, the type of behavior in which people hold back their wheat as soon as there is notice of a poor harvest. So, the sudden price rise will take place, but it will very quickly slow down or reach a ceiling inasmuch as everyone will give their wheat in view of the possibly massive exports that will arrive after six months.[20]

There will be the same phenomenon on the side of the foreign exporters, that is to say, if they learn of a shortage in France, the English, German, and other exporters will want to profit from the price rise. But they do not know how much wheat will enter France in this way. They do not know how much wheat their competitors have available, or when, at what point, and in what proportions they will bring their wheat, and so they do not know themselves if they might not make a bad deal by waiting too long. Hence their tendency to profit from the immediate price rise to launch their wheat on the foreign market and, as a result, wheat

---

* Old measure of capacity; G.B.

will flow in to the same extent as it is scarce.[21] This means that the phenomenon of scarcity-dearness induced by a poor harvest at a given moment will lead, through a series of mechanisms that are both collective and individual (we will come back to this shortly), to ways by which this phenomenon is gradually corrected, compensated for, checked, and finally nullified. It means that it is the rise that produces the fall. The scarcity will be nullified on the basis of the reality of the movement that leads to scarcity. So, with a technique like that of the pure and simple freedom of grain circulation, there cannot be any scarcity. As Abeille says, scarcity is a chimera.

This conception of market mechanisms is not just the analysis of what happens. It is at once an analysis of what happens and a program for what should happen. Now there are certain necessary conditions for making this analysis-program. You will have been able to identify them as we have proceeded. The analysis* had to be considerably broadened. First, it had to be broadened on the side of production. Once again, we must consider not only the market, but also the entire cycle from the initial actions of producers up to the final profit. The farmer's profit is part of this whole that must be taken into account, dealt with, or allowed to develop. Second, the analysis was broadened on the side of the market, for it is not just a matter of considering one market, the internal French market; the world grain market must be taken into account and connected with every market on which grain may be put on sale. It is not enough therefore to think about the people who buy and sell on a given market in France. We must think of all the grain that may be put on sale on all the markets in all the countries of the world. So, the analysis must be broadened on the side of production and on the side of the market. [Third,] the analysis must be broadened also on the side of the protagonists, inasmuch as instead of subjecting them to obligatory rules, we will try to identify, understand, and know how and why they act, what calculation they make when, faced with a price rise, they hold back grain, and what calculation they make when, on the other hand, they know there is freedom, when they do not know how much

---

* Foucault adds: the taking into consideration

grain will arrive, when they hesitate so as to know whether there will be a rise or fall in the amount of grain. All of this, that is to say that completely concrete element of the behavior of *homo œconomicus*, must also be taken into account. In other words, it is an economics, or a political-economic analysis, that integrates the moment of production, the world market, and, finally, the economic behavior of the population, of producers and consumers.

This is not all. This new way of conceiving and programming things implies something very important in relation to the event of scarcity, in relation to this event-scourge of scarcity-dearness with its possible consequence, revolt. At bottom, the scourge, scarcity, as it was conceived until then, was both an individual and collective phenomenon, and in the same way that people suffered hunger, so entire populations and the nation suffered hunger, and it was precisely this kind of immediate solidarity, the massiveness of the event, that constituted its character as a scourge. Now what will happen in the analysis that I have just been making and in the political-economic program that is its immediate result? Basically, the event will be split into two levels. Actually, we can say that thanks to these measures, or rather thanks to the suppression of the juridical-disciplinary straitjacket that framed the grain trade, all in all, as Abeille said, scarcity becomes a chimera. It seems that, on the one hand, it cannot exist and that, when it existed, far from it being a reality, a natural reality as it were, it was no more than the aberrant result of a number of artificial measures that were themselves aberrant. So, from now on, no more scarcity. There will no longer be any scarcity as a scourge, there will no longer be this phenomenon of scarcity, of massive, individual and collective hunger that advances absolutely in step and without discontinuity, as it were, in individuals and in the population in general. Now, there will be no more food shortage at the level of the population. But what does this mean? It means that we succeed in curbing scarcity by a sort of "*laisser-faire*," a certain "freedom of movement (*laisser-passer*),"[22] a sort "[*laisser*]-*aller*," in the sense of "letting things take their course." It means allowing prices to rise where their tendency is to rise. We allow the phenomenon of dearness-scarcity to be produced and develop on such and such a market, on a whole series of markets, and this phenomenon, this reality which we have allowed to develop, will itself entail precisely its own self-curbing and self-regulation. So there will no longer be any scarcity in general, on condition that for a whole series of people, in a whole series of markets, there was some scarcity, some dearness, some difficulty in buying wheat, and consequently some hunger, and it may well be that some people die of hunger after all. But by letting these people die of hunger one will be able to make scarcity a chimera and prevent it occurring in this massive form of the scourge typical of the previous systems. Thus, the scarcity-event is split. The scarcity-scourge disappears, but scarcity that causes the death of individuals not only does not disappear, it must not disappear.

We have two levels of phenomena therefore. Not a level of the collective and a level of the individual, for after all it is not just an individual who will die, or at any rate suffer, from this scarcity. But we will have an absolutely fundamental caesura between a level that is pertinent for the government's economic-political action, and this is the level of the population, and a different level, which will be that of the series, the multiplicity of individuals, who will not be pertinent, or rather who will only be pertinent to the extent that, properly managed, maintained, and encouraged, it will make possible what one wants to obtain at the level that is pertinent. The multiplicity of individuals is no longer pertinent, the population is. This caesura within what constituted the totality of the subjects or inhabitants of a kingdom is not a real caesura. There is not a real distinction between some and others. But within the system of knowledge-power, within the economic technology and management, there is this break between the pertinent level of the population and the level that is not pertinent, or that is simply instrumental. The final objective is the population. The population is pertinent as the objective, and individuals, the series of individuals, are no longer pertinent as the objective, but simply as the instrument, relay, or condition for obtaining something at the level of the population.

I will try to return to this fundamental caesura next week, because I think that all that is involved in this notion of population appears very clearly here. The population as a political subject, as a new collective subject absolutely foreign to the juridical and political thought of earlier centuries is appearing here in its complexity, with its caesuras. You can already see it appearing as an object, that is to say as that on which and towards which mechanisms are directed in order to have a particular effect on it, as well as a subject, since it is called upon to conduct itself in such and such a fashion. The population covers the old notion of people, but in such a way that in comparison with that notion the phenomena are spread out, some levels being retained while others are not, or are considered differently. In order just to point out the thing I will come back to next week, because it is fundamental, I would like— and I will finish here with Abeille's text—to indicate that we find a very curious distinction in this text. Because, when Abeille has finished his analysis, he nonetheless has a scruple. He says: That's all very well. The scarcity-scourge is a chimera, agreed. It is a chimera when, in fact, people conduct themselves properly, that is to say when some accept to endure scarcity-dearness, others sell their wheat at the right moment, that is to say very soon, and when exporters send their product when prices begin to rise. This is all very well and we have here, I don't say the good elements of the population, but behavior such that every individual functions well as a member, as an element of the thing we want to manage in the best way possible, namely the population. They really act as members of the population. But suppose that precisely in a given market, in a given town, instead of waiting, instead of putting up with scarcity, instead of accepting costly grain, instead of accepting consequently to buy little, instead of accepting hunger, and instead of [waiting]* for the wheat to arrive in sufficient quantity so that prices fall or the rise is at any rate attenuated or slows down a bit, suppose that instead of all this, on the one hand, the people throw themselves on the supplies, that they even seize them without paying, and, on the other hand, suppose some people hold back grain irrationally on the basis of bad calculations, and everything jams. The result will be revolt on the one hand, and monopolization on the other, or monopolization and revolt. Fine, says Abeille, all this proves that these people do not really belong to the population. What are they? Well, this is the people. The people comprise those who conduct themselves in relation to the management of the population, at the level of the population, as if they were not part of the population as

---

* Word omitted by Foucault.

a collective subject-object, as if they put themselves outside of it, and consequently the people are those who, refusing to be the population, disrupt the system.[23]

We have here an analysis that is barely sketched by Abeille, but which is very important to the extent that, on the one hand, you can see that in some respects it is fairly close to, echoes, and has a kind of symmetry with the juridical thought that said, for example, that every individual who accepts the laws of his country is in the position of having subscribed to the social contract, accepting and renewing it at every moment by his own behavior, while, on the other hand, the person who violates the laws, breaks the social contract and thereby becomes a foreigner in his own land, consequently falling under the jurisdiction of the penal laws that punish him, exile him, and in a way kill him.[24] In relation to the collective subject created by the social contract, the delinquent really breaks the contract and falls outside the collective subject. Here too, in this sketch that begins to outline the notion of population, we see a division being made in which the people are generally speaking those who resist the regulation of the population, who try to elude the apparatus by which the population exists, is preserved, subsists, and subsists at an optimal level. This people/population opposition is very important. Next week I will try to show you how in fact, despite the apparent symmetry with the collective subject of the social contract, something completely different is involved, [that] the population-people relationship is not like the obedient subject/delinquent opposition, and that the population as a collective subject is very different from the collective subject constituted and created by the social contract.[25]

In any case, and to end with this, I would like to show you that, if we want a better grasp of the characteristics of the kind of apparatus (*dispositif*) that the physiocrats and eighteenth century economists conceived with regard to scarcity, then I think we should compare it to the disciplinary mechanisms found not only in earlier periods, but in the same period that apparatuses of security were being deployed. Basically, I think we can say this. Discipline is essentially centripetal. I mean that discipline functions to the extent that it isolates a space, that it determines a segment. Discipline concentrates, focuses, and encloses. The first action of discipline is in fact to circumscribe a space in which its power and the mechanisms of its power will function fully and without limit. And precisely, if we take again the example of the disciplinary police of grain as it existed until the middle of the eighteenth century, as set out in hundreds of pages in Delamare's *Traité de la police*,[26] we see that the disciplinary police of grain is in actual fact centripetal. It isolates, it concentrates, it encloses, it is protectionist, and it focuses essentially on action on the market or on the space of the market and what surrounds it. In contrast, you can see that the apparatuses of security, as I have tried to reconstruct them, have the constant tendency to expand; they are centrifugal. New elements are constantly being integrated: production, psychology, behavior, the ways of doing things of producers, buyers, consumers, importers, and exporters, and the world market. Security therefore involves organizing, or anyway allowing the development of ever-wider circuits.

There is a second major difference. By definition, discipline regulates everything. Discipline allows nothing to escape. Not only does it not allow things to run their course, its principle is that things, the smallest things, must not be abandoned to themselves. The smallest infraction of discipline must be taken up with all the more care for it being small. The apparatus of security, by contrast, as you have seen, "lets things happen."* Not that everything is left alone, but *laisser-faire* is indispensable at a certain level: allowing prices to rise, allowing scarcity to develop, and letting people go hungry so as to prevent something else happening, namely the introduction of the general scourge of scarcity. In other words, discipline does not deal with detail in the same way as apparatuses of security. The basic function of discipline is to prevent everything, even and above all the detail. The function of security is to rely on details that are not valued as good or evil in themselves, that are taken to be necessary, inevitable processes, as natural processes in the broad sense, and it relies on these details, which are what they are, but which are not considered to be pertinent in themselves, in order to obtain something that is considered to be pertinent in itself because situated at the level of the population.

---

* In inverted commas in the manuscript, p. 7: "Security 'laisse faire,' in the positive sense of the expression."

Third difference. How basically does discipline, like systems of legality, proceed? Well, they divide everything according to a code of the permitted and the forbidden. Then, within these two fields of the permitted and the forbidden, they specify and precisely define what is forbidden and what is permitted, or rather, what is obligatory. We can say that, within this general schema, the basic function of the system of legality, the system of law, is to give greater definition to things that are prohibited. Basically, what the law says is, don't do this, don't do that, stop doing that, and so on. So that the movement of specification and definition in a system of legality always focuses with greatest precision on what is to be prevented, what is to be prohibited. In other words, order is to be established by taking the point of view of disorder and analyzing it with increasing subtly, that is to say, order is what remains. Order is what remains when everything that is prohibited has in fact been prevented. I think this negative thought and technique is typical of a legal code.

The disciplinary mechanism also constantly codifies in terms of the permitted and forbidden, or rather the obligatory and the forbidden, which means that the point on which the disciplinary mechanism focuses is not so much the things one must not do as the things that must be done. A good discipline tells you what you must do at every moment. If we take monastic life as a model of disciplinary saturation, and monasticism was actually the point of departure and matrix of discipline, then what the monk does is entirely regulated, from morning to night and from night to morning, and the only thing undetermined is what is not said and what is therefore forbidden. In the system of the law, what is undetermined is what is permitted; in the system of disciplinary regulation, what is determined is what one must do, and consequently everything else, being undetermined, is prohibited.

It seems to me that in the apparatus of security, as I have presented it, what is involved is precisely not taking either the point of view of what is prevented or the point of view of what is obligatory, but standing back sufficiently so that one can grasp the point at which things are taking place, whether or not they are desirable. This means trying to grasp them at the level of their nature, or let's say—this word not having the meaning we now give it[27]—grasping them at the level of their effective reality. The mechanism of security works on the basis of this reality, by trying to use it as a support and make it function, make its components function in relation to each other. In other words, the law prohibits and discipline prescribes, and the essential function of security, without prohibiting or prescribing, but possibly making use of some instruments of prescription and prohibition, is to respond to a reality in such a way that this response cancels out the reality to which it responds—nullifies it, or limits, checks, or regulates it. I think this regulation within the element of reality is fundamental in apparatuses of security.

We could even say that the law works in the imaginary, since the law imagines and can only formulate all the things that could and must not be done by imagining them. It imagines the negative. Discipline works in a sphere that is, as it were, complementary to reality. Man is wicked, bad, and has evil thoughts and inclinations, etcetera. So, within the disciplinary space a complementary sphere of prescriptions and obligations is constituted that is all the more artificial and constraining as the nature of reality is tenacious and difficult to overcome. Finally security, unlike the law that works in the imaginary and discipline that works in a sphere complementary to reality, tries to work within reality, by getting the components of reality to work in relation to each other, thanks to and through a series of analyses and specific arrangements. So, I think we arrive at this idea that is essential for the thought and organization of modern political societies: that the task of politics is not to see to the establishment within men's behavior of the set of laws imposed by God or necessitated by men's evil nature. Politics has to work in the element of a reality that the physiocrats called, precisely, physics, when they said that economics is a physics.[28] When they say this, they are not aiming so much at materiality in the, if you like, post-Hegelian sense of the word "matter," but are actually aiming at the reality that is the only datum on which politics must act and with which it must act. Only ever situating oneself in this interplay of reality with itself is, I think, what the physiocrats, the economists, and eighteenth century political thought understood when it said that we remain in the domain of physics, and that to act in the political domain is still to act in the domain of nature.

And you can see at the same time that the postulate, I mean this fundamental principle that political technique must never get away from the interplay of reality with itself is profoundly linked to the general principle of what is called liberalism. The game of liberalism—not interfering, allowing free movement, letting things follow their course; *laisser faire, passer et aller*—basically and fundamentally means acting so that reality develops, goes its way, and follows its own course according to the laws, principles, and mechanisms of reality itself. So this problem of freedom, [to which] I hope to return next week,[29] can, I think, be considered and grasped in different ways. For sure, we can say—and I don't think it would be false, it cannot be false—that this ideology of freedom really was one of the conditions of development of modern or, if you like, capitalist forms of the economy. This is undeniable. The problem is whether, in the deployment of liberal measures like those we have seen concerning the grain trade, this was what was really aimed at or sought after in the first instance. In any case, there is a problem. Second, I said somewhere that we could not understand the establishment of liberal ideologies and a liberal politics in the eighteenth century without keeping in mind that the same eighteenth century, which made such a strong demand for freedoms, had all the same ballasted these freedoms with a disciplinary technique that, taking children, soldiers, and workers where they were, considerably restricted freedom and provided, as it were, guarantees for the exercise of this freedom.[30] Well, I think I was wrong. I was not completely wrong, of course, but, in short, it was not exactly this. I think something completely different is at stake. This is that this freedom, both ideology and technique of government, should in fact be understood within the mutations and transformations of technologies of power. More precisely and particularly, freedom is nothing else but the correlative of the deployment of apparatuses of security. An apparatus of security, in any case the one I have spoken about, cannot operate well except on condition that it is given freedom, in the modern sense [the word]* acquires in the eighteenth century: no longer the exemptions and privileges attached to a person, but the possibility of

---

* M.F.: that it

movement, change of place, and processes of circulation of both people and things. I think it is this freedom of circulation, in the broad sense of the term, it is in terms of this option of circulation, that we should understand the word freedom, and understand it as one of the facets, aspects, or dimensions of the deployment of apparatuses of security.

The idea of a government of men that would think first of all and fundamentally of the nature of things and no longer of man's evil nature, the idea of an administration of things that would think before all else of men's freedom, of what they want to do, of what they have an interest in doing, and of what they think about doing, are all correlative elements. A physics of power, or a power thought of as physical action in the element of nature, and a power thought of as regulation that can only be carried out through and by reliance on the freedom of each, is, I think, something absolutely fundamental. It is not an ideology; it is not exactly, fundamentally, or primarily an ideology. First of all and above all it is a technology of power, or at any rate can be read in this sense. Next week I will try to finish what I have been saying about the general form of mechanisms of security by talking about procedures of normalization.

1. Louis-Paul Abeille, *Lettre d'un négociant sur la nature du commerce des grains* (1763, republished 1911) p. 91, emphasis in the original. On this work see below, note 17.

2. See, in particular, Niccolò Machiavelli, *Il Principe*, ch. 25: "*Quantum fortuna in rebus humanis possit et quomodo illi sit occurrendum*"; French translation by J.-L. Fournel and J.-Cl. Zancarini, *Le Prince* (Paris: PUF, 2000) p. 197; English translation by Russell Price, *The Prince*, eds. Quentin Skinner and Russell Price (Cambridge: Cambridge University Press, 1988) ch. 25: "How much power fortune has over human affairs, and how it should be resisted."

3. See, for example, N. Delamare, *Traité de la police* (Paris: M. Brunet, 1722, 2nd edn.) vol. II, pp. 294-295: "It is often one of those salutary scourges that God employs to punish us and make us return to our duty. (…) God often makes use of secondary causes in order to exercise his Justice here below (…). Also, whether they [scarcity, famine] are sent to us by heaven with a view to correcting us, or they arrive in the usual way by nature, or through men's malice, in appearance they are always the same, but always part of the order of Providence." On this author, see below note 26.

4. On this "greed" imputed to monopolizing merchants who, according to an explanation frequently invoked by the police and the people under the Ancien Régime, were the essential cause of shortages and sudden price rises, see, for example, N. Delamare, ibid. p. 390, with regard to the subsistence crisis of 1692-1693: " 'But,' reported Delamare, [although a blight in the Spring of 1692 had only ruined half of the prospective harvest] 'since only a pretext is necessary to determine evil-intentioned Merchants, always avid for gain, to exaggerate matters pertaining to dearth, they did not fail to profit from this one; they were immediately observed resuming their ordinary style and putting into use again all their bad practices for making the price of grain go up; associations, dashes into the Provinces, false rumors spread about, monopolies through purchases of all the grain, overbidding in the markets, downpayments on grain still uncut or in the barns and granaries, retention in the magazines; thus the whole commerce was reduced to a certain number among them who made themselves its master'," quoted by S.L. Kaplan, *Bread, Politics and Political Economy in the Reign of Louis XV* (The Hague: Martinus Nijhoff, 1976) vol. 1, pp. 55-56; French translation by M.-A. Revellat, *Le Pain, le Peuple et le Roi* (Paris: Perrin, "Pour l'histoire," 1986).

5. This notion is the guiding thread of Quesnay's thought, from the "Maximes de gouvernement économique," which concludes the article "Grains" (1757) in *F. Quesnay et la physiocratie* (INED, 1958) vol. 2, pp. 496-510, to the "Maximes générales du gouvernement économique d'un royaume agricole" (1767) ibid. pp. 949-976.

6. See, for example, F. Quesnay's article "Impôts" (1757) ibid. vol. 2, p. 582: "The annual wealth that constitutes the nations revenues are the products that, all expenses returned, form the profits drawn from landed property."

7. This is the system of the bonus to the outflow of grain on English vessels, so long as they did not exceed the prices fixed by law. See E. Depitre's introduction to Cl.-J. Herbert, *Essai sur la police générale des grains* (1755) (Paris: L. Geuthner, "Collection des économistes et des réformateurs sociaux de la France," 1910) p. xxxiii. This text is one of Foucault's documentary sources.

8. Prohibition of the import of foreign grains "so long as their current price is kept below that fixed by the statutes." See E. Depitre, ibid.

9. See, for example, Claude-Jacques Herbert (1700-1758), *Essai sur la police générale des grains* (London: 1753) pp. 44-45: "Based on the same principles [as Holland], England seems to have no fear of running out and to be on guard only against superfluity. For sixty years it has adopted a method that seems strange at first sight and which nonetheless, during this time, has preserved it from the unfortunate consequences of scarcity. There are customs duties only on inflow, there are none at all on outflow; quite the reverse, they encourage and reward it." There is a more detailed analysis in the second, 1755 edition, cited above in note 7, pp. 43-44. A disciple of Gournay, Herbert was one of the first, along with Boisguilbert (*Détail de la France* and *Traité de la nature, culture, commerce et intérêt des grains*, 1707), Dupin (*Mémoire sur les Bléds*, 1748) and Plummart de Dangeul (*Remarques sur les avantages et les désavantages de la France et de la Grande-Bretagne par rapport au commerce et aux autres sources de la Puissance des États*, 1754) to defend the principle of the free circulation of grain according to the English model. It is his treatise, however, that has the most profound influence. On the "innumerable

Memoirs, Essays, Treatises, Letters, Observations, Responses or Dialogues" that will strike public opinion on the question of grain and grain trade from the middle of the eighteenth century, see J. Letaconnoux, "La question des subsistances et du commerce des grains en France au XVIIIe siècle: travaux, sources et questions à traiter" in *Revue d'histoire moderne et contemporaine*, March 1907, an article to which Depitre refers in Herbert's *Essai sur la police générale des grains* (1755) p. vi.

10. Edict of 17 September 1754, signed by the general auditor), Moreau de Séchelles (but conceived by his predecessor Machault d'Arnouville), establishing the free circulation of grain and flour within the kingdom and authorizing export in years of plenty. The text was prepared by Vincent de Gournay (see below, note 15).

11. See G. Weulersse, *Le Mouvement physiocratie en France de 1756 à 1770*, in 2 volumes (Paris: Félix Alcan, 1910). For the years 1754-1764, vol. 1, pp. 44-90: "Les débuts de l'École."

12. See G.-F. Letrosne, *Discours sur l'état actuel de la magistrature et sur les causes de sa décadence* (1764) p. 68: "The Declaration of May 25 1763 razed these interior barriers erected by timidity, maintained for such a long time by habit, so favorable to monopoly, and so dear to the eyes of arbitrary authority. *But there still remains to take the most essential step*" (i.e., freedom of export, completely necessary to internal freedom), quoted in S.L. Kaplan, *Bread, Politics and Political Economy*, p. 141. Letrosne (or Le Trosne) is also the author of an opuscule on the free trade in grain (see below, note 14).

13. In actual fact, July 1764: "The May Declaration treated the grain trade as a national affair. The Edict of July 1764, by permitting the export of grain and flour, added an internal dimension," S.L. Kaplan, *Bread, Politics and Political Economy*, p. 93. For more details, see p. 94.

14. See, G. Weulersse, *Les Physiocrates* (Paris: G. Doin, 1931) p. 18: "It was [Trudaine de Montigny, the counselor of the general auditor Laverdy, who was] the true author of the liberating Edict of 1764, to whom did he appeal in its drafting? To Turgot, and even to Dupont, whose text ended up almost completely prevailing. It is through his care, no doubt, that Le Trosne's opuscule, *La liberté [du commerce] des grains toujours utile et jamais nuisible* [Paris: 1765] is widespread in the provinces and it is from there that the general auditor will draw weapons to defend his policy."

15. Vincent de Gournay (1712-1759), merchant at Cadiz for fifteen years, then Intendant of commerce (1751-1758), following various voyages in Europe, is the author, with his student Cliquot-Blervache, of *Considérations sur le commerce* (1758), numerous memoranda drafted for the Bureau du commerce, and a translation of Josiah Child's *A new discourse of trade* (Glasgow: 1693) as *Traités sur le commerce* (Amsterdam and Berlin: 1754). His commentary on Child could not be printed in his lifetime and the first edition was edited by Takumi Tsuda, *Traites sur le commerce de Child et Remarques inedites de Gourney* (Tokyo: Kinokuniya Company Ltd., 1983). "His influence on the development of economic thought in France [was] considerable thanks to his role in French commercial administration, his work directing economic studies at the Amiens Academy, and above all his unofficial role in the publication of economic works" A. Murphy, "Le développement des idées économiques en France (1750-1756)," *Revue d'histoire moderne et contemporaine*, vol. XXXIII, Oct.-Dec. 1986, p. 523. He contributed to the spread of Cantillon's ideas and ensured the success of the phrase (the paternity of which, since Dupont de Nemours, was often attributed to him): "*laissez faire, laissez passer.*" (On the origin of this phrase, see the note on d'Argenson in *Naissance de la biopolitique*, lecture of 10 January 1979, note 13). See Turgot, "Éloge de Vincent de Gournay," *Mercure de France*, August 1759; G. Schelle, *Vincent de Gournay* (Paris: Guillaumin, 1897); G. Weulersse, *Le Mouvement physiocratie*, vol. 1, pp. 58-60, and *Les Physiocrates*, p. xv; and the reference work, henceforth, by S. Meysonnier, *La Balance et l'Horloge. La genèse de la pensée libérale en France au XVIIIe siècle* (Montreuil: Les Éditions de la passion, 1989) pp. 168-236: "Vincent de Gournay or putting a new economic politics to work" (detailed biography pp. 168-187). Gournay's principal disciple, with Turgot, was Morellet; see G. Weulersse, *Le Mouvement physiocratie*, vol. 1, pp. 107-108, and *Les Physiocrates*, p. 15.

16. See E. Depitre's introduction to Herbert, *Essai sur la police générale des grains* (1755) p. viii: "(. . .) it is then a period of intense publication and lively polemics. But the position of the *Économistes* is not so good and they find themselves having to pass from the offensive to

the defensive; they reply in numbers to the *Dialogues* of the abbot Galiani [*Dialogues sur le commerce des blés*, London, 1770]."

17. Louis-Paul Abeille (1719-1807), *Lettre d'un négociant sur la nature du commerce des grains* (Marseille: 8 October 1763) republished in L.-P. Abeille, *Premiers Opuscules sur le commerce des grains: 1763-1764*, introduction and analytical table, Edgar Depitre (Paris: P. Geuthner, "Collection des économistes et des réformateurs sociaux de la France," 1911) pp. 89-103. When he published the text Abeille was secretary to the Society of Agriculture of Brittany, founded in 1756 with Gournay present. Won to physiocratic theses, he was named secretary of the Bureau of Commerce in 1768, but then distanced himself from the school. On his life and writings, see J.-M. Quérard, *La France littéraire, ou Dictionnaire bibliographique des savants, historiens et gens de lettres de la France*, vol. 1 (Paris: Didot, 1827) pp. 3-4; G. Weulersse, *Le Mouvement physiocratie*, vol. 1, pp. 187-188: on Abeille's break with the physiocrats in 1769 ("Abeille will later support Necker against Dupont"). He is also the author of *Réflexions sur la police des grains en France* (1764), republished by Depitre in *Premiers Opuscules*, pp. 104-126, and the pamphlet *Principes sur la liberté du commerce des grains* (Amsterdam-Paris: Desaint, 1768) appeared under his name and was the object of an immediate counter-attack by F. Véron de Forbonnais, "Examen des *Principes sur la liberté du commerce des grains*" in *Journal de l'agriculture*, August 1768, to which the physiocrat journal, *Éphémérides du citoyen*, will reply in December of the same year. See G. Weulersse, *Le Mouvement physiocratie*, vol. 1, bibliographic index, p. xxiv.

18. On this notion see G. Weulersse, ibid. vol. 1, pp. 261-268: "For the Physiocrats (...), there is no true income, any income strictly speaking, except the net income or net product, and by net product they understand the surplus of the total product, or gross product, over and above the costs of production."

19. L.-P. Abeille, *Lettre d'un négociant*, 1763 edn. p. 4; 1911 edn. p. 91: "Dearth, that is to say the actual insufficiency of the quantity of grain necessary for a nation's subsistence, is obviously a chimera. The harvest would have had to have been nil, in the strict sense of that term. We have not seen any People that hunger has made disappear from the face of the Earth, even in 1709." This conception is not specific to Abeille. See S.L. Kaplan, *Bread, Politics and Political Economy*, pp. 87-88: "... some of the men who dealt with subsistence problems in the eighteenth century, as well as some who wrote about them, were not convinced that these scarcitys were 'real.' They conceded that some so-called scarcitys resembled real scarcitys in their immediate consequences, but they contended that no genuine grain shortages were involved. The most vocal debunkers were the physiocrats, who were also the most determined critics of the police regime. 'Everyone knows that the one in Paris in 1725 was artificial,' wrote Lemercier de la Rivière. Roubaud concurred and added 1740 to the list of 'phony scarcitys.' Quesnay and Dupont both believed that most scarcitys were 'scarcitys of opinion' rather than 'real scarcitys.' Even Galiani, who reviled the physiocrats, claimed that 'scarcity is, for three quarters [of the cases], a malady of the imagination.'" In November 1764, although riots broke out at Caen, Cherbourg, and in the Dauphiné, the *Journal économique*, warmly welcoming the new era of liberal politics, mocked the "chimerical fear of falling into scarcity" (quoted in ibid. p. 187).

20. L.-P. Abeille, *Lettre d'un négociant*, 1763 edn. pp. 9-10; 1911 edn. p. 94: "It is true that liberty will not prevent the market price from being maintained; but far from increasing it, it could perhaps contribute to making it fall, because it will be continually threatened by foreign competition, and those who have competitors to fear must hasten to sell, so limiting their profit, so as not to run the risk of having to be satisfied with even less profit."

21. Ibid. 1763 edn. pp. 7-8; 1911 edn. p. 93: "I see clearly that interest will be sole motor of those foreign merchants. They hear there is a lack of wheat in a country; that consequently they sell easily and at a good price there; from that moment all the speculations are made: that is where the grain must be sent, and sent promptly, so as to profit from the time favorable to selling."

22. On the origin of the formula "Laissez faire, laissez passer," see above, note 15, on Vincent de Gournay, and *Naissance de la biopolitique*, lecture of 10 January 1979, note 13.

23. L.-P. Abeille, *Lettre d'un négociant*, 1763 edn. pp. 16-17; 1911 edn. pp. 98-99: "When need makes itself felt, that is to say, when the price of wheat rises too high, the people become restless. Why increase its anxiety by declaring the government's anxiety with prohibitions on export? (...) If one joins to this prohibition, which in itself is to say the least

pointless, orders to make declarations, etc., the evil could quickly reach its peak. Have we not everything to lose by embittering those who are governed against those who govern; and by making the people bold against those who daily provide it with the means of subsistence? This is to kindle a civil war between proprietors and the people." See also, 1763 edn. p. 23; 1911 edn. p. 203: "Nothing will be more harmful to them [nations] than to overturn the rights of property and to reduce those who are the strength of a state to be only the providers of a restless people, who envisage only what favors its greed and are incapable of judging what proprietors must do by what they can."

24. See, for example, J.-J. Rousseau, *Du contrat social*, 1762, II, 5, in *Œuvres complètes* (Paris: Gallimard, "Bibliothèque de la Pléiade," 1964) vol. 3, pp. 376; English translation by G.D.H. Cole, *The Social Contract* in *The Social Contract and Discourses* (London: J.M. Dent, 1993) p. 209: "Again, every malefactor, by attacking social rights, becomes on forfeit a rebel and a traitor to his country; by violating its laws he ceases to be a member of it; he even makes war upon it. In such a case the preservation of the State is inconsistent with his own, and one or the other must perish; in putting the guilty to death, we slay not so much the citizen as an enemy. The trial and judgment are the proofs that he has broken the social treaty, and is in consequence no longer a member of the State. Since, then, he has recognized himself to be such by living there, he must be removed by exile as a violator of the compact, or by death as a public enemy; and in such case the right of war is to kill the vanquished."

25. See below, lecture of 25 January, pp. 65-66 (3rd comment concerning the three examples of the town, food shortage, and the epidemic).

26. Nicolas Delamare (de La Mare) (1639-1723), *Traité de la police, où l'on trouvera l'histoire de son établissement, les fonctions et les prérogatives de ses magistrats, touts les loix et tous les règlemens qui la concernent*, 3 volumes, Paris, 1705-1719, vol. 4, by A.-L. Lecler du Brillet, 1738 (see below, lecture of 5 April, note 1 for more information). Delamare was superintendent (*commissaire*) at Châtelet from 1673 to 1710, under the lieutenancy of La Reynie—first magistrate responsible for the lieutenancy of police since its creation by the edict of March 1667—and then under d'Argenson. See P.-M. Bondois, "Le Commissaire N. Delamare and the *Traité de la police*" in *Revue d'histoire moderne*, 19, 1935, pp. 315-351. On the police of grain, see volume II, which, according to L.S. Kaplan, *Bread, Politics and Political Economy*, p. 2, note 1, is "the richest single source for questions of subsistence administration." (*Traité de la police*, vol. II, Book V: "On supplies"; see in particular the heading 5: "On the police of France, concerning the grain trade," pp. 55-89, and 4: "On the police of grain, and on that of Bread, in times of scarcity or famine," pp. 294-447.)

27. For a detailed analysis of the different senses of the word "nature" in the eighteenth century, see the classic work by J. Ehrard (who knew Foucault), *L'Idée de nature en France dans la première moitié du XVIIIᵉ siècle* (Paris: SEVPEN, 1963; republished, Paris: Albin Michel, "Bibliothèque de l'évolution de l'humanité," 1994).

28. See Dupont de Nemours, *Journal de l'agriculture, du commerce et des finances*, September 1765, preface: "[Political economy] is not a science of opinion in which one argues between likelihoods and probabilities. The study of physical laws, all of which are reduced to calculation, decide its least results" (quoted by G. Weulersse, *Le Mouvement physiocratique*, vol. 2, p. 122; Le Trosne, *Journal de l'agriculture*, June 1766, pp. 14-15: "Economic science, being nothing other than the application of the natural order to the government of societies, is as constant in its principles and as capable of demonstration as the most certain physical sciences" (quoted by Weulersse, ibid. note 3). The name "Physiocracy," which sums up this conception of economic government, appeared in 1768, with the anthology *Physiocratie ou Constitution naturelle du gouvernement le plus avantageux au genre humain*, published by Dupont de Nemours.

29. Foucault does not return to this subject in the following lecture.

30. See *Surveillir et Punir*, pp. 223-225; *Discipline and Punish*, pp. 221-224.

three

25 JANUARY 1978

General features of apparatuses of security (III). ∼ *Normation* (normation) *and normalization.* ∼ *The example of the epidemic* (*smallpox*) *and inoculation campaigns in the eighteenth century.* ∼ *The emergence of new notions: case, risk, danger, and crisis.* ∼ *The forms of normalization in discipline and in mechanisms of security.* ∼ *Deployment of a new political technology: the government of populations.* ∼ *The problem of population in the mercantilists and the physiocrats.* ∼ *The population as operator* (operateur) *of transformations in domains of knowledge: from the analysis of wealth to political economy, from natural history to biology, from general grammar to historical philology.*

IN PREVIOUS YEARS* I have tried to bring out something of what seems to me to be specific in disciplinary mechanisms in comparison with what we can call, broadly speaking, the system of the law. This year my plan was to bring out what is specific, particular, or different in the apparatuses of security when we compare them with the mechanisms of discipline I have tried to identify. So I wanted to emphasize the opposition, or at any rate the distinction, between security and discipline. The immediate, and immediately perceptible and visible, aim of this, of course, is to put a stop to repeated invocations of the master as well as to

---

* Foucault adds: in short, the previous years, one or two years, let's say those that have just passed

the monotonous assertion of power. Neither power nor master, neither Power nor the master, and neither one nor the other as God. In the first lecture I tried to show how the distinction between discipline and security could be grasped by considering the different ways in which they dealt with and planned spatial distributions. Last week I tried to show you how discipline and security each dealt differently with what we can call the event, and today, briefly, because I would like to get to the heart, and in a sense the end, of the problem, I would like to try to show you how each deals differently with what we call normalization.

You know better than me the unfortunate fate of this word "normalization." What is not normalization? I normalize, you normalize, and so on. However, let's try to identify some of the important points in all this. First, some people, prudently re-reading Kelsen in these times,[1] have noticed that he said, demonstrated, or wanted to show that there was and could not fail to be a fundamental relationship between the law and the norm, and that every system of law is related to a system of norms. I think it really is necessary to show that the relationship of the law to the norm does in fact indicate that there is something that we could call a normativity intrinsic to any legal imperative, but this normativity intrinsic to the law, perhaps founding the law, cannot be confused with what we are trying to pinpoint here under the name of procedures, processes, and techniques of normalization. I would even say instead that, if it is true that the law refers to a norm, and that the role and function of the law therefore—the very operation of the law—is to codify a norm, to carry out a codification in relation to the norm, the problem that I am trying to mark out is how techniques of normalization develop from and below a system of law, in its margins and maybe even against it.

Let's now take discipline. I think it is indisputable, or hardly disputable, that discipline normalizes. Again we must be clear about the specificity of disciplinary normalization. You will forgive me for summarizing very roughly and schematically things that have been said a thousand times. Discipline, of course, analyzes and breaks down; it breaks down individuals, places, time, movements, actions, and operations. It breaks them down into components such that they can be seen, on the one hand, and modified on the other. It is this famous disciplinary, analytical-practical grid that tries to establish the minimal elements of perception and the elements sufficient for modification. Second, discipline classifies the components thus identified according to definite objectives. What are the best actions for achieving a particular result: What is the best movement for loading one's rifle, what is the best position to take? What workers are best suited for a particular task? What children are capable of obtaining a particular result? Third, discipline establishes optimal sequences or co-ordinations: How can actions be linked together? How can soldiers be deployed for a maneuver? How can schoolchildren be distributed hierarchically within classifications? Fourth, discipline fixes the processes of progressive training (*dressage*) and permanent control, and finally, on the basis of this, it establishes the division between those considered unsuitable or incapable and the others. That is to say, on this basis it divides the normal from the abnormal. Disciplinary normalization consists first of all in positing a model, an optimal model that is constructed in terms of a certain result, and the operation of disciplinary normalization consists in trying to get people, movements, and actions to conform to this model, the normal being precisely that which can conform to this norm, and the abnormal that which is incapable of conforming to the norm. In other words, it is not the normal and the abnormal that is fundamental and primary in disciplinary normalization, it is the norm. That is, there is an originally prescriptive character of the norm and the determination and the identification of the normal and the abnormal becomes possible in relation to this posited norm. Due to the primacy of the norm in relation to the normal, to the fact that disciplinary normalization goes from the norm to the final division between the normal and the abnormal, I would rather say that what is involved in disciplinary techniques is a normation (*normation*) rather than normalization. Forgive the barbaric word, I use it to underline the primary and fundamental character of the norm.

Now, from the point of view of normalization, what happens with this set of apparatuses that I have called, with a word that is certainly not satisfactory and to which we will have to return, apparatuses of security? How does one normalize? After the examples of the town and scarcity, I would like to take the example, which is almost necessary in this series, of the epidemic, and of smallpox in particular, which was an endemic-epidemic disease in the eighteenth century.[2] It was an important problem, of course, first of all because smallpox was definitely the most widely endemic of all the diseases known at this time, since every newborn child had a 2 out of 3 chance of getting it. As a general rule, and for the whole population, the [mortality]* rate [for] smallpox was 1 in 7.782, almost 1 in 8. So, it was a widely endemic phenomenon with a very high mortality rate. Second, it was a phenomenon that also had the feature of sudden, very strong and intense epidemic outbursts. In London in particular, at the end of the seventeenth and the start of the eighteenth century there were very intense epidemic outbursts at intervals of rarely more than five or six years. Third, finally, smallpox is evidently a privileged example since, from 1720, with what is called inoculation or variolization,[3] and then from 1800 with vaccination,[4] techniques were available with the fourfold characteristic, which was absolutely out of the ordinary in the medical practices of the time, of first, being absolutely preventative, second, having almost total certainty of success, third, being in principle able to be extended to the whole population without major material or economic difficulties, and fourth, and above all, variolization first of all, but still vaccination at the start of the nineteenth century, had the considerable advantage of being completely foreign to any medical theory. The practice of variolization and vaccination, the success of variolization and vaccination were unthinkable in the terms of medical rationality of this time.[5] It was a pure matter of fact,[6] of the most naked empiricism, and this remained the case until the middle of the nineteenth century, roughly with Pasteur, when medicine was able to provide a rational understanding of the phenomenon.

We have, then, techniques that can be generalized, are certain, preventative, and absolutely inconceivable in the terms of medical theory. What happened and what were the effects of these purely empirical techniques in the domain of what could be called medical police?[7] I think that variolization first of all, and then vaccination, benefited from two supports that made possible [their] insertion in the real practices of population and government of Western Europe. First, of course, thanks to the statistical instruments available, the certain and generally

---

* M.F.: morbidity

applicable character of vaccination and variolization made it possible to think of the phenomena in terms of the calculus of probabilities.[8] To that extent, we can say that variolization and vaccination benefited from a mathematical support that was at the same time a sort of agent of their integration within the currently acceptable and accepted fields of rationality. Second, it seems to me that the second support, the second factor of the importation, of the immigration of these practices into accepted medical practices—despite its foreignness, its heterogeneity with regard to medical theory—was the fact that variolization and vaccination were integrated, at least analogically and through a series of important resemblances, within the other mechanisms of security I have been talking about. What seemed to me important and very typical of mechanisms of security concerning scarcity, was precisely that whereas the juridical-disciplinary regulations that reigned until the middle of the eighteenth century tried to prevent the phenomenon of scarcity, from the middle of the eighteenth century, with the physiocrats as well as many other economists, there was the attempt to find a point of support in the processes of scarcity themselves, in the kind of quantitative fluctuation that sometimes produced abundance and sometimes scarcity: finding support in the reality of the phenomenon, and instead of trying to prevent it, making other elements of reality function in relation to it, in such a way that the phenomenon is canceled out, as it were. Now what was remarkable with variolization, and more especially with variolization than with vaccination, is that it did not try to prevent smallpox so much as provoke it in inoculated individuals, but under conditions such that nullification of the disease could take place at the same time as this vaccination, which thus did not result in a total and complete disease. With the support of this kind of first small, artificially inoculated disease, one could prevent other possible attacks of smallpox. We have here a typical mechanism of security with the same morphology as that seen in the case of scarcity. There is a double integration, therefore, within different technologies of security, and within the rationalization of chance and probabilities. This is no doubt what made these new techniques acceptable, if not for medical thought, at least for doctors, administrators, those responsible for the medical police, and finally for the people themselves.

Now, I think that through this typical practice of security we see a number of elements emerging that are absolutely important for the later extension of apparatuses of security. First, what do we see in all the processes of the practice of inoculation: in the supervision of those inoculated, in the set of calculations made in the attempt to determine whether or not it really is worth inoculating people, whether one risks dying from the inoculation, or dying from the smallpox itself? First of all we see that the disease is no longer apprehended in terms of the notion of "prevailing disease (*maladie régnante*)," which was still a very sound category, consistent with the medical thought and practice of the time.[9] As defined or described in seventeenth and still in eighteenth century medicine, a prevailing disease is a kind of substantial disease, if you like, which is united with a country, a town, a climate, a group of people, a region, a way of life. The prevailing disease was defined and described in terms of this mass, overall relationship between a disease and a place, a disease and a group of people. When quantitative analyses are made of smallpox in terms of success and failure, defeats and successful outcomes, when the different possibilities of death or contamination are calculated, the result is that the disease no longer appears in this solid relationship of the prevailing disease to its place or milieu, but as a distribution of cases in a population circumscribed in time or space. Consequently, the notion of case appears, which is not the individual case, but a way of individualizing the collective phenomenon of the disease, or of collectivizing the phenomena, integrating individual phenomena within a collective field, but in the form of quantification and of the rational and identifiable. So, there is the notion of case.

Second, the following fact appears: If the disease is accessible in this way at the level of the group and at the level of each individual, in this notion, this analysis of the distribution of cases, then with regard to each individual or group we will be able to identify the risk for each of [catching]* smallpox, of dying from it or being cured. For each individual, given his age and where he lives, and for each age group, town, or profession, we will be able to determine the risk of morbidity and the

* M.F.: taking

risk of mortality. Thus, we will know the specific risk for each age group—here I refer to the text published by Duvillard right at the start of the nineteenth century, *Analyse de l'influence de la petite vérole*,[10] which is, as it were, the summation of all this quantitative research, which establishes all these quantitative facts accumulated [in the] eighteenth century and shows that for every child born there is a risk of getting smallpox that can be established as of the order of 2 in 3. If one catches smallpox, we can determine the risk of dying from it according to age group, if one is young or old, belongs to a particular milieu, if one follows a certain profession, and so on. We can also establish the risk of vaccination or variolization provoking the disease, and the risk of getting smallpox later despite variolization. So, there is the absolutely crucial notion of risk.

Third, this calculation of risk shows straightaway that risks are not the same for all individuals, all ages, or in every condition, place or milieu. There are therefore differential risks that reveal, as it were, zones of higher risk and, on the other hand, zones of less or lower risk. This means that one can thus identify what is dangerous. [With regard to] the risk of smallpox, it is dangerous to be less than three years old. It is more dangerous to live in the town than in the country. So, after the notions of case and risk, there is the third important notion of danger.

Finally, phenomena of sudden worsening, acceleration, and increase of the disease can be identified that do not fall within the general category of epidemic, but are such that its spread at a particular time and place carries the risk, through contagion obviously, of multiplying cases that multiply other cases in an unstoppable tendency or gradient until the phenomenon is effectively checked by either an artificial or an enigmatic natural mechanism. This phenomenon of sudden bolting, which regularly occurs and is also regularly nullified, can be called, roughly—not exactly in medical terminology, since the word was already used to designate something else—the crisis. The crisis is this phenomenon of sudden, circular bolting that can only be checked either by a higher, natural mechanism, or by an artificial mechanism.

Case, risk, danger, and crisis are, I think, new notions, at least in their field of application and in the techniques they call for, because a series of interventions will have the aim of precisely not following the previous practice of seeking purely and simply to nullify the disease in all the subjects in which it appears, or to prevent contact between the sick and the healthy. What, basically, was the aim of the disciplinary mechanisms, of the disciplinary system applied in epidemic regulations, or in regulations applied to endemic diseases like leprosy? It was, of course, first of all to treat the disease in each patient, insofar as they could be cured, and then to prevent contagion by isolating the sick from the healthy. What does the apparatus that appears with variolization-vaccination consist in? It is not the division between those who are sick and those who are not. It takes all who are sick and all who are not as a whole, that is to say, in short, the population, and it identifies the coefficient of probable morbidity, or probable mortality, in this population, that is to say the normal expectation in the population of being affected by the disease and of death linked to the disease. In this way it was established—and on this point all the statistics in the eighteenth century agree—that the rate of mortality from smallpox (*la petite vérole*)* was 1 in 7.782. Thus we get the idea of a "normal"† morbidity or mortality. This is the first thing.

The second thing is that with regard to the morbidity or mortality considered to be normal, one tries to arrive at a finer analysis that will make it possible to disengage different normalities in relation to each other. One will get the "normal" distribution;‡ of cases of and deaths due to smallpox (*la petite vérole*)§ for every age, in each region, town, and different areas of the town, and in terms of different occupations. Thus one will have the normal, overall curve, and different curves considered to be normal. What technique will be used in relation to this? It will be to try to reduce the most unfavorable, deviant normalities in relation to the normal, general curve, to bring them in line with this normal, general curve. In this way, for example, when it was very quickly discovered that children under three years are affected by smallpox much more quickly, much more easily, much more strongly, and with a much higher rate of morbidity, the problem arose of how to reduce this infant

---

* M.F.: variola (smallpox; *variole*).
† normal is in inverted commas in the manuscript, p. 7.
‡ normal is in inverted commas in the manuscript, p. 7.
§ M.F.: variola

morbidity and mortality so that it tends to fall in line with the average level of morbidity and mortality, which will itself be altered moreover by the fact that a section of individuals within this general population has a lower morbidity and mortality. It is at this level of the interplay of differential normalities, their separation out and bringing into line with each other, that—this is not yet epidemiology, the medicine of epidemics—the medicine of prevention will act.

We have then a system that is, I believe, exactly the opposite of the one we have seen with the disciplines. In the disciplines one started from a norm, and it was in relation to the training carried out with reference to the norm that the normal could be distinguished from the abnormal. Here, instead, we have a plotting of the normal and the abnormal, of different curves of normality, and the operation of normalization consists in establishing an interplay between these different distributions of normality and [in] acting to bring the most unfavorable in line with the more favorable. So we have here something that starts from the normal and makes use of certain distributions considered to be, if you like, more normal than the others, or at any rate more favorable than the others. These distributions will serve as the norm. The norm is an interplay of differential normalities.* The normal comes first and the norm is deduced from it, or the norm is fixed and plays its operational role on the basis of this study of normalities. So, I would say that what is involved here is no longer normation, but rather normalization in the strict sense.

So, over three weeks, the first two weeks and today, I have taken three examples: the town, scarcity, and the epidemic, or, if you like, the street, grain, and contagion. We can see straightaway that there is a very visible and clear link between these three phenomena: They are all linked to the phenomenon of the town itself. They all come back down to the first of the problems I tried to outline, for in the end the problem of scarcity and grain is the problem of the market town, and the problem of contagion and epidemic diseases is the problem of the town as the home of disease. The town as market is also the town as the place of revolt; the town as a

---

* Foucault repeats here: and the operation of normalization consists in establishing an interplay between these different distributions of normality.

center of diseases is the town as the site of miasmas and death. Anyway, it really is the problem of the town that is, I think, at the heart of these different examples of mechanisms of security. And if it is true that the outline of the very complex technology of securities appeared around the middle of the eighteenth century, I think that it is to the extent that the town posed new and specific economic and political problems of government technique. Very roughly, since this would all have to be refined, let's say again that the town was always an exception within an essentially territorial system of power founded and developed on the basis of a territorial domination defined by feudalism. What's more, the town was par excellence the free town. Up to a point, to a certain extent and within some clearly defined limits, it was the town that had the possibility, which had been given the right, to govern itself. But the town also represents a sort of autonomous zone in relation to the major organizations and mechanisms of territorial power typical of a power developed on a feudal basis. I think the integration of the town within central mechanisms of power, or better, the inversion that made the town the primary problem, even before the problem of the territory, is a phenomenon, a reversal, typical of what took place between the seventeenth and the beginning of the eighteenth century. It was a problem to which it really was necessary to respond with new mechanisms of power whose form is no doubt found in what I call mechanisms of security. Basically, the fact of the town and legitimate sovereignty had to be reconciled. How can sovereignty be exercised over the town? It was not that easy and a whole series of transformations were required of which I have obviously only indicated a bare outline.

Second, I would like to note that these three phenomena, or three problems rather—the street, grain, and contagion, or the town, scarcity, and epidemics—share the fact that they all more or less turn on the problem of circulation. I mean, of course, circulation in the very broad sense of movement, exchange, and contact, as form of dispersion, and also as form of distribution, the problem being: How should things circulate or not circulate? We could say that if the traditional problem of sovereignty, and so of political power linked to the form of sovereignty, had in the past always been either that of conquering new territories or holding on to conquered territory, then its problem was in a way: How can it not change, or how can I advance without it changing? How can the territory be demarcated, fixed, protected, or enlarged? In other words, it involved something that we could call precisely the safety (*sûreté*) of the territory, or the safety (*sûreté*) of the sovereign who rules over the territory. In the end this is Machiavelli's problem in fact. In a given territory, either conquered or inherited[11]—whether the power is legitimate or not is not important—Macchiavelli's problem was precisely how to ensure that the sovereign's power is not endangered, or at any rate, how can it keep at bay, with full certainty, the threats hanging over it. The Prince's problem, the political problem of sovereignty, was, I think, the Prince's safety in the reality of his territorial power. But far from thinking that Machiavelli opens up the field of political thought to modernity, I would say that he marks instead the end of an age, or anyway that he reaches the highest point of a moment in which the problem was actually that of the safety of the Prince and his territory. Now it seems to me that through the obviously very partial phenomena that I have tried to pick out we see the emergence of a completely different problem that is no longer that of fixing and demarcating the territory, but of allowing circulations to take place, of controlling them, sifting the good and the bad, ensuring that things are always in movement, constantly moving around, continually going from one point to another, but in such a way that the inherent dangers of this circulation are canceled out. No longer the safety (*sûreté*) of the Prince and his territory, but the security (*sécurité*) of the population and, consequently, of those who govern it. I think this is another very important change.

These mechanisms share [another,] third characteristic. Whether they are new forms of urban research, ways of preventing or at least controlling food shortages, or ways of preventing epidemics, they all have the following in common: They do not attempt, at least not primarily or in a fundamental way, to make use of a relationship of obedience between a higher will, of the sovereign, and the wills of those subjected to his will. In other words, the mechanism of security does not function on the axis of the sovereign-subjects relationship, ensuring the total and as it were passive obedience of individuals to their sovereign. They are connected to what the physiocrats called physical processes, which could be called natural processes, and which we could also call elements of reality. These mechanisms do not tend to a nullification of phenomena in the form of the prohibition, "you will not do this," nor even, "this will not happen," but in the form of a progressive self-cancellation of phenomena by the phenomena themselves. In a way, they involve the delimitation of phenomena within acceptable limits, rather than the imposition of a law that says no to them. So mechanisms of security are not put to work on the sovereign-subjects axis or in the form of the prohibition.

Finally—and here I think we come to the central point of all this—all these mechanisms, unlike those of law or of discipline, do not tend to convey the exercise of a will over others in the most homogeneous, continuous, and exhaustive way possible. It is a matter rather of revealing a level of the necessary and sufficient action of those who govern. This pertinent level of government action is not the actual totality of the subjects in every single detail, but the population with its specific phenomena and processes. The idea of the panopticon[12] is a modern idea in one sense, but we can also say that it is completely archaic, since the panoptic mechanism basically involves putting someone in the center—an eye, a gaze, a principle of surveillance—who will be able to make its sovereignty function over all the individuals [placed] within this machine of power. To that extent we can say that the panopticon is the oldest dream of the oldest sovereign: None of my subjects can escape and none of their actions is unknown to me. The central point of the panopticon still functions, as it were, as a perfect sovereign. On the other hand, what we now see is [not] the idea of a power that takes the form of an exhaustive surveillance of individuals so that they are all constantly under the eyes of the sovereign in everything they do, but the set of mechanisms that, for the government and those who govern, attach pertinence to quite specific phenomena that are not exactly individual phenomena, even if individuals do appear in a way, and there are specific processes of individualization (and we will have to come back to this, because it is very important). The relation between the individual and the collective, between the totality of the social body and its elementary fragments, is made to function in a completely different way; it will function differently in what we call population. The government of populations is, I think, completely different from the exercise of sovereignty over the fine grain of individual behaviors. It seems to me that we have two completely different systems of power.

So, I would now like to begin to analyze this. Through the examples of the town, scarcity, and epidemics I have merely tried to grasp some mechanisms, which are new, I think, in this period. Through these examples we can see that what is involved is, on the one hand, a completely different economy of power and, on the other hand—and I would now like to say a few words about this—an absolutely new political personage that I do not think existed previously, that had not been perceived or recognized, as it were, or singled out, and this new personage that makes a remarkable entrance and, what's more, is very quickly noted in the eighteenth century, is the population.

To be sure, this is not the first appearance of the problem and concern with the population, not only in political thought in general, but in the techniques and conduct of government. If we look at the use of the word "population" in the oldest texts,[13] we can see that the problem of population was raised, almost continually, for a long time, but in an essentially negative way. What was called the population was basically the contrary of depopulation. That is to say, "population" was understood as the movement by which a deserted territory was repopulated after a great disaster, be it an epidemic, war, or food shortage, after one of these great dramatic moments in which people died with spectacular rapidity and intensity. Let's say that the problem of population was posed in relation to the desert or desertification due to major human catastrophes. Moreover, it is entirely in keeping with this that the famous mortality tables—you know that eighteenth century demography could only begin inasmuch as some countries, and England in particular, had established mortality tables that made a quantification and knowledge of the causes of death possible[14]—had not always existed, of course, and above all were not always continuous. In England, which was the first country to draw up these mortality tables, in the sixteenth century and still at the start of the seventeenth century I think—I no longer know when things changed—at any rate, throughout the sixteenth century, these mortality tables were only drawn up at the time of the major epidemics when that scourge made mortality so dramatic that there was an interest in knowing how many people were dying, where they died, and of what cause.[15] In other words, the question of the population was not at all grasped in its positivity and generality. The question of knowing what the population is and how one could repopulate arose in relation to dramatic mortality.

Nor does the positive value of the notion of population date from the middle of the eighteenth century to which I have been referring until now. We only need to read the texts of chroniclers, historians, and travelers to see that the population always figures in their descriptions as one of the factors or elements of a sovereign's strength. For a sovereign to be powerful he had, of course, to rule over an extensive territory. The importance of his finances were also measured, estimated, or calculated. So, size of territory, the importance of finances, and also population, which figured under three aspects moreover: A large population, a population that could thus appear on the blazon of a sovereign's power, made its presence felt by the fact that it provided many troops, that the towns were populated, and that the markets were busy. This large population could only be a characteristic feature of the sovereign's power on two supplementary conditions that, on the one hand, it is obedient, and, on the other, it is animated by zeal, by a taste for work, and by activity, which enable the sovereign to be really strong, that it is to say, obeyed, on the one hand, and rich on the other. All of this belongs to the most traditional way of conceiving the population.

Things begin to change in the seventeenth century, at the time distinguished by cameralism[16] and mercantilism,[17] not so much as economic doctrines as a new way of posing the problems of government. Maybe we will come back to this. Anyway, for the mercantilists of the seventeenth century, the population was no longer simply a positive feature that allowed it to appear in the emblems of the sovereign's power, but appeared within a dynamic, or rather, not within, but as the very source of a dynamic, and of the dynamic of the strength of the state and sovereign. The population is a fundamental element, that is to say one that conditions all the others. Why does it condition the other elements? Because the population provides manpower for agriculture, that is to say, it guarantees abundant harvests, since there will be many cultivators, extensive cultivated land, abundant harvests, and so a low price of grain and agricultural products. It also provides manpower for manufacture, that is to say, as far as it is possible, it enables one to do without imports and everything for which one has to pay foreign countries with good currency, in gold or silver. [Finally], the population is a fundamental component of the state's power because it ensures competition within the possible workforce within the state, which of course ensures low wages. Low wages mean low prices of products and the possibility of export, and hence a new guarantee, a new source of the state's strength.

The population can only be the basis of the state's wealth and power in this way on condition, of course, that it is framed by a regulatory apparatus (*appareil*) that prevents emigration, calls for immigrants, and promotes the birth rate, a regulatory apparatus that also defines useful and exportable products, fixes the objects to be produced, the means of their production, as well as wages, and which prevents idleness and vagrancy. In short, it requires an apparatus that will ensure that the population, which is seen as the source and the root, as it were, of the state's power and wealth, will work properly, in the right place, and on the right objects. In other words, mercantilism was concerned with the population as a productive force, in the strict sense of the term, and I do not think it is in the eighteenth century, after the mercantilists, nor, obviously, in the nineteenth century, that the population is seen as essentially and fundamentally a productive force. It was the mercantilists, or the cameralists, who basically saw the population in this way, on condition, of course, that it is effectively trained, divided up, distributed, and fixed by disciplinary mechanisms. The population as the source of wealth, as a productive force, and disciplinary supervision are all of a piece within the thought, project, and political practice of the mercantilists.

It seems to me that from the eighteenth century, in the years I have been taking as my reference point, things change. It is usually said that, in contrast to the mercantilists of the earlier period, the physiocrats were anti-populationist.[18] That is to say, whereas the mercantilists thought that population should be increased as much as possible because it was the source of wealth and power, the physiocrats are said to have adopted a much more qualified position. In actual fact, I do not think that the difference hangs on the value or lack of value of expanding the population. I think the physiocrats are distinct from the mercantilists, or from the cameralists, because they consider population in a different way.[19] Because when the mercantilists and cameralists talk about population as, on the one hand, the source of wealth, and, on the other, as having to be framed by a regulatory system, they basically still only see it as the collection of a sovereign's subjects on which a number of laws and regulations can be imposed from above in an entirely voluntarist manner telling it what it must do, and where and how it must do it. In other words, the mercantilists considered the problem of population essentially in terms of the axis of sovereign and subjects. The mercantilist, cameralist, or, if you like, Colbertian project was situated within the relationship of the sovereign's will to the subjected will of the people, in relation to subjects of right, subjects subject to a law, subjects who can be framed by regulations. Now with the physiocrats and, more generally, with the eighteenth century economists, I think the population no longer appears as a collection of subjects of right, as a collection of subject wills who must obey the sovereign's will through the intermediary of regulations, laws, edicts, and so on. It will be considered as a set of processes to be managed at the level and on the basis of what is natural in these processes.

But what does this "naturalness"* of the population signify? What is it that means that the population will henceforth be seen, not from the standpoint of the juridical-political notion of subject, but as a sort of technical-political object of management and government? What is this naturalness? To put it very briefly, I think it appears in three ways. First, as problematized in thought, but [also] in eighteenth century governmental practice, the population is not the simple sum of individuals inhabiting a territory. Nor is it solely the result of their will to reproduce. Nor is it the vis-à-vis of a sovereign will that may encourage or shape it. In fact, the population is not a primary datum; it is dependent on a series of variables. Population varies with the climate. It varies with the material surroundings. It varies with the intensity of commerce and activity in the circulation of wealth. Obviously it varies according to the laws to which it is subjected, like tax or marriage laws for example. It also varies with people's customs, like the way in which daughters are given a dowry, for example, or the way in which the right of primogeniture is ensured, with birthright, and also with the way in which

---

* naturalness: in inverted commas in the manuscript, p. 13.

children are raised, and whether or not they are entrusted to wet nurses. Population varies with the moral or religious values associated with different kinds of conduct; the ethical-religious value, for example, of the celibacy of priests and monks. Above all, of course, it varies with the condition of means of subsistence, and here we encounter Mirabeau's famous aphorism that population will never vary beyond and cannot in any circumstance exceed the limits fixed by the quantity of means of subsistence.[20] These analyses, by Mirabeau, by the abbot Pierre Jaubert,[21] or by Quesnay in the article "Hommes" in the *Encylopédie*,[22] all show that it is obvious to this way of thinking that the population is not that kind of original datum, that kind of material on which the sovereign's action is to be exercised, that vis-à-vis of the sovereign. The population is a datum that depends on a series of variables, which means that it cannot be transparent to the sovereign's action and that the relation between the population and sovereign cannot simply be one of obedience or the refusal of obedience, of obedience or revolt. In fact, the variables on which population depends are such that to a very considerable extent it escapes the sovereign's voluntarist and direct action in the form of the law. If one says to a population "do this," there is not only no guarantee that it will do it, but also there is quite simply no guarantee that it can do it. If we restrict ourselves to the sovereign-subject relationship, the limit of the law is the subject's disobedience; it is the "no" with which the subject opposes the sovereign. But when it is a question of the relationship between government and population, then the limit of the sovereign's or government's decision is by no means necessarily the refusal of the people to whom the decision is addressed.

The population appears therefore as a kind of thick natural phenomenon in relation to the sovereign's legalistic voluntarism. To say that population is a natural phenomenon that cannot be changed by decree does not mean, however, that it is an inaccessible and impenetrable nature, quite the contrary. And this is where the analysis of the physiocrats and economists becomes interesting, in that the naturalness identified in the fact of population is constantly accessible to agents and techniques of transformation, on condition that these agents and techniques are at once enlightened, reflected, analytical, calculated, and calculating. Not only must voluntary changes in the law be considered if the laws are unfavorable to the population, but above all, if one wants to encourage population, or achieve the right relationship between the population and the state's resources and possibilities, then one must act on a range of factors and elements that seem far removed from the population itself and its immediate behavior, fecundity, and desire to reproduce. For example, one must act on the currency flows that irrigate the country, knowing their directions and whether they really reach all the elements of the population or leave some regions inert. One will have to act on exports: the greater the demand for exports, the greater the possibility of work, of course, and so of wealth, and so of population. The problem of imports arises: Do imports encourage or discourage population? If one imports, one takes jobs from people here, but one also gives them food. So there is the problem of the regulation of imports, which was crucial in the eighteenth century. In any case, it is possible to act effectively on the population through the interplay of all these remote factors. So you can see that a completely different technique is emerging that is not getting subjects to obey the sovereign's will, but having a hold on things that seem far removed from the population, but which, through calculation, analysis, and reflection, one knows can really have an effect on it. I think a very important mutation in the organization and rationalization of methods of power takes place with reference to this penetrable naturalness of population.

We could also say that the naturalness of the population appears in a second way in the fact that this population is of course made up of individuals who are quite different from each other and whose behavior, within a certain limit at least, cannot be accurately predicted. Nevertheless, according to the first theorists of population in the eighteenth century, there is at least one invariant that means that the population taken as a whole has one and only one mainspring of action. This is desire. Desire is an old notion that first appeared and was employed in spiritual direction (to which, possibly, we may be able to return),[23] and it makes its second appearance within techniques of power and government. Every individual acts out of desire. One can do nothing against desire. As Quesnay says: You cannot stop people from living where they think they will profit most and where they desire to live, because they desire that profit. Do not try to change them; things will not change.[24] However—and it is here that this naturalness of desire thus marks the population and becomes accessible to governmental technique—for reasons to which we will have to come back and which are one of the important theoretical elements of the whole system, this desire is such that, if one gives it free play, and on condition that it is given free play, all things considered, within a certain limit and thanks to a number of relationships and connections, it will produce the general interest of the population. Desire is the pursuit of the individual's interest. In his desire the individual may well be deceived regarding his personal interest, but there is something that does not deceive, which is that the spontaneous, or at any rate both spontaneous and regulated play of desire will in fact allow the production of an interest, of something favorable for the population. The production of the collective interest through the play of desire is what distinguishes both the naturalness of population and the possible artificiality of the means one adopts to manage it.

This is important because you can see that with this idea of a management of populations on the basis of the naturalness of their desire, and of the spontaneous production of the collective interest by desire, we have something that is completely the opposite of the old ethical-juridical conception of government and the exercise of sovereignty. For what was the sovereign for the jurists, for medieval jurists but also for the theorists of natural law, for Hobbes as well as for Rousseau? The sovereign is the person who can say no to any individual's desire, the problem being how to legitimize this "no" opposed to individuals' desire and found it on the will of these same individuals. Now through the economic-political thought of the physiocrats we see a completely different idea taking shape, which is that the problem of those who govern must absolutely not be how they can say no, up to what point they can say no, and with what legitimacy they can say no. The problem is how they can say yes; it is how to say yes to this desire. The problem is not therefore the limit of concupiscence or the limit of self-esteem in the sense of love of oneself, but concerns rather everything that stimulates and encourages this self-esteem, this desire, so that it can produce its necessary beneficial effects. We have here therefore the matrix of an entire, let's say, utilitarian philosophy.[25] And just as I think that Condillac's Ideology,[26] or, in short, what has been called sensualism, was the theoretical instrument by which the practice of discipline could be underpinned,[27] I would say that utilitarian philosophy was the theoretical instrument that underpinned the government of populations, which was something new at this time.*

Finally, the naturalness of the population, which appears in this universal benefit of desire, and also in the fact that the population is always dependent upon complex and modifiable variables, appears again in a third way. It appears in the constancy of phenomena that one might expect to be variable since they depend on accidents, chance, individual conduct, and conjunctural causes. Now it is enough to observe these phenomena that should be irregular, it is enough to look at them and count them, to realize that in actual fact they are regular. This was the great discovery of the Englishman Graunt[28] at the end of the seventeenth century, who, precisely with reference to mortality tables, not only managed to establish that there was a constant number of deaths every year in a town, but also that there was a constant proportion of different accidents, however varied, that produce this death. The same proportion of people die from consumption, the same proportion from fevers, or from the kidney stone, gout, or jaundice.[29] What clearly astonished Graunt is that in the London mortality tables the proportion of suicides is exactly the same from one year to the next.[30] We also see other regular phenomena such as, for example, a higher birth rate for males, but boys suffering from more accidents of varied kinds than girls, so that proportion is re-established after a certain time.[31] Child mortality is always greater than adult mortality for both boys and girls.[32] Mortality is always higher in the town than in the country,[33] and so on. We have then a third surface of emergence for the naturalness of the population.

The population is not, then, a collection of juridical subjects in an individual or collective relationship with a sovereign will. It is a set of elements in which we can note constants and regularities even in accidents, in which we can identify the universal of desire regularly producing the benefit of all, and with regard to which we can identify a number of modifiable variables on which it depends. Taking the effects

---

* Manuscript, p. 17: "What is also important is that 'utilitarian philosophy' is to the government of populations a bit what Ideology was to the disciplines."

specific to population into consideration, making them pertinent if you like, is, I think, a very important phenomenon: the entry of a "nature"* into the field of techniques of power, of a nature that is not something on which, above which, or against which the sovereign must impose just laws. There is not nature and then, above nature and against it, the sovereign and the relationship of obedience that is owed to him. We have a population whose nature is such that the sovereign must deploy reflected procedures of government within this nature, with the help of it, and with regard to it. In other words, with the population we have something completely different from a collection of subjects of right differentiated by their status, localization, goods, responsibilities, and offices: [We have]† a set of elements that, on one side, are immersed within the general regime of living beings and that, on another side, offer a surface on which authoritarian, but reflected and calculated transformations can get a hold. The dimension in which the population is immersed amongst the other living beings appears and is sanctioned when, for the first time, men are no longer called "mankind (*le genre humaine*)" and begin to be called "the human species (*l'espèce humaine*)."[34] With the emergence of mankind as a species, within a field of the definition of all living species, we can say that man appears in the first form of his integration within biology. From one direction, then, population is the human species, and from another it is what will be called the public. Here again, the word is not new, but its usage is.[35] The public, which is a crucial notion in the eighteenth century, is the population seen under the aspect of its opinions, ways of doing things, forms of behavior, customs, fears, prejudices, and requirements; it is what one gets a hold on through education, campaigns, and convictions. The population is therefore everything that extends from biological rootedness through the species up to the surface that gives one a hold provided by the public. From the species to the public; we have here a whole field of new realities in the sense that they are the pertinent elements for mechanisms of power, the pertinent space within which and regarding which one must act.

---

* nature: in inverted commas in the manuscript, p. 18.
† M.F.: but

We could add something else. While I have been speaking about population a word has constantly recurred—you will say that this was deliberate, but it may not be entirely so—and this is the word "government." The more I have spoken about population, the more I have stopped saying "sovereign." I was led to designate or aim at something that again I think is relatively new, not in the word, and not at a certain level of reality, but as a new technique. Or rather, the modern political problem, the privilege that government begins to exercise in relation to rules, to the extent that, to limit the king's power, it will be possible one day to say, "the king reigns, but he does not govern,"[36] this inversion of government and the reign or rule and the fact that government is basically much more than sovereignty, much more than reigning or ruling, much more than the *imperium*, is, I think, absolutely linked to the population. I think that the series, mechanisms of security—population—government and the opening up of the field that we call politics, should be analyzed.

I would like to take five more minutes to add something, and maybe you will see why. It is a bit marginal to all of this.[37] So there is the emergence of this absolutely new thing, the population, with the mass of juridical, political, and technical problems that it gives rise to. Now, if we take a completely different series of domains, [those] we could call domains of knowledge (*savoirs*), we see—and I am not putting forward a solution here, but a problem—that this same problem of population appears in a whole series of knowledges.

More precisely, let us take the case of political economy. Basically, for those who were concerned with finances—since in the seventeenth century it was still a question of this—insofar as it was a question of quantifying wealth, measuring its circulation, determining the role of currency, and knowing whether it was better to devalue or revalue a currency, insofar as it was a question of establishing or supporting the flows of external commerce, I think "economic analysis"* remained at the level of the analysis of wealth.[38] On the other hand, when it became possible not only to introduce population into the field of economic theory, but also into economic practice, when it became possible to introduce into

---

* Foucault adds: in inverted commas.

the analysis of wealth this new subject, this new subject-object, with its demographic aspects, but also with the aspect of the specific role of producers and consumers, owners and non-owners, those who create profit and those who take it, when the entry of this subject-object, of population, became possible within the analysis of wealth, with all its disruptive effects in the field of economic reflection and practice, then I think the result was that one ceased analyzing wealth and a new domain of knowledge, political economy, was opened up. After all, one of Quesnay's fundamental texts is in fact the article "Hommes" in the *Encyclopédie*,[39] and throughout his work Quesnay never stopped saying that real economic government was government that concerned itself with the population.[40] But then, the well-known opposition between Malthus and Marx[41] would be proof that in the nineteenth century the problem of population is still really central in all political economic thought. After all, on a Ricardian basis[42] that is absolutely common to them both, what is the source of their disagreement? For Malthus, the problem of population basically has to be thought as a bio-economic problem, whereas Marx tried to circumvent the problem and to get rid of the very notion of population, but only to rediscover it in the no longer bio-economic form, but in the specifically historical-political form of class, of class confrontation and class struggle. That is the source of their disagreement: either population or classes, that is where the split occurs, on the basis of an economic thought, a political economic thought, that was only possible as such with the introduction of the subject-population.

Consider now the case of natural history and biology. Basically, as you know, the essential role and function of natural history was to determine the classificatory characteristics of living beings that would enable them to be distributed to this or that case of the table.[43] In the eighteenth and the beginning of the nineteenth century, a whole series of transformations take place that take us from the identification of classificatory characteristics to the internal organization of the organism,[44] and then from the organism in its anatomical-functional coherence to the constitutive or regulatory relationships with the milieu in which it lives. Roughly speaking, this is the Lamarck-Cuvier problem,[45] to which Cuvier provides the solution, in which the principles of rationality are found in Cuvier.[46] Finally, in the transition from Cuvier to Darwin,[47] from the milieu of life, in its constitutive relationship to the organism, we pass to the population that Darwin succeeded in showing was, in fact, the element through which the milieu produces its effects on the organism. To think about the relationships between the milieu and the organism, Lamarck resorted to something like the idea of the organism being acted on directly and shaped by the milieu. Cuvier resorted to what appear to be more mythological things—like catastrophes, God's creative acts, and so on—but which actually organized the field of rationality much more carefully. Darwin found that population was the medium between the milieu and the organism, with all the specific effects of population: mutations, eliminations, and so forth. So in the analysis of living beings it is the problematization of population that makes possible the transition from natural history to biology. We should look for the turning point between natural history and biology on the side of population.

I think we could say the same thing with regard to the transition from general grammar to historical philology.[48] General grammar was the analysis of the relations between linguistic signs and representations of any speaking subject whomsoever, or of the speaking subject in general. The birth of philology became possible when a series of investigations in different countries, particularly in central Europe, and also in Russia for political reasons, succeeded in identifying the relationship between a population and a language, and in which, as a result, the problem was how in the course of history, and in terms of the specific regularities, not of the population, but of its language, the population, as collective subject, could transform the language it spoke. Here again, I think it is the introduction of the subject-population that makes possible the transition from general grammar to philology.

To sum up, I think that if we look for the operator (*opérateur*) of transformation for the transition from natural history to biology, from the analysis of wealth to political economy, and from general grammar to historical philology, if we look for the operator that upset all these systems of knowledge, and directed knowledge to the sciences of life, of labor and production, and of language, then we should look to population. Not in a way that would amount to saying that, finally understanding the importance of the population, the ruling classes set naturalists to work in this area, who mutated into biologists as a result, grammarians who were consequently transformed into philologists, and financiers who became economists. It did not take place like this, but in the following form: A constant interplay between techniques of power and their object gradually carves out in reality, as a field of reality, population and its specific phenomena. A whole series of objects were made visible for possible forms of knowledge on the basis of the constitution of the population as the correlate of techniques of power. In turn, because these forms of knowledge constantly carve out new objects, the population could be formed, continue, and remain as the privileged correlate of modern mechanisms of power.

Hence the theme of man, and the "human sciences"* that analyze him as a living being, working individual, and speaking subject, should be understood on the basis of the emergence of population as the correlate of power and the object of knowledge. After all, man, as he is thought and defined by the so-called human sciences of the nineteenth century, and as he is reflected in nineteenth century humanism, is nothing other than a figure of population. Or let us say again: If, on the one hand, it is true that man could not exist, and that only the juridical notion of the subject of right could exist when the problem of power was formulated within the theory of sovereignty, on the other hand, when population becomes the vis-à-vis of government, of the art of government, rather than of sovereignty, then I think we can say that man is to population what the subject of right was to the sovereign. There you are, all wrapped up and loose ends tied.

---

* human sciences: in inverted commas in the manuscript.

1. Hans Kelsen (1881-1973). Born in Prague, Kelsen taught public law and philosophy at Vienna from 1919 to 1929, then at Cologne from 1930 to 1933. Dismissed by the Nazis, he pursued his career at Geneva (1933-1938) and Berkeley (1942-1952). He was a founder of the Vienna School (around the *Zeitschrift für öffentliches Recht* created in 1914) which radicalized the doctrine of juridical positivism, and in his *Reine Rechtslehre* (Vienna: 1960, 2nd edn.); French translation by H. Thévenaz, *Théorie pure du droit*, 1st edn. (Neuchâtel: La Baconnière, 1953), 2nd edn., trans. Ch. Eisenmann (Paris: Dalloz, 1962); English translation by Max Knight, *Pure Theory of Law* (Berkeley: University of California Press, 1967) he defended a normativist conception of law, according to which the law constitutes a hierarchical and dynamic system of norms connected to each other by a relationship of imputation (distinct from the relationship of causality on which scientific reasoning is based), that is to say, "the relation between a certain behavior as condition and a sanction as consequence" (*General Theory of Norms*, ch. 7, § II, p. 24). To avoid infinite regress (every juridical power can only derive from higher juridical authorization), this system gets its validity from a basic norm (*Grundnorm*), not posited like other norms, but presupposed and thereby suprapositive, which "represents the ultimate reason for the validity of all the legal norms forming the legal order" (ibid. ch. 59, p. 255). See also his posthumous work, *Allgemeine Theorie der Normen* (Vienna: Manz Verlag, 1979); English translation by Michael Hartney, *General Theory of Norms* (Oxford: Oxford University Press, 1991). On Kelsen, see the comments of G. Canguilhem, *Le Normal et le Pathologique* (Paris: PUF, 1975, 3rd edn.) pp. 184-185; English translation, *On the Normal and the Pathological*, trans. Carolyn R. Fawcett (Dordrecht and London: D. Reidel, 1978) p. 153.

2. See the doctoral medical thesis of Anne-Marie Moulin, *La Vaccination anti-variolique. Approche historique de l'évolution des idées sur les maladies transmissibles et leur prophylaxie* (Paris: Université Pierre et Marie Curie (Paris 6)-Faculté de Médecine Pitié Salpétrière, 1979). The author of this thesis gave an account of "the campaigns of variolization in the eighteenth century," in 1978 in Foucault's course (see below, Course Summary, p. 367). See also, J. Hecht, "Un débat médical au XVIIIᵉ siècle, l'inoculation de la petite vérole," *Le Concours médical*, 18, 1 May 1959, pp. 2147-2152, and the two works that appeared the year before this course: P.E. Razzell, *The Conquest of Smallpox: The impact of inoculation on smallpox mortality in the 18th century* (Firle: Caliban Books, 1977) and G. Miller, *The Adoption of Inoculation for Smallpox in England and France* (Philadelphia: University of Philadelphia Press, 1977) that Foucault was able to consult.

3. The first word was employed in the eighteenth century with reference to processes of plant graft. The second was only used in the nineteenth century.

4. From 1800 Jenner's vaccination progressively replaces inoculation. See E. Jenner, *An Inquiry into the Causes and Effects of the Variolae Vaccinae* (1798) (London: Dawson, 1966, reproduction of the 1st edition); R. Le Droumaguet, *À propos du centenaire de Jenner. Notes sur l'histoire des premières vaccinations contre la variole*, Medical thesis, Belfort-Mulhouse, 1923; A-M. Moulin, *La Vaccination anti-variolique*, pp. 33-36.

5. See A.-M. Moulin, *La Vaccination anti-variolique*, p. 36: "[At the end of the eighteenth century] medicine had not elucidated the profound meaning of inoculations," and p. 42, this quotation of Berthollet concerning the "modification" introduced into the organism by the vaccine: "What is the nature of this difference and this change? No-one knows; experience alone proves its reality" (*Exposition des faits recueillis jusqu'a présent concernant les effets de la vaccination*, 1812).

6. Inoculation was practiced in China from the seventeenth century and in Turkey (see A.-M. Moulin, *La Vaccination anti-variolique*, pp. 12-22). For Chinese practice see the letter of Father La Coste in 1714 which appeared in the *Mémoires de Trévoux*, and, for Turkey, the debate on inoculation in the Royal Society, in England, drawing on merchant's reports of the East India Company. On 1 April 1717, Lady Montaigu, wife of the English ambassador in Istanbul and one of the most zealous propagandists of inoculation in her country, wrote to a correspondent: "Smallpox, so fatal and frequent among us, is here rendered inoffensive by the discovery of inoculation (...). There is a group of old women here who are specialists in this operation" (quoted by Moulin, ibid. pp. 19-20).

7. On this notion, see the article by M. Foucault, "La politique de la santé au XVIIIe siècle" in *Les Machines à guérir. Aux origines de l'hôpital moderne; dossiers et documents* (Paris: Institut de l'environnement, 1976) pp. 11-21; *Dits et Écrits*, 3, pp. 15-27 (see pp. 17-18); English translation by Colin Gordon, "The Politics of Health in the Eighteenth Century" in M. Foucault, *Essential Works*, 3, pp. 90-110 (see pp. 94-95).

8. See A.-M. Moulin, *La Vaccination anti-variolique*, p. 26: "In 1760, the mathematician Bernoulli imparts the statistics more rigorously [than J. Jurin's tables, in the *Philosophical Transactions* of the Royal Society, in 1725], which is in fact the only theoretical justification for inoculation. (...) If inoculation is adopted, the result will be a gain of several thousand persons for civil society; even if it is deadly, as it kills children in the cradle, it is preferable to smallpox that causes the death of adults who have become useful to society; if it is true that the generalization of inoculation risks replacing the great epidemics with a permanent state of endemic disease, the danger is less because smallpox is a generalized eruption and inoculation affects only a small part of the surface of the skin." Bernoulli concludes with the demonstration that if one neglects the point of view of the individual, "it will always be geometrically true that the interest of Princes is to favor inoculation" (D. Bernoulli, "Essai d'une nouvelle analyse de la mortalité causée par la petite vérole et des avantages de l'inoculation pour la prévenir," *Histoires et Mémoires de l'Académie des sciences*, 2, 1766). This essay, which dates from 1760, aroused the hostile reaction of D'Alembert, 12 November 1760, at the Academy of Sciences. For a detailed analysis of Bernoulli's method of calculation and of the quarrel with D'Alembert, see H. Le Bras, *Naissance de la mortalité* (Paris: Gallimard-Le Seuil, "Hautes Études," 2000) pp. 335-342.

9. On this notion, see M. Foucault, *Naissance de la clinique* (Paris: PUF "Galien," 1963) p. 24 (reference to L.S.D. Le Brun, *Traité théorique sur les maladies épidémiques* [Paris: Didot le jeune, 1776] pp. 2-3) and p. 28 (reference to F. Richard de Hautersierck, *Recueil d'observations. Médecine des hôpitaux militaires* [Paris: Imprimerie royale, 1766] vol. 1, pp. xxiv-xxvii); English translation by A.M. Sheridan Smith, *The Birth of the Clinic. An Archeology of Medical Perception* (London: Tavistock Publications, 1973) p. 25 and p. 29 [where "maladies régnantes" is translated as "common diseases"; G.B.].

10. Emmanuel Étienne Duvillard (1755-1832), *Analyse et Tableaux de l'influence de la petite vérole sur la mortalité à chaque âge, et de celle qu'un préservatif tel que la vaccine peut avoir sur la population et la longévité* (Paris: Imprimerie impériale, 1806). On Duvillard, a "specialist of population statistics, but also a theorist of insurance and the calculation of annuities," see G. Thuillier, "Duvillard et la statistique en 1806," *Études et Documents* (Paris: Imprimerie nationale, Comité pour l'histoire économique et financière de la France, 1989) vol. 1, pp. 425-435; A. Desrosières, *La Politique des grands nombres. Histoire de la raison statistique* (Paris: La Découverte, 2000 [1993]) pp. 48-54.

11. On this distinction, which founds the entire problematic of the "new prince" in Machiavelli, see *The Prince*, ch. 1: "The different kinds of principality and how they are acquired" and ch. 2: "Hereditary principalities."

12. See below, lecture of 8 February, p. 117.

13. Foucault is alluding here to the writings of Francis Bacon, credited by a number of dictionaries with the invention of the word "population." See, for example, *Dictionnaire historique de la langue française. Le Robert*. In reality this word cannot be found in Bacon and only appears in some late translations [see end of this note; G.B.]. The first occurrence of the English word seems to go back to the *Political Discourses* (1751) of David Hume, and the French term only began to circulate in the second half of the eighteenth century. Montesquieu was still unaware of it in 1748. He speaks of the "number of men" in *De l'esprit des lois*, Book XVIII, ch. 10, in *Œuvres complètes* (Paris: Gallimard, "Bibliothèque de la Plèiade," 1958) vol. 2, p. 536; English translation by Anne Cohler, Basia Miller, Harold Stone, *The Spirit of The Laws* (Cambridge: Cambridge University Press, 1989) p. 290, or of inhabitants, of "propagation of the species" (ibid. Book XXIII, ch. 26) p. 710 and p. 711; trans., ibid. p. 453. See *Lettres persanes* (1721), CXXII, ibid. p. 313; English translation by C.J. Betts, *Persian Letters* (Harmondsworth: Penguin, 1973) Letter 120, p. 219. On the other hand, from *Persian Letters* he uses the negative form of the word, "depopulation" (Letter CXVII, ibid. p. 305; trans., ibid. Letter 117, p. 211); *De l'esprit des lois*, XXIII, ch. 19, p. 695, and ch. 28, p. 711; *The Spirit of the Laws*, pp. 439-440 and p. 454. The use of the

word goes back to the fourteenth century (see Littré, *Dictionnaire de la langue française* [Paris: J.-J. Pauvert, 1956] vol. 2, p. 1645) in the active sense of the verb "se dépeupler." Absent from the first edition of Herbert's *Essai sur la police générale des grains* in 1753, "population" appears in the 1755 edition. For a recent clarification of the question, see H. Le Bras, his preface to H. Le Bras, ed., *L'Invention des populations* (Paris: Odile Jacob, 2000), and I. Tamba, "Histoires de démographe et de linguiste: le couple population/dépopulation," *Linx*, Paris X, 47, 2002, pp. 1-6. [It is not true that the word "population" cannot be found in Bacon. The word appears in his *Essays*, and precisely in the essay discussed by Foucault in some detail in the lecture of 15 March 1978, "Of Seditions and Troubles." G.B.]

14. On John Graunt, see below, note 28.

15. See E. Vilquin, Introduction to J. Graunt, *Observations naturelles ou politiques répertoriés dans l'Index ci-après et faites sur les bulletins de mortalité de John Graunt citoyen de Londres, en rapport avec le gouvernement, la religion, le commerce, l'accroissement, l'atmosphère, les maladies et les divers changements de ladite cité*, trans. E. Vilquin (Paris: INED, 1977) pp. 18-19: "The bills of mortality of London are among the first published demographic statements, but their origin is not well known. The earliest bill that has been discovered responds to a question on 21 October 1532 from the Royal Council to the Mayor of London concerning the number of deaths due to the plague (...). In 1532 and 1533 there were series of weekly bills indicating for every parish the total number of deaths and the number due to the plague. Obviously, the only reason for these bills was to give the London authorities an idea of the extent and development of the plague and therefore appear and disappear with it. The plague of 1563 gave rise to a long series of bills from 12 June 1563 to 26 July 1566. There was another series in 1754, another, continuous series, from 1578 to 1583, then from 1592 to 1595, and from 1597 to 1600. It is not impossible that the regularity of weekly bills goes back to 1563, it is only certain from 1603."

16. See above, lecture of 11 January, note 25.

17. Ibid.

18. On this question, see G. Weulersse, *Le Mouvement physiocratique*, vol. 2, Book V, ch. 1, pp. 268-295: "Discussion des principes du populationnisme," and, *Les Physiocrates*, pp. 251-254; Joseph J. Spengler, *French Predecessors of Malthus. A Study in Eighteenth-Century Wage and Population Theory* (Durham, North Carolina: Duke University Press, 1942) pp. 170-211; A. Landry, "Les idées de Quesnay sur la population," *Revue d'Histoire des doctrines économiques et sociales*, 1909, republished in *F. Quesnay et la physiocratie*, vol. 1, pp. 11-49; J.-Cl. Perrot, *Une histoire intellectuelle de l'économie politique*, pp. 143-192: "Les économistes, les philosophes et la population."

19. The essential position of the physiocrats on the subject consists in the introduction of wealth as mediating between population and subsistence. See Quesnay's article, "Hommes" in *F. Quesnay et la physiocratie*, vol. 2, p. 549: "One would like to increase the population in the countryside, and one does not know that the increase of population depends beforehand on the increase of wealth." See G. Weulersse, *Les Physiocrates*, pp. 252-253: "It is not that they were indifferent to the increase of population: because men contribute to the enrichment of the State in two ways, as producers and consumers. But they will only be useful producers if they produce more than they consume, that is to say if their work is accomplished with the assistance of the necessary capitals; and their consumption, similarly, will only be advantageous if they pay a good price for the commodities on which they live, that is to say equal to what foreign purchasers would pay for them: otherwise, a strong national population, far from being a resource, becomes a burden. But you begin by increasing the revenues of the land: men, called to life as it were by the abundance of wages, will multiply proportionately by themselves; this is the true populationism, but indirect of course." There is an excellent clarification also in J.J. Spengler, *French Predecessors of Malthus*, pp. 172-175. On the analysis of the role of population in the physiocrats and economists, see M. Foucault, *Histoire de la folie*, pp. 429-430; *Madness and Civilization*, pp. 231-232.

20. See Victor Riquet[t]i, Marquis de Mirabeau (1715-1789), known as Mirabeau the Elder, *L'Ami des hommes, ou Traité de la population*, published under the author's name (Avignon: 1756) 3 vols. See, L. Brocard, *Les Doctrines économiques et sociales du marquis de Mirabeau dans l' "Ami des hommes"* (Paris: Giard et Brière, 1902). Mirabeau's aphorism, taken from *L'Ami des Hommes*—"the measure of subsistence is that of the population" (vol. 1, p. 37)—finds its

counterpart in the work of A. Goudart, *Les Intérêts de la France mal entendues, dans les branches de l'agriculture, de la population, des finances* ... published the same year (Amsterdam: Jacques Cœur, 1756) 3 vols: "The number of men always depends upon the general degree of subsistence" and is taken up, even in its formulation in imagery (men will multiply "like mice in a barn if they have unlimited means of subsistence") in Richard Cantillon, *Essai sur la nature du commerce en général* (London: Fletcher Gyles, 1755; facsimile re-publication, Paris: INED, 1952 and 1997) ch. 15, p. 47.

21. Abbé Pierre Jaubert, *Des causes de la dépopulation et des moyens d'y remédier*, published under the author's name (London-Paris: Dessain junior, 1767).

22. This article, written for the *Encylopédie*, the publication of which was prohibited in 1757 and only taken up again in 1765, remained unpublished until 1908 (*Revue d'histoire des doctrines économiques et sociales*, 1). It is republished in *François Quesnay et la physiocratie*, vol. 2, in *Œuvres*, pp. 511-575. It was however partially recopied and distributed by Henry Patullo in his *Essai sur l'amelioration des terres* (Paris: Durand, 1758). See J.-Cl. Perrot, *Une histoire intellectuelle de l'économie politique*, p. 166. Quesnay's article was replaced in the *Encyclopédie* by Diderot's article "Hommes" (Politics) and Damilaville's, "Population." The manuscript of the article, deposited in the Bibliothèque Nationale, was only rediscovered in 1889. This is why it was not reproduced in E. Daire's collection, *Les Physiocrates* (Paris: Guillaumin, 1846). See L. Salleron, in *F. Quesnay et la physiocratie*, vol. 2, p. 511, note 1.

23. Foucault is alluding here to a question he discussed in the 1975 Collège de France lectures, *Les anormaux; Abnormal*. See below, lecture of 22 February, note 43.

24. See the article "Hommes," p. 537: "Men gather together and multiply wherever they can acquire wealth, live comfortably, possess securely and as owners the wealth that their work and their industry can procure them."

25. On this notion see *Naissance de la biopolitique*, lecture of 17 January 1979, p. 42 (utilitarianism as "technology of government").

26. Étienne Bonnot de Condillac (1715-1780), author of *Essai sur l'origine des connaissances humaines* (Paris: P. Mortier, 1746); English translation by Hans Aarsleff, *Essay on the Origin of Human Knowledge*, ed. Hans Aarsleff (Cambridge: Cambridge University Press, 2001), of the *Traité des sensations* (Paris: De Bure, 1754); English translation by Geraldine Carr, *Condillac's Treatise on the Sensations* (London: Favil Press, 1930), and *Traité des animaux* (Paris: De Bure, 1755). In the *Traité des sensations* he maintains that there is no operation of the soul that is not a transformed sensation—hence the name of sensualism given to his doctrine—and that any sensation, whatever it is, suffices to engender all the faculties, imagining, in defense of his thesis, a statue on which he separately and successively confers the five senses. Ideology designates the philosophical movement deriving from Condillac, which begins in 1795 with the creation of the Institute (of which the Academy of moral and political sciences, to which the followers of Condillac belonged, was part). The main representative of this school was Destutt de Tracy (1754-1836), author of *Élements d'idéologie*, 4 vols. (Paris: Courcier, 1804-1815). Foucault, who devoted several pages to the *Idéologues* in *Les Mots et les Choses* (Paris: Gallimard, "Bibliothèque des sciences humaines," 1966) ch. VII, pp. 253-255; English translation by A. Sheridan, *The Order of Things* (London: Tavistock and New York: Pantheon, 1970) ch. 7, pp. 240-243, already connected Condillac's genetic conception with Bentham's panoptic apparatus in his 1973-1974 lectures, *Le Pouvoir psychiatrique*, ed. J. Lagrange (Paris: Gallimard-Le Seuil, "Hautes Études," 2003), lecture of 28 November 1973, p. 80; English translation by Graham Burchell, *Psychiatric Power. Lectures at the Collège de France 1973-1974*, English series ed. Arnold Davidson (New York: Palgrave Macmillan, 2006) p. 78. On Condillac, see also *Les Mots et les Choses*, ch. III, pp. 74-77; *The Order of Things*, pp. 60-63.

27. See *Surveiller et Punir*, p. 105; *Discipline and Punish*, p. 102: "[The discourse of the *Idéologues*] provided, in effect, by means of the theory of interests, representations and signs, by the series and geneses that it reconstituted, a sort of general recipe for the exercise of power over men: the 'mind' as a surface of inscription for power, with semiology as its tool; the submission of bodies through the central control of ideas; the analysis of representations as a principle in a politics of bodies that was much more effective than the ritual anatomy of torture and execution. The thought of the *Idéologues* was not only a theory of the individual

and society; it developed as a technology of subtle, effective, economic powers, in opposition to the sumptuous expenditure of the power of the sovereign."

28. John Graunt (1620-1674), *Natural and Political Observations Mentioned in Following Index, and Made upon the Bills of Mortality. With reference to the Government, Religion, Trade, Growth, Ayre, Disease, and the Several Changes of the Said City* (London: John Martin, 1662, 5th edition 1676) republished in *The Economic Writings of Sir William Petty*, ed. C.H. Hull (Cambridge: Cambridge University Press, 1899) vol. 2; French translation by H. Dussauze and M. Pasquier, *Œuvres économiques de Sir William Petty* (Paris: Giard et Brière, 1905) vol. 2, pp. 351-467; new translation by E. Vilquin, J. Graunt, *Observations naturelles ou politiques* (see above, note 15). An autodidact, a master draper by trade, and a friend of William Petty, Graunt had the idea of drawing up chronological tables on the basis of bills of mortality published on the occasion of the great plague that decimated London in the seventeenth century. This text is seen as the starting point of modern demography. See P. Lazersfeld, *Philosophie des sciences sociales* (Paris: Gallimard, "Bibliothèque des sciences humaines," 1970) pp. 79-80: "(...) the first mortality tables, published in 1662 by John Graunt who is considered to be the founder of modern demography." The attribution of the *Natural and Political Observations* to Graunt was challenged, however, in the seventeenth century in favor of Petty. See H. Le Bras, *Naissance de la mortalité*, p. 9, for whom "the balance swings clearly against Graunt's paternity and in favor of that of Petty." The counter thesis is defended by P. Kraeger, "New light on Graunt," *Population Studies*, 42 (1), March 1988, pp. 129-140.

29. J. Graunt, *Natural and Political Observations* ch. 2, § 19, in Petty, *Economic Writings*, vol. 2, p. 352: "... among the several *Casualties* some bear a constant proportion unto the whole number of *Burials*; such are *Chronical* Diseases, and the Diseases whereunto the City is most subject; as for Example, *Consumptions, Dropsies, Jaundice, Gout, Stone, Palsie, Scurvy, Rising of the Lights* or *Mother, Rickets, Aged, Agues, Fevers, Bloody Flux* and *Scowring*."

30. Ibid. "nay, some Accidents, as *Grief, Drowning, Men's making away themselves*, and being *Kill'd by several Accidents etc.* do the like." On the probability of suicide, see ch. 3, § 13, p. 355.

31. Ibid. ch. 8, § 4, p. 375: "We have hitherto said, There are more *Males* than *Females* [see § 1 of same chapter]; we say next, That the one exceed the other by about a thirteenth part. So that although more Men die violent deaths than Women, that is, more are *slain* in *Wars, killed by Mischance, drowned* at *Sea*, and die by the *Hand of Justice*; moreover, more Men go to the *Colonies*, and travel into Foreign parts, than Women; and lastly, more remain unmarried than of Women, as *Fellows* of *Colleges*, and *Apprentices* above eighteen, *etc.* and yet the said thirteenth part difference bringeth the business to such a pass, that every Women may have an Husband, without the allowance of *Polygamy*."

32. Ibid. ch. 11, § 9, p. 386: "Whereas we have found, [see ch. 2, § 12-13, p. 349] that of 100 quick Conceptions, about 36 of them die before they be six years old, and that perhaps but one surviveth 76" (there follows what a number of commentators improperly call Graunt's "mortality table").

33. Ibid. ch. 12, § 12, p. 393: "although Men die more regularly, and less *per saltum* in London, than in the Country, yet, upon the whole matter, there die fewer *per rata*; so as the Fumes, Steams, and Stenches above-mentioned, although they make the air of *London* more equal, yet not more *Healthful*." Foucault's allusion to Durkheim here is obvious. On the interest of nineteenth century sociology in suicide, see *La Volonté de savoir*, p. 182; *The History of Sexuality, vol. 1: An Introduction*, p. 139: "This determination to die, strange and yet so persistent and constant in its manifestations, and consequently so difficult to explain as being to particular circumstances or individual accidents (...)."

34. "The species, systematic unity, as for a long time the naturalists understood it, was defined for the first time by John Ray [in his Historia planarum (London: Faithorne)] in 1686 [a 'set of individuals who, through reproduction, engender other individuals similar to themselves']. Previously, the word was employed with very varied meanings. For Aristotle it designated small groups. Later it was confused with that of genus (*genre*)." E. Guyénot, *Les Sciences de la vie aux XVIIe et XVIIIe. L'idée d'évolution* (Paris: Albin Michel, "L'Évolution de l'humanité," 1941) p. 360. In 1758, in the 10th edition of his *Systema naturae*, Linneaus includes the genus *Homme* in the order of *Primates*, distinguishing two species: *Homo sapiens* and *Homo troglodytes* (in *Systema Naturae per Regna Tria Naturae*, 12th edition, vol. 1, [Stockholm: Salvius, 1766] p. 28 *sq.*). On the birth of the concept of

species in the seventeenth century, see also François Jacob, *La Logique du vivant* (Paris: Gallimard, "Bibliothèque des sciences humaines," 1970) pp. 61-63; English translation by Betty E. Spillman, *The Logic of Living Systems* (London: Allen Lane, 1974) pp. 50-52. The expression "human species" is a current expression in the eighteenth century. It is frequently found in Voltaire, Rousseau, and d'Holbach. See, for example, George Louis de Buffon (1707-1788), *Des époques de la nature* (Paris: Imprimerie royale, 1778) pp. 187-188: "(...) man is actually the great and final effect of creation. It will be said that the analogy seems to demonstrate that the human species has followed the same steps and that it dates from the same time as the other species, that it is even more universally distributed; and that if the period of its creation is later than that of the animals, nothing proves that man has not at least been subjected to the same laws of nature, the same alterations, and the same changes. We will acknowledge that the human species does not differ fundamentally from other species in its physical faculties, and that in this respect its fate has been more or less the same as that of the other species; but can we doubt that we differ prodigiously from the animals by the sovereign being's divine light?"

35. In the new usage of the word "public," see the fundamental work of J. Habermas, *Strukturwandel der Öffentlichkeit* (Neuwied-Berlin: H. Luchterhand, 1962) the French translation of which, by M. de Launay, *L'Espace public. Archéologie de la publicité comme dimension constitutive de la société bourgeoise* appeared in 1978 (Paris: Payot); English translation by Thomas Burger and Patrick Lawrence, *The Structural Transformation of the Public Sphere: Inquiry into a Category of Bourgeois Society* (Cambridge, Mass.: MIT Press, 1989). Foucault returns at greater length to the question of the public at the end of the lecture of 15 March.

36. The famous phrase of Thiers in an article in the *National*, 4 February 1830.

37. In the light of the phenomenon of population, Foucault puts the three large epistemic domains studied in *The Order of Things* in a different perspective: the transition from the analysis of wealth to political economy, from natural history to biology, and from general grammar to historical philology, while noting that this is not a "solution," but a "problem" to be investigated more deeply. For a first "genealogical" summary of these three fields of knowledge, on the basis of the tactical generalization of historical knowledge at the end of the eighteenth century, see, "*Il faut défendre la société*," lecture of 3 March 1976, p. 170; "*Society must be defended*," p. 190.

38. See, *Les Mots et les Choses*, ch. VI: "Échanger," pp. 177-185 (1. L'analyse des richesses, II. Monnaie et prix); *The Order of Things*, ch. 6: "Exchanging": 1. The analysis of wealth, and 2, Money and prices, pp. 166-174.

39. See above, note 22.

40. See Quesnay's article, "Hommes," p. 512: "The condition of the population and the employment of men are (...) the main objects of the economic government of states; for the fertility of the land, the monetary value of products, and the good use of financial wealth are the result of the work and industry of men. Here are the four sources plenty: they mutually contribute to the increase of each other; but it can only be sustained by the operation of the general administration of men, possessions, and products (...)." On economic government, see, for example, *Despotisme de la Chine* (1767), ch. 8, in F. *Quesnay et la physiocratie*, vol. 2, p. 923: "The economic government of the cultivation of the land is an example of the general government of the nation". According to C. Larrère, who quotes this passage in his *L'Invention de l'économie au XVIIIᵉ siècle* (Paris: PUF, "Léviathan," 1992), p. 194, it is therefore around government that the unity of doctrine takes shape in which one must be able to find "those laws and conditions that must govern the general administration of the government of society" (*Despotisme de la Chine*). See A. Landry, "Les idées de Quesnay," above, note 18, and below, lecture of 1 February, note 23.

41. See the texts collected in K. Marx and F. Engels, *Critique de Malthus*, eds., R. Dangeville and others (Paris: Maspero, 1978); see K. Marx and F. Engels, *Marx and Engels on Malthus*, ed. R.L. Meek, trans. D.L. Meek and R.L. Meek (London: Lawrence and Wishart, 1953).

42. David Ricardo (1772-1823), British economist and author of *On the Principles of Political Economy and Taxation* (London: J. Murray, 1817). From 1809 he formed a friendship with Malthus that did not affect their theoretical disagreements. On the relationship between Malthus and Ricardo, see, *Les Mots et les Choses*, p. 269; *The Order of Things*, pp. 256-257: "What makes economics possible, and necessary, then, [for Ricardo] is a perpetual and

fundamental situation of scarcity: confronted by a nature that in itself is inert and, save for one very small part, barren, man risks his life. It is no longer in the interplay of representation that economics finds its principle, but near that perilous region where life is in confrontation with death. And thus economics refers us to that order of somewhat ambiguous considerations which may be termed anthropological: it is related, in fact, to the biological properties of a human species, which, as Malthus showed in the same period as Ricardo, tends always to increase unless prevented by some remedy or constraint (...)."

43. See, *Les Mots et les Choses*, ch. V: "Classer," pp. 140-144 (II. L'histoire naturelle) and pp. 150-158 (IV. Le caractère); *The Order of Things*, ch. 5: "Classifying": II. Natural history, pp. 128-132, and IV. Character, pp. 138-145.

44. Ibid. ch. VII: "Les limites de la représentation," pp. 238-245 (III. L'organisation des êtres); trans. ibid. ch. 7: "The limits of representation": III. The organic structure of beings, pp. 226-232, especially the pages devoted to Larmarck, who is credited with having "brought the era of natural history to a close" and half-opened that of biology, not with his transformist theses, but the distinction he establishes between "the space of organic structure and that of nomenclature."

45. See ibid. pp. 287-288; trans. ibid. pp. 274-276. The problem Foucault refers to here concerns the respective places that should be attributed to Lamarck and Cuvier in the history of the nascent biology. Was Lamarck, with his transformist intuitions "which seem to 'prefigure' what was to be evolutionism," more modern than Cuvier, attached to an "old fixism, impregnated through and through with traditional prejudices and theological postulates" (p. 287; trans. p. 274)? Rejecting the summary opposition, the result of a "whole series of amalgams, metaphors, and inadequately tested analogies" (ibid.), between the "progressive" thought of the former and the "reactionary" thought of the latter, Foucault shows that, paradoxically, "[h]istoricity (...) has now been introduced into nature" (p. 288; trans. p. 276) with Cuvier—as a result of discovery of the discontinuity of living forms, which broke with the ontological continuity still accepted by Lamarck—and that in this way the possibility of evolutionist thought is opened up. A broadly convergent analysis of the problem is presented by F. Jacob in *La Logique du vivant*, pp. 171-175; *The Logic of Living Systems*, pp. 156-157, that Foucault praised in a review, "Croître et multiplier," *Le Monde*, no. 8037, 15-16 November 1970: *Dits et Écrits*, 2, pp. 99-104.

46. See *Les Mots et les Choses*, ch. VIII: "Travail, vie, langage," pp. 275-292 (III. Cuvier); *The Order of Things*, ch. 8: "Labour, life, language": III. Cuvier, pp. 263-280. See also the lecture given by Foucault at the "Journées Cuvier" at the Institut d'histoire des sciences, in May 1969: "La situation de Cuvier dans l'histoire de la biologie," *Revue d'histoire des sciences et de leurs applications*, vol. XXIII (1), January-March 1970, pp. 63-92; *Dits et Écrits*, 2, pp. 30-36, with discussion pp. 36-66.

47. Foucault does not deal with this question in *Les Mots et les Choses*; *The Order of Things*. See, "La situation de Cuvier," p. 36.

48. See, *Les Mots et les Choses*, ch. IV: "Parler," pp. 95-107 (II. La grammaire générale), ch. VIII: "Travail, vie, langage," pp. 292-307 (V. Bopp); *The Order of Things*, ch. 4: "Speaking": II General grammar, pp. 81-92, and ch. 8, "Labour, life, language": V. Bopp, pp. 280-294, and Foucault's introduction to A. Arnauld and C. Lancelot, *Grammaire générale et raisonnée* (Paris: Republications Paulet, 1969) pp. iii-xxvi; *Dits et Écrits*, 1, pp. 732-752.

four

1 FEBRUARY 1978*

The problem of "government" in the sixteenth century. ∼ *Multiplicity of practices of government (government of self, government of souls, government of children, etcetera).* ∼ *The specific problem of the government of the state.* ∼ *The point of repulsion of the literature on government: Machiavelli's* The Prince. ∼ *Brief history of the reception of* The Prince *until the nineteenth century.* ∼ *The art of government distinct from the Prince's simple artfulness.* ∼ *Example of this new art of government: Guillaume de la Perrière* Le Miroir politique *(1555).* ∼ *A government that finds its end in the "things" to be directed.* ∼ *Decline of law to the advantage of a variety of tactics.* ∼ *The historical and institutional obstacles to the implementation of this art of government until the eighteenth century.* ∼ *The problem of population an essential factor in unblocking the art of government.* ∼ *The triangle formed by government, population, and political economy.* ∼ *Questions of method: the project of a history of "governmentality."* *Overvaluation of the problem of the state.*

* A first transcription of this lecture was published in the Italian journal, *Aut-Aut*, no. 167-168, Sept.-Dec. 1978, reproduced in *Actes*, special issue, 54, *Foucault hors les murs*, Summer 1986, pp. 6-15, and reproduced in the same form, according to the editors' criteria, in *Dits et Écrits*, 3, pp. 635-657, with the title "La 'gouvernementalité.'" Our version has been completely revised on the basis of the recordings and manuscript. [A first English version, translated from the Italian by Rosi Braidotti, appeared in the English journal *I&C*, no. 6, Autumn 1979, and was republished, revised by Colin Gordon, in Graham Burchell, Colin Gordon, Peter Miller, eds. *The Foucault Effect. Studies in Governmentality* (Hemel Hempstead: Harvester Wheatsheaf, 1991; republished in Foucault, *Essential Writings, 3: Power*). I have consulted and benefited from this version in making this new translation; G.B.]

THROUGH THE ANALYSIS OF some mechanisms of security I have tried to see how the specific problems of population emerged, and last week, looking more closely at these problems we were quickly led to the problem of government. In short, in the last lectures we were concerned with the establishment of the series security—population—government. I would now like to begin to make a bit of an inventory of this problem of government.

There was, of course, no shortage of treatises in the Middle Ages and in Greco-Roman antiquity that presented themselves as advice to the prince, concerning how he should conduct himself, exercise power, and obtain the acceptance or respect of his subjects, on the love of God and obedience to him, the enforcement of his law in the cities of men,[1] and so on. But I think it is quite striking that, from the sixteenth century, and throughout the period going roughly from the middle of the sixteenth to the end of the eighteenth century, there is a flourishing development of a significant series of treatises that do not exactly present themselves as advice to the prince, nor yet as political science, but which, between advice to the prince and treatises of political science, are presented as arts of government. I think that the general problem of "government"* suddenly breaks out in the sixteenth century with respect to many different problems at the same time and in completely different aspects. There is the problem of the government of oneself, for example. The sixteenth century return to Stoicism revolves around this reactualization of the problem of how to govern oneself. There is also the problem of the government of souls and of conduct, which was, of course, the problem of Catholic or Protestant pastoral doctrine. There is the problem of the government of children, with the emergence and development of the great problematic of pedagogy in the sixteenth century. And then, perhaps only the last of these problems, there is that of the government of the state by the prince. How to govern oneself, how to be governed, by whom should we accept to be governed, how to be the best possible governor? It seems to me that all these problems, both in their intensity and multiplicity, are typical of the sixteenth century and, putting it very schematically, are at the point of intersection of two movements, two processes. There is, of course, the process that, dismantling feudal

---

* In inverted commas in the manuscript, p. 2.

structures, organizes and sets up the great territorial, administrative, and colonial states. Then there is a completely different movement, but with complex interactions with the first—there is no question of analyzing all this here—that, with the Reformation and then the Counter Reformation, questions how one wishes to be spiritually directed here on earth for one's salvation. On the one hand, there is the movement of state centralization, and, on the other, one of religious dispersion and dissidence: I think it is at the meeting point of these two movements that the problem arises, with particular intensity in the sixteenth century, of "how to be governed, by whom, to what extent, to what ends, and by what methods." A general problematic of government in general is, I think, the dominant feature of this question of government in the sixteenth century.

Within this enormous literature on government, which gets going then, or anyway breaks out, explodes in the middle of the sixteenth century, and extends until the end of the eighteenth century with the transformation I will try to identify, I would like to pick out just some noteworthy points in what is an immense, as well as monotonous, literature. I would like to pick out the points concerning the actual definition of the government of the state, of what we would call, if you like, the political form of government. The simplest way of identifying some of these noteworthy points would no doubt be to compare this mass of literature on government with a text that from the sixteenth to the eighteenth century was a sort of constant point of repulsion (*point de répulsion*) for this literature on government. This abominable text, in relation to which, by opposition [to which], and [through the] rejection of which the literature of government situated itself, is obviously Machiavelli's *The Prince*.[2] The history of this text is interesting; or rather, it would be interesting to trace the relationships between this text and all those that followed it, criticized it, and rejected it.

[We should remember first of all] that, rather than being immediately abominated, Machiavelli's *The Prince* was honored by his contemporaries and immediate successors, and was again honored at the end of the eighteenth century, or rather right at the start of the nineteenth century, precisely when all this literature on the art of government is disappearing. Macchiavelli's *The Prince* reappears at the beginning of the nineteenth century, especially in Germany moreover, where it is translated, prefaced, and commented upon by people like Rehberg,[3] Leo,[4] Ranke,[5] and Kellerman,[6] and in Italy also with Ridolfi,[7] and I think—this will have to be analyzed, I am putting it in a completely summary way—in the context of, on the one hand, Napoleon, of course, but also in a context created by the Revolution and the problem of the Revolution, that is to say[8]: How and under what conditions can a sovereign maintain his sovereignty? This is also a context of the emergence, with Clausewitz, of the problem of the relations between politics and strategy, of the political importance, evident at the 1815 Congress of Vienna,[9] of relationships of force and of the calculation of relationships of force as the principle of intelligibility and rationalization of international relations. Finally, it is a context of the problem of the territorial unity of Italy and Germany, since you know that Machiavelli was precisely one of those who sought to define the conditions for the territorial unification of Italy.

This is the climate then in which Machiavelli reappears at the beginning of the nineteenth century. However, between the honor accorded Machiavelli at the beginning of the sixteenth century and this rediscovery and re-evaluation at the beginning of the nineteenth century, it is clear that there was an extensive body of anti-Machiavelli literature. Sometimes this was explicit: there are a number of books that generally came from Catholic milieus, often from the Jesuits. There is, for example, Ambrogio Politi's *Disputationes de libris a Christiano detestandis*,[10] that is to say, as far as I know, *Discussion of books that Christians must detest*; there is the book of someone who had the misfortune to have the name Gentillet, and the first name Innocent, who wrote one of the first texts against Machiavelli called, *Discours d'Estat sur les moyens de bien gouverner contre Nicolas Machiavel*;[11] and, in this explicitly anti-Machiavellian literature, we find the later text of Frederick the Great in 1740.[12] But there is also an implicit literature taking the position of hidden and muted opposition to Machiavelli. For example, there is the English book by Thomas Elyot, *The Governor*, published in 1580,[13] Paruta's *La Perfection de la vie politique*,[14] and maybe one of the first, which I shall look at, Guillaume de La Perrière's

Le Miroir politique, published in 1555.*[15] Whether this anti-Machiavellianism is overt or surreptitious, the important thing is that its function is not just the negative one of a barrier against, or the censure and rejection of the unacceptable, and, notwithstanding our modern taste for this kind of analysis—you know: faced with such a powerful and subversive thought, so in advance of itself, every run-of-the-mill discourse has to obstruct it by essentially repressive means—I don't think this is what is interesting in the anti-Machiavelli literature.[16] I would like to consider this anti-Machiavelli literature as a positive genre, with its specific object, concepts, and strategy.

So, let's look at this implicitly or explicitly anti-Machiavellian literature. What do we find in it? Obviously, negatively, we find a sort of shallow representation of Machiavelli's thought. An adverse Machiavelli is given or reconstructed, whom the author needs, moreover, in order to say what he has to say. How does this literature characterize this more or less reconstructed Prince, against whom one struggles, or against whom one wants to say something else? (Obviously, I am not raising the question of in what respects, or to what extent, this Prince really does resemble Machiavelli's *Prince*.)

First, the Prince is characterized by a single principle: For Machiavelli, the Prince exists in a relationship of singularity and externality, of transcendence, to his principality. Machiavelli's Prince receives his principality either through inheritance, or by acquisition, or by conquest; in any case, he is not a part of it, but external to it. It makes no difference whether the link that binds him to his principality is one of violence, or tradition, or one established through the compromise of treaties and the complicity or agreement of other princes, it is, in any case, a purely synthetic link; there is no fundamental, essential, natural, and juridical connection between the Prince and his principality: externality, the Prince's transcendence, is the principle. A corollary of this principle is, of course, that inasmuch as it is an external relationship, it is fragile and constantly under threat. It is threatened from outside, by the Prince's enemies who want to take, or re-conquer, his principality, and it is also threatened internally, for there is no a priori or immediate

---

* M.F.: 1567

reason for the Prince's subjects to accept his rule. Third, an imperative is deduced from this principle and its corollary, which is that the objective of the exercise of power is, of course, to maintain, strengthen, and protect the principality. More exactly, it will be to protect the principality understood as the relationship of the Prince to what he possesses, to the territory he has inherited or acquired, and to his subjects, rather than the principality as the whole, the objective territory, if you like, constituted by the subjects and the territory. What is to be protected is the principality as the relationship of the Prince to his subjects and his territory, and not directly, immediately, fundamentally, or primarily, the territory and its inhabitants. The object of the art of governing, the art of being Prince that Machiavelli puts forward, must be this fragile link between the Prince and his principality.

One consequence of this is that the mode of analysis has two aspects. On the one hand, it involves the identification of dangers: where they come from, in what they consist, and their comparative severity; what is the greater danger, and what the lesser? The second aspect is the art of manipulating relations of force that enable the Prince to protect his principality, the link binding him to his subjects and his territory. Broadly speaking, from between the lines of these implicitly or explicitly, anti-Machiavellian treatises, The Prince emerges as a treatise on the Prince's ability to hold on to his principality. The anti-Machiavellian literature wanted to replace this ability, this know-how, with something different and new: an art of government. Being able to hold on to one's principality is not the same as possessing the art of governing; the art of government is something else. What does it comprise?

To pick out things in their still crude state, I will take one of the first texts in this large anti-Machiavellian literature, Guillaume de La Perrière's, *Le Miroir politique, contenant diverses manières de gouverner*,[17] from 1555.* In this text, which is disappointing, especially in comparison with Machiavelli himself, some important things are nevertheless outlined. First, what does La Perrière understand by "to govern" and "governor"; how does he define these terms? On page 23 of his text he

---

* M.F.: 1567 [*same date in the manuscript*].

says: "Governor may be applied to any monarch, emperor, king, prince, lord, magistrate, prelate, judge, and the like."[18] Like La Perrière, others who write about the art of government also recall that we also talk about "governing" a household, souls, children, a province, a convent, a religious order, and a family.

These comments, which seem to be and are purely terminological, actually have important political implications. Machiavelli's Prince, or how he is represented in this literature, is by definition, in terms of what was seen as the book's fundamental principle, unique in his principality and in a position of externality and transcendence in relation to it. However, in these authors we see that governing, the people who govern, and the practice of government, are multifarious since many people govern—the father of a family, the superior in a convent, the teacher, the master in relation to the child or disciple—so that there are many governments in relation to which the Prince governing his state is only one particular mode.* On the other hand, all these governments are internal to society itself, or to the state. It is within the state that the father governs his family, the superior governs the convent, and so on. There is then both a plurality of forms of government and the immanence of practices of government to the state, a multiplicity and immanence of this activity that radically distinguishes it from the transcendent singularity of Machiavelli's Prince.

Certainly, among all these forms of government that are caught up, intertwined, and tangled together within society and the state, there is a specific form that has to be identified, that of the government to be applied to the state as a whole. Thus, a bit later than La Perrière, in the following century, trying to produce a typology of different forms of government, François de La Mothe Le Vayer, in a series of pedagogical texts written for the French Dauphin, will say that there are basically three types of government, each of them falling under a science or particular form of reflection: the government of oneself, which falls under morality; the art of properly governing a family, which is part of economy; and finally, the "science of governing well" the state, which belongs to

---

* Foucault adds: whereas there is only one modality [*some inaudible words*] the principality, to be prince.

politics.[19] It is quite clear that politics has its own particular character in comparison with morality and economy, and La Mothe Le Vayer points out that politics is not exactly economy or entirely morality. What is important here is that, notwithstanding this typology, these arts of government refer to and postulate an essential continuity from one to the other. Whereas the doctrine of the Prince or the juridical theory of the sovereign constantly try to make clear the discontinuity between the Prince's power and any other form of power, which involves explaining, asserting, and founding this discontinuity, in these arts of government one must try to identify both an upward and a downward continuity.

There is upward continuity in the sense that whoever wants to be able to govern the state must first know how to govern himself, and then, at another level, his family, his goods, his lands, after which he will succeed in governing the state. This kind of ascending line is typical of all the pedagogies of the Prince that are so important in this period, and of which La Mothe Le Vayer is an example. For the Dauphin, he first writes a book of morality, then a book of economy [. . .*], and finally a treatise of politics.[20] It is the education of the Prince, therefore, that will assure the upward continuity of the different forms of government. Then there is continuity in the opposite, downward direction in the sense that when a state is governed well, fathers will know how to govern their families, their wealth, their goods, and their property well, and individuals will also conduct themselves properly. This descending line, which means that the good government of the state affects individual conduct or family management, is what begins to be called "police" at this time. The education of the Prince assures the upward continuity of forms of government, and police assures their downward continuity.

In any case, you can see that the essential component, the central element in this continuity, both in the Prince's education and in police, is the government of the family, which is called precisely "economy." The art of government essentially appears in this literature as having to answer the question of how to introduce economy—that is to say, the proper way of managing individuals, goods, and wealth, like the management of a family by a father who knows how to direct his wife, his children, and

---

* Some inaudible words.

his servants, who knows how to make his family's fortune prosper, and how to arrange suitable alliances for it—how to introduce this meticulous attention, this type of relationship between father and the family, into the management of the state? The essential issue of government will be the introduction of economy into political practice. And if this is true in the sixteenth century, it is still the case in the eighteenth. In his article on "Political Economy," it is quite clear that Rousseau still poses the problem in the same terms, saying roughly: The word "economy" originally designates "the wise government of the house for the common good of the whole family."[21] The problem, Rousseau says, is how to introduce this wise government of the family, *mutatis mutandis*, and with the discontinuities that we will note, within the general management of the state.[22] To govern a state will thus mean the application of economy, the establishment of an economy, at the level of the state as a whole, that is to say, [exercising]* supervision and control over its inhabitants, wealth, and the conduct of all and each, as attentive as that of a father's over his household and goods.

An expression that was important in the eighteenth century describes this very well. Quesnay speaks of good government as "economic government."[23] In Quesnay, and I will come back to this later, we find the moment [of birth]† of this notion of economic government, which is basically tautological since the art of government is precisely to exercise power in the form, and according to the model, of economy. But if Quesnay says "economic government," the reason is that the word "economy," for reasons I shall try to elucidate shortly, is already beginning to acquire its modern meaning, and it is becoming apparent at this moment that the essence of this government, that is to say, of the art of exercising power in the form of economy, will have what we now call the economy as its principal object. The word "economy" designated a form of government in the sixteenth century; in the eighteenth century, through a series of complex processes that are absolutely crucial for our history, it will designate a level of reality and a field of intervention for government. So, there you have what is governing and being governed.

---

* M.F.: having
† Some words difficult to hear.

Second, still in Guillaume de La Perrière's text, there is the following [phrase]*: "Government is the right disposition of things arranged so as to lead to a suitable end."[24] I would like to make some further remarks with regard to this second sentence, different from those concerning the definition of the governor and of government. "Government is the right disposition of things": I would like to dwell a little on this word "things," because when we look for what characterizes the objects on which power bears in Machiavelli's The Prince, we see that the object, the target of power is, on the one hand, a territory, and, [on the other], its inhabitants. What's more, in this respect Machiavelli only takes up, for his own uses and for the specific ends of his analysis, the same juridical principle that characterized sovereignty in public law. From the Middle Ages to the sixteenth century, sovereignty is not exercised on things, but first of all on a territory, and consequently on the subjects who inhabit it. In this sense we can say that the territory really is the fundamental element both of Machiavelli's principality and of the juridical sovereignty of the sovereign as defined by philosophers or legal theorists. Obviously, these territories may be fertile or barren, they may be densely or sparsely populated, the people may be rich or poor, active or idle, but all these elements are only variables in relation to the territory that is the very foundation of the principality or of sovereignty.

Now we can see that in La Perrière's text the definition of government does not refer to the territory in any way: one governs things. What does La Perrière mean when he says that government governs "things"? I do not think it is a matter of an opposition between things and men, but rather of showing that government is not related to the territory, but to a sort of complex of men and things. The things government must be concerned about, La Perrière says, are men in their relationships, bonds, and complex involvements with things like wealth, resources, means of subsistence, and, of course, the territory with its borders, qualities, climate, dryness, fertility, and so on. "Things" are men in their relationships with things like customs, habits, ways of acting and thinking. Finally, they are men in their relationships with things like accidents, misfortunes, famine, epidemics, and death.

---

* M.F.: text

1 February 1978   97

That government is concerned with things understood in this way as the intrication of men and things is readily confirmed by the inevitable metaphor of the ship that is always invoked in these treatises on government.[25] What is it to govern a ship? It involves, of course, being responsible for the sailors, but also taking care of the vessel and the cargo; governing a ship also involves taking winds, reefs, storms, and bad weather into account. What characterizes government of a ship is the practice of establishing relations between the sailors,* the vessel, which must be safeguarded, the cargo, which must be brought to port, and their relations with all those eventualities like winds, reefs, storms and so on. It is the same for a household. Governing a family is not fundamentally directed toward the aim of safeguarding the family property, but essentially means having the individuals who compose it, their wealth and prosperity, as the objective, the target; it means taking possible events, like deaths and births, into account; it means considering the things one can do, such as alliances with other families. It is this general management that is characteristic of government and in comparison with which the problem of landed property for the family, or of the acquisition of sovereignty over a territory for the Prince, are ultimately only relatively secondary elements. The essential, the main element, then, is this complex of men and things, the territory and property being only variables.

This theme in La Perrière's curious definition of government as the government of things is found again in the seventeenth and eighteenth centuries. Frederick the Great has some illuminating pages on the subject in his *Anti-Machiavel*, when he says, for example: Compare Holland and Russia. Russia may well have the longest borders of any European state, but what does it consist of? It is mostly marshes, forests, and deserts; it is sparsely populated by bands of poor, miserable people who lack activity and industry. Holland, on the other hand, is quite small and also largely marshland, but Holland has such a population, wealth, commercial activity, and fleet as to ensure that it is an important country in Europe, which Russia is hardly beginning to become.[26] So, to govern means to govern things.

---

* Foucault adds: whom one must safeguard

I come back again to the text I quoted a moment ago, where La Perrière said: "Government is the right disposition of things that one arranges so as to lead them to a suitable end." Government therefore has a purpose, it arranges things, in the sense I have been talking about, and it arranges things [for an end]*. Here again I think government is very clearly distinguished from sovereignty. Of course, sovereignty is never presented in philosophical and juridical texts as a pure and simple right. Neither jurists, nor, a fortiori, theologians ever said that a legitimate sovereign was simply entitled to exercise his power, without further qualification. The sovereign, to be a good sovereign, must always propose an end, that is to say, as the texts regularly say, the common good and the salvation of all. For example, in a text from the end of the seventeenth century Pufendorf says: "Sovereign authority has only been conferred on them [these sovereigns; M.F.] in order that they make use of it to obtain and preserve the public utility [...]. A sovereign must on no account consider his own advantage, unless it be also advantageous for the state."[27] Now what does this common good, or this salvation of all, which is regularly invoked by jurists and laid down as the very end of sovereignty, comprise? What do jurists and theologians say when we look at the real content that they give to this common good? They say that the common good exists when all subjects obey the law without fail, perform their appointed tasks well, practice the trades to which they are assigned, and respect the established order, insofar as this order conforms to the laws imposed by God on nature and men. That is to say, the public good is essentially obedience to the law, either to the earthly sovereign's law, or to the law of the absolute sovereign, God. In any case, what characterizes the end of sovereignty, this common or general good, is ultimately nothing other than submission to this law. This means that the end of sovereignty is circular; it refers back to the exercise of sovereignty. The good is obedience to the law, so that the good proposed by sovereignty is that people obey it. There is an essential circularity that, whatever its theoretical structure, moral justification, or practical effects, is not so far removed from Machiavelli saying that the Prince's main objective must be to preserve his principality; we always come

---

* Conjecture; words inaudible.

back to this circular relationship of sovereignty, or the principality, to itself.

Now, with La Perrière's new definition, with his search for a definition of government, I think we see the emergence of a new type of finality. Government is defined by La Perrière as a right way of arranging (*disposer*) things in order to lead (*conduire*) them, not to the form of the "common good," as the texts of the jurists said, but to a "suitable end," an end suitable for each of the things to be governed. This implies, first of all, a plurality of specific ends. For example, the government will have to ensure that the greatest possible amount of wealth is produced, that the people are provided with sufficient means of subsistence, and that the population can increase. So, the objective of government will be a series of specific finalities. And one will arrange (*disposer*) things to achieve these different ends. This word "*disposer*" is important because, what enabled sovereignty to achieve its aim of obedience to the laws, was the law itself; law and sovereignty were absolutely united. Here, on the contrary, it is not a matter of imposing a law on men, but of the disposition of things, that is to say, of employing tactics rather than laws, or, of as far as possible employing laws as tactics; arranging things so that this or that end may be achieved through a certain number of means.

I think this marks an important break. Whereas the end of sovereignty is internal to itself and gets its instruments from itself in the form of law, the end of government is internal to the things it directs (*diriger*); it is to be sought in the perfection, maximization, or intensification of the processes it directs, and the instruments of government will become diverse tactics rather than laws. Consequently, law recedes; or rather, law is certainly not the major instrument in the perspective of what government should be. Here again we find the theme that recurs throughout the seventeenth century and is quite explicit in the eighteenth century texts of the *économistes* and physiocrats, which explain that the ends of government cannot be effectively achieved by means of the law.

Finally, a fourth remark or bearing taken on this text by Guillaume de La Perrière, but on a simple, elementary, and very quick point. La Perrière says that someone who knows how to govern well, a good governor, must possess "patience, wisdom, and diligence."[28] What does he mean by "patience"? Well, when he wants to explain the word patience he takes the example of what he calls "the king of the honey bees," the bumblebee, and he says: The bumblebee reigns over the hive—this is not true, but it's not important—without need of a sting.[29] Through this, God wished to show, in a "mystical" way, he says, that the true governor should not need a sting, that is, a weapon for killing, a sword, in order to exercise his government. He must have patience rather than anger, and it is not the right to kill, to assert his strength, that should be essential in the figure of the governor. What positive content is to be given to this absence of a sting? It will be wisdom and diligence. The wisdom required of someone who governs is not exactly the wisdom of tradition, in the form of the knowledge of human and divine laws, of justice and equity, but rather wisdom as, precisely, the knowledge of things, of the objectives that can and must be attained, and the "disposition (*disposition*)" one must employ in order to attain them: this is the knowledge that constitutes the sovereign's wisdom. As for diligence, this is precisely what ensures that the sovereign, or rather one who governs, should govern only in a way such that he will consider himself and act as if he were in the service of those who are governed. Here again La Perrière refers to the example of the father: The father is someone who rises earlier than anyone else, who is the last to go to bed, and who watches over everything because he thinks of himself as being in the service of his household.[30]

You can see straightaway how different this description of government is from the description of the Prince found, or thought to be found, in Machiavelli. For sure, despite some novel aspects, this notion of government is still very crude. I think that this first little sketch of the notion and theory of the art of government did not remain up in the air in the sixteenth century; it was not just a concern of political theorists. We can identify its correlations in reality. On the one hand, from the sixteenth century the theory of the art of government was linked to the development of the administrative apparatus of the territorial monarchies (the emergence of government apparatuses and relays, etcetera). It was also linked to a set of analyses and forms of knowledge that began to develop at the end of the sixteenth century and increased in scope in the seventeenth century; essentially knowledge of the state in its different elements, dimensions, and the factors of its strength, which was called, precisely, "statistics," meaning science of the state.[31] Finally, third, we cannot fail to link this search for an art of government with mercantilism and cameralism, which are efforts to rationalize the exercise of power, precisely in terms of the knowledge acquired through statistics, and also, at the same time, a doctrine, or rather a set of doctrinal principles concerning how to increase the power and wealth of the state. This art of government is not therefore just an idea of philosophers and advisors of the Prince; in fact it was only formulated insofar as the great apparatus of the administrative monarchy and its correlative forms of knowledge were being organized.

However, in truth, this art of government could not acquire its full scope and consistency before the eighteenth century. It remained imprisoned, as it were, within the forms of the administrative monarchy. There are, I think, a number of reasons why this art of government remained somewhat wrapped up in itself or, at any rate, the prisoner of structures [...*]. First, this art of government was blocked for historical reasons, in the strict sense of the word "historical reason," which are easy to identify. Speaking in very broad terms, of course, I think this is quite simply the series of major crises of the seventeenth century: first, the Thirty Years War, with its devastation and ruin; second, [in the middle]† of the century, the great peasant and urban uprisings; and finally, the financial crisis, as well as the crisis of means of subsistence, which weighed on the policy of all the Western monarchies at the end of the seventeenth century. Basically, the art of government could only spread, be reflected, and take on and increase its dimensions in a period of expansion free from the great military, economic, and political emergencies that plagued the seventeenth century from beginning to end.

So, massive, elementary historical reasons, if you like, blocked this art of government. I think that the art of government formulated in the sixteenth century was also blocked in the seventeenth century for other

* A few unintelligible words. All the preceding passage, from "which are efforts to...", is strangely missing from the transcription of the course published in *Dits et Écrits* (see above, footnote at start of this lecture), p. 648, and is replaced by a paragraph of 19 lines of which there is no trace either in the recording or in the manuscript. [The same is true of the previous English translation of the Italian version published in *Aut-Aut*, see, *The Foucault Effect*, pp. 96–97; *Essential Writings*, 3, pp. 212–213; G.B.]
† Words difficult to hear. Manuscript: "which occupy all the middle of the century"

reasons, which could be called, in terms that I don't much care for, institutional and mental structures. At any rate, let's say that the preeminence of the problem of the exercise of sovereignty, both as a theoretical question and as a principle of organization, was a fundamental factor in blocking the art of government. So long as sovereignty was the major problem and the institutions of sovereignty were the fundamental institutions, and so long as the exercise of power was thought of as the exercise of sovereignty, the art of government could not develop in a specific and autonomous way, and I think that we have an example of this in, precisely, mercantilism. Mercantilism was the first effort, I was going to say the first sanctioned effort, of this art of government at the level of political practices and knowledge of the state; in this sense we can say that mercantilism is a first threshold of rationality in this art of government for which Perrière's text indicated only some moral rather than realistic principles. Mercantilism is the first rationalization of the exercise of power as a practice of government; it is the first time that a knowledge of the state began to be formed that can be employed for tactics of government. This is absolutely true, but I think that mercantilism was blocked and halted precisely because it took the sovereign's might as its essential objective: how to ensure not only that the country is rich, but that the sovereign has wealth and funds at his disposal, and can build up an army with which to pursue his policies? The objective of mercantilism is the might of the sovereign. What are its instruments? They are laws, edicts, and regulations, that is to say, the traditional weapons of sovereignty. Objective: sovereignty; instruments: those of sovereignty. Mercantilism tried to introduce the possibilities given by a reflected art of government within an institutional and mental structure of sovereignty that blocked it. Thus, throughout the seventeenth century, and until the great liquidation of mercantilist themes at the beginning of the eighteenth century, the art of government was marking time, as it were, trapped between two things. On the one hand, was the excessively large, abstract, and rigid framework of sovereignty as a problem and an institution. The art of government had tried to combine with the theory of sovereignty by trying to deduce the guiding principles of an art of government from a renewed theory of sovereignty. This is where the jurists of the seventeenth century intervene with the formulation or bringing up to date of the theory of the contract. The theory of the contract—of the founding contract and the reciprocal commitment of sovereign and subjects—will be a kind of framework for bringing together the general principles of an art of government. But if the theory of the contract, this reflection on the relationships between the sovereign and his subjects, played a very important role in the theory of public law, [in reality]— and the example of Hobbes clearly shows this—notwithstanding the fact that ultimately it was looking for the guiding principles of an art of government, it always remained at the level of the formulation of general principles of public law.

So, the art of government was caught between an excessively large, abstract, and rigid framework of sovereignty on the one hand, and, on the other, a model of the family that was too narrow, weak, and insubstantial. The art of government either tried to join up with the general form of sovereignty, or—or rather, at the same time—it relied, and could not fail to rely, on the kind of complete model provided by the government of the family.[32]* How can one ensure that the state can be governed as well, as precisely, and as meticulously as a family? And by the same token it was blocked by this idea of economy, which at that time only ever referred to the management of a small *ensemble* comprising the family and the household. With the household and father on the one hand, and the state and sovereignty on the other, the art of government could not find its own dimension.

How was the art of government released from this blocked situation? The process of its release, like the blockage itself, should be situated within a number of general processes: the demographic expansion of the eighteenth century, which was linked to the abundance of money, which was itself linked in turn to the expansion of agricultural production through circular processes with which historians are familiar and so will not be discussed here. This being the general framework, I think we can say more precisely that the unblocking of the art of government was

---

* The manuscript adds, p. 17: "For it is in fact the government of the family that best corresponds to the art of government that was sought: a power immanent to society (the father being part of the family), a power over 'things' rather than territory, a power with multiple finalities all of which concern the well-being, happiness, and wealth of the family, a peaceful, vigilant power."

linked to the emergence of the problem of population. Or, let's say that there is a quite subtle process, which we should try to reconstruct in detail, in which we can see how the science of government, the re-focusing of the economy on something other than the family, and the problem of population are all interconnected. It is through the development of the science of government that the economy could be re-focused on a level of reality that we now describe as the economic; and it is again through the science of government that the specific problem of population could be identified. But we could also say that it is thanks to the perception of the specific problems of the population, and thanks to the isolation of the level of reality that we call the economy, that it was possible to think, reflect, and calculate the problem of government outside the juridical framework of sovereignty. And the same statistics, which, within the framework of mercantilism, had only ever been able to function within and, in a way, for the benefit of a monarchical administration that itself functioned according to the form of sovereignty, now becomes the main technical factor, or one of the main technical factors, in unblocking the art of government.

How in fact did the problem of population make possible the release of the art of government? The perspective of population, the reality of phenomena specific to population, makes it possible to eliminate the model of the family and to re-focus the notion of economy on something else. In fact, statistics, which had hitherto functioned within administrative frameworks, and so in terms of the functioning of sovereignty, now discovers and gradually reveals that the population possesses its own regularities: its death rate, its incidence of disease, its regularities of accidents. Statistics also shows that the population also involves specific, aggregate effects and that these phenomena are irreducible to those of the family: major epidemics, endemic expansions, the spiral of labor and wealth. Statistics [further] shows that, through its movements, its customs, and its activity, population has specific economic effects. Statistics enables the specific phenomena of population to be quantified and thereby reveals that this specificity is irreducible [to the] small framework of the family. Apart from some residual themes, such as moral or religious themes, the family disappears as the model of government.

On the other hand, the family now appears as an element within the population and as a fundamental relay in its government. In other words, prior to the emergence of the problematic of population, the art of government could only be conceived on the basis of the model of the family, in terms of economy understood as management of the family. When, however, the population appears as absolutely irreducible to the family, the result is that the latter falls to a lower level than the population; it appears as an element within the population. It is therefore no longer a model; it is a segment whose privilege is simply that when one wants to obtain something from the population concerning sexual behavior, demography, the birth rate, or consumption, then one has to utilize the family. The family will change from being a model to being an instrument; it will become a privileged instrument for the government of the population rather than a chimerical model for good government. The shift from the level of model to that of instrument in relation to the population is absolutely fundamental. And in actual fact, from the middle of the eighteenth century, the family really does appear in this instrumental relation to the population, in the campaigns on mortality, campaigns concerning marriage, vaccinations, and inoculations, and so on. What enables population to unblock the art of government is that it eliminates the model of the family.

Second, population will appear above all as the final end of government. What can the end of government be? Certainly not just to govern, but to improve the condition of the population, to increase its wealth, its longevity, and its health. And the instruments that government will use to obtain these ends are, in a way, immanent to the field of population; it will be by acting directly on the population itself through campaigns, or, indirectly, by, for example, techniques that, without people being aware of it, stimulate the birth rate, or direct the flows of population to this or that region or activity. Population, then, appears as the end and instrument of government rather than as the sovereign's strength: it is the subject of needs and aspirations, but also the object of government manipulation; vis-à-vis government, [population] is both aware of what it wants and unaware of what is being done to it. Interest as the consciousness of each of the individuals making up the population, and interest as the interest of the population, whatever the individual interests and aspirations may be of those who comprise the population, will be the ambiguous fundamental target and instrument of the government of populations. This is the birth of an art, or anyway, of absolutely new tactics and techniques.

Finally, population will be the point around which what the sixteenth century texts called the "sovereign's patience" is organized. This means that the population will be the object that government will have to take into account in its observations and knowledge, in order to govern effectively in a rationally reflected manner. The constitution of a knowledge (*savoir*) of government is absolutely inseparable from the constitution of a knowledge of all the processes revolving around population in the wider sense of what we now call "the economy." Last week I said that the constitution of political economy was made possible when population emerged as a new subject from the different elements of wealth. Well, a new science called "political economy" and, at the same time, a characteristic form of governmental intervention, that is, intervention in the field of the economy and population, will be brought into being by reference to this continuous and multiple network of relationships between the population, the territory, and wealth.* In short, the transition from an art of government to political science,[33] the transition in the eighteenth century from a regime dominated by structures of sovereignty to a regime dominated by techniques of government revolves around population, and consequently around the birth of political economy.

I am not saying that sovereignty ceased to play a role when the art of government becomes a political science. Rather, I would say that the problem of sovereignty was never more sharply posed than at this moment, precisely because it was no longer a question, as in the sixteenth and seventeenth centuries, of how to deduce an art of government from theories of sovereignty, but rather, given the existence and deployment of an art of government, what juridical form, what institutional form, and what legal basis could be given to the sovereignty typical of a state.

Read the two texts by Rousseau—the first, chronologically, is the article for the *Encyclopédie*, "Political economy"[34]—and you can see how Rousseau poses the problem of government and of the art of government by noting (and the text is quite typical from this point of view) that the

---

* The manuscript clarifies, p. 20: "Physiocrats: a science of government is a science of the relations between wealth and population."

word "economy" essentially designates the father's management of the family's goods;[35] but this model can no longer be accepted, even if it was valid in the past. We know, he says, that nowadays political economy is no longer family economy, and, without explicit reference to either the physiocrats or statistics, or to the general problem of population, he clearly registers this break and the fact that "economy," "political economy," has a completely new meaning that can no longer be reduced to the old model of the family.[36] At any rate, in this article he takes on the task of defining an art of government. Then he writes *The Social Contract*[37] in which the problem is how, with notions like those of "nature," "contract," and "general will," one can give a general principle of government that will allow for both the juridical principle of sovereignty and the elements through which an art of government can be defined and described. So sovereignty is absolutely not eliminated by the emergence of a new art of government that has crossed the threshold of political science. The problem of sovereignty is not eliminated; on the contrary, it is made more acute than ever.

As for discipline, this is not eliminated either. Obviously, its organization and deployment, and all the institutions within which it flourished in the seventeenth and beginning of the eighteenth century— schools, workshops, armies—are part and parcel of, and can only be understood on the basis of, the development of the great administrative monarchies. But discipline was never more important or more valued than when the attempt was made to manage the population: managing the population does not mean just managing the collective mass of phenomena or managing them simply at the level of their overall results; managing the population means managing it in depth, in all its fine points and details.

Consequently, the idea of a government as government of population makes the problem of the foundation of sovereignty even more acute (and we have Rousseau) and it makes the need to develop the disciplines even more acute (and we have the history of the disciplines that I have tried to analyze elsewhere).[38] So we should not see things as the replacement of a society of sovereignty by a society of discipline, and then of a society of discipline by a society, say, of government. In fact we have a triangle: sovereignty, discipline, and governmental management, which has population as its main target and apparatuses of security as its essential mechanism. Anyway, I wanted to show you the profound historical link between the movement that overturns the constants of sovereignty consequent upon the major problem of good choices of government; the movement that reveals the population as a given, as a field of intervention, and as the end of government techniques; and, [finally,] the process that isolates the economy as a specific domain of reality, with political economy as both a science and a technique of intervention in this field of reality.* I think we should note that, from the eighteenth century, these three movements—government, population, political economy—form a solid series that has certainly not been dismantled even today.

I would like to add just one word [. . .†]. Basically, if I had wanted to give the lectures I am giving this year a more exact title, I certainly would not have chosen "security, territory, population." What I would really like to undertake is something that I would call a history of "governmentality." By this word "governmentality" I mean three things. First, by "governmentality" I understand the ensemble formed by institutions, procedures, analyses and reflections, calculations, and tactics that allow the exercise of this very specific, albeit very complex, power that has the population as its target, political economy as its major form of knowledge, and apparatuses of security as its essential technical instrument. Second, by "governmentality" I understand the tendency, the line of force, that for a long time, and throughout the West, has constantly led towards the pre-eminence over all other types of power—sovereignty, discipline, and so on—of the type of power that we can call "government" and which has led to the development of a series of specific governmental apparatuses (*appareils*) on the one hand, [and, on the other]‡ to the development of a series of knowledges (*savoirs*). Finally, by "governmentality" I think we should understand the process, or rather, the result of the process by which the state of justice of the

---

* The manuscript adds, p. 22: "the one [process] that will assure the management of populations by a body of functionaries."
† Some unintelligible words follow.
‡ M.F.: the development also

Middle Ages became the administrative state in the fifteenth and sixteenth centuries and was gradually "governmentalized."

We know the fascination that the love or horror of the state exercises today; we know our attachment to the birth of the state, to its history, advance, power, and abuses. I think this overvaluation of the problem of state is basically found in two forms. An immediate, affective, and tragic form is the lyricism of the cold monster[39] confronting us. But there is a second way of overvaluing the problem of the state that is paradoxical because apparently reductive. This analysis consists in reducing the state to a number of functions like, for example, the development of the productive forces and the reproduction of the relations of production. But this reductive view of the relative importance of the state in comparison with something else nonetheless makes the state absolutely essential as the target to be attacked and, as you well know, as the privileged position to be occupied. But the state, doubtless no more today than in the past, does not have this unity, individuality, and rigorous functionality, nor, I would go so far as to say, this importance. After all, maybe the state is only a composite reality and a mythicized abstraction whose importance is much less than we think. Maybe. What is important for our modernity, that is to say, for our present, is not then the state's takeover (*étatisation*) of society, so much as what I would call the "governmentalization" of the state.

We live in the era of a governmentality discovered in the eighteenth century. Governmentalization of the state is a particularly contorted phenomenon, since if the problems of governmentality and the techniques of government have really become the only political stake and the only real space of political struggle and contestation, the governmentalization of the state has nonetheless been what has allowed the state to survive. And it is likely that if the state is what it is today, it is precisely thanks to this governmentality that is at the same time both external and internal to the state, since it is the tactics of government that allow the continual definition of what should or should not fall within the state's domain, what is public and what private, what is and is not within the state's competence, and so on. So, if you like, the survival and limits of the state should be understood on the basis of the general tactics of governmentality.

And maybe, in a completely general, rough, and therefore inexact way, we could reconstruct the major forms, the major economies of power in the following way: first, the state of justice, born in a feudal type of territoriality and broadly corresponding to a society of customary and written law, with a whole interplay of commitments and litigations; second, the administrative state that corresponds to a society of regulations and disciplines; and finally, a state of government that is no longer essentially defined by its territoriality, by the surface occupied, but by a mass: the mass of the population, with its volume, its density, and, for sure, the territory it covers, but which is, in a way, only one of its components. This state of government, which essentially bears on the population and calls upon and employs economic knowledge as an instrument, would correspond to a society controlled by apparatuses of security.

There, if you like, are some remarks on the deployment of this, important I think, phenomenon of governmentality. I will now try to show you how this governmentality was born, [first], from the archaic model of the Christian pastorate and, second, by drawing support from a diplomatic-military model, or rather, technique, and finally, third, how it could only acquire its present dimensions thanks to a set of very specific instruments, the formation of which is exactly contemporaneous with the art of government, and which is called, in the old, seventeenth and eighteenth century sense of the word, police. I think the pastoral, the new diplomatic-military technique, and finally, police, were the three major points of support on the basis of which that fundamental phenomenon in the history of the West, the governmentalization of the state, could be produced.

1. On this tradition of the "mirrors of princes," see P. Hadot, "Fürstenspiegel" in *Reallexikon für Antike und Christentum*, vol. 8, ed. Th. Klauser (Stuttgart: A. Heisemann, 1972) col. 555-632.
2. N. Macchiavelli, *Il Principe* (1513), (Rome: B. Di Giunta, 1532).
3. A.W. Rehberg, *Das Buch vom Fürsten von Niccolo Macchiavelli*, übersetzt und mit Einleitung und Ammerkungen begleitet (Hanover, bei den Gebrüdern Hahn, 1810; 2nd edn., Hanover: Hahnschen Hofbuchhandlung, 1824). See S. Bertelli and P. Innocenti, *Bibliografia machiavelliana* (Verona: Edizioni Valdonega, 1979) p. 206 and pp. 221-223.
4. Heinrich Leo published the first German translation of Machiavelli's informal letters in 1826, preceded by an introduction, *Die Briefe des Florentinischen Kanzlers und Geschichtsschreiber Niccolò di Bernado dei Machiavelli an seine* (Dümmler, 1828). See, G. Procacci, *Machiavelli nella cultura europea dell'eta moderna* (Bari: Laterza, 1995) pp. 385-386; S. Bertelli and P. Innocenti, *Bibliografia*, pp. 227-228.
5. Leopold von Ranke (1795-1886), *Zur Kritik neuerer Geschichtsschreiber* (Leipzig and Berlin: G. Reimer, 1824) pp. 182-202. In this work Ranke only devotes a "brief but substantial" appendix to Machiavelli (Procacci). On its importance, see P. Villari, *Niccolò Machiavelli e i suoi tempi* (Milan: U. Hoepli, 1895) vol. 2, p. 463 *sq.*; G. Procacci, *Machiavelli nella cultura europea*, pp. 383-384: "After Fichte, Ranke was the first among the German interpreters (do not forget that the Hegelian pages of the essay *Über Verfassung Deutschlands* were still unpublished) to pose the problem of the unity of Machiavelli's work in a consistent way and to attempt to resolve it on a purely historical basis." See also, Friedrich Meinecke (1862-1954), *Die Idee der Staatsräson in der neueren Geschichte* (Munich-Berlin: R. Oldenbourg, 1924); French translation by M. Chevallier, *L'Idée de la raison d'État dans l'histoire des temps modernes* (Geneva: Droz, 1973) p. 343; English translation by Douglas Scott, *Machiavellism. The Doctrine of Raison d'État and its Place in Modern History* (Boulder and London: Westview Press, 1984) p. 380: "It is one of the most intelligent and fruitful estimates of Machiavelli that has ever been written, and it broke new ground for all those who followed him. Fifty years later, he supplemented it with additions which throw a particular light on his attitude towards Machiavelli, whereas the first edition was carried out purely from a historical point of view, and only hinted lightly at a moral judgment." This second edition appeared in 1874 and is reproduced in the *Sämtliche Werke* (Leipzig, 1877) XXXIII-XXXIV, p. 151 *sq.*
6. This author is not cited in any bibliography. No trace of his name is found in the article by A. Elkan, "Die Entdeckung Machiavellis in Deutschland zu Beginn des 19. Jahrhunderts," *Historische Zeitschrift*, 119, 1919, pp. 427-458.
7. Angelo Ridolfi, *Pensieri intorno allo scopo di Niccolò Machiavelli nel libro Il Principe* (Milan: 1810). See G. Procacci, *Machiavelli nella cultura europea*, pp. 374-377.
8. And not, "in the United States" as in the Italian *Aut-Aut* version of the text (*Dits et Écrits*, 3, p. 637) and the English version based on this.
9. Congress held at Vienna from November 1814 until June 1815 in order to establish a durable peace after the Napoleonic wars and to redraw the political map of Europe. This was the most important European congress since that of Westphalia in 1648. See below, lecture of 29 March 1978, note 9.
10. Lancellotto Politi (entered the Dominican order in 1517 under the name of Ambrogio Catarino), *Enarrationes R.P.F. Ambrossi Catharini Politi Senensis Archiepiscopi campani in quinque priora capital libri Geneses. Adduntur plerique alii tractatus et quaestiones rerum variarum* (Rome: Antonium Bladum Camerae apostolicae typographum, 1552). According to Luigi Firpo, "La prima condanna del Machiavelli," Turin University of Studies, *Annuario dell'anno accademico 1966-67* (Turin: 1967) p. 28, the work could have been printed in 1548. The paragraph in this book entitled "Quam execrandi Machiavelli discursus & instituito sui principis" (pp. 340-344) immediately follows the paragraph in which the author deals with "de libris a Christiano detestandis & a Christianismo penitus eliminandis" (p. 339)—not only pagan works, but also those of their imitators, such as Petrarch and Boccacio. See G. Procacci, *Machiavelli nella cultura europea*, pp. 89-91.
11. I. Gentillet, *Discours sur les moyens de bien gouverner et maintenir en bonne paix un Royaume ou autre Principauté, divisez en trois parties à savoir du Conseil, de la Religion et Police, que doit tenir*

un Prince. Contre Nicolas Machiavel Florentin (Geneva: 1576), republished as *Anti-Machiavel*, edited with commentary and notes by C.E. Rathé (Geneva: Droz, "Les Classiques de la pensée politique," 1968). See C.E. Rathé, Innocent Gentillet and the first " 'Antimachiavel'," *Bibliothèque d'Humanisme et Renaissance*, XXVII, 1965, pp. 186-225. Gentillet (c.1535-1588) was a Huguenot jurisconsult who took refuge in Geneva after Saint Bartholomew's Day Massacre. Between 1576 and 1655 there were 24 editions of his book (ten in French, eight in Latin, two in English, one in Dutch, and three in German). The title given by Foucault (*Discours d'Estat...*) corresponds to the Leyden edition that appeared in 1609.

12. Frederick II (Frederick the Great), *Anti-Machiavel* (The Hague: 1740) is Voltaire's revised version of the *Réfutation du Prince* of Machiavelli written by the young heir to the Prussian throne in 1739, the text of which will only be published in 1848 (republished, Paris: Fayard, "Corpus des œuvres de philosophie en langue française," 1985); English translation, *Anti-Machiavel: Or, an Examination of Machiavel's* Prince. *With notes historical and Political. Published by Mr. de Voltaire* (London: T. Woodward, MDCCXLI).

13. The first edition of Thomas Elyot's *The Boke Named the Governour* appeared in London and is actually dated 1531; critical edition ed. D.W. Rude (New York: Garland, 1992).

14. Paolo Paruta, *Della perfettione della vita politica* (Venice: D. Nicolini, 1579).

15. Guillaume de La Perrière (1499?-1553?), *Le Miroire politique, œuvre non moins utile que necessaire à tous monarches, roys, princes, seigneurs, magistrats, et autres surintendants et gouverneurs de Republicques* (Lyon: Macé Bonhomme, 1555; 2nd edn., Paris: V. Norment and J. Bruneau, 1567; 3rd edn., Paris: Robert Le Magnier, 1567); English edition, *The Mirror of Police* (London: Adam Islip, 1589 and 1599). See G. Dexter, "Guillaume de La Perrière," *Bibliothèque d'Humanisme et Renaissance*, XVII (1), 1955, pp. 56-73; E. Sciacca, "Forme di governo e forma della società nel *Miroire Politicque* di Guillaume de La Perrière," *Il Pensiero politico*, XXII, 1989, pp. 174-197. The posthumous work could have been written in 1539 on the request of the Toulouse *Capitolz*, who will ask the author to "compose in one volume, in suitable order, illustrating and enriching municipal edicts and statutes, concerning the act of political government" (3rd dedication, p. 9).

16. The last part of this sentence, from "notwithstanding the taste...," does not appear in the Italian *Aut-Aut* version [or English version; G.B.] of the text.

17. Title of the first Paris edition of 1567: *Le Miroir politique, contenants diverses manières de gouverner & policer les Republiques qui sont, & ont esté par cy-devant*, to which Foucault's citations refer. See above, note 15.

18. G. de La Perrière, *Le Miroir politique*, folio p. 23r.

19. François de La Mothe Le Vayer (1588-1672), *L'Œconomique du Prince* (Paris: A. Courbé, 1653), reprinted in *Œuvres*, vol. 1, part II (Dresden: Michel Groell, 1756) pp. 287-288: "Morality, which is the science of conduct, is divided into three parts. In the first, which is called ethics, or morality par excellence, and on which your Majesty has already conversed, we learn to govern ourselves by the rules of reason. There are two other parts that naturally follow this, one of which is œconomic and the other political. This order is quite natural, since it is absolutely necessary that a man knows how to govern himself before commanding others, either as father of a family, which is œconomic, or as sovereign, magistrate, or minister of the State, which concerns politics." See also the prologue to *La Politique du Prince* in *Œuvres*, p. 299: "After the first two parts of morality, one teaching self-control and the other stewardship, that is to say conducting a family properly, the third part, which is politics, or the science of governing well." These writings, composed between 1651 and 1658, are grouped together in the *Œuvres* of Le Vayer under the title: *Sciences dont la connaissance peut devenir utile au Prince.* They make up the set of the Instruction of Monseigneur le Dauphin, which dates from 1640. See, N. Choublier-Myskowski, *L'Éducation du prince au XVIIe siècle d'après Heroard et La Mothe Le Vayer* (Paris: Hachette, 1976).

20. F. de La Mothe Le Vayer, *La Géographie et la Morale du Prince* (Paris: A. Courbé, 1651 [*Œuvres*, vol. 1, part II, pp. 3-174 for the first treatise and pp. 239-286 for the second]); *L'Œconomique du Prince. La Politique du Prince* (Paris: A. Courbé, 1653 [*Œuvres*, ibid., pp. 287-298 for the first treatise, and pp. 299-360 for the second]).

21. Jean-Jacques Rousseau, *Discours sur l'économie politique* (1755), in *Œuvres complètes*, vol. 3 (Paris: Gallimard, "Bibliothèque de la Pléiade," 1964) p. 241; English translation by

G.D.H. Cole, *A Discourse on Political Economy* in *The Social Contract and Discourses*, p. 128: "The word Economy, or Œconomy, is derived from οἶκός, a house, and νόμος, law, and meant originally only the wise and legitimate government of the house for the common good of the whole family."

22. Ibid.: "The meaning of the term was then extended to the government of that great family, the State." A few lines later Rousseau notes that "the rules of conduct proper for one of these societies" would not be "also proper for the other. They differ too much in extent to be regulated in the same manner; and there will always be a great difference between domestic government, in which a father can see everything for himself, and civil government, where the chief sees hardly anything save through the eyes of others."

23. See, François Quesnay (1694-1774), *Maximes générales du gouvernement économique d'un royaume agricole*, in Du Pont de Nemours, ed., *Physiocratie ou Constitution naturelle du Gouvernement le plus avantageux au genre humain* (Paris: Merlin, 1768) pp. 99-122; republished in F. *Quesnay et la physiocratie*, vol. 2, pp. 949-976. See above, lecture of 25 January, note 40.

24. G. de La Perrière, *Le Miroir politique*, folio 23r: "Gouvernement est droicte disposition des choses, desquelles on prent charge pour les conduire jusques à fin convenable."

25. On the classical use of this metaphor, see Plato, *Euthyphro*, 14b, *Protagoras*, 325c, *The Republic*, 389d, 488a-489d, 551c, 573d, *The Statesman*, 296e-297a, 297e, 301d, 302a, 304a, *The Laws*, 737a, 942b, 945c, 961c, etcetera (see P. Louis, *Les Métaphores de Platon* [Paris: Les Belles Lettres, 1945] p. 156); Aristotle, *Politics*, III, 4, 1276b, 20-30; Cicero, *Ad Atticum*, 3, 47; Thomas Aquinas *De regno*, I, 2, II, 3. In the next lecture Foucault returns to this metaphor on the basis of Sophocles' *Oedipus the King*.

26. Frederick II (the Great), *Anti-Machiavel* (Amsterdam: 1741); English, *Anti-Machiavel: or, an Examination of* Machiavel's *Prince*, commentary on chapter 5 of *The Prince*, pp. 17-19. Foucault probably used the Garnier edition of the text, published after Machiavelli's *The Prince* by R. Naves, 1941, pp. 117-118. See also the critical edition of the work by C. Fleischauer in, *Studies on Voltaire and the Eighteenth Century* (Geneva: E. Droz, 1958) vol. 5, pp. 199-200. Foucault's paraphrase is, however, inexact: Frederick the Great did not say Russia was made up of marshes, etcetera, but of land that "produces all sorts of corn."

27. Samuel von Pufendorf (1632-1694), *De officio hominis et civis iuxta Legem naturalem* (ad Junghans, Londini Scanorum 1673) Book II, ch. 11, § 3; French translation, *Les Devoirs de l'homme et du citoyen tels qu'ils sont prescrits par la loi naturelle*, trans. J. Barbeyrac (Amsterdam: Pierre du Coup, 1718, 4th edn.) vol. 1, pp. 361-362; English translation by Michael Silverthorne, *On the Duty of Man and Citizen according to Natural Law*, ed. James Tully (Cambridge: Cambridge University Press, 1991) p. 151: "This is the general rule for sovereigns: the safety of the people is the supreme law. For authority has been given them to achieve the end for which states were instituted. Princes must believe that nothing is good for them privately which is not good for the state." [The French translation of this passage is a bit different: "The good of the people is the sovereign law: it is also the general maxim that sovereigns [*Puissances*] must keep constantly in mind, since Sovereign authority has only been conferred on them in order that they make use of it to obtain and preserve the public utility that is the natural end of the establishment of civil societies. A sovereign therefore must on no account hold to what is to his own advantage, unless it be also advantageous for the State"; G.B.]; see also, *De jure naturae et gentium* (Lund: A. Junghaus, 1672) VII, IX, § 3; French translation by J. Barbeyrac, *Le Droit de la nature et des gens, ou Système général des principes les plus importants de la Morale, de la Jurisprudence et de la Politique*, trans. J. Barbeyrac (Amsterdam: H. Schelte and J. Kuyper, 1706); English translation by Basil Kennet and others, *Of the Law of Nature and Nations* (Oxford: 1703).

28. G. de La Perrière, *Le Miroir politique*, f. 23r: "Every governor of a Kingdom or Republic must possess in himself wisdom, patience, and diligence."

29. Ibid. f. 23v: "Every governor must also have patience, following the example of the King of the honey bees, who has no sting at all, by which nature wanted to show mystically that Kings and governors of Republics must employ much more clemency than severity towards their subjects, and more equity than harshness."

30. Ibid.: "What must a good governor of a Republic possess? He must have extreme diligence in the government of his city, and if the good father (in order to be a good steward, that is

to say head of the household) must be the first to rise and the last to go to bed in his private household, what must the governor do in a city in which there are several households, and the King in the Kingdom of several cities?"

31. On the history of statistics, see the classical work of V. John, *Geschichte der Statistik* (Stuttgart: F. Encke, 1884), reference to which appears in Foucault's notes. He may also have been familiar with the volume published by the INSEE, *Pour une histoire de la statistique* (Paris: INSEE, 1977; republished, Paris: Éd. Economica/INSEE, 1987).

32. See, for example, Richelieu, *Testament politique* (Amsterdam: H. Desbordes, 1688); ed., L. André (Paris: R. Laffont, 1947) p. 279: "Private families are the true models of Republics."

33. See the subtitle of the book on cameralism by P. Schiera, *Il Cameralismo e l'assolutismo tedesco: Dall'Arte di Governo alle Scienze dello Stato* (Milan: A. Giuffré, 1968). Foucault never cites this book, which marks a milestone in the recent history of *Polizeiwissenschaft*, but he probably knew of it, at least indirectly, through Pasquale Pasquino, who was then very close to him. Foucault comes back to the word "science," which he rejects, at the start of the next lecture.

34. See above, note 21.

35. See, ibid.

36. Jean-Jacques Rousseau, *Discours sur l'économie politique*, p. 241 and p. 244; *A Discourse on Political Economy*, p. 128 and p. 131. "But how could the government of the State be like that of the family, when the basis on which they rest is so different? (...) From all that has just been said, it follows that *public* economy, which is my subject, has been rightly distinguished from *private* economy, and that, the State having nothing in common with the family except the obligations which their heads lie under of making both of them happy, the same rules of conduct cannot apply to both."

37. *Du Contract social, ou Principe du droit politique* (Amsterdam: M. Rey, 1762).

38. See *Surveiller et Punir; Discipline and Punish*.

39. See Friedrich Nietzsche, *Thus Spoke Zarathustra*, trans. R.J. Hollingdale (Harmondsworth: Penguin, 1969) p. 75: "The state is the coldest of all cold monsters [*das kälteste aller kalten Ungeheuer*]. Coldly it lies, too; and this lie creeps from its mouth: 'I, the state, am the people.'" Nietzsche's expression is frequently taken up in anarchist discourse.

five

8 FEBRUARY 1978

Why study governmentality? ∿ The problem of the state and population. ∿ Reminder of the general project: triple displacement of the analysis in relation to (a) the institution, (b) the function, and (c) the object. ∿ The stake of this year's lectures. ∿ Elements for a history of "government." Its semantic field from the thirteenth to the sixteenth century. ∿ The idea of the government of men. Its sources: (A) The organization of a pastoral power in the pre-Christian and Christian East. (B) Spiritual direction (direction de conscience). ∿ First outline of the pastorate. Its specific features: (a) it is exercised over a multiplicity on the move; (b) it is a fundamentally beneficent power with salvation of the flock as its objective; (c) it is a power which individualizes. Omnes et singulatim. The paradox of the shepherd (berger). ∿ The institutionalization of the pastorate by the Christian Church.

I MUST APOLOGIZE, BECAUSE I will be more muddled than usual today. I've got the flu and don't feel very well. I was bothered all the same, since I had some misgivings about letting you come here and then telling you at the last minute that you could leave again. So, I will talk for as long as I can, but you must forgive me for the quantity as well as the quality.

I would like to begin to go over the dimension that I have called by the ugly word "governmentality."* Assuming that "governing" is different

---

* In inverted commas in the manuscript.

from "reigning or ruling," and not the same as "commanding" or "laying down the law," or being a sovereign, suzerain, lord, judge, general, landowner, master, or a teacher, assuming therefore that governing is a specific activity, we now need to know something about the type of power the notion covers. In short, we need to analyze the relations of power on which the sixteenth century arts of government set their sights, which are also the target of seventeenth century mercantilist theory and practice, and which, finally, are the aim—and maybe reach a certain threshold of, I think last week I said science,[1] but this is a thoroughly bad and disastrous word; let's say a certain level of political competence—in, broadly speaking, the physiocratic doctrine of "economic government."[2]

First question: Why should one want to study this insubstantial and vague domain covered by a notion as problematic and artificial as that of "governmentality"? My immediate answer will be, of course, in order to tackle the problem of the state and population. Straightaway there is a second question: This is all very well, but we know what the state and population are, or, at any rate, we think we do. The notions of the state and of the population have their definitions and histories. Broadly speaking, we are more or less familiar with the domain to which these notions refer, or anyway, if there is a submerged or obscure part, there is another visible part. So, since it involves studying this, at best, or worst, semi-obscure domain of the state and population, why should one want to approach it through such a thoroughly obscure notion as that of "governmentality"? Why attack the strong and the dense with the feeble, diffuse, and lacunary?

Well, I will give you the reason in a few words and by recalling a somewhat more general project. When in previous years we talked about the disciplines, about the army, hospitals, schools, and prisons, basically we wanted to carry out a triple displacement, shifting, if you like, to the outside, and in three ways. First, moving outside the institution, moving off-center in relation to the problematic of the institution or what could be called the "institutional-centric" approach. Consider the example of the psychiatric hospital. For sure, we can start from the psychiatric hospital as it is given in its structure and institutional density and try to discover its internal structures, to identify the logical necessity of each of its constituent components, and to show what type of medical power is organized within it and how it develops a certain psychiatric knowledge. But—and here I refer specifically to Robert Castel's clearly fundamental and essential work, *L'Ordre psychiatrique*,[3] which really should be read— we can proceed from the outside, that is to say, show how the hospital can only be understood as an institution on the basis of something external and general, that is, the psychiatric order, precisely insofar as the latter is connected up with an absolutely global project, which we can broadly call public hygiene, which is directed towards society as a whole.[4] As Castel does, we can show how the psychiatric institution gives concrete expression to, intensifies, and gives density to a psychiatric order rooted in the definition of a non-contractual regime for individuals reduced to the status of minors.[5] Finally, we can show how a whole battery of multifarious techniques concerning the education of children, assistance to the poor, and the institution of workers' tutelage are coor- dinated through this psychiatric order.[6] This kind of method entails going behind the institution and trying to discover in a wider and more overall perspective what we can broadly call a technology of power. In the same way, this analysis allows us to replace a genetic analysis through filiation with a genealogical analysis—genealogy should not be confused with genesis and filiation—which reconstructs a whole net- work of alliances, communications, and points of support. So, the first methodological principle is to move outside the institution and replace it with the overall point of view of the technology of power.[7]

The second shift, the second transfer to the outside, concerns the function. Take the case of the prison, for example. We could of course analyze the prison on the basis of the functions we expect it to perform, those defined as its ideal functions, and of the optimal way of exercising them (which is, broadly speaking, what Bentham did in his *Panopticon*[8]). Starting from there, we could see what real functions were assured by the prison and establish an historical balance sheet of func- tional pluses and minuses, or anyway of what was intended and what was actually achieved. But, here again, studying the prison from the angle of the disciplines involved short-circuiting, or rather moving out- side in relation to the functional point of view, and putting the prison back in a general economy of power. As a result, we noticed that the real history of the prison is undoubtedly not governed by the successes and failures of its functionality, but is in fact inserted within strategies and tactics that find support even in these functional defects themselves. So, the second principle is to substitute the external point of view of strategies and tactics for the internal point of view of the function.

Finally, the third de-centering, the third shift to the outside, concerns the object. Taking the point of view of the disciplines involved refusing to give oneself a ready-made object, be it mental illness, delinquency, or sexuality. It involved not seeking to measure institutions, practices, and knowledges in terms of the criteria and norms of an already given object. Instead, it involved grasping the movement by which a field of truth with objects of knowledge was constituted through these mobile technologies. We can certainly say that madness "does not exist,"[9]* but this does not mean it is nothing. All in all, it was a matter of doing the opposite of what phenomenology had taught us to say and think, the phenomenology that said, roughly: Madness exists, which does not mean that it is a thing.[10]

In short, the point of view adopted in all these studies involved the attempt to free relations of power from the institution, in order to analyze them from the point of view of technologies; to distinguish them also from the function, so as to take them up within a strategic analysis; and to detach them from the privilege of the object, so as to resituate them within the perspective of the constitution of fields, domains, and objects of knowledge. If this triple movement of a shift to the outside was tried out with regard to the disciplines, I would now like to explore this possibility with regard to the state. Can we cross over to the outside of the state as we could, without great difficulty, with regard to these different institutions? Is there an encompassing point of view with regard to the state as there was with regard to local and definite institutions? I think this type of question cannot fail to arise, be it only as the result, the necessity implied by precisely what I have just been saying. After all, do not these general technologies of power, which we have attempted to reconstruct by moving outside the institution, ultimately fall under a global, totalizing institution that is, precisely, the state?

---

* In inverted commas in the manuscript.

By stepping outside these local, regional, and precise institutions of the hospital, the prison, or families, are we not referred back, quite simply, to another institution, so that we will have abandoned institutional analysis only to be enjoined to enter into another type of institutional analysis in which, precisely, the state is the stake? It is all very well to emphasize confinement, for example, as a general procedure that enveloped the history of psychiatry; but in the end is not confinement a typical operation of the state, or one that broadly falls under the action of the state? We may well single out the disciplinary mechanisms of sites such as the prison, workshops, and the army, where there were attempts to put these mechanisms to work. But, in the last instance, is not the state ultimately responsible for their general and local application? It may be that the extra-institutional, non-functional, and non-objective generality of the analysis I have been talking about confronts us with the totalizing institution of the state.*

---

* No doubt due to the fatigue that he refers to at the start of the lecture, Foucault leaves out the exposition of pages 8 to 12 of the manuscript:
"Hence the second reason for raising the question of the state: Is not the method of analyzing localized powers in terms of procedures, technologies, tactics, and strategies just a way of passing from one level to another, from the micro to the macro? And consequently, would it not have only provisional value: for the stage of this transition? It is true that no method should be a stake in itself. A method should be made in order to get rid of it. But it is less a question of method than of point of view, of an adaptation of the gaze, a way of turning round the [support?] of things by moving the person observing them. Now it seems to me that such a shift produces effects that are at least worth maintaining for as long as one can, if not holding on to them at any price.
What are these effects?
a. By de-institutionalizing and de-functionalizing relations of power we can grasp their genealogy, i.e., the way they are formed, connect up with each other, develop, multiply, and are transformed on the basis of something other than themselves, on the basis of processes that are something other than relations of power. Example of the army: We may say that the disciplinarization of the army is due to its control by the state (*étatisation*). However, when disciplinarization is connected, [not] with a concentration of state control, but with the problem of floating populations, the importance of commercial networks, technical inventions, models [several illegible words] community management, a whole network of alliance, support, and communication constitutes the "genealogy" of military discipline. Not the genesis: filiation. If we want to avoid the circularity that refers the analysis of relations of power from one institution to another, it is by grasping them at the point where they constitute techniques with operative value in multiple processes.
b. By de-institutionalizing and de-functionalizing relations of power we can [see] the respect in which and why they are unstable.
—Permeability to a whole series of different processes. Technologies of power are not immobile: they are not rigid structures aiming to immobilize living processes by their very immobility. Technologies of power are endlessly modified by the action of numerous factors. And when an institution breaks down it is not necessarily because the power that underpins

So, in short, the challenge of the lectures I would like to give this year will be this. Just as in the examination of the relationships between reason and madness in the modern West we tried to question the general procedures of confinement and segregation, thus going behind the asylum, the hospital, therapies, and classifications,* and just as for the prison we tried to go behind penitentiary institutions in the strict sense so as to seek out the general economy of power, can we carry out the same reversal for the state? Is it possible to move outside? Is it possible to place the modern state in a general technology of power that assured its mutations, development, and functioning? Can we talk of something like a "governmentality" that would be to the state what techniques of segregation were to psychiatry, what techniques of discipline were to the penal system, and what biopolitics was to medical institutions? These are the kind of questions that are at stake [in these lectures].†

So, this notion of government. A bit of orientation in the history of the word, in a period in which it had not yet acquired the political, rigorous statist meaning, it begins to take on in the sixteenth and seventeenth centuries. What do we get from looking at some historical dictionaries of the French language?[11] We see that in the thirteenth,

---

it has been put out of play. It may be because it has become incompatible with some fundamental mutations of these technologies. Example of penal reform (neither popular revolt, nor even extra-popular pressure).

—But also accessibility to struggles or attacks that inevitably find their theater in the institution.

This means that it is entirely possible to arrive at overall effects, not by concerted confrontations, but also by local or lateral or diagonal attacks that bring into play the general economy of the whole. Thus: marginal spiritual movements, multiplicities of religious dissidence, which did not in any way attack the Catholic Church, ultimately toppled not only a whole section of the ecclesiastical institution, but the way in which religious power was exercised in the West.

These theoretical and practical effects suggest that it may be worth the effort to continue with experiment."

* The manuscript adds here (p. 13): "just as to examine the status of illness and the privileges of medical knowledge in the modern world it was also necessary to go behind the hospital and medical institutions in order to attempt to connect up with the general procedures for taking charge of life and illness in the West, with 'biopolitics.'"

† Inaudible words. Foucault adds: I would now like to, in order to excuse the character [an inaudible word] of what I am trying to say to you between two fits of coughing . . .

The manuscript contains this complementary note: "NB. I am not saying that the state was born from the art of government, or that the techniques for governing men were born in the seventeenth century. The state as the set of institutions of sovereignty has existed for millennia. The techniques of the government of men also existed for millennia. But it is on the basis of a new general technology [of] the government of men that the state took the form that we know."

fourteenth, and fifteenth centuries the word "to govern (*gouverner*)" actually covers a considerable number of different meanings. First, we find the purely material, physical, and spatial meaning, of to direct, move forward, or even to move forward oneself on a track, a road. "To govern" is to follow a path, or put on a path. In Froissart, for example, you find a text like this: "A [...] path so narrow that [...] two men *ne s'y pourraient gouverner*,"[12] that is to say, could not go forward walking abreast. It also has the material but much wider meaning of supporting by providing means of subsistence. For example, in a text from 1421: "enough wheat to govern (*gouverner*) Paris for two years,"[13] or again, from the same period: "a man did not have the wherewithal to live or govern (*gouverner*) his wife who was ill."[14] So, "to govern" in the sense of support, provide for, and give means of subsistence. "A wife of excessive government (*gouvernement*)"[15] is a wife who consumes too much and is difficult to support. "To govern" also has a meaning close to this, but a little different, of the source of one's means of subsistence. Froissart talks of a town "which is governed (*se gouverne*) by its drapery,"[16] that is to say, getting its means of subsistence from this activity. These are a set of reference points, or some specifically material references anyway, of this word "to govern (*gouverner*)."

There are meanings of a moral kind. "To govern" may mean "to conduct someone," either in the specifically spiritual sense of the government of souls—a completely classical sense that will endure and subsist for a very long time—or, in a way that deviates a bit from this, "to govern" may mean "to impose a regimen," on a patient for example: the doctor governs the patient, or the patient, who imposes treatment on himself, governs himself. Thus, a text says: "A patient who, after having left the Hôtel-Dieu, passed away as a result of his bad government."[17] He had followed a bad regimen. "To govern," or "government," may refer to conduct in the specifically moral sense of the term: a daughter who was of "bad government,"[18] that is to say, whose conduct was bad. "To govern" may refer also to a relationship between individuals that can take many forms, be it the relationship of command and control—directing, dealing with someone—or having a verbal relationship with someone: "governing someone" may mean "speaking with him," "conversing with him" in the sense of holding someone in a conversation. Thus, a text from the fifteenth century says: "He ate well with all those who conversed with him (*le gouvernaient*) during his supper."[19] To govern (*gouverner*) someone during his supper is to speak with him. But it may also refer to a sexual relationship: "A fellow who had a sexual relationship with (*gouvernait*) the wife of his neighbor, and saw her regularly."[20]

This is both a very empirical and unscientific set of reference points established through dictionaries and various references. All the same, I think it allows us to situate one of the dimensions of the problem. Before it acquires its specifically political meaning in the sixteenth century, we can see that "to govern," covers a very wide semantic domain in which it refers to movement in space, material subsistence, diet, the care given to an individual and the health one can assure him, and also to the exercise of command, of a constant, zealous, active, and always benevolent prescriptive activity. It refers to the control one may exercise over oneself and others, over someone's body, soul, and behavior. And finally it refers to an intercourse, to a circular process or process of exchange between one individual and another. Anyway, one thing clearly emerges through all these meanings, which is that one never governs a state, a territory, or a political structure. Those whom one governs are people, individuals, or groups. When one speaks of a town that governs itself (*se gouverne*), and which is governed on the basis of its drapery, it means that people get their means of subsistence, their food, their resources, and their wealth from drapery. It is not therefore the town as a political structure, but the people, individuals, or group. Those whom one governs are people.*

I think this may put us on the track of something that is undoubtedly of some importance. To start with, and fundamentally, at least through this first set of references, those whom one governs are people. Now the idea of governing people is certainly not a Greek idea, and nor do I think it is a Roman idea. In Greek literature at least, there is the fairly frequent metaphor of the rudder, the helmsman, the pilot, and the person who steers the ship, to designate the activity of the person who is the head of the city-state and who has a number of duties and responsibilities with regard to the city. Take, for example, *Oedipus the King*.[21] In *Oedipus the*

---

* The manuscript adds: "History of governmentality. Three major vectors of the governmentalization of the state: the Christian pastoral = old model; the new regime of diplomatic-military relations = supporting structure; the problem of the internal police of the state = internal support." See above, the last lines of the previous lecture, 1 February.

King, frequently, or at several points, there is the metaphor of the king who is responsible for the city-state and must conduct it as a good pilot properly governs his ship, avoiding reefs and guiding it to port.[22] But in these metaphors, which identify the king as a helmsman and the city as a ship, we should note that what is governed, what the metaphor designates as the object of government, is the city-state itself, which is like a ship threatened by reefs, a ship caught in the storm, a ship that has to steer a course avoiding pirates and enemies, and a ship that must be led to safe harbor. Individuals are not the object of government; the action of government is not brought to bear on individuals. The captain or pilot of the ship does not govern the sailors; he governs the ship. In the same way, the king governs the city-state, but not the men of the city. The object or target of government is the city-state in its substantial reality, its unity, and its possible survival or disappearance. Men are only governed indirectly, insofar as they have boarded the ship. And men are governed through the intermediary or relay of boarding the ship. But it is not men themselves who are directly governed by the person who is the head of the city-state.*

So I do not think that the idea that one could govern men, or that one did govern men, was a Greek idea. If I have the time and courage I will come back to this problem, either at the end of these lectures or in the next series of lectures, basically around Plato and *The Statesman*. But, generally speaking, I think we can say that the origin of the idea of a government of men should be sought in the East, in a pre-Christian East first of all, and then in the Christian East, and in two forms: first, in the idea and organization of a pastoral type of power, and second, in the practice of spiritual direction, the direction of souls.

First, the idea and organization of a pastoral power. The theme of the king, god, or chief as a shepherd (*berger*) of men, who are like his flock, is frequently found throughout the Mediterranean East. It is found in Egypt,[23] Assyria,[24] Mesopotamia,[25] and above all, of course, in the Hebrews. In Egypt, for example, but also in the Assyrian and Babylonian

---

* The manuscript adds, p. 16: "This does not exclude there being those among the rich and powerful who had a status that allowed them to manage the affairs of the city-state, and allowed others (citizens, not slaves or metics) multiple and closely woven modes of action: clientelism, euergetism."

monarchies, the king is actually designated, in a completely ritual way, as the shepherd (*berger*) of men. On his coronation, for example, the Pharaoh receives the insignia of the shepherd. The shepherd's crook is placed in his hands and he is declared the shepherd of men. The title of shepherd (*pâtre*) or pastor (*pasteur*) of men, is one of the royal titles for the Babylonian monarchs. It was also a term designating the relationship of the gods, or god, with men. God is the pastor of men. In an Egyptian hymn, we can read something like this: "Oh Ra who keeps watch when all men sleep, who seeks what is good for your flock . . ."[26] God is the shepherd (*berger*) of men. In a word, this metaphor of the shepherd, this reference to pastorship allows a type of relationship between God and the sovereign to be designated, in that if God is the shepherd of men, and if the king is also the shepherd of men, then the king is, as it were, the subaltern shepherd to whom God has entrusted the flock of men and who, at the end of the day and the end of his reign, must restore the flock he has been entrusted with to God. Pastorship is a fundamental type of relationship between God and men and the king participates, as it were, in this pastoral structure of the relationship between God and men. An Assyrian hymn addressed to the king says: "Radiant companion who shares in God's pastorship (*pastorat*), who cares for the land and provides for it, O shepherd of plenty."[27]

Obviously, the theme of pastorship is especially developed and intensified in the Hebrews,[28] with the particular characteristic that in the Hebrews the shepherd-flock relationship is essentially, fundamentally, and almost exclusively a religious relationship. Only the relations between God and his people are defined as relations between a shepherd (*pasteur*) and a flock. No Hebrew king, with the exception of David, the founder of the monarchy, is explicitly referred to by name as a shepherd (*berger*).[29] The term is reserved for God.[30] But some prophets are thought to have received the flock of men from God, to whom they must return it,[31] and, on the other hand, the bad kings, those who are denounced for having betrayed their task, are designated as bad shepherds, not in relation to individuals, but always in reference to the whole, as those who have squandered and dispersed the flock, who have been unable to feed it and take it back to its land.[32] The pastoral relationship in its full and positive form is therefore essentially the relationship of God to men. It is a religious type of power that God exercises over his people.

I think there is something in this that is fundamental, and probably specific, to the Mediterranean East, and which is very different from what is found in the Greeks. You never find the Greeks having the idea that the gods lead men like a pastor, a shepherd, leads his flock. Whatever the intimacy between the Greek gods and their city, and it is not necessarily very great, it is never that kind of relationship. The Greek god founds the city, he or she indicates its site, helps in the construction of walls, guarantees its soundness, gives his or her name to the town, and issues oracles through which he or she gives advice. The god is consulted; he or she protects and intervenes; he or she is sometimes angry, and then makes peace; but the Greek god never leads the men of the city like a shepherd leads his sheep.

What is it, then, that characterizes this power of the shepherd, which we can see is foreign to Greek thought, but present and intense in the Mediterranean East, especially in the Hebrews? What are its specific features? I think we can summarize them in the following way. The shepherd's power is not exercised over a territory but, by definition, over a flock, and more exactly, over the flock in its movement from one place to another. The shepherd's power is essentially exercised over a multiplicity in movement. The Greek god is a territorial god, a god *intra muros*, with his privileged place, his town or temple. The Hebrew God, on the other hand, is the God moving from place to place, the God who wanders. The presence of the Hebrew God is never more intense and visible than when his people are on the move, and when, in his people's wanderings, in the movement that takes them from the town, the prairies, and pastures, he goes ahead and shows his people the direction they must follow. The Greek god, rather, appears on the walls to defend his town. The Hebrew God appears precisely when one is leaving the town, when one is leaving the city walls behind and taking the path across the prairies. "O God, when you set out at the head of your people," say the Psalms.[33] In the same way, or in a somewhat similar way, Amon, the Egyptian shepherd-god, is defined as the one who leads people on every path. If there is a reference to the territory in the direction God gives to a multiplicity on the move, it is to where the shepherd-god knows fertile grasslands can be found, the best routes to take, and the places suitable for resting. In Exodus, it is said to Yahweh: "In your faithful love you led out the people you had redeemed; in your strength you have guided them to your holy pastures."[34]* So, in contrast with the power exercised on the unity of a territory, pastoral power is exercised on a multiplicity on the move.

Second, pastoral power is fundamentally a beneficent power. You will say that this is part of all religious, moral, and political descriptions of power. What kind of power would be fundamentally wicked? What kind of power would not have the function, purpose, and justification of doing good? It is a universal feature, except that, nonetheless, in Greek thought anyway, and I think also in Roman thought, the duty to do good was ultimately only one of the many components characterizing power. Power is characterized as much by its omnipotence, and by the wealth and splendor of the symbols with which it clothes itself, as by its beneficence. Power is defined by its ability to triumph over enemies, defeat them, and reduce them to slavery. Power is also defined by the possibility of conquest and by the territories, wealth, and so on it has accumulated. Beneficence is only one of a whole bundle of features by which power is defined.

However, pastoral power is, I think, entirely defined by its beneficence; its only *raison d'être* is doing good, and in order to do good. In fact the essential objective of pastoral power is the salvation (*salut*)† of the flock. In this sense we can say that we are assuredly not very far from the objective traditionally fixed for the sovereign, that is to say, the salvation of one's country, which must be the *lex suprema* of the exercise of power.[35] But the salvation that must be assured to the flock has a very precise meaning in this theme of pastoral power. Salvation is first of all essentially subsistence. The means of subsistence provided, the food assured,

---

* [Foucault's French version of this verse is slightly different from the King James version: "thou has guided them in thy strength unto thy holy habitation," and from that of the New Jerusalem Bible: "in your strength you have guided them to your holy dwelling"; G.B.]

† The French *salut* can, of course, mean both "safety" and "salvation" in its religious sense. I have chosen to translate it as salvation, bearing in mind that the English word, in addition to the specifically religious sense, also includes the sense of preserving from harm, whereas "safety" does not include the religious sense: G.B.

is good pasture. The shepherd is someone who feeds and who feeds directly, or at any rate, he is someone who feeds the flock first by leading it to good pastures, and then by making sure that the animals eat and are properly fed. Pastoral power is a power of care. It looks after the flock, it looks after the individuals of the flock, it sees to it that the sheep do not suffer, it goes in search of those that have strayed off course, and it treats those that are injured. A rabbinic commentary, which is a bit late but which absolutely reflects this, explains how and why Moses was chosen by God to lead the flock of Israel. It was because when Moses was a shepherd in Egypt he knew how to graze his sheep and knew, for example, that when he came to pasture he had to send the youngest sheep first to eat the most tender grass, then those a little older, and then the eldest and most robust who could eat the toughest grass. In this way each category of sheep had the grass it needed and enough to eat. Moses presided over this just, calculated, and reflected distribution of food, and Yahweh, seeing this, said to him: "Since you know how to pity the sheep, you will have pity for my people, and I will entrust them to you."[36]

The shepherd's (*pasteur*) power manifests itself, therefore, in a duty, a task to be undertaken, so that—and I think this is also an important characteristic of pastoral power—the form it takes is not first of all the striking display of strength and superiority. Pastoral power initially manifests itself in its zeal, devotion, and endless application. What is the shepherd (*berger*)? Is he someone whose strength strikes men's eyes, like the sovereigns or gods, like the Greek gods, who essentially appear in their splendor? Not at all. The shepherd is someone who keeps watch. He "keeps watch" in the sense, of course, of keeping an eye out for possible evils, but above all in the sense of vigilance with regard to any possible misfortune. He will keep watch over the flock and avoid the misfortune that may threaten the least of its members. He will see to it that things are best for each of the animals of his flock. This is true for the Hebrew God and equally for the Egyptian god, of whom it is said: "Oh Ra who keeps watch when all men sleep, who seeks what is beneficial for your flock . . ."[37] But why? He keeps watch because he has an office, which is not primarily defined as an honor, but rather as a burden and effort. The shepherd (*pasteur*) directs all his care towards others and never towards himself. This is precisely the difference between the good and the bad shepherd. The bad shepherd only thinks of good pasture for his own profit, for fattening the flock that he will be able to sell and scatter, whereas the good shepherd thinks only of his flock and of nothing else. He does not even consider his own advantage in the well-being of his flock. I think we see here the appearance, the outline, of a power with an essentially selfless and, as it were, transitional character. The shepherd (*pasteur*) serves the flock and must be an intermediary between the flock and pasture, food, and salvation, which implies that pastoral power is always a good in itself. All the dimensions of terror and of force or fearful violence, all these disturbing powers that make men tremble before the power of kings and gods, disappear in the case of the shepherd (*pasteur*), whether it is the king-shepherd or the god-shepherd.

Finally, the last feature, which confirms some of things I have been saying, is the idea that pastoral power is an individualizing power. That is to say, it is true that the shepherd directs the whole flock, but he can only really direct it insofar as not a single sheep escapes him. The shepherd counts the sheep; he counts them in the morning when he leads them to pasture, and he counts them in the evening to see that they are all there, and he looks after each of them individually. He does everything for the totality of his flock, but he does everything also for each sheep of the flock. And it is here that we come to the famous paradox of the shepherd, which takes two forms. On the one hand, the shepherd must keep his eye on all and on each, *omnes et singulatim*,[38] which will be the great problem both of the techniques of power in Christian pastorship, and of the, let's say, modern techniques of power deployed in the technologies of population I have spoken about. *Omnes et singulatim*. And then, in an even more intense manner, the second form taken by the paradox of the shepherd is the problem of the sacrifice of the shepherd for his flock, the sacrifice of himself for the whole of his flock, and the sacrifice of the whole of his flock for each of the sheep. What I mean is that, in this Hebrew theme of the flock, the shepherd owes everything to his flock to the extent of agreeing to sacrifice himself for its salvation.[39] But, on the other hand, since he must save each of the sheep, will he not find himself in a situation in which he has to neglect the whole of the flock in order to save a single sheep? This theme, with Moses at its center, is endlessly repeated in all the different sedimentations of the Biblical text from Genesis up to the rabbinical commentaries. Moses really was prepared to abandon the whole of the flock in order to save a single sheep that had gone astray. Finally he found the sheep and brought it back on his shoulders, and at that moment, it turns out that the flock he was prepared to sacrifice was nonetheless saved, symbolically, precisely by the fact that he was prepared to sacrifice it.[40] This is central to the challenge, to the moral and religious paradox of the shepherd, or what could be called the paradox of the shepherd: the sacrifice of one for all, and the sacrifice of all for one, which will be at the absolute heart of the Christian problematic of the pastorate.

To sum up, we can say that the idea of a pastoral power is the idea of a power exercised on a multiplicity rather than on a territory. It is a power that guides towards an end and functions as an intermediary towards this end. It is therefore a power with a purpose for those on whom it is exercised, and not a purpose for some kind of superior unit like the city, territory, state, or sovereign [...*]. Finally, it is a power directed at all and each in their paradoxical equivalence, and not at the higher unity formed by the whole. I think the structures of the Greek city-state and the Roman Empire were entirely foreign to this type of power. You will say that there are a number of texts in Greek literature in which there is a very explicit comparison between political power and the power of the shepherd. There is *The Statesman*, which, as you know, is engaged in precisely this type of research. What is the one who rules? What is it to rule? Is it not exercising power over a flock?

Good, listen, I feel really lousy. I cannot go into all this, and ask you if we can stop now. I really am too tired. I will talk about this again, the problem of *The Statesman* in Plato next week. I would just like to indicate roughly—well, if I have given you this very clumsy schema, it is because it seems to me that we have a very important phenomenon, which is that the idea of a pastoral power, which is entirely foreign, or at any rate considerably foreign to Greek and Roman thought, was introduced into the Western world by way of the Christian Church. The Christian Church

---

* An inaudible word.

coagulated all these themes of pastoral power into precise mechanisms and definite institutions, it organized a pastoral power that was both specific and autonomous, it implanted its apparatuses within the Roman Empire, and at the heart of the Empire it organized a type of power that I think was unknown to any other civilization. This really is the paradox and the subject on which I would like to focus in the next lectures. Of all civilizations, the Christian West has undoubtedly been, at the same time, the most creative, the most conquering, the most arrogant, and doubtless the most bloody. At any rate, it has certainly been one of the civilizations that has deployed the greatest violence. But, at the same time, and this is the paradox I would like to stress, over millennia Western man has learned to see himself as a sheep in a flock, something that assuredly no Greek would have been prepared to accept. Over millennia he has learned to ask for his salvation from a shepherd (*pasteur*) who sacrifices himself for him. The strangest form of power, the form of power that is most typical of the West, and that will also have the greatest and most durable fortune, was not born in the steppe or in the towns. This form of power so typical of the West, and unique, I think, in the entire history of civilizations, was born, or at least took its model from the fold, from politics seen as a matter of the sheep-fold.

1. See the previous lecture, 1 February, p. 104 and p. 106 concerning economy as "science of government," and p. 107: "an art of government that has now crossed the threshold of political science."
2. On this notion, see above, lecture of 18 January, p. 33.
3. R. Castel, *L'Ordre psychiatrique. L'âge d'or de l'aliénisme* (Paris: Minuit, "Le sens commun," 1976; English translation by W.D. Halls, *The Regulation of Madness, the origins of incarceration in France* (Berkeley and Los Angeles: University of California Press, 1988).
4. See, ibid. ch. 3, pp. 138-152 ("L'aliéniste, l'hygiéniste et la philanthrope"); trans., ibid. pp. 112-124 ("The Mental Health Specialist, the Hygienist and the Philanthropist"). See on pp. 142-143 (trans. pp. 116-117), the quotations from the prospectus presenting the *Annales d'hygiène publique et de médecine légale*, founded in 1829 by Marc and Esquirol ("public hygiene, which is the art of preserving the health of people gathered together in society and which is destined to be very greatly developed and to provide numerous applications for the improvement of our institutions").
5. Ibid. ch. 1, pp. 39-50 ("Le criminel, l'enfant, le mendiant, le prolétaire et le fou"); trans., ibid. pp. 28-38 ("Criminal, Child, Beggar, Poor Wage-earner and Mad person").
6. Ibid. ch. 5, pp. 208-215 ("Les opérateurs politiques"); trans., ibid. pp. 171-180 ("The Political Operators").
7. In the 1973-1974 lectures, *Le Pouvoir psychiatrique*; *Psychiatric Power*, going back over various points in *Histoire de la folie*; *Madness and Civilization*, that according to him could be challenged, Foucault questions for the first time the criticism of psychiatric power in terms of the institution and sets against it a criticism founded on the analysis of relations of power, or the micro-physics of power. See the lecture of 7 November 1973, p. 16; p. 15: "I no longer think that the institution is a very satisfactory notion. It seems to me that it harbors a number of dangers, because as soon as we talk about institutions we are basically talking about both individuals and the group, we take the individual, the group, and the rules which govern them as given, and as a result we can throw in all the psychological or sociological discourses. [...] What is important [...] is not institutional regularities, but much more the practical dispositions of power, the characteristic networks, currents, relays, points of support, and differences of a form of power, which are, I think, constitutive of, precisely, both the individual and the group." See the lecture of 14 November 1973, p. 34; p. 33: "Let's be really anti-institutionalist." See too, *Surveiller et Punir*, p. 217; *Discipline and Punish*, p. 215: " 'Discipline' may be identified neither with an institution nor with an apparatus (*appareil*)."
8. Jeremy Bentham (1748-1832), *Panopticon, or the Inspection House . . .* , in *Works*, ed., J. Bowring (Edinburgh: Tait, 1838-1843) vol. IV, pp. 37-66; French translation, *Panoptique, Mémoire sur un nouveau principe pour construire des maisons d'inspection, et nommément des maisons de force*, trans. E. Dumont (Paris: Imprimerie nationale, 1791), republished in *Œuvres de Jérémy Bentham*, ed., E. Dumont (Brussels: Louis Hauman and Co., 1829) vol. 1, pp. 245-262. The French translation is reproduced in J. Bentham, *Le Panoptique*, preceded by M. Foucault, "L'œil du pouvoir"; "The eye of power" and followed by a translation by M. Sissung of the first part of the original version of *Panopticon*, as published by Bentham in England in 1791. The most recent English edition is, Jeremy Bentham, *The Panopticon Writings*, ed. M. Božovič (New York and London: Verso, 1995). See *Surveiller et Punir*, pp. 201-206; *Discipline and Punish*, pp. 200-209.
9. See, "L'éthique du souci de soi comme pratique de la liberté" (January 1984) *Dits et Écrits*, 4, p. 726; English translation by P. Aranov and D. McGrawth, "The Ethics of the Concern for Self as a Practice of Freedom" in *Essential Works of Foucault 1954-1984, Vol. 1: Ethics: subjectivity and truth*, ed. Paul Rabinow (New York: The New Press, 1997) p. 297: "I have been seen as saying that madness does not exist, whereas the problem is absolutely the converse: it was a question of knowing how madness, under the various definitions that have been given, was at a particular time integrated into an institutional field that constituted it as a mental illness occupying a specific place alongside other illnesses." According to Paul Veyne, this was how Raymond Aron, for example, understood *Histoire de la folie*; *Madness and Civilization*.
10. See Paul Veyne, "Foucault révolutionne l'histoire" (1978) in Paul Veyne, *Comment on écrit l'histoire* (Paris: Le Seuil, "Points Histoire," 1979) p. 229. Veyne's essay on Foucault is not

included in the English translation of the first, 1971 edition of his book, *Writing History: Essay on Epistemology*, trans. Mina Moore-Rinvolucri (Middletown, Conn.: Wesleyan University Press, 1984). The essay is translated by Catherine Porter, "Foucault Revolutionizes History" in Arnold I. Davidson, ed., *Foucault and his Interlocutors* (Chicago and London: University of Chicago Press, 1997) p. 170: "When I showed the present text to Foucault, he responded roughly as follows: 'I personally have never written that *madness does not exist*, but it can be written; because, for phenomenology, madness exists, but is not a thing, whereas one has to say on the contrary that madness does not exist, but that it is not therefore nothing.'"

11. The manuscript (unnumbered page inserted between pages 14 and 15) refers to the *Dictionnaire de l'ancienne langue française et de tous ses dialectes du IXe au XVe* of Frédéric Godefroy (Paris: F. Vieweg, 1885) vol. IV.

12. "Un petit chemin si estroit, qu'un home a cheval seroit assez empesché d passer outre, ne deux hommes ne s'y pourroyent gouverner" Froissart, *Chroniques*, 1559, Book I, p. 72, cited by F. Godefroy, *Dictionnaire*, p. 326.

13. "Si y avoit a Paris plus de blé que homme qui fust ne en ce temp y eust oncques voeu, car on tesmoignoit qu'il y en avoit pour bein gouverner Paris pour plus de 2 ans entiers," *Journal de Paris sous Charles VI*, p. 77, cited by F. Godefroy, *Dictionnaire*, p. 325.

14. "Il n'avoit de quoy vivre ni gouverner sa femme qui estoit malade" 1425, Arch. JJ 173, pièce 186, cited by Godefroy, ibid.

15. "Pour ces jours avait ung chevalier et une dame de trop grand gouvernement, et se nommoit li sires d'Aubrecicourt" Froissart, *Chroniques*, vol. II, p. 4, cited by Godefroy, ibid.

16. "Une grosse ville non fermee qui s'appelle Senarpont et se gouverner toute de la draperie" Froissart, *Chroniques*, Book V, cited by Godefroy, ibid. p. 326.

17. "De laquelle bateure icellui Philipot a esté malade par l'espace de trois semaines ou environ, tant a l'Ostel Dieu ou il fu porté comme en son hostel, et depuis, par son mauvais gouvernement, est alé de vie a trespassement" 1423, Arch. JJ 172; pièce 186, cited by Godefroy, ibid. p. 325.

18. "Une fille qui avoit esté de mauvais gouvernement" H. Estienne, *Apol. P. Hérod.*, c. 15, cited by Godefroy, ibid.

19. "Il fit bonne chera a tous, voire aux principaux des Seize, qui le gouvernerent pendant son souper" Pasq., *Lett.*, XVII, 2, cited by Godefroy, ibid.

20. "Un quidam qui gouvernait la femme de son voisin et l'alloit voir si souvent qu'a la fin le mary s'en aperçut" G. Bouchet, *Serées*, 1.III, p. 202, cited by Godefroy, ibid. This is also cited by Littré, *Dictionnaire de la langue française* (Paris: J.-J. Pauvert, 1957) vol. 4, p. 185.

21. Foucault frequently took an interest in this drama in the years between 1970 and 1980. See the lectures of 1970-1971, "La Volonté de savoir," 12th lecture (summarized in a lecture at Cornell in October 1972); "La vérité et les formes juridiques," (1974) *Dits et Écrits*, 2, pp. 553-568; English translation by Robert Hurley, "Truth and Juridical Forms," *Essential Works of Foucault*, 3, pp. 1-89; the first lectures of the 1979-1980 series, "Du gouvernement des vivants" (16 and 23 January, and 1 February: the Louvain seminar of May 1981, "Mal faire, dire vrai. Fonction de l'aveu" (unpublished).

22. In fact the image only appears once in *Oedipus the King*. See the French translation by R. Pignarre (Paris: Garnier, 1964) p. 122: "My king, I have said to you before, and I say it again, / I would prove mad and foolish / if I were to abandon you, you / who, when my country was beset by storm, / was the good wind that guided it. Ah! Once again, / if you can, lead us to safe harbor today." [Cf. the English translation by David Grene, which refers to "you who steered the country," but not explicitly to harbor or port; "Oedipus the King" in David Grene and Richmond Lattimore, eds, *Sophocles I* (Chicago: The University of Chicago Press, 1991) pp. 40-41; G.B.] It is, however, a recurrent theme in Sophocles: *Ajax*, 1082, *Antigone*, 162, 190. See P. Louis, *Les Métaphores de Platon*, p. 156, n. 18.

23. The Pharaohs were designated as the shepherds (*bergers*) of their people from the 12th dynasty, under the Middle Empire at the beginning of the 2nd millennium. See D. Müller, "Der gute Hirt. Ein Beitrag zur Geschichte ägyptischer Bildrede," *Zeitschrift für Ägypt. Sprache*, 86, 1961, pp. 126-144.

24. The description of the king as pastor (*re'ü*) goes back to Hammurabi (around 1728-1686). Most of the Assyrian kings, up to Assurbanipal (669-626) and the neo-Babylonian

monarchs, will adopt this custom. See L. Dürr, *Ursprung und Ausbau der israelitisch-jüdischen Heilandserwartung. Ein Betrag zur Theologies des Alten Testaments* (Berlin: C.A. Schwetschke & Sohn, 1925) pp. 116-120.

25. See I. Seibert, *Hirt–Herde–König. Zur Herausbildung des Königtums in Mesopotamien* (Berlin: Deutsche Akademie der Wissenschaft zu Berlin. Schriften der Sektion für Altertumwissenschaft, 53, 1969).

26. "Hymne à Amon-Rê" (Le Caire, c.1430 B.C.E) in A. Barucq and F. Daumas, *Hymnes et Prières de l'Éypte ancienne*, no. 69 (Paris: Le Cerf, 1980) p. 198.

27. Source unidentified. On the divine origin of royal power, which expresses the image of the shepherd (*pasteur*), see I. Seibert, *Hirt–Herde–König*, pp. 7-9.

28. There is a considerable literature on this subject. See, W. Jost, *Poimen. Das Bild vom Hirten in der biblischen Überlieferung und seine christologische Bedeutung* (Giessen: Otto Kindt, 1939); G.E. Post, "Sheep," in *Dictionary of the Bible* (Edinburgh: 1902) vol. 4, pp. 486-487; V. Hamp, (i) "Das Hirtmotiv im Alten Testament," in *Festschrift Kard. Faulhaber* (Munich: J. Pfeiffer, 1949) pp. 7-20, and (ii) "Hirt," in *Lexikon für Theologie und Kirche* (Freiburg im Breisgau: 1960) col. 384-386. On the New Testament: Th. H. Kempf, *Christus der Hirt. Ursprung und Deutung einer altchristlichen Symbolgestalt* (Rome: Officium Libri Catholici, 1942); J. Jeremias, "Ποψήν," in *Theologisches Wörterbuch zum Neuen Testament*, Bd. 6, 1959, pp. 484-501. Among more recent studies we note the article by P. Grelot, "Berger," in *Dictionnaire de spiritualité ascétique et mystique* (Paris: Bauchesne) 1984) vol. 12, col. 361-372, and the good synthesis accompanied by a very rich bibliography, by D. Peil, *Untersuchungen zur Staats- und Herrschaftsmetaphorik in literarischen Zeugnissen von der Antike bis zur Gegenwart* (Munich: W. Fink, 1983) pp. 29-164 ("Hirt und Herde").

29. This title is not applied directly to him in the historical and sapiential books. See the second book of Samuel, 5, 2; 24, 17; Psalms, 78, 70-72: God entrusts the "grazing (*paître*)" of the people of Israel to him and David designates the latter as a "flock." On the other hand, the designation is more frequent in the prophetic books: see, for example, Ezekiel, 34, 23; 37, 24 ("My servant David will reign over them, one shepherd for all" (New Jerusalem Bible). As Foucault suggests, the image of the shepherd is sometimes used to designate pagan kings: see Isaiah, 44, 28 (with reference to Cyrus); Jeremiah, 25, 34.

30. See Genesis, 48, 15; Psalms, 23, 1-4; 80, 2; Isaiah, 40, 11; Jeremiah, 31, 10; Ezekiel, 34, 11-16; Zechariah, 11, 4-14. See W. Jost, *Poimen*, p. 19 *sq*. Obviously there are many more occurrences of the application of pastoral vocabulary to Yahweh ("to guide," "to lead," "to herd," "to lead to pasture," etcetera). See, J. Jeremias, "Ποψήν," p. 486.

31. See, Jeremiah, 17, 16 (but the translation of this passage has been questioned); Amos, 1, 1; 7, 14-15; See W. Jost, *Poimen*, p. 16.

32. See, Isaiah, 56, 11; Jeremiah, 2, 8; 10, 21; 12, 10; 23, 1-3; Ezekiel, 34, 2-10 ("Disaster is in store for the shepherds of Israel who feed themselves! Are not shepherds meant to feed a flock? Yet you have fed on milk, you have dressed yourselves in wool, you have sacrificed the fattest sheep, but failed to feed the flock. You have failed to make weak sheep strong, or to care for the sick ones, or bandage the injured ones. You have failed to bring back strays or look for the lost. On the contrary you have ruled them cruelly and harshly" New Jerusalem Bible); Zechariah, 10, 3; 11, 4-17; 13, 7.

33. Psalms, 68, 7.

34. Exodus, 15, 13.

35. Foucault is alluding here to the maxim "Salus populi suprema lex esto," the first occurrence of which is found—with a quite different meaning—in Cicero, *De legibus*, 3, 3, 8, with regard to the duty of magistrates to apply the law zealously, and which was taken up from the sixteenth century by most of the theorists of absolutism. See above, lecture of 1 February, note 27, the quotation from Pufendorf's *De officio hominis et civis*; *On the Duty of Man and Citizen*.

36. See, J. Engemann, "Hirt" in *Reallexikon für Antike und Christentum* (Stuttgart: 1991) vol. 15, col. 589: "Andererseits bleibt ihnen (= den Rabbinen) dennoch bewußt, daß Mose, gerade weil er ein guter Hirt war, von Gott erwählt wurde, das Volk Israël zu führen (Midr. Ex. 2, 2); L. Ginzberg, *The legends of the Jews*, 7, trans. from the German manuscript by Henrietta Szold (Philadelphia: Jewish Publ. Soc. of America, 1938) Reg. s.v. shepherd." See also Philo of Alexandria, *Di vita Mosis*, I. 60 (according to D. Peil, *Untersuchungen*, p. 43, n. 59); Justin Martyr, *Apologies*, 62, 3 (according to W. Jost, *Poimen*, p. 14, n. 1).

37. Phrase already quoted above, p. 124.

38. See the lectures, "'*Omnes et singulatim*': Toward a critique of political reason," given by Foucault at the University of Stanford in October 1979, in *Essential Works of Foucault*, 3, pp. 298-325; French translation by P.-E. Dauzat, "'Omnes et singulatim': vers une critique de la raison politique," *Dits et Écrits*, 4, pp. 134-161.

39. See, John, 11, 50; 18, 14: "... it was better for one man to die for the people."

40. See the next lecture, 15 February, p. 152.

six

15 FEBRUARY 1978

*Analysis of the pastorate (continuation). ∽ The problem of the
shepherd-flock relationship in Greek literature and thought: Homer,
the Pythagorean tradition. Rareness of the shepherd metaphor in
classical political literature (Isocrates, Demosthenes). ∽ A major
exception: Plato's* The Statesman. *The use of the metaphor in
other Plato texts (*Critias, Laws, The Republic*). The critique of
the idea of a magistrate-shepherd in* The Statesman. *The pastoral
metaphor applied to the doctor, farmer, gymnast, and teacher. ∽
The history of the pastorate in the West, as a model of the
government of men, is inseparable from Christianity. Its
transformations and crises up to the eighteenth century. Need for a
history of the pastorate. ∽ Characteristics of the "government of
souls": encompassing power coextensive with the organization of the
Church and distinct from political power. ∽ The problem
of the relationships between political power and pastoral power
in the West. Comparison with the Russian tradition.*

IN EXPLORING THIS THEME of governmentality I have begun
an extremely vague sketch, not of the history, but of some reference
points that allow us to shed a little light on what I believe has been so
important in the West and that we can call, and is in fact called, the
pastorate. All of these reflections on governmentality, this very vague sketch
of the pastorate, should not be taken as gospel truth. This is not finished
work, it is not even work that's been done; it is work in progress, with

all that this involves in the way of inaccuracies and hypotheses—in short, it amounts to possible tracks for you, if you wish, and maybe for myself, to follow.

So, last week I laid some stress on this theme of the pastorate and tried to show you that the use of shepherd-flock relationship to designate the relationship of either God, of the divinity, to men, or of the sovereign to his subjects, was undoubtedly a frequent theme in Pharaonic Egyptian literature, but also in Assyrian literature, and in any case was a very insistent theme for the Hebrews, while on the other hand it did not seem that this shepherd-flock relationship had such importance for the Greeks. It even seems to me that the shepherd-flock relationship was not a good political model for the Greeks. I think a number of objections can be made to this, and last week someone approached me to say that he did not agree with me on this theme, on this point. So, if it's okay with you, I would like to spend some time and try to plot out a bit this problem of the shepherd-flock relationship in Greek literature and thought.

It seems to me that the theme of the shepherd-flock relationship, for designating the relationship of the sovereign or political official with his subjects or fellow citizens, is present in the Greeks, and we can support this assertion on three main groups of references. The first, of course, is Homeric vocabulary. Everyone knows that in the *Iliad*, essentially with reference to Agamemnon, but also in the *Odyssey*, there are a number of references that designate the king as the shepherd (*pasteur*) of nations, the *poimēn laon*, a ritual title.[1*] This is undeniable and I think it is easily explained by the fact that this is a ritual title of the sovereign in all Indo-European literature, which we find precisely in Assyrian literature; it is a ritual title consisting in addressing oneself to the sovereign by calling him "shepherd of peoples (*berger des peuples*)." There are a number of studies of this. You can look at a German book by Rüdiger Schmitt, for example, on poetry and poetic expressions in the Indo-European epoch. It was published in 1967.[2] On pages 283-284 there are a whole series of references to this expression *poimēn laon*, shepherd of

---

* In the manuscript, Foucault cites the following references: *Iliad*, II, 253; *Odyssey*, III, 156; XIV, 497.

peoples, which is archaic but also appears later, since it is found, for example, in the Old English poems of *Beowulf*,[3] where the sovereign is designated as shepherd (*pasteur*) of the people, or shepherd (*pasteur*) of the country.

The second series of texts refer explicitly to the Pythagorean tradition in which, from the beginning until the neo-Pythagoreans, to the texts of the pseudo-Archytas cited by Stobaeus,[4] there is also reference to the model of the shepherd. Basically this focuses on two or three themes. First the etymology traditionally accepted by the Pythagoreans derived *nomos*, the law, from *nomeus*, that is to say, the shepherd. The shepherd is the lawmaker insofar as he distributes food, directs the flock, indicates the right direction, and says how the sheep must mate so as to have good offspring. All this is the function of the shepherd who gives the law to his flock. Hence the title of Zeus as *Nomios*. Zeus is the god-shepherd, the god who provides his sheep with the food they need. Finally, still in this Pythagorean type of literature, there is the idea that the magistrate is not characterized by his power, strength, and decision-making ability so much as by the fact that he is above all the *philanthrōpos* who loves those under his jurisdiction, the men subject to him, and who is not egoistic. The magistrate is by definition full of zeal and solicitude, like the shepherd. "The law is not made for him," the magistrate, but first and foremost "for those under his jurisdiction."[5] So there is certainly a fairly coherent and durable tradition throughout Antiquity that maintained this fundamental theme that the magistrate, the decision-maker in the city-state, is essentially a shepherd. But of course, this Pythagorean tradition is, if not marginal, at least limited.

What is the situation in the third set of texts, those of classical political vocabulary? Well, there are two theses if you like. The German Gruppe, in his edition of the fragments of Archytas,[6] explains that actually the metaphor of the shepherd is hardly found in the Greeks, except where there could have been an oriental influence, and precisely a Hebrew influence; that the texts where the shepherd is represented as the model of the good magistrate are revealing, dense texts, which refer to a typically oriental ideology or type of political representation; and that this theme is entirely confined to the Pythagoreans: where there is a reference to the shepherd, a Pythagorean and therefore oriental influence should be seen.

In opposition to this, Delatte, in *La Politique des pythagoriciens*,[7] says: No, not at all, the theme of the shepherd as a political model or figure is a commonplace. It is not at all specific to the Pythagoreans. It does not express an oriental influence and is ultimately a relatively unimportant theme, a sort of commonplace way of thinking, or rather a commonplace in the vocabulary, in the political rhetoric of the classical epoch.[8] In actual fact, this thesis, the assertion that the theme of the shepherd is a commonplace in the political thought or vocabulary of the classical epoch, is just baldly stated by Delatte and is not supported by any precise reference. And then, if we consult the different indexes that could record the use of words like "shepherd," "herdsman," and "father" in Greek literature—words like *poimēn* and *nomeus*—we are completely surprised. For example, the *Index isokrateon* gives absolutely no references for the words *poimēn* and *nomeus*. That is to say, it seems that the expression shepherd or herdsman cannot be found in Isocrates. And in a precise text, the *Areopagiticus*, in which Isocrates describes the duties of the magistrate with great precision,[9] it is surprising to note that Isocrates gives a very precise, prescriptive, and dense description of the good magistrate who, above all, must watch over the good education of youth. A whole series of duties and tasks are incumbent on the magistrate. He must look after the young people and constantly supervise them, he must watch over not only their education but also their food, how they behave, how they develop, and even how they marry. We are close here to the metaphor of the shepherd, but it does not arise. This type of metaphor is also practically absent from Demosthenes. So, the metaphor of the shepherd is rare in what is called the classical political vocabulary of Greece.[10]

It is rare, with the one obvious, major and crucial exception of Plato. There you have a whole series of texts in which the good magistrate, the ideal magistrate is seen as the shepherd (*berger*). To be a good shepherd (*pasteur*) is to be not only the good magistrate, but quite simply the true, ideal magistrate. You find this in *Critias*,[11] *The Republic*,[12] *The Laws*,[13] and *The Statesman*.[14] I think *The Statesman* should be examined separately. Let us leave it aside for a moment and take up the other texts in which

Plato employs the metaphor of the shepherd-magistrate. What do we see? I think in these other texts, apart from *The Statesman* that is, the metaphor of the shepherd is employed in three ways.

First of all it is used to designate the specific, full and blessed power of the gods over humanity in the earliest time of its existence, before the time of misfortune or harshness changed its condition. The gods really were the original shepherds (*pâtres*) of humanity, its pastors. It was the gods who nurtured [men],* who guided them, provided them with food, gave them their general principles of conduct, and watched over their happiness and well-being. This is what you find in the *Critias*,[15] and it is found again in *The Statesman*, and you will see what, in my view, this means.

Second, there are also texts in which the magistrates of the present, hard time following the great happiness of humanity presided over by the gods, is also seen as a shepherd. But we should note that this magistrate-shepherd is never considered to be the founder of the city-state or the one who has given it its basic laws, but as the principal magistrate. The magistrate-shepherd—this is completely typical and entirely clear in *The Laws*—is in fact a subordinate magistrate. He is something between a watchdog strictly speaking, let's say brutally, a policeman, and someone who is the real master or legislator of the city-state. In Book 10 of *The Laws*, the magistrate-shepherd is, on the one hand, opposed to the beasts of prey he must keep away from his flock, but on the other hand, he is equally distinct from the masters at the summit of the state.[16] So, he is a functionary-shepherd, of course, but only a functionary. That is to say, it is not so much the very essence of the political function, the very essence of power in the city-state, that the shepherd represents, but merely a lateral function that in *The Statesman* is called, precisely, auxiliary.[17]

Finally, the third series of texts, still from Plato, but with the exception of *The Statesman*, is taken from *The Republic*, particularly the discussion with Thrasymachus in Book One, in which Thrasymachus says, as if it were obvious, or a commonplace, a familiar theme at least: Yes, of course, we will say that the good magistrate is one who is a genuine shepherd. But then, let's take a look at what the shepherd does.

---

* M.F.: who nurtured them

Do you really think, says Thrasymachus, that the shepherd is the man who is essentially and even exclusively concerned with the good of his flock? The shepherd only troubles himself insofar as it profits him; he only puts himself out for his animals in view of the day when he will be able to sacrifice them, cut their throats, or at any rate sell them. The shepherd acts as he does from egoism and pretends to devote himself to his animals. So, Thrasymachus says, comparison with the shepherd really is not appropriate for describing the virtue necessary for the magistrate.[18] Thrasymachus is answered: But you are not defining the good shepherd, the true shepherd, or even the shepherd at all, but the caricature of the shepherd. An egoistic shepherd is a contradiction in terms. The true shepherd is precisely someone who devotes himself entirely to his flock and does not think of himself.[19] It is certain . . . well probable anyway, that this is an explicit reference, if not to that commonplace that does not seem to be so common in Greek thought, then at least to a theme familiar to Socrates, Plato, and [Platonist] circles, to the Pythagorean theme. I think it is the Pythagorean theme of the magistrate-shepherd, of politics as shepherding, that clearly surfaces here in Book One of The Republic.

This is precisely the theme that is debated in the great text of The Statesman, for I think the function of this text is precisely to pose directly and head on, as it were, the problem of whether one can really describe and analyze, not this or that magistrate in the city-state, but the magistrate par excellence, or rather the very nature of the political power exercised in the city-state, on the basis of the model of the shepherd's action and power over his flock. Can politics really correspond to this form of the shepherd-flock relationship? This is the fundamental question, or anyway one of the fundamental dimensions of The Statesman. The whole text answers "no" to this question, and with a no that seems to me sufficiently detailed for us to see it as a full rebuttal of what Delatte called, wrongly it seems to me, a commonplace, but which should be recognized as a familiar theme in Pythagorean philosophy: The chief in the city-state must be the shepherd of the flock.

So, the rebuttal of this theme. I will just run through schematically the development of the argument in The Statesman. You know broadly how this objection to the metaphor of the shepherd is made. What is a politician; what is the politician? He can only be defined, of course, by the specific knowledge (*connaissance*) and particular art that allows him to exercise his action as a politician effectively, properly, as he should. The politician's characteristic knowledge, his characteristic art is the art of prescribing, of commanding. But then a seer who passes on the orders of the god, a messenger or herald who brings the results of the deliberations of an assembly, and the chief of the rowers in a boat, also command and give orders. So, from among all those who actually give orders, we must recognize the one who is really the politician and the specifically political art that corresponds to the function of the magistrate. Hence, the first move in the analysis of what it is to prescribe takes place in the following way. There are two ways of giving orders, Plato says. One can give orders that one issues oneself, or one can give orders issued by someone else, as in the case of the messenger or herald, the chief of the rowers, and also the seer. It is clear that the politician passes on his own orders.[20] To whom does he give these orders that he makes and passes on in his own name? Orders may concern inanimate things. This is what the architect does, for example, when he imposes his will and decisions on inanimate things like wood and stone. One can also impose orders on animate things, and fundamentally on living beings. The politician must obviously be put on this, rather than the architect's side. He therefore prescribes to living beings.[21] One can prescribe to living beings in two ways, either by prescribing to particular individuals—to one's horse or to a pair of oxen under one's command—or by giving prescriptions to a group of animals, living in a flock or formed into a herd. Clearly, the politician belongs on the latter side. He will therefore command living beings in a herd or flock.[22] Finally, one can give orders either to those living beings that are animals of any kind, to all animals, or to that particular species of living beings, human beings. Obviously the politician will be found on the latter side. Now what is it to give orders to a herd or flock of living beings, animals or men? Obviously, it is to be their shepherd or herdsman. So we have this definition: The politician is the shepherd (*berger*) of men, he is the shepherd (*pasteur*) of that flock of living beings that constitutes a population in a city-state.[23] In its evident clumsiness it is fairly clear that this result registers, if not a commonplace, then at least a familiar opinion, and the problem of the dialogue will precisely be how one extricates oneself from this familiar theme.

The movement of freeing oneself from this familiar theme of the politician as the shepherd of the flock takes place, I think, in four stages. First the method of division, so crude and simplistic in its first moves, is taken up again. In fact, straightaway there is an objection. What does it mean to oppose all the animals of whatever kind, on the one hand, to men, on the other? This is a bad division, Plato says, referring to the problem of method [. . . *].[24] We cannot put all animals on one side and all men on the other. We must make divisions that are really complete on both sides, good divisions by equivalent halves. With regard to the theme that the magistrate is someone who watches [over] a flock, we will thus have to distinguish between different types of animal, between wild animals and peaceful, domestic animals.[25] Men belong to the second category. Among the domestic or peaceful animals, there are those who live in water and those who live on the land. Man belongs to those who live on the land. Those who live on the land must be divided between those that fly and those that walk, those with or without horns, those with or without cloven hooves, and those that can or cannot interbreed. And so the division gets lost in its own subdivisions, thereby showing that one gets nowhere this way, that is to say, by starting from this familiar theme: the magistrate is a shepherd, but the shepherd of who? In other words, if we take "the magistrate = the shepherd" as the invariant of the definition, and if we then vary the object on which this relationship, the shepherd's power, bears, then we can have all the classifications we like of possible animals—aquatic and not aquatic, walking and not walking, cloven hoofed and not cloven hoofed, and so on—and we will have a typology of animals, but we will make no advance at all in the fundamental question: What then is this art of prescribing? The theme of shepherd as the invariant is completely sterile and all we ever refer to are possible variations in the categories of animals.[26]

Hence the need to take up the argument again, and this is the second moment in this critique of the theme. It consists in saying: We must now look at what it is to be a shepherd. That is to say, we must now vary the

---

* Some inaudible words.

hitherto accepted invariant of the analysis. What is it to be a shepherd; in what does it consist? We can answer in this way: Being a shepherd means first of all that, as a shepherd, one is on one's own in a flock. There are never several shepherds for a flock; there is only one. On the other hand, with regard to forms of activity, we see that the shepherd has to do a whole range of things. He must assure food for the flock. He must look after the young. He must cure those who are ill or injured. He must lead them down paths by giving them orders or possibly by playing music to them. He must arrange their mating in order to produce the most vigorous and fertile sheep that produce the best lambs. So, there is a single shepherd and a series of different functions.[27] Now, let's take this up and apply it to humans or the city-state. What will we [say]*? We are agreed that the human shepherd must be alone; there must be only one magistrate or king. But who in the city-state will be responsible for all these activities of feeding, care, therapy, and the regulation of mating; who can be in charge, and who in fact is in charge of this? It is at this point that the principle of the singleness, the uniqueness of the shepherd, is immediately challenged, and we see the birth of what Plato calls the rivals of the king, the rivals of the king in shepherding. If the king is in fact defined as shepherd (*pasteur*), why not say that the farmer who feeds men, or the baker who makes bread and provides them with food, is just as much the shepherd of humanity as the shepherd who leads the flock of sheep to grass or gets them to drink? The farmer and the baker are rivals of the king as shepherds of humanity. But the doctor who takes care of those who are sick is equally a shepherd (*berger*), he performs the function of shepherd (*pâtre*); the gymnastics master and the teacher, who watch over the good education and health of children, over the vigor of their bodies and their abilities, are also equally shepherds in relation to the human flock. All may lay claim to being shepherds (*pasteurs*) and are therefore rivals of the politician.[28]

So, to start with we had an invariant: The magistrate is the shepherd. We vary the series of beings on which the shepherd's power bears, we get a typology of animals, and the division becomes endless. So once more

---

* Inaudible word.

we take up the analysis of what it is to be a shepherd, and then we see the proliferation of a series of functions that are not political functions. So, on the one hand, there is the series of all the possible divisions in animal species and, on the other, the typology of all the possible activities that may be related to the shepherd's activity in the city-state. Politics has disappeared. Hence the problem has to be taken up anew.

The third stage of the analysis: How will we capture the very essence of politics? It is at this point that myth comes in. You are familiar with the myth of *The Statesman*. This is the idea that the world turns on itself, first in the right direction, or anyway in the direction of happiness, the natural direction, and then, when it has run its course, this is followed by a movement in the opposite direction, which is the movement of difficult times.[29] Humanity lives in happiness and felicity so long as the world turns on its axis in the first direction. This is the age of Chronos. This is an age, Plato says, "that does not belong to the present constitution of the world, but to its earlier constitution."[30] What happens at this point? There is a whole series of animal species and each one appears as a flock. At the head of this flock there is a shepherd. This shepherd (*berger*) is the divine pastor (*génie pasteur*) who rules over each of the animal species. Among these animal species there is a particular flock, the human flock. This human flock also has its divine pastor. What is this pastor? It is, Plato says, "the deity himself."[31] The deity himself is the pastor of the human flock in this period of humanity that does not belong to the present constitution of the world. What does this pastor do? In truth, his task is infinite, exhaustive, and, at the same time, easy. It is easy inasmuch as the whole of nature provides man with everything he needs: food is provided by the trees; the climate is so mild that man does not have to build houses, he can sleep beneath the stars; and he is no sooner dead than he returns to life. And it is this happy flock, with abundant food and endlessly living anew, this flock without dangers or difficulties, over which the deity rules. The deity is their pastor and, Plato's text says, "because the deity was their pastor, they had no need of a political constitution."[32] Politics begins, therefore, precisely when this first age, during which the world turns in the right direction, comes to an end. Politics begins when the world turns in the opposite direction. When the world turns in the opposite direction, in fact, the deity withdraws, and difficult times begin. For sure, the gods do not completely abandon men, but they only help them in an indirect way, by giving them fire, the [arts],* and so forth.³³ They are no longer really the shepherds who were everywhere and immediately present in the first phase of humanity. The gods have withdrawn and men are obliged to direct each other, that is to say, they need politics and politicians. However, and here again Plato's text is very clear, these men who are now in charge of other men are not above the flock in the way in which the gods are above humanity. They are themselves a part of humanity and therefore cannot be seen as shepherds.³⁴

Now, the fourth stage of the analysis: Since politics, the political, and politicians only arise when the old constitution of humanity has disappeared, that is to say, when the age of the deity-pastor has come to an end, how will the role of the politician be defined, and in what will this art of giving orders to others consist? At this point, as an alternative to the model of the shepherd, the model of weaving, endlessly famous in political literature, is put forward.³⁵ The politician is a weaver. Why is the model of weaving the good one? (I am going very quickly here because these are familiar things.) First of all, this model of weaving enables us to make a coherent analysis of the different modalities of political action in the city-state. Against the, as it were, invariable and global theme of the shepherd, which can only lead back to either the earlier state of humanity or to the crowd of people who may claim to be shepherds of humanity, the model of the weaver gives us instead an analytical schema of precisely those processes within the city-state that concern being in charge of men. To start with, we will be able to put aside everything that constitutes the auxiliary arts of politics, that is to say, the other forms in terms of which one may prescribe things that are not specifically political. In fact, the art of politics is like the art of the weaver; it is not concerned with everything overall, as the shepherd is supposed to be concerned with the whole flock. Politics, like the art of the weaver, can only develop on the basis of and with the help of certain auxiliary or preparatory actions. For the weaver to carry out his task,

---

* Inaudible word.

the wool must have been sheared, the yarn must have been twisted, and the carder must have done his work. Similarly, a whole series of auxiliary arts are required to help the politician. Making war, giving good judgments in tribunals, as well as persuading assemblies with the art of rhetoric, are not exactly politics but the conditions of its practice.[36] What then is political action in the strict sense, the essence of the political, the politician, or rather the politician's action? It will be to join together, as the weaver joins the warp and the weft. The politician will bind the elements together, the good elements formed by education; he will bind together the virtues in their different forms, which are distinct from and sometimes opposed to each other; he will weave and bind together different contrasting temperaments, such as, for example, spirited and moderate men; and he will weave them together thanks to the shuttle of a shared common opinion. So the royal art is not at all that of the shepherd, but the art of the weaver, which is an art that consists in bringing together these lives "in a community [I am quoting; M.F.] that rests on concord and friendship."[37] In this way, with his specific art, very different from all the others, the political weaver forms the most magnificent fabric and "the entire population of the state, both slaves and free men," Plato goes on to say, "are enveloped in the folds of this magnificent fabric."[38] In this way we are led to all the happiness a state is capable of.

In this text I think we have the bona fide rebuttal of the theme of the pastorate. Not that Plato in any way says that the theme of the pastorate should be entirely eliminated or abolished. But what is involved is showing precisely that if there is a pastorship, according to him it can only be in minor activities that are no doubt necessary for the city-state, but that are subordinate with respect to the political order, such as the activities of, for example, the doctor, the farmer, the gymnast, and the teacher. All of these may in fact be likened to a shepherd, but the politician, with his particular and specific activities, is not a shepherd. There is a very clear text on this in The Statesman, in paragraph 295a, which says: Do you think that the politician could lower himself, could quite simply have the time, to act like the shepherd, or like the doctor, the teacher, or the gymnast, and sit down beside every citizen to advise, feed, and look after him?[39] The activities of the shepherd exist, and they are necessary. Let us leave them there where they are, where they have their value and effectiveness, with the doctor, gymnast, and teacher. Above all, let's not say that the politician is a shepherd (*berger*). The royal art of prescribing cannot be defined on the basis of pastorship. The demands of pastorship are too trifling to be suitable for a king. It is too little also because of the very humbleness of its task, and consequently the Pythagoreans are deceived in wanting to emphasize the pastoral form, which may really function in small religious and pedagogical communities; they are wrong in wanting to emphasize it at the level of the whole city-state. The king is not a shepherd (*pasteur*).

With all the negative signs given by the absence of the theme of the shepherd in classical Greek political vocabulary, and by the explicit criticism of the theme by Plato, I think we have a fairly clear indication that Greek thought, Greek reflection on politics, excludes this positive valuation of the theme of the shepherd. You find it in the East and in the Hebrews. In the ancient world there were no doubt forms of support that, from a certain moment, precisely with "Christianity" (and I put "Christianity" in inverted commas), allowed the form of pastorship to spread. But this needs much more research, and more precise research. But I do not think these points of support for the later spread of pastorship should be looked for in political thought or in the major forms of organization of the city-state. We should no doubt look for them in small communities and restricted groups with their specific social forms, such as philosophical or religious communities like the Pythagoreans, or in pedagogical communities, gymnastics schools, and maybe also, I will come back to this next week, in certain forms of spiritual direction. We could see, if not the explicit establishment of the shepherd theme, at least a number of configurations, techniques, and reflections that allowed the subsequent spread of the theme of pastorship, imported from the East, throughout the Hellenic world. At any rate, I do not think that the positive analysis of power on the basis of the form of shepherding and of the pastor-flock relationship is truly found in major political thought.

Given this, in the Western world I think the real history of the pastorate as the source of a specific type of power over men, as a model and matrix of procedures for the government of men, really only begins with

Christianity. And—referring to what Paul Veyne has often said[40]—the word "Christianity" is no doubt not correct and in truth covers a whole series of different realities. We should no doubt say, if not with more precision, at least a bit more accurately, that the pastorate begins with a process that is absolutely unique in history and no other example of which is found in the history of any other civilization: the process by which a religion, a religious community, constitutes itself as a Church, that is to say, as an institution that claims to govern men in their daily life on the grounds of leading them to eternal life in the other world, and to do this not only on the scale of a definite group, of a city or a state, but of the whole of humanity. The Church is a religion that thus lays claim to the daily government of men in their real life on the grounds of their salvation and on the scale of humanity, and we have no other example of this in the history of societies. With this institutional-ization of a religion as a Church, fairly rapidly, at least in its broad out-line, an apparatus was formed of a kind of power not found anywhere else and which was constantly developed and refined over fifteen cen-turies, from the second and third century after Jesus Christ up to the eighteenth century. This pastoral power, absolutely bound up with the organization of a religion as a Church, with the Christian religion as the Christian Church, no doubt underwent considerable transformations during these fifteen centuries of its history. It was no doubt shifted, broken up, transformed, and integrated in various forms, but basically it has never been truly abolished. And I am very likely still mistaken when I situate the end of the pastoral age in the eighteenth century, for in fact pastoral power in its typology, organization, and mode of functioning, pastoral power exercised as power, is doubtless something from which we have still not freed ourselves.

This does not mean that pastoral power has remained an invariant and fixed structure throughout fifteen, eighteen, or twenty centuries of Christian history. We may even say that the importance, vigor, and depth of implantation of this pastoral power can be measured by the intensity and multiplicity of agitations, revolts, discontent, struggles, battles, and bloody wars that have been conducted around, for, and against it.[41] The immense dispute over the gnosis that divided Christianity for centuries is to a large extent a dispute over the mode of exercising pastoral power.[42] Who will be pastor? How, in what form, with what rights, and in order to do what? The great debate, linked to the gnosis moreover, between the asceticism of the anchorites and the regulation of monastic life in its cenobite form,[43] is again an affair [... *] of the pastorate in the first centuries of our era. After all, all or a great part of the struggles that permeated not only the Christian Church but the Christian world, that is to say the entire Western world from the thirteenth to the seventeenth and eighteenth century, were struggles around and concerning pastoral power. From Wyclif[44] to Wesley,[45] from the thirteenth to the eighteenth century, all these struggles that culminated in the Wars of Religion were fundamentally struggles over who would actually have the right to govern men, and to govern them in their daily life and in the details and materiality of their existence; they were struggles over who has this power, from whom it derives, how it is exercised, the margin of autonomy for each, the qualification of those who exercise it, the limits of their jurisdiction, what recourse is possible against them, and what control is exercised over each other. This great battle of pastorship traversed the West from the thirteenth to the eighteenth century, and ultimately without ever really getting rid of the pastorate. For if it is true that the Reformation was undoubtedly much more a great pastoral battle than a great doctrinal battle, if it is true that what was at issue with the Reformation was actually the way in which pastoral power was exercised, then the two worlds or series of worlds that issue from the Reformation, that is to say, a Protestant world, or a world of Protestant churches and the Counter Reformation, were not worlds without a pastorate. What resulted from the Reformation was a formidable reinforcement of the pastorate in two different types. On the one hand there was the, let's say, Protestant type, or the type developed by different Protestant sects, with a meticulous pastorate, but one that was all the more meticulous as it was hierarchically supple, and, on the other hand, there was the Counter Reformation with a pastorate entirely brought back under control, a hierarchized pyramid, within a strongly

---

* One or two inaudible words.

centralized Catholic Church. But anyway, these great revolts—I was going to say anti-pastoral revolts, but no, these great revolts around the pastorate, around the right to be governed and to know how and by whom one will be governed—were actually bound up with a profound reorganization of pastoral power. I would say that the feudal type of political power undoubtedly experienced revolutions or, at any rate, came up against a series of processes that, apart from a few traces, well and truly eliminated it and chased it from the history of the West. There have been anti-feudal revolutions; there has never been an anti-pastoral revolution. The pastorate has not yet experienced the process of profound revolution that would have definitively expelled it from history.

There is obviously no question of undertaking the history of this pastorate here. I would just like to note—with all due reserve, one would have to consult the competent people, that is to say, historians, not me—that it seems to me that the history of the pastorate has never really been undertaken. The history of ecclesiastical institutions has been written. The history of religious doctrines, beliefs, and representations has been written. There have also been attempts to produce the history of real religious practices, namely, when people confessed, took communion, and so on. But it seems to me that the history of the techniques employed, of the reflections on these pastoral techniques, of their development, application, and successive refinements, the history of the different types of analysis and knowledge linked to the exercise of pastoral power, has never really been undertaken. And yet, after all, from the beginning of Christianity, the pastorate has not been perceived just as a necessary institution; it has not been reflected simply as a set of prescriptions imposed on some and privileges accorded to others. In actual fact, there has been an enormous reflection on the pastorate that straightaway appeared, again, not only as a reflection on laws and institutions [... *], but as a theoretical reflection with philosophical status. At any rate, we should not forget that Saint Gregory Nazianzen was the first to define this art of governing men by the pastorate as the *technē technōn, epistemē*

---

* An inaudible word.

epistemōn, the "art of arts," the "science of sciences."[46] This will be echoed down until the eighteenth century in the familiar traditional form of *ars artium, regimen animarum*:[47] the "regimen of souls," the "government of souls," is the *ars artium*. Now this phrase should not only be understood as a fundamental principle, but also in its polemical force, since what was the *ars artium*, the *technē technōn*, the *epistemē epistemōn*, before Gregory Nazianzen? It was philosophy. That is to say, well before the seventeenth and eighteenth centuries, what took over from philosophy in the Christian West was not another philosophy, and it was not even theology; it was the pastorate. This was the art by which some people were taught the government of others, and others were taught to let themselves be governed by certain people. It was this game of the government of some by others, of everyday government, of pastoral government, that was reflected for fifteen centuries as the science par excellence, the art of all arts, the knowledge (*savoir*) of all knowledges (*savoirs*).

If one wanted to pick out some of the characteristics of this knowledge of all knowledges, this art of governing men, we could straightaway note the following.* Remember what we said last week concerning the Hebrews. God knows that the theme of the pastor, linked to religious life and to the Hebrew people's historical perception of themselves, was important; much more important than in the Egyptians, and even more so than in the Assyrians. Everything unfolded in the pastoral form, since God was the pastor and the wanderings of the Jewish people were wanderings in search of its pasture. In a sense, everything was pastoral. Two things, however. First, the shepherd-flock relationship was ultimately only one aspect of the multiple, complex, and permanent relationships between God and men. God was a shepherd, but he was also something other than a shepherd. For example, he was a legislator, or he turned away from his flock in anger and abandoned it to itself. In both the history and organization of the Hebrew people the shepherd-flock relationship was not the only dimension, the only form in which the relationships between God and his people could be seen. Second, and

---

* Foucault adds: this is what characterizes the institutionalization of the pastorate in the Christian Church, it is this:

especially, among the Hebrews there was no pastoral institution strictly speaking. Within Hebrew society, no one occupied the position of pastor in relation to the others. Even better, the Hebrew kings (remember what was said last week) were not designated specifically as pastors of men, with the exception of David, the founder of the Davidian monarchy. As for the others, they were designated as pastors precisely only when it was a question of denouncing their negligence and showing the extent to which they were bad shepherds. In the Hebrews the king is never designated positively, directly, or immediately as a shepherd. There is no shepherd outside of God.

On the other hand, in the Christian Church we see instead the, as it were, autonomization of the shepherd theme in relation to other themes, as not merely one of the dimensions or aspects of God's relationship to men. It will become the fundamental, essential relationship, not just one alongside others but a relationship that envelops all the others and, second, a relationship that will, of course, be institutionalized in a pastorate with its laws, rules, techniques, and procedures. So, the pastorate will be autonomous, encompassing, and specific. From top to bottom of the Church, relationships of authority are based upon the privileges, and at the same time on the tasks, of the shepherd in relation to his flock. Christ, of course, is the pastor, and a pastor who sacrifices himself in order to bring back to God the flock that has lost its way; who sacrifices himself not only for the flock in general, but also for each sheep in particular. Here we find again the Mosaic theme, as you know, of the good shepherd who accepts the sacrifice of his entire flock in order to save the single sheep at risk.[48] But what was only one theme in the Mosaic literature will now become the keystone of the whole organization of the Church. The first pastor is obviously Christ. The Epistle to the Hebrews already said it: "God has brought back from the dead our Lord Jesus Christ, the great shepherd of the sheep (...)."[49] Christ is the shepherd (*pasteur*). The apostles are also shepherds, the pastors who one after the other visit the flocks confided to them, and who, at the end of the day and at the end of their life, when the dreadful day arrives, will have to account for all that has happened in their flock. In the Gospel according to Saint John, 21, 15-17: Jesus Christ commands Peter to feed his lambs and sheep.[50] The apostles are pastors. The bishops, those in charge who, to quote the eighth letter of Saint Cyprian, are put in front to "*custodire gregam*," "guard the flock,"[51] or in letter 17, *"fovere oves,"* "look after the sheep,"[52] are pastors. In the basic text of the pastoral throughout the Middle Ages, the Bible, if you like, of the Christian pastorate, in Gregory the Great's frequently republished *Regula pastoralis* (The rule of pastoral life),* often called the *Liber pastoralis* (The pastoral book),[53] Gregory the Great frequently calls the bishop "pastor." Abbots at the head of communities are seen as pastors. Look at the basic *Rules* of Saint Benedict.[54]

Finally, there remains the problem, or rather, when Christianity had established the organization and precise territoriality of parishes during the Middle Ages,[55] the problem arises of whether parish priests can be seen as pastors. You know that this was one of the problems that, if they did not exactly give rise to the Reformation, at least provoked a series of crises, challenges, and debates that finally led to the Reformation. The parishes had no sooner been set up than the problem arose of whether parish priests were pastors. Yes, said Wyclif.[56] A whole series of Protestant Churches will say yes, each in their way. The Jansenists of the seventeenth and eighteenth century will also say yes.[57] To which the Catholic Church will obstinately reply: No, parish priests are not pastors.[58] Still in 1788† Marius Lupus published *De parochiis*, which fundamentally challenged the thesis that parish priests are pastors, which would broadly be accepted in a pre- and post-council atmosphere.[59]

In any case—leaving the problem of priests open—we can say that the whole organization of the Church, from Christ to the abbots and bishops, presents itself as a pastoral organization. The powers held by the Church are given, I mean both organized and justified, as the shepherd's power in relation to the flock. What is sacramental power? Of baptism? It is calling the sheep into the flock. Of communion? It is giving spiritual nourishment. Penance is the power of reintegrating those sheep that have left the flock. A power of jurisdiction, it is also a power of the pastor, of the shepherd. It is this power of jurisdiction, in fact, that allows the bishop as pastor, for example, to expel from the flock those sheep that by disease or scandal are liable to contaminate the whole flock. Religious power, therefore, is pastoral power.

---

* Foucault gives the title in the plural: *Regulae pastoralis vitae*, The rules of pastoral life.
† M.F.: 1798

Finally, the absolutely fundamental and essential feature of this overall pastoral power is that throughout Christianity it remained distinct from political power. This does not mean that religious power only took on the task of caring for individual's souls. On the contrary, pastoral power—and this is one of its fundamental features, and one of its paradoxes, to which I will come back next week[60]—is only concerned with individual souls insofar as this direction (*conduite*) of souls also involves a permanent intervention in everyday conduct (*conduite*), in the management of lives, as well as in goods, wealth, and things. It concerns not only the individual, but [also] the community, and a text of Saint John Chrysostom says that the bishop must watch over everything; the bishop must have a thousand eyes since he must be concerned not just with individuals, but with the whole town and ultimately—the text is found *De sacerdotio*—[with] the *orbis terrarum*, [with the] whole world.[61] It is, then, a form of power that really is a terrestrial power even though it is directed towards the world beyond. And yet, despite this, and leaving aside the Eastern Church, in the Western Church it has always remained a power that is completely distinct from [political]* power. Doubtless we should hear this separation resonating in Valentinian's famous apostrophe to Saint Ambrose when he sent the latter to govern Milan. He sent him to govern Milan, "not as a magistrate, but as a pastor."[62] I think the formula will remain as a sort of principle or fundamental law throughout the history of Christianity.

I will make two remarks here. First of all, between the pastoral power of the Church and political power there will, of course, be a series of conjunctions, supports, relays, and conflicts, on which I will not dwell because they are well known, such that the intertwining of pastoral and political power will in fact be an historical reality throughout the West. However, the fundamental point is that despite these conjunctions, this intertwining, and these supports and relays, I think pastoral power, its form, type of functioning, and internal technology, remains absolutely specific and different from political power, at least until the eighteenth century. It does not function in the same way, and even when the same figures exercise

---

* M.F.: religious

pastoral power and political power, and God knows this has happened in the Christian West, even with every imaginable kind of alliance between Church and state, Church and political power, I think this specificity remained as an absolutely typical feature of the Christian West.

My second remark is that the reason for this distinction is a big problem of history and, for me at least, an enigma. Anyway, I make absolutely no claim to resolve the problem, or even to set out its complex dimensions, either now or next week. How did it come about that these two types of power, political and pastoral, thus maintained their specificity and their own physiognomies? My impression is that if we examined Eastern Christianity we would have a quite different process, a quite different development, a much stronger intrication, and perhaps some form of loss of specificity on both sides. I don't know. At any rate, one thing seems to be quite clear, which is that despite all the conjunctions and interferences, the specificity remained. The king, whose definition, specificity, and essence was sought by Plato, remained the king, even when certain linking or bridging mechanisms were established, such as the coronation of kings in England and France, for example, and the fact that for a time the king was seen as a bishop and what's more consecrated as a bishop. But despite all of this, the king remained king, and the pastor a pastor. The pastor remained a figure exercising power over the mystical world; the king remained someone who exercised power over the imperial world. The distinction, the heterogeneity of a Christlike (*christique*) pastorate and imperial sovereignty seems to me [to be] a feature of the West. Again, I do not think that we would find exactly the same thing in the East. I am thinking, for example, of Alain Besançon's book of twelve or so years ago that was devoted to the sacrificed Tsarevich, in which he develops a number of religious themes peculiar to the Russian monarchy, to the Russian Empire, and in which he shows the extent of the presence of Christlike (*christiques*) themes in political sovereignty as, if not actually organized, at least lived, perceived, and deeply experienced in ancient Russian, and even still in modern Russian society.[63]

I would just like to read you a text from Gogol which I came across the other day quite by chance in Sinyavsky's recently published book on Gogol.[64] To define what the Tsar is and must be, Gogol, in a letter to

Joukovski in 1846, evokes the future of the Russian Empire, and he evokes the day when the Empire will have reached its perfect form and the affective intensity that the political relationship, the relationship of mastery between the sovereign and his subjects, requires, and this is what he says on this finally reconciled Empire: "Man will swell with [a] love never previously felt towards [the whole] of humanity. We others, taken individually, will not be inflamed at all by [this] love. [It] will remain ideal, chimerical, [and] unfulfilled. Only those whose intangible rule is to love all men as a single man can be penetrated [by this love]. Because he will have loved everyone in his realm down to the last subject of the lowest class, and because he will have converted his whole realm into his body, suffering, crying, and imploring for his people night and day, the sovereign [the Tsar] acquires that all-powerful voice that alone is able to makes itself heard by humanity, able to touch wounds without irritating them, and to bring appeasement to the different social classes and harmony to the state. The people will only truly be healed when the [Caesar] [will have fulfilled] his supreme destiny: to be the image on earth of He who is Love."[65] We have here, I think, an admirable image and an admirable evocation of a Christlike (*christique*) sovereign. This Christlike sovereign does not appear to me to be typical of the West. The Western sovereign is Caesar, not Christ; the Western pastor is not Caesar, but Christ.

Next week I will try to go into this comparison between political power and pastoral power a bit more and show you the specificity of the form of pastoral power.

1. According to K. Stegmann von Pritzwald, *Zur Geschichte der Herrscherbezeichnungen von Homer bis Platon* (Leipzig: "Forschungen zur Völker-Psyhologie u. Soziologie," 7, 1930) pp. 16-24, the title ποιμήν λαῶνϕ appears 44 times in the *Illiad* and 12 times in the *Odyssey* (according to J. Engemann, "Hirt," *Realexikon für Antike und Christentum*, col. 580). P. Louis, *Métaphores de Platon*, p. 162, records 41 references in the *Illiad* and 10 in the *Odyssey*. See H. Ebeling, ed., *Lexikon Homericum* ([Leipzig: 1885] Hildesheim: Olms, 1963) vol. 2, p. 195. W. Jost, *Poimen*, p. 8, points out that the expression is also employed as a royal title in *Le Bouclier d'Héraclès*, 41, an apocryphal poem the start of which was for a long time attributed to Hesiod.

2. R. Schmitt, *Dichtung und Dichtersprache in indogermanischer Zeit* (Wiesbaden: O. Harrassowitz, 1967).

3. Ibid. p. 284: "Längst hat man auch auf die germanische Parallele hingewisen, die uns das altenglische *Beowulf*-Epos in den Verbindungen *folces hyrde* 'Hirte des Volkes' (v. 610, 1832, 1849, 2644, 2981) und ähnlichem *rīces hyrde* 'Hirte des Reiches' (v. 2027, 3080) bietet." Schmitt notes that this expression was not unknown to people outside the Indo-Germanic area: "So bezeichnet etwa Hammurabi sich selbst als (akkad.) *re 'ū nīšī* 'Hirte des Volkes.'" On this last, see above, lecture 8 February, note 24. *Beowulf*: anonymous Anglo-Saxon poem from the pre-Christian era, reworked between the eighth and tenth centuries, the manuscript of which was published for the first time in 1815 (the first French translation by L. Botkine [Le Havre: Lepelletier, 1877]).

4. This is the fragments of a Περί νομού χαί διχαιοσύνς attributed by Antiquity to Archytas of Taranto, but certainly apocryphal; written in Dorian dialect, they were preserved by Stobaeus, *Florilegium*, 43, 129; 43, 132; 43, 133 *a* and *b*; 43, 134; and 46, 61 (= Wachsmuth and Hense, eds, *Anthologion*, IV, 132; 135; 136 and 137; 138; and IV, 5, 61) in A.E. Chaignet, *Pythagore et la Philosophie pythagoricienne, contenant les fragments de Philolaüs et d'Archytas* (Paris: Didier, 1874).

5. On the different elements of the tradition see, A. Delatte, *Essai sur la politique pythagoricienne* (Liège: Vaillant-Carmanne, "Bibliothèque de la Faculté de philosophie et lettres de l'Université de Liège," 1922; republished, Geneva: Slatkine, 1979).

6. O.F. Gruppe, *Ueber die Fragmente des Archytas und der älteren Pythagorer* (Berlin: G. Eichler, 1840) p. 92. See, A. Delatte, *Essai*, p. 73: "the magistrate is identified as a shepherd: [according to Gruppe] this conception is specifically Jewish," and p. 121, note 1: "I do not know why Gruppe (*Fragm. Des Arch.*, p. 92) wants to see in this simple comparison [of the magistrate with the shepherd] an identification, and in this the indication of a Hebrew influence."

7. A. Delatte, *Essai*.

8. Ibid. p. 121 (with regard to the following passage: "To command well the true magistrate must not only be wise and powerful, but also human (ϕιλάνθρωπον). For it would be odd for a shepherd to hate his flock or be malevolent towards it"): "The comparison of the magistrate with a shepherd is classical in the political literature of the 4th century. But here it is not an empty formula nor a commonplace: it is justified by the etymology of the word νομεύς, put forward in the previous fragment [see p. 118: 'The Law must penetrate the mores and habits of the citizens: only on this condition will it make them independent and distribute to each what he deserves and what is due to him. So the Sun, advancing in the circle of the Zodiac, distributes to all terrestrial beings the share of birth, food, and life that is due to them, producing the beautiful blend of the seasons as a *eumonia*. This is also the reason why Zeus is called Νόμιος and Νεμήϊος and that the one who distributes food to the sheep is called νομεύς. Just as we give the name of "nomes" to the songs of the cithara players, for they also put order in the soul because they are sung according to harmony, rhythm, and meter']. The author rediscovers in this word the same root and the same notion as in διανέμεν, which for him describes the action of the Law."

9. Isocrates, *Areopagiticus*, § 36, § 55, § 58, French translation by G. Mathieu, in *Discours*, vol. III (Paris: Les Belles Lettres, "Collection des universités de France," 1942); English translation by George Norlin, "On the Peace" in *Isocrates*, vol. 2 (Cambridge, Mass. and London: Harvard and Heinemann, 1968).

10. See Xénophon, *Cyropaedia*, VIII, 2, 14 and I, 1, 1-3, in which the identification of the king with a shepherd is clearly designated as being of Persian origin (references indicated by A. Diès in Platon, *Le Politique* in *Œuvres complètes* (Paris: Les Belles Lettres, "Collection des universités de France," 1935) vol. 9, p. 19.

11. Plato, *Critias*, 109b-c.

12. Plato, *The Republic*, I, 343a-345e; III, 416a-b, 440d.

13. Plato, *The Laws*, V, 735b-e

14. Plato, *The Statesman*, 267c-277d. Foucault uses the translations of Léon Robin in Platon, *Œuvres complètes* (Paris: Gallimard, "Bibliothèque de la Pléiade," 1950). [English translations in the text are from the French, in consultation with a number of English versions of Plato; G.B.]

15. *Critias*, 109b-c.

16. *The Laws*, X, 906b-c: "It is clear moreover that there are men living on earth who have the souls of beasts of prey and are in possession of ill-gotten gains, souls which, when by chance they come up against the souls of the watchdogs, or of the shepherds, or the souls of the Masters who are at the top of the scale, they try to persuade them with flattery, and in enchantments mingled with vows, that they are permitted [...] to enrich themselves at the cost of their fellows, without any inconvenience to themselves."

17. *The Statesman*, 281d-e (distinction made by the Stranger between a "true cause" and an "auxiliary cause").

18. *The Republic*, I, 343b-344c.

19. Ibid. I, 345c-e.

20. *The Statesman*, 260e.

21. Ibid. 261a-d.

22. Ibid. 261d.

23. Ibid. 261e-262a.

24. See, ibid. 262a-263e.

25. Ibid. 264a.

26. Ibid. 264b-267c.

27. Ibid. 268a.

28. Ibid. 267e-268a.

29. Ibid. 268e-270d.

30. Ibid. 271c-d: "(...) this is a time that does not belong to the present constitution of the course of the world: it too belongs to the earlier constitution."

31. Ibid. 271e: "(...) It was the Divinity himself who was their shepherd and who directed their life."

32. Ibid. "(...) since [the Deity] was their shepherd, they had no need of a political constitution."

33. Ibid. 274c-d: "Such, therefore, is the origin of the benefits that, according to old legends, were given to us by the Gods, together with the teaching and learning they required: fire, the gift of Prometheus; the arts from Hephaistos and the goddess who is his collaborator; and finally, seeds and plants from other deities."

34. Ibid. 275b-c: "(...) the figure of the divine pastor is, I think, too great even for a king, whereas politicians here and now are by nature much more similar to those of whom they are the chiefs, just as they are more like them through their shared culture and education."

35. Ibid. 279a-283b.

36. Ibid. 303d-305e.

37. Ibid. 311b.

38. Ibid. 311c: "(...) we have completed a correctly woven fabric and political activity when it [the royal art] has fashioned the most magnificent and excellent fabric, with a view to common life, when all the population of the state, slaves and free men, are enveloped in its folds, and political activity holds together the two modes of being in question by means of this weaving (...)."

39. Ibid. 295a-b: "How, Socrates, could someone sit beside each individual at every moment of life, in order to prescribe exactly what is right for him?"

40. Foucault is alluding here to an article, "La famille et l'amour sous le Haut-Empire romain," in *Annales ESC*, 1, 1978, reprinted in Paul Veyne, *La Société romaine* (Paris: Le Seuil, "Des travaux," 1991) pp. 88-130, as well as, no doubt, to a paper on love in Rome given by

Paul Veyne, at which Foucault was present, at a seminar of George Duby at the Collège de France, and about which he spoke again with him. (I am grateful to P. Veyne for these clarifications.)

41. On the revolts of conduct that, from the Middle Ages, express resistance to the pastorate, see below, the lecture of 1 March, pp. 201-202.

42. See, ibid.

43. See, ibid.

44. John Wyclif (c.1324-1384), English theologian and reformer, the author of *Du dominio divino* (1376), *Du veritate Scripturae sanctae* (1378), and *De ecclesia* (1378). His doctrine is at the origin of the "Lollards" movement, which attacked ecclesiastical customs and called for a return to poverty. He was a supporter of the separation of Church and state, asserted the autonomy of Scripture, independently of the *magisterium* of the Church, and rejected the sacraments and priests, all being equal and only dispensers of the Word. See, H.B. Workman, *John Wyclif* (Oxford: Clarendon Press, 1926) 2 vols.; L. Cristiani, "Wyclif" in *Dictionnaire de théologie catholique*, 1950, vol.15/2, col. 3585-3614; K.B. McFarlane, *John Wycliffe and English Nonconformity* (Harmondsworth: Penguin, 1972).

45. John Wesley (1703-1791), founder of the Methodists, one of the major currents of the *Revival of Religion* movement that, in the eighteenth century, advocated the restoration of the original faith at the heart of Protestantism. See, G.S. Wakefield, "Wesley" in *Dictionnaire de spiritualité ascétique et mystique*, vol. 16, 1994, col. 1374-1392.

46. Grégoire de Nazianze, *Discours* 2, 16, trans. J. Laplace (Paris: Cerf, "Sources chrétiennes," 1978) p. 110-111; English translation by Charles Gordon Browne, Gregory Nazianzen, *Orations*, in *A Select Library of Nicene and Post-Nicene Fathers*, vol. 7 (Grand Rapids: W.B. Eerdmans, 1893) p. 208: "For the guiding of man, the most variable and manifold of creatures, seems to me in very deed to be the art of arts [*technē technōn*] and the science of sciences [*epistemē epistemōn*]."

47. The formula appears in the first lines of *The Book of Pastoral Rule* of Gregory the Great (who was familiar with the *Orations* of Gregory Nazianzen through Rufin's Latin translation, *Apologetica*): "ars est artium regimen animarum (the government of souls is the art of arts)" *Règle pastorale*, trans. Ch. Morel, with introduction and notes by B. Judic (Paris: Cerf, "Sources chrétiennes," 1992) pp. 128-129; *The Book of Pastoral Rule*, p. 1, trans. James Barmby, in *A Select Library of Nicene and Post-Nicene Fathers of The Christian Church*, vol. 12 (Oxford: James Parker and Company, 1895).

48. See, Luke, 15, 4: "Which one of you with a hundred sheep, if he lost one, would fail to leave the ninety-nine in the desert and go after the missing one till he found it?" See Ezekiel, 34, 4, and the same text in Mathew, 18, 12, and John, 10, 11: "I am the good shepherd: the good shepherd lays down his life for his sheep."

49. Paul, *Epistle to the Hebrews*, 13, 20.

50. John, 21, 15-17: "When they had eaten, Jesus said to Simon Peter, 'Simon son of John, do you love me more than these others do?' He answered, 'Yes, Lord, you know I love you.' Jesus said to him, 'Feed my lambs.' A second time he said to him, 'Simon son of John, do you love me?' He replied, 'Yes, Lord, you know I love you.' Jesus said to him, 'Look after my sheep.' Then he said to him a third time, 'Simon son of John, do you love me?' Peter was hurt that he asked him a third time, 'Do you love me?' and said, 'Lord, you know everything; you know I love you.' Jesus said to him, 'Feed my sheep'."

51. Saint Cyprian (c.200-258), *Correspondance*, text established and translated by the canon Bayard (Paris: Les Belles Lettres, CUF, 1961) vol. 1, Letter 8, p. 19: "(...) incumbat nobis qui videmur praeposit esse et vice pastorum custodire gregem"; English translation *The Epistles of S. Cyprian* (Oxford: John Henry Parker, "Library of the Fathers," 1844) p. 17: "And since it is incumbent on us, who seem to be set over the flock, to guard it instead of the shepherd."

52. Ibid. Letter 17, p. 49: "Quod quidem nostros presbyteri et diaconi monere debuerant, ut commendatas sibi oves foverent..."; *The Epistles*, p. 43: "This our Presbyters and Deacons ought indeed to have advised you, that so they might tend the sheep committed to them..."

53. Or just, the *Pastoral*. Gregory the Great, *Regula pastoralis*, written between September 590 and February 591; *Patrologia Latina*, ed., J.-P. Migne, 77, col. 13-128; English translation by James Barmby, *The Book of Pastoral Rule*, in *A Select Library of Nicene and Post-Nicene Fathers*.

54. Saint Benedict, *Regula sancit Benedicti*; French translation, *La Règle de Saint Benoît* (sixth century), introduction, translation and notes by A. De Vogüé (Paris: Cerf, "Sources chrétiennes," 1972); English translation Oswald Hunter Blair, *The Rule of Saint Benedict*, in Emmanuel Heufelder, *The Way to God according to the Rule of Saint Benedict*, trans. Luke Eberle (Kalamazoo, Mich.: Cistercian Publications, 1983). See ch. 2, 7-9, p. 225: "And let him [the abbot] know that to the fault of the shepherd shall be imputed any lack of profit which the father of the household may find in his sheep. Only then shall he be acquitted, if he shall have bestowed all pastoral diligence on his unquiet and disobedient flock, and employed all his care to amend their corrupt manner of life."

55. On the canonical definition of parishes, their development from the fifth century, and the juridical conditions of their establishment, see R. Naz, "Paroisse" in *Dictionnaire de droit canonique* (Paris: Librairie Letouzey et Ané, 1957) vol. VI, col. 1234-1247. Foucault's immediate source here is the article by B. Dolhagaray, "Curés" in *Dictionnaire de théologie catholique* (Paris: Letouzey et Ané, 1908) vol. III, 2, col. 2429-2453.

56. See, Dolhagaray, "Curés," col. 2430, § 1 (concerning the question: "Are priests of divine institution?"): "Some heretics, called presbyterians, then Wyclif, Jean Hus, Luther, Calvin, etcetera, wanted to establish that simple priests were of the same rank as bishops. The Council of Trent condemned this error."

57. Ibid. col. 2430-2431: "The Sorbonnists of the thirteenth and fourteenth centuries, and the Jansenists of the seventeenth century wanted to establish (. . .) that priests really were of divine institution, having received from God authority over the faithful; so that the priest being instituted spouse of his church, like the bishop of his cathedral, being pastor, charged with the direction of his people, in both the internal forum and external forum, no-one could exercise the holy functions in a parish without the priest's authorization. These, they claimed, were the exclusive, divine rights of the parochial system (*parochiat*)."

58. Ibid. col. 2432 § 2 (question: "Are priests pastors in the strict sense of the word?"): "Strictly speaking, the denomination pastor applies solely to bishops. The prerogatives contained in this expression are fulfilled in the princes of the Church. The divine power to graze Christ's flock, to instruct and govern the faithful, has been entrusted to the bishops, in place of the apostles. The evangelical texts prove this; the commentators have no hesitations on this point; traditional teaching is unanimous. (. . .) When the people attributes the title of pastor to its parish priests, it knows very well that they are such only thanks to the bishops and so long as they remain in union with them, subject to their jurisdiction."

59. Marius Lupus, *De Parochiis ante annum Christi millesium* (Bergomi: apud V. Antoine, 1788): "Certum est pastoris titulum parochis non quadrare; unde et ipsum hodie nunquam impartit Ecclesia romana. Per pastores palam intelliguntur soli episcopi. Parochiales presbyterii nequaquam a Christo Domino auctoritatem habent in plebem suam, sed ab episcopo (. . .) hic enim titulus solis episcopisdebetur" (cited by B. Dolhagaray, "Curés," col. 2432, from Venice edition of 1789, vol. II, p. 314. The canons 515, § 1, and 519 of the new code of Canon law promulgated after the council of Vatican II clearly notes the pastoral function of priests: "The parish is the precise community of the faithful that is constituted in a stable way in the particular Church, the pastoral function of which is entrusted to the parish priest, as to its ówn pastor, under the authority of the diocesan Bishop"; "The parish priest is pastor of the parish that has been handed over to him (. . .)."

60. In the next lecture Foucault does not return to this material aspect of the *regimen animarum*.

61. John Chrysostom (c.345-407), ΠΕΡΙ ΙΕΡΩΣΝΗΣ, *De Sacerdotio*, French translation, *Sur le sacerdoce*, introd., trans., and notes, A.-M. Malingrey (Paris: Cerf, "Sources chrétiennes," 1980, 6th part, ch.4, title, pp. 314-315: "To the priest is entrusted the direction of the whole world [τῆςοίχουμένης] and other formidable missions"; *Patrologia Graeca*, ed., J.-P. Migne, vol. XLVII, 1858, col. 677: "Sacerdotem terrarum orbi aliisque rebus tremendis praepositum esse"; English translation by Graham Neville, *Six Books on the Priesthood* (London: SPCK, 1964) p. 140.

62. The original phrase does not contain the word "pastor." It is found in Paulin's life of Saint Ambrose, *Vita sancti Ambrosii mediolanensis episcopi, a Paulino ejus notario ad beatum Augustinum conscripta*, 8, PL 14, col. 29D: "Qui inventus [Ambrose, until then the governor

(*judex*) of the provinces of North Italy, had tried to flee in order to avoid his election as bishop], cum custodiretur a populo, missa relatio est ad clementissimum imperatorem tun Valentinianum, qui summo gaudio accepit quod judex a se directus ad sacerdotium peteretur. Laetabatur etiam Probus praefectus, quod verbum ejus impleretur in Ambrosio; dixerat enim proficiscenti, cum mandata ab eodem darentur, ut moris est: *Vade, age non ut judex, sed ut episcopus*" (my emphasis; M.S.). On this episode, see for example, H.[F.] von Campenhausen, *Lateinische Kirchenväter* (Stuttgart: Kohlhammer, c.1960); French translation, *Les Pères latins*, trans. C.A. Moreau (Paris: Le Seuil, "Livre de vie," 1969) pp. 111-112.

63. A. Besançon, *Le Tsarévitch immolé. La symbolique de la loi dans la culture russe* (Paris: Plon, 1967) ch. 2: "La relation au soverain," pp. 80-87.

64. A. Siniavski (Andrei Sinyavsky), *Dans l'ombre de Gogol*, trans. from Russian, G. Nivat (Paris: Le Seuil, "Pierres vives," 1978). See the translation of this (fictional) letter of Gogol to Joukovski, "Sur le lyrisme de nos poètes," trans. J. Johannet, *Passages choisis de ma correspondance avec mes amis*, 1846, Letter X, in Nicolas Gogol, *Œuvres complètes* (Paris: Gallimard, "Bibliothèque de la Pléiade," 1967) pp. 1540-1541 (on Gogol's mystical and political "grand design" to which this work corresponded, see the translator's note, p. 1488). In 1966 the Soviet dissident, Andrei Sinyavsky (1925-1997), was condemned to seven years in a camp for publishing, under the pseudonym Abram Tertz, a lively satire of the regime, *Récits fantastiques* (Paris, 1964). He lived in Paris from 1973. *Dans l'ombre de Gogol* was basically written during his imprisonment, as were *A Voice from the chorus*, trans. Kyril Fitzlyon and Max Hayward (New Haven and London: Yale University Press, 1995) and *Strolls with Pushkin*, trans. Catherine Theimer Nepomnyashchy and Slava I. Yastremski (New Haven and London: Yale University Press, 1993) Foucault met Sinyavsky in June 1977 when an evening was organized at the Récamier theater to protest against Leonid Brezhnev's visit to France. (See the "Chronologie" produced by D. Defert in *Dits et Écrits*, 1, p. 51.) On Soviet dissidence, see below, lecture of 1 March, note 27.

65. André Siniavski, *Dans l'ombre de Gogol*, p. 50. The text read by Foucault has some minor additions in comparison with the original, indicated by words in brackets.

seven

22 FEBRUARY 1978

Analysis of the pastorate (end). ~ *Specificity of the Christian pastorate in comparison with Eastern and Hebraic traditions.*
~ *An art of governing men. Its role in the history of governmentality.* ~ *Main features of the Christian pastorate from the third to the sixth century (Saint John Chrysostom. Saint Cyprian, Saint Ambrose, Gregory the Great, Cassian, Saint Benedict): (1) the relationship to salvation. An economy of merits and faults: (a) the principle of analytical responsibility; (b) the principle of exhaustive and instantaneous transfer; (c) the principle of sacrificial reversal; (d) the principle of alternate correspondence.*
(2) The relationship to the law: institution of a relationship of complete subordination of the sheep to the person who directs them. An individual and non-finalized relationship. Difference between Greek and Christian apatheia. *(3) The relationship to the truth: the production of hidden truths. Pastoral teaching and spiritual direction.* ~ *Conclusion: an absolutely new form of power that marks the appearance of specific modes of individualization. Its decisive importance for the history of the subject.*

TODAY I WOULD LIKE to finish with these histories of the shepherd, the pastor, and the pastoral, which must seem to you a bit long-winded, and return next week to the problem of government, of the art of government, of governmentality from the seventeenth and eighteenth centuries. Let's finish with the pastoral.

Last week, when I tried to contrast the shepherd of the Bible with Plato's weaver, the Hebraic pastor with the Greek magistrate, I did not want to show that there was a Greek or Greco-Roman world on one side that was entirely unaware of the pastor theme and the pastoral form of directing men, and then, arriving from the more or less near East, and especially from Hebraic culture, there was on the other side the form of a pastoral power that Christianity took over and, on the basis of Jewish theocracy, imposed, either with its consent or by force, on the Greco-Roman world. I merely wanted to show that Greek thought hardly resorted to the model of the shepherd to analyze political power and that the theme of the shepherd, so often employed and so highly valued in the East, was employed in Greece either as a ritual designation in ancient texts, or, in the classical texts, to describe ultimately local and circumscribed forms of power exercised, not by magistrates over the whole city, but by certain individuals over religious communities, in pedagogical relationships, in the care of the body, and so on.

What I would now like to show is that the Christian pastorate, institutionalized, developed, and reflected from around the third century, is actually completely different from a pure and simple revival, transposition, or continuation of what we have been able to identify as an above all Hebraic and Eastern theme. I think that the Christian pastorate is absolutely, profoundly, I would almost say essentially different from the pastoral theme we have already identified.

In the first place, it is completely different because, of course, the theme was enriched, transformed, and complicated by Christian thought. It is completely different also, and this is something entirely new, inasmuch as the Christian pastorate, the pastoral theme in Christianity, gave rise to an immense institutional network that we find nowhere else and was certainly not present in Hebraic civilization. The God of the Hebrews is indeed a pastor-God, but there were no pastors within the political and social regime of the Hebrews. So, the pastorate in Christianity gave rise to a dense, complicated, and closely woven institutional network that claimed to be, and was in fact, coextensive with the entire Church, and so with Christianity, with the entire Christian community. Hence the institutionalization of the pastorate is a much more complicated theme. Finally, and above all, the third difference, and it is this that I would like to stress, is that in Christianity the pastorate gave rise to an art of conducting, directing, leading, guiding, taking in hand, and manipulating men, an art of monitoring them and urging them on step by step, an art with the function of taking charge of men collectively and individually throughout their life and at every moment of their existence. For the historical background of this governmentality that I would like to talk about, this seems to me to be an important, decisive phenomenon, no doubt unique in the history of societies and civilizations. From the end of antiquity to the birth of the modern world, no civilization or society has been more pastoral than Christian societies. And I do not think that this pastorate, this pastoral power, can be assimilated to or confused with the methods used to subject men to a law or to a sovereign. Nor can it be assimilated to the methods used to train children, adolescents, and young people. It cannot be assimilated to the formulae employed to convince, persuade, and lead men more or less in spite of themselves. In short, the pastorate does not coincide with politics, pedagogy, or rhetoric. It is something entirely different. It is an art of "governing men,"* and I think this is where we should look for the origin, the point of formation, of crystallization, the embryonic point of the governmentality whose entry into politics, at the end of the sixteenth and in the seventeenth and eighteenth centuries, marks the threshold of the modern state. The modern state is born, I think, when governmentality became a calculated and reflected practice. The Christian pastorate seems to me to be the background of this process, it being understood that, on the one hand, there was a huge gap between the Hebraic theme of the shepherd and the Christian pastorate and, on the other, that there will of course be a no less important and wide gap between the government or pastoral direction of individuals and communities, and the development of arts of government, the specification of a field of political intervention, from the sixteenth and seventeenth centuries.

Today I do not want to study how this Christian pastorate took shape, was institutionalized, and how, in its development, it was far

---

* "governing men": in inverted commas in the manuscript.

from being the same as a political power, despite a series of conjunctions and entanglements. So I do not want to undertake the history of the pastorate, of Christian pastoral power; it would be ridiculous to want to do so [given] my level of competence and the time available. I would just like to indicate some of the features that were formed, from the outset, in the practice and reflection that has always accompanied pastoral practice, and which I do not think have ever been obliterated.

For this very vague, rudimentary, and elementary sketch I will take some old texts from around the third to the sixth century that redefine the pastorate in communities of the faithful, in churches, since the Church really does not exist until relatively late on; a few texts then, which are either basically Western, or are Eastern texts that had great importance and influence in the West, like John Chrysostom's *De sacerdotio*, for example.[1] I will take, the *Epistles* of Saint Cyprian,[2] the crucial treatise by Saint Ambrose entitled, *De officiis ministrorum* (the responsibilities, the offices of ministers),[3] and then the *Liber pastoralis*,*[4] which will be used until the end of the seventeenth century as the basic text of the Christian pastoral. I will also take some texts that refer to a, as it were, more dense, more intense form of the pastoral, which is not implemented in churches or communities of the faithful, but in monastic communities: John Cassian's text, *Conferences*,[5] which basically transmitted to the West the first experiences of communal life in the Eastern monasteries, and the *Cenobite Institutes*,[6] then the *Letters* of Saint Jerome,[7] and finally, of course, the *Rule* or *Rules* of Saint Benedict,[8] which is the great founding text of Western monasticism.

How does the pastorate appear [on the basis] of elements taken from these texts? What specifies the pastorate and distinguishes it both from the Greek magistrate and from the Hebraic theme of the pastor, of the shepherd, the good shepherd? If we take the pastorate in its abstract, general, and completely theoretical definition, we can see that it is connected to three things. The pastorate is connected to salvation, since its essential, fundamental objective is leading individuals, or at any rate,

---

* M.F.: *Regulae pastoralis vitae.* Same title in the manuscript.

allowing individuals to advance and progress on the path of salvation. This is true both for individuals and for the community. The pastorate therefore guides individuals and the community on the way to salvation. Second, the pastorate is connected to the law, since for individuals and communities to earn their salvation, it must make sure that they really submit to the order, command, or will of God. Finally, third, the pastorate is connected to the truth, since in Christianity, as in all scriptural religions, earning one's salvation and submission to the law are, of course, conditional upon acceptance, belief, and profession of a particular truth. So, there is a connection to salvation, the law, and to truth; the pastor guides to salvation, prescribes the law, and teaches the truth.

Clearly, if the pastorate was no more than this and it was sufficient to describe it in these terms and at this single level, then the Christian pastorate would have no kind of specificity or originality at all, because, when it comes to it, guiding, prescribing, and teaching, saving, enjoining, and educating, fixing the common end, formulating the general law, and stamping true and correct opinions on minds, proposing or imposing them, are all activities of any power whatsoever and the definition of the pastorate would not be distinct from, would be of the same type as, and isomorphic with the definitions of the city-state, or of the magistrates of the city-state in Plato. So I do not think the specificity of the Christian pastorate is exactly characterized or indicated by the connection to salvation, the law, and truth, taken as such in this general form. In actual fact, I do not think the pastorate is defined at the level of its connection with these three fundamental elements of salvation, law, and truth. It is defined, well it is specified at least at a different level, and that is what I will now try to show you.

Let's take salvation first of all. How does the Christian pastorate claim to lead individuals to salvation? Let's consider it in its most general, most banal form. A common feature of the Greek city-state and the Hebraic theme of the flock is that a common destiny envelops the people and the person who is their chief or guide. If the chief leads his flock astray, or if the magistrate does not direct the city-state well, the magistrate loses the city-state, or the shepherd his flock, but they too are lost along with it. They are saved with it and they are lost with it. This common destiny—again, the theme is found in the Greeks and the

Hebrews—is justified by a sort of moral reciprocity in the sense that, when misfortunes rain down on the city-state, or when famine scatters the flock, who is responsible? Where, at any rate, should we look for its cause; what was the starting point for this misfortune? We should look, of course, to the shepherd, chief, or sovereign. If you look and search for the source of the plague at Thebes you find Oedipus; the king, the chief, the shepherd is the very source of the city's misfortune. Conversely, what is the reason for a bad king or an unwise shepherd at the head of the flock or the city? The reason is that fortune, or destiny, or the god, Yahweh, wanted to punish the people for its ingratitude or the city for its injustice. The reason and justification for the historical event of a bad king or a bad shepherd is the sins or faults of the community or city. So in all of this we have a sort of total relationship, a common destiny, and reciprocal responsibility between the community and the person who is responsible for it.

In the Christian pastorate there is also a series of relations of reciprocity between pastor and sheep, pastor and flock, but I think this relationship is much more complex and elaborate than the kind of global reciprocity I have just been [talking about]. The Christian pastor and his sheep are bound together by extremely complex and subtle relationships of responsibility. The first characteristic of these non-global relationships is that they are fully and paradoxically distributive. Here again, you will see that we are not far from the Hebraic theme of the shepherd, or even from connotations found in Plato. But we must proceed step by step. So, what does fully and paradoxically distributive mean? Fully distributive means that the pastor must assure the salvation of all. To assure the salvation of all means two things that must in fact be linked. On the one hand, the pastor must assure the salvation of everyone, that is to say, of the whole community, of the community as a whole, as a unity. "The pastor," says Chrysostom, "must take care of the whole town and even of the *orbis terrarum*."[9] In one sense this is the salvation of all, but it is equally the salvation of each. No individual sheep is a matter of indifference. Not one sheep must escape this movement, this operation of direction and guidance leading to salvation. The salvation of each is absolutely, not relatively important. Saint Gregory tells us in the *The Book of Pastoral Rule*, Book 2, chapter 5: "That the pastor has compassion for each sheep in particular."[10] And in Saint Benedict's *Rule*, chapter 27, the abbot must show extreme concern for each of his monks, for each member of his community: "He must strive with all his sagacity and know-how not to lose one of the sheep entrusted to him."[11] All means to save everyone: to save the whole and to save each. Here we encounter the endlessly repeated and revived metaphor of the pomegranate, the pomegranate that was symbolically attached to the high priest's robe at Jerusalem.[12] The unity of the pomegranate, under its solid envelope, does not exclude the singularity of the seeds, but rather is made up from them, and each seed is as important as the pomegranate.[13]

This is where we encounter the paradoxically distributive side of the Christian pastorate. It is paradoxically distributive since, of course, the necessity of saving the whole entails, if necessary, accepting the sacrifice of a sheep that could compromise the whole. The sheep that is a cause of scandal, or whose corruption is in danger of corrupting the whole flock, must be abandoned, possibly excluded, chased away, and so forth.[14] On the other hand, and this is the paradox, the salvation of a single sheep calls for as much care from the pastor as does the whole flock; there is no sheep for which he must not suspend all his other responsibilities and occupations, abandon the flock, and try to bring it back.[15] "Bringing back the stray and bleating sheep" was not just a theoretical theme; from the first centuries of Christianity it was a fundamental practical problem when one needed to know what to do about the *lapsi*, those who had renounced the Church.[16] Should one abandon them once and for all or go in search of them wherever they were or had fallen? In short, there was this whole problem of the paradox of the shepherd that I have already talked about,[17] because in fact it was already present, not just sketched out, but even expressed in the Bible and in Hebraic literature.

Now I think Christianity added four more absolutely specific and unprecedented principles to that of the full and paradoxical distributive character of pastoral power. First there is the principle of what I will call analytical responsibility. That is to say, at the end of the day, at the end of life in the world, the Christian shepherd, the Christian pastor, will of course have to account for every sheep. A numerical and individual distribution will make it possible to know if he really has concerned himself with every one of his sheep, and any missing sheep will be counted against him. But also—and this is where the principle of analytical responsibility comes in—he will have to account for every act of each of his sheep, for everything that may have happened between them, and everything good and evil they may have done at any time. So it is not just a responsibility defined by a numerical and individual distribution, but also a responsibility defined by a qualitative and factual distribution. The pastor will be questioned and examined, and, Saint Benedict says, he will have to account for everything that every single sheep has done.[18] Saint Cyprian, in Letter 8, says that on the fearful day, "if we, the pastors, are found negligent, it will be said that we did not search for the lost sheep"—principle of numerical distribution—"but also that we did not return to the straight path those who strayed, or bandaged their broken feet, although we drank their milk and wore their wool."[19] So we have to go beneath this individual responsibility and consider the pastor responsible for each and every one.

The second principle, which is also completely specific to Christianity, I will call the principle of exhaustive and instantaneous transfer. On the dreadful day, not only will the pastor have to account for the sheep and for what they have done, but he will also have to consider everything a sheep has done, every merit or fault, as his own act. When anything good happens to a sheep, the pastor will have to experience it as his own good. The pastor will also have to consider an evil that happens to a sheep, or which occurs through or because of a sheep, as an evil that is happening to him or that he has done himself. He must take delight in the good of the sheep with a particular and personal joy, and grieve or repent for the evil due to his sheep. In the Letter 58, Saint Jerome says: "Make the salvation of others, *lucrum animae suae*, the profit of your soul."[20] So, this is the principle of the exhaustive and instantaneous transfer to the pastor of the merits and faults of the sheep.

The third principle is that of sacrificial reversal, which is once again completely specific to the Christian pastorate. In fact, if it is true that the pastor is lost along with his sheep—according to the general form of that kind of global solidarity I have been talking about—he must also lose himself for his sheep, and in their place. That is to say, the pastor must be prepared to die to save his sheep. "The pastor," writes Saint John, "defends the sheep against wolves and wild beasts. He gives his life for them."[21] The commentary on this fundamental text says that, of course, in the temporal sense of the expression, the pastor must be prepared to die a biological death if his sheep are at risk, he must defend them against their temporal enemies, but he must also be prepared to die in the spiritual sense, that is to say, the pastor must risk his soul for the souls of others. He must agree to take the sins of the sheep on his shoulders so that they do not have to pay, and so that he is the one who pays. So, if it comes to it, the pastor must expose himself to temptation, taking upon himself everything the sheep could shed if, through this kind of transfer, it freed itself both from temptation and the risk it had of spiritual death. This theme, which appears decidedly theoretical and moral, assumed concrete actuality with the problem of spiritual direction, which I will talk about later. What, in some if not all its aspects, did spiritual direction involve? The question was this: Will not the person who directs and explores the recesses of someone else's conscience, the person to whom one confides one's sins and the temptations to which one has been exposed, will not this person who is called upon to see, observe, and discover evil, be exposed to temptation? Will not the evil of which he relieves the conscience of the person he directs, by the very act of relieving it, expose [him] to temptation? Will not learning of such horrible sins, seeing such beautiful sinners, precisely expose him to the risk of the death of his own soul at the moment he saves the soul of this sheep?[22] So, this is the problem, which, from the thirteenth century, was widely discussed and is precisely the implementation of this paradox of the reversal of values; sacrificial reversal involves the pastor accepting the danger of dying in order to save the souls of others. And it is precisely when he accepts dying for others that the pastor is saved.

The fourth principle, the fourth mechanism that we find in the definition of the Christian pastor is what could be called, again in a completely schematic and arbitrary way, the principle of alternate correspondence. If in fact it is true that the sheep's merit constitutes the shepherd's merit, then can we not also say that the shepherd's merit would not amount to much if all the sheep were always perfectly worthy of merit? Is not the shepherd's merit due, at least in part, to the sheep being recalcitrant, exposed to danger, and always about to fall? And the shepherd's merit, which earns his salvation, will be precisely that he has constantly struggled against these dangers, brought back the stray sheep, and that he has had to struggle against his own flock. Thus, Saint Benedict says: "If his subordinates are unruly, then the pastor will be absolved."[23] Conversely, we can also say, equally paradoxically, that the pastor's weaknesses may contribute to the salvation of the flock. How can the pastor's frailties contribute to the flock's salvation? Certainly, the pastor should be perfect, as far as possible. The pastor's example is fundamental; it is essential for the virtue, merit, and salvation of the flock. As Saint Gregory says in *The Book of Pastoral Rule*, II [2]*: "Should not the hand that would clean the dirt from others be proper and clean?"[24] So, the pastor must be proper and clean. But if the pastor has no weaknesses, if he is too proper or too clean, will he not take something like pride in this perfection, and, again from Saint Gregory's *Liber pastoralis*, "will not the loftiness that he conceives as due to [his own perfection] constitute a precipice from which he will fall in the eyes of God?"[25]† It is good, then, for the pastor to have imperfections, to know them, and not to hide them hypocritically from his faithful. It is good that he repents of them explicitly and is humbled by them, so as to maintain himself in a self-abasement that will edify the faithful, just as carefully hiding his own frailties would produce a scandal.[26] Consequently, just as on one side the pastor's merit and salvation are due to the weaknesses of his sheep, so too the pastor's faults and weaknesses contribute to the edification of his sheep and are part of the movement, the process, of guiding them towards salvation.

This analysis of the subtleties of the bond between the pastor and his sheep could be continued indefinitely, or anyway for a very long time. What I wanted to show you is, in the first place, that instead of that community, of that complete and mass reciprocity of salvation and peace between sheep and pastor, but working on and developing this general relationship without ever entirely calling it into question, developing it and working on it from within, there is the idea that the Christian

---

* M.F.: II, 1.
† Foucault adds: The pastor's perfection is a school [*one or two inaudible words*].

pastor does what? The Christian pastor acts in a subtle economy of merit and fault, an economy that presupposes an analysis into precise elements, mechanisms of transfer, procedures of reversal, and of the interplay of support between conflicting elements; in short, a whole detailed economy of merits and faults between which, in the end, God decides. For here too there is a fundamental element: In the end, neither the pastor's nor his sheep's certain and definitive salvation is guaranteed by this economy of merits and faults that the pastor constantly has to manage. In the end, the actual production of salvation eludes one's grasp; it is entirely in God's hands. Whatever the pastor's skill, merit, virtue, or holiness, he is not the one who brings about either his sheep's or his own salvation. On the other hand, without any final certainty, he has to manage the trajectories, circuits, and reversals of merit and fault. We are always within the general horizon of salvation, but with a completely different mode of action, type of intervention, ways of doing things, styles, and pastoral techniques from those that would lead the whole flock to the Promised Land. So, distinguishing itself from the general theme of salvation, we have something specific in Christianity that I will call the economy of faults and merits.

Consider now the problem of the law. I think we could carry out a somewhat similar analysis and show that the pastor is not fundamentally a man of the law, or at any rate, it is in no way typical and specific about the pastor that he speaks the law. Very broadly speaking, in a schematic and caricatural way, the Greek citizen—and obviously I am talking about the citizen and not the slave or those who, for whatever reason, are minors in relation to the right of citizenship and the effects of the law—basically does not let himself be directed, and is only prepared to be directed by two things: by the law and by persuasion, that is to say, by the injunctions of the city-state or by the rhetoric of men. Again, very roughly I would say that the general category of obedience does not exist in the Greeks, or in any case that there are distinct spheres that do not belong entirely to the realm of obedience. There is, then, the sphere of respect for the laws, for the decisions of the assembly, for the sentences of the magistrates, and, in short, for orders that are addressed either to all in the same way or to particular individuals in the name of all. So there is this zone of respect, and then there is the zone, I was going to say of ruse, let's say of insidious actions and effects: the set of processes by which men let themselves be led, persuaded, or seduced by someone else. These are the processes by which the orator, for example, will convince his audience, the doctor will persuade his patient to follow a particular treatment, and the philosopher will persuade someone who consults him to do this or that in order to arrive at the truth, self-control, and so on. These are the processes by which the master who teaches something to his student will succeed in convincing him of the importance of arriving at a particular result and of the means he must employ to do so. So, there is respect for the laws and letting oneself be persuaded by someone: law or rhetoric.

The Christian pastorate has, I think, organized something completely different that seems to me to be foreign to Greek practice, and this is what we could call the insistence on "pure obedience,"* that is to say, on obedience as a unitary, highly valued type of conduct in which the essence of its *raison d'être* is in itself. What I mean is this. Everyone knows—and here again, to start with, we do not go much beyond the Hebraic theme—that Christianity is not a religion of the law; it is a religion of God's will, a religion of what God wills for each in particular. Hence, of course, the fact that the pastor will not be the man of the law or even its representative, his action will always be conjunctural and individual. We can see this with regard to the famous *lapsi*, those who have renounced God. We should not, says Saint Cyprian, treat them all in the same way by applying a single general measure and condemning them in the way a civil court might. Each must be treated as a particular case.[27] The idea that the pastor is not a man of the law is also seen in the very early and constant comparison with the doctor. The pastor is not fundamentally or primarily a judge; he is essentially a doctor who has to take responsibility for each soul and for the sickness of each soul. We see it in a whole series of texts, like that of Saint Gregory, for example, who says: "One and the same method is not applied to all men because all are not governed by the same nature of character. Procedures that benefit some are frequently harmful to others."[28] So, the pastor may well have to make the law known, to make known the will of God

---

* "pure obedience" in inverted commas in the manuscript, p. 15.

applied to all men; he will have to make known the decisions of the Church or community that are applied to all the members of that community. However, the Christian pastor's mode of action is individualized. Here again we are not very far from what is found in the Hebrews, even if, however, the Jewish religion is essentially a religion of the law. But the Biblical texts always say that the pastor is someone who is concerned with each sheep individually and he sees to their salvation by [giving]* the necessary care that is peculiar to each one. In addition to this theme of the pastor as someone who treats each case according to its specific characteristics, rather than as a man of the law, I think the relationship of the sheep to the person who directs it is one of complete subordination, which is again specific to the Christian pastorate and I do not think is found anywhere else.

Complete subordination means three things. First, it is a relationship of submission, but not submission to a law or a principle of order, and not even to a reasonable injunction, or to some reasoned principles or conclusions. It is a relationship of the submission of one individual to another. The relationship of submission of one individual to another individual, correlating an individual who directs and an individual who is directed, is not only a condition of Christian obedience, it is its very principle. And the person who is directed must accept submission and obey within this individual relationship and because it is an individual relationship. The Christian puts himself in his pastor's hands for spiritual matters, but equally for material things and for everyday life. Here again, the Christian texts constantly take up what is no doubt a passage from the Psalms, which says: "Who is not guided falls like a dead leaf."[29] This is true for the laity, but of course it is also much more intensely true for monks, and in this case we see the implementation of the fundamental principle that Christian obedience is not obedience to a law, a principle, or any rational element whatsoever, but subordination to someone because he is someone.

This subordination of someone to someone else is, of course, institutionalized in monastic life in the relationship to the abbot or superior, or to the master of the novices. One of the fundamental points in the

---

* M.F.: taking

organization and planning of cenobite life from the fourth century was that every individual entering a monastic community be put in the hands of someone—the superior, the master of novices—who takes total charge of him and tells him what he must do at every moment. The novice's perfection and merit ultimately consists in considering it a fault to do anything without having received an explicit order to do it. His entire life must be codified by the fact that each of its episodes and moments must be commanded, ordered by someone. This is illustrated by a number of what could be called tests of good obedience, of immediate action without thought. We have a series of accounts of this reported by Cassian in the *Cenobite institutes*, and which are also found in *The Lausiac History*,[30] such as the test which consists in this: As soon as an order is given to a monk, he must immediately stop whatever he happens to be doing at that time and carry out the order without wondering why he has been given this order or whether it wouldn't be more worthwhile to continue with what he was doing. As an example of this virtue of obedience, he refers to a novice who was copying a text, and even a text of Holy Scripture, and who interrupted his copying, not at the end of a paragraph or a sentence, and not even in the middle of a word, but in the middle of a letter, and who left this letter in suspense in order to obey the stupidest order he could be given.[31] This is also the test of absurdity. The perfection of obedience consists in obeying an order, not because it is reasonable or because it entrusts you with an important task, but rather because it is absurd. This is the endlessly repeated story of the monk John, who was ordered to water a dried out stick planted far from his cell in the middle of the desert, and who went to water it twice a day.[32] The stick did not flower as a result of this, but John's saintliness, however, was assured. It is also the test of the cantankerous master. The more sour the master, the less he acknowledges the disciple, the less he shows gratitude, and the less he congratulates the disciple on his obedience, the more the obedience is recognized as meritorious. And finally, it is above all the test of breaking the law, that is to say, having to obey even when the order is contrary to everything one might think of as law. This is the test of Lucius reported in *The History Lausiac*. Lucius arrives at a monastery after having lost his wife, but with a son who was left to him, a 12-year-old child. Lucius is subjected to a series of tests at the end of which he is told to drown his son in the river.³³ And Lucius, because it is an order that he must carry out, will actually drown his son in the river. Christian obedience, the sheep's obedience to his pastor, is therefore a complete obedience of [one] individual to another individual. What's more, the person who obeys, the person who is subject to the order, is called the *subditus*, literally, he who is dedicated, given to someone else, and who is entirely at their disposition and subject to their will. It is a relationship of complete servitude.

Second, it is a relationship that is not finalized, in the sense that when a Greek entrusted himself to a doctor or a philosopher, it was in order to arrive at a particular result. This result could be knowledge of a craft, or some kind of perfection, or a cure, and obedience is only the necessary and not always agreeable route to this result. So in Greek obedience, or anyway in the fact that a Greek submits himself at a given moment to the will or orders of someone, there is always an objective—health, virtue, the truth—and an end, that is to say, there will be a point when this relationship of obedience is suspended and even turned around. When one submits oneself to a philosophy professor, in Greece, it is in order to succeed in becoming master of oneself at a certain moment, that is to say, to reverse this relationship of obedience and to become one's own master.³⁴ Now in Christian obedience, there is no end, for what does Christian obedience lead to? It leads quite simply to obedience. One obeys in order to be obedient, in order to arrive at a state* of obedience. I think this notion of a state of obedience is also something completely new and specific that is absolutely unprecedented. The end point towards which the practice of obedience aims is what is called humility, which consists in feeling oneself the least of men, in taking orders from anyone, thus continually renewing the relationship of obedience, and above all in renouncing one's own will. Being humble is not a matter of knowing that one has committed many sins, and it is not merely accepting being given and submitting to the orders given by anyone whomsoever. Being humble is basically, and above all, knowing that any will of one's own is a bad will. So if there is an end to obedience, it is a state of obedience defined by the definitive and complete renunciation of one's own will. The aim of obedience is the mortification of one's will; it is to act so that one's will, as one's own will, is dead, that is to say, so that there is no other will but not to have any will. And this is how Saint Benedict defines good monks, in chapter 5 of his *Rule*: "They no longer live by their free will, *ambulantes alieno judicio et imperio*, in marching under the judgment and the *imperium* of another, they always desire that someone command them."[35]

Obviously, this should all be investigated, because the institutionalization of the Christian pastorate is very important for Christian morality, both in the history of ideas and for the practice itself, as also for all the problems of what is called the "flesh" in Christianity. As you can see, it involves the difference in the successive meanings given to the same word *apatheia*, the *apatheia* to which, precisely, obedience strives. When a Greek disciple comes to see a philosophy master and places himself under his direction and guidance, he does so in order to arrive at something called *apatheia*: the absence of *pathē*, or the absence of passions. But what does this absence of passions mean and in what does it consist? Not having passions is no longer having any passivity. I mean that it is to eliminate from oneself all those impulses, forces, and storms of which one is not the master and which thus lay you open to being the slave of what takes place in you, or in your body, or possibly of what happens in the world. Greek *apatheia* guarantees mastery of oneself. In a way, it is the other side of self-mastery. One obeys, and one renounces certain things, and in Stoic philosophy and late Epicureanism one even renounces the pleasures of the flesh and the body, in order to assure *apatheia*, which is only the other side, the negative hollow, as it were, of the positive thing, self-mastery, to which one strives. Thus one will become master through renunciation. The word *apatheia*, transmitted to Christianity by Greek or Greco-Roman moralists,[36] [will take on] a completely different meaning, and renunciation of pleasures of the body, of sexual pleasures, of the desires of the flesh, will have a completely different effect in Christianity. What does the absence of *pathē*, of passions, mean for Christianity? Essentially it means renunciation of egoism, of my own singular will. The charge against the pleasures of the flesh is not that they make one passive—which was the Stoic and even Epicurean theme—but rather that an individual, personal, and egoistic activity is deployed within them. The charge is that the self, that I myself, am directly interested in them, and through them maintain a frenzied assertion of the self as the essential, fundamental thing, and the greatest value. Consequently, the *pathos* to be kept at bay through practices of obedience is not passion but the will, a will directed on oneself, and the absence of passion, *apatheia*, will be the will that has renounced itself and continually renounces itself.[37]

We could add here (but I will pass over it quickly) that in this theory and practice of Christian obedience, the one who commands, in this case the pastor, whether abbot or bishop, obviously does not command in order to command, but only because he has been ordered to command. The proof that qualifies someone as pastor is that he refuses the pastorate for which he is given responsibility. He refuses because he does not want to command, but insofar as his refusal would be the assertion of a particular will, he must give up his refusal; he must obey, and command. So we have a sort of generalized field of obedience that is typical of the space in which pastoral relationships are deployed.

Just as the analysis or definition of the pastorate distinguished it from the theme of the common relationship and revealed the complex economy of the circulation, transfer, and exchange of merits and faults, so too, in the same way, in relation to the general principle of the law, the pastorate reveals an entire practice of submission of individual to individual, under the sign of the law, for sure, but outside its field, in a subordination that never has any generality, does not guarantee any freedom, and does not lead to any mastery, either of oneself or of others. It is a field of generalized obedience, strongly individualized in each of its manifestations, always instantaneous and limited, and such that even the points where there is mastery are still effects of obedience.

We should, of course, note a further problem here that I will just mention: the organization of the series, or rather the couple, of servitude-service. The sheep, the one who is directed, must live his relationship to his pastor as a relationship of complete servitude. But conversely, the pastor must experience his responsibility as a service, and one that makes him the servant of his sheep. Then, we should compare this relationship of servitude-service with Greek and Roman conceptions of office, of the *officium*, and you can see another fundamental problem, that of the self. That is to say, in pastoral power (I will come to this shortly), we have a mode of individualization that not only does not take place by way of affirmation of the self, but one that entails destruction of the self.

Finally, third, there is the problem of truth, and here I will be very quick since I have already spoken about this elsewhere in a different way. Here again, expressed in the most schematic way, and if we do not look at it in detail, the relationship of the pastorate to truth is inscribed in a kind of curve and outline that does not distinguish it greatly from possible forms of Greek teaching. What I mean is that the pastor has a teaching task vis-à-vis his community. We can even say that this is his primary and principal task. In one of the first sentences of the *De officiis ministorum*, Saint Ambrose says: "*Episcopi proprium munus docere*," "the proper responsibility of the bishop is to teach."[38] Clearly, this teaching task is not one-dimensional; it is a more complicated affair than just giving a lesson to others. The pastor must teach by his example, by his own life, and what's more the value of this example is so strong that if he does not give a good example by his own life, then any theoretical, verbal teaching he gives will be nullified. In the *Book of Pastoral Rule*, Saint Gregory says that pastors who teach the good doctrine, but give a bad example, are a bit like shepherds who drink the clear water but whose dirty feet muddy the water that the sheep in their charge must drink.[39] The pastor also does not teach in a global, general way. He does not teach everyone in the same way, for the minds of the listeners are like the strings of a cithara, which are stretched differently and cannot be touched in the same way. In the *Liber pastoralis*, Saint Gregory gives thirty-six distinct ways of teaching, according to whether one is addressing people who are married or single, rich or poor, sick or healthy, happy or sad, and so on.[40] All this is far removed from the traditional conception of teaching. But in relation to this there are, I think, two fundamental new things that continue to characterize the Christian pastorate.

First, there is the fact that this teaching must be a direction of daily conduct. It is not just a matter of teaching what one must know and what one must do. It is not just a matter of teaching by general principles, but rather by a daily modulation, and this teaching must also pass through an observation, a supervision, a direction exercised at every moment and with the least discontinuity possible over the sheep's whole, total conduct. The perfection, merit, or quality of daily life must not be just the result of a general teaching or even of an example. The pastor must really take charge of and observe daily life in order to form a never-ending knowledge of the behavior and conduct of the members of the flock he supervises. Concerning the pastor in general, Saint Gregory says: "In pursuing heavenly things, the pastor must not abandon the needs of his neighbor, nor should he lose his taste for higher things by condescending to the material needs of his neighbors."[41] And he refers to Saint Paul who, he says: "while ecstatic in the contemplation of the invisible, lowered his mind to the marital bed. He taught spouses the conduct they should follow in their intimate relations." Saint Paul had indeed penetrated the heavens with contemplation, but he did not exclude from his concerns the bed of those who are still carnal.[42] So we have an integral teaching that at the same time involves the pastor's exhaustive observation of the life of his sheep.

The second aspect, which is also very important, is spiritual direction (*direction de conscience*).[43] That is to say, the pastor must not simply teach the truth. He must direct the conscience. What does this mean? Here again, we have to look back a bit. Strictly speaking, the practice of spiritual direction is not a Christian invention. There were forms of spiritual direction in Antiquity,[44] but we can describe it, very schematically, in the following way. [First,] spiritual direction in Antiquity is voluntary, that is to say, the person who wishes to be directed finds someone whom he asks to direct him. What's more, in its very early forms, and even in later forms, spiritual direction was paid for. One saw someone who said: I would very much like to direct you, but you must give me some money. The Sophists had spiritual direction shops on the public square. One had to pay for a consultation.

Second, spiritual direction in Antiquity was circumstantial, that is to say, one did not let the whole of one's life be directed or let oneself be directed for all of one's life, but one sought out a spiritual director when going through a bad time, or experiencing a hard and difficult episode. If one had suffered bereavement, had lost one's children or one's wife, was ruined, or exiled by a prince, one sought out someone who basically helped as a comforter. So, spiritual direction was voluntary, episodic, consolatory, and at certain times it took place through the examination of conscience. That is to say, direction often involved the director saying to the person being directed, inviting him, and even constraining him, if there could be constraint, to examine his own conscience and each day, in the evening, to undertake an examination of what he had done, of the good or bad things he may have done, of what had happened to him, and, in short, to put the life of the day, a fragment of life, through the filter of discourse in such a way as to fix in truth what had happened and the merits, virtue, and progress of the person thus examined. But this examination of conscience had a fundamental aim. This was precisely that the person who examined himself could take control and become master of himself by knowing exactly what he had done and in what respect he had made progress. It was therefore a condition of self-mastery.

Christian practice will involve a completely different spiritual direction and examination of conscience because, in the first place, spiritual direction will not exactly be voluntary. At any rate, it is not always voluntary, and in the case of monks, for example, spiritual direction is absolutely obligatory and one has to have a spiritual director. Second, spiritual direction is not circumstantial; it is not a matter of responding to a misfortune, a crisis, or a difficulty. Spiritual direction is absolutely permanent, and one is directed with regard to everything and for the whole of one's life. Finally, third, the function of the examination of conscience, which is really a part* of these instruments of spiritual direction, is not to assure the individual's mastery of himself, in compensation, as it were, for his subordination to the director in this examination. On the contrary, it will be quite the opposite. One will only examine one's conscience in order to tell the director what one has done, what one is, what one has experienced, the temptations to which one has been subject, and the bad thoughts that inhabit one's mind, that is to say, one examines one's conscience the better to mark and fix more firmly the relationship of subordination to the other. In classical

---

* M.F. adds: of this arsenal, in short

antiquity examination of conscience was an instrument of mastery, here it will be an instrument of subordination. And so, at every moment, a particular discourse of truth on the self will be formed through the examination of conscience. Starting from oneself, one will extract and produce a truth which binds one to the person who directs one's conscience. Here again you can see that the type of relationship to truth in the Christian pastorate is not at all the same as that found in Greco-Roman antiquity, [and that it is] also very different from what was set out in the Hebraic theme of the pastor.

So, the Christian pastorate is not fundamentally or essentially characterized by the relationship to salvation, to the law, and to the truth. The Christian pastorate is, rather, a form of power that, taking the problem of salvation in its general set of themes, inserts into this global, general relationship an entire economy and technique of the circulation, transfer, and reversal of merits, and this is its fundamental point. Similarly with regard to the law, Christianity, the Christian pastorate, is not simply the instrument of the acceptance or generalization of the law, but rather, through an oblique relationship to the law, as it were, it establishes a kind of exhaustive, total, and permanent relationship of individual obedience. This is something quite different from the relationship to the law. And finally, if Christianity, the Christian pastor, teaches the truth, if he forces men, the sheep, to accept a certain truth, the Christian pastorate is also absolutely innovative in establishing a structure, a technique of, at once, power, investigation, self-examination, and the examination of others, by which a certain secret inner truth of the hidden soul, becomes the element through which the pastor's power is exercised, by which obedience is practiced, by which the relationship of complete obedience is assured, and through which, precisely, the economy of merits and faults passes. It is not salvation, the law, and the truth, but these new relationships of merits and faults, absolute obedience, and the production of hidden truths, which constitute, I think, what is essential and the originality and specificity of Christianity.

I will end by saying that with the Christian pastorate we see the birth of an absolutely new form of power. Also, and this will be my second and final conclusion, we see the emergence of what could be called absolutely specific modes of individualization. Individualization in the Christian pastorate will be carried out in a completely specific way that we have been able to see at work in relation to the themes of salvation, the law, and truth. In fact, the individualization assured by the exercise of pastoral power in this way will no longer be defined by an individual's status, birth, or the splendor of his actions. It will be defined in three ways. First, it will be defined by a game of dissection that defines the balance, interplay, and circulation of merits and faults at each moment. Let's say that this is not individualization by status, but by analytical identification. Second, it is a mode of individualization that is not brought about by the designation or marking of an individual's place in a hierarchy. Nor will it be brought about by the assertion of the self's mastery of self, but by a whole network of servitude that involves the general servitude of everyone with regard to everyone and, at the same time, the exclusion of the self, of the ego, and of egoism as the central, nuclear form of the individual. It is therefore a mode of individualization by subjection (*assujettissement*). Finally, third, it is a form of individualization that will not be acquired through the relationship to a recognized truth, [but] will be acquired instead through the production of an internal, secret, and hidden truth. Analytical identification, subjection, and subjectivation (*subjectivation*) are the characteristic procedures of individualization that will in fact be implemented by the Christian pastorate and its institutions. What the history of the pastorate involves, therefore, is the entire history of procedures of human individualization in the West. Let's say also that it involves the history of the subject.

The pastorate seems to me to sketch out, or is the prelude to what I have called governmentality as this is deployed from the sixteenth century. It is the prelude to this governmentality in two ways. First, it is the prelude through the procedures peculiar to the pastorate, through the way in which, fundamentally, it does not purely and simply put the principles of salvation, law, and truth into play, but rather, through all these kinds of diagonals, establishes other types of relationships under the law, salvation, and truth. So, the pastorate is a prelude to governmentality in that way. And it is also a prelude to governmentality through the constitution of a specific subject, of a subject whose merits are analytically identified, who is subjected in continuous networks of obedience, and who is subjectified (*subjectivé*) through the compulsory extraction of truth. Well, I think this typical constitution of the modern Western subject makes the pastorate one of the decisive moments in the history of power in Western societies. There you are. We will have finished with the pastorate now, and next week I will take up again the theme of governmentality.

1. See the previous lecture, 15 February, note 61.
2. Saint Cyprian, *The Epistles of S. Cyprian*.
3. Ambrose of Milan (bishop of Milan from 374 to 397), *De officiis ministrorum*, written in 389. The correct title of the work is *De officiis*. See the French translation, Saint Ambroise, *Des devoirs*, trans. and note M. Testard (Paris: Les Belles Lettres, CUF, 1984) vol. 1, Introduction, pp. 49-52. Foucault uses the Migne edition, *De officiis ministrorum: Epist. 63 ad Vercellensem Ecclesiam*, in *Patrologia Latina*, ed., J.-P. Migne, 16, col. 23-184.
4. See above, lecture of 15 February, note 53.
5. John Cassian, *Collationes*; French translation by E. Pichery, *Les Conférences* (Paris: Cerf, "Sources chrétiennes," 1966, 1967, 1971) vols 1-3; English translation by Colm Luibheid, *Conferences* (New York: Paulist Press, 1985). On Cassian, who spent several months alongside the Egyptian monks and then, ordained as a priest at Rome around 415, founded and directed two convents in the Marseilles region, one for men and the other for women, see the course summary for 1979-1980, "Du gouvernement des vivants," *Dits et Écrits*, 4, pp. 127-128, concerning the practice of confession (*exagoreusis*); English translation, "On the government of the living," *Essential Works*, 1, pp. 83-84; " '*Omnes et Singulatim*' " pp. 308-309; (French trans.) " 'Omnes et Singulatim' " pp. 144-145, concerning obedience and the relationship between the pastor and his sheep conceived of in Christianity as a relationship of individual and complete subordination; "Sexuality and Solitude" (1981) in *Essential Works*, 1, p. 183; French translation by F. Durand-Bogaert, "Sexualité et solitude" in *Dits et Écrits*, 4, p. 177; "Le combat de la chasteté" (1982) in *Dits et Écrits*, 4, pp. 295-308; English translation by Anthony Forster, "The Battle for Chastity" in *Essential Works*, 1, pp. 185-205, on the spirit of fornication and the ascesis of chastity; "Résumé du cours" in *L'Herméneutique du sujet, Cours au Collège de France. 1981-1982*, ed. Frédéric Gros (Paris: Gallimard/Le Seuil, 2001) p. 483; English translation by Graham Burchell, "Course summary" in *The Hermeneutics of the Subject. Lectures at the Collège de France 1981-1982*, English series ed. Arnold Davidson (New York: Palgrave Macmillan, 2005) p. 503; "L'écriture de soi" (1983) in *Dits et Écrits*, 4, p. 416; English translation by Robert Hurley, "Self Writing" in *Essential Works*, 1, p. 208; and "Technologies of the Self" in *Essential Works*, 1, pp. 240-241, 246-248; French translation by F. Durand-Bogaert, "Les techniques de soi" in *Dits et Écrits*, 4, pp. 802-803, 809-812.
6. J. Cassian, *De institutis coenobiorum et de octo principium vitiorum remediis* (written around 420-424); French translation by J.-C. Guy, *Institutions cénobitiques* (Paris: Cerf, "Sources chrétiennes," 1965); English translation by Jerome Bertram, *The Monastic Institutes* (London: The Saint Austin Press, 1999).
7. Saint Jerome (Hieronymus Stridonensis), *Epistolae* in *Patrologia Latina*, 22, col. 325-1224; French translation by J. Labourt, *Lettres* (Paris: Les Belles Lettres, CUF, 1949-1961) vols. I-VII.
8. Saint Benedict, *Regula sancti Benedicti*; *La Règle de saint Benoît*; *The Rule of Saint Benedict*.
9. Saint John Chrysostom, *De Sacerdotio*; *Sur le sacerdoce*, pp. 314-315; English translation by Graham Neville, *Six Books on the Priesthood* (London: SPCK, 1964) p. 140.
10. Gregory the Great, *Regula pastoralis*, II, 5, trans. B. Judic (Paris: Cerf, "Sources chrétiennes," 1992); *The Book of Pastoral Rule*: "Sit rector singulis compassione procimus"; "That the ruler should be a near neighbour to every one in compassion . . ."
11. *The Rule of Saint Benedict*, ch. 27, "How careful the abbot should be of the excommunicate": "Debet abbas (. . .) omni sagacitate et industria currere, ne aliquam de ovibus sibi creditis perdat"; "For the abbot is bound to use the greatest care, and to strive with all possible prudence and zeal, not to lose any one of the sheep committed to him."
12. Exodus, 28, 34.
13. See, for example, Gregory the Great, *Regula pastoralis*, II, 4, p. 193; *The Book of Pastoral Rule*, p. 12: "Hence in the priest's vestment, according to Divine precept, to bells are added pomegranates. For what is signified by pomegranates but the unity of the faith? For, as within a pomegranate many seeds are protected by one outer rind, so the unity of the faith comprehends the innumerable peoples of holy Church, whom a diversity of merits retains within her."

14. See *The Rule of Saint Benedict*, ch. 28, p. 256: " 'If the faithless one depart, let him depart', lest one diseased sheep should taint the whole flock." This theme of the black sheep, already present in Origen, is a commonplace of patristic literature.

15. Ibid. ch. 27, p. 255: "Let him imitate the loving example of the Good Shepherd, who, leaving the ninety and nine sheep on the mountains, went to seek one which had gone astray ..." See Luke, 15, 4, and Matthew 8, 12.

16. The problem arose notably, and on a particular scale, as a result of the persecutory measures of the Emperor Decius in 250, who wanted to oblige citizens of the Empire to participate in his favor in an act of worship towards the gods. Many Christians, not having been able to escape from the law, submitted more or less fully to the imperial will (some, rather than perform the idolatrous act, limited themselves to a vague gesture or procured a certificate of compliance). Most wanting to be reintegrated within the Church, two tendencies confronted each other in the clergy, one favorable to indulgence, the other to rigorism (hence the rigorist schism of Novatian at Rome denounced by Saint Cyprian in his Epistle 69). In the eyes of the bishops, reconciliation of the *lapsi* had to be preceded by an appropriate penance. See Saint Cyprian, *Liber de lapsis* in *Patrologia Latina*, 4, col. 463-494; French translation, *De ceux qui ont failli*, trans. D. Gorce, in *Textes* (Namur: Éd. du Soleil levant, 1958) pp. 88-92, to which Foucault refers in "Technologies of the Self" p. 244; "Les techniques de soi" p. 806, with regard to *exomologēsis* (public confession). On this subject, see also the 1979-1980 course, "Du gouvernement des vivants" and the Louvain seminar of May 1981 (unpublished).

17. See above, lecture of 8 February, pp. 128-130.

18. *The Rule of Saint Benedict*, ch. 2, pp. 227-228, "What kind of man the abbot ought to be": "And let him know that he who has undertaken the government of souls, must prepare himself to render an account of them. And whatever may be the number of the brethren under his care, let him be certainly assured that on the day of judgment he will have to given an account to the Lord of all these souls, as well as of his own. And thus, being ever fearful of the coming inquiry which the Shepherd will make into the state of the flock committed to him."

19. Saint Cyprian, *Correspondance*, Letter 8, p. 19: "Et cum incumbat nobis qui videmur praepositi esse et vice pastorum custodire gregem, si neglegentes inveniamur, dicetur nobis quod et antecessoribus nostris dictum est, qui tam neglegentes praepositi erant, quoniam 'perditum non requisivimus et errantem non correximus et claudum non colligavimus et lactem eorum edebamus et lanis eorum operiebamur' [see Ezekiel, 34, 3]"; *The Epistles of S. Cyprian*, p. 17: "And since it is incumbent on us, who seem to be set over the flock, to guard it instead of the shepherd; the same will be said to us if we be found to be negligent, as to our predecessors, who were such negligent guardians; that *we have not sought that which was lost; and have not brought back that which was strayed; and have not bound up that which was broken; but have eaten their milk, and clothed ourselves with their wool.*"

20. Saint Jerome, *Epistolae*, in *Patrologia Latina*, 22, Letter 58, col. 582: "Si officium vis exercere Presbyteri, si Episcopatus, te vel opus, vel forte honor delectat, vive in urbibus et castellis; et aliorum salutem, fac lucrum animae tuae"; French translation by Labourt, *Lettres*, pp. 78-79: "If you wish to exercise the function of priest, if perhaps the episcopacy—work or honor—pleases you, live in the towns and castles; make the salvation of others the profit of your soul."

21. John, 10, 11-12: "I am the good shepherd: the good shepherd lays down his life for his sheep. The hired man, since he is not the shepherd and the sheep do not belong to him, abandons the sheep as soon as he sees a wolf coming, and runs away, and then the wolf attacks and scatters the sheep" (*New Jerusalem Bible*).

22. See Gregory the Great, *Regula pastoralis*, II, 5, p. 203; *The Book of Pastoral Rule*, p. 14: "And for the most part it comes to pass that, while the ruler's mind becomes aware, through condescension, of the trials of others, it is itself also attacked by the temptations whereof it hears; since the same water of the laver in which a multitude of people is cleansed is undoubtedly itself defiled. For, in receiving the pollutions of those who wash, it loses, as it were, the calmness of its own purity." See *Les anormaux*, lecture of 19 February 1975, p. 166; *Abnormal*, p. 179, concerning the problem of the "holiness" of the priest who hears confessions, as analyzed by the theorists of the Tridentine pastoral.

23. *The Rule of Saint Benedict*, ch. 2: "What kind of man the abbot ought to be" p. 225: "(...) if he shall have bestowed all pastoral diligence on his unquiet and disobedient flock, and employed all his care to amend their corrupt manner of life: then shall he be absolved in the judgment of the Lord."

24. Gregory the Great, *Regula pastoralis*, II, 2; *The Book of Pastoral Rule*, p. 9: "(...) necesse est ut esse munda studeat manus, quae diluere sordes curat"; "(...) for the hand that would cleanse from dirt must needs be clean."

25. Ibid. II, 6, pp. 14-15: "(...) and those whom he has surpassed in the accident of power he believes himself to have transcended also in the merits of his life (...). Wherefore, through a marvellous judgment he finds a pit of downfall within himself, while outwardly he exalts himself on the summit of power. For he is indeed made like unto the apostate angel, when, being a man, he disdains to be like unto men."

26. Ibid. p. 15: "But still let even their subjects perceive, by certain signs coming out becomingly, that in themselves they are humble; so as both to see something to be afraid of in their authority, and to acknowledge something to imitate with respect to humility."

27. See, Saint Cyprian, *Correspondance*, Letter 17 (III, 1), p. 50: "(...) vos itaque singulos regite et consilio ac moderatione vestra secundum divina praecepta lapsorum animos temperate"; *The Epistles of S. Cyprian*: "(...) guide them individually, and by your advice and restraint temper the minds of the lapsed in accordance with the divine precepts." On the question of the *lapsi*, see the introduction of the Canon Bayard to the *Correspondance*, pp. xviii-xix; see also, above, note 16.

28. Gregory the Great, *Regula pastoralis*, III, prologue; *The Book of Pastoral Rule*, p. 24: "Ut enim longe ante nos reverendae memoriae Gregorius Nazanzinus edocuit, nonuna eademque cunctis exhortatio congruit, quia nec cunctos per morum qualitas astringit. Saepe namque aliis officiunt, quae aliis prosunt"; "For, as long before us Gregory Nazianzen of reverend memory has taught [see *Orations*, 2, 28-33], one and the same exhortation does not suit all, inasmuch as neither are all bound together by similarity of character. For the things that profit some often hurt others."

29. In the unpublished Louvain seminar, "Mal dire, mal faire," Foucault gives Proverbs as the source of this phrase, but it cannot be found there any more than it can in Psalms. The phrase probably derives from a combination of two passages, according to the Vulgate text: (1) Proverbs, 11, 14: "Ubi non est gubernator, populus corruet" (In the absence of direction, a people succumbs), and (2) Isaiah, 64, 6: "Et cecidimus quasi folium universal" (We all fade like dead leaves"—literally, according to the Latin text, "we fell"). Foucault cites this phrase again, without giving a precise reference, in *L'Herméneutique du sujet*, p. 381; *The Hermeneutics of the Subject*, p. 398.

30. τό Λαυσιαχον/*The Lausiac History*, work written by Palladius (c.363-c.425), bishop of Helenopolis of Bithnyia (Asia Minor), reputed to have Origenist tendencies. After staying several years with the monks of Egypt, he published this collection of biographies dedicated to Lausius or Lausus, Great Chamberlain of Theodosius II (408-450), and is an important source for knowledge of ancient monasticism. Palladius, *Histoire lausiaque (Vies d'ascètes et de Pères du désert)*, Greek text, translated and introduced by A. Lucot (Paris: A. Picard et fils, "Textes et Documents pour l'histoire du christianisme," 1912), based on the critical edition of Dom Butler, *Historia Lausiaca* (Cambridge: Cambridge University Press, "Texts and Studies," 6, 1904); Pallade d'Hélénopolis, *Les Moines du désert. Histoire lausiaque*, trans. du Carmel de la Paix (Paris: Desclée de Brouwer, "Les Pères dans la foi," 1981); English translation, *Palladius: The Lausiac History*, trans. R.T. Meyer (New York: Newman Press, Ancient Christian Writers, 34, 1964); See, R. Draguet, "L'*Histoire lausiaque*, une œuvre écrite dans l'esprit d'Evagre," *Revue d'histoire ecclésiastique*, 41, 1946, pp. 321-364, and 42, 1947, pp. 5-49.

31. Cassian, *Institutions cénobitiques*, Book IV, ch. 12; *The Monastic Institutes*, p. 46: The passage does not indicate what text the scribe is copying. Obedience here corresponds to the sound of "the knocker" which is "the summons to prayer or some other duty."

32. Ibid. Book IV, ch. 24. John the Visionary—Abba John—(died around 395 after forty years as a recluse at Lycopolis) is one of the most famous figures of fourth century Egyptian monasticism. The story, with John Colobos rather than John of Lycopolis as the protagonist, is taken up notably in the *Apophtegmata Patrum* (*Patrologia Graeca*, 65, col.

204C) with the important difference that the stick ends up taking root and bearing fruit. See, J.-Cl. Guy, *Paroles des Anciens. Apophtegmes des Pères du désert* (Paris: Le Seuil, "Points Sagesses," 1976) p. 69.

33. The episode is not from *The History Lausiac*, but is reported by Cassian in the *Institutions cénobitiques*; *The Monastic Institutes*, Book IV, ch. 27, with regard to the abbot Patermutus and his son aged 8 (some brethren, stationed in advance to watch, take the child from the river, thus preventing full execution of command of the superior, who was satisfied with the father's devotion) and is found in various collections of apothegms. In the Louvain seminar, Foucault in fact refers to Cassian when recounting this story.

34. On the function of the master in Greco-Roman culture, see *L'Herméneutique du sujet*, lecture of 27 January, pp. 149-158; *The Hermeneutics of the Subject*, pp. 154-164.

35. *The Rule of Saint Benedict*, ch. 5, "Of obedience," pp. 232-234: "These, therefore, choose the narrow way, of which the Lord says: 'Narrow is the way which leads to life'; so that living not by their own will, nor obeying their own desires and pleasures, but walking according to the judgment and command of another [*ut non suo arbitrio viventes vel desideriis suis et voluptatibus oboiedientes, sed ambulantes alieno iudicio et imperio*], and dwelling in community [*coenobia*], they desire to have an abbot over them [*attbatem sibi praeesse desideraant*]." See, " *'Omnes et singulatim'* " p. 309; " *'Omnes et singulatim'* " (French) pp. 145-146.

36. On the difficulty of finding a Latin equivalent for *apatheia* and the ambiguity created by its translation as *impatientia*, see Seneca, *Letters to Lucilius*, 9.2; the Latin fathers will translate the word by *imperturbatio* (Sainte Jerome, in Jer. 4, proem.), or more frequently by *impassibilitas* (Saint Jerome, *Epistolae*, 133, 3); Saint Augustine, *Civitas Dei*, 14, 9, 4; English translation by Henry Bettenson, *City of God*, ed. David Knowles (Penguin: Harmondsworth, 1972) p. 564: "that condition which in Greek is called *apatheia*, which might be translated in Latin by *impassibilitas* (impassibility) if such a word existed."

37. Is this brief exposition of *apatheia* an implicit criticism of the pages devoted to this notion by Pierre Hadot in his article, "Exercises spirituels antiques et 'philosophie chrétienne' " in *Exercises spirituels et Philosophie antique* (Paris: Études augustiniennes, 1981) pp. 59-74; English translation by Michael Chase, "Ancient Spiritual Exercises and 'Christian Philosophy' " in P. Hadot, *Philosophy as a Way of Life*, ed. Arnold I. Davidson (Oxford: Blackwell, 1995) pp. 126-144. Emphasizing the crucial role of *apatheia* in monastic spirituality, Hadot traces a continuous line through Stoicism, Neo-Platonism, and the doctrine of Evagrius of Pontius and Doretheus of Gaza (pp. 70-72; pp. 136-140). On the *apatheia* of the Christian ascetics, see the next lecture, 1 March, pp. 205-207.

38. These first words of the subtitle of chapter 1, in the Migne edition (*Patrologia Latina*, 16, col. 23A) are not taken up in more recent editions and are therefore probably due to the editor. The same idea, however, is expressed later on by Saint Ambrose, *De officiis*, 1, 2, ed. J. Testard, p. 96: "(...) cum iam effugere non possimus officium docendi quod nobis refugientibus imposuit sacerdotii necessitudo"; "(...) and we cannot evade the duty of teaching, which the responsibility of priesthood has imposed on us against our will."

39. Gregory the Great, *Regula pastoralis*, I, 2; *The Book of Pastoral Rule*, p. 2: "For indeed the shepherds drink most pure water, when with a right understanding they imbibe the streams of truth. But to foul the same water with their feet is to corrupt the studies of holy meditation by evil living. And verily the sheep drink the water fouled by their feet, when any of those subject to them follow not the words which they hear, but only imitate the bad examples which they see" (commentary of the Scripture quotation from Ezekiel, 34, 18-19).

40. See the third part of the *The Book of Pastoral Rule*, ch. 24-59 ("thirty-six ways" in the strict sense).

41. Ibid. II, 5, p. 13: "(...) lest either in seeking high things he despise the weak things of his neighbours, or in suiting himself to the weak things of his neighbours he relinquish his aspiration after high things."

42. Ibid. "For hence it is that Paul is caught up into Paradise and explores the secrets of the third heaven, and yet, though borne aloft in that contemplation of things invisible, recalls the vision of his mind to the bed of the carnal, and directs how they should have intercourse with each other in their hidden privacy."

43. The Christian practice of spiritual direction was already examined by Foucault in *Les anormaux*, the lectures of 19 February, p. 170 *sq.*, and 26 February, p. 187 *sq.*: *Abnormal*, p. 183 *sq.*, and p. 201 *sq.*, but in a different chronological framework—the sixteenth and seventeenth centuries—and a different analytical perspective—the appearance of the "body of desire and pleasure" within penitential practices. As D. Defert notes in his "Chronologie," Foucault was working in January 1978 on the second volume of the *History of Sexuality*, which was to have traced "a genealogy of concupiscence through the practice of confession in Western Christianity, and of spiritual direction as it develops from the Council of Trent," *Dits et Écrits*, 1, p. 53. This manuscript was subsequently destroyed.

44. On spiritual direction in Antiquity, see P. Rabbow, *Seelenführung Methodik der Exerzitien in der Antike* (Munich: Kösel, 1954). No doubt Foucault had also read the work of I. Hadot, *Seneca und die grieschisch-römische Tradition der Seelenleitung* (Berlin: Walter De Gruyter and Co., 1969) that he cites in 1984 in *Le Souci de Soi. Histoire de la Sexualité*, vol. 3 (Paris: Gallimard, "Bibliothèque des histoires," 1984); English translation by Robert Hurley, *The Care of the Self. Volume 3 of The History of Sexuality* (New York: Pantheon, 1986). He will come back to this comparison of ancient and Christian practices of spiritual direction in the lectures, "Du gouvernement des vivants," lectures of 12, 19, and 26 March 1980, and in *L'Herméneutique du sujet*, lectures of 3 March 1982, pp. 345-348, and 10 March, p. 390; *The Hermeneutics of the Subject*, pp. 362-366 and p. 408.

eight

1 MARCH 1978

*The notion of "conduct." ∼ The crisis of the pastorate. ∼ Revolts of conduct in the field of the pastorate. ∼ The shift of forms of resistance to the borders of political institutions in the modern age: examples of the army, secret societies, and medicine. ∼ Problem of vocabulary: "Revolts of conduct," "insubordination (*insoumission*)," "dissidence," and "counter-conduct." Pastoral counter-conducts. Historical reminder: (a) asceticism; (b) communities; (c) mysticism; (d) Scripture; (e) eschatological beliefs. ∼ Conclusion: what is at stake in the reference to the notion of "pastoral power" for an analysis of the modes of exercise of power in general.*

LAST WEEK I TALKED a bit about the pastorate and its specificity. Why have I talked about this and at such length? Let's say, for two reasons. The first is to try to show you—and this won't have escaped you, of course—that there is no Judeo-Christian morality*; [Judeo-Christian morality] is a false unity. The second reason is that if there really is a relationship between religion and politics in modern Western societies, it may be that the essential aspect of this relationship is not found in the interplay between Church and state, but rather between the pastorate and government. In other words, in modern Europe at least, the fundamental problem is undoubtedly not the Pope and the

---

* An almost entirely inaudible phrase follows: notion (. . .) anti-Semitic. Foucault adds: there is then no Judeo-Christian morality

Emperor, but rather that mixed figure, or the two figures who in our language, and also in others, share one and the same name of minister. The minister, with all the ambiguity of this word, is perhaps the real problem and where the relationship between religion and politics, between government and the pastorate, is really situated. So that is why I have insisted somewhat on this theme of the pastorate.

I have tried to show you that the pastorate constituted a set of techniques and procedures and have merely indicated some of their fundamental elements. Of course, these techniques go well beyond what I have been able to indicate. Now, I would like to point out straightaway, in passing, so that we can take it up again later, that this set of techniques and procedures typical of the pastorate were given a name by the Greeks, the Greek fathers, and precisely by Gregory Nazianzen, and it is a quite remarkable name since [Gregory] called the pastorate, *oikonomia psuchōn*, that is to say, the economy of souls.[1] In other words, this Greek notion of economy,[2] which was found in Aristotle and at that time designated the typical management of the family, of its goods and wealth, the management or direction of slaves, of the wife, and of children, and possibly the *management*,* if you like, of clients, takes on a completely different dimension and a completely different field of references with the pastorate. It assumes a different dimension since in comparison with the fundamentally family economy in the Greeks—*oikos* is habitat—[the economy of souls] will take on the dimension, if not of all humanity, at least of the whole of Christendom. The economy of souls must bear on the whole Christian community and on each Christian in particular. As well as a change of dimension, there is a change of references, since it will be a matter not just of the prosperity and wealth of the family or household, but of the salvation of souls. I think all these changes are very important and next week I will try to show you the nature of the second mutation of this notion of economy in the sixteenth and seventeenth centuries.

"Economy" is evidently not the French word best suited to translate *oikonomia psuchōn*. The Latins translated it as *regimen animarum*, "government or regimen (*régime*) of souls," which is not bad, but it is clear that

---

* English in original; G.B.

in French we either benefit from or are the victims of, have the advantage or disadvantage, as you prefer, of possessing a word whose ambiguity is nonetheless quite interesting for translating this economy of souls. What's more, the word, with its ambiguity, was introduced relatively recently and we only begin to find it in the two meanings I am now going to talk about from the end of the sixteenth and [the start of] the seventeenth century;* there are some citations in Montaigne.[3] The word, obviously, is "conduct (*conduite*)," since the word "conduct" refers to two things. Conduct is the activity of conducting (*conduire*), of conduction (*la conduction*) if you like, but it is equally the way in which one conducts oneself (*se conduit*), lets oneself be conducted (*se laisse conduire*), is conducted (*est conduit*), and finally, in which one behaves (*se comporter*) as an effect of a form of conduct (*une conduite*) as the action of conducting or of conduction (*conduction*).[†] I think the least bad translation for the *oikonomia psuchōn* Gregory Nazianzen spoke about could perhaps be the conduct of souls, and I think that this notion of conduct, with the field it covers, is doubtless one of the fundamental elements introduced into Western society by the Christian pastorate.

Having said that, I would now like to try to identify a little how the crisis of the pastorate opened up and how the pastorate burst open, broke up, and assumed the dimension of governmentality, or how the problem of government, of governmentality, was able to arise on the basis of the pastorate. Of course, this will only amount to a few reference points and some very discontinuous probes. There is absolutely no question of undertaking the history of the pastorate here, and in particular I leave

---

* The French has: "from the end of the seventeenth and [beginning of] the seventeenth century," which is clearly an error; G.B.

† Usually *conduire*, *conduite*, etcetera, would be translated into English by a variety of terms—lead, direct, guide, take, run, manage, behave, etcetera—as well as conduct. However, despite the resulting occasional awkwardness, since Foucault specifically draws attention to and exploits its two meanings in the French, in translating *conduite* I have often used the English conduct, and its various forms where normally another English word would be used. The meaning of "conduction," in both English and French (*la conduction*), seems to be exclusively scientific or technical; Foucault adopts the word as a process noun for the practice of conducting (the process of producing conduct), along the lines perhaps of his coinage "*veridiction*" for the practice of truth (see "Table ronde du 20 mai 1978," *Dits et Écrits*, *IV* and the second lecture of *Naissance de la biopolitique*, 17 January 1979). Finally, when Foucault speaks of "a conduct" (*une conduite*) the sense often embraces the activity by which some conduct others, the way in which some are conducted by others, and the way in which individuals conduct themselves within this form of "conduct."

to one side all of what could be called the great external blockages that
the Catholic and Christian pastorate came up against throughout the
Middle Ages and finally in the sixteenth century. By external blockages
I mean a number of things that I will disregard, not because they did not
exist or had no effect, but because this is not what I want to highlight or
that most interests me. By external blockages I mean, of course, the passive resistance of populations still undergoing conversion to Christianity
in the late Middle Ages. Even when converted, for a long time these
populations were resistant to a number of obligations imposed on them
by the pastorate. There was the long-standing resistance to the obligatory practice of confession imposed by the Lateran Council in 1215, for
example. The pastorate also clashed head-on with active resistance,
whether these were what may be called extra-Christian practices, such
as witchcraft—the extent to which they were extra-Christian is another
question—or the great heresies, in truth *the* great heresy in the Middle
Ages, which is broadly speaking the dualist, Cathar heresy.[4] As another
external blockage, we could also mention the relations [of the pastorate]*
with political power, and the problem [it] encountered with the development of economic structures in the second half of the Middle Ages,
and so on.

But this is not what I want to talk about. I would like to try to
identify some of the points of resistance, some of the forms of attack and
counter-attack that appeared *within* the field of the pastorate. What is at
issue? If it is true that the pastorate is a highly specific form of power
with the object of conducting men—I mean, that takes as its instrument
the methods that allow one to direct them (*les conduire*), and as its target
the way in which they conduct themselves, the way in which they
behave—if the objective of the pastorate is men's conduct, I think
equally specific movements of resistance and insubordination appeared
in correlation with this that could be called specific revolts of conduct,
again leaving the word "conduct" in all its ambiguity.[5] They are movements whose objective is a different form of conduct, that is to say:
wanting to be conducted differently, by other leaders (*conducteurs*) and
other shepherds, towards other objectives and forms of salvation, and

---

* M.F.: of its relations

through other procedures and methods. They are movements that also seek, possibly at any rate, to escape direction by others and to define the way for each to conduct himself. In other words, I would like to know whether the specificity of refusal, revolts, and forms of resistance of conduct corresponded to the historical singularity of the pastorate. Just as there have been forms of resistance to power as the exercise of political sovereignty, and just as there have been other, equally intentional forms of resistance or refusal that were directed at power in the form of economic exploitation, have there not been forms of resistance to power as conducting?

I will make three remarks. First, in presenting things in this way are we not assuming that first of all there was the pastorate and then, afterwards, counter-movements, what I have called counter-attacks, or kinds of reaction? Are we not merely dealing with the same phenomena in reverse, from the negative or reactive side? Obviously, this needs to be examined more closely and straightaway we should note that from the start the pastorate developed in reaction to, or at any rate with hostility towards and in confrontation and war with what we can hardly call a revolt of conduct, since a clear pastoral form of conduct did not yet exist. The pastorate was formed against a sort of intoxication of religious behavior, examples of which are found throughout the Middle East in the second, third, and fourth centuries, and to which certain Gnostic sects in particular bear striking and indisputable testimony.[6] In at least some of these Gnostic sects, in fact, the identification of matter with evil, the fact that matter was seen, recognized, and qualified as evil, and as absolute evil, obviously entailed certain consequences. This might be, for example, a kind of vertigo or enchantment provoked by a sort of unlimited asceticism that could lead to suicide: freeing oneself from matter as quickly as possible. There is also the idea, the theme, of destroying matter through the exhaustion of the evil it contains, of committing every possible sin, going to the very end of the domain of evil opened up by matter, and thus destroying matter. Let us sin, then, and sin to infinity. There is also the theme of the nullification of the world of the law, to destroy which one must first destroy the law, that is to say, break every law. One must respond to every law established by the world, or by the powers of the world, by violating it, systematically breaking the law and, in effect, overthrowing the reign of the one who created the world. To the creator of the material world, Yahweh, who accepted Abel's sacrifices and refused Cain's, who loved Jacob and hated Esau, and who punished Sodom, we must respond by preferring Cain's sacrifices, loving Esau and hating Jacob, and by glorifying Sodom. The Western and Eastern Christian pastorate developed against every- thing that, retrospectively, might be called disorder. So we can say that there was an immediate and founding correlation between conduct and counter-conduct.

My second remark is that these revolts of conduct have their specificity. What I would like to show you is that they are distinct from political revolts against power exercised by a form of sovereignty, and they are also distinct [from economic revolts against power]* inasmuch as it maintains or guarantees exploitation. They are distinct in their form and in their objective.[7] There are revolts of conduct. After all, the greatest revolt of conduct the Christian West has known was that of Luther, and we know that at the outset it was neither economic nor political, notwithstanding the connections that were immediately established with economic and political problems. But the specificity of these struggles, of these resistances of conduct, does not mean that they remained separate or isolated from each other, with their own partners, forms, dramaturgy, and distinct aim. In actual fact they are always, or almost always, linked to other conflicts and problems. Throughout the Middle Ages resistances of conduct are linked to struggles between the bourgeoisie and feudalism, in the Flemish towns,[8] for example, or in Lyon at the time of the Waldensians.[9] They are also linked to the uncou- pling of the urban and rural economies that is particularly noticeable from the twelfth century. There are the Hussites and Calixtines[10] on the one hand, and the Taborites on the other.[11] You also find revolts, or resistances of conduct linked to the completely different but crucial problem of the status of women. These revolts of conduct are often linked up with the problem of women and their status in society, in civil

---

* M.F.: from power
See the manuscript, p. 5: "These 'revolts of conduct' have their specificity: they are distinct from political or economic revolts in their objective and form."

society or in religious society. You see these revolts of conduct flourish in convents, in the movement that is called Rhenish *Nonnenmystik* in the twelfth century.[12] There are also all those groups formed around women prophets in the Middle Ages, like Jeanne Dabenton,[13] Marguerite Porete,[14] and so on. Later, you see them in those curious semi-fashionable and semi-popular groups of conduct, or rather of spiritual direction, in six-teenth century Spain with Isabel de la Cruz,[15] or in France with Armelle Nicolas,[16] Marie des Vallées,[17] and Madame Acarie.[18] The revolts are also linked to the phenomena of different cultural levels. For example, the opposition or conflict between Doctors of the Church and pastors, which clearly breaks out with Wyclif,[19] with the Amaurians in Paris,[20] and with John Huss in Prague.[21] So, these revolts of conduct may well be specific in their form and objective, but whatever the identifiable charac-ter of their specificity, they are never autonomous, they never remain autonomous. And then, from start to finish, the English Revolution of the seventeenth century, with all the complexity of its institutional con-flicts, class confrontations, and economic problems, allows us to see a quite special dimension of the resistance of conduct, of conflicts around the problem of conduct. By whom do we consent to be directed or con-ducted? How do we want to be conducted? Towards what do we want to be led? This is my second remark on the non-autonomous specificity of these resistances, these revolts of conduct.[22]

Finally, my third remark is that it is clear that in their religious form, these revolts of conduct are linked to the pastorate, to the great age of the pastorate extending from the tenth and eleventh centuries up to the sixteenth and the end of the seventeenth century. Revolts and resistances of conduct then take a different form. We can say that to a certain extent they diminish in intensity and number, although the Methodist movement in the second half of the eighteenth century is a magnificent example of a revolt or resistance of conduct that is extremely important economically and politically.[23] However, from the end of the seventeenth and the beginning of the eighteenth century, generally speaking I think that inasmuch as many pastoral functions were taken up in the exercise of governmentality, and inasmuch as government also begins to want to take responsibility for people's conduct, to conduct people, then from then on we see revolts of conduct arising less from the religious institution and much more from political institutions. Conflicts of conduct will occur on the borders and edge of the political institution. I will just give you some examples as types of possible analysis or research.

First, waging war. For a long time, let's say in the seventeenth and eighteenth centuries, apart from those for whom being a man of war was a status (broadly speaking the nobility), waging war was more or less, often less rather than more, a voluntary occupation, and to that extent military recruitment allowed scope for a whole series of resistances, refusals, and desertions. Desertion was an absolutely ordinary practice in all the armies of the seventeenth and eighteenth centuries. But when waging war became not just a profession or even a general law, but an ethic and the behavior of every good citizen of a country; when being a soldier was a form of political and moral conduct, a sacrifice, and devotion to the common cause and common salvation directed by a public conscience and public authority within the framework of a tight discipline; when being a soldier was therefore no longer just a destiny or a profession but a form of conduct, then, in addition to the old desertion-offence I was just talking about, you see a different form of desertion that I will call desertion-insubordination. Refusing to be a soldier and to spend some time in this profession and activity, refusing to bear arms, appears as a form of conduct or as a moral counter-conduct, as a refusal of civic education, of society's values, and also as a refusal of a certain obligatory relationship to the nation and the nation's salvation, as a refusal of the actual political system of the nation, and as a refusal of the relationship to the death of others and of oneself. You see then that a phenomenon of resistance of conduct appears here that no longer has the old form of desertion and that is not without analogy with some of the phenomena of resistance of religious conduct [that we have seen in the]* Middle Ages.

Let's take another example. In the modern world, from the eighteenth century, you see the development of secret societies. In the eighteenth century these are still basically close to forms of religious dissidence. As you know, they have their dogmas, rituals, hierarchy, postures, ceremonies, and forms of community. Freemasonry is, of course, a privileged example of this. Then, in the nineteenth century, they become increasingly

---

* Some words which are difficult to hear.

composed of political elements and take on clearer political objectives—plots, political or social revolutions—but always with an aspect of the pursuit of a different form of conduct: to be led differently, by other men, and towards other objectives than those proposed by the apparent and visible official governmentality of society. Its clandestine character is no doubt a necessary dimension of this political action, but at the same time it includes and offers this possibility of an alternative to governmental direction in the form of another form of conduct with its unknown chiefs and specific forms of obedience, etcetera. We could say that in contemporary societies, in our societies, there still exist basically two types of political parties. There are those that are no more than ladders to the exercise of power or to access to functions and responsibilities, and then there are political parties, or rather there is a political party, which has ceased being clandestine for a long time however, but which continues to have the aura of an old project that it has evidently abandoned but to which its destiny and name remain linked, and which is the project of giving birth to a new social order and creating a new man. That being the case, it cannot fail to function to a certain extent as a counter-society, another society, even if in fact it only reproduces the society that exists, and consequently it appears and functions internally as a sort of different pastorate, a different governmentality with its chiefs, its rules, and its principles of obedience, and to that extent it possesses, as you know, a considerable capacity both to appear as a different society, a different form of conduct, and to channel revolts of conduct, take them over, and control them.[24]

I will take a third example. In its modern forms, the pastorate is deployed to a great extent through medical knowledge, institutions, and practices. We can say that medicine has been one of the great powers that have been heirs to the pastorate. And to that extent it too has given rise to a whole series of revolts of conduct, what we could call a strong medical *dissent*, from the end of the eighteenth century and still today, which extends [from] the refusal of certain medications and certain preventive measures like vaccination, to the refusal of a certain type of medical rationality: the attempt to constitute sorts of medical heresies around practices of medication using electricity, magnetism, herbs, and traditional medicine; [the] refusal of medicine *tout court*, which is frequently found in certain religious groups. Here we can see how movements of religious dissidence were able to link up with resistance to medical conduct.

I won't dwell on this further. I would just like to raise a problem of simple vocabulary. Could we not try to find a word to designate what I have called resistance, refusal, or revolt? How can we designate the type of revolts, or rather the sort of specific web of resistance to forms of power that do not exercise sovereignty and do not exploit, but "conduct"*? I have often used the expression "revolt of conduct," but I have to say that I am not very satisfied with it, because the word "revolt" is both too precise and too strong to designate much more diffuse and subdued forms of resistance. The secret societies of the eighteenth century are not revolts of conduct; the mysticism of the Middle Ages I was just talking about is not exactly a revolt. Second, the word "disobedience" is, on the other hand, too weak no doubt, although the problem of obedience is in fact at the center of all this. A movement like Anabaptism,[25] for example, was much more than disobedience. Furthermore, these movements that I have tried to pick out definitely have a productivity, forms of existence, organization, and a consistency and solidity that the purely negative word of disobedience does not capture. "Insubordination (*insoumission*)," perhaps, although we are dealing with a word that in a way is localized and attached to military insubordination.

There is, to be sure, a word that comes to mind, but I would rather cut my tongue out than use it. I will just mention it therefore. It is, as you will have guessed, the word "dissidence."[26] In fact, maybe the word "dissidence" is exactly suited for these forms of resistance that concern, set their sights on, and have as their objective and adversary a power that assumes the task of conducting men in their life and daily existence. The word would be justified for two reasons, both of them historical. The first is that in fact the word "dissidence" has often been employed to designate religious movements of resistance to pastoral organization. Second, its current application could in fact justify its use since, after all, what we [call]† "dissidence" in the East and the Soviet Union,[27] really

---

* Word in inverted commas in the manuscript.
† M.F.: designate by

does designate a complex form of resistance and refusal, which involves a political refusal, of course, but in a society where political authority, that is, the political party, responsible for defining both the country's characteristic form of economy and structures of sovereignty, is at the same time responsible for conducting individuals in their daily life through a game of generalized obedience that takes the form of terror, since terror is not when some command and strike fear into others. There is terror when those who command tremble with fear themselves, since they know that the general system of obedience envelops them just as much as those over whom they exercise their power.[28] We could speak, moreover, of the pastoralization of power in the Soviet Union. Certainly there is bureaucratization of the Party. There is also pastoralization of the Party, and dissidence, the political struggles that we put together under the name of dissidence, certainly have an essential, fundamental dimension that is refusal of this form of being conducted. "We do not want this salvation, we do not wish to be saved by these people and by these means." The whole pastoral practice of salvation is challenged. It is Solzhenitsyn.[29] "We do not wish to obey these people. We do not want this system where even those who command have to obey out of terror. We do not want this pastoral system of obedience. We do not want this truth. We do not want to be held in this system of truth. We do not want to be held in this system of observation and endless examination that continually judges us, tells us what we are in the core of ourselves, healthy or sick, mad or not mad, and so on." So we can say [that] this word dissidence really does cover a struggle against those pastoral effects I talked about last week. And it is precisely because the word dissidence is too localized today in this kind of phenomena that it cannot be used without drawback. After all, who does not have his theory of dissidence today?

So let's give up this word, and what I will propose to you is the doubtless badly constructed word "counter-conduct"—the latter having the sole advantage of allowing reference to the active sense of the word "conduct"—counter-conduct in the sense of struggle against the processes implemented for conducting others; which is why I prefer it to "misconduct (*inconduite*)," which only refers to the passive sense of the word, of behavior: not conducting oneself properly. And then maybe this word "counter-conduct" enables us to avoid a certain substantification allowed by the word "dissidence." Because from "dissidence" we get "dissident," or the other way round, it doesn't matter, in any case, dissidence is the act of one who is a dissident, and I am not sure that this substantification is very useful. I fear it may even be dangerous, for there is not much sense in saying, for example, that a mad person or a delinquent is a dissident. There is a process of sanctification or hero worship which does not seem to me of much use. On the other hand, by using the word counter-conduct, and so without having to give a sacred status to this or that person as a dissident, we can no doubt analyze the components in the way in which someone actually acts in the very general field of politics or in the very general field of power relations; it makes it possible to pick out the dimension or component of counter-conduct that may well be found in fact in delinquents, mad people, and patients. So, an analysis of this immense family of what could be called counter-conducts.

After this rapid survey of the general theme of counter-conduct in the pastorate and in governmentality, I would now like to try to identify what happened in the Middle Ages and to what extent and how far these counter-conducts were able to put in question, work on, elaborate, and erode the pastoral power I spoke about last week, that is to say, how over a long period an internal crisis of the pastorate was opened up by the development of counter-conducts. I would like us to keep in mind some well-known facts, and so you will forgive me for summarizing them in this purely academic way. First, of course, with reference to the sketch of the pastorate I gave last week, from the first centuries of Christianity we witness a whole development, an extreme complication of pastoral techniques and procedures: an extremely rigorous and dense institutionalization of the pastorate. Second, and, if you like, characterizing this institutionalization of the pastorate in a very specific, particular, and important way, we should note the development of a dimorphism, a binary structure within the pastoral field, distinguishing the clergy from the laity.[30] The whole of medieval Christianity, and Catholicism from the sixteenth century, is characterized by the existence of these two clearly distinguished categories of individuals, clergy and laity, who do not have the same civil rights, obligations, or privileges, of course, but who do not even have the same spiritual privileges.[31] This dimorphism and the problem it posed, the disquiet it introduced into the Christian community by the existence of clerics who not only have economic and civil privileges, but also spiritual privileges, who are broadly speaking closer than others to paradise, heaven, and salvation, will be one of the major problems, and one of the points of collision of pastoral counter-conduct.[32] A further fact that we should recall in this institutionalization of the pastorate is the definition of a theory and practice of the priest's sacramental power. Here again, like the appearance of the dimorphism between clergy and laity, this is a relatively late phenomenon; the *presbyteros*, or bishop or pastor[33] of the first Christian communities did not have sacramental power. He receives the power to implement the sacraments, that is to say, have direct effectiveness in the salvation of the sheep through his action, his words, in the wake of a whole series of developments.[34] These are the major purely religious transformations of the pastorate.

From the external, political point of view we should speak of the intrication of the pastorate, civil government, and political power. We should speak of the feudalization of the Church, of the secular clergy, but also of the regular clergy. And then finally, third, at the border of this strictly internal and religious evolution and this external, political and economic evolution, we should, I think, emphasize the appearance of something important, basically around the eleventh and twelfth century. This is the introduction of an essentially and fundamentally secular model, namely the judicial model, into the usual pastoral practice. In truth, it would be wrong to say this dates from the eleventh and twelfth centuries, since in fact the Church had already acquired and exercised judicial functions from the seventh and eighth centuries, as is proven by the penitentials of this time. But the important thing is the development of the practice of confession in the eleventh and twelfth centuries and it becoming obligatory in 1215[35]—it was, in fact, already fairly generalized—that is to say, the existence of a permanent court before which every faithful had to regularly present him or herself. We see the appearance and development of belief in Purgatory,[36] that is to say, a system of modulated, provisional punishment in which justice, the pastorate in short, has a role. This role is performed by the system of indulgences, that is to say, the possibility, for the pastor, for the Church, of attenuating penalties to some extent on certain, basically financial, conditions. So, from the twelfth century, the Church was penetrated by a judicial model that was a major reason for anti-pastoral struggles.

I won't dwell further on this. One word more to say that these anti-pastoral struggles took very different forms. Here again I will not list them. I would like to talk to you about more specific things. We should just recall that these [anti-]pastoral struggles are found at a specifically doctrinal level, as in theories of the Church, for example, in the ecclesiology of Wyclif or John Huss.[37] You also find these anti-pastoral struggles in the form of individual behavior, which may be either strictly individual, or individual but serial, through contagion, as in the case of mysticism, for example, with the formation of groups that break up almost as soon as they are constituted. On the other hand, you find these anti-pastoral struggles in strongly organized groups, some of them as appendages to, or in the margins of, the Church, without involving very violent conflict, such as the third orders or devotional societies, for example. Others are groups in open breach with the Church, like the Waldensians,[38] the Hussites,[39] the Anabaptists,[40] and some swinging from obedience to refusal and revolt, like the Beghards[41] and especially the Beguines.[42] And then you also find these anti-pastoral struggles, these pastoral counter-conducts, in a whole new attitude, religious comportment, way of doing things and being, and a whole new way of relating to God, obligations, morality, as well as to civil life. This diffuse and crucial phenomenon is what has been called the *devotio moderna*.[43]

Now with regard to the history of the relations between pastoral conduct and pastoral counter-conducts, what points can we hold on to in these very different phenomena? It seems to me that the Middle Ages developed five main forms of counter-conduct, all of which tend to redistribute, reverse, nullify, and partially or totally discredit pastoral power in the systems of salvation, obedience, and truth, that is to say, in the three domains that we talked about last week and which characterize, I think, the objective, the domain of intervention of pastoral power. [What are] these five forms of counter-conduct developed by the Middle Ages (and once again please excuse the dry and schematic character of the analysis)?

First asceticism. You will say that it is a bit paradoxical to present asceticism as counter-conduct when we are accustomed to linking asceticism with the very essence of Christianity, contrasting it with ancient religions by making it a religion of ascesis. Nonetheless, we should recall that in the third and fourth centuries, the pastorate in the Eastern and Western Church, and I alluded to this earlier, developed essentially—well, to a not inconsiderable extent—against ascetic practices, or at any rate against what were retrospectively called the excesses of monachism, of Egyptian and Syrian *anachōrēsis*.[44] The organization of monasteries with obligatory communal life; the organization of a hierarchy around the abbot and subordinates who relay his power; the appearance of a communal and hierarchized life according to a rule imposed in the same way on everyone, or anyway on each category of monks in a specific way, but on all the members of that category, according to whether they are novices or elders; the existence of the superior's absolute, unchallenged authority with the rule of unquestioning obedience; the assertion that real renunciation is not renunciation of one's body or flesh, but essentially renunciation of one's will, in other words, the fact that the supreme sacrifice demanded of the monk in this form of spirituality is essentially obedience, all clearly show that what was at stake was limiting anything that could be boundless in asceticism, or at any rate everything incompatible with the organization of power.[45]

What was there, in fact, in asceticism that was incompatible with obedience, or what was there in obedience that was essentially anti-ascetic? In the first place, I think that ascesis is an exercise of self on self; it is a sort of close combat of the individual with himself in which the authority, presence, and gaze of someone else is, if not impossible, at least unnecessary. Second, asceticism is a progression according to a scale of increasing difficulty. It is, in the strict sense of the term, an exercise,[46] an exercise going from the easier to the more difficult, and from the more difficult to what is even more difficult. And what is the criterion of this difficulty? It is the ascetic's own suffering. The criterion of difficulty is the difficulty that the ascetic actually experiences in moving on to the following stage and doing the next exercise, so that the ascetic with his suffering, with his own refusals, his own disgust, and his own impossibilities, the ascetic at the point when he recognizes his limits, becomes the guide of his own asceticism and it is through his immediate and direct experience of the block and the limit that he feels pushed to overcome it. Third, asceticism is also a form of challenge, or rather it is a form of internal challenge, if one can put it like that, which is also a challenge to the other. The accounts describing the lives of ascetics and Eastern, Egyptian, and Syrian anchorites, are full of these stories passing from ascetic to ascetic, anchorite to anchorite, in which we learn of one making an extremely difficult exercise, to which the other responds with an even more difficult exercise: fasting for a month, fasting for a year, fasting for seven years, fasting for fourteen years.[47] So, asceticism has a form of both internal and external challenge. Fourth, asceticism strives for a state that, to be sure, is not a state of perfection, but which is nonetheless a state of tranquility, of appeasement, a state of that *apatheia* I talked about last week,[48] and which is at bottom another kind of asceticism. It is different in the pastoral practice of obedience, but the ascetic's *apatheia* is the mastery he exercises over himself, his body, and his own sufferings. He reaches a stage in which he no longer suffers from what he suffers and in which anything he inflicts on his own body no longer troubles him, no longer disturbs him, and provokes no passion or strong sensation. Again we have a number of examples, like the Abbot Jean I spoke about last week,[49] who reached a point of asceticism such that a finger could be poked in his eye and he would not move.[50] There is something in this that is clearly very close to Buddhist asceticism and monachism.[51] All in all, it is a matter of overcoming oneself, of vanquishing the world, the body, matter, or even the devil and his temptations. Hence the importance of temptation is not so much that the ascetic must suppress it, as that he must constantly master it. The ascetic's ideal is not the absence of temptations but to reach a point of mastery where he is indifferent to temptation. Finally, the fifth feature of asceticism is that either it refers to a refusal of the body, and so of matter, and therefore to that kind of acosmism (*acosmisme*) that is one of the dimensions of the gnosis and of dualism, or else it refers to the identification of the body with Christ. Being an ascetic, accepting the sufferings, refusing to eat, whipping oneself, and taking the iron to one's own body, one's own flesh, means turning one's own body into the body of Christ. This identification is found in all the forms of asceticism, in Antiquity of course, but also in the Middle Ages. Recall the famous text by Suso,[52] in which he recounts how, in the glacial cold of a winter morning, he flogged himself with a whip with iron hooks that removed lumps of flesh from his body until he reached the point of tears and cried over his own body as if it were the body of Christ.[53]

You can see a number of typical elements of asceticism here which refer to the athletic contest, or to mastery of oneself and the world, or to refusal of matter and Gnostic acosmism, or to glorifying identification with Christ's body. This is clearly incompatible with a pastoral structure that (as I said last week) involves permanent obedience, renunciation of the will, and only of the will, and the deployment of the individual's conduct* in the world. There is no refusal of the world in the pastoral principle of obedience; there is never any access to a state of beatitude or to a state of identification with Christ, to a sort of final state of perfect mastery, but instead a definitive state, acquired from the outset, of obedience to the orders of others; and finally, in obedience there is never anything of this joust with others or with oneself, but permanent humility instead. There is, I think, a profound difference between the structures of obedience and asceticism. This is why, whenever and wherever pastoral counter-conducts develop in the Middle Ages, asceticism was one of their points of support and instruments against the pastorate. Asceticism developed in a number of orthodox religious circles, like the Benedictines and the Rhenish Benedictines, or openly heterodox circles, like the Taborites[54] and the Waldensians, or just intermediary circles like the Flagellants.[55] This asceticism, if it is not literally foreign to Christianity, is certainly foreign to the structure of pastoral power around which Christianity was organized. And it was activated as an element of struggle throughout the history of Christianity, and certainly with particular intensity from the eleventh or twelfth century. So, the conclusion is that Christianity is not an ascetic religion. Insofar as the pastorate characterizes its structures of power, Christianity is fundamentally anti-ascetic, and asceticism is rather a sort of tactical element, an element of reversal by which certain themes of Christian theology or religious experience are utilized against these structures of power. Asceticism is a sort of exasperated and reversed obedience that

---

* Foucault adds: in the first place

has become egoistic self-mastery. Let's say that in asceticism there is a specific excess that denies access to an external power.

If you like, the Christian pastorate added to the Jewish or Greco-Roman principle of the law a further excessive and completely exorbitant element of continuous and endless obedience of one man to another. In relation to this pastoral rule of obedience, asceticism adds another exaggerated and exorbitant element. Asceticism stifles obedience through the excess of prescriptions and challenges that the individual addresses to himself. You can see that there is a level of respect for the law. The pastorate adds to this the principle of submission and obedience to another person. Asceticism turns this around again by making it a challenge of the exercise of the self on the self. So, the first element of anti-pastoral or pastoral counter-conduct is asceticism.

The second element is communities. There is in fact another, to a certain extent opposite way of refusing submission to pastoral power, which is the formation of communities. Asceticism has an individualizing tendency. The community is something completely different. On what is it based? First, there is a sort of theoretical background that is found in most of the communities formed during the Middle Ages. This is the refusal of the pastor's authority and its theological or ecclesiological justifications. In particular, the communities, or some of them, the most violent and virulent, those most openly in breach with the Church, start from the principle that the Church itself, and in particular its fundamental and central body, namely Rome, is a new Babylon and represents the Antichrist. This is a moral and apocalyptic theme. More subtly, in the more learned groups, this endless and always recommenced activity of the formation of communities depended upon important doctrinal problems. The first was that of the pastor in a state of sin. Is the pastor's privilege of power or authority due to a definitive and ineradicable sign? In other words, is it because he is a priest and has been ordained that he wields a power that ultimately cannot be taken from him, except possibly by a higher authority? Is the pastor's power independent of his moral character, of what he is internally, of his way of life and conduct? You can see that this is a problem that concerns the whole system of merits and faults I talked about last week. Some people, essentially Wyclif, and then John Huss, replied to this in strictly theoretical, theological, or ecclesiological terms. Wyclif laid down the principle: "*Nullus dominus civilis, nullus episcopus dum est in peccato mortali*," which means: "No civil master, but equally no bishop, no religious authority, *dum est in peccato mortali*, if he is in a state of mortal sin."[56] In other words, the sole fact of a pastor being in a state of mortal sin suspends any power he may have over the faithful. This is the principle taken up by John Huss in a text that is called *De ecclesia* in which he says . . . no, it is not in *De ecclesia*. He had this principle written, carved, or painted on the walls of the church of Bethlehem in Prague:[57] "Sometimes it is good not to obey prelates and superiors." John Huss even spoke of "the heresy of obedience."[58] When one obeys someone in a state of mortal sin, when one obeys a pastor who is unfaithful to the law, or who is unfaithful to the principle of obedience, one becomes a heretic. The heresy of obedience, says John Huss.

The other doctrinal aspect is the problem of the priest's sacramental power. What does the priest's power to administer the sacraments consist of? From the start, Church doctrine never ceased to single out, back up, give weight to, and intensify the priest's sacramental power.[59] In the first place, the priest can control entry into the community through baptism; he can unbind in heaven what he unbinds on Earth in confession; and he can give Christ's body through the Eucharist. The development of different religious communities constantly challenged all these aspects of the priest's sacramental power gradually established by the Church.[60] There is refusal, for example, of the obligatory baptism of children whose effect is entirely that of a priest's act on someone who has no will.[61] So, there is refusal of the baptism of children and a tendency towards adult, voluntary baptism, that is to say, baptism that is voluntary for the individual as well as for the community that accepts the individual. And all this ends up with Anabaptism,[62] of course, but it was already found in the Waldensians, the Hussites, and so on. There is [also] mistrust of confession, which, until the tenth to eleventh century, was still an activity, a practice that could take place between one layperson and another, and which later, from the eleventh to twelfth century, was reserved essentially, exclusively to priests. So we see a practice of lay confession and mistrust of confession to a priest developing in these communities. For example, in the accounts given by the Oberland Friends of God there is the famous story of a woman who went to a priest to tell him of her experience of carnal temptations, and the priest told her that these are not very serious temptations, not to worry about them, and that all things considered this is natural. Then, the following night, God, Christ appeared to her and said: Why have you confided your secrets to a priest? You must keep your secrets to yourself.[63] So, there is refusal of confession, or a tendency to refuse confession.

Finally, there is the Eucharist, with the problem of the real presence and all those practices developed in communities of counter-conducts in which the Eucharist once again takes the form of the communal meal, with consumption of bread and wine, but generally speaking without the dogma of the real presence.

This is the kind of theoretical foundation on which these communities developed. Positively, the formation of these communities is characterized by the suppression, or tendency to suppress the priests-laity dimorphism that was typical of the organization of the Christian pastorate. What replaces this clergy-laity dimorphism? It is replaced by a number of things, such as the designation of the pastor by way of election and provisionally, as in the Taborites, for example. In this case, being elected provisionally, the pastor or person in charge, the *praepositus*, evidently does not possess any definitive distinguishing characteristic. He does not receive a sacrament; the community's will gives him certain tasks and responsibilities for a time, and it confers a provisional authority on him that he will never possess by virtue of having being given some kind of sacrament. The dimorphism of clergy and laity will often be replaced by another, very different dimorphism, which is that of the opposition or distinction between the elect and others. We find this, of course, in all the Cathars, and it is also found in the Waldensians. However, this is a very different kind of distinction, because the priest no longer has any effect in one's salvation when one becomes one of the elect. The elect no longer need the pastor's intervention to guide them on the path to salvation, since they have already completed it. Conversely, those who are not and never will be members of the elect also have no need of the pastor's power. To that extent, the dimorphism of the elect and the non-elect excludes the organization of pastoral power, the effectiveness of pastoral power that is found in, let's say, the official, general Church.

Again, there may be the principle of absolute equality between all members of the community, either in a religious form, that is to say, each is a pastor, a priest, or a shepherd, which is to say nobody is, [or in the] strict economic [form]* that you find in the Taborites, in which there is no personal possession of goods and anything acquired is acquired by the community, with an egalitarian division or a communal utilization of wealth.

This does not mean that the principle of obedience was wholly unrecognized or suppressed in these communities. There were some communities in which no form of obedience was recognized. For some pantheistic groups of the Brethren of the Free Spirit, for example,[64] more or less inspired by Amaury de Bène[65] and Ulrich de Strasbourg,[66] God was matter itself. Consequently, all individuality was only illusion. The division between good and evil could not exist and was only a chimerical effect, and consequently all appetites were legitimate. To that extent it was, at least in principle, a system that excluded all obedience or, at any rate, asserted the legitimacy of all conduct. But then we find many other ways of asserting schemas of obedience in these communities, but in a way that is completely different from the pastoral schema. There are, for example, relationships of reciprocal obedience. In the Oberland Friends of God there were rules, or oaths rather, pledges of reciprocal obedience of one individual to another. Thus Rulman Merswin[67] and the anonymous Oberland Friend of God[68] made a pact of reciprocal obedience for twenty-eight years. For twenty-eight years each agreed that they would obey the other's orders as if he were God Himself.[69] We also find phenomena of hierarchical reversal. In these groups you have systematic reversals of hierarchy. That is to say, the most ignorant or poorest person, or someone with the lowest reputation or honor, the most debauched, the prostitute, was chosen as leader of the group.[70] This is what happened, for example, with the Society of the Poor and Jeanne Dabenton, who was reputed to have led the most dissolute life and who, precisely because of this, became the group's pastor. Somewhat as asceticism had this aspect of almost ironic exaggeration in relation to the pure and simple rule of obedience, we could say that in some of these communities there was a

---

* M.F.: and again, equality

counter-society aspect, a carnival aspect, overturning social relations and hierarchy. In short, we would have to study (... it's a whole problem) the carnival practice of overturning society and the constitution of these religious groups in a form that is the exact opposite [of] the existing pastoral hierarchy. The first really will be the last, but the last will also be the first.

The third element, a third form of counter-conduct is mysticism,* that is to say, the privileged status of an experience that by definition escapes pastoral power. Basically, pastoral power developed a system of truth that, as you know, went from teaching to examination of the individual; a truth conveyed as dogma to all the faithful, and a truth extracted from each of them as a secret discovered in the depths of the soul. Mysticism is a completely different system. In the first place, it has a completely different game of visibility. The soul is not offered to the other for examination, through a system of confessions (*aveux*). In mysticism the soul sees itself. It sees itself in God and it sees God in itself. To that extent mysticism fundamentally, essentially, escapes examination. Second, as immediate revelation of God to the soul, mysticism also escapes the structure of teaching and the passing on of truth from someone who knows it to someone to whom it is taught, who passes it on in turn. Mystical experience short-circuits this hierarchy and the slow circulation of the truths of teaching. Third, while it is true that mysticism accepts and functions according to a progressive principle like teaching, it has a completely different principle of progress, since teaching follows a regular progression from ignorance to knowledge through the successive acquisition of cumulative elements, whereas the mystical path passes through a play of alternations—night/day, dark/light, loss/return, absence/presence—which are continually reversed. Better still, mysticism develops on the basis of, and in the form of, absolutely ambiguous experiences, in a sort of equivocation, since the secret of the night is that it is an illumination. The secret, the force of illumination, is precisely that it blinds. In mysticism ignorance is a knowing, and

---

* M.F. adds: "But then, I realize that I have gone on too long. I would like to stop here ... You must be tired. I don't know. I don't know what to do. On the other hand, it's necessary to see the end of this. We will go quickly, because these are things that are known, basically. We will go quickly, and then in that way we will be rid of it and we will move on to something else next week ... Fine. The third element of counter-conduct, mysticism.

knowledge has the very form of ignorance. To that extent you can see how far we are from the typical form of pastoral teaching. In the pastorate, the pastor's direction of the individual soul was necessary, and no communication between the soul and God could take place that was not either ruled out or controlled by the pastor. The pastorate was the channel between the faithful and God. In mysticism there is an immediate communication that may take the form of a dialogue between God and the soul, of appeal and response, of the declaration of God's love of the soul, and of the soul's love of God. There is the mechanism of perceptible and immediate inspiration that makes the soul recognize God's presence. There is also communication through silence. There is communication through the physical clinch, when the mystic's body really feels the presence, the urgent presence of the body of Christ Himself. So here again you can see the distance separating mysticism from the pastoral.

[The fourth element], my penultimate point—and here I can go very quickly—is the problem of Scripture. That is to say, it is not that the privileges of Scripture did not exist in the system of pastoral power, but it is quite clear that it was as if Scripture was relegated to the background of the essential presence, teaching, intervention, and speech of the pastor himself. In the movements of counter-conduct that develop throughout the Middle Ages, it is precisely the return to the texts, to Scripture, that is used against and to short-circuit, as it were, the pastorate.[71] Because the Scripture is a text that speaks for itself and has no need of the pastoral relay, or if a pastor must be called in, it can only be, as it were, within Scripture, in order to enlighten and establish a better relationship between the faithful and Scripture. The pastor can comment on Scripture, he can explain what is obscure, and he can point out what is important, but this will be so that the reader can read the Scripture himself. Reading is a spiritual act that puts the faithful in the presence of God's word and which consequently finds its law and guarantee in this inner illumination. Reading the text given by God to man, the reader sees the very word of God, and his understanding of it, even when confused, is nothing other that what God wanted to reveal of Himself to man. So, here again, we can say that the return to Scripture, one of the major themes of all the pastoral counter-conducts of the Middle Ages, is an essential component.

Finally, [the fifth element], and I will stop here, is eschatological beliefs. After all, the other way of disqualifying the pastor's role is to claim that the times are fulfilled or in the process of being fulfilled, and that God will return or is returning to gather his flock. He will be the true shepherd. Consequently, since he is the true shepherd coming to gather his flock, he can give notice to the pastors of history and time, and it is for him now to make the division, to give nourishment to the flock, and to guide it. The pastors are given notice, since Christ is returning, or again, another form of eschatology that developed along a line that more or less stems from Joachim of Fiore,[72] is the assertion of the advent of a third time or third age in history. The first age is that of the incarnation of the first person of the Trinity in a prophet, Abraham, and at that point the Jewish people needed pastors who were the other prophets. The second time, period, or age, is that of the incarnation of the second person. But the second person of the Trinity does not act like the first; he does better. The first sent a pastor, the second is incarnated in person, and this is Christ. But when Christ returned to Heaven he entrusted his flock to pastors who were supposed to represent him. But, says Joachim of Fiore, the third time, the third period, the third phase in the history of the world is coming, and the Holy Spirit will descend on Earth. Now the Holy Spirit is not incarnated in a prophet, and he is not incarnated in a person; he is spread over the entire world. That is to say, there will be a particle, a fragment, a spark of the Holy Spirit in each of the faithful and so they will no longer need a shepherd.

All this is to say that in this development of movements of counter-conduct in the Middle Ages I think we can find five fundamental themes, which are those of eschatology, Scripture, mysticism, the community, and ascesis. That is to say, Christianity in its real pastoral organization is not an ascetic religion, it is not a religion of the community, it is not a mystical religion, it is not a religion of Scripture, and, of course, it is not an eschatological religion. This is the first reason for wanting to talk to you about all this.

The second reason is that I wanted to show you that generally speaking these themes that have been fundamental elements in these counter-conducts are clearly not absolutely external to Christianity, but are actually border-elements, if you like, which have been continually re-utilized, re-implanted, and taken up again in one or another direction, and these elements, such as mysticism, eschatology, [or] the search for community, for example, have been continually taken up by the Church itself. This appears very clearly in the fifteenth and sixteenth centuries when, threatened by all these movements of counter-conduct, the Church tries to take them up and adapt them for its own ends, until the great separation takes place, the great division between the Protestant churches, which basically opt for a certain mode of re-implantation of these counter-conducts, and the Catholic Church, which tries to re-utilize them and re-insert them in its own system through the Counter Reformation. This is the second point. So, if you like, the struggle was not conducted in the form of absolute exteriority, but rather in the form of the permanent use of tactical elements that are pertinent in the anti-pastoral struggle, insofar as they fall within, in a marginal way, the general horizon of Christianity.

Finally, third, I wanted to stress this in order to try to show you that my reason for taking the point of view of pastoral power was, of course, in order to try to find the inner depth and background of the governmentality that begins to develop in the sixteenth century. It was also to show you it is not a question of undertaking anything like an endogenous history of power that develops on the basis of itself in a sort of paranoiac and narcissistic madness. Rather, the point of view of power is a way of identifying intelligible relations between elements that are external to each other. Fundamentally the problem is why and how political or economic problems that arose in the Middle Ages, such as the movements of urban revolt and peasant revolt, the conflicts between feudalism and the merchant bourgeoisie, were translated into a number of religious themes, forms, and concerns that finally result in the explosion of the Reformation, of the great religious crisis of the sixteenth century. If we do not take the problem of the pastorate, of the structures of pastoral power, as the hinge or pivot of these different elements external to each other—the economic crises on one side and religious themes on the other—if we do not take it as a field of intelligibility, as the principle establishing relations between them, as the switch-point between these elements, then I think we are forced to return to the old conceptions of ideology, [and]* to say that the aspirations of a group, a class, and so forth, are translated, reflected, and expressed in something like a religious belief. The point of view of pastoral power, of this analysis of the structures of power, enables us, I think, to take up these things and analyze them, no longer in the form of reflection and transcription, but in the form of strategies and tactics.[†] There you are. Forgive me for having taken too long, and next time, this is a promise, we won't speak any more about pastors.

---

* M.F.: that is to say

[†] For fear of going on "too long," Foucault summarizes in a few sentences the conclusion that is more fully developed in the manuscript in which he opposes the identification of "tactical *entrées*" to the interpretation of religious phenomena in terms of ideology:

"[If I have emphasized] these tactical elements that gave precise and recurrent forms to pastoral insubordinations, it is not in any way so as to suggest that it is a matter of internal struggles, endogenous contradictions, pastoral power devouring itself or encountering the limits and barriers of its operations. It is in order to identify the 'points of entry' ('*les entrées*') through which processes, conflicts, and transformations—which concern the status of women, the development of a market economy, the decoupling of the urban and rural economies, the raising or extinction of feudal rent, the status of urban wage-earners, the spread of literacy—can enter into the field of the exercise of the pastorate, not to be transcribed, translated, and reflected there, but to carry out divisions, valorizations, disqualifications, rehabilitations, and redistributions of every kind. (...) Rather than say that each class, group, or social force has its ideology that allows it to translate its aspirations into theory, aspirations and ideology from which corresponding institutional reorganizations are deduced, we should say: every transformation that modifies the relations of force between communities or groups, every conflict that confronts them or brings them into competition calls for the utilization of tactics which allows the modification of relations of power and the bringing into play of theoretical elements which morally justify and give a basis to these tactics in rationality."

1. This expression does not seem to appear in the *Orations*. However, in the passage of the second oration concerning the differentiated application of the medicine of souls (τὴν τῶν ψυκῶν ἰατρείαν) according to categories of the faithful, Gregory writes: "For these classes differ sometimes more widely from each other in their desires and passions than in their physical characteristics; or, if you will, in the mixtures and blendings of the elements of which we are composed, and, therefore to regulate them is no easy task," this last verb translating "τὴν οἰκονομίαν" (Gregory Nazianzen, *Orations*, 2, 29, p. 211). It is thus likely that Foucault coined the expression he cites on the basis of this usage of the word οἰκονομία to designate the pastoral government of sheep as beings of desires and appetites.

2. "Seeing then that the state is made up of households, before speaking of the state we must speak of the management of the household (οἰκονομία). The parts of household management (οἰκονομία) correspond to the persons who compose the household, and a complete household consists of slaves and freemen. Now we should begin by examining everything in its fewest possible elements; and the first and fewest possible parts of a family are master and slave, husband and wife, father and children. We have therefore to consider what each of these three relations is and ought to be." Aristotle, *Politics*, 1, 3, 1253b, trans. B. Jowett, in *The Complete Works of Aristotle. The Revised Oxford Translation* (Princeton: Princeton University Press/Bollingen Series LXXI.2, 1984) vol. 2, p. 1988.

3. See, for example, *Essais*, I, 26, ed. A. Tournon (Paris: Imprimerie nationale, 1998) vol. 1, p. 261: English translation by Donald M. Frame, *Essays*, in Michel de Montaigne, *The Complete Works* (London: Everyman's Library, 2003) p. 134: "If, as is our custom, the teachers undertake to regulate many minds of such different capacities and forms with the same lesson and a similar measure of guidance [*conduite*], it is no wonder if in a whole race of children they find barely two or three who reap any proper fruit from their teaching."

4. Manichean dualism (from Manes, or Mani, 216-277) underwent a wide diffusion in Asia and North Africa from the third century. Its repression in the Empire led to it splintering into a multitude of small clandestine communities. After an eclipse of several centuries, some "Manichean" sects—Bogomil, Cathar—reappear in Medieval Europe, but their link with Manicheism is problematic. From the twelfth to the thirteenth century, the Cathar "heresy" spread into Lombardy, central Italy, Rhineland, Catalonia, Champagne, Burgundy, and above all the French Midi ("Albigensians"). The struggle against the latter was carried out firstly by preaching and the Inquisition, and then by a crusade, summoned by Innocent III in 1208, which degenerated into a veritable war of conquest.

5. This analysis of revolts of conduct correlative to the pastorate forms part of the extension of the thesis presented by Foucault in *La Volonté de savoir*, pp. 125-127; *The History of Sexuality. Volume 1: An Introduction*, pp. 95-98, according to which: "Where there is power, there is resistance," the latter never being "in a position of exteriority in relation to power," but constituting "the other term in relations of power," their "irreducible vis-à-vis." In 1978, the notion of resistance remains at the heart of Foucault's conception of politics. In a series of manuscript pages inserted between two lectures of the course, he writes in fact: "The analysis of governmentality (...) implies that 'everything is political.' (...) Politics is nothing more and nothing less than that which is born with resistance to governmentality, the first revolt, the first confrontation." The idea of "counter-conduct," in the expression advanced below, represents an essential stage in Foucault's thought, between the analysis of techniques of subjection and that, developed from 1980, of practices of subjectivation.

6. In the first centuries of Christianity, representatives of Gnostic movements opposed official ecclesiastical teaching in the name of a higher knowledge, or gnosis (γνῶσις). This tendency asserted itself especially in the second century and spread in a multitude of sects. Whereas the ecclesiastical authors of Antiquity saw in Gnosticism a Christian heresy—a thesis accepted for a long time by modern research: see, A. von Harnack, for whom Gnosticism was a radical Hellenization of Christianity—the works produced at the start of the last century by the comparativist school (*religionsgeschichtliche Schule*) have highlighted the extreme complexity of the Gnostic phenomenon and shown that it was not a product of Christianity, but the outcome of a multitude of influences (Hellenistic religious philosophy, Iranian dualism, doctrines of the mystery cults, Judaism, and Christianity). A good synthesis is found in M. Simon, *La Civilisation de l'Antiquité et le Christianisme* (Paris: Arthaud, 1972) pp. 175-186.

See also, F. Gros, in *L'Herméneutique du sujet*, pp. 25-26, note 49; *The Hermeneutics of the Subject*, pp. 23-24, note 49, which refers to the work of H.-C. Puech, *Sur le manichéisme et Autres Essais* (Paris: Flammarion, 1979). Foucault may also have consulted H. Jones, *The Gnostic Religion* (Boston, Mass.: Beacon Press, 1972).

7. Compare this analysis with that developed by Foucault in *Le Pouvoir psychiatrique*, lecture of 28 November 1973, p. 67 *sq*.; *Psychiatric Power*, p. 65 *sq*.: the formation of relatively egalitarian communal groups in the Middle Ages and on the eve of the Reformation is described there in terms of "disciplinary apparatuses (*dispositifs*)" in opposition to the "system of differentiation of the apparatuses of sovereignty." Taking the example of the mendicant monks, the Brothers of the Common Life, and popular or bourgeois communities, which immediately preceded the Reformation, Foucault identifies in their mode of organization a critique of the relationship of sovereignty rather than a form of resistance to the pastorate.

8. In the fourteenth century the Netherlands was one of the regions where the heresy of the Free Spirit (see below, notes 41-42) was most strongly rooted.

9. Originally close to the attitude of the mendicant orders, the Waldensian movement stemmed from the fraternity of the Poor of Lyon, founded in 1170 by Pierre Valdès (Peter Waldo, 1140-1206), who preached poverty and return to the Gospels, rejecting the sacraments and ecclesiastical hierarchy. At first associated with anti-Cathar preaching organized by the Church (Lateran Council, 1179), it was not long before it came into conflict with this and the Waldenses found themselves associated with Cathar Manicheism, to which they were strongly opposed however, in the Pope's anathema at the Verona synod of 1184. The doctrine spread to Provence, the Dauphiné, Piedmont, and as far as Spain and Germany. Some Waldenses reached Bohemia where they joined the Hussites. See L. Cristiani, "Vaudois" in *Dictionnaire de théologie catholique*, vol. XV, 1950, col. 2586-2601.

10. The Calixtines were a component of the moderate tendency of the Hussites, alongside the Utraquists. Whereas the latter called for communion in the two kinds, bread and wine, the former demanded only the chalice. See N. Cohn, *The Pursuit of the Millennium* (London: Secker and Warburg, 1957) p. 220. See below, note 39.

11. It was at Tabor (founded in 1420 in South Bohemia, and named after Mount Tabor, which the New Testament gives as the site of Christ's resurrection) that the radical Hussites, intransigent defenders of the *Four Articles* of Prague (see below, note 39), established their camp. Stemming from the July 1419 insurrection against the Catholic administration of the Ville Nouvelle quarter in Prague, imposed by King Wenceslas, this movement, originally made up of artisans, rapidly recruited from the lower strata of the population. "Whereas the Utraquists clung in most respects to traditional Catholic doctrine, the Taborites affirmed the right of every individual, layman as well as priest, to interpret the Scriptures according to his lights" (N. Cohn, *The Pursuit of the Millenium*, p. 223). Calling for the massacre of all sinners in order to purify the Earth, the most extreme members announced the imminent arrival of the Millennium, which will be characterized by "a return of the lost anarcho-communistic order. Taxes, dues, rents were to be abolished and so was private property of all kinds. There was to be no human authority of any kind: 'All shall live together as brothers, none shall be subject to another.' 'The Lord shall reign, and the Kingdom shall be handed over to the people of the earth'" (ibid. p. 228). This battle entailed a merciless struggle against *Dives* (the Rich), "that old ally of Antichrist," identified with the feudal lord, but especially with the rich citizen, merchant, or absentee landlord (ibid.). The Taborite army was defeated at Lipan in 1434 by Utraquist troops, "and from then onwards the strength of the Taborite wing of the Hussite movement rapidly declined. After the town of Tabor itself was taken over by the Utraquists in 1452, a coherent Taborite tradition survived only in the sect known as the Bohemian or Moravian Brethren" (ibid. p. 237). See below, note 39.

12. *Nonnenmystik*, the mysticism of nuns: a disparaging expression used by some German scholars with regard to the spirituality of the Rhenish-Flemish Beguines. On this ecstatic feminine movement, see the introduction by Brother J.-B. P., in Hadewijch d'Anvers, ed., *Écrits mystiques des Béguines* (Paris: Le Seuil, "Points Sagesses," 1954) pp. 9-34.

13. See N. Cohn, *The Pursuit of the Millennium*, pp. 176-177; "In 1372 certain male and female heretics who called themselves 'the Society of the Poor', but who were popularly known by the obscene nickname of Turlupins, were captured at Paris. Their leader was also a woman,

Jeanne Dabenton. She was burnt; and so were the body of her male assistant, who had died in prison, and the writings and peculiar costumes of her followers. Nothing is known of the teachings of this group, but the name 'Turlupin' was normally given only to the Brethren of the Free Spirit."

14. Marguerite Porete (died 1310), a Beguine of Hainaut, was the author of *Mirouer des Simples Ames Anienties et qui seulement demourent en Vouloir et Désir d'Amour*, bilingual edition by R. Guarnieri (Turnhout: Brepols, "Corpus christianorum. Continuatio Mediaevalis," 69, 1986). The text, which was rediscovered in 1876, was for a long time attributed to Marguerite of Hungary. It was only in 1946 that the true identity of the author was established. See R. Guarnieri, *Il Movimento del Libero Spirito. Testi e Documenti* (Rome: Ed. di storia e lettaratura, 1965). *Le Mirouer*, which teaches the doctrine of pure love, was burnt on the public square of Velenciennes at the beginning of the fourteenth century. Declared a relapsed heretic by the tribunal of the Inquisition, Marguerite Porete died at the stake, place de Grève, Paris, 1 June 1310. On the two propositions which earned her this condemnation, see Brother J.-B. P., in Hadewijch d'Anvers, ed., *Écrits mystiques des Béguines*, p. 16, note 5. The work has been translated several times into modern French, in addition to the translation by Guarnieri already cited (Albin Michel, 1984; Jérôme Millon, 1991). See, "Frères du Libre Spirit" in *Dictionnaire de spiritualité*, 1964, vol. 5, col. 1252-1253 and 1257-1268, and 1978, vol. 10, col. 343; N. Cohn, *The Pursuit of the Millennium*, pp. 176-177.

15. The main inspiration for the visionaries of New Castille in the 1520s, Isabel de la Cruz was a nun of the Franciscan third order. From Guadalajara, where she preached the principles of mystical abandon—the *dejamiento*, distinct from the simple *recogimiento* (meditation)—the source of impeccability through the love God infuses, her teaching soon spread throughout New Castile. Arrested in 1524 by the Inquisition she was sentenced to be flogged and then imprisoned for life. See M. Bataillon, *Érasme et l'Espagne* (Geneva: Droz, 1998) pp. 182-183, 192-193, and 469; C. Guilhem, "L'Inquisition et la dévaluation des discours féminins" in B. Bennassar, ed., *L'Inquisizione espagnole, XVᵉ-XVIᵉ siècle* (Paris: Hachette, 1979) p. 212. On the details of her biography and trial, see J.E. Longhurst, *Luther's Ghost in Spain (1517-1546)* (Lawrence, Mass.: Coronado Press, 1964) pp. 93-99, and by the same author, "La beata Isabel de la Cruz ante la Inquisición, 1524-1529" in *Cuadernos de historia da España* (Buenos Aires) vols XXV-XXVI, 1957.

16. Armelle Nicolas (called the Good Armelle, 1606-1671): a laywoman of peasant origin who, after years of internal struggles, penances, and mystical ecstasies, took the vow of poverty and gave all her goods to the poor. Her life was written by a nun of the monastery of Saint Ursule de Vannes (Jeanne de la Nativité) *Le Triumphe de l'amour divin dans la vie d'une grande servante de Dieu, nommée Armelle Nicolas* (1683) (Paris: printed by A. Warin, 1697). See, *Dictionnaire de spiritualité*, 1937, vol. 1, col. 860-861; H. Bremond, *Histoire littéraire du sentiment religieux en France depuis la fin de guerres de Religion jusqu'à nos jours* (Paris: A. Colin, 1967) vol. 5, pp. 120-138.

17. Marie des Vallées (1590-1656): laywoman, also of peasant origin, who from her nineteenth year was prey to torments, convulsions, and physical and moral sufferings that lasted until her death. She was denounced as a witch but in 1614 was acquitted, declared innocent, and really possessed. Jean Eudes, who tried to exorcise her in 1641, acknowledged her as being possessed, but also as holy. In 1655 he wrote, in three volumes, "La Vie admirable de Marie des Vallées et des choses prodigieuses qui se sont passées en elle," which was not published but passed from hand to hand. See, H. Bremond, *Histoire littéraire du sentiment religieux en France*, vol. 3, pp. 583-628; P. Milcent, "Vallées (Marie des)" in *Dictionnaire de spiritualité*, 1992, vol. 16, col. 207-212.

18. Madame Acarie, born Barbe Avrillot (1565-1618): belonging to the Parisian high, institutional bourgeoisie, she was one of the most remarkable figures of female mysticism in France at the time of the Counter Reformation. In 1604, with the support of her cousin Pierre de Bérulle (1575-1629), she introduced the Spanish Carmelite order in France. See Bremond, *Histoire littéraire du sentiment religieux en France*, vol. 2, pp. 192-262; P. Chaunu, *La Civilisation de l'Europe classique* (Paris: Arthaud, 1966) pp. 486-487.

19. On Wyclif, see above lecture of 15 February, note 44.

20. Disciples of Amaury de Bène (?1150-1206): the latter, who taught dialectics at Paris, was condemned by Pope Innocent III for his conception of the incorporation of the Christian in Christ, understood in a pantheistic sense. He did not leave any writings. It seems that the group of priests, scholars, and lay people of both sexes claiming to be his followers only came together after his death. Ten of them were burned in 1210 following the council of Paris that condemned eight of their propositions. The main source concerning Amaurianism is Guillaume le Breton (died 1277), *Gesta Philippi Aiugusti/Vie de Philippe Auguste* (Paris: J.-L. Brière, 1825).

Beyond the pantheism (*Omnia sunt Deus, Deus est omnia*), the Amaurians, professing the advent of the Holy Spirit, after the age of the Father and of the Son, denied all the sacraments and affirmed that each can be saved by the sole internal grace of the Spirit, that heaven and hell are only imaginary places, and that the only resurrection consists in knowledge of the truth. They thereby denied the existence of sin: "If someone, they said, possessing the Holy Spirit, commits an immodest act, he does not sin, for the Holy Spirit, which is God, cannot sin, and man cannot sin inasmuch as the Holy Spirit, which is God, lives in him," Césaire de Heisterbach (died 1240), *Dialogus miraculorum*. See, C. Capelle, *Amaury de Bène. Étude sur son panthéisme formel* (Paris: J. Vrin, 1932); A. Chollet, "Amaury de Bène" in *Dictionnaire de théologie catholique*, 1900, vol. 1, col. 936-940; F. Vernet, "Amaury de Bène et les Amauriciens" in *Dictionnaire de spiritualité*, 1937, vol. 1, col. 422-425; Dom F. Vandenbroucke, in Dom J. Leclercq, Dom F. Vandenbroucke, and L. Bouyer, *La Spiritualité du Moyen Âge* (Paris: Aubier, 1961) p. 324; N. Cohn, *The Pursuit of the Millennium*, pp. 156-161.

21. John Huss (Jan Hus) (?1370-1415). Ordained priest in 1400, dean of the Prague Faculty of Theology the following year, he is the most illustrious representative of the reforming tendency arising from the crisis of the Czech Church in the middle of the fourteenth century. He translated the Gospels into Czech and, according to him, these are the only infallible rule of faith and preach evangelical poverty. An admirer of Wyclif, whose condemnation he refused to accept, he lost the support of King Wenceslas IV and, excommunicated (1411, then 1412), he withdrew into southern Bohemia where, among other writings, he wrote *De ecclesia* (1413). Having refused to retract during the Council of Constance, he died at the stake in 1415. See, Cohn, *The Pursuit of the Millennium*, pp. 219-221; Jean Boulier, *Jean Hus* (Paris: Club français du Livre, 1958); P. De Vooght, *L'Hérésie de Jean Huss* (Louvain: Bureau de la *Revue d'histoire ecclésiastique*, 1960 [followed by an appendix volume *Hussiana*]); M. Spinka, *John Hus' Concept of the Church* (Princeton, NJ: Princeton University Press, 1966).

22. On these revolts of conduct based on the interpretation of Scripture, see Foucault's lecture, "Qu'est-ce que la critique? [Critique et *Aufklärung*]" given on 27 May 1978, *Bulletin de la Société française de philosophie*, 84 (2), April-June 1990, pp. 38-39.

23. See above, lecture of 15 February, note 45.

24. The perfectly transparent criticism of the Communist Party should be linked to the project Foucault evokes in the 1978-1979 course of studying "party governmentality (...) at the historical origin of something like the totalitarian regimes," *Naissance de la biopolitique*, lecture of 7 March 1979, p. 197. If this project was not carried out within the framework of the course, it was nonetheless not abandoned. During his last stay at Berkeley, in 1983, Foucault constituted an interdisciplinary working group on new political rationalities in the period between the two World Wars that would have studied, among other subjects, political militantism in parties of the left, and notably Communist Parties, in terms of "styles of life" (the ethic of asceticism in revolutionaries, etcetera). See, *History of the Present*, 1, February 1985, p. 6.

25. On the Anabaptist movement (from Greek, ἀνά, again, and βαπτίζειν, dive in water), an outcome of the Peasants' War (see below, lecture 8 March, note 1), for which the faithful, baptized as children, had to have a second baptism when adult, and which broke up into many sects. See N. Cohn, *The Pursuit of the Millennium*, pp. 273-306; E.G. Léonard, *Histoire générale du protestantisme* (Paris: PUF, [1961] 1988) vol. 1, pp. 88-91.

26. The word was used shortly before with regard to religious forms of the refusal of medicine.

27. It was at the start of the 1970s that the word "dissidence" established itself to designate the movement of intellectual opposition to the communist system in the U.S.S.R. and the

Soviet bloc. "Dissidents" corresponds to the Russian word *inakomysliachtchie*, "those who think differently." The movement develops following the condemnation of Andrei Sinyavksy and Yuly Daniel in 1966 (see above, lecture of 15 February, note 64). Its main representatives in the U.S.S.R., beyond Solzhenitsyn (see below, note 29), were the physicist Andrei Sakharov, the mathematician Leonid Plioutch (whom Foucault met when he arrived in Paris in 1976), the historian Andrei Amalrik, the writers Vladimir Bukovsky, author of *Une nouvellelle maladie mentale en URSS: l'opposition*, trans. F. Simon and J.-J. Marie (Paris: Le Seuil, 1971), Alexander Ginzburg, Victor Nekrasov, and Alexander Zinoviev. See *Magazine littéraire*, 125, June 1977: URSS: *les écrivains de la dissidence*. In Czechoslovakia, dissidence was organized around Charter 77, published in Prague, the spokesmen of which were Jiri Hajek, Václav Havel, and Jan Patoćka.

28. See Foucault's interview with K.S. Karol, "Crimes et châtiments en URSS et ailleurs..." *Le Nouvel Observateur*, 585, 26 January-1 February 1976, reprinted in *Dits et Écrits*, 3, p. 69: "(...) basically terror is not the culmination of discipline but its failure. In the Stalinist regime, the Chief of Police could himself be executed one fine day after leaving the Council of Ministers. No NKVD chief has died in his bed."

29. On Alexander Isayevich Solzhenitsyn (born 1918), emblematic figure of anti-Soviet dissidence, see *Naissance de la biopolitique*, lecture of 14 February 1979, p. 156, note 1.

30. On the origin of this distinction, see J. Zeiller, "L'organisation ecclésiastique aux deux premiers siècles" in A. Fliche and V. Martin, *Histoire de l'Église depuis les origines jusqu'à nos jours. I. L'Église primitive* (Paris: Bloud & Gay, 1934) pp. 380-381.

31. On the differences of status between these two kinds of Christian (to which a third "estate" will be added, that of the religious, members of an order) in the Middle Ages, see G. Le Bras in J.-B. Duroselle and E. Jarry, *Histoire de l'Église depuis les origines jusqu'á nos jours. XII. Institutions ecclésiastiques de la Chrétienté médiévale* (Paris: Bloud and Gay, 1959) pp. 149-177.

32. Allusion to the thesis of the "universal priesthood" supported by Wyclif and Huss, and then taken up by Luther.

33. On the synonymy of these terms ("elder," πρεσβύτερος, and "supervisor" or "overseer," ἐπίσκοπος) in the first century and their progressive differentiation, see F. Prat, "Évêque. 1: Origine de l'épiscopat" in *Dictionnaire de théologie catholique*, 1913, vol. V, col. 1658-1672. See for example, Acts of the Apostles, 20: 17 and 28; I Peter, 5: 1-2, etcetera. This synonymy in the apostolic writings is invoked by Protestants in support of the thesis that the minister is a simple member of the lay community, delegated by the community for preaching and the administration of the sacraments.

34. See, A. Michel, "Sacrements" in *Dictionnaire de théologie catholique*, 1939, vol. XIV, col. 594.

35. The 4th Lateran Council (1215) instituted the obligation to confess regularly, at least once a year, at Easter, for the laity, and each month, or even each week, for the clergy. On the importance of this event in the development of "tariffed" penance, based on a judicial and penal model, see *Les Anormaux*, lecture of 19 February 1975, pp. 161-163; *Abnormal*, pp. 174-176.

36. At the time of these lectures, Jacques Le Goff's fundamental book, *La Naissance du purgatoire* (Paris: Gallimard, "Bibliothèque des histoires," 1981) had not yet appeared. But Foucault was able to read, amongst other studies, the article by A. Michel, "Purgatoire" in *Dictionnaire de théologie catholique*, 1936, vol. 13, col. 1163-1326. See the bibliography of works on Purgatory in Le Goff, pp. 487-488.

37. See the *De ecclesia* written by both of these authors, one in 1378 and the other in 1413: Iohannis Wyclif, *Tractatus de ecclesia*, ed. I. Loserth (London: Trübner Co., 1886 [reprinted, New York and London/Frankfurt: Johnson Reprint Corporation, Minerva, 1966]); Magistri Johanis Hus, *Tractatus de ecclesia*, ed. S.H. Thomson (Cambridge: University of Colorado Press, W. Heffer and Sons, 1956).

38. See above, note 9.

39. After the death of John Huss (see above, note 21), the Diet of the lords of Bohemia vehemently protested against his condemnation. The "defenestration" of Prague in July 1419 gave the signal for the Hussite insurrection, definitively repressed in 1437. During these eighteen years, Europe organized five crusades, on the appeal of the Pope and the Emperor Sigismond, in order to overcome the "heresy." The Hussite program was summarized in the

Four Articles of Prague (1420): free preaching of the Scripture, communion in both kinds or species, confiscation of the clergy's goods, repression of mortal sins (see N. Cohn, *The Pursuit of the Millennium*, p. 220). Their movement, however, was divided into two enemy camps: the moderate part, Utraquist or Calixtine (see above, note 10), open to a compromise with Rome, who got satisfaction on the first two articles in 1433 (*Compactata* of Basle), and that of the radicals, or Taborites (see above, note 11). The Utraquists allied with Rome in 1434 to crush the Taborites. See E. Denis, *Huss et la guerre des hussites* (Paris: E. Leroux, [1878] 1930); J. Macek, *Le Mouvement hussite en Bohême* (Prague: Orbis, 1965).

40. See above, note 25.

41. See N. Cohn, *The Pursuit of the Millennium*, p. 164: "The heresy of the Free Spirit, after being held in check for half a century, began to spread rapidly again towards the close of the thirteenth century. From then onwards until the close of the Middle Ages it was disseminated by men who were commonly called Beghards and who formed an unofficial lay counterpart to the Mendicant Orders. (...) These self-appointed 'holy beggars' were full of contempt for the easy-going monks and friars, fond of interrupting church services, impatient of ecclesiastical discipline. They preached much, without authorisation but with considerable popular success." On the condemnation of the Beghards and Beguines *in regno Alemania* by the Vienna Council in 1311, see Dom F. Vandenbroucke, in Dom J. Leclerq and others, *La Spiritualité du Moyen Âge*, pp. 427-428.

42. See Cohn, *The Pursuit of the Millennium*, pp. 166-167: "(...) the movement [of the Free Spirit] owed much to the women known as Beguines—women of the towns, and often from well-to-do families, who dedicated themselves to a religious life whilst continuing to live in the world. During the thirteenth century Beguines became very numerous in the area which is now Belgium, in northern France, in the Rhine valley—Cologne had two thousand Beguines—and in Bavaria and central German towns such as Magdeburg. As a sign of their status these women adopted a religious dress—a hooded robe of grey or black wool and a veil; but there was no single way of life which was common to them all. Some of them (...) lived with their families, or enjoyed private incomes, or supported themselves by work. Others lived unattached lives as wandering mendicants: true female counterparts to the Beghards. Most Beguines, however, formed themselves into unofficial religious communities, living together in a house or group of houses. (...) The Beguines had no positive heretical intentions but they did have a passionate desire for the most intense forms of mystical experience. This desire was of course shared by many nuns; only for Beguines mysticism held temptations against which nuns were protected. Beguines lacked the discipline of a regular order; and at the same time they received no adequate supervision from the secular clergy, who had scant sympathy for this new-fangled and audacious religiosity." See Fr. J.-B. P., in Hadewijch d'Anvers, ed., *Écrits mystiques des Béguines*.

43. The spirituality developed by the Brethren of the Common Life, grouped in the Windesheim monastery and baptized by Jean Busch, chronicler of Windesheim. It found its most complete expression in *The Imitation of Christ*, attributed to Thomas à Kempis. See P. Debongnie, "Dévotion moderne" in *Dictionnaire de spiritualité*, 1957, vol. 3, col. 727-747; P. Chaunu, *Les Temps des réformes. La crise de la chrétienté, l'éclatement* (Paris: Fayard, 1975) p. 257 and pp. 259-260, which refers to E. Delaruelle, E.R. Labande, and P. Ourliac, *Histoire de l'Église*, eds., Fliche and Martin, vol. XIV, especially p. 926: "The first feature to catch the eye in the *devotio moderna*, when we compare it with traditional monastic devotion, is that it lays more emphasis on the personal internal life than on the liturgy" (p. 259). See A. Hyma, *The Christian Renaissance: A History of the "Devotio moderna"* (Grand Rapids, Mich.: 1924) 2 volumes.

44. The restriction of anchorite isolation was the object, in the West, of several Council canons from 465 (Council of Vannes; dispositions repeated at the Council of Agde [506] and at the council of Orléans [511]). See N. Gradowicz-Pancer, "Enfermement monastique et privation d'autonomie dans les règles monastiques (v^e-vi^e siècles)," *Revue historique*, CCLXXXVIII/I, 1992, p. 5. On Egyptian *anachōrēsis*, P. Brown, *The Making of Late Antiquity* (Cambridge, Mass., and London: Harvard University Press, 1978), ch. 4, "From the Heavens to the Desert: Anthony and Pachomius." At this time Foucault was no doubt familiar with Peter Brown's first articles on the question (for example, "The Rise and Function of the Holy Man in Late Antiquity," *Journal of Roman Studies*, LXI, 1971, pp. 80-101;

reprinted in P. Brown, *Society and the Holy in Late Antiquity* [London: Faber and Faber, 1982] pp. 103-152) as well as the book by A. Voöbus, *A History of Ascetism in the Syrian Orient* (Louvain: CSCO, 1958-1960). See also, E.A. Judge, "The earliest use of 'Monachos'," *Jahrbuch für Antike und Christentum*, 20, 1977, pp. 72-89.

45. See Cassian, *Conferences*, 18, ch. 4 and 8. On the question of the choice between anchorite and monastic life in Cassian, see in particular the introduction of E. Pichery, pp. 52-54 of the French translation, Cassien, *Conférences*, which evokes the position of Saint Basil, favorable to the cenobite form. (N. Gradowicz-Pancer, "Enfermement monastique et privation d'autonomie dans le règles monastiques" p. 5, note 13, also refers to Cassian, 18, 8, pp. 21-22, with regard to solitaries considered as false hermits); *The Rule of Saint Benedict*, ch. 1, "Of the several kinds of monks and their way of life." The author distinguishes the cenobites, living in a monastery under a rule and an abbot; the anchorites, well prepared, through the discipline acquired within the monastery, for the "single-handed combat of the desert"; the sarabaites who "make a law to themselves in the pleasure of their own desires," and the gyrovagues, "ever roaming, with no stability" (pp. 223-224). On the transition from the "desert," as site of the perfect life, to the eulogy of the cenobite life in Cassian's thought, see R.A. Markus, *The End of Ancient Christianity* (Cambridge: Cambridge University Press, 1990) ch. 11: "City or Desert? Two models of community."

46. On ascesis, in the strict sense of *askēsis*, or exercise, see *L'Herméneutique du sujet*, lecture of 24 February 1982, pp. 301-302; *The Hermeneutics of the Subject*, pp. 315-316.

47. These examples are not found in the *Apophtegmata Patrum* (*Patrologia Graeca*, 65); English translation, *The Sayings of the Desert Fathers*, trans. B. Ward (Oxford: Oxford University Press, 1975); French, incomplete, translation, *Paroles des Anciens*; and complete French translation by L. Regnault, *Les Sentences des Pères du Désert* (Solesmes, 1981).

48. See above, lecture of 22 February, pp. 178-179.

49. See ibid. p. 176.

50. The anecdote is not found in Cassian's *Institutions*, or in the *Apophtegmata Patrum*, or in the *Histoire lausiaque*.

51. Reading these words, it will be recalled that some weeks after this session Foucault spent some time in Japan during which he had the opportunity for discussion, in Kyoto, "with specialists on Zen Buddhist mysticism compared with techniques of Christian mysticism" (Daniel Defert, "Chronologie," *Dits et Écrits*, 1, p. 53). See "Michel Foucault et le zen: un séjour dans un temple zen" (1978), *Dits et Écrits*, 3, pp. 618-624; see in particular p. 621, on the difference between Zen and Christian mysticism, which "aims at individualization"; "Zen and Christian mysticism are two things that cannot be compared, whereas the technique of Christian spirituality and that of Zen are comparable."

52. Henri Suso (1295?-1366), Dominican beatified in 1831, author of the *Horologium sapientiae* and several works written in German, the *Vie*, the *Livre de la Sagesse éternelle*, the *Livre de la Verité*, and the *Petit Livre des lettres*. He entered the convent of Constance when he was 13, followed the teaching of Eckhart at Cologne, and devoted his life to preaching and directing cloistered nuns. See J.-A. Bizet, *Le Mystique allemand Henri Suso et le déclin de la scolastique* (Paris: F. Aubier, 1946); *Mystiques allemands du XIVe siècle: Eckhart, Suso, Tauler* (Paris: Aubier, no date [c.1957]) pp. 241-289, reprinted (Paris: Aubier-Montaigne, "Bibliothèque de philologie germanique," 1971); and "Henri Suso" in *Dictionnaire de spiritualité*, 1968, vol. 7, col. 234-257; Dom F. Vandenbroucke in Dom J. Leclerq and others, *La Spiritualité du Moyen Âge*, pp. 468-469.

53. *Vie*, XVI, in Bienheureux Henri Suso, *Œuvres complètes*, trans. and notes J. Ancelet-Hustache (Paris: Le Seuil, 1975) p. 185: "On Saint Clement's day, when Winter begins, he once made a general confession and, as it was in secret, he closed himself in his cell, stripped to his hair shirt, took his barbed scourge (*discipline*) and struck his body, arms, and legs so that blood ran everywhere as when one scarifies. Having a point like a fish hook, the scourge bit into and ripped his flesh. He struck himself so hard that the scourge broke into three pieces, one remained in his hand and the points were thrown against the walls. When he stood up, covered in blood, he observed himself, and the sight was so pitiable that he resembled in some way the beloved Christ when he was cruelly flogged. He so pitied himself that he cried with all his heart, knelt in the cold, naked and bloody, and prayed to God that, with a gentle gaze, he wipe away his sins."

54. See above, note 11.

55. The movement of the Flagellants—whose members practiced self-flagellation in a spirit of penance—appeared in Italy in the middle of the thirteenth century and spread into Germany where it underwent an important expansion during the Black Death of 1348-1349. Describing the ritual of their processions in detail, N. Cohn stresses the population's benevolent attitude towards them. "The flagellants were regarded as they regarded themselves—not simply as penitents who were atoning for their own sins but as martyrs who were taking upon themselves the sins of the world and thereby averting the plague and, indeed, the annihilation of mankind," *The Pursuit of the Millennium*, p. 133. Flagellation was thus lived as a collective *imitatio Christ*. From 1349 the movement evolved towards a revolutionary millenarianism, violently opposed to the Church, and took an active part in the massacre of Jews. The Papal Bull of Clement VI (October 1349), condemning its errors and excesses, lead to its rapid decline. See P. Bailly, "Flagellants" in *Dictionnaire de spiritualité*, 1962, vol. 5, col. 392-408; N. Cohn, *The Pursuit of the Millennium*, pp. 121-143.

56. J. Wyclif, *De Ecclesia*. The thesis was taken up by John Huss, who asserted that a priest in the state of mortal sin is no longer a genuine priest (an assertion valid also for bishops and the Pope): "Priests living in vice of any kind soil sacerdotal power (...). No-one is the representative of Christ or Peter if he does not also imitate their morals"; propositions taken from the writings of Huss, according to the Bull of Martin V of 22 July 1418, cited by J. Delumeau, *Naissance et Affirmation de la Réforme* (Paris: PUF, "Nouvelle Clio," 2nd edn., 1968) p. 63.

57. The chapel of the Holy Innocents of Bethlehem, commonly called the Church of Bethlehem, in which, from March 1402, John Huss undertook his preaching in the Czech language.

58. We have not been able to find the source of these two quotations.

59. See above, this lecture, p. 203.

60. See A. Michel, "Sacrements" col. 593-614.

61. Ibid. col. 594: "The letter of Innocent III to Ymbert d'Arles (1201), inserted in the *Decretals*, 1. III, tit. III, 42, *Majores*, censures those who claim that baptism of children is pointless, saying that faith or charity and the other virtues cannot be infused in them, even as *habitus*, because they are unable to consent."

62. See above, note 25.

63. See A. Jundt, *Les Amis de Dieu au quatorzième siècle* (Paris: Sandoz and Fischbacher, 1879) p. 188. This is the story of Ursule, a young girl of Brabant, who, on the advice of a Beguine, chose in 1288 the cloistered and solitary life. After ten years of giving herself up "to the most painful practices of asceticism, (...) she was warned by God to suspend the 'external practices that she imposed on herself through her own will,' and to let her heavenly spouse alone direct her spiritual life by means of 'internal exercises.' She obeyed and was immediately assailed 'by the most dreadful and impure temptations.' After vainly imploring God's help, she revealed part of her torments to her confessor, who tried to abuse her naive confidence in him, counseling her, 'by subtle discourses full of mystery and obscurity,' to satisfy her carnal desires so as to get rid of the temptations that prevented God's action in her and put her soul in peril. Indignant, she dismissed the priest from her presence. The following night, God sharply rebuked the fault she had committed by revealing to a man the secrets of her internal life that only her spouse should know; He accused her of having made an honest man fall into sin through her imprudent 'chatter.' Called back by her the following day, the confessor mended his ways and became once again a man of piety and exemplary conduct."

64. See N. Cohn, *The Pursuit of the Millennium*, pp. 156-161; G. Leff, *Heresy in the Later Middle Ages: The Relation of Heterodoxy to Dissent, c.1250-c.1450* (Manchester: Manchester University Press, 1967) pp. 308-407, which questions, pp. 309-311, the filiation suggested here by Foucault; R.E. Lerner, *The Heresy of the Free Spirit in the Later Middle Ages* (Berkeley: University of California Press, 1972).

65. See above, note 20, with regard to the Amaurians.

66. Ulrich Engelbert of Strasbourg (1220/25-1277) was a fervent disciple of Albert the Great whose courses he followed at Paris and then Cologne. He is the author of a massive œuvre,

the *Summa de summo bono* that is one of the great founding texts of Rhenish theology. See J. Daguillon, *Ulrich de Strasbourg, O.P. La Summa de Bono. Livre I. Introduction et édition critique* (Paris: "Bibliothèque thomiste," XII, 1930); E. Gilson, *La Philosophie au Moyen Âge* (Paris: Payot, 1922; republished in "Petite Bibliothèque Payot") pp. 516-519; A. de Libera, *La Mystique rhénane. D'Albert le Grand à Maître Eckhart* (Paris: ŒIL, "Sagesse chrétienne," 1984; republished, Paris: Le Seuil, "Points Sagesses," 1994) pp. 99-161.

67. See J. Ancelet-Hustach, introduction to Suso, *O.C.*, p. 32: "(...) Rulman Merswin (1307-1382), a layman, banker, and man of affairs, to whom is no doubt due the apocryphal literature attributed for a long time to the Oberland Friend of God: he is therefore, if you like, a pious forger, but in the end he devotes his wealth to the foundation of the Johannites of the Ile vert, at Strasbourg, and withdaws from the world at the age of forty to dedicate himself entirely to the spiritual life." See A. Jundt, *Rulman Merswin et l'Ami de Dieu de l'Oberland. Un problème de psychologie religieuse* (Paris: Fischbacher, 1890); P. Strauch, "Rulman Merswin und die Gottesfreunde" in *Realenzyklopädie fürprotestantische Theologie und Kirche*, vol. 17, Leipzig, 1906, p. 203 *sq.*; J.M. Clark, *The Great German Mystics: Eckhart, Tauler and Suso* (Oxford: Blackwell, 1949) ch. 5; F. Rapp, "Merswin (Rulman)" in *Dictionnaire de spiritualité*, vol. 10, 1979, col. 1056-1058.

68. This legendary character of the mystical literature of the fourteenth century undoubtedly never existed. Since P. Denifle demonstrated his fictional character ("Der Gottesfreund im Oberland und Nikolaus von Basel. Eine kritische Studie" in *Histor.-polit. Blätter*, vol. LXXV, Munich 1875, against C. Schmidt, who identified him with the Begard Nicholas of Basle and published under this name several works attributed to the anonymous author) historians have wondered who is hiding behind this figure and his writings. According to A. Chiquot, "Ami de Dieu de l'Oberland" in *Dictionnaire de spiritualité*, vol. 1, 1937, col. 492, everything inclines one to think that it was Rulman Merswin himself. On this debate, see Dom F. Vandenbroucke, in Dom J. Leclerq and others, *La Spiritualité du Moyen Âge*, p. 475. See also, in addition to the works cited in the previous note, W. Rath, *Der Gottesfreund vom Oberland, ein Menscheitsführer an der Schwelle der Neuzeit: sein Leben geschildert auf Grundlage der Urkundenbücher des Johanniterhauses "Zum Grünen Wörth" in Strasbourg* (Zurich: Heitz, 1930; republished Stuttgart: 1955) to whom H. Corbin gives homage in the fourth volume of *En islam iranien* (Paris: Gallimard, "Bibliotheque des idées," 1978) p. 395, note 2, for having "safeguarded the specific nature of the spiritual fact," without resorting to the hypothesis of the literary hoax. Foucault, who takes the anecdote of the pact of obedience from A. Jundt's book (see the next note), published in 1879, does not distinguish clearly the two characters. In 1890, in *Rulman Merswin et l'Ami de Dieu de l'Oberland*, Jundt replied to Denifle's criticisms, accepting the thesis that the Oberland Friend of God never existed, but rejecting the arguments that tended to establish that the history of the latter was only a deception by Merswin (pp. 69-93).

69. See A. Jundt, *Les Amis de Dieu au quatorzième siècle*, p. 175: "In the Spring of 1352 a solemn pact of friendship was sealed between the two men that was to be so fertile in consequences for their later history. The commitments into which they entered were nonetheless not so unilateral as Rulman Merswin's account seems to suggest [see p. 174, the account of his first meeting with the Oberland Friend of God]. The truth is that they each submitted to the other 'in God's place,' that is to say they promised to mutually uplift each other in everything as though under obedience to God Himself. This relationship of mutual submission lasted for 28 years, until the Spring of 1380."

70. See above, note 13. N. Cohn, however, does not refer to the dissolute life of Jeanne Dabenton.

71. See, "Qu'est-ce que la critique?" pp. 38-39.

72. Joachim of Fiore (c.1132-1202): Cistercian monk born in Calabria. In 1191 he founded a new order, the hermetical Congregation of Fiore, which was approved by the Pope in 1196. Based on an allegorical exegesis of Scripture, his doctrine of "three ages" or "three states" of humanity—the Age of the Father (time of the law and servile obedience, the Old Testament), the Age of the Son (time of grace and filial obedience, the New Testament), and the Age of the Spirit (time of more abundant grace and freedom)—is

set out notably in his *Concorde des deux Testaments* (*Concordia Novi ac Veteris Testamenti*). The advent of the third Age, the fruit of the spiritual intelligence of the two Testaments, had to be the work of spiritual men (*viri spirituales*) for whom the present monks were only the predecessors. For the priestly and hierarchical Church would be substituted the monastic reign of pure charity. See N. Cohn, *The Pursuit of the Millennium*, pp. 99-102; Dom F. Vandenbroucke, in Dom J. Leclerq and others, *La Spiritualité du Moyen Âge*, pp. 324-327.

nine

8 MARCH 1978

*From the pastoral of souls to the political government of
men. ∿ General context of this transformation: the crisis of the
pastorate and the insurrections of conduct in the sixteenth century.
The Protestant Reformation and the Counter Reformation. Other
factors. ∿ Two notable phenomena: the intensification of the religious
pastorate and the increasing question of conduct, on both private
and public levels. ∿ Governmental reason specific to the exercise
of sovereignty. ∿ Comparison with Saint Thomas. ∿ Break-up of
the cosmological-theological continuum. ∿ The question of the art
of governing. ∿ Comment on the problem of intelligibility in
history. ∿ Raison d'État (1): newness and object of scandal.
∿ Three focal points of the polemical debate around raison d'État:
Machiavelli, "politics" (la "politique"), and the "state."*

TODAY I WOULD FINALLY like to move on from the pastoral of souls
to the political government of men. It should be understood, of course,
that I will not try even to sketch the series of transformations that actually brought about the transition from this economy of souls to the government of men and populations. In the following lectures I would like
to talk about some of the overall redistributions that confirmed this
transition. All the same, since it is necessary to pay a minimum of
homage to causality and the traditional principle of causality, I would
just add that this transition from the pastoral of souls to the political
government of men must be situated in a certain familiar context. In the

first place, of course, the context was that of the great revolt, or rather the great series of pastoral revolts in the fifteenth century, and obviously especially in the sixteenth century, of what I call those "insurrections of conduct,"* the most radical form of which, and the form in which they were brought back under control, was the Protestant Reformation. So, there were these insurrections of conduct, whose history, what's more, it would be very interesting to trace.† If the main dimension of the great processes of political and social upheaval at the end of the fifteenth and the beginning of the sixteenth century was insurrections of conduct, we should not forget that this dimension of the revolt of conduct has also always been present in upheavals and revolutionary processes with completely different objectives and stakes. This is still very evident, of course, in the English Revolution of the seventeenth century, in which the explosion of different forms of religious community and religious organization was one of the major axes and one of the great stakes of all the struggles. And still in the French Revolution there was an entire axis, a whole dimension of the revolt or insurrection of conduct, in which the clubs of course played an important role, but which undoubtedly had other dimensions. In the Russian Revolution of 1917 also, there was a whole aspect of insurrections of conduct, [of which]‡ the Soviets, the workers' councils, were one, but only one, expression. It would be interesting to see how these series of insurrections, these revolts of conduct, spread and what effects they have had on revolutionary processes themselves, how they were controlled and taken in hand, and what was their specificity, form, and internal law of development. Well, this would be an entire field of possible research. Anyway, I just want to note that this transition from the pastoral of souls to the political government of men should be situated in this general context of resistances, revolts, and insurrections of conduct.§

Second, we should of course recall the two major types of reorganization of the religious pastoral, either in the form of the different

---

* In inverted commas in the manuscript.
† Foucault adds: for after all there has not been . . . [unfinished sentence]
‡ M.F.: in which
§ M.F.: at the origin of conduct

Protestant communities, or, of course, in the form of the Catholic Counter Reformation. Both the Protestant churches and the Catholic Counter Reformation re-integrated many of the typical elements of those counter-conducts I have talked about. Spirituality, intense forms of devotion, recourse to Scripture, and the at least partial re-qualification of asceticism and mysticism, are all part of a kind of re-integration of counter-conduct within a religious pastorate organized either in the Protestant churches or in the Counter Reformation. Certainly, we should also refer to the great social struggles that drove, sustained, and prolonged these pastoral insurrections. The Peasants' War is an example of this.[1] We should also mention the inability of feudal structures, and of the forms of power connected to them, to cope with these struggles and put an end to them; and of course—this is all very well-known—we should talk again about the new economic, and consequently political relations for which feudal structures were no longer a sufficient and effective framework; and finally we should mention the disappearance of the two great poles of historical-religious sovereignty that dominated the West and promised salvation, unity, and the fulfillment of time, those two great poles of the Empire and the Church that represented a sort of great spiritual and temporal pastorate above princes and kings. The break up of these two great complexes was one of the factors of the transformation I was talking about.

Anyway—and I will bring this brief introduction to an end on this— I think we should note that the pastorate does not disappear in the sixteenth century. There is not even a massive, comprehensive transfer of pastoral functions from Church to state. What we see in reality is a much more complex phenomenon. On the one hand, we can say that there is an intensification of the religious pastorate in its spiritual forms, but also in its extension and temporal efficiency. The Reformation as well as the Counter Reformation gave the religious pastorate much greater control, a much greater hold on the spiritual life of individuals than in the past: an increase in devotional conduct and of spiritual controls, and an intensification of the relationship between individuals and their guides. The pastorate had never before intervened so much, had never had such a hold on the material, temporal, everyday life of individuals; it takes charge of a whole series of questions and problems concerning material life, property, and the education of children. So, there is an intensification of the religious pastorate in its spiritual dimensions and in its temporal extensions.

On the other hand, in the sixteenth century we also see a development of forms of the activity of conducting men outside of ecclesiastical authority, and here again in two aspects, or more exactly in a whole series of aspects that form a wide range, starting from the development of specifically private forms of the problem of conduction: How to conduct oneself, one's children, and one's family? We should not forget that at this time we see the appearance, or rather reappearance, of the function that philosophy had in, let's say, the Hellenistic period, and which had effectively disappeared in the Middle Ages, that is to say, philosophy as the answer to the fundamental question of how to conduct oneself. What rules must one give oneself in order to conduct oneself properly in daily life, in relation to others, in relation to those in authority, to the sovereign or the lord,* and in order to direct one's mind as well, and to direct it in the right direction, to its salvation, certainly, but also to the truth?[2] If Descartes' philosophy is taken as the foundation of philosophy, we should also see it as the outcome of this great transformation that brought about the reappearance of philosophy in terms of the question: "How to conduct oneself?"[3] *Regulae ad directionem ingenii*,[4] *meditationes*,[5] are categories, forms of philosophical practice that reappeared in the sixteenth century as a result of this intensification of the problem of conduct, of the reappearance of the problem of conducting/conducting oneself as a fundamental problem, or at any rate as a result of it taking a form then that was not specifically religious or ecclesiastical.

The theme of conduction also appears in what I will call the public domain. The opposition between the private and the public is still not really pertinent, although it is no doubt the problematization of conduct and the specification of different forms of conduct that begins to establish the opposition between private and public in this period. Anyway, in the public domain, in what will later be called the political domain, the problem also arises of how and to what extent the exercise of the sovereign's power can and must take upon itself these previously unacknowledged

---

* Foucault adds: in order to conduct oneself also in an acceptable and decent way, properly.

tasks of conduction. The sovereign who rules and exercises his sovereignty now finds himself responsible for, entrusted with, and assigned new tasks of conducting souls.* So there was not a transition from the religious pastorate to other forms of conduct, conduction, or directing. In fact there was an intensification, increase, and general proliferation of this question and of these techniques of conduct. With the sixteenth century we enter the age of forms of conducting, directing, and government.

You will see why there is a problem here that assumed an even greater intensity than others in this period, probably because it was precisely at the point of intersection of these different forms of conduction: conduction of oneself and one's family, religious conduction, and public conduction through the concerns or under the control of government. This is the problem of the education of children. The pedagogical problem of how to conduct children—how to conduct them so that they are useful to the city, so that they will be able ensure their salvation, and so that they will be able to conduct themselves—was probably surcharged and over-determined by this explosion of the problem of conduct in the sixteenth century. The education of children was the fundamental utopia, crystal, and prism through which problems of conduction were perceived.[6†]

---

* Given that Foucault is talking about the theme of conduct in the public domain, that is as an exercise of political sovereignty, "conducting souls" may be a slip and should perhaps be read as "conducting men"; G.B.

† Foucault omits here a long passage from the manuscript (pp. 4-6):
"Lay stress on the fact that these counter-conducts did not have as their objective how to get rid of the pastorate in general, of any pastorate, but rather: how to benefit from a better pastorate, how to be guided better, more certainly saved, maintain obedience better, and approach truth better. Several reasons. This: that the pastorate had individualizing effects: it promised the salvation of each and in an individual form; it entailed obedience, but as an individual to individual relationship and it guaranteed individuality by obedience itself; it allowed each to know the truth, better: his truth. Western man is individualized through the pastorate insofar as the pastorate leads him to his salvation that fixes his identity for eternity, subjects him to a network of unconditional obedience, and inculcates in him the truth of a dogma at the very moment it extorts from him the secret of his inner truth. Identity, subjection, interiority: the individualization of Western man throughout the long millennium of the Christian pastorate was carried out at the price of subjectivity. By subjectivation. To become individual one must become subject (in all the senses of "subject"). Now, to the same extent as the pastorate was a factor and agent of individualization, it created a formidable appeal, an appetite for the pastorate: [*some illegible words*] how to become subject without being subjected? Enormous desire for individuality, well before the bourgeois consciousness and radically distinguishing Christianity from Buddhism (absence of the pastorate/mysticism [*an illegible word*], de-individualization). The great crisis of the pastorate and the onslaughts of the counter-conducts that fueled this crisis did not lead to an overall rejection of all forms of conduct, but to an increased pursuit of being conducted, but properly and appropriately? Hence the increase in 'needs of conduct' in the sixteenth century."

Obviously, I do not want to talk about all of this but about the particular point I have touched on, namely: To what extent must whoever exercises sovereign power now be responsible for the new and specific tasks of the government of men? There are two problems straightaway. First, according to what rationality, calculation, or type of thought can one govern men within the framework of sovereignty? So this is a problem of the type of rationality. Second, there is a problem of the domain and objects: What are the specific objects and domains of application of a government of men that is not a government of the Church, of the religious pastorate, and is not government in the private domain, but which is the task and responsibility of the political sovereign? That is to say, according to what rationality must the sovereign govern? And to speak Latin, because you know that I really like speaking Latin, I will say: What must be the *ratio gubernatoria* as distinct from the *ratio pastoralis*?*

Good, governmental reason then. In order to try to explain this a little, I would like to return for a moment to scholastic thought, and specifically to Saint Thomas and the text in which he explains the nature of royal power.[7] It is important to remember that Saint Thomas never said that the sovereign was only a sovereign, that he only had to rule and governing was not one of his tasks. On the contrary, he always said that the king had to govern. He even gives a definition of the king: the king is "he who governs the people of a single city and a single province, and who does so with a view to the common good."[8] The king is the one who governs the people. But what I think is important is that according to Saint Thomas, the monarch's government has no specificity with respect to the exercise of sovereignty. There is no discontinuity, no specificity, and no division between the two functions of being sovereign and governing. On the other hand, Saint Thomas draws support from a whole series of external models, which I will call analogies of government, to define what is comprised by this government that the monarch, the sovereign, must ensure.

What is meant by analogies of government? Insofar as he governs, the sovereign does nothing other than reproduce a model [that] is quite

---

* Foucault adds: Those who know Latin ... *[end of sentence inaudible]*

simply that of God's government on Earth. Saint Thomas explains: In what does the excellence of an art consist? To what extent is an art excellent? An art will be excellent insofar as it imitates nature.[9] Now nature is ruled by God, for God created nature and continues to govern it all the time.[10] The king's art will be excellent insofar as it imitates nature, that is to say, insofar as it operates like God. And just as God created nature, the king will be the founder of the state or city, and just as God governs nature, the king will govern his state, city, or province. So, the first analogy is with God.

The second analogy, the second continuity, is with nature itself. There is nothing in the world, Saint Thomas says, or at any rate no living animal, whose body would not be exposed to loss, separation, and decomposition, if there were not some vital, guiding force within it holding together the different elements of which living bodies are composed and ordering them in terms of the common good. If there were not a living force, the stomach would go its way and the legs another, etcetera.[11] The same applies to a kingdom. Each individual in a kingdom would strive for his own good, since one of man's characteristics, one of his essential features, is precisely that he strives for his own good. Everyone would strive for their own good and thus neglect the common good. Therefore there must be something in the kingdom that corresponds to the vital, guiding force in the organism, and this is the king, who turns each individual's tendency back from his own good towards the common good. "As in any multitude," says Saint Thomas, "a direction is necessary that is responsible for regulating and governing."[12] This is the second analogy, the analogy of the king with an organism's vital force.

Finally, the third analogy, the third continuity is with the pastor and the father of a family, for, Saint Thomas says, the final end of man is evidently not to be rich, nor even is it to be happy on Earth, or in good health. Ultimately, man strives for eternal bliss, the enjoyment of God. What, then, is the royal function? It must procure the common good of the multitude in accordance with a method that can obtain for it heavenly blessedness.[13] To that extent the king's function is not substantially different from that of the pastor with regard to his flock, nor even of the father with regard to his family. In his terrestrial and temporal decisions he must act in such a way that not only is the individual's eternal salvation not compromised, but also that it is possible. With the analogy with God, the analogy with nature, and the analogy with the pastor and father of a family, there is a sort of theological-cosmological continuum in the name of which the sovereign is authorized to govern and which provides models in accordance with which he must govern. If the sovereign can and must govern in the extension and uninterrupted continuity of the exercise of his sovereignty, it is insofar as he is part of this great continuum extending from God to the father of a family by way of nature and the pastors. There is no break therefore. This great continuum from sovereignty to government is nothing else but the translation of the continuum from God to men in the—in inverted commas— "political" order.

In the sixteenth century this great continuum in Saint Thomas's thought, which justifies the king's government of men, is broken. By this I do not want in any way to say that the relationship of the sovereign, or of a person who governs, to God, to nature, to the father of a family, and to the religious pastor is broken. On the contrary, we constantly see [. . .*]. And we will find them laid down all the more precisely inasmuch as they undergo re-evaluation and are established on a different basis and according to a completely different system, because a characteristic feature of political thought at the end of the sixteenth and the beginning of the seventeenth century is precisely the pursuit and definition of a specific form of government with respect to the exercise of sovereignty. Briefly, standing back a bit by means of some grand fictions, let's say that there was a sort of chiasmus, a sort of fundamental crossover. Basically, the astronomy of Copernicus and Kepler, Galileo's physics, the natural history of John Ray,[14] the Port Royal grammar[15] . . . well, one of the major effects of all these discursive practices, all these scientific practices—I am only talking about one of the innumerable effects of these sciences†—was to show that ultimately God only rules the world through general, immutable, and universal laws, through simple and intelligible laws that are accessible either in the form of

---

* Some inaudible words.
† Foucault adds: one of the effects of these new configurations of knowledge (*savoir*).

measurement and mathematical analysis, or in the form of classificatory analysis in the case of natural history, or in the form of logical analysis in the case of general grammar. What does it mean to say that God only rules the world through general, immutable, universal, simple, and intelligible laws? It means that God does not "govern" * the world; he does not govern it in the pastoral sense. He reigns over the world in a sovereign manner through principles.

What is it to govern the world in a pastoral sense? If we refer to what I was saying two weeks ago concerning the specific economy of pastoral power,[16] the specific system bearing on salvation, obedience, and truth, and if we apply this schema to God, then God's pastoral government of the world meant that the world was subject to an economy of salvation, that is to say, that it was made in order for man to earn his salvation. More precisely, it meant that the things of the world were made for man and that man was not made to live in this world, at any rate not definitively, but only in order to pass into another world. The world governed in a pastoral fashion according to a system of salvation was [therefore] a world of final causes that culminated in man who had to earn his salvation in this world. Final causes and anthropocentrism was one of the forms, one of the manifestations, one of the signs of God's pastoral government of the world.

[Second,] pastoral government of the world meant that the world was subject to a system of obedience. Whenever God wished to intervene in the world for any particular reason—for you know that pastoral obedience fundamentally takes the form of the individual relationship—whether with regard to someone's salvation or loss, or in a particular circumstance or conjuncture, he intervened according to the system of obedience. That is to say, he forced beings to show his will through signs, prodigies, marvels, and monstrosities that were so many threats of chastisement, promises of salvation, or marks of election. A pastoral government of nature was therefore a nature peopled by prodigies, marvels, and signs.

Finally, third, a world subject to pastoral government, as in the pastorate, was a world in which there was an entire system of truth: truth

---

* In inverted commas in the manuscript, p. 10.

taught, on the one hand, and truth hidden and extracted on the other. That is to say, in a world subject to a pastoral government there were forms of teaching. The world was a book, an open book in which one could discover the truth, or rather in which truths taught themselves, and they taught themselves essentially in the form of their reciprocal cross-references, that is to say, in the form of resemblance and analogy. At the same time it was also a world in which it was necessary to decipher hidden truths that showed themselves by hiding and hid by showing themselves, that is to say, it was a world that was filled with ciphers to be decoded.

An entirely finalist world, an anthropocentric world, a world of prodigies, marvels, and signs, and finally a world of analogies and ciphers,[17] constitute the manifest form of God's pastoral government of the world. This is what disappeared. When? Precisely between 1580 and 1650, at the same time as the foundation of the classical *episteme*.[18] This is what disappeared, or, if you like, the unfolding of an intelligible nature in which final causes gradually disappear and anthropocentrism is called into question, of a world purged of its prodigies, marvels, and signs, and of a world that is laid out in terms of mathematical or classificatory forms of intelligibility that no longer pass through analogy and cipher, corresponds to what I will call, in short—please excuse the word—a de-governmentalization of the cosmos.

Now in the same period, from 1580 to 1660, the following, completely different theme is developed. The sovereign's exercise of sovereignty over his subjects is not distinguished simply by his extension of a divine sovereignty over Earth that would somehow be reflected in the continuum of nature: he has a specific task to perform that is no-one else's. His task is not that of God in relation to nature, or of the soul in relation to the body, or of the pastor in relation to his flock, or of the father in relation to his children. His task is absolutely specific: it consists in governing, and its model is found neither in God nor in nature. At the end of the sixteenth century, the emergence of the specificity of the level and form of government is expressed by the new problematization of what was called the *res publica*, the public domain or state (*la chose publique*). The sovereign is required to do more than purely and simply exercise his sovereignty, and in doing more than exercise sovereignty he is called upon for something other than God's action in relation to nature, the pastor's in relation to his flock, the father's in relation to his children, or the shepherd's in relation to his sheep. In short, in relation to his sovereignty, and in relation to the pastorate, something more is demanded from him, something different, something else. This is government. It is more than sovereignty, it is supplementary in relation to sovereignty, and it is something other than the pastorate, and this something without a model, which must find its model, is the art of government. When we have found the art of government we will know the rationality in accordance with which we will be able to carry out this operation that is neither sovereignty nor the pastorate. Hence the point at issue, the fundamental question at the end of the sixteenth century: What is the art of government?

Let us summarize all this. On the one hand we have a level at which* nature is severed from the governmental theme. There is now a nature that no longer tolerates government and that only allows the reign of a reason that is ultimately the common reason of God and men. This is a nature that only allows a reason that has fixed once and for all—what? We would not say "laws" (well okay, we see the appearance of the word "law" when we adopt a juridical-epistemological point of view), it is not yet what are called "laws", [but] "principles," *principia naturae*. On the other hand there is a sovereignty over men that is required to take upon itself something specific that is not directly contained in it, which conforms to another model and another type of rationality, and this something extra is government, the government that must seek out its reason. So, on the one hand *principia naturae*, and, on the other, the reason of this government—you are familiar with the expression—*ratio status*. This is *raison d'État*. Principles of nature and *raison d'État*. And since the Italians are always one step ahead of us, and of everyone, they were the first to define *raison d'État*. At the end of the sixteenth century Botero writes:[19] "The state is a firm domination over peoples"—you see that there is no territorial definition of the state, it is not a territory, it

---

* These three words—*niveau par lequel*—are barely audible.

is not a province or a realm, it is only peoples and a firm domination—
"The state is a firm domination over peoples." *Raison d'État*—and he
does not give it the narrow definition that we now give it—"is the
knowledge of the appropriate means for founding, preserving, and
expanding such a domination." However, Botero adds (we will come
back to this later), "this *ragion di stato* embraces preserving the state
much more than its foundation or expansion, and its expansion more
than its foundation strictly speaking."[20] That is to say, he makes *raison
d'État* the type of rationality that will allow the maintenance and preservation of the state once it has been founded, in its daily functioning, in
its everyday management. With *principia naturae* and *ratio status*, principles of nature and *raison d'État*, nature and state, the two great references
of the knowledge (*savoirs*) and techniques given to modern Western man
are finally constituted, or finally separated.

A purely methodological comment. You may say that it's all very well
to point to the appearance of these two elements, their correlation,
crossover, and the chiasmus that takes place, but you do not explain it.
To be sure I do not explain it, for a whole range of reasons. Except, I too
would like to put a question. If explanation means that I am asked to
exhibit the single source from which nature and the state, the separation
of nature and the state, and the separation of the *principiae naturae*
and the *ratio status* would supposedly stem, if in short I were asked to
find the one that divides into two, I would immediately give up. But are
there no other means for constituting the intelligibility that we need to
establish or maybe should establish in history? Must intelligibility arise
in no other way than through the search for the one that splits into two
or produces the two? Could we not, for example, start not from the
unity, and not even from this nature-state duality, but from the multiplicity of extraordinarily diverse processes in which we would find
precisely these resistances to the pastorate and these insurrections of
conduct, in which we would find urban development, the development
of algebra, experiments on falling bodies [...*]? This would involve
establishing the intelligibility of the processes I am talking about by

---

* Two or three inaudible words.

showing phenomena of coagulation, support, reciprocal reinforcement, cohesion, and integration. In short, it would involve showing the bundle of processes and the network of relations that ultimately induced as a cumulative, overall effect, the great duality, both breach and symmetry, of, on one side, a nature that cannot be understood if one assumes it is governed, a nature therefore that can only be understood if we relieve it of pastoral government and, if we want to direct it, in which we recognize only the sovereignty of some fundamental principles, and, on the other side, a republic that can only be maintained if it is endowed with a government, and with a government that goes well beyond sovereignty. At bottom, maybe intelligibility in history does not lie in assigning a cause that is always more or less a metaphor for the source. Intelligibility in history would perhaps lie in something that we could call the constitution or composition of effects. How are overall, cumulative effects composed? How is nature constituted as an overall effect? How is the state effect constituted on the basis of a thousand diverse processes, some of which I have simply tried to point out to you? The problem is discovering how these two effects are constituted in their duality and in terms of the essential opposition between the a-governmentality of nature and the governmentality of the state. There is the chiasmus, the crossover, and the overall, global effect, but this global character is only an effect, and it is on this composition of cumulative effects that historical analysis should be put to work. I do not need to tell you that in all of this, in these few barely sketched methodological reflections, as well as in the general problem of the pastorate and governmentality I have been talking about, I have been inspired and owe a number of things to the works of Paul Veyne—whose book, *Le Pain et le Cirque,* [21] you know, or anyway you really should know—whose study of the phenomena of euergetism in the ancient world is currently the model that inspires my attempt to talk about these problems of the pastorate and governmentality.[22]

So, let's talk about this *raison d'État*, this *ratio status*. Some preliminary remarks. *Raison d'État*, in the full, broad sense that we see emerging in Botero's text, was immediately perceived as an invention, or as an innovation anyway, which had the same sharp and abrupt character as the discovery of heliocentricism fifty years earlier and the later discovery of the law of falling bodies. In other words, it really was seen as something new. This is not a retrospective view, of the kind that one might say: Ah, something finally happened then that is undoubtedly important. No. The contemporaries themselves, that is to say, everyone at the end of the sixteenth and the beginning of the seventeenth century saw that there was a reality, or at any rate something, a problem, that was absolutely new. In an absolutely fundamental text by Chemnitz— under the pseudonym of Hippolite a Lapide, Chemnitz published a text that was actually intended for those negotiating the Treaty of Westphalia,[23] and which dealt with the relations between the German Empire and the different states (the historical background of all this, one of the essential historical backgrounds, is the problem of the Empire and its administration),[24]—and in this text, which appeared in Latin with the title *Ratio status* and was translated into French much later, in 1711 or 1712, so in a different historical context and still concerning the Empire, with the title *Les Intérêts des princes allemands* (the translation seems a distortion, but actually it is not; the *ratio status* is in fact the interest of the German princes), Chemnitz writes, during the peace of Westphalia, 1647-1648: "Every day we hear an infinite number of people speaking of *raison d'État*. Everyone joins in, those buried in the dust of the schools as well as those with the responsibilities of public office."[25] So in 1647 it was still something new, a fashionable novelty. A false novelty, some will say, because, in fact *raison d'État* has always been at work. You only need to read the historians of Antiquity to see that it was only ever a question of *raison d'État* at that time. What does Tacitus talk about? *Raison d'État.*[26] Of what does he show the operations? *Raison d'État.* Hence that extraordinary re-investment of political thought in historical material—[in] the Latin historians and especially Tacitus—in order to see whether one could really find in them a model of *raison d'État* and whether one could extract from these texts a little known, buried secret that was forgotten throughout the Middle Ages and which a good reading of Tacitus would restore to us. Tacitus as the bible of *raison d'État.* Hence the formidable return to history in these years.

Others, on the other hand, said: No, there is something new, a radical novelty, and if we want to know what is happening we should not be looking at the historians, but well and truly around us, or in foreign countries; it is the analysis of contemporary reality that will allow us to determine how *raison d'État* functions [...*]. Here we should cite Chemnitz, because he really is one of the most interesting, the one who clearly saw the relationship between, or at any rate envisaged an analogy between what was taking place in the domain of the sciences and what was taking place in the domain of *raison d'État*. He says: Certainly, *raison d'État* has always existed, if by this we understand the mechanism by which states can function,[27] but an absolutely new intellectual instrument was needed to detect and analyze it, just as we had to wait for the appearance of certain instruments and telescopes before we could see stars that existed but had never been seen. "With their telescopes," says Chemnitz, "modern mathematicians have discovered new stars in the firmament and spots on the sun. With their telescopes, the new *politiques* have discovered what the Ancients did not know or which they carefully hid from us."[28]

Raison d'État is an innovation, therefore, which is immediately perceived as such; it is an innovation and scandal, and just as Galileo's discoveries—there is no point returning to this—provoked the scandal in the field of religious thought that you all know about, so too, in the same way, *ratio status* caused at least as great a scandal. Certainly, the real historical and political functioning of this scandal was completely different inasmuch as behind it all was the problem of the division between the Protestant and Catholic Churches and the problem of the management of states, like France, with sovereigns claiming to be Catholic but in which there was tolerance. What's more, the fact, in France at least, that the most rigorous and ardent supporters of *raison d'État* were people like Richelieu and Mazarin, who maybe were not intensely pious but were at least draped in the purple, meant that the religious scandal provoked by the appearance of the notion, the problem, the question of *raison d'État* was completely different from the case of Galilean physics. There was scandal anyway, to the point that Pope Pius V said that the *ratio status* is not at all *raison d'État*; *ratio status* is *ratio diaboli*, the devil's reason.[29] In France, there was a literature opposed to *raison d'État* which was inspired, on the one hand, by a sort of, I was going to say, fundamentalist

---

* Some inaudible words.

Catholicism, anyway by an ultramontane, pro-Spanish Catholicism, and, [on the other], which was opposed to Richelieu's politics. This series of pamphlets has been organized and studied in depth by Thuau in his book on political thought under Richelieu.[30] I refer you to it and I have just taken from it this quotation of a reverend father Claude Clément, who I think was a Jesuit and linked, but I do not know how far and to what extent, with the Spanish—did he go to Spain, was he just a Spanish agent, I do not know—in any case in 1637 he writes a book entitled, *Machiavellianism's throat cut (Le Machiavélisme égorgé), Machiavellismus jugulatus*, in which he says, at the start: "Reflecting on the sect of the *Politiques*, I do not know what I should say about it, about what I should keep silent, and by what name I should call it. Shall I designate it as a Polytheism? Yes, no doubt, because the *Politique* respects everything and anything only through political reason. Shall I call it Atheism? This would be just, because the *Politique* has a respect for command that determines the sole *raison d'État*; he changes his color and skin and is capable of more transformations than Proteus. Shall I name it [still this sect of the *Politiques*; M.F.] Statolatry? This would be the fairest name. If in his general indifference the *Politique* respects something, it is in order to give men over to I know not what divinity, God, or Goddess that the ancient Greeks invoked with the name of City, the Romans with the name of Republic or Empire, and people today with the name of State. This is the only divinity of the *Politiques*, this is the most just name by which to designate them."[31] There is an immense literature and again you will find it in Thuau, and I will give you just the title of a later text, from 1667, which was written by Raymond de Saint-Martin. The title is simply this: *The True Religion in its true light against all the contrary errors of the atheists, libertines, mathematicians and all the others*[32] *who establish Destiny and Fatality, the pagans, Jews, Mohammedans, heretical sects in general, schismatics, Machiavellians and politiques.*[33]

I would like to hold on to three words in these diatribes. First, the word "Machiavelli," second, the word "*politique*," and third, of course, the word "state." Machiavelli first of all. In a previous lecture[34] I tried to show you that the art of government that was so eagerly sought after in the sixteenth and seventeenth centuries could not be found in Machiavelli for the excellent reason that it was not there, and it was not there precisely because Machiavelli's problem is not the preservation of the state in itself. I think this will be clearer next week when we tackle this problem of *raison d'État* internally. What Machiavelli sought to save, to safeguard, is not the state but the relationship of the Prince to that over which he exercises his domination, that is to say, it is a matter of saving the principality as the Prince's relation of power to his territory or population. So it is something completely different. I do not think there is an art of government in Machiavelli. It remains the case that Machiavelli is at the center of the debate, and my earlier statement that Machiavelli was ultimately rebutted at the time of the art of government should be considerably qualified; things are more complicated and this was ultimately false. He is at the center of the debate with different, sometimes negative, sometimes positive values. In actual fact, he is at the center of the debate throughout this period from 1580 to 1650-1660. He is not at the center of debate insofar as it takes place because of what he said, but insofar as the debate is conducted through him. The debate does not take place because of what he said, and an art of government will not be found through or in him. He did not define an art of government, but an art of government will be looked for in what he said. This phenomenon in which one searches in a discourse for what is taking place, while actually only seeking to force it to say something, is not unique. From this point of view, Marx is our Machiavelli: the discourse does not stem from him, but it is through him that it is conducted.

Well, how is the debate conducted through him? The adversaries of *raison d'État*, the pro-Spanish, anti-Richelieu Catholics, say to the supporters of *raison d'État* and those who are looking for the specificity of an art of government: You claim there is a really autonomous and specific art of government that is different both from the exercise of sovereignty and from pastoral management. But if you take a look, this art of government that you claim exists, that must be found, that is rational, organized for the good of all, and of another type than the laws of God or nature, in actual fact does not exist, it has no substance. At the most it can only define the Prince's whims or interests. However thoroughly you examine your idea of a specific art of government, you will only ever find Machiavelli. You will only find Machiavelli, that is to say, the whims or laws of the Prince. Outside of God, outside of His laws, outside of the

great models given by nature, that is to say, ultimately, by God, and outside of the principle of sovereignty, there is nothing, only the Prince's
whim, only Machiavelli. At this point Machiavelli plays the role of the
counter-example, of critique, of the example of the reduction of the art of
government to nothing other than the salvation, not of the state, but of
the principality. Governmentality does not exist. This is what the adversaries of *raison d'État* mean when they say: You are only Machiavellians.
You will not find this art of government. And on top of all that (this is
what Innocent Gentillet, about whom I have already spoken, says[35]), we
can even say that employing Machiavelli's principles is not only not on
the track of an art of government, but it is a very bad instrument for the
Prince himself who will risk losing his throne and his principality if he
applies them.[36] So, Machiavelli not only allows the reduction of what is
being sought in the specificity of *raison d'État*, but he also shows that it is
immediately contradictory and harmful. And then, even more radically,
there is another argument that consists in saying: Where in fact will we
end up when we do without God and the fundamental principle of
God's sovereignty over the world, nature, and men in order to seek out a
specific form of government? We will end up with the Prince's whims, as
I have [already] said, and then also with the impossibility of justifying
any form of higher obligation. If you remove God from the system and tell
people that one must obey, and that one must obey a government, then in
the name of what must one obey? No more God, no more laws. No more
God, no more obligations. And there is someone who said: "If God does
not exist, everything is permitted." This is not who you think it is.[37] It is
the reverend father Contzen in the *Politicorum libri decem*, the *Book of les
politiques*, of 1620.[38] In 1620 he said*: If God does not exist, everything
is permitted. You can see how the appearance of the questions of the
state, of governmentality, in mid(-nineteenth)† century Russia did not
provoke the same question, the same problem‡. If God does not exist,
everything is permitted. So, God really must exist [...§].

---

* Foucault adds: in terms *[inaudible word]*, since it was in Latin.
† M.F.: seventeenth
‡ Foucault adds: the same *[inaudible word]*
§ The end of the sentence is inaudible (last word: a state).

As for the supporters of *raison d'État*, some will say: In actual fact, we have nothing to do with Machiavelli. Machiavelli does not give us what we are looking for. Machiavelli is actually no more than a Machiavellian, someone who calculates solely in terms of the Prince's interests, and we deny this and him. So you can see that the objection to Machiavelli comes from two sides. It comes from those who criticize *raison d'État* by saying that in the end it is nothing but Machiavelli; and it comes from the supporters of *raison d'État* who say: What we are actually after has nothing to do with Machiavelli; he can be thrown to the dogs. Among the supporters of *raison d'État*, however, some will pick up the challenge and say: Well yes, Machiavelli, at least Machiavelli of the *Commentaries*,[39] if not of *The Prince*, may actually serve us insofar as he tried to identify, without any natural model or theological foundation, the necessary relationships between governors and governed intrinsic to the city. This is the form in which you find some apologists for Machiavelli, obviously not among the adversaries of *raison d'État*, but in some, and only some, of those who are in favor of *raison d'État*. There is Naudé, Richelieu's agent, for example, who writes a work in which he praises Machiavelli,[40] and there is also, in a paradoxically Christian sense, a book by someone called Machon,[41] who explains that Machiavelli is in complete conformity with what is found in the Bible.[42] He does not seek to show that the Bible is full of horrors, but that even in the people led by God and his prophets, there really is an irreducible specificity of government, a certain *ratio status*, a *raison d'État* that functions for itself and outside of any general laws given by God to the world or nature. So, that's it for Machiavelli.*

Second, the word "*politique*." You have seen that in these diatribes against *raison d'État* we [find] the word "*politique*." You will have noticed, [first of all], that the word is always used negatively, and [then] that it does not refer to some thing, domain, or type of practice, but to people. These are "*les politiques*." The *politiques* are a sect, something that

---

* The manuscript (p. 20) gives here an exposition on the theory of the contract as a means of "stopping Contzen's insidious question": "Even if God does not exist, man is obliged. By whom? By himself." Taking Hobbes as an example, Foucault adds: "The sovereign instituted in this way, being absolute, will not be bound by anything. He will therefore be able to be fully a 'ruler' (*gouvernant*)."

smells of or verges on heresy. The word *"politique[s]"* appears then to designate people who share a particular way of thinking, a way of analyzing, reasoning, calculating, and conceiving of what a government must do and on what form of rationality it can rest. In other words, it was not politics (*la politique*) as a domain, set of objectives, or even as a profession or vocation that first appeared in the sixteenth and seventeenth century West, but the *politiques*, or, if you like, a particular way of positing, thinking, and programming the specificity of government in relation to the exercise of sovereignty. As opposed to the juridical-theological problem of the foundation of sovereignty, the *politiques* are those who try to think the form of government rationality for itself. And [it is] just in the middle of the seventeenth century that you see the appearance of politics (*la politique*), of politics understood then as a domain or type of action. You find the word "politics (*la politique*)" in some texts, in particular in the marquis du Chastelet,[43] and also in Bossuet. And you can see that politics is certainly no longer a heresy when Bossuet speaks of "politics drawn from Holy Scripture."[44] Politics ceases being a way of thinking or particular way of reasoning peculiar to some individuals. It really has become a domain, and one that is positively valued insofar as it is fully integrated at the level of institutions, practices, and ways of doing things within the system of sovereignty of the French absolute monarchy. It is precisely Louis XIV who introduces the specificity of *raison d'État* into the general forms of sovereignty. What fixes the absolutely singular place of Louis XIV in this history is precisely that he succeeded in showing, at the level of his practice as well as at the level of the manifest and visible rituals of his monarchy (I will come back to this next week*), the bond and connection between sovereignty and government, and at the same time their specificity and the difference of their level and their form. Louis XIV really is in fact *raison d'État*, and when he says "The State is me," it is precisely this stitching together of sovereignty and government that is being put forward. At any rate, when Bossuet says "politics drawn from Holy Scripture," politics thus becomes something that has lost its negative connotations. It has become

---

* Foucault adds: we will try *[some inaudible words]*
See his comments in the next lecture on the political role of the theater under Louis XIV.

a domain, a set of objects, a type of organization of power. [Finally], it is drawn from Holy Scripture, which means that reconciliation with the religious pastoral or, at any rate, the modality of relations with the religious pastoral has been established. And if we add that in Bossuet this politics drawn from Holy Scripture leads to the justification of Gallicanism, that is to say, that *raison d'État* can be used against the Church, we can see what reversals have been carried out between, on the one hand, the time when anathemas were thrown at the *politiques*, associating them with Mohammedans or heretics, [and], on the other, the bishop of Tours drawing from Holy Scripture the right of Louis XIV to have a politics governed by *raison d'État* that is consequently specific, different from, and indeed opposed to that of the absolute monarchy of the Church. The Empire is indeed dead.

Finally, third, after Machiavelli and politics, the state. (I will be very brief, because I will talk about this at greater length next week.) Obviously, it would be absurd to say that the set of institutions we call the state date from this period of 1580 to 1650. It would be meaningless to say that the state was born then. After all, big armies had already emerged and been organized in France with Francis I. Taxation was established before this, and justice even earlier. So, all these apparatuses existed. But what is important, what we should hold on to, and what is at any rate a real, specific, and incompressible historical phenomenon is the moment this something, the state, really began to enter into reflected practice. The problem is knowing when, under what conditions, and in what form the state began to be projected, programmed, and developed within this conscious practice, at what moment it became an object of knowledge (*connaissance*) and analysis, when and how it became part of a reflected and concerted strategy, and at what point it began to be called for, desired, coveted, feared, rejected, loved, and hated. In short, it is the entrance of the state into the field of practice and thought that we should try to grasp.

What I would like to show you, and will try to show you, is how the emergence of the state as a fundamental political issue can in fact be situated within a more general history of governmentality, or, if you like, in the field of practices of power. I am well aware that there are those who say that in talking about power all we do is develop an internal and circular ontology of power, but I say: Is it not precisely those who talk of the state, of its history, development, and claims, who elaborate on an entity through history and who develop the ontology of this thing that would be the state? What if the state were nothing more than a way of governing? What if the state were nothing more than a type of governmentality? What if all these relations of power that gradually take shape on the basis of multiple and very diverse processes which gradually coagulate and form an effect, what if these practices of government were precisely the basis on which the state was constituted? Then we would have to say that the state is not that kind of cold monster in history that has continually grown and developed as a sort of threatening organism above civil society. What we would have to show would be how, from the sixteenth century, a civil society, or rather, quite simply a governmentalized society organized something both fragile and obsessive that is called the state. But the state is only an episode in government, and it is not government that is an instrument of the state. Or at any rate, the state is an episode in governmentality. That's it for today. Next week I will talk more precisely about *raison d'État*.

1. *Bauernkrieg* (1524-1526): the revolt of German peasants in Swabia, Franconia, Thuringia, Alsace, and the Austrian Alps. This movement, which, in the continuation of fifteenth century peasant revolts, were first of all directed against excesses of the corvée system, usurpation of outbuildings, and the abuse of seigniorial jurisdictions, took on a religious character at the beginning of 1525 under the influence, notably, of the Anabaptists of Müntzer (see above, lecture of 1 March, note 25). The repression undertaken by Catholic and Lutheran princes led to more than 100,000 deaths. See E. Bloch, *Thomas Münzer als Theologe der Revolution* (Berlin: Aufgebau-Verlag, 1960); French translation, *Thomas Münzer, théologien de la Révolution*, trans. M. de Gandillac (Paris: Julliard, 1964); K.G. Walter, *Thomas Munzer (1489-1525) et les luttes sociales à l'époque de la Réforme* (Paris: A. Picard, 1927); M. Pianzola, *Thomas Munzer, ou la Guerre des paysans* (Paris: Le Club français du livre, "Portraits d'histoire," 1958); and E.G. Léonard, *Histoire générale du protestantisme*, vol. 1, pp. 93-97.

2. We should connect this periodization of the history of philosophy with that set out by P. Hadot the previous year in his article "Exercices spirituels," *Annuaire de l'École pratique des hautes études, V^e section*, t. LXXXIV, 1977, p. 68, reprinted in P. Hadot, *Exercices spirituels et Philosophie antique* (Paris: Études augustiniennes, 1981) p. 56; English translation by Michael Chase, "Spiritual Exercises" in *Philosophy as a Way of Life* (Oxford: Blackwell, 1995) p. 107: whereas in its original aspect philosophy appears as "a method for training people to live and look at the world in a new way (...) an attempt to transform mankind," it is in the Middle Ages, with its reduction "to the rank of a 'handmaid of theology' " that it came to be considered as a "purely theoretical and abstract approach." We know the importance this re-reading of ancient philosophy in terms of spiritual exercises will have for Foucault's work from 1980.

3. On this reading of the Cartesian meditations, see "Mon corps, ce papier, ce feu" (1972), *Dits et Écrits*, 2, pp. 257-258; English translation by Geoff Bennington, "My Body, This Paper, This Fire," *Essential Works of Foucault 1954-1984. Volume Two: Aesthetics, Method, and Epistemology*, ed. James Faubion (New York: The New Press, 1998) pp. 405-406 (Cartesian meditation as an exercise modifying the subject himself) and *L'Herméneutique du sujet*, pp. 340-341; *The Hermeneutics of the Subject*, p. 358: "(...) this idea of meditation, not as the game the subject plays with his thought but as the game thought plays on the subject, is basically exactly what Descartes was still doing in the *Meditations*." In 1983, in his long inter-view with Dreyfus and Rabinow, "On the Genealogy of Ethics: An Overview of Work in Progress" (in *Essential Works of Foucault*, 1), Foucault no longer considers Descartes as heir to a conception of philosophy founded on the primacy of the conduct of self, but rather as the first to break with this conception: "(...) we must not forget that Descartes wrote 'medita-tions'—and meditations are a practice of the self. But the extraordinary thing in Descartes's texts is that he succeeded in substituting a subject as founder of practices of knowledge for a subject constituted through practices of the self. (...) In Western culture up to the sixteenth century, asceticism and access to truth are always more or less obscurely linked. (...) After Descartes, we have a nonascetic subject of knowledge" pp. 278-279; French translation by G. Barbeddere and F. Durand-Bogaert, "À propos de la généalogie de l'éthique: un aperçu du travail en cours," *Dits et Écrits*, 4, pp. 410-411.

4. *Regulae ad directionem ingenii/Les Règles pour la direction de l'esprit*, was written by Descartes in 1628 and published after his death in Amsterdam in 1701 (after the appearance of a Flemish translation in 1684) in *R. Descartes opuscula posthuma*. The standard modern edition is that of Ch. Adam and P. Tannery, *Œuvres de Descartes* (Paris: Léopold Cerf, 1908) vol. X, pp. 359-469 (reprinted Paris: Vrin, 1966); English translation, *Rules for the Direction of the Mind*, trans. Dugald Murdoch, in *The Philosophical Writings of Descartes*, trans. J. Cottingham, R. Stootfoff, and D. Murdoch (Cambridge: Cambridge University Press, 1985) vol. 1, pp. 7-78.

5. *Meditationes Metaphysicae* (or *Meditationes de Prima Philosophia in qua Dei existentia et animae immortalitas demonstrantur*) (Paris: Michel Soly, 1641); French translation by the Duc de Luynes, *Les Méditations métaphysiques de Descartes* (Paris: Vve J. Camusat & Le Petit, 1647); Adam and Tannery, *Œuvres de Descartes*, 1904; English translation by John Cottingham, *Meditations on First Philosophy*, in *The Philosophical Writings of Descartes*, trans. John Cottingham, Robert Stoothoff, and Dugald Murdoch (Cambridge: Cambridge University Press, 1984) vol. 2.

6. Maybe we should see in this exposition an allusion to the works of Philippe Ariès, *L'Enfant et la vie familiale sous l'Ancien Régime* (Paris: Plon, 1960; republication, Paris: Seuil, "L'univers historique," 1973; abridged edition, "Points Histoire," 1975); English translation by Robert Baldick, *Centuries of Childhood* (Harmondsworth: Penguin, 1979), who wrote the preface to *La Civilité puérile d'Erasme* (Paris: Ramsay, "Reliefs," 1977) situating the text in the tradition of manuals of courtesy: "These manuscripts of courtesy are in the fifteenth century, for the way of conducting oneself, the equivalent of the compilations of customs for the law; in the sixteenth century they are compilations of customary rules of behavior ("codes of behavior" say R. Chartier, M.-M. Compère, and D. Julia in *L'Éducation en France du XVIe au XVIIIe* [Paris: Sedes, 1976]), which defined how each should conduct himself in every circumstance of everyday life" (p. x). The text by Erasmus in this volume is preceded by a long note by Alcide Bonneau, taken from the edition of Isidore Lisieux (Paris: 1877), on "books of civility since the sixteenth century." See also, on the sources and posterity of the work of Erasmus, N. Elias, *Über den Process der Zivilisation. Soziogenetische und psychogenetische Untersuchungen* (Berne: Francke, 1939); French translation, *La Civilisation des mœurs* (Paris: Calman-Lévy, 1973; republished, Le Livre de Poche, "Pluriel," 1977) pp. 90-140; English translation by Edmund Jephcott, *The Civilizing Process: Sociogenetic and Psychogenetic Investigations* (Oxford: Blackwell, 2000, revised edition). In the article devoted to Ariès after his death in 1984, "Le souci de la vérité," *Dits et Écrits*, 4, Foucault wrote: "Max Weber was interested above all in economic conducts; Ariès was interested in conducts that concern life" p. 647.

7. Saint Thomas Aquinas, *De regno*, in *Opera omnia*, vol. 42 (Rome: 1979) pp. 449-471; English translation by R.W. Dyson in Saint Thomas Aquinas *Political Writings* (Cambridge: Cambridge University Press, 2002).

8. Ibid. Book I, ch. 2, p. 10: "(...) a king is one who rules over the community [*multitudo*] of a city or province, and for the common good."

9. Ibid. Book I, ch. 13, p. 36: "And because it is true that art imitates nature ... it would seem best to infer the duties of a king from the forms of government which occur in nature. Now among natural things there is found both a universal and a particular form of government. The universal form is that according to which all things are contained under the government of God, Who governs all things by his Providence."

10. Ibid. Book I, ch. 14, p. 37: "Now God's work in relation to the world must be considered under two general aspects. First, He made the world; second, He governs the world that He has made."

11. Ibid. Book I, ch. 1, p. 7: "the body of a man and of any other animal would fall apart if there were not some general ruling force to sustain the body and secure the common good of all its parts."

12. Ibid. p. 8: "(...) in every multitude there should be some ruling principle."

13. Ibid. Book I, ch. 16, p. 43: "And because the end of our living well at this present time is the blessedness of heaven, the king's duty is therefore to secure the good life for the community [*multitudo*] in such a way as to ensure that it is led to the blessedness of heaven."

14. See lecture of 25 January, note 34.

15. See lecture of 25 January, note 48.

16. See above, lecture of 22 February, p. 167 *sq.*

17. On this description of the medieval and Renaissance cosmos, see *Les Mots et les Choses*, ch. 2, pp. 32-46; *The Order of Things*, pp. 17-45.

18. Ibid. pp. 64-91; ibid., pp. 58-77.

19. Giovanni Botero (1540-1617), *Della ragion de Stato libri dieci* (Venice: Giolitti, 1589; 4th enlarged edition, Milan: 1598); French translation, *Raison et Gouvernement d'Estat en dix livres*, trans. G. Chappuys (Paris: Guillaume Chaudière, 1599). There have been two recent editions of the work, one edited by L. Firpo (Turin: UTET, "Classici politici," 1948), the other by C. Continisio (Rome: Donzelli, 1997). Reference below is to the latter edition.

20. Botero, *Ragion di stato*, p. 7: "Ragione di Stato si è notizia de' mezzi atti a fondare, conservare e ampliare un dominio. Egli è vero che, sebbene assolutamente parlando, ella si stende alle tre parti sudette, nondimeno pare chepiù strettamente abbracci la conservazione che l'altre, e dall'altre due più l'ampliazione che la fondazione"; French translation, p. 4: "Estat est

une ferme domination sur les peuples; & la Raison d'Estat est la cognoissance des moyens propres à fonder, conserve, & agrandir une telle domination & seigneurie. Il est bien vray, pour parler absolument, qu'encore qu'elle s'estende aux trois susdites parties, il semble ce neantmoins qu'elle embrasse plus estroictement la conservation que les autres: & des autres l'estendue plus que la fondation."

21. P. Veyne, *Le Pain et le Cirque. Sociologie historique d'un pluralisme politique* (Paris: Le Seuil, "L'Univers historique," 1976; republished, "Points Historie," 1995); (Abridged) English translation by Brian Pearce, *Bread and Circuses. Historical Sociology and Political Pluralism* (London: Allen Lane The Penguin Press, 1990).

22. It may seem strange that Foucault renders homage here to a book that is explicitly inserted in the sphere of influence of historical sociology according to Raymond Aron and of which its author avows that he would have written it completely differently if he had then understood the meaning of Foucault's methodology (see, "Foucault révolutionne l'histoire" p. 212; "Foucault Revolutionizes History" p. 154: "(...) I once believed and wrote, wrongly, that bread and circuses were aimed at establishing a relation between the governed the governors, or that they were a response to the objective challenge constituted by the governed"). According to Veyne, to whom I put the question, we should take Foucault's humor into account in his reference to his book. Nevertheless, it is clear that the analysis of euergetism put forward by Veyne ("gifts from an individual to the community" p. 9, or "private liberality for public benefit" p. 20), his distinction between free and statutory forms of *euergesia*, the link established between different practices (patronage, generosity *ob honorem*, and funerary liberalities) and social categories or actors (notables, senators, emperors), and the prominence given to multiple motives (piety, desire to be honored, patriotism), and so forth, could, in Foucault's eyes, constitute the model of a historian's practice which is hostile to a causal type of explanation and concerned with individualizing events. See P. Veyne, *Comment on écrit l'histoire* (Paris: Le Seuil, "L'Univers historique," 1971) p. 70; *Writing History*, p. 91: "The problem of causality in history is a survival of the paleoepistemological era." As D. Defert notes, the nominalist theses developed by Paul Veyne in "Foucault révolutionne l'histoire" (but already present in *Comment on écrit l'histoire*) were discussed by Foucault with the group of researchers who met in his office "during the two years he was dealing with governmentality and liberal political reason" ("Chronologie," *Dits et Écrits*, 1, p. 53).

23. On this treaty, or rather these treaties, which mark the birth of modern political Europe, see below, lecture of 22 March, note 9.

24. Son of a high German functionary, Martin Chemnitz, who had been chancellor of two princes of the Empire, Bogislaw Philipp von Chemnitz (1606-1678) studied law and history at Rostock and Jena. It was in this university that he came under the influence of the Calvinist jurist, Dominicus Arumaeus (1579-1637), considered to be the creator of the science of German public law, the school of which played a determinant role in the critique of the imperial ideology. Having interrupted his studies around 1627, for reasons that remain obscure, Chemnitz served as an officer in the Dutch army, and then in the Swedish army where he followed his army career until 1644, and became the historian of Christine of Sweden. The *Dissertatio de ratione status in Imperio nostro Romano-Germanico* appeared in 1640 under the pseudonym of Hippolithus a Lapide. (The date of publication is in dispute and may be 1642 or 1643. See R. Hoke, "Staatsräson und Reichsverfassung bei Hippolithus a Lapide" in R. Schnur, ed., *Staatsräson. Studien zur Geschichte einen politischen Begriffs* [Berlin: Duncker & Humblot, 1975] pp. 409-410, n. 12 and p. 425; M. Stolleis, *Histoire du droit public en Allemagne, 1600-1800*, p. 303, n. 457 on the state of the discussion.) There have been two French translations of the work, one by Bourgeois du Chastenet, *Interets des Princes d'Allemagne*, 2 volumes (Freistade: 1712), based on the first edition dated 1640, and the other, more complete, by S. Formey, *Les Vrais Intérêts de l'Allemagne*, 3 volumes (The Hague: 1762) based on the second, 1647, edition. Foucault, who here mixes up the dates of the two editions, refers to the first translation. A new edition of the work, by R. Hoke, is in preparation for the "Bibliothek des deutschen Staatsdenkens," edited by H. Maier and M. Stolleis (Frankfurt: Insel Verlag).

25. *Dissertatio*, vol. 1, 1712 edn., p. 1 (1647 Latin edn., p. 1). Cited by E. Thuau, *Raison d'État et Pensée politique à l'époque de Richelieu* (Paris: Armand Colin, 1966; reprinted, Paris: Albin

Michel, "Bibliothèque de l'évolution de l'humanité," 2000) pp. 9-10, n. 2. This is the first sentence of the *Dissertatio* which opens the work ("General considerations of *Raison d'État*"). The translator, however writes: "la poussière de l'école" [in the singular] (*in pulvere scholastico*), an expression directed against the Aristotelianism then dominant in German universities.

26. See E. Thuau, *Raison d'État et Pensée politique*, ch. 2: "L'accueil à Tacite et à Machiavel ou les deux raisons d'État," pp. 33-102. For a problematization of the relations between Tacitus, Machiavelli, and *raison d'État*, see A. Stegman, "Le tacitisme: programme pour un nouvel essai de définition," *Il Pensiero politico*, II (Florence: Olschki, 1969) pp. 445-458.

27. *Dissertatio*, vol. 1, 1712 edn., p. 6 (1647 edn. p. 4): "The cause and origin of *Raison d'État* are those of the state itself where it has taken birth."

28. Ibid. pp. 6-7 (1647 edn., p. 4).

29. Pius V (1504-1572) was elected pope in 1566. The phrase is attributed to him, from the end of the sixteenth century, by many authors. See notably Girolamo Frachetta, *L'Idea del Libro de' governi di Stato e di guerra* (Venice: Damian Zenaro, 1592) p. 44b: "*Ragion di stato* (...) was justly called by Pius V of happy and holy memory, Reason of the Devil." Other examples are given by R. De Mattei, *Il Problema della "ragion di stato" nell'età della controriforma* (Milan-Naples: R. Ricciardi, 1979) pp. 28-29.

30. E. Thuau, *Raison d'État et Pensée politique*. See ch. 3: "L'opposition à la 'raison d'enfer' " pp. 103-152.

31. R.P. Claude Clément (1594-1642/43), *Machiavellismus jugulatus a Christiana Sapientia Hispanica et Austriaca* [The throat of Machiavellianism cut by the Christian Wisdom of Spain and Austria] (Compluti: apud A. Vesquez, 1637) pp. 1-2; quoted by E. Thuau, *Raison d'État et Pensée politique*, pp. 95-96. Foucault slightly modifies the end of the text, which appears in this form: "(...) that the Greeks invoked as the City, the Romans as Republic and Empire, and people today as the State."

32. Original title: *or others* (instead of "*and all the others*").

33. R.P. Raymond de Saint-Martin's book was published at Montauban in 1667. See E. Thuau, *Raison d'État et Pensée politique*, p. 92 and p. 443.

34. See above, lecture of 1 February, pp. 91-92.

35. Ibid. p. 90.

36. E. Thuau, *Raison d'État et Pensée politique*, pp. 62-65.

37. Foucault is alluding to the famous expression of Ivan Karamazov in Dostoevsky's novel, *The Brothers Karamazov* (1879-1880), English translation by Richard Pevear and Larissa Volokhonsky (New York: Farrar, Straus and Gioux), Book 5, ch. 5, "The Grand Inquisitor" p. 263 (see also p. 69).

38. R.P. Adam Contzen, S.J., *Politicorum libri decem, in quibus de perfectae reipublicae forma, vitutibus et vitiis tractatur* (Maguntiae: B. Lippius, 1620) p. 20: "Si Deus non est aut non regit mundum, sine metu sunt omnia scelera" (quoted by E. Thuau, *Raison d'État*, p. 94).

39. Foucault designates by this, of course, Machiavelli's *Discourses on the First Ten Books of Titus Livy* (manuscript, p. 19: "Machiavelli (at least the Machiavelli of the Commentaries on T.L.) sought the autonomous principles of the art of government").

40. Gabriel Naudé (1600-1653), secretary of the cardinal de Bagni at Rome from 1631 to 1641, was recalled to France by Richelieu on the latter's death, then became Mazarin's librarian until 1651. Foucault refers to the *Considérations politiques sur les coups d'État*, published under the author's name ("by G.P.N.") in 1639 (reprinted, Hildesheim: Olms, 1993, with introduction and notes by F. Charles-Daubert). This first edition, limited to a dozen copies, was followed in the seventeenth century by several posthumous editions: in 1667, without indication of place ("on the copy of Rome"); in 1673 at Strasbourg, under the title *Sciences des Princes, ou Considérations politiques sur les coups d'État*, with commentaries by Louis De May, secretary of the Elector of Mainz; in 1676 at Paris (republished Bibliothèque de philosophie politique et juridique de l'Université de Caen, 1989), etcetera. The 1667 text has been re-edited by Louis Marin (Paris: Éditions de Paris, 1988) with an important introduction, "Pour une théorie baroque de l'action politique." See E. Thuau, *Raison d'État*, pp. 318-334.

41. Louis Machon (1603-?), "Apologie pour Machiavelle en faveur des Princes et des Ministres d'Estat," 1643, definitive version 1668 (manuscript 935 of the Bibliothèque of

the town of Bordeaux). This work, composed in the first place under the impulse of Richelieu, remained unpublished, apart from a fragment representing the first third of the final text, published according to a 1653 manuscript in the introduction to the *Œuvres complètes de Machiavel* by J.A.C. Buchon in 1852 (Paris: Bureau du Panthéon littéraire). See E. Thuau, *Raison d'État*, pp. 334-350 (biographical note, p. 334, n. 2); G. Procacci, *Machiavelli nella cultura europea*, pp. 464-473.

42. "My first intention concerning this *Apologie* was to place the text of our *Politique* [Machiavelli] on one side of this book, and those of the Bible, of the doctors of the Church, and of the canonists (. . .) on the other; and to show, without further reasoning or artifice that this great man wrote nothing that may not be drawn word for word, or at least that may not correspond to all that these learned persons have said before him or approved since (. . .)" L. Machon, *Apologie*, 1668 texts, pp. 444-448, quoted by K.T. Butler, "Louis Machon's 'Apologie pour Machiavelle'," *Journal of the Warburg and Courtauld Institutes*, vol. 3, 1939-1940, p. 212.

43. Paul Hay, marquis du Chastelet, *Traitté de la politique de France* (Cologne: Pierre du Marteau, 1699). This work, which strongly displeased Louis XIV, was constantly republished until the end of the seventeenth century and was one of the main sources of inspiration for Vauban's *Dîme royale* (1707). Hay du Chastelet defined politics (*la politique*) in this way (enlarged 1677 edition, same editor, p. 13): "*La Politique* is the art of governing states, the ancients said that it was a royal and very divine science, the most excellent and mistress of all the others, and among the practical disciplines they gave it the same advantage that metaphysics and theology have among the speculative disciplines."

44. Jacques-Bénigne Bossuet (bishop of Meaux, 1627-1704), *Politique tirée des popres paroles de l'Écriture Sainte* (Paris: Pierre Cot, 1709; critical edition by J. LeBrun, Geneva: Droz, "Les Classiques de la pensée politique," 1967); English translation by Patrick Riley, *Politics drawn from the Very Words of Holy Scripture* (Cambridge: Cambridge University Press, 1990).

ten

15 MARCH 1978

[
Raison d'État *(II): its definition and principal characteristics
in the seventeenth century.* ∼ *The new model of historical
temporality entailed by* raison d'État. ∼ *Specific features of* raison
d'État *with regard to pastoral government: (1) The problem of
salvation: the theory of* coup d'État *(Naudé). Necessity, violence,
theatricality.* ∼ *(2) The problem of obedience. Bacon: the question
of sedition. Differences between Bacon and Machiavelli.* ∼ *(3) The
problem of truth: from the wisdom of the prince to knowledge of the
state. Birth of statistics. The problem of the secret.* ∼ *The reflexive
prism in which the problem of the state appeared.* ∼ *Presence-absence
of "population" in this new problematic.*
]

TODAY I WOULD LIKE to talk very quickly about what is understood
by *raison d'État* at the end of the sixteenth and the beginning of the
seventeenth century, making use of texts from Italy (Palazzo), England
(Bacon), France, and again the text by Chemnitz that I talked about last
week[1] and which seems to me to be particularly important. What is
understood by *raison d'État*? I will start by referring to two or three
pages of Palazzo's treatise, published in Italian right at the end of the
sixteenth century, or maybe in the first years of the seventeenth century.[2]
There is a 1606 edition in the [Bibliothèque] Nationale, which may not
be the first, but anyway the French translation, at least the first French
translation, dates from 1611. The treatise is entitled *Discourse on government
and the true raison d'État*, and in the first pages Palazzo simply puts the

question: What should we understand by "reason" and what should we understand by "state"? "Reason," he says—and you will see how, let's say, scholastic, in the banal and trivial sense of the term, all this is—what is "reason"? Well, "reason" is a word used in two senses: Reason is the entire essence of a thing, which constitutes the union, the combination of all its parts; it is the necessary bond between the different elements that constitute a thing.[3] That is reason. But "reason" is also employed in another sense. Subjectively, reason is a certain power of the soul that enables it to know the truth of things, that is to say, precisely that bond, that integrity of the different parts that constitutes a thing. Reason is therefore a means of knowledge, but it is also something that allows the will to adjust itself to what it knows, that is to say, to adjust itself to the very essence of things.[4] So reason will be the essence of things, knowledge of the reason of things, and that kind of force that enables, and up to a point obliges [the will] to go to the very essence of things.[5] So much for the definition of the word "reason."

Now the definition of the word "state." "State," says Palazzo, is a word understood in four senses.[6] A state is a domain,* *dominium*. Second, he says it is a jurisdiction, a set of laws, rules, and customs, if you like, something like what we call—of course, he does not use this word—an institution, a set of institutions. Third, he says (the translator says, whose word I am following here) "state" is a condition of life, that is to say, a kind of individual status, or a profession: the state of magistrate, or the state of celibacy, or the religious state. And finally, fourth, the "state," he says, is something that renders things, if not completely immobile—and here I skip the detail, because, he says, some forms of immobility would be contrary to the thing's rest, and some things must move so as to be able to remain really at rest—in any case this state is a quality that means that the thing remains what it is.

What is the republic? The republic is a state in the four senses I have just given. A republic is first of all a domain, a territory. It is then a milieu of jurisdiction, a set of laws, rules, and customs. If it is not one state, the republic is at least a set of states in the sense of individuals defined by their status. And finally, the republic is a certain stability of

* In French, *domaine*; the original Italian is *dominio*: dominion, property, domain (G.B.).

these three preceding things, domain, jurisdiction, and institution or the status of individuals.[7]

What is "*raison d'État,*" in the two, objective and subjective senses of the word "reason"? Objectively, we will call *raison d'État*, in the four senses of the word "state," that which is necessary and sufficient for the republic to preserve its integrity. Consider the territorial aspect of the republic, for example. If this fragment of the territory, this town within the territory, or this fortress defending it, really is indispensable for maintaining the integrity of the state, then we will say that this element, territory, fragment of territory, citadel, or these towns are part of the *raison d'État*.[8] Now, what is "*raison d'État*" if we consider the [subjective]* side of the word "reason"? Well, it is "a rule or an art"—I am quoting Palazzo's text—"a rule or an art (...) which makes known to us the means for obtaining the integrity, tranquility, or peace of the republic."[9] This formal definition, this scholastic definition in the trivial sense of the word, is not peculiar to Palazzo, and you find it in practically most of the theorists of *raison d'État*. I would like to quote from a much later text by Chemnitz, from 1647.[10] Chemnitz says: What is *raison d'État*? It is "a certain political consideration that is necessary in all public matters, councils and plans, which must strive solely for the preservation, expansion, and felicity of the state, and for which we must employ the most ready and swift means."[11]

You can see that Palazzo's definition, which is confirmed by others, by Chemnitz and many theorists of *raison d'État*, immediately presents some very clear characteristics. In the first place, nothing in this definition refers to anything other than the state itself. There is no reference to a natural order, an order of the world, fundamental laws of nature, or even to a divine order. Nothing of the cosmos, nature, or the divine is present in the definition of *raison d'État*. Second, you can see that this *raison d'État* is strongly articulated around the essence-knowledge (*savoir*) relation. *Raison d'État* is the very essence of the state, and it is equally the knowledge (*connaissance*) that enables us to follow, as it were, the weave of this *raison d'État*, and comply with it. It is therefore an art, with its practical

---

* M.F.: positive

aspect and its aspect of knowledge. Third, *raison d'État* is essentially . . . I was going to say: conservative, let's say: protective. In *raison d'État*, and by *raison d'État*, what is involved is essentially identifying what is necessary and sufficient for the state to exist and maintain itself in its integrity if, in the event of it being damaged, it is necessary to re-establish this integrity. But *raison d'État* is not in any way a principle of the state's transformation, or even of its development I would say. Certainly, you find the word "increase," to which I will return shortly. But this is basically only the increase, the perfecting of features and characteristics that already actually constitute the state and is in no way its transformation. *Raison d'État* is therefore conservative. In the second half of the seventeenth century, the marquis du Chastelet will say that it is a matter of arriving at a "just mediocrity."[12] Finally, and this is doubtless the most typical feature, there is no prior, external purpose, or even a purpose subsequent to the state itself. Certainly, one will speak of felicity. This is in Chemnitz.[13] But to what must this felicity, happiness, and perfection be attributed and related? To the state itself. You recall the way in which Saint Thomas spoke of the nature of the republic and of royal government. Royal government did indeed fall under a particular terrestrial art, but its final objective was to ensure that on leaving their terrestrial status, and freed from this human republic, men can arrive at eternal bliss and the enjoyment of God. This means that, in the end, the art of governing or ruling in Saint Thomas was always organized for this extra-terrestrial, extra-state, I was going to say extra-republican purpose, outside the *res publica*, and, in the last and final instance, it was for this end that the *res publica* had to be organized.[14] There is nothing of this here. The end of *raison d'État* is the state itself, and if there is something like perfection, happiness, or felicity, it will only ever be the perfection, happiness, or felicity of the state itself. There is no last day. There is no ultimate point. There is nothing like a uniform and final temporal organization.

Palazzo immediately raises objections. Were they objections he had encountered or did he think them up himself? It doesn't matter, they are interesting, because Palazzo says: If, in following *raison d'État*, government, the art of government basically has no end foreign to the state itself, if we cannot offer men anything beyond the state, and if *raison d'État* basically has no purpose, can we not dispense with it? Why would men feel obliged to obey a government that offers them no personal end external to the state? Second objection: If it is true that *raison d'État* only has a conservative aim, or at any rate a conservative objective, if these ends are internal to the very maintenance of the state, is it not sufficient for *raison d'État* to intervene simply when the state's existence is compromised by an accident, which may occur in some cases, but not all the time? In other words, should not *raison d'État*, the art of government, and government itself intervene simply when it is a matter of correcting a defect or warding off an immediate danger? So, can we not have a discontinuous government and a *raison d'État* intervening only at certain points and particular dramatic moments?[15] Palazzo answers: Not at all, the republic would not survive for a moment and would have no continuance if it were not reviewed at every moment and maintained by an art of government assured by *raison d'État*. "The republic itself," he says, "would not be able or sufficient to maintain itself in peace for one hour."[16] The weakness of human nature and men's wickedness mean that nothing could be maintained in the republic if there were not at every point, at every moment, and in every place a specific action of *raison d'État* assuring a concerted and reflected government. So, government is always necessary and has been necessary from time immemorial: government as the continuous act of creation of the republic.

I think that this general theme posed by Palazzo in his definition of *raison d'État* is important for several reasons. I will stick to just one of them. With this analysis of *raison d'État* we see the emergence of a historical and political temporality with specific characteristics in comparison with the temporality that dominated the thought of the Middle Ages, and even of the Renaissance, because it is an indefinite temporality, the temporality of a government that is both never-ending and conservative. Consequently, to start with there is no problem of origin, of foundation, or of legitimacy, and no problem of dynasty either. Even Machiavelli's problem of how to govern in view of how one acquired power—one cannot govern in the same way when one has inherited power as when one has usurped or conquered power[17]—no longer arises, or does so only secondarily. The art of government and *raison d'État* no longer pose a problem of origin: we are always already in a world of government, *raison d'État*, and the state.

Second, not only is there no point of origin that is pertinent for modifying the art of government, but the problem of the endpoint must not be posed, and this is undoubtedly more important. This means that the state—*raison d'État* and the government commanded by *raison d'État*—will not have to concern itself with individual salvation. It will not even have to pursue something like the end of history, either as a fulfillment or as the point at which historical time and eternity join together. Consequently there is nothing like the dream of the last Empire that dominated medieval religious and historical perspectives. The time of the Middle Ages was still one that, at a certain moment, had to become unified as the universal time of an Empire in which all differences would be effaced, and this universal Empire will herald and be the theater of Christ's return. The Empire, the last Empire, the universal Empire, whether of the Caesars or of the Church, was something that haunted the medieval perspective, and to that extent there was no indefinite government. There was no state or kingdom destined to indefinite repetition in time. Instead, we now find ourselves in a perspective in which historical time is indefinite, in a perspective of indefinite governmentality with no foreseeable term or final aim. We are in open historicity due to the indefinite character of the political art.

Subject obviously to correction by things to which we will return, the idea of perpetual peace, which already existed in the Middle Ages, but always as an aspect of the final Empire or of the Empire of the Church, replaces, I think, the idea of the final Empire, and whereas in the Middle Ages the final Empire was the fusion of all particularities and kingdoms in a single form of sovereignty, the idea of perpetual peace will be the dream of a link between states that remain states. That is to say, universal peace will not be the consequence of unification in a temporal or spiritual empire, but, if things actually work out, it will be the way in which different states are able to co-exist with each other according to a balance that prevents one dominating the others. Universal peace is the stability acquired in and through a balanced plurality, and is therefore completely different from the idea of the final Empire. This idea of an indefinite governmentality will subsequently be corrected by the idea of progress, that is, by the idea of progress in man's happiness. But this is another matter that precisely implies something that you will note is absent from this analysis, namely the notion of population.

Having said this, in order to situate the general horizon of *raison d'État* I would now like to continue with some of the features of the government of men that is no longer practiced as pastoral art therefore, but where the key theme is *raison d'État*. I do not want to make an exhaustive analysis, but—I was going to say, some surveys, but the word is unfortunate—some sections (*coupes*), that's all, by relating *raison d'État* to some of the important themes we have come across in the analysis of the pastorate, that is to say, the problems of salvation, obedience, and truth.

I will take the precise example of the theory of *coup d'État* to study the way in which salvation is thought, reflected, and analyzed by *raison d'État*. The *coup d'État* is a very important notion at the start of the seventeenth century, and entire treatises were devoted to [it]. For example, in 1639 Naudé writes *Considérations sur les coups d'État*.[18] Some years earlier there was Sirmond's more polemical text, the *Coup d'État de Louis XIII*,[19] which was more immediately linked to events, but which was not at all a polemic against Louis XIII, [quite] the opposite. For at the beginning of the seventeenth century the term "*coup d'État*" did not in any way signify someone's seizure of the state at the cost of those who had previously held it and are then dispossessed. The *coup d'État* is something else entirely.* What is the *coup d'État* in political thought at the start of the seventeenth century? In the first place it is a suspension of, a temporary departure from, laws and legality. The *coup d'État* goes beyond ordinary law. *Excessus iuris communis*, says Naudé.[20] Or again, it is an extraordinary action against ordinary law, an action retaining no order or form of justice.[21] Is the *coup d'État* foreign to *raison d'État* in this? Is it an exception with regard to *raison d'État*? Absolutely not, because, and I think this is an essential point to note, *raison d'État* and a system of legality or legitimacy are not in any way homogeneous. What is *raison d'État*? Well, Chemnitz says, for example, it is something that allows departure from all "the public, particular, and fundamental laws of whatever kind they may be."[22] In fact, *raison d'État* must command, not by "sticking to the laws," but, if necessary, it must command "the laws themselves, which must adapt to the present state of the republic."[23]

---

* William King's 1711 translation of Naudé's work renders *coups d'état* as "master-strokes of state"; G.B.

So, the *coup d'État* does not break with *raison d'État*. It is an element, an event, a way of doing things that, as something that breaches the laws, or at any rate does not submit to the laws, falls entirely within the general horizon, the general form of *raison d'État*.

But what, then, is specific in the *coup d'État* that makes it more than just one expression among others of *raison d'État*? Well, *raison d'État*, which by its nature does not have to abide by the laws, and which in its basic functioning is always exceptional in relation to public, particular, and fundamental laws, usually does respect the laws. It does not respect them in the sense of yielding to positive, moral, natural, and divine laws because they are stronger, but it yields to them and respects them insofar as, if you like, it posits them as an element of its own game. In any case, *raison d'État* is fundamental with regard to these laws, but it makes use of them in its usual functioning precisely because it deems them necessary or useful. However, there will be times when *raison d'État* can no longer make use of these laws and due to a pressing and urgent event must of necessity free itself from them. In the name of what? In the name of the state's salvation. It is this necessity of the state with regard to itself that, at a certain moment, will push *raison d'État* to brush aside the civil, moral, and natural laws that it had previously wanted to recognize and had incorporated into its game. Necessity, urgency, the need to save the state itself will exclude the game of these natural laws and produce something that in a way will only be the establishment of a direct relationship of the state with itself when the keynote is necessity and safety. The *coup d'État* is the state acting of itself on itself, swiftly, immediately, without rule, with urgency and necessity, and dramatically. The *coup d'État* is not therefore a takeover of the state by some at the expense of others. It is the self-manifestation of the state itself. It is the assertion of *raison d'État*, of [the *raison d'État*] that asserts that the state must be saved, whatever forms may be employed to enable one to save it. The *coup d'État*, therefore, is an assertion of *raison d'État*, and a self-manifestation of the state.

I think there are a number of important elements in this locating of the notion of the state. In the first place, there is this notion of necessity. There is then a necessity that is over and above the law. Or rather, the law of this reason peculiar to the state, and which is called *raison d'État*, is that the state's salvation must prevail over any other law. This fundamental law of necessity, which at bottom is not a law, thus goes beyond all natural law, positive law, and even the law of God's commandments, which the theorists dare not call exactly divine law, but call instead "philosophical," so as to mask things a little. Naudé will say: The *coup d'État* does not comply with "natural, universal, noble and philosophical justice" (the word "noble" is ironic and the word "philosophical" covers something else), it complies with "an artificial, particular, political justice (...) concerning the necessity of the state."[24] Politics, therefore, is not something that has to fall within a form of legality or a system of laws. Politics is concerned with something else, although at times, when it needs them, it uses laws as an instrument. Politics is concerned with necessity. You find a whole kind of, not philosophy, but, how to put it . . . praise and glorification of necessity in political writings at the start of the seventeenth century. Someone like Le Bret, for example, will say: "So great is the force of necessity that, like a sovereign goddess, having nothing sacred in the world but the firmness of its irrevocable decrees, it ranks everything divine and human beneath its power. Necessity silences the laws. Necessity puts an end to all privileges in order to make itself obeyed by everyone" (which is quite strange in relation to the scientific thought of the time, and in direct opposition to this thought).[25] So, we do not have government connected with legality, but *raison d'État* connected with necessity.

The second important notion is, of course, that of violence. For the nature of the *coup d'État* is to be violent. The usual, habitual exercise of *raison d'État* is not violent precisely because it readily avails itself of laws as its framework and form. But when necessity demands it, *raison d'État* becomes *coup d'État*, and then it is violent. This means that it is obliged to sacrifice, to sever, cause harm, and it is led to be unjust and murderous. As you know, this principle is completely at variance with the pastoral theme that the salvation of each is the salvation of all, and the salvation of all is the salvation of each. We now have a *raison d'État* for which the pastoral will be one of selection and exclusion, of the sacrifice of some for the whole, of some for the state. In a phrase taken up by Naudé, Charron said: "To retain justice in big things it is sometimes necessary to turn away from it in small things."[26] As a fine example of the necessary violence of *coups d'État*, Chemnitz cites Charlemagne's actions against the Saxons when he made war [on them] and occupied their territories. Chemnitz says that Charlemagne established judges to suppress Saxon revolt and agitation, and the first peculiarity of these judges was that they were unknown to the public, so one did not know who one's judges were. Second, these judges judged without knowledge of the facts, that is to say, without doing anything to establish the facts held against those they sentenced. Third, their judgment did not take the form of a trial, that is to say, there was no judicial ritual. In other words, for Chemnitz this is a polite way of saying that Charlemagne planted assassins among the Saxons, who killed whomsoever they wished, as they wished, and without giving a reason. Whom did they have to kill? Disturbers of the public peace and of the state. We could also have analyzed the idea of crimes of state, because this is a very important notion that appeared and took on very particular dimensions at this time. Chemnitz says, certainly there were injustices and innocents were sentenced in Charlemagne's *coup d'État*, but the system did not last and the Saxons' fury was restrained.[27] So, the *coup d'État* is violent. Now as the *coup d'État* is nothing other than the manifestation of *raison d'État*, we arrive at the idea that there is no antinomy between violence and reason, in things concerning the state at least. Creating an opposition— which you will no doubt recognize if you read the article by Genet in *Le Monde* last September[28]—an anonymous text from the first half of the seventeenth century (written under Richelieu) said that one must distinguish between violence and brutality, because brutality is violence "committed only on the whim of particular individuals," while acts of violence "committed by the wise in concert" are *coups d'État*.[29] Bossuet also took up the contrast between brutality and violence, and Genet in turn, simply reverses the tradition and calls the violence of the state brutality, and calls violence what the seventeenth century theorists called brutality.

After necessity and violence, I think the third important notion is the necessarily theatrical character of the *coup d'État*. In fact, insofar as a *coup d'État* is the irruptive assertion of *raison d'État*, it must be recognized immediately. It must be recognized immediately according to its real features, by extolling the necessity that justifies it. But to win support, and so that the suspension of laws with which it is necessarily linked do not count against it, the *coup d'État* must break out in broad daylight and in so doing reveal on the very stage where it takes place the *raison d'État* that brings it about. No doubt the *coup d'État* must hide its preparatory processes and moves, but it must appear solemnly in its effects and in the reasons that defend it. Hence the need to stage the *coup d'État*, and we find this in the political practice of the period as, for example, in the day of the Dupes,[30] the arrest of the prince,[31] and the imprisonment of Fouquet.[32] All of this means that the *coup d'État* is a particular way for the sovereign to demonstrate in the most striking way possible the irruption of *raison d'État* and its prevalence over legitimacy.

We touch here on an apparently marginal problem that I think is nevertheless important, and this is the problem of theatrical practice in politics, or again the theatrical practice of *raison d'État*. The theater, theatrical practice, this dramatization, must be a mode of manifestation of the state and of the sovereign as the holder of state power. In contrast with and in opposition to traditional ceremonies of royalty, which, from anointment to coronation up to the entry into towns or the funerals of sovereigns, marked the religious character of the sovereign and articulated his power on religious power and theology, I think we could set this modern kind of theater in which royalty wanted to be shown and embodied, with one of its most important manifestations being the practice of the *coup d'État* carried out by the sovereign himself. So there is the appearance of a political theater along with, as the other side of this, the function of theater in the literary sense as the privileged site of political representation, and of representation of the *coup d'État* in particular. For after all, a part of Shakespeare's historical drama really is the drama of the *coup d'État*. Corneille, even Racine, are only ever representations . . . well, I exaggerate saying that, but quite often, almost always, they are representations of *coups d'État*. *Andromaque*[33] and *Athalie*[34] are *coups d'État*. Even *Bérénice* is a *coup d'État*.[35] I think Classical drama is basically organized around the *coup d'État*.[36] Just as in politics *raison d'État* manifests itself in a kind of theatricality, so theater is organized around the representation of this *raison d'État* in its dramatic, intense, and violent form of the *coup d'État*. We could say that the court, as organized by Louis XIV, is precisely the point of articulation, the place where *raison d'État* is dramatized in the form of intrigues, disgraces, preferences, exclusions, and exiles, and also the place, precisely, where the theater represents the state itself.

In a few words, at a time when the quasi-imperial unity of the cosmos is breaking up, when nature is being made less dramatic, freed from the event and from the tragic, I think something like the reverse of this is taking place in the political order. In the seventeenth century, at the end of the wars of religion—precisely at the time of the Thirty Years War, ever since the great treaties, the great pursuit of the European balance—a new historical perspective opens up of indefinite governmentality and the permanence of states that will have neither final aim nor term, a discontinuous set of states appears doomed to a history without hope since it has no term, states that are not organized by reference to a reason whose law is that of a dynastic or religious legitimacy, but rather by reference to the reason of a necessity that it must face up to with *coups* that, although they must always be concerted, are always risky. State, *raison d'État*, necessity, and risky *coups d'État* will form the new tragic horizon of politics and history. At the same time as the birth of *raison d'État*, I think a certain tragic sense of history is born that no longer has anything to do with lament for the present or the past, with the lament of the chronicles, which was the form in which the tragic sense of history had previously appeared, but is linked rather to political practice itself, and, in a way, the *coup d'État* brings this tragedy into play on the stage of reality itself. In an astonishing text in which he gives his definition or description of the *coup d'État*, Naudé describes this tragedy of the *coup d'État*, of history, and of a governmentality that has no term but can only appear, when necessary, in this theatrical and violent form. You will see that there is something very Napoleonic in this text, something that quite remarkably makes one think of Hitlerian nights, of the night of the long knives. Naudé says: "(...) with *coups d'État*, we see the thunderbolt before we hear it rumbling in the clouds"; in *coups d'État* "Matins are said before the bells are rung, the execution precedes the sentence; everything becomes Jewish; (...) who thought to strike receives the blow, who thought himself safe dies, another suffers what he never dreamed of, everything is done at night, in the dark, in the fog and shadows."[37] To the great promise of the pastorate, which required every hardship, even the voluntary ones of asceticism, there now succeeds this theatrical and tragic harshness of the state that in the name of its always threatened and never certain salvation, requires us to accept acts of violence as the purest form of reason, and of *raison d'État*. That is what I wanted to say about the problem of salvation with regard to the state, simply from the point of view of the *coup d'État*.

And now, second, the problem of obedience. Here I will take a completely different question and a completely different text. The question is that of revolts and sedition, which until the end of the seventeenth century were, of course, a major political problem, and for which there is a quite remarkable text written by the Lord Chancellor Francis Bacon,[38] whom no one studies any more and who is certainly one of the most interesting figures at the start of the seventeenth century. I am not much in the habit of giving you advice concerning university work, but if any of you wanted to study Bacon, I don't think that you would be wasting your time.[39]

So, Bacon writes an essay entitled "Of Seditions and Troubles."[40] In this essay he gives a complete description, a quite remarkable analysis— I was going to say, a physics—of sedition and the precautions to be taken against it, and of government of the people. First, sedition should not be seen as extraordinary so much as an entirely normal, natural phenomenon, immanent as it were to the life of the *res publica*, of the republic. Seditions, he says, are like tempests, they arise precisely when they are least expected, in the greatest calm, in periods of stability or equinox. In moments of equality and calm, something may very well be brewing, or rather being born, or swelling like a tempest.[41] The sea secretly swells, he says, and it is precisely this way of signaling, this semiotics of revolt that must be worked out. How can we locate the possible formation of sedition in a period of calm? Bacon, and here I am going very quickly, gives some signs. First, rumors, that is to say the circulation of libels, pamphlets, and discourses against the state and those who govern. Second, what I will call a reversal of values, or anyway of evaluations. Whenever the government does something praiseworthy, it is taken badly by the malcontents. Third, the poor circulation of orders, which is seen in two things: first, in the tone adopted by those in the chain of command. That is to say, those passing on orders speak timidly and those receiving them speak boldly. Well, one should watch out when this reversal of tone occurs. Another thing concerning the circulation of orders is the problem of interpretation, when the person who receives an order, instead of receiving it and executing it, begins to interpret it and insert his own discourse, as it were, between the injunction he receives and the obedience that should normally follow it.[42]

So much for the signs that come from below and seem to prove that a tempest is brewing, even at times of the equinox and calm. Then there are signs that come from above, and it is also necessary to pay attention to these. The first is when the great and the powerful, those around the sovereign, those who are his officers or close to him, clearly show that they are not obeying the sovereign's orders so much as their own interest, and that they are acting on their own initiative. Instead of being, as Bacon says, "like planets that move quickly on the impulse of the first mover," the sovereign in this case, the great are like planets lost in a sky without stars, going no matter where, or rather going where they will instead of being held in the orbit fixed for them.[43] Finally, the prince gives another sign, in spite of himself, when he cannot, or no longer wants to take a point of view either external to or above the different contending parties struggling with each other within the republic, but spontaneously takes the side of one party and supports their interests against the others. Thus, he says, when Henry III took the side of the Catholics against the Protestants, he should have taken care that in so doing he clearly showed that his power was such that it no longer conformed to the dictates of *raison d'État* but simply followed the reason of a party and thus gave the clear sign to everyone, both the great and the people, that his power was weak and consequently one could revolt.[44]

So, seditions have signs. They [also] have causes, and here again, in a scholastic way if you like, anyway in a very traditional way, Bacon says: There are two sorts of causes of seditions, material and occasional.[45] The material causes of sedition are not difficult, Bacon says, and there are not many, only two. The material of seditions is in the first place poverty, or at least excessive poverty, that is to say, a level of poverty that ceases to be bearable. And, Bacon says, "rebellions arising from the belly are the worst of all."[46] The second material of sedition, apart from the belly, is the head, that is to say, discontent. This is a phenomenon of opinion, of perception, and Bacon stresses that this is not necessarily correlative with the first, that is to say, with the condition of the belly. One may well be discontented when there is no great poverty, for the phenomena of discontent may arise for a number of reasons and causes—to which we will come back—which do not correspond with reality itself. In fact, Bacon says, one of the properties, one of the characteristics of the naivety of the people is to be indignant with regard to things that are not worth troubling about and to accept things that should not be tolerated.[47] But things being what they are, one must take account of both the belly and the head, of poverty and the state of opinion. Hunger and opinion, belly and head, are the two materials of sedition. They are, Bacon says, like two inflammable materials, that is to say, these two conditions, the belly and opinion, are absolutely indispensable for sedition.[48]

As for the [occasional]* causes, these are like burning elements falling on the combustible material. What is more, we do not have a clear knowledge of where they come from and it may be anything. Bacon lists these occasional causes without giving them any order. It may be a change in religion, a modification in the distribution of privileges, an upheaval in the laws and customs, a change in the tax regime, the fact that the sovereign promotes unworthy people to important posts, the presence and too evident enrichment of too many strangers, or it may the be scarcity of grain or means of subsistence and a rise in prices. In any case, Bacon says, it is all that which "by offending unites."[49] That is to say, there are occasional causes of sedition when previously separated and indifferent elements are brought to a level of conscious discontent, when the same type of discontent is produced in different people, which, as a result, leads them to unite despite the divergence of their interests.

So, sedition has causes. It also has remedies. One absolutely must not apply these remedies to the series of occasional causes, since these latter are very numerous, and if this or that occasional cause is suppressed, there will always be another to ignite the inflammable material. In reality, remedies must be brought to bear on the inflammable materials, that is to say, on the belly or the head, or on poverty and discontent. I am going

---

* Word omitted.

very quickly, but what I think is interesting is the actual nature of these proposed remedies. Remedies against poverty: the removal of want and poverty, Bacon says, involves the repression of luxury and the prevention of idleness, vagrancy, and begging. It involves the promotion of internal trade and increasing the circulation of money by reducing the rate of interest, avoiding excessively large estates, raising living standards— well, he does not use this expression, but says: it is better that many people spend little than that few spend a great deal[50]—promoting exter- nal commerce by increasing the value of raw materials through work, and assuring provision of transport to foreign countries. It is necessary too, he says, to balance population and the resources available to the state. It is also necessary to balance the proportions between the pro- ductive population and non-productive parts of the population constituted by the clergy and the powerful. So all this must be done to prevent, to extinguish the material cause of revolt constituted by poverty.[51]

A whole series of techniques and processes are also needed on the side of discontent. Bacon says that there are basically two categories of indi- viduals within the state. There are the common people and the nobility. Now, in fact, there is only real and really dangerous sedition when the common people and the nobility unite. For the people in itself, he says, is too slow and will never engage in revolt unless instigated by the nobility. As for the nobility, being obviously few in number, it is weak, and it will remain weak as long as the people are not disposed to unrest. A slow people and a weak nobility mean that sedition can be prevented and discontents stopped from contaminating each other. Now, Bacon says, there is basically no real problem when we consider things on the side of the grand and the nobility because one can always come to an arrange- ment with them. One either buys them or executes them.[52] A noble is beheaded, or he betrays his cause, so a noble is always on our side and will not be the problem. However, the discontent of the people is a much greater, much more serious problem, and more difficult to resolve. One must see to it, first of all, that the people's discontent never arrives at a point where its only outlet is explosion in revolt and sedition. Second, one must ensure that the people, which is slow and can do nothing by itself, never finds a leader in the nobility. It is therefore necessary always to establish a breach, a rivalry of interests, between the nobility and the people so as to prevent a coagulation of discontents.[53]

I have quoted all this, in fact, because I think if we compare this text with Machiavelli's, which in some respects it resembles, a difference between them soon becomes apparent. We should note straightaway that Bacon refers to Machiavelli and cites him with praise.[54] Notwithstanding this, I think we can see the difference. What was the problem posed by Machiavelli? Basically it was the problem of the Prince in danger of being dispossessed. What should the Prince do to avoid being dispossessed? So the question raised by Machiavelli was basically the acquisition or loss of the principality. Here, rather, the problem of the dispossession of the king, the possibility that he may be driven out and lose his kingdom, is never evoked.[55] What is evoked instead is a sort of constantly present possibility within the state that in some way belongs to the daily life of states, or at any rate belongs to the intrinsic virtualities of the state. This virtuality is sedition and riot. The possibility of sedition and riot is something with [which] one must govern. And one aspect of government will precisely be taking responsibility for this possibility of riot and sedition.

Second, Machiavelli clearly distinguished between what arises from the people and what from the nobles. It is also a Machiavellian idea that one should take good care that the discontent of the nobility and the discontent of the people never go hand in hand and reinforce each other.[56] But for Machiavelli the essential danger came from the nobles, from the Prince's enemies anyway, from those who schemed and plotted.[57] For Machiavelli, the people were essentially passive and naive and had to be the instrument of the Prince or else they would be the instrument of the nobles. The problem was the debate between the Prince and his external or internal rivals, those who formed military alliances against him and those who wove internal plots against him. You can see that the nobles are not the problem for Bacon. The problem is the common people. For Bacon, the people are equally naive as they are for Machiavelli. But for the state it is precisely the people who must be the object of government. When, as with Machiavelli, it was a matter of maintaining a principality, one could think of the nobles and rivals. Now that it is a matter of governing according to *raison d'État*, one must think about the people and have them constantly in mind. The problem for government is not the Prince's rivals but the people, for, once again, the nobles are either bought or beheaded. They are close to the government, whereas the people are both close and distant. The people are really difficult and really dangerous. Governing will basically be governing the people.

The third difference between Bacon and Machiavelli is that Machiavelli's calculations seem to me to be brought to bear on, how to put it? . . . the Prince's real or apparent attributes. Machiavelli's problem is whether the Prince should be just or unjust. Should he appear to be just or unjust? How should he appear to be fearsome? How should he hide his weakness?[58] What is at stake in Machiavellian calculation is basically always the Prince's epithets. With Bacon, on the contrary, we are dealing with a calculation that does not bear on the Prince's epithets, on his real or apparent attributes. It is a calculation that concerns both crucial and real elements, that is to say—and I refer to Bacon's proposed remedies for seditions—the economy. The calculation of government, says Bacon, must be brought to bear on wealth, its circulation, duties, taxes, and so forth, all of which must be the object of government. It is a calculation that concerns the elements of the economy, and it is also a calculation concerning opinion, that is to say, not how the Prince appears, but what is going on in the minds of the governed. I think the two major elements of reality that government will have to handle are economy and opinion.

Implicit in this, barely sketched out in Bacon, is in actual fact the political practice of the time, since it is from this period that we see the development of, on the one hand, a politics of economic calculation with mercantilism, which is not theory but above all and essentially a political practice, and [on the other hand] the first great campaigns of opinion that are a feature of Richelieu's government in France. Richelieu invented the political campaign by means of lampoons and pamphlets, and he invented those professional manipulators of opinion who were called at the time "publicistes."[59] Birth of the économistes, birth of the publicistes. Economy and opinion are the two major aspects of the field of reality, the two correlative elements of the field of reality that is emerging as the correlate of government.

Finally, third, there is the problem of *raison d'État* and truth. I will be very quick, because an hour has gone by and these are things that are much more familiar, although they are absolutely essential. Just like the pastorate, the *ratio status*, the rationality intrinsic to the art of government, involves a production of truth, but its circuits and types are very different from those of the pastorate. You recall that in the pastorate there first had to be a taught truth. In the system of truth of the pastorate, the pastor had to know what he passed on to his community. Then each of the pastor's sheep had to discover a truth in himself that he brings to light and of which the pastor is, if not the judge and guarantor, then at least the constant witness. This was the characteristic cycle of truths of the pastorate. There will also be a field of truth with *raison d'État* and this new way of governing men, but clearly it will be of an entirely different type. First of all, at the level of content, what must be known in order to be able to govern? I think we see an important phenomenon here, an essential transformation. In the images, the representation, and the art of government as it was defined up to the start of the seventeenth century, the sovereign essentially had to be wise and prudent. What did it mean to be wise? Being wise meant knowing the laws: knowing the positive laws of the country, the natural laws imposed on all men, and, of course, the laws and commandments of God himself. Being wise also meant knowing the historical examples, the models of virtue, and making them rules of behavior. On the other hand, the sovereign had to be prudent, that is to say, to know in what measure, when, and in what circumstances it was actually necessary to apply this wisdom. When, for example, should the laws of justice be rigorously applied, and when, rather, should the principles of equity prevail over the formal rules of justice? Wisdom and prudence, that is to say, in the end an ability to handle laws.

At the start of the seventeenth century I think we see the appearance of a completely different description of the knowledge required by someone who governs. What the sovereign or person who governs, the sovereign inasmuch as he governs, must know is not just the laws, and it is not even primarily or fundamentally the laws (although one always refers to them, of course, and it is necessary to know them). What I think is new, crucial, and determinant is that the sovereign must know those elements that constitute the state, in the sense that Palazzo, in the text with which I began, spoke of the state. That is to say, someone who governs must know the elements that enable the state to be preserved in its strength, or in the necessary development of its strength, so that it is not dominated by others or loses its existence by losing its strength or relative strength. That is to say, the sovereign's necessary knowledge (*savoir*) will be a knowledge (*connaissance*) of things rather than knowledge of the law, and this knowledge of the things that comprise the very reality of the state is precisely what at the time was called "statistics."* Etymologically, statistics is knowledge of the state, of the forces and resources that characterize a state at a given moment. For example: knowledge of the population, the measure of its quantity, mortality, natality; reckoning of the different categories of individuals in a state and of their wealth; assessment of the potential wealth available to the state, mines and forests, etcetera; assessment of the wealth in circulation, of the balance of trade, and measure of the effects of taxes and duties, all this data, and more besides, now constitute the essential content of the sovereign's knowledge. So, it is no longer the corpus of laws or skill in applying them when necessary, but a set of technical knowledges that describes the reality of the state itself.

Technically, of course, this knowledge of the state raised a great many difficulties. And we know that statistics were first developed in smaller states, or where there was a favorable situation, as in Ireland, for example, where in view of the smallness of the country and its military occupation by England it was possible to know exactly what was there and what its resources were.[60] Statistics also develops in the small German states,[61] since the units of research, so to speak, were smaller. Because of these technical difficulties it was also necessary to think about an administrative apparatus that did not yet exist but which would be such that it would be possible to know exactly what is taking place in the realm at any moment, an administrative apparatus which would not just be the agent for executing the sovereign's orders, or for raising the taxes, wealth, and men needed by the sovereign, but one that at the same time

---

* In the manuscript, p. 23, Foucault writes: "*Statistik*." On the origin of this word, which dates from the eighteenth century, see below, this lecture, note 61.

would be an apparatus of knowledge, and here again, as an essential dimension of the exercise of power.[62]*

We could add other elements to this, such as the problem of the secret, for example. Actually, the knowledge that the state must develop of itself, and on the basis of itself, would be in danger of losing some of its effects and not having its expected consequences if everyone were to know what was going on. In particular, the state's enemies and rivals must not know the real resources available in terms of men, wealth, and so on, hence the need for secrecy. Consequently, inquiries are needed that are in a way coextensive with the exercise of administration, but a precise codification of what can be and what must not be published is also necessary. At the time this was an explicit part of *raison d'État* called the *arcana imperii*, the secrets of power,[63] and for a long time statistics in particular were considered as secrets of power not to be divulged.[64]

Finally, third, and still in this domain of the practice of truth, there is the problem of the public. That is to say, *raison d'État* must act on the consciousness of people, not just to impose some true or false beliefs on them, as when, for example, sovereigns want to create belief in their own legitimacy or in the illegitimacy of their rival, but in such a way that their opinion is modified, of course, and along with their opinion their way of doing things, their way of acting, their behavior as economic subjects and as political subjects. This work of public opinion will be one of the aspects of the politics of truth in *raison d'État*.[†]

---

* In the manuscript, p. 24, after analyzing the "content" of the knowledge required by *raison d'État*, Foucault rapidly describes the "form":
(1) "continuous inquiries and reports," first of all, allowing the constitution of a "specific knowledge (*savoir*) continuously arising in the exercise itself of government power, which is coextensive with it, lights its way at each step, and indicates not what must be done, but what exists [and] what is possible. The knowledge that was previously demanded for politics was the product of practical reason. It was always 'what to do' (in terms of skill, prudence, wisdom, and virtue). Essentially prescriptive, articulated on the basis of *exemplum*, from which positive/ negative advice was drawn. Now, government will cram itself with a factual, contemporary knowledge articulated around a reality (the state), with a field of possibility and impossibility around it. The state: that instance of the real that defines the possibilities of government"; (2) the secret: "this knowledge of forces (real + possibility) is in many cases only an instrument of government on condition of not being divulged." Only this second point is taken up in the lecture.
† The manuscript, p. 25, adds: "The public as subject-object of a knowledge (*savoir*): subject of a knowledge that is 'opinion' and object of a knowledge that is of a different type, since it has opinion as its object and the question for this knowledge of the state is to modify opinion, or to make use of it, to instrumentalize it. We are far from the 'virtuous' idea of communication between monarch and subjects in the shared knowledge of human, natural, and divine laws. Far too from the 'cynical' idea of a prince who lies to his subjects the better to establish and preserve his power."

In saying all this, it is clearly understood that in no way have I wanted to undertake the genealogy of the state itself or the history of the state. I have simply wanted to show some sides or edges of what we could call the practico-reflexive prism, or just simply the reflexive prism, in which the problem of the state appeared in the sixteenth century, at the end of the sixteenth and the beginning of the seventeenth century. It is a bit as if I were to say to you: My aim has not been to give you the history of the planet Earth in terms of astrophysics, but to give you the history of the reflexive prism that, at a certain moment, allowed one to think that the Earth was a planet. It is the same kind of thing, but with a difference however. The difference is that when one simply does the history of the sciences, of the way in which we learned, the way in which we constituted a knowledge (*savoir*) in which the Earth appears as a planet in relation to the sun, then it is quite clear that in doing a history like that one is doing the history of a completely autonomous and independent series that has nothing to do with the evolution of the cosmos itself. It goes without saying that the fact that since a certain point in time we have known that the Earth is a planet has had no influence on the Earth's position in the cosmos. However, the appearance of the state on the horizon of a reflected practice at the end of the sixteenth and the beginning of the seventeenth century has been of absolutely capital importance in the history of the state and in the way in which the institutions of the state actually crystallized. The reflexive event, the set of processes by which the state effectively entered into the reflected practice of people at a given moment, the way in which, at a given moment, the state became for those who governed, for those who advised the governors, for those who reflected on governments and the action of governments as they saw it [. . .*], was without a doubt not the absolutely determinant factor in the development of the state apparatuses, which in truth existed well before—the army, taxation, justice all existed well before—but it was absolutely essential, I think, for the entry of all these elements into the field of an active, concerted, and reflected practice that was, precisely, the state. We cannot speak of the

---

* Part of the sentence unfinished.

state-thing as if it was a being developing on the basis of itself and imposing itself on individuals as if by a spontaneous, automatic mechanism. The state is a practice. The state is inseparable from the set of practices by which the state actually became a way of governing, a way of doing things, and a way too of relating to government.

So I have tried to isolate this kind of reflexive prism and I will now end by making just one remark (I would like to make others, but I will keep quiet and make them next week). In this analysis of *raison d'État*, as seen from the angle of salvation and the *coup d'État*, from the angle of obedience and submission, and from the angle of truth, the inquiry, and the public, there is nonetheless an element that is both . . . I was going to say, present and absent—present in a way, but even more absent than present, and this element is the population. The population is present inasmuch as if we ask what the purpose of the state is, and if the reply is that it is the state itself, but the state itself inasmuch as this state must be happy and prosperous, etcetera, then we can say that the population, as the subject or object of this felicity, is faintly sketched out. When one speaks of obedience, and the fundamental element of obedience in government is the people who may engage in sedition, you can see that the notion of "population" is virtually present. When one speaks of the public on whose opinion one must act in such a way as to modify its behavior, one is already very close to the population. But I think population as a really reflected element, the notion of population, is not present and is not operative in this first analysis of *raison d'État*. For example, when Chemnitz defines *raison d'État*, he says "felicity of the state" and never "felicity of the population."[65] It is not men who must be happy or prosperous, and ultimately it is not men who must be rich; it is the state itself. This is in fact one of the fundamental features of mercantilist politics at this time. The problem is the wealth of the state and not that of the population. *Raison d'État* is a relationship of the state to itself, a self-manifestation in which the element of population is hinted at but not present, sketched out but not reflected. Similarly, when, with Bacon, one speaks of seditions, of poverty and discontent, we are very close to population, but Bacon never envisages the population as constituted by economic subjects who are capable of autonomous behavior. One will speak of wealth, the circulation of wealth, and the balance of trade, but one will not speak of population as an economic subject. And with regard to truth, when theorists of *raison d'État* lay stress on the public and the need for a public opinion, the analysis is conducted, as it were, in purely passive terms. It is a question of giving individuals a certain representation, an idea, of imposing something on them, and not in the least of actively making use of their attitudes, opinions, and ways of doing things. In other words, I think *raison d'État* really did define an art of government in which there was an implicit reference to the population, but precisely population had not yet entered into the reflexive prism. From the beginning of the seventeenth to the middle of the eighteenth century there is a series of transformations thanks to which and through which this notion of population, which will be a kind of central element in all political life, political reflection, and political science from the eighteenth century, is elaborated. It is elaborated through an apparatus (*appareil*) that was installed in order to make *raison d'État* function. This apparatus is police. It is the intervention of this field of practices called police that brings to light this new subject in this, if you like, general absolutist theory of *raison d'État*. Well, this is what I will try to explain to you next time.

1. See previous lecture, 8 March, pp. 240-241.
2. Giovanni Antonio Palazzo, *Discorso del governo e della ragion vera di Stato* (Naples: for G.B. Sottile, 1604). We know almost nothing about this author, other than that he followed the profession of lawyer for a time in Naples, without great success, and was secretary to the lord of Vietri, Don Fabrizio Di Sangro. His book was translated twice into French: *Discours du gouvernement et de la raison vraye d'Estat*, by Adrien de Vallières (Douai: printed by De Bellire, 1611) and *Les politiques et vrays remèdes aux vices volontaires qui se comettent ez cours et republiques* (Douai: printed by B. Bellère, 1662). It was also translated into Latin: *Novi discursus de gubernaculo et vera status ratione nucleus, ab Casparo Janthesius*, by Casparo Janthesius (Danzig: sumptibus G. Rhetii, 1637).
3. *Discours du gouvernement*, Part I, ch. 3 ("Of *raison d'État*") p. 13: "Reason is often taken for the essence of each thing, which is nothing other than the entire being of the thing that consists in the union of all the parts."
4. Ibid.: "Further reason signifies the intellectual power of the soul, which understands and knows the truth of things, and well and duly regulates the will in its actions."
5. Ibid.: "Reason thus being understood in its first signification is the entire essence of things, and in the other it is a just rule of the same things and a measure of our operations." See also, IV, 17, p. 363.
6. Ibid. I, 2 ("Of the state of the republic, and of princes, final cause of government") pp. 10-11, and IV, 17 ("Of *raison d'État*") p. 362. The second text is both more concise and precise so we quote it in full: "We use the word state to signify four things. First, it signifies a limited place of the domain (*dominio*), which being exercised in it cannot go beyond its borders. Second, state signifies the same jurisdiction, which is called state, insofar as the prince strives to conserve it and to render it always firm and stable; thus such a state is nothing other than a constant and stable domain of the prince. Third, state signifies a permanent choice of life, either not to marry, to be religious, or to marry; or truly it signifies a choice of office, of art, and of exercise, which are differently named degree (*grado*) and condition, and this choice is called state, for that the man must be immutable in it and constant in the observation of its rules and reasons introduced for its firmness. Finally state signifies a quality of things contrary to movement. For just as it is always the property of imperfect things that they are now and afterwards are no longer, are now good and now bad, now of one quality and then of another, this being caused by the contrariness and distinction of the same things; similarly to the contrary peace is nothing other than a rest, a perfection and an establishment of the same things, caused by their simplicity and union raised to a same end, already acquired; and from this property of rendering things firm and stable, this rest comes to be called state."
7. Ibid. I, 2; IV, 18-21.
8. Ibid. I, 3, pp. 13-14: "First, *raison d'État* is the entire essence of things and all that is required by all the arts and offices in the republic. This description can be verified by examples, for if some province or town fails, or a castle of the kingdom is occupied, the integrity of its essence will cease. And for this we can and must use suitable means for restoring it in its entirety, and this usage and employment of means is done for *raison d'État*, that is to say for its integrity."
9. Ibid. p. 14: "But according to the other meaning, I say that *raison d'État* is a rule and an art that teaches and observes the due and suitable means for obtaining the artisan's intended end, which definition is verified in government; for it is this that makes known to us the means, and teaches us their exercise, for obtaining the tranquility and good of the republic (. . .)."
10. On this dating, see the previous lecture, 8 March, note 24.
11. B. Chemnitz, *Interets des Princes d'Allemagne*, 1712 edition, vol. 1, p. 12 (Latin 1647 edition, p. 8). Some pages before, Chemnitz criticizes Palazzo's definition—"*raison d'État* is a rule and a level with which we measure every thing, and which leads them to the end to which they must be taken"—as "too general and obscure" to explain clearly the nature of *raison d'État* (ibid. p. 10; 1647 edition, pp. 6-7). Foucault is therefore only justified in saying that Chemnitz confirms this definition by adopting a point of view external to the academic debates on the meaning of the term.

12. Paul Hay, marquis du Chastelet, *Traité de la politique de France*, 1677 edition, pp. 13-14: "The means of Politics consist in the exact observance of Religion, being just in all things, acting in such a way that the people can maintain themselves in time, and ridding the State of poverty and Wealth, maintaining a just and praiseworthy mediocrity."

13. The 1712 translation, quoted by Foucault above—"a certain political consideration that we must have in all public matters, in all councils and plans, and which must strive solely for the preservation, increase, and felicity of the state, for which we must employ the most ready and swift means" (p. 12)—distorts the Latin text, which defines *raison d'État* as a certain political point of view, to which, as to a rule, every decision and action in a republic referred, in order to attain the supreme end, which is the safety and growth of the republic (*summum finem, qui est salus & incrementum Reipublicae*), by most felicitous (*felicius*) and swift means. "Felicity" pertains therefore to the means rather than the ends.

14. See the previous lecture, pp. 232-234.

15. Giovanni Antonio Palazzo, *Discours du gouvernement*, I, 5 ("Of the necessity and excellence of government") pp. 28-29.

16. Ibid. p. 31: "(...) now our Prince being our Captain and leader (Fr., *conducteur*; It., *duce*) in this war of the world, the republic has continual need of him, for the wicked disorders to be put right are infinite. It would not be much if he did not have to conserve with great vigilance the health that the republic has acquired; for otherwise the disorders of men will be so many that the republic itself would be neither able nor sufficient to maintain itself in peace for the space of one hour."

17. See Machiavelli, *The Prince*, ch. 2-7.

18. See previous lecture, 8 March, note 40.

19. Jean Sirmond (1589-1649), *Le Coup d'Estat de Louis XIII* (Paris: 1631). See E. Thuau, *Raison d'État et Pensée politique*, pp. 226-227 and 395. This lampoon is part of the *Recueil de diverses pièces pour servir à l'Histoire* [1626-1634] composed by Hay du Chastelet in 1635 (Paris).

20. G. Naudé, *Considérations politiques sur les coups d'État* (1667) ch. 2, p. 93 and p. 103 (1988, p. 99 and p. 101). See E. Thuau, *Raison d'État et Pensée politique*, p. 324. Naudé applies to *coups d'État* this definition that he contrasts right at the start to Botero's definition of *raison d'État*: "(...) which accords less with my view than those who define it, *excessum juris communis propter bonum commune* (Abuse of common law for the sake of the common good)"; "Coups d'État (...) can go under the same definition that we have already given to the Maxims and to *raison d'État, ut sint excessus juris communis propter bonum commune*." This definition is taken from Scipion Ammirato (1531-1600), *Discorsi sopra Cornelio Tacito* (Fiorenza: G. Giunti, 1594) XII, 1; French translation, *Discours politiques et militaires sur C. Tacit*, trans. L. Melliet (Rouen: Jacques Caillove) VI, 7, p. 338: "*Raison d'État* is nothing other than a contravention of ordinary reasons for the sake of the common good, or (...) of a greater and more universal reason."

21. G. Naudé, *Considérations politiques*, p. 103 (1988, p. 101), immediately after the definition given above: "(...) or so that I am a bit better understood in French, *bold and extraordinary actions that Princes are constrained to execute in difficult and desperate circumstances, in breach of common law, without even keeping to any method or form of justice, risking particular interests for the public good*." See Thuau, *Raison d'État et Pensée politique*, p. 324.

22. B. Chemnitz, *Interets des Princes d'Allemagne*, vol. 1, pp. 25-26: "*Raison d'État* held within the bounds we have just been talking about (Religion, faithfulness, honesty, and justice) does not recognize any others: the public, particular, or fundamental laws, or of whatever other kind they may be, do not hinder it at all; and when it is a matter of saving the state, it can boldly depart from them."

23. Ibid. p. 26: "(...) it is necessary to command, not by following the laws, but commanding the laws themselves, which must adapt to the present state of the republic, and not the state to the laws."

24. G. Naudé, *Considérations politiques*, ch. 5, pp. 324-325 (1988, pp. 163-164). The passage concerns justice, the second virtue of the counselor-minister, along with strength and prudence: "But inasmuch as this natural, universal, noble and philosophical justice is sometimes out of use and inconvenient in the practical world, in which *veri juris germanaeque justitiae solidam & expressam effigiem nullam tenemus, umbria & imaginibus utimur* [we have no solid and distinct effigy of the true law and of true justice, we make use of

their shadows], it will often be necessary to make us of the artificial, particular, and political kind, made and adapted to the needs and the necessity of Police and States, since it is loose and soft enough to accommodate itself like the Lesbian rule to human and popular weakness, and to diverse times, people, affairs, and accidents." See E. Thuau, *Raison d'État et Pensée politique*, p. 323. These formulae are taken almost literally from Charron, *De la sagesse* (1601) (Paris: Fayard, 1986) III, 5, p. 626, as A.M. Battista notes in "Morale 'privée' et utilitarisme politique en France, au XVIIe" (1975), in C. Lazzeri and D. Reynié, *Le Pouvoir et la raison d'État* (Paris: PUF, "Recherches politiques," 1992) pp. 218-219.

25. Cardin Le Bret (1558-1655), *De la souveraineté du roi, de son domaine et de sa couronne* (Paris: 1632); see E. Thuau, *Raison d'État et Pensée politique*, pp. 275-278, and p. 396 for the quotation taken from R. von Albertini, *Das politische Denken in Frankreich zur Zeit Richelieus* (Giessen: Bruhl, 1951) p. 181.

26. G. Naudé, *Considérations politiques*, ch. 1, p. 15 (1988, p. 76): "Many hold that the wise and well-advised Prince must not only command according to the laws, but command the laws themselves if necessity requires it. To retain justice in big things, says Charron, it is sometimes necessary to turn away from it in small things, and in order to do right overall, it is permissible to cause harm in detail." See E. Thuau, *Raison d'État et Pensée politique*, p. 323. The quotation from Charron is taken from the treatise *De la sagesse*.

27. B. Chemnitz, *Interets des Princes d'Allemagne*, vol. 1, pp. 27-28: "It is true that these people sometimes committed injustices, and that this way of punishing the criminals was not too good in itself, since the innocent could be included among the guilty. Also this arrangement did not last for long and was only suffered for as long as was thought necessary in relation to the fury of the Saxons that could only be restrained in such an extraordinary way."

28. J. Genet, "Violence et brutalité" (With reference to the "Rote Armee Fraktion"), *Le Monde*, no. 10137, 2 September 1977, pp. 1-2. Asserting right at the start that "violence and life are roughly synonymous," Genet wrote: "(...) putting violence on trial is brutality. And the greater the brutality, the more infamous the trial, the more violence becomes urgent and necessary. The more peremptory the brutality, the more demanding will be the violence of life, calling even for heroism." He concluded the first part of his article thus: "We are indebted to Andreas Baader, Ulrike Meinhof, Holger Meine, and the R.A.F. in general, for having made us understand, not only with words, but through their actions, outside prison and in prison, that only violence can bring an end to men's brutality." The reference to this text is all the more interesting in that it may appear as an apology for terrorism ("[the word] 'terrorism' [...] should be applied as much, if not more to the brutalities of bourgeois society"), against the "casual leftists," the offspring by May 1968, described as angelic, spiritualist, and humanist—"heroism," Genet writes, "is not within the reach of any militant whomsoever"—whereas Foucault, from 1977, clearly registered his hostility towards every form of terrorist action ("I did not accept the terrorism and the blood, I did not approve of Baader and his gang" he will later confide to Claude Mauriac. See C. Mauriac, *Les Temps immobile* (Paris: Grasset, 1986) vol. IX, p. 388, cited by D. Eribon, *Michel Foucault* (Paris: Flammarion, 1989) p. 276.

29. *La Vérité prononçant ses oracles sans flatteries*, cited by E. Thuau, *Raison d'État et Pensée politique*, p. 395: "Acts of violence are brutality when committed only on the whim of a particular individual, when committed by the wise in concert, they are *coups d'État*."

30. 11 September 1630 when the "dupes" were Richelieu's adversaries who thought they were the victors when it was nothing of the kind. Louis XIII, who was ill, had promised Marie de Médicis, Gaston d'Orléans, and Anne of Austria, who were in league with each other, to dismiss the cardinal, but after a meeting with the latter at Versailles he changed his mind and handed over his enemies to him (*Petit Robert des noms propres*, 1996, p. 630).

31. Possible allusion to the arrest of the prince of Condé, who was close to members of the Fronde after the peace of Rueil in 1649.

32. In 1661. Superintendant of Finances from 1653, Nicolas Fouquet (1615-1680?) acquired a prodigious fortune. Accused of embezzlement, he was confined in the dungeon of Pignerol after a long trial tainted with irregularities.

33. Jean Racine, *Andromaque* (1668), in *Théâtre complet*, ed., Maurice Rat (Paris: Garnier, 1960) pp. 112-171.

34. *Athalie* (1691), ibid., pp. 648-715.

35. *Bérénice* (1671), ibid., pp. 296-350.

36. Compare these remarks with those Foucault makes in 1976 on the political function of the tragedies of Shakespeare, Corneille, and Racine in *"Il faut défendre la société,"* lecture of 25 February 1976, pp. 155-157; *"Society Must Be Defended,"* pp. 174-177.

37. G. Naudé, *Considérations politiques*, p. 105 (1988, p. 101). See E. Thuau, *Raison d'État et Pensée politique*, p. 324.

38. Francis Bacon (1561-1626), Lord Verulam, Privy Councillor in 1616, Lord Keeper of the Great Seal in 1617, and then Lord Chancellor from 1618 to 1621 when, accused of taking bribes, he was stripped of his posts.

39. Has this advice been taken? The study of Bacon has enjoyed an important expansion in France since the end of the 1970s, with the translation of the *Essais* (Aubier, 1979), *La Nouvelle Atlantide* (Payot, 1983; GF, 1995), *Novum Organum* (PUF, 1986), *De dignitate et augmentis scientiarum/Du progrès et de la promotion des savoirs* (Gallimard, "Tel," 1991), and *La Sagesse des Anciens* (Vrin, 1997).

40. This essay, not included in the first two editions of the *Essays* (1597 and 1612), appears in the third edition published in 1625 (London: printed by John Haviland) one year before Bacon's death.

41. F. Bacon, *The Essays or Counsels Civil and Moral*, ed. Brian Vickers (Oxford: Oxford University Press) "Of Seditions and Troubles": "Shepherds of people had need know the calendars of tempests in state, which are commonly greatest, when things grow to equality; As natural tempests are greatest about the *Equinoctia*. And as there are certain hollow blasts of wind and secret swellings of seas before a Tempest, so are there in States" p. 31.

42. Ibid. pp. 31-32.

43. Ibid. pp. 32-33: "For the motions of the greatest persons in a government ought to be as the motions of the planets under *Primum Mobile* (according to the old opinion), which is, that every of them is carried swiftly by the highest motion, and softly in their own motion. And therefore, when great ones, in their own particular motion, move violently, (...) it is a sign the orbs are out of frame."

44. Ibid. pp. 31-33. Allusion to the attitude of the Catholic League, after the peace of Monsieur (1576), that it judged too favorable to the Huguenots. It pushed Henry III to resume the war against the latter, while aiming to dethrone him to the advantage of their head, Duke Henri de Guise. The king had him killed in 1588, after the day of the Barricades, in Paris, where the League had risen up in his support.

45. This distinction appears in a less scholastic form in Bacon's original text, which speaks of "the Materials of Seditions; Then, (...) the Motives of them," ibid. p. 33.

46. Ibid. p. 33: "(...) the rebellions of the belly are the worst."

47. Ibid.: "And let no prince measure the danger of them by this, whether they be just or unjust. For that were to imagine people to be too reasonable, who do often spurn at their own good; Nor yet by this, whether the griefs, whereupon they rise, be in fact great or small; for they are the most dangerous discontentments, where the fear is greater than the feeling."

48. Ibid. p. 32: "(...) the surest way to prevent seditions (if the times do bear it) is to take away the matter of them. For if there be fuel prepared, it is hard to tell whence the spark shall come that shall set it on fire. The matter of seditions is of two kinds; much poverty and much discontentment."

49. Ibid. p. 34: "(...) whatsoever in offending people, joineth and knitteth them in a common cause."

50. Ibid. "For a smaller number, that spend more and earn less, do wear out an estate sooner than a greater number, that live lower and gather more."

51. Ibid. pp. 33-35 [See above, lecture of 25 January 1978, note 13; G.B.].

52. The text does not exactly say this (p. 36): "(...) which kind of persons are either to be won and reconciled to the state, and that in a fast and true manner; or to be fronted with some other of the same party, that may oppose them, and so divide the reputation." The remedy proposed, as the following sentence clarifies, is therefore that of "the dividing and breaking of all factions," and not of executing the leaders.

53. Ibid. pp. 35-36.
54. Ibid. p. 32: "(...) as Machiavel noteth well; when princes that ought to be common parents, make themselves as a party and lean to a side, it is as a boat that is overthrown by uneven weight on the one side." There then follows the example of Henry III.
55. See, however, p. 32, concerning the example of Henry III: "(...) when the authority of princes, is made but an accessary to a cause, and that there be other bands that tie faster than the band of sovereignty, kings begin to be put almost out of possession."
56. See *The Prince*, ch. 9.
57. On the danger of conspiracies, see ibid., ch. 19.
58. Ibid. ch. 15-19.
59. See E. Thuau, *Raison d'État et Pensée politique*, pp. 169-178, on the "government of minds" according to Richelieu and the employment of the principle "to govern is to create belief (*faire croire*)."
60. Foucault is alluding to the works of William Petty (1623-1684), founder of political arithmetic, *Political Arithmetick or a Discourse Concerning, The Extent and Value of Lands, People, Buildings: Husbandry, Manufacture, Commerce, Fishery, Artizans, Seamen, Soldiers; Publick Revenues, Interest, Taxes, Superlucration, Registries, Banks Valuation of Men, Increasing of Seamen, of Militia's, Harbours, Situation, Shipping, Power at Sea, &c. As the same relates to every Country in general, but more particularly to the Territories of His Majesty of Great Britain, and his Neighbours of Holland, Zealand, and France* (London: R. Clavel, 1691) in Sir William Petty, *The Economic Writings*, vol. 1, ed., C.H. Hull (Cambridge: Cambridge University Press, 1899); French translation, by Dussauze and Pasquier, in *Les Œuvres économiques de William Petty*, vol. 1, pp. 263-348. After establishing the cadaster of the island, Petty, who was employed as a doctor in the government of Ireland, was asked to divide up the land taken from the Catholics and distribute it to the English troops and their sponsors. From this experience came his work, *The Political Anatomy of Ireland* (London: D. Brown, 1691) in *The Economic Writings*, vol. 1; French translation, *L'Anatomie politique de l'Irlande*, in *Œuvres économiques*, vol. 1, pp. 145-260.
61. On the development of German statistics, see V. John, *Geschichte der Statistik*, pp. 15-154. The most representative works of this tradition are the writings of H. Conring devoted to the "notitia rerum publicarum," *Opera*, vol. IV (Braunschweig: F.W. Meyer, 1730), and Gottried Achenwall's treatise, *Notitiam rerum publicarum Academiis vindicatum* (Göttingen: J.F. Hager, 1748), to which we owe the invention of the word *Statistik* in 1749. See, R. Zehrfeld, *Hermann Conrings (1606-1681) Staatenkunde. Ihre Bedeutung für die Geschichte der Statistik unter besonderer Berücksichtigung der Coringischen Bevölkerungslehre* (Berlin and Leipzig: W. De Gruyter, 1926), and F. Felsing, *Die Statistik als Methode er politischen Ökonomie im 17. und 18. Jahrhundert* (Leipzig: 1930).
62. See below, pp. 317-318.
63. This concept, which goes back to Tacitus, was introduced into the modern political vocabulary by Bodin in *Methodus ad facilem Historiarum cognitionem* (Paris: apud Martinum Juvenem, 1566) ch. 6; French translation by P. Mesnard, *La Méthod de l'histoire* (Paris: PUF, 1951); English translation by Beatrice Reynolds, *Method for the Easy Comprehension of History* (New York: Columbia University Press, 1945). The first major treatise devoted to this theme is that of the German jurist, Arnold Clapmar (Clapmarius), *De arcanis rerum publicarum* (Bremen: 1605, republished Amsterdam: apud Ludovicum Elzevirium, 1644).
64. See, for example, the anonymous manuscript of Colbertian inspiration, *Discours historique à Monseigneur le Dauphin sur le Gouvernement intérieur du Royaume* (1736): "The more the forces of the state are unknown, the more they deserve respect" (cited by E. Brian, *La Mesure de l'État*, [Paris: Albin Michel, "L'Évolution de l'humanité," 1994] p. 155). This tradition of the secret of the administration, as Brian shows, extends up to the second half of the eighteenth century.
65. See above, note 13.

eleven

22 MARCH 1978

> Raison d'État *(III)*. ∼ *The state as principle of intelligibility and as objective.* ∼ *The functioning of this governmental reason: (A) In theoretical texts. The theory of the preservation of the state. (B) In political practice. Competition between states.* ∼ *The Treaty of Westphalia and the end of the Roman Empire.* ∼ *Force, a new element of political reason.* ∼ *Politics and the dynamic of forces.* ∼ *The first technological ensemble typical of this new art of government: the diplomatic-military system.* ∼ *Its objective: the search for a European balance. What is Europe? The idea of "balance."* ∼ *Its instruments: (1) war; (2) diplomacy; (3) the installation of a permanent military apparatus* (dispositif).

I HAVE TRIED TO show you something of how what could be called the breakthrough of a "governmental reason"* took place in Europe. I do not mean by this that this art of governing men, some of whose features I have pointed out in connection with pastoral practice, became one of the attributes of sovereign power by a simple process of copying, transfer, or translation. The king does not become the shepherd of bodies and lives in the way that the spiritual shepherd was the shepherd of souls and afterlives. I tried to show you that an absolutely specific art of government came into being, with its own reason, its own rationality, its own *ratio*. This is an event in the history of Western reason, of Western

---

* In inverted commas in the manuscript.

rationality, which is undoubtedly no less important than the event associated with Kepler, Galileo, Descartes, and so on at exactly the same time, that is to say, at the end of the sixteenth and in the course of the seventeenth century. We are dealing with a very complex phenomenon of the transformation of Western reason. I have tried to show you how this appearance of a governmental reason gave rise to a certain way of thinking, reasoning, and calculating. This is what was called politics at the time, and it should never be forgotten that this was initially seen and recognized, and immediately disturbed its contemporaries, as something heterodox: a different way of thinking; a different way of thinking power, the kingdom, the fact of ruling and governing; a different way of thinking the relations between the kingdom of Heaven and the kingdom on Earth. This heterodoxy was identified and called politics; politics would be to the art of government something like what *mathesis* was to the science of nature in the same period.

I have also tried to show you that this governmental *ratio*, this governmental reason delineated the state as both its principle and its objective, as both its foundation and its aim. The state would be, if you like, I am not too sure what to say ... a principle of intelligibility and strategic schema, or, to use an anachronistic word in relation to the period we are talking about, let's say, a regulatory idea.[1] The state is the regulatory idea of governmental reason. By this I mean that the state was first of all a principle of intelligibility of reality for this political thought that was seeking the rationality of an art of government; it was a way of thinking the specific nature, connections, and relations of certain already given elements and institutions. What is a king? What is a sovereign? What is a magistrate? What is a constituted body? What is a law? What is a territory? What are the inhabitants of this territory? What is the wealth of the prince? What is the wealth of the sovereign? All these things began to be thought of as elements of the state. The state was a way of conceiving, analyzing, and defining the nature and relations of these already given elements. The state is therefore a schema of intelligibility for a whole set of already established institutions, a whole set of given realities. We see the king defined as a character with a particular role, not so much with regard to God or with regard to men's salvation, but with regard to the state: he is magistrate, judge, etcetera. So the state appears as the principle of intelligibility of an absolutely given reality, of an already established institutional whole.

Second, the state functions as an objective in this political reason in the sense that it is that which must result from the active interventions of this reason or rationality. The state is what must exist at the end of the process of the rationalization of the art of government. What the intervention of *raison d'État* must arrive at is the state's integrity, its completion, consolidation, and its re-establishment if it has been compromised, or if a revolution has overturned it or momentarily suspended its strength and specific effects. The state is therefore the principle of intelligibility of what is, but equally of what must be; one understands what the state is in order to be more successful in making it exist in reality. The state is the principle of intelligibility and strategic objective that frames the governmental reason that is called, precisely, *raison d'État*. I mean that the state is essentially and above all the regulatory idea of that form of thought, that form of reflection, of that form of calculation, and that form of intervention called politics: politics as *mathesis*, as rational form of the art of government. Governmental reason thus posits the state as the principle for reading reality and as its objective and imperative. The state is what commands governmental reason, that is to say, it is that which means one can govern rationally according to necessity; it is the function of intelligibility of the state in relation to reality, and it is that which makes it rational, necessary, to govern. Governing rationally because there is a state and so that there is a state. That is something of what I have tried to say in the previous lectures.

Obviously this is all completely insufficient for pinning down the real function of *raison d'État*, of this governmental reason. In fact, if we look again at these definitions of *raison d'État* I have spoken about, it seems to me that there is not exactly an ambiguity, but always a sort of blur, something a bit shaky, a fluctuation in the definition. I don't know if you [remember] how *raison d'État* was defined in the text by Palazzo written, edited, and published in Italian in 1606, and translated into French in 1611.[2] Palazzo said that *raison d'État* is that which assures the integrity of the state. It is, he said, and here I quote his own words, "the very essence of peace, the rule of living at rest, the perfection of things."[3] In other words, Palazzo gives an absolutely essentialist definition of *raison d'État. Raison d'État* must ensure that the state really conforms to what it is, that is to say, remains at rest, close to its essence, its reality exactly true to what it should be at the level of its ideal necessity. *Raison d'État* will thus align the state's reality with its eternal, or at any rate immutable essence. In a word: *Raison d'État* is what allows the state to be maintained in good order (*en état*). Moreover, Palazzo—I have quoted the text[4]—played on the word *status*, which means both "state," in the sense of the state (*l'État*), and at the same time the thing's immobility. Preserving the state (*l'État*) in good order (*en état*), is what Palazzo was saying.

However, in the definitions given by Palazzo and others in more or less the same period, there is at the same time another characteristic feature of *raison d'État* that I cannot say functions in an absolutely secret way, but let's say functions discreetly. Palazzo says that *raison d'État* is the rule that makes possible the acquisition of this peace, rest, and perfection of things; the acquisition, preservation, and development of this peace. Botero, the first in Italy to produce the theory of *raison d'État*, says that it is "a perfect knowledge of the means by which states are formed, preserved, strengthened, and expanded."[5] Much later, at the time of the Treaty of Westphalia, Chemnitz says that *raison d'État* is what allows the establishment, preservation, and expansion of a republic.[6] And if it is true that most of the theorists lay stress on the fact that *raison d'État* is what makes it possible to preserve the state—the word "*manutention*," preserving, maintaining, is used—they all add that as well as this, maybe in something of a subordinate way, it is also necessary to increase or expand it. What, then, is this growth of the state that forms part of all the definitions given of *raison d'État*? The definitions, well most of the texts I have cited—Botero's and Palazzo's certainly, that of Chemnitz a bit less no doubt, because it was more linked to a precise political situation—are somewhat theoretical and speculative, and they still have something like a Platonic odor in the sense that, according to them, *raison d'État* must be characterized by the preservation of the state in accordance with its essence as state. What are to be avoided are, of course, those quasi-necessary, or anyway always threatening events that Bacon spoke about with regard to seditions.[7] What must be avoided according to Botero, Palazzo, and the others, are those practically inevitable or anyway always threatening processes that, after having taken the state to the peak of history, risk provoking its decadence, causing it to disappear and die. What basically is to be avoided, and it is in and for this that *raison d'État* functions according to Botero and Palazzo, is the cycle of birth, growth, perfection, and then decadence that was undergone by the kingdom of Babylon, the Roman Empire, and Charlemagne's Empire. In the terminology of the time this cycle was called "revolutions." Revolution, revolutions, is that kind of quasi-natural, half natural and half historical phenomenon that forces states into a cycle that, after taking them up to the light and plenitude, causes them to disappear and die. This is revolution. And what Botero and Palazzo basically understand by *raison d'État* is essentially preserving states against these revolutions. You can see that in this sense we are close to Plato, as I just said, but for this one difference however: Plato proposed a good constitution, good laws, and virtuous magistrates as means for preventing the decadence always threatening city-states, whereas the men of the sixteenth century, Botero, Palazzo, do not propose laws, a constitution, or even the virtue of magistrates against this quasi-inevitable threat of revolutions, but rather an art of government, and so a sort of skill, at any rate a rationality in the means employed to govern. But this art of government still has basically the same objective as Plato's laws: a single state (*État*) in a permanent state (*état*) of perfection.

However, I think we find something quite different in fact in texts that are less theoretical, speculative, moralistic, or moral than those of Botero and Palazzo. We find it in texts coming from people who were certainly closer to political practice, who were directly involved in politics themselves, that is to say, in the texts left by Sully, published under the title *Économies Royales*,[8] or by Richelieu, and also in the *Instructions* given to ambassadors, for example, or to officials or royal officers. Here we see that the theory of the preservation of the state is completely insufficient to cover the real practice of politics and the implementation of *raison d'État*. This other thing, the real support of what Botero and the others call simply the "expansion" of the state, seems to me to be a very important phenomenon. It is the observation that states are situated alongside other states in a space of competition. And I think that at the time this idea was at once fundamental, new, and extremely fruitful with regard to everything that we may call political technology. Why is it a new idea? We can consider things under two aspects, one specifically theoretical, and the other referring to the historical reality of the state.

First, the theoretical point of view: the idea that states are in competition with each other is basically the direct, almost ineluctable consequence of the theoretical principles posited by *raison d'État* I spoke about last week. When I tried to describe how *raison d'État* was conceived, it turned out that theorists of *raison d'État* defined the state as always being its own end. The state is organized only by reference to itself. No positive law, of course, no moral or natural law, and in the end perhaps no divine law—but this is another question—at any rate, no law can be imposed on the state from outside. The state is organized only by reference to itself: it seeks its own good and has no external purpose, that is to say, it must lead to nothing but itself, neither to the sovereign's salvation, of course, nor to men's eternal salvation, nor to any form of fulfillment or eschatology towards which it should strive. I reminded you last week that with *raison d'État* we exist within a world of indefinite historicity, in an open time without end. In other words, through *raison d'État* a world is sketched out in which, necessarily, inevitably, there will forever be a plurality of states that have their law and end in themselves. In this perspective, the plurality of states is not a transitional phase between a first unitary kingdom and a final empire in which unity will be restored. The plurality of states is not a transitional phase imposed on men for a time and as a punishment. In fact, the plurality of states is the very necessity of a history that is now completely open and not temporally oriented towards a final unity. The theory of *raison d'État* I talked about last week entails an open time and a multiple spatiality.

But it is no doubt true that these theoretical consequences would not have been enough to crystallize something like a political technology* if they were not, in fact, connected to a historical reality for which they were precisely the principle of intelligibility. What is this historical reality on which the idea of a temporally open history and, I was going to say, a multiple state space is articulated? It is, of course, the final

---

* Foucault adds: if, in fact, they were not able to be invested

disappearance in the course of the sixteenth century of the old forms of universality offered to and imposed on Europe throughout the Middle Ages practically since the Roman Empire and as its heritage. This disappearance took place in an absolutely noticeable, tangible, and definitive way that was recognized at the time, and what's more was institutionalized in the seventeenth century in the famous treaty of Westphalia,[9] to which we will return. The end of the Roman Empire should be situated exactly in [1648],* that is to say, when [it] is finally recognized that the Empire is not the ultimate vocation of all states, when it is no longer the form into which it is hoped or dreamed that states will one day merge. At the same time, the treaty of Westphalia established the division of the Church arising from the Reformation as an accepted, institutionalized, and recognized fact,[10] as well as that states, in their politics, choices, and alliances no longer have to band together in accordance with their religious adherence. Catholic states may perfectly well form alliances with Protestant states, and vice versa; Catholic states may employ Protestant armies, and vice versa.[11] In other words, Empire and Church, the two great forms of universality that, in the case of the Empire at least, for a number of years, for decades and maybe centuries, had no doubt become a sort of empty envelope, an empty shell, but which still retained their power of focalization, attraction, and intelligibility, these two great forms of universality had lost their vocation and meaning, at least at the level of this universality. This is the reality on which the principle that we exist within a [politically]† open and multiple state space is articulated. We are now dealing with absolute units, as it were, with no subordination or dependence between them, at least for the major states, and—this is the other aspect or side of the historical reality on which all this is articulated—these units assert themselves, or anyway seek to assert themselves, in a space of increased, extended, and intensified economic exchange. They seek to assert themselves in a space of commercial competition and domination, in a space of monetary circulation, colonial conquest, and control of the seas, and all this gives each state's self-assertion not just the form of each

---

* M.F.: 1647
† M.F.: temporally

being its own end that I spoke about last week, but also this new form of competition. To use somewhat anachronistic words for this reality, a state can only assert itself in a space of political and economic competition, which is what gives meaning to the problem of the state's expansion as the principle, the main theme of *raison d'État*.

Even more concretely, I think we can say that the appearance, or development rather, of a *raison d'État* that can only preserve the state by increasing its forces in a space of competition, assumes immediate and concrete shape in the problem, broadly speaking, of Spain, or of Spain and Germany. It is true that *raison d'État* is born in Italy; it was formulated in Italy on the basis of specific problems of the relations between small Italian states. But if it developed and really became an absolutely fundamental category of thought for all the European states, if it did not remain an instrument of analysis and reflection, an instrument of action and a strategic form in the small Italian states, it is because of these phenomena I have been talking about, which are materialized in the shape of Spain. They are materialized in Spain, which, through the dynastic channels of the Empire and the family in command of it, finds itself heir to the claim of universal monarchy; which from the sixteenth century, after the absorption of Portugal at least, finds itself in possession of a more or less worldwide quasi-monopolistic colonial and maritime empire; and finally, which finds itself the example for all Europe of an astounding phenomenon that will focus the reflection of chroniclers, historians, politicians, and economists for dozens and dozens of years—namely, that Spain, precisely because of this quasi-monopoly, in short, precisely because of the extent of its empire, was enriched in a spectacular fashion for some years and then, during the seventeenth century, and maybe even from the start of the sixteenth century, was impoverished in an even more spectacular fashion and even more quickly.

So, with Spain we are faced with a set of processes that completely crystallized all these reflections on *raison d'État* and the competitive space in which one was now living. First, any state, provided it has the means, the extent, and can really define its claim, will seek, like Spain, to occupy a dominant position vis-à-vis other states. It will no longer lay direct claim to the Empire, but to a de facto domination over other countries. Second, the exercise of this domination, of the quasi-monopolistic situation that Spain, if it had not acquired, had at least dreamed of and almost achieved for a time, is nevertheless constantly threatened by precisely that which made it possible and kept it going. That is to say, a state may become impoverished from becoming rich, it may become exhausted by its excess of power, and the situation of domination may become the casualty of something that will now be called revolution, but in a completely different sense of revolution as the set of real mechanisms by which the very thing that assured the state's strength and domination will in turn produce the loss, or at any rate the diminution of its strength. Spain was the privileged object, the classic example around which the analysis of *raison d'État* developed. And we can see why all these analyses of *raison d'État*, and of this new, emerging field of politics are especially developed in the enemies and rivals of Spain: in France, in Germany, which was trying to get free from the yoke of imperial preeminence, and in Tudor England. In short, from an idea of time that I think still dominated sixteenth century political thought and served as its horizon, a time with a unifying tendency and punctuated, threatened by essential revolutions, we pass to an open time traversed by phenomena of competition that may bring about real revolutions, that is to say, revolutions at the same level of the mechanisms that assure the wealth and power of nations.

Having said that, is all this so new? Can we really say that the opening up of a space of competition between states was a phenomenon that suddenly appeared at the end of the sixteenth and the beginning of the seventeenth century and thus crystallized a series of new aspects and developments of *raison d'État*? Certainly, it goes without saying that there had long been rivalries, confrontations, and phenomena of competition. But, once again, I would like to be very clear that what I am talking about, what is at issue in what I am saying, is the point at which all these phenomena actually enter a reflexive prism that allows them to be organized into strategies. The problem is when these phenomena of confrontation and rivalry, which can be observed at any time, actually began to be perceived in the form of competition between states in an open economic and political field, and in an indefinite time. When did one begin to codify all these phenomena in terms of an idea and strategy of competition? This is what I would like to try to grasp, and it really does seem to me that it is from the sixteenth and seventeenth centuries that relations between states were no longer perceived in the form of rivalry, but in the form of competition. And here—obviously I can only indicate the problem—I think we should try to identify how it was possible to see, recognize, and talk about, as well as think and calculate confrontations between kingdoms in terms of rivalries, and essentially dynastic rivalries, and then at what point they came to be thought in terms of competition.

Very roughly and schematically, we could say that inasmuch as a form of confrontation was reflected as rivalry between princes, as dynastic rivalry, the relevant element was of course the prince's wealth, either in the form of his treasure or in the form of the fiscal resources available to him. The first transformation took place when possible confrontations and their outcomes were no longer thought, calculated, and gauged in terms of the prince's wealth, the treasure available to him, and his monetary resources, and when there was the attempt instead to think about them in terms of the wealth of the state itself, that is to say, with the transition from seeing the prince's wealth as a factor of power to seeing the state's wealth as the very force of the kingdom. The second transformation was the transition from estimating a prince's power by the extent of his possessions to an investigation of the more solid, although more secret forces that characterize a state, that is to say, [no] longer the possessions themselves, [but] the state's intrinsic wealth, its available resources, natural resources, commercial possibilities, balance of trade, and so forth. Third, when confrontations were thought of in terms of rivalry between princes, the prince's power was characterized by his system of alliances, in the familial sense or in the sense of familial obligations linked to it, and the third transformation was when one began to think of confrontations in terms of competition, that is to say, [through] alliance as a provisional combination of interests. This transition from the rivalry of princes to the competition of states is undoubtedly one of the most fundamental mutations in both the form of Western political life and the form of Western history.

Obviously, the transition from dynastic rivalry to competition between states is a lengthy and complex process, the overlaps continue for a long time, and I completely caricature it by pointing out some of its characteristics in this way. For example, at the beginning of the eighteenth century, the War of Spanish Succession[12] is still completely impregnated with the problems, techniques, and processes, the ways of acting and thinking, of dynastic rivalry. However, with the War of Spanish Succession, and the block, the failure it encountered, I think we have the last moment, the last form of confrontation in which the dynastic rivalry of princes still impregnates and to a certain extent governs the competition between states, which in subsequent wars appears in the free, naked state. At any rate, in passing from the rivalry of princes to competition between states, to thinking of confrontation in terms of competition between states, it is clear that we expose and lay bare an absolutely essential and fundamental notion that previously did not appear and was not formulated in any of the theoretical texts of *raison d'État* I have been talking about, and this notion is, of course, that of force. No longer territorial expansion, but the development of the state's forces; no longer the extension of possessions or matrimonial alliances, [but] increase of the state's forces; no longer the combination of legacies through dynastic alliances, but the composition of state forces in political and provisional alliances: all this will be the raw material, the object, and, at the same time, the principle of intelligibility of political reason. If we no longer take political reason as it appears in those somewhat theoretical, still somewhat essentialist and Platonic texts I spoke about last week, and if instead we consider it in its formulations at the end of the sixteenth and the beginning of the seventeenth century, especially around the Thirty Years War,[13] and in people who were practitioners rather than theorists of politics, then we find a new theoretical strata. This new theoretical and analytical strata, this new element of political reason, is force. It is force, the force of states. We enter a politics whose principal object will be the employment and calculation of forces. Politics, political science, encounters the problem of dynamics.

Obviously there is a problem here that I leave completely in abeyance and merely point out to you. You can see that this development that takes place entirely on the basis of a historical reality and identifiable historical processes—the discovery of America, the constitution of colonial empires, the disappearance of the Empire, and the withdrawal, the erosion of the universal functions of the Church—in short, all these

phenomena, which are what they are and which have their own necessity and intelligibility, lead to the appearance in political thought of the
fundamental category of force. All these phenomena lead to a mutation
that means that for the first time we are faced with political thought
that aspires to be, at the same time, a strategy and a dynamics of forces.
Now you are well aware that at the same time, and by completely different processes, the sciences of nature, and physics in particular, will
also encounter this notion of force. So the dynamics of politics and the
dynamics of physics are more or less contemporaneous. And we should
see how all of this is connected through Leibniz,[14] who is the general
theorist of force as much from the historical-political point of view as
from the point of view of physical science. Why is it like this? What is
this contemporaneousness? I confess I know absolutely nothing about
it, but I think the problem inevitably arises insofar as Leibniz is proof
that the homogeneity of the two processes was not entirely foreign to
the thought of the time.

Let's summarize all this. The real problem of this new governmental
rationality is not therefore just the preservation of the state within a
general order so much as the preservation of a relation of forces; it is the
preservation, maintenance, or development of a dynamic of forces. In
order to implement a political reason that is now essentially defined in
terms of the dynamic of forces, I think the West, or Western societies, set
up two assemblages that can only be understood on this basis of the
rationalization of forces. These two great assemblages, which I want to
talk about today and next week, are, of course, a military-diplomatic
apparatus, on the one hand, and the apparatus of police, in the sense the
word had at the time, on the other. What essentially did they have to
ensure? First they had to maintain a relation of forces, and then the
growth of each of the forces without the break-up of the whole. This
maintenance of the relation of forces and development of the internal
forces of each element, linking them together, is precisely what will later
be called a mechanism of security.

First, the new military-diplomatic type of techniques. If states exist
alongside each other in a competitive relationship, a system must be
found that will limit the mobility, ambition, growth, and reinforcement
of all the other states as much as possible, but nonetheless leaving each

state enough openings for it to maximize its growth without provoking its adversaries and without, therefore, leading to its own disappearance or enfeeblement. This system of security was outlined, and to tell the truth was fully installed at the end of the Thirty Years War, at the end of the one hundred years of religious and political struggles[15] that led to the clear and definitive disappearance of both the imperial dream and ecclesiastical universalism, and which ranged a number of states against each other, all of which could lay claim to their self-assertion and the self-purpose of their own policy. What did the system installed at the end of the Thirty Years War comprise? It consisted of an objective and some instruments. The objective was the balance of Europe. Here again, just like *raison d'État*, the balance of Europe is of Italian origin; the idea of a balance is of Italian origin. I think it is in Guicciardini that we find the analysis of this policy by which each of the Italian princes tried to maintain a state of equilibrium in Italy.[16] Let's leave the Italian case and return to Europe. What does the balance of Europe mean? When the diplomats, the ambassadors who negotiated the treaty of Westphalia, received instructions from their government,[17] they were explicitly advised to ensure that the new frontiers, the distribution of states, the new relationships to be established between the German states and the Empire, and the zones of influence of France, Sweden, and Austria be established in terms of a principle: to maintain a balance between the different European states.

First of all, what is Europe? At the start, or in the first half of the seventeenth century, the idea of Europe is absolutely new. What is Europe? First, it is precisely a unit that no longer has the universal vocation of Christianity, for example. Christianity, by definition, by vocation, aimed to cover the entire world. Europe, on the other hand, is a geographical division that at the time did not include Russia, for example, and only included England in a somewhat ambiguous way, since England was not actually a party to the treaty of Westphalia. So, Europe is a quite limited geographical division, without universality. Second, Europe is not a hierarchical form of states more or less subordinate to each other and culminating in a final, single form of the Empire. Every sovereign—I am speaking very roughly here, as you will see, and we will have to correct it straightaway—every sovereign is emperor in his own domain, or at any rate the main sovereigns are emperors in their realm, and there is no indication that a single sovereign of a particular state has a superiority that would make Europe a kind of single whole. Europe is fundamentally plural. Obviously, and this is where I immediately correct what I have been saying, this does not mean that there were no differences between the states.* [The fact was very clearly marked],† for example, even before the treaty of Westphalia, in what Sully tells us about Henri IV and what he called the "grand design."[18] The grand design that Sully attributes to Henri IV's political thought consisted in constituting a Europe, a plural Europe therefore, as a limited geographical division, without universality and without a culminating unity, of course, but in which fifteen states would be stronger than the others and take decisions for them.[19] So, it is a geographical division, a multiplicity of states without unity, [within] which however there is a major, if not constitutive, interlinked difference between the big and the small. Finally, the fourth characteristic of Europe is that while it is a geographical division, a plurality, it is not cut off from the whole world, but its relationship with the whole world marks the very specificity of Europe in relation to the world, since the only type of relationship that Europe must have and begins to have with the rest of the world is that of economic domination or colonization, or at any rate commercial utilization. The idea formed at the end of the sixteenth and beginning of the seventeenth century, which crystallized in the middle of the seventeenth century with the set of treaties signed at that time, and which is the historical reality that is still not behind us, is that of Europe as a geographical region of multiple states, without unity but with differences between the big and the small, and having a relationship of utilization, colonization, and domination with the rest of the world. That is what Europe is.

Second, balance. What is the balance of Europe?[20] The Latin term is *trutina Europae*.‡ The word "balance" is used with several meanings in the

---

* M.F.: and, on the contrary, was very clearly marked
† M.F.: we find it
‡ Manuscript p. 14: "*trutina sive bilanx Europeae*" (the expression is quoted by L. Donnadieu, *La Théorie de l'équilibre. Étude d'histoire diplomatique et de droit international*, doctoral thesis in political science, University of Aix-Marseille (Paris: A. Rousseau, 1900) p. 3.

texts of this period. In different countries, in different policies, and at different moments, the balance of Europe primarily meant the impossibility of the strongest state laying down the law to any other state. In other words, the balance of Europe will be maintained if we make sure that the difference between the strongest state and those behind it is not such that the strongest can impose its law on all the others. Thus there is a limitation of the gap between the strongest and the others.* That's the first point. Second, European balance, European equilibrium, was thought of as the constitution of a limited number of the strongest states, between which equality will be maintained so that each of them will be able to prevent any other from taking the lead and getting the upper hand. In other words, this means the constitution of an aristocracy of states, and of an egalitarian aristocracy that will take the form, for example, of an equality of forces between England, Austria, France, and Spain. In such a quadriga,† clearly none of the four can take a considerable lead over the others, since if this were to happen the first reaction of the other three would obviously be to prevent it somehow. Finally, the third definition of European balance is the one that can most easily be found in the jurists and which subsequently has the series of consequences that you may imagine. In the eighteenth century you find it in Wolff in the *Jus gentium*, in which he says that European equilibrium must consist in the following: "the mutual Union of several nations" must be able to ensure "that the preponderant power of one or several countries is equal to the combined power of the others."[21] In other words, things must be such that the combination of several small powers can counterbalance the force of a superior power that might threaten one of them. Consequently, there is the possibility of coalition whose effect, at a given moment and in a given place, can counterbalance any established preponderance. The absolute limitation of the force of the strongest, the equalization of the strongest, and the possibility of the combination of the weaker against the stronger are the three forms conceived and devised to constitute European equilibrium, the balance of Europe.

---

* In the manuscript Foucault refers here to "Sully, 'the grand design.'" See below, this lecture, note 18.

† Two-wheeled chariot drawn by four horses abreast; G.B.

With these different procedures, instead of a sort of absolute eschatology that posits an empire, a universal monarchy as the culminating
point of history, we have what could be called a relative eschatology, a
precarious and fragile eschatology, but towards which it really is
necessary to strive, and this fragile eschatology is, in short, peace. It is
universal peace, relatively universal and relatively definitive peace, of
course, but the peace one dreams of at this time is no longer expected to
come from a finally united and definitively unchallenged supremacy like
that of the Empire or the Church. Rather, this universal and relatively
universal peace, this definitive but relatively definitive peace, is expected
from a plurality without major unitary effects of domination. Peace will
no longer come from unity, but from non-unity, from plurality maintained as plurality. You can see the extent to which we are now situated
within an historical perspective, but also in a form of diplomatic technique, very different from what was possible in the Middle Ages, for
example, when peace was expected to come from the Church because it
was the single, unique, and unifying power. Peace is now expected to
come from the states themselves, and from their plurality. This is a
major change. The objective will now be to ensure the security in which
each state can effectively increase its forces without bringing about the
ruin of other states or of itself.

Second, the instruments. *Raison d'État*, whose framework is diplomatic
and so essentially defined by the constitution of a Europe, of a European
balance, makes use of three instruments. It goes without saying that war
is the first instrument of this precarious, fragile, and provisional universal
peace that takes on the aspect of a balance and equilibrium between a plurality of states. That is to say, henceforth it will be possible to wage war,
or better it will be necessary to wage war, precisely in order to preserve
this balance. And here we see the functions, forms, justifications, and
juridical thought concerning war, as well as the objectives of war, completely overturned. What, after all, was war in medieval conceptions?
I was going to say that war was basically a juridical behavior; I mean it was
basically a judicial behavior. Why did one go to war? One waged war
when there was injustice, when there was a violation of right, or anyway
when someone claimed a right that was challenged by someone else. In the
medieval world there was no discontinuity between the world of right and

the world of war. There was not even any discontinuity between the universe of private law, in which it was a matter of settling disputes, and the world of confrontations between princes, which was not, and could not be called international and public law. One was always in the realm of disputes, of the settlement of disputes—you have taken my inheritance, you have seized one of my lands, you have repudiated my sister—and one fought, wars developed, within this juridical framework of public war and private war. It was public war as private war, or private war that took on a public dimension. It was a war of right, and the war was settled moreover exactly like a juridical procedure, by a victory, which was like a judgment of God. You lost, therefore right was not on your side. On this continuity of law and war, on this homogeneity between the battle and the victory and God's judgment, I refer you to Duby's book on *Le Dimanche de Bouvines*,[22] in which there are some illuminating pages on the judicial function of war.

War now functions differently, because, on the one hand, it is no longer a question of a war of right, but of a war of the state, of *raison d'État*. Basically, one no longer needs a juridical reason for starting a war. One is fully entitled to have a purely diplomatic reason for starting a war: the balance is jeopardized, it must be re-established, there is too much power on one side, and this can no longer be tolerated. For sure, the juridical pretext will be found, but war is detached from that pretext. Second, if war loses its continuity with law, you can see that it gets back another continuity, which is, of course, its continuity with politics. At a given moment, politics—the function of which is precisely to preserve and assure the balance between states in the European framework—will order war to be waged, against this or that state, up to a certain point and only that point, without jeopardizing the balance too much, with a system of alliances, and so on. As a consequence of this the well-known principle appears which, almost two hundred years later, is formulated by someone who says: "War is politics continued by other means."[23] But in saying this he did no more than observe a mutation that was actually established at the start of the seventeenth century, [with the constitution]* of the new diplomatic reason, the new

---

* M.F.: at the moment of that great constitution

political reason, at the time of the treaty of Westphalia. We should not forget that on the bronze of the French king's canons was written: *Ultima ratio regum*, "the last, the final reason of kings."[24]* So, this is the first instrument for getting the system of European security, of European balance, to work.

The second instrument, the diplomatic instrument, is just as old as war, and it too is profoundly renewed. Something relatively new appears at this time—but here we should clarify things—anyway, something like the treaty of Westphalia is a multilateral treaty in which one does not settle a dispute between several persons, but in which the totality of states that constitute the new system of Europe, with the exception of England, sort out their problems and settle their conflicts.[25] Now sorting out their problems and settling their conflicts does not mean following the juridical lines prescribed by the laws and traditions. It does not mean following the lines prescribed by the rights of inheritance, or by the rights of the victor, with clauses of ransom, marriage, and transfer. The lines of force followed by the diplomats in this multilateral treaty are those determined by the need for a balance. On what basis, in what terms will territories, towns, bishoprics, ports, abbeys, and colonies be exchanged, haggled over, and transferred? Not, then, according to the old right of inheritance or the old right of the victor, but in terms of physical principles, since it will involve joining one territory to another, transferring this revenue to that prince, and granting this port to that territory, in accordance with the principle that an inter-state balance with the greatest possible stability must be established. The fundamental principle of this new diplomacy will be a physics of states, and no longer a right of sovereigns. In connection with this, of course, and still in the domain of diplomacy, we see the creation of what are not yet called permanent diplomatic missions, but at any rate the organization of practically permanent negotiations and a system of information concerning the state of forces in each country (I will come back to all this shortly). The institution of permanent ambassadors also has a long

---

* A partly inaudible phrase follows: (...) the political reason that is now inscribed on the canon (...)

genesis in fact, and was set up at the end of the fifteenth and the start of the sixteenth century, but the conscious, reflected, and absolutely permanent organization of a diplomacy of constant negotiation dates from this period. That is to say, there is the idea of a permanent apparatus of relations between states that is not an apparatus of imperial unity or ecclesiastical universality. It is the idea of a veritable society of nations, and I am not employing a word retrospectively here. The idea was well and truly formulated at this time. You find it in someone called Crucé who wrote a sort of utopia at the beginning of the seventeenth century called *Le Nouveau Cynée*,[26] in which, on the one hand, he envisions a police[27] (I will come back to this in more detail next week[28]) and, on the other, at the same time and, essentially correlated with this—which explains why, while promising to talk about police, I felt the need to speak beforehand about military-diplomatic organizations—a permanent organization of consultation between states with ambassadors permanently assembled in a town. The town would be Venice, a territory that he says is neutral and indifferent to all the princes,[29] and the ambassadors permanently assembled in Venice would be responsible for settling disputes and contentions and for ensuring that the principle of equilibrium is well and truly maintained.[30]

The idea that between themselves states form something like a society in the European space, the idea that states are like individuals who must have certain relations between them that the law must fix and codify, gave rise at this time to the development of what has been called the law of nations (*droit des gens*), the *jus gentium*, which becomes one of the fundamental points, one of the particularly intense focal points of the activity of juridical thought, since it involves defining juridical relations between these new individuals, the states of Europe, coexisting in a new space, or society of nations. Then you find the idea that the states are a society clearly expressed in a text from right at the start of the eighteenth century, by the greatest theorist of the law of nations, Burlamaqui, his *Les Principes du droit de la nature et des gens*,[31] which says: "Europe today is a political system, a body in which everything is linked by the relations and varied interests of the nations that inhabit this part of the world. It is no longer, as previously, a confused mass of isolated pieces in which each thinks it has little interest in the fate of the others and is rarely troubled by what does not immediately affect it"—which is historically false, but it's not important, this is not how things were before, but this is how he defines the current situation: "The continuous attention of sovereigns to all that happens in their own and other nations, permanently resident ministers [reference to permanent diplomats;[32] M.F.], and continual negotiations make modern Europe a kind of republic the members of which, independent but bound by common interest, come together to maintain order and liberty."

This, then, is how the idea of Europe and European balance was born. It is crystallized, of course, with the treaty of Westphalia,[33] the first complete, conscious, explicit expression of a politics of European balance, the main function of which, as you know, is to reorganize the Empire, to define its status and its rights in relation to the German principalities, and the zones of influence of Austria, Sweden, and France on German territory, all according to the laws of equilibrium, which actually explains why Germany could become, and actually became, the center for the elaboration of the European republic. We should never forget that Europe as a juridical-political entity, as a system of diplomatic and political security, is the yoke that the most powerful countries (of this Europe) imposed on Germany every time they tried to make it forget the dream of the sleeping emperor, whether Charlemagne, Barbarossa, or the little man who was burnt between his dog and his mistress one May evening* on the chancellery premises. Europe is the way of making Germany forget the Empire. So, if the emperor never really wakes up, we should not be surprised that Germany sometimes gets up and says: "I am Europe. I am Europe since you wished it that I be Europe." And it says this precisely to those who wanted it to be Europe and nothing but Europe, namely French imperialism, English domination, or Russian expansionism. In Germany they wanted to substitute the obligation of Europe for the desire for Empire. "Fine," Germany replies therefore, "that's no problem, since Europe will be my empire. It is just that Europe be my empire," says Germany, "since you only created

---

* An obvious slip. Hitler killed himself on 30 April 1945 in the underground bunker of the Reich chancellery in Berlin.

Europe in order to impose the domination of England, France, and Russia on Germany." We should not forget this little anecdote from 1871, when Thiers was arguing with the German plenipotentiary, who was called Ranke, I think, and said to him: "But who are you fighting against? We no longer have an army, no one can resist you, France is exhausted, the Commune was the final blow against any possibility of resistance, so against whom are you waging war?" Ranke answered: "But let's see, against Louis XIV."

The third instrument of this military-diplomatic system for maintaining European balance—the first was a new form, a new conception of war, [second] was a diplomatic instrument—the third instrument will be the constitution of another fundamental and new element, which is the deployment of a permanent military apparatus (*dispositif*) that comprises: [first] professionalization of the soldier, setting up a military career; second, a permanent armed structure that can serve as the framework for exceptional wartime recruitment; third, an infrastructure of back-up facilities of strongholds and transport; and finally, fourth, a form of knowledge, a tactical reflection on types of maneuver, schemas of defense and attack, in short an entire specific and autonomous reflection on military matters and possible wars. So there is the appearance of this military dimension that is far from being solely and entirely taken up in the practice of war. The existence of a permanent, costly, large, and scientific military apparatus within the system of peace itself has, of course, been one of the indispensable instruments for the constitution of the European balance. How could one maintain this balance in fact if each of the states, or at least the most powerful, did not have this military apparatus and did not in fact broadly maintain it, overall, at more or less the same level as that of its main rival? So the constitution of a permanent military apparatus, which is not so much the presence of war in peace as the presence of diplomacy in politics and the economy, is an essential component of a politics governed by the calculation of balances and the maintenance of a force obtained through war, or through the possibility or threat of war. In short, it is an essential element in this competition between states in which, of course, each seeks to turn the relation of force in its favor, but which all seek to maintain as a whole. Here again we can see how the Clausewitzian principle that war is the continuation of politics had a support, a precise institutional support, in the institutionalization of the military. War is no longer a different aspect of human activity. At a given moment, war will mean bringing into play politically defined resources, of which the military is one of the fundamental and constitutive dimensions. We have then a political-military complex that is absolutely necessary to the constitution of this European balance as a mechanism of security; this political-military complex will be continually brought into play and war will be only one of its functions. [Thus we can understand]* that the relation between war and peace, between the military and the civil, will be redeployed around this complex.†

Good, I have gone on a bit too long, forgive me. Next week I will talk about another great mechanism of security that was installed in this *raison d'État* that is henceforth organized by reference to the problem of force and strength, and this other instrument, this other great technology is not the military-diplomatic apparatus, but the political apparatus of police.

---

* Conjecture; some inaudible words.
† The manuscript adds, p. 20: "4. Fourth instrument: an information apparatus (*appareil*). Knowing one's own forces (and what's more hiding them), knowing those of the others, allies and adversaries, and hiding the fact that one knows them. Knowing them implies that one knows what the force of states consists in. Where is the secret in which it resides: the mystery of Spain, which lost its power, and the mystery of the United Provinces, one of the important states of Europe.

1. On this Kantian concept, of which Foucault makes a fairly free use here, see I. Kant, *Critique of Pure Reason*, trans. Norman Kemp Smith (London: Macmillan, 1933) I, Second Division, "Appendix to the Transcendental Dialectic: The Regulative Employment of the Ideas of Pure Reason," p. 533: "(. . .) transcendental ideas (. . .) have an excellent, and indeed indispensably necessary, regulative employment, namely, that of directing the understanding towards a certain goal upon which all the routes marked out by all its rules converge, as upon their point of intersection (. . . [which]) serves to give to these concepts the greatest [possible] unity combined with the greatest [possible] extension."

2. See previous lecture, 15 March, pp. 255-257.

3. A. Palazzo, *Discours du gouvernement et de la raison d'Estat*, IV, 24, pp. 373-374: "Finally, *raison d'État* is the very essence of peace, the rule of living at rest, and the perfection of things (. . .)."

4. See the previous lecture, 15 March, pp. 255-257.

5. See above, lecture of 8 March, pp. 237-238.

6. See previous lecture, 15 March, p. 257.

7. See previous lecture, 15 March, p. 267 *sq.*

8. Maximilien de Béthune, baron de Rosny, duc de Sully (1559-1641), *Économies Royales*, ed. J. Chailley-Bert (Paris: Guillaumin, c.1820). See below, note 18.

9. The peace of Westphalia, definitively signed at Münster on 24 October 1648 at the end of the Thirty Years War, was the result of five years of intense and difficult negotiations between the major European powers. Historians distinguish three major periods: (1) from January 1643 to November 1645, when procedural questions were at the center of discussions, (2) from November 1645 to June 1647, which allowed most of the differences between the Germans and the Dutch to be settled, and (3) 1648, which will come to end with the signing of the two treaties, between the Empire and France at Münster (*Instrumentum Pacis Monstieriense*), and between the Empire and Sweden at Osnabrück (*Instrumentum Pacis Osnabrucense*). See G. Parker, *The Thirty Years War*. The states of the Empire shift to recognizing in right the "territorial superiority" (*Landeshoheit*) that for a century a great number of them were already exercising in fact. The Empire itself, stripped of its Holy character, continued to survive as a state, but at the cost of some constitutional modifications. For further clarification of these points, see M. Stolleis, *Histoire du droit public en Allemagne, 1600-1800*, pp. 335-343.

10. The treaties, in fact, effectively sanction the recognition of Calvinism as the third legal religion of the Empire, along with Catholicism and Lutheranism.

11. In the wake of the *politiques*, this was already the attitude adopted by Richelieu towards the Spanish House, which ended up with entry into open war in 1635. "The interests of state that link princes are different from the interests of the salvation of our souls," Richelieu, in D.L.M. Avenel, ed., *Lettres, Instructions diplomatiques et Papiers d'État du cardinal du Richelieu*, vol. 1, *1608-1624* (Paris: Imprimerie impériale, 1854) p. 225. This politics, based solely upon the criterion of "interests of state," found its first defense in the treatise of Henri de Rohan, *De l'inérêt des princes et des États de la chrétienté* (1638) ed., C. Lazzeri (Paris: PUF, 1995). See F. Meinecke, *Machiavellism*, Book 1, ch. 6: "The doctrine of the best interest of the state at the time of Richelieu" (on Rohan, see pp. 162-195).

12. This conflict, which ranges France and Spain against a European coalition (the Quadruple Alliance) from 1701 to 1714, following the accession to the Spanish throne of Philip V, grandson of Louis XIV, ended with the treaties of Utrecht and Rastadt. See L. Donnadieu, *La Théorie de l'équilibre. Étude d'histoire diplomatique et de droit international*, doctoral thesis in Political Science, University of Aix-Marseille (Paris: A. Rousseau, 1900) pp. 67-79.

13. The Thirty Years War (1618-1648), which gradually transforms Germany into the battlefield of Europe (Sweden enters in 1630, France, after a "hidden war," in 1635), was at the same time both a civil war and the first great international conflict in the seventeenth century that brings the logic of force into play. On the treaties of Westphalia that put an end to the war, see above, note 9.

14. Gottfried Wilhelm Leibniz (1646-1717), jurist, mathematician, philosopher, and diplomat, the author of *Theodicy* (1710) and *Monadology* (1714). On "force" as the physical expression of the unity of substance, see in particular, *Specimen dynamicum* (1695), ed., H.G. Dorsch (Hamburg: F. Meiner, 1982). Leibniz is also the author of historical-political writings: see *Opuscules contre la paix de Ryswick*, in *Die Werke von Leibniz gemäss seinem handschriftlichen Nachlass in der Bibliothek zu Hannover* (Hanover: Klindworth, 1864-1884) vol. VI, section B. On Leibnizian dynamics, see: M. Guéroult, *Leibniz. Dynamique et métaphysique* (Paris: Aubier-Montaigne, 1967); W. Voisé, "Leibniz's model of political thinking," *Organon*, 4, 1967, pp. 187-205. On the juridical-political implications his metaphysical positions, see A. Robinet, *G.W. Leibniz. Le meilleur des mondes par la balance de l'Europe* (Paris: PUF, 1994), especially pp. 235-236: "What is 'the balance of Europe'? It is the idea of *a political-military physics of nations* in which variable antagonistic forces are exercised in terms of random violent clashes of some with others, of some against others. (...) The balance of Europe is not a problem of statics, but of dynamics."

15. One hundred years, if we take the period going from the Peace of Augsbourg (1555), which recognized the right of each state within the Empire to practice the religion, Catholic or Lutheran, that it confessed—a principle later called *cujus regio, ejus religio*—thereby consecrating the end of the medieval Empire, up to the peace of Westphalia (1648).

16. Francesco Guicciardini (1483-1540), *Storia d'Italia*, I, 1 (Fiorenzo: appresso Lorenzo Torrentino, 1561, incomplete edition; Geneva: Stoer, 1621; Turin: Einaudi, ed. Silvana Seidel Menchi) pp. 6-7: "E conoscendo che alla republica fiorentina e a sé proprio sarebbe molto pericoloso se alcuno de' maggiori potentati ampliasse più la sua potenza, procurava con ogni studio che le cose d'Italia in modo bilanciate si mantenessino che più in una che in un'altra parte non pendessino: il che, senza la conservazione della pace e senza vegghiare con somma diligenza ogni accidente benché minimo, succedere non poteva." ["And knowing that it would be very dangerous for the Florentine Republic and for himself if one of the more powerful were to increase their strength further, he [Lorenzo de' Medici] took every effort to maintain a balance in Italian affairs so that they did not lean in one or another direction; this could not be achieved without preserving the peace and without diligently supervising the least accident."] French translation, *Histoire d'Italie*, trans. J.-L. Fournel and J.-C. Zancarini (Paris: Robert Laffont, "Boquins," 1996, p. 5.

17. See, *Recueil des instructions données aux ambassadeurs et ministres de France, depuis les traités de Westphalie jusqu'à la Révolution française*, XXVIII, États allemands, vol. 1: *L'Électorat de Mayence*, ed., G. Livet (Paris: Éd. du CNRS, 1962); vol. 2: *L'Électorat de Cologne*, 1963; vol. 3: *L'Électorat de Trèves*, 1966. See also the collection of the *Acta Pacis Westphalicae*, being published since 1970, edited by K. Repgen, in the framework of the Nordrhein-Westfälische Akademie der Wissenschaften (Serie II. Abt. B: *Die französischen Korrespondenzen* [Münster: Aschendorff, 1973]).

18. Maximilien of Béthune, baron of Rosny, duc de Sully, *Mémoires des sages et royales œconomies d'Estat, domestiques, politiques et militaires de Henri le Grand*, ed., Michaud and Poujoulat (Paris: "Nouvelle Collection des mémoires pour servir à l'histoire de France," 1837) vol. 2, ch. 2, pp. 355b-356a. See E. Thuau, *Raison d'État et Pensée politique*, p. 282, which refers to the article by C. Pfister, "Les 'Œconomies royales' de Sully et le Grand Dessein de Henri IV," *Revue historique*, 1894, vol. 54, pp. 300-324, vol. 55, pp. 67-82 and pp. 291-302, and vol. 56, pp. 39-48 and pp. 304-339. The expression "grand design (*magnifique dessein*)" is quoted by L. Donnadieu, *La Théorie de l'équilibre*, p. 45, followed by the following extract from the *Œconomies royales* (ed., Petito, VII, 94): "Rendering all the fifteen major powers of Christian Europe roughly equal in strength, realm, wealth, extent, and domination and giving them well-adjusted and moderated bounds and limits so that those whose desires and greed would be the biggest and most ambitious do not think of expanding, and the others are not offended, jealous, and fearful of being oppressed."

19. See the second and third of the king's designs set out by Sully, p. 356a: "(...) to associate as many sovereign powers as possible with his design to reduce all these hereditary monarchies to an almost equal strength, as much in the size of the country as in wealth, so that those with too much do not think of oppressing the weak, and the latter do not fear oppression by the power"; "(...) to try to introduce between the fifteen dominations, from which the Christianity of Europe must be composed, some well-adjusted boundaries

between those bordering each other, and to regulate so equitably the diversity of their rights and claims that they may never more enter into dispute."

20. On this question see Donnadieu's thesis, which is Foucault's main source. See E. Thuau, *Raison d'État et Pensée politique,* pp. 307-309, and the article by G. Zeller to which Thuau refers: "Le principe d'équilibre dans la politique internationale avant 1789," *Revue historique,* 215, January-March 1956, pp. 25-27.

21. Christian von Wolff, *Jus gentium methodo scientifica pertractatum* (Halle: in officina libraria Rengeriana, 1749) ch. VI, § 642, quoted by L. Donnadieu, *La Théorie de l'équilibre,* p. 2, note 5, which adds: "Talleyrand is close to Wolff: 'Equilibrium is a relationship between the reciprocal forces of resistance and aggression of different political bodies' ('Instruction for the Congress of Vienna,' Angeberg, p. 227)."

22. G. Duby, *Le Dimanche de Bouvines* (Paris: Gallimard, "Trente journées qui ont fait la France," 1973); English translation by Catherine Tihanyi, *The Legend of Bouvines. War, Religion and Culture in the Middle Ages* (Berkeley and Los Angeles: University of California Press, 1990).

23. C. von Clausewitz, *Vom Kriege,* ed. W. Hahlweg (Bonn: Dümmlers Verlag, 1952) Book I, ch. 1, § 24; French translation, *De la guerre* (Paris: Minuit, 1955; trans. De Vatry, revised and completed, Paris: Lebovici, 1989); English translation, *On War,* edited with an introduction by Anotol Rapoport (Harmondsworth: Penguin, 1982). Compare this analysis with that in the 1975-1976 lectures, *"Il faut défendre la société"* pp. 146-147; *"Society Must Be Defended"* p. 165. Clausewitz's expression is analyzed in these lectures, not as the extension of the new diplomatic reason, but as the reversal of the relationship between war and politics defined in the seventeenth and eighteenth centuries by the historians of the war between races.

24. On this phrase, see the declaration of the princes of the Empire (the 23rd observation in answer to the circular sent by the French plenipotentiaries, 6 April 1644, inviting them to send representatives to the conference at Münster) quoted by G. Livet, *L'Équilibre européen* (Paris: PUF, 1976) p. 83: "We have seen inscriptions, portraits of the French king, where he is named the conqueror of the Universe, we have seen on his canons this thought, *the final reason of kings,* which fully expresses his usurping spirit."

25. "At Münster, around the nuncio and the representative of Venice, apart from the powers at war in Germany [France and Sweden], are in session Spain, the United Provinces, Portugal, Savoy, Tuscany, Mantua, the Swiss Cantons, and Florence." G. Livet, *La Guerre de Trente Ans* (Paris: PUF, 1963) p. 42.

26. Emeric Crucé (Emery La Croix, 1590?-1648), *Le Nouveau Cynée, ou Discours d'Estat representant les occasions & moyens d'établir une paix generalle & la liberté du commerce par tout le monde* (Paris: Jacques Villery, 1623, republished 1624; reprinted Paris: Éditions d'histoire sociale, 1976). See L.-P. Lucas, *Un plan de paix générale et de liberté du commerce au XVIIᵉ siècle, Le Nouveau Cynée d'Emeric Crucé* (Paris: L. Tenin, 1919); H. Pajot, *Une rêveur de paix sous Louis XIII* (Paris: 1924); E. Thuau, *Raison d'État et Pensée politique,* p. 282. Crucé does not speak of a "society of nations" but of "human society" (*Le Nouveau Cynée,* preface, no page number): "(...) human society is a body in which all the members have a sympathy, such that it is impossible for the maladies of one not to be communicated to the others," ibid. p. 62.

27. Ibid. preface (no page numbers): "(...) this little book contains a universal police, equally useful for all nations, and agreeable to those who have some light of reason" (see the text starting from p. 86).

28. Foucault will return to the question of police in the next lecture, but not to Crucé's analysis of it.

29. *Le Nouveau Cynée,* p. 61: "Now the most convenient place for such an assembly is the territory of Venice, because it is neutral and indifferent to all princes: it is also close to the most illustrious Monarchs of the earth, to those of the Pope, the two Emperors, and the King of Spain."

30. A fairly free interpretation of Crucé's text. See, ibid. p. 78: "(...) nothing can assure an Empire except a general peace, the mainspring of which consists in the limitation of monarchies, so that every prince is contained and limited to the lands he presently possesses and that he does not exceed them for any claim. And if he is offended by such a regulation, let him consider that the bounds of kingdoms and seigniories are in the hands of

God, who takes them away and transfers them when and where seems good to Him." This respect for the *statu quo*, in conformity with divine will, is very far from the dynamic principle of balance.

31. Jean-Jacques Burlamaqui (1694-1748), *Principes du droit de la nature et des gens*, posthumous ed. De Felice (Yverdon: 1767-1768, 8 volumes) Part IV, ch. II; new edition revised and corrected by M. Dupin (Paris: B. Warée, 1820, 5 volumes), quoted in L. Donnadieu, *La Théorie de l'équilibre*, p. 46, who adds: "Burlamaqui's ideas are found word for word in Vattel, *Droit des gens*." See E. de Vattel, *Le Droit des gens, ou Principes de la loi naturelle* . . . , III, 3, § 47, "De l'Équilibre politique" (London: 1758) vol. 2, pp. 39-40.

32. As Donnadieu clarifies, *La Théorie de l'équilibre*, p. 27, note 3: "The treaties of Westphalia established the use of ambassadors. From this comes in part their great influence on the Balance."

33. On the peace of Westphalia, which in reality comprises several treaties, see above, this lecture, note 9.

twelve

29 MARCH 1978

The second technological assemblage characteristic of the new art of government according to raison d'État: police. *Traditional meanings of the word up to the sixteenth century. Its new sense in the seventeenth and eighteenth centuries: calculation and technique making possible the good use of the state's forces.* ∼ *The triple relationship between the system of European balance and police.* ∼ *Diversity of Italian, German, and French situations.* ∼ *Turquet de Mayerne,* La Monarchie aristodémocratique. ∼ *The control of human activity as constitutive element of the force of the state.* ∼ *Objects of police: (1) the number of citizens; (2) the necessities of life; (3) health; (4) occupations; (5) the coexistence and circulation of men.* ∼ *Police as the art of managing life and the well-being of populations.*

[*Foucault apologizes for his lateness, due to a traffic jam.*]

I WILL HAVE SOME more bad new news for you, but I will tell you at the end of the lecture. So, I have tried to show you that this new art of government became—this is the first point—one of the functions, attributes, or tasks of sovereignty, and it found its principle of calculation in *raison d'État*. Last week I tried to show you that the essential novelty of this new art of government is based on something else. That is to say, from the end of the sixteenth and the beginning of the seventeenth century it was no longer a matter of this art of government, which obviously existed in outline for a long time, following the old formula and conforming to, approaching, or remaining true to the essence of a perfect government. Henceforth the art of government will not consist in restoring an essence or in remaining faithful to it, but in manipulating, maintaining, distributing, and re-establishing relations of force within a space of competition that entails competitive growths. In other words, the art of government is deployed in a field of relations of forces. I think this is the great threshold of modernity of this art of government.

Concretely, deployment in a field of relations of forces means setting up two major assemblages of political technology. One, which I talked about last week, is constituted by the procedures necessary and sufficient for maintaining what was already called the balance of Europe, European equilibrium, that is to say, in short, the technique that consists in organizing and developing the composition of forces and an inter-state compensation of forces through a double instrumentation: a diplomatic instrumentation of permanent and multilateral diplomacy, on the one hand, and the organization of a professional army on the other. This is the first great technological assemblage typical of the new art of government in a competitive field of forces.

The second great technological assemblage, which I want to talk about today, is what at the time was called "police," which it must be understood has very little, no more than one or two elements, in common with what we should call police from the end of the eighteenth century. In other words, from the seventeenth to the end of the eighteenth century, the word "police" had a completely different meaning from the one it has today.[1] I want to make three sets of remarks concerning this police.

First, of course, some remarks on the meaning of the word. In the fifteenth and sixteenth centuries the word "police" is already frequently used to designate a number of things. In the first place, one calls "police," quite simply, a form of community or association governed by a public authority; a sort of human society when something like political power or public authority is exercised over it. Very often you find series of expressions or listings like the following: states, principalities, towns, police (*les polices*). Or again, you often find the two words, republics and police (*les polices*), associated. A family, or a convent won't be said to be a police, precisely because they lack the characteristic exercise of a public authority over them. All the same, it is a sort of relatively poorly defined society, a public body. The use of the word "police" in this sense will last practically until the beginning of the seventeenth century. Second, still in the fifteenth and sixteenth centuries, one also calls "police" precisely the set of actions that direct these communities under public authority. Thus you find the almost traditional expression "police and regiment (*régiment*)," "regiment" used in the sense of a way of directing, of governing, and which is associated with "police." Finally, there is the third sense of the word "police," which is quite simply the result, the positive and valued result of a good government. These are broadly the three somewhat traditional meanings that we come across up to the sixteenth century.

From the seventeenth century it seems to me that the word "police" begins to take on a profoundly different meaning. I think we can briefly summarize it in the following way. From the seventeenth century "police" begins to refer to the set of means by which the state's forces can be increased while preserving the state in good order.[2] In other words, police will be the calculation and technique that will make it possible to establish a mobile, yet stable and controllable relationship between the state's internal order and the development of its forces. There is a word, moreover, which more or less covers this object, this domain, designating the relationship between the increase of the state's forces and its good order. We come across this rather strange word for describing the object of police several times. You find it at the start of the seventeenth century in a text to which I will have frequent occasion to return, a text from 1611 written by Turquet de Mayerne with the curious title of *La Monarchie aristodémocratique*.[3] You find it again fifty years later in 1776 in a German text by Hohenthal.[4] This word is quite simply "splendor." Police must ensure the state's splendor. In 1611, Turquet de Mayerne says that police must be concerned with "Everything that gives ornament, form, and splendor to the city."[5] And in 1776, Hohenthal, taking up the traditional definition, says: "I accept the definition of those who call police the set of means that serve the splendor of the entire state and the happiness of all its citizens."[6] What is splendor? It is both the visible beauty of the order and the brilliant, radiating manifestation of a force. Police therefore is in actual fact the art of the state's splendor as visible order and manifest force. In a more analytical form, this type of definition of police is found in the author who was ultimately the greatest theorist of police, a German called von Justi,[7] who, in the middle of the eighteenth century, in his *Éléments généraux de police*, gave the following definition of police: It is the set of "laws and regulations that concern the interior of a state and which endeavor to strengthen and increase the power of this state and make good use of its forces."[8] The good use of the state's forces, this is the object of police.

The second comment I want to make is that you can see the close relations between this traditional, canonical definition of police in the seventeenth and eighteenth centuries, and the problems of the equilibrium, the balance of Europe. There is a morphological relation first of all, since, in what basically did the European equilibrium, this military-diplomatic technique of balance, consist? Well, it consisted in maintaining a balance between different, multiple forces each of which strove to increase according to its own development. Police will also be, but in an opposite direction as it were, a way of increasing the state's forces to the maximum while preserving the state's good order. In one case, the problem of European equilibrium has as its main objective the maintenance of a balance despite the growth of the state, as it were; in the other, the problem of police is how to ensure the maximum growth of the state's forces while maintaining good internal order. So, the first relation is between police and European equilibrium.

Second, there is a relation of conditioning, for at the end of the sixteenth century the space of inter-state competition has opened out considerably and taken over from dynastic rivalries, and it is quite clearly understood that in this space of, not generalized competition, but European competition between states, the maintenance of equilibrium is only gained insofar as each state is able to increase its own force to an extent such that it is never overtaken by another state. One can only effectively maintain the balance and equilibrium in Europe insofar as each state has a good police that allows it to develop its own forces. There will be imbalances if the development between each police is not relatively parallel. Each state must have a good police so as to prevent the relation of forces being turned to its disadvantage. One quickly arrives at the, in a way, paradoxical and opposite consequence, which consists in saying: In the end, there will be imbalance if within the European equilibrium there is a state, not my state, with bad police. Consequently one must see to it that there is good police, even in other states. European equilibrium begins to function as a sort of inter-state police or as right. European equilibrium gives the set of states the right to see to it that there is good police in each state. This is the conclusion drawn explicitly and systematically in 1815 with the Vienna treaty and the policy of the Holy Alliance.[9]

Finally, third, there is a relationship of instrumentation between European equilibrium and police, in the sense that there is at least one common instrument. This instrument common to European equilibrium and the organization of police is statistics. The effective preservation of European equilibrium requires that each state is in a position, first, to know its own forces, and second, to know and evaluate the forces of the others, thus permitting a comparison that makes it possible to uphold and maintain the equilibrium. Thus a principle is needed for deciphering a state's constitutive forces. For each state, one's own and the others, one needs to know the population, the army, the natural resources, the production, the commerce, and the monetary circulation— all the elements that are in fact provided by the science, or domain of knowledge, statistics, which is founded and developed at this time. How can one establish statistics? It can be established precisely by police, for police itself, as the art of developing forces, presupposes that each state exactly identifies its possibilities, its virtualities. Police makes statistics necessary, but police also makes statistics possible. For it is precisely the whole set of procedures set up to increase, combine, and develop forces, it is this whole administrative assemblage that makes it possible to identify what each state's forces comprise and their possibilities of development. Police and statistics mutually condition each other, and statistics is a common instrument between police and the European equilibrium. Statistics is the state's knowledge of the state, understood as the state's knowledge both of itself and also of other states. As such, statistics is the hinge of the two technological assemblages.

There is a fourth element of the essential, fundamental relation between police and equilibrium, which is the problem of commerce, but I will try to talk about this next week. Let's leave it for the moment.

The third set of remarks I wanted to make is that this project of police, the idea anyway that in each state there must be a concerted art for increasing its constitutive forces, clearly did not take the same form, have the same theoretical characteristics, or provide itself with the same instruments in the different states. Whereas the elements I have talked about until now, the theory of *raison d'État*, for example, or the apparatus of European equilibrium, were all in all common notions or apparatuses found in most European countries, obviously with modulations, in the case of police I think things took a quite different course, and police is neither reflected nor institutionalized in the same way in different European countries. Obviously, this needs to be studied in detail. As indications, hypotheses, in outline, if you like, I think we can say this.

What happened in Italy? Well, quite strangely, although the theory of *raison d'État* was developed in Italy, and although equilibrium was an important and frequently remarked problem, police, on the other hand, was lacking. It was absent both as an institution and as a form of analysis and reflection. The reason for this may have been the combined effect of the territorial division of Italy, the relative economic stagnation it experienced from the seventeenth century, foreign political and economic domination, as well as the presence of the Church as both a universalist and localized institution, dominant in the peninsula and territorially anchored in a precise part of Italy, which meant perhaps that the problematic of the growth of forces was never really able to establish itself, or rather, that it was constantly permeated and blocked by another problem, dominant for Italy, which was precisely the balance of this plurality of forces that were not unified and maybe could not be unified. Basically, since the great dividing up of Italy the question has always been first of all that of the composition and compensation of forces, that is to say, the primacy [of] diplomacy. The problem of the growth of forces, of the concerted, reflected, and analytical development of the forces of the state could only come afterwards. This was undoubtedly true before Italian unity, and it is no doubt also true after the realization of Italian unity and the constitution of something like an Italian state, a state that has never really been a state of police, in the seventeenth and eighteenth century sense of course, and which has always been a state of diplomacy, that is to say, a set of plural forces between which an equilibrium must be established, between political parties, trade unions, clienteles, the Church, the North, the South, the mafia, and so on, which resulted in Italy being a state of diplomacy without being a state of police. This, perhaps, has meant that precisely something like war, or guerilla war, or quasi-war, is the permanent form of existence of the Italian state.

In the case of Germany, territorial division paradoxically produced a completely different effect. This was an "over-problematization"* of police, an intense theoretical and practical development of what police should be as a mechanism for increasing the forces of the state. We should try to identify the reasons why territorial division had the kind of effect it did in Italy, and an exactly opposite effect in Germany. Let's leave aside the reasons. What I would just like to indicate is that we can think of these German states, which were constituted, reorganized, and sometimes even fabricated at the time of the treaty of Westphalia in the middle of the seventeenth century, as veritable small, micro-state laboratories that could serve both as models and sites of experiment. Between feudal structures recombined by the treaty of Westphalia and the imperial idea beyond Germany—hovering over its territory, but weakened, if not nullified by this same treaty—we see the constitution of these, if not modern, at least new states which are privileged spaces for state experiment occupying an intermediate position between feudal structures and the big states. This laboratory aspect was no doubt reinforced by the fact that, coming out of a feudal structure, Germany completely lacked what France possessed: an already constituted administrative personnel. This meant that in order to undertake this experimentation it really had to provide itself with a new personnel. Where did it go to find this new personnel? It was found in an institution that existed throughout Europe, but which in a divided Germany, and divided especially between Protestants and Catholics, had become much more

---

* Word in inverted commas in the manuscript.

important than anywhere else, that is to say, the university. Whereas in France the universities were constantly losing their weight and influence, for reasons arising from both administrative development and also the dominant character of the Catholic Church, in Germany they became places both for the training of those administrators who had to secure the development of the state's forces, and at the same time for reflection on the techniques to be employed to increase the state's forces. From this stems the fact that you see the development in German universities of something with practically no equivalent in Europe: the *Polizeiwissenschaft*, the science of police,[10] which from the middle or end of the seventeenth century to the end of the eighteenth century is an absolutely German specialty that spreads throughout Europe and exerts a crucial influence. Theories of police, books on police, and manuals for administrators will produce an enormous bibliography of *Polizeiwissenschaft* in the eighteenth century.[11]

I think the situation in France is neither that of Germany nor Italy. The rapid, early development of territorial unity, of monarchical centralization, and also of administration, means that the problematization of police is not carried out in the theoretical and speculative mode we see in Germany. In a way police was conceived of within administrative practice, but without theory, system, or concepts, and so it was practiced and institutionalized through measures, rulings, collections of edicts, and also through critiques and projects that did not come from the university at all, but from individuals hovering around the administration, either administrators themselves, or those who wanted to enter or had been dismissed from the administration. We also find it in teachers, and in the prince's teachers in particular: there is a theory of police in Fénelon, for example,[12] another very interesting one in Fleury,[13] and in all the private tutors of the dauphins. So in France there are not those great constructions like the [German] *Polizeiwissenschaft*, [nor even] the notion of *Polizeistaat*, police state, which was so important in Germany. Subject to correction, I think it will be found in other texts, I have found the notion once. In Montchrétien's *Traité d'économie politique* I found the expression police state (*État* de police*), which exactly corresponds to the German's *Polizeistaat*.[14]

---

* With capital letter in the manuscript.

So much for the general situation of this problem of police. Now then, a question: If its general objective is to increase the state's forces in such a way that it reinforces rather than compromises the order of this state, what in fact is police concerned with? I will take a text I have already referred to, which is a very early text written right at the start of the seventeenth century, and which is a sort of utopia of precisely what the Germans would have immediately called a *Polizeistaat*, a police state, and for which the French did not have the word. This utopia of a police state from 1611 was written by someone called Turquet de Mayerne, and in this text, entitled *La Monarchie aristodémocratique*, Turquet de Mayerne begins by defining police as "everything that gives [I have given this quotation; M.F.] ornament, form, and splendor to the city."[15] It is "the order of everything that one can see" in the city.[16] Consequently, at this level, police really is the entire art of government. For Turquet de Mayerne, the art of government and the exercise of police is the same thing.[17] But if we now want to know how in fact to exercise police, well, says Turquet de Mayerne, every good government would have four great offices and four great officers:[18] the Chancellor, concerned with justice, the Constable, concerned with the army, and the Superintendent, concerned with finance—all of these being already existing institutions—plus a fourth great officer who, he says, will be the "Commisioner (*Conservateur*) and general reformer of police." What is his role? His role is to maintain [and I quote; M.F.] "a particular practice of modesty, charity, loyalty, industry, and domestic order" in the people.[19] I will come back to this shortly.

Now, in the different regions and provinces of the country, who will be subject to the orders of this great officer, this police Commissioner, who is thus at the same level as the Chancellor and is not subject to a supervisor? In every province there will be four offices under the Commissioner's authority, and these will therefore be direct branches and subordinates of the Commissioner of police. What is the first, which has the name Bureau of Police strictly speaking, responsible for? First, the instruction of children and young people. The Bureau of Police will have to ensure that children acquire literacy, and Turquet de Mayerne says literacy involves everything necessary to fill all the offices of the kingdom, and so all that is required for exercising an office in the kingdom.[20] Obviously they must learn devotion, and finally they must receive military training.[21] So the Bureau of Police, which is concerned with the instruction of children and young people, will also have to be concerned with the profession of each. That is to say, when his training is finished and he reaches the age of 25, the young man will have to present himself to the Bureau of Police. He will have to say what type of occupation he wants in life, whether or not he is rich, whether he wishes to increase his wealth or simply enjoy it. In any case, he must say what he wants to do. He will be entered in a register with his choice of profession, his chosen mode of life, and he will be entered once and for all. Those who, by chance, do not to want to be entered under one of the headings—I pass over the headings proposed[22]—must be held to be not citizens, but "dregs, crooks and without honor."[23] So much for the Bureau of Police.

Still under the responsibility and direction of the great officer, the general Reformer of police, alongside the Bureau of Police in the strict sense, there will be bureaus of police in a different sense, namely the Bureau of Charity. The Bureau of Charity will be concerned with the poor, with the able-bodied poor of course, who will be given or forced to take work, and the sick and disabled poor, who will be given grants.[24] The Bureau of Charity will also be concerned with public health in times of epidemic and contagion, and also at other times. It will be concerned with accidents of fire, floods, deluges, and anything that may cause impoverishment, "which puts families in indigence and poverty."[25] It will try to prevent these accidents, and to repair them and help their victims. Finally, the Bureau of Charity will lend money "to humble artisans and laborers" who need it to practice their profession, and in order to protect them from the "plunder of usurers."[26]

After police, in the strict sense, and charity, a third bureau will be concerned with markets and—passing over this very quickly—will regulate the problems of the market, of manufacture and the mode of manufacture, and will have to promote trade throughout the province.[27] Finally, a fourth bureau, the Bureau of the Domain, will be concerned with landed property: avoiding the crushing weight of seigniorial rights on the people, checking on the sale of landed property and the way in which it is bought and sold, monitoring sale prices, recording inheritances, and finally seeing to the king's domain and to the roads, rivers, public buildings, and forests.[28]

So, what do we see when we examine Turquet de Mayerne's project? In the first place we see that, at a first level, police is identified with the whole of government, and at a second level—its first distinction with regard to this general function—it appears as a function of the state that is distinct from the three other traditional institutions: justice, the army, and finance. These were the traditional institutions, and now a fourth must be added, police, which is administrative modernity par excellence. Second, we should note that when Turquet de Mayerne defines the role of the general Reformer of police he says that the Reformer must see to the loyalty and modesty of citizens, and so he has a moral function. But he must equally be concerned with wealth and household management, that is to say, with the way in which people conduct themselves with regard to their wealth, their way of working, and consuming. He is therefore concerned with a mixture of morality and work. But what particularly strikes me as essential and typical is that when we look at the very heart of police, at the object and concern of the bureaus of police in the strict sense, we see that it is education on the one hand, and then the profession, the professionalization of individuals, on the other; it is concerned with the education that must train individuals so that they can have a profession, and then the profession, or at any rate, the type of activity to which they will devote themselves and be committed to devote themselves. So, we have a set of controls, decisions, and constraints brought to bear on men themselves, not insofar as they have a status or are something in the order, hierarchy, and social structure, but insofar as they do something, are able to do it, and undertake to do it throughout their life. Moreover, Turquet de Mayerne himself notes that what matters to police is not the distinction between the nobility and the common people; what matters is different occupations, not differences in status.[29] I would like to read you this remarkable passage that is at the start, in the first pages of Turquet de Mayerne's book. With regard to police magistrates, he says: "To the magistrates who will be its directors"—so it's a matter of police—"I have proposed man as the true subject on whom virtue and vice are impressed, in order that, by degrees, he is led from childhood to his perfection, and so that, having led him to a certain perfection, in terms of true political and social virtue, he, in himself and his actions, is held to something to which he devotes himself."[30]

I think one of the most fundamental and typical elements of what will henceforth be understood by "police" is this having "man as the true subject," and as the true subject of "something to which he devotes himself," inasmuch as he has an activity that must characterize his perfection and thus make possible the perfection of the state. Police is directed towards men's activity, but insofar as this activity has a relationship to the state. What interested the sovereign, prince, or republic in the traditional conception, was what men were, either in terms of their status, their virtues, or their intrinsic qualities. It was important for them to be virtuous, it was important for them to be obedient, and it was important for them to be workers and not idlers. The good quality of the state depended upon the good quality of its elements. It was a relationship of being, of the quality of being, a relationship of virtue. In this new conception, what interests the state is not what men are, or even their disputes, as in a state of justice. What interests the state is not even their money, which is typical of, let's say, a fiscal state. What is characteristic of a police state is its interest in what men do; it is interested in their activity, their "occupation."* The objective of police is therefore control of and responsibility for men's activity insofar as this activity constitutes a differential element in the development of the state's forces. I think this is at the very heart of the organization of what the Germans call the police state and what the French actually establish without giving it that name. Through Turquet de Mayerne's project we can see that the project of police hangs on the activity of men as a constitutive element of the state's strength.

What, then, are the concrete tasks of police? As its instrument, it will have to provide itself with whatever is necessary and sufficient for

---

* Word in inverted commas in the manuscript. Foucault notes in the margin of the manuscript: "Cf. Montchrétien, p. 27." The latter writes: "The most competent man in matters of police is not he who exterminates brigands and thieves by rigorous torture, but he who, by the occupation he gives those committed to his government, prevents there being any," *Traité de l'œconomie politique* (1615), ed., Th. Funck-Brentano (Paris: E. Plon, 1889) p. 27.

effectively integrating men's activity into the state, into its forces, and into the development of these forces, and it will have to ensure that the state, in turn, can stimulate, determine, and orientate this activity in such a way that it is in fact useful to the state. In a word, what is involved is the creation of a state utility on the basis of and through men's activity; the creation of a public utility on the basis of men's occupation and activity, on the basis of what they do. On this basis, and by taking from this the modern idea of police, I think we can easily deduce the objects that police will henceforth claim are its concern.

The first concern of police will be the number of men, since, for men's activity as much as for their integration within a state utility, it is important to know how many there are and to ensure that there are as many as possible. The state's strength depends on the number of its inhabitants. This thesis was already formulated in the Middle Ages and was repeated throughout the sixteenth century, but it begins to take on a precise meaning in the seventeenth century insofar as the question immediately arises of how many men are really needed and what the relationship should be between the number of men and the size of the territory, and its wealth, for the best and most certain development of the state's strength. The thesis, or assertion, that the state's force depends on the number of its inhabitants is obstinately repeated throughout the seventeenth century, and still at the beginning of the eighteenth century before the physiocrats' great critique and re-problematization, but I will take a text from the end of the seventeenth and the beginning of the eighteenth century. In the published notes of lessons given to the Dauphin, the priest Fleury said:[31] "We cannot render justice, wage war, raise finance, and so on, without an abundance of living, healthy, and peaceful men. The more there are of them, the more the rest is easy, and the stronger the state and prince will be." Again, it must be said straightaway that it is not the absolute number of the population that counts, but its relationship with the set of forces: the size of the territory, natural resources, wealth, commercial activities, and so on. It is again Fleury who says in his course notes; "(...) it is not expanse of land that contributes to the greatness of the state, but fertility and the number of men. What is the difference between Holland, Muscovy, and Turkey? Desert expanse harms commerce and government. Rather

500,000 men in a small space than a scattered million: the land of Israel."[32] From this stems the first object of police: the number of men, the quantitative development of the population in relation to the resources and possibilities of territory occupied by this population. This is what Hohenthal will call the *copia civium*, in his *Traité de police*, the quantity, the abundance of citizens.[33] So, the first object of police is the number of citizens.

The second object of police is the necessities of life. For people are not enough, they must also be able to live. Consequently police will be concerned with these immediate necessities. First and foremost, of course, is the provision of food, the so-called basic needs. Here again Fleury says: "Prince means father: feeding his children, seeking the means to provide the people with food, clothing, housing, heating. (...) Foodstuffs useful to life cannot be increased too much."[34] This objective of police—seeing that people can in fact support the life given to them by birth— obviously entails an agricultural policy: increasing the number of people in the countryside by reducing the *taille*,* services, the militia, bringing land under cultivation, and so on. This is all in Fleury.[35] So, it entails an agricultural policy. It also entails tight control of the marketing and circulation of foodstuffs, and of provisions made for times of shortage; in short, all that police of grains that I spoke about at the start,[36] and which was, according to Argenson, the police that is the "most precious and important for public order."[37] This not only implies supervision of the marketing of foodstuffs and provisions, but also supervision of their quality at the time of sale, ensuring their good quality and that they are not spoiled, and so on.

Here we touch on a third objective of police. After the number of people and the necessities of life we come to the problem of health. Health becomes an object of police inasmuch as health is also a necessary condition for the many who subsist thanks to the provision of foodstuffs and bare necessities, so that they can work, be busy, and occupied. So health is not just a problem for police in cases of epidemics, when plague is declared, or when it is simply a matter of avoiding the contagious,

---

* French tax, pre-1789, levied by king or overlord on his subjects; G.B.

such as those suffering from leprosy; henceforth the everyday health of everyone becomes a permanent object of police concern and intervention. Thus it is necessary to keep an eye on anything that may support disease in general. The air, aeration, ventilation, especially in towns, will all be linked, of course, with the theory of miasmas,[38] and a whole new politics of amenities, of new urban space, will be organized by reference to and subordinated to concerns and principles of health: the width of roads, the dispersion of elements that may produce miasmas and poison the atmosphere, butchers, abattoirs, cemeteries.

When there is a large population that can subsist and is in good health, the fourth objective of police, after health, will be to see to the activity of this population. By activity is understood, first of all, preventing idleness. With regard to the able-bodied, the policy will be to put to work those who can work, and only to provide for the needs of the disabled poor. Much more important will be seeing to the different types of activity men are capable of, ensuring that the different professions needed by the state are in fact practiced, and ensuring that the kind of products manufactured are such that the country can benefit from them. The regulation of professions is hence another object of police.

Finally, the last object of police is circulation, the circulation of goods, of the products of men's activity. This circulation should be understood first of all in the sense of the material instruments with which it must be provided. Thus police will be concerned with the condition and development of roads, and with the navigability of rivers and canals, etcetera. In his *Traité de droit public*, Donat devotes a chapter [to this question] which is called "Of police," the full title being: "Of police for the use of seas, rivers, bridges, roads, public squares, major routes and other public places."[39] So the space of circulation is a privileged object for police.[40] But by "circulation" we should understand not only this material network that allows the circulation of goods and possibly of men, but also the circulation itself, that is to say, the set of regulations, constraints, and limits, or the facilities and encouragements that will allow the circulation of men and things in the kingdom and possibly beyond its borders. From this stem those typical police regulations, some of which seek to suppress vagrancy, others to facilitate the circulation of goods in this or that direction, [and] others that want to prevent qualified workers from leaving their place of work, or especially the kingdom. After health and the objects of bare necessity, after the population itself, this whole field of circulation will become the object of police.

Generally speaking, what police has to govern, its fundamental object, is all the forms of, let's say, men's coexistence with each other. It is the fact that they live together, reproduce, and that each of them needs a certain amount of food and air to live, to subsist; it is the fact that they work alongside each other at different or similar professions, and also that they exist in a space of circulation; to use a word that is anachronistic in relation to the speculations of the time, police must take responsibility for all of this kind of sociality (*socialité*). The eighteenth century theorists will say this: Police is basically concerned with society.[41] But Turquet de Mayerne had already said that the vocation of men—he does not use the word "vocation," well, I no longer know—is to associate with each other, to seek each other out, and it is this "communication," "the provision and maintenance" of this communication that is the proper object of police.[42] The coexistence and communication of men with each other is ultimately the domain that must be covered by the *Polizeiwissenschaft* and the institution of police that people of the seventeenth and eighteenth centuries were talking about.

So what police thus embraces is basically an immense domain that we could say goes from living to more than just living. I mean by this that police must ensure that men live, and live in large numbers; it must ensure that they have the wherewithal to live and so do not die in excessive numbers. But at the same time it must also ensure that everything in their activity that may go beyond this pure and simple subsistence will in fact be produced, distributed, divided up, and put in circulation in such a way that the state really can draw its strength from it. In a word, let's say that this economic, social system, we could even say this new anthropological system installed at the end of the sixteenth and the beginning of the seventeenth century, is no longer commanded by the immediate problem of surviving and not dying, but is now commanded by the problem of living and doing a bit better than just living, and this is where police is inserted, inasmuch it is the set of techniques that ensure that living, doing better than just living, coexisting, and communicating can in fact be converted into forces of the state. Police is the set of interventions and means that ensure that living, better than just living, coexisting will be effectively useful to the constitution and development of the state's forces. So with police there is a circle that starts from the state as a power of rational and calculated intervention on individuals and comes back to the state as a growing set of forces, or forces to be developed, passing through the life of individuals, which will now be precious to the state simply as life. This was basically already established; it was well known that a king, a sovereign, was more powerful the more subjects he had. This circle will pass through the life of individuals, but it will also pass through their more than just living, that is to say, through what at the time was called men's convenience (*commodité*), their amenity, or even felicity. That is to say, this circle, with all that this implies, means that police must succeed in linking together the state's strength and individual felicity. This felicity, as the individual's better than just living, must in some way be drawn on and constituted into state utility: making men's happiness the state's utility, making men's happiness the very strength of the state. That is why in these definitions of police to which I have just been alluding there is an element that I have been careful to put to one side, which is men's happiness. In Delamare, for example, you find this assertion that the sole object of police "consists in leading man to the most perfect felicity that he can enjoy in this life."[43] Or again, Hohenthal, only the first part of whose definition of police I have already quoted,[44] says that police is the set of means that ensure "*reipublicae splendorem*, the splendor of the republic, *et externam singulorum civilium felicitatem*, and the external felicity of each individual."[45] Splendor of the republic and the felicity of each. I will take up again Justi's fundamental definition, which is, once again, the clearest and most articulate, most analytical. Von Justi says: "Police is the set of laws and regulations that concern the interior of a state, which endeavor to strengthen and increase its power, to make good use of its forces"—I have already quoted this—"and finally to procure the happiness of the subjects."[46] It is this connection between strengthening and increasing the powers of the state, making good use of the forces of the state, and procuring the happiness of its subjects, that is specific to police.

There is a word that designates the concern of police even better than those of amenity, convenience, and felicity. It is rarely found before the end of the eighteenth century. It was however used at the beginning of the seventeenth century and, quite uniquely, it seems to me, without being used again in the French literature, although you will see its echoes and how it leads on to a series of absolutely fundamental problems. The word is found in Montchrétien's *L'Économie politique.* Montchrétien says: "Basically, nature can only give us being, but we get well-being (*bien-être*) from discipline and the arts."[47] Discipline, which must be equal for all, important as it is for the good of the state as for all who live well and honestly within it, and the arts, which since the fall are indispensable for providing us with—and I quote again—"the necessary, the useful, the proper, and the pleasant."[48] So, it seems to me that the objective of police is everything from being to well-being, everything that may produce this well-being beyond being, and in such a way that the well-being of individuals is the state's strength.*

Fine, on the one hand I was late, by fifteen minutes, and, on the other, I am in any case far from having finished what I wanted to say. So—and this was the second bad news—I am certainly going to give another lecture next week, Wednesday, when, starting from this general definition of police, I will try to see how it was criticized, how one got free from it in the course of the eighteenth century, how political economy was born from it, and how the specific problem of population was detached from it, [which will] link up with the problem of "security and population" I spoke about last week. So, if this won't bore you . . . In any case, I will give this lecture next week. Since in any case you are not forced to be here, you may do as you wish.

---

* In the manuscript, p. 28, Foucault adds: "The 'good (*bien*)' in the definition of government given by Saint Thomas—ensure that men conduct themselves well (*bien*) so as to be able to accede to the supreme good (*bien*)—completely changes meaning."

1. See the definition Foucault gives in 1976 in "La politique de la santé au XVIIIe siècle," p. 17; "The Politics of Health in the Eighteenth Century," p. 94: "Down to the end of the ancien régime, the term 'police' does not signify (at least not exclusively) the institution of police in the modern sense; 'police' is the ensemble of mechanisms serving to ensure order, the properly channeled growth of wealth, and the conditions of preservation of health 'in general.' " (A brief description of Delamare's *Treatise* follows.) Foucault's interest in Delamare goes back to the 1960s. See *Histoire de la folie*, pp. 89-90; *Madness and Civilization*, p. 63 [but the precise reference to, and long quotation from, Delamare's *Treatise* is omitted from the English translation; G.B.].

2. In a series of manuscript pages on police, joined to the preparatory dossier for the lectures, Foucault quotes this from the *Instructions* of Catherine II (see below, lecture of 5 April 1978, note 18), concerning the transformation of the meaning of the word police ("from effect to cause"): "Everything that serves to preserve the good order of society is a matter for police."

3. Louis Turquet de Mayerne (1550-1615), *La Monarchie aristodémocratique, ou le Gouvernement composé et meslé des trois formes de legitimes Republiques* (Paris: Jean Berjon and Jean le Bouc, 1611). In his lecture " 'Omnes et singulatim' " Foucault notes: "It's one of the first utopian programs for a policed state. Louis Turquet de Mayerne drew it up and presented it in 1611 to the Dutch States General. In his book *Science and Rationalism in the Government of Louis XIV* [Baltimore: The Johns Hopkins Press, 1949] "J. King draws attention to the importance of this strange work (...)" *Essential Works of Foucault*, 3, p. 317; *Dits et Écrits*, 4. See especially pp. 31-32, 56-58, and 274 of King's work (King has "Louis Turquet-Mayerne"). See also R. Mousnier, "L'opposition politique bourgeoise à la fin du XVIe et au début du XVIIe siècle. L' œuvre de Turquet de Mayerne," *Revue historique*, 213, 1955, pp. 1-20.

4. Peter Carl Wilhelm, Reichsgraf von Hohenthal, *Liber de politia, adspersis observationibus de causarum politiae et justitiae differentiis* (Leipzig: C.J. Hilscherum, 1776) § 2, p. 10. Being written in Latin, we should understand "a text by the German Hohenthal." On this treatise, see " 'Omnes et singulatim' " pp. 321-322; (French trans.) p. 158.

5. Louis Turquet de Mayerne, *La Monarchie aristodémocratique*, Book 1, p. 17: "(...) under Police must be included everything that gives ornament, form, and splendor to the city, and this is in fact the order of everything that one can see in it."

6. P.C.W. Hohenthal, *Liber de politia*, § II, p. 10: "Non displicet vero nobis ea definitio, qua politiam dicunt congeriem mediorum (s. legum et institutorum), quae universae reipublicae splendori atque externae singulorum civium felicitati inserviunt." In support of this definition, Hohenthal cites J.J. Moser, *Commentatio von der Landeshoheit in Policy-Sachen* (Frankfurt-Leipzig: 1773) p. 2, § 2, and J.S. Pütter, *Institutiones Iuris publici germanici* (Göttingen, 1770) p. 8. Neither of these, however, lays stress on the happiness or security of the subjects, nor employs the word "splendor."

7. Polygraph of the eventful career and whose life contains many shadowy zones, Johann heinrich Gottlob von Justi (1720-1771) was both a professor and a practitioner. He taught first of all cameralistics at the Theresianum of Vienna, an establishment founded in 1746, intended for the education of young nobles, and then, after various episodes that take him from Leipzig to Denmark, he settled in Berlin in 1760 where Frederic II entrusted him, some years later, with the office of Berghauptmann, a sort of general administrator of the mines. Accused, doubtless falsely, of having misappropriated public money, he was imprisoned in 1768 in the fortress of Küstrin where, blind and ruined, he died without being able to prove his innocence. The works corresponding to the two periods of his life, in Vienna and Berlin, have a quite distinct tonality. The first, of which the *Grundsätze der Policey-Wissenschaft*, 1756, taken from the lectures at the Theresianum and translated into French as *Élément généraux de police*, 1769, are basically organized around the good of the state, while the second (*Grundriß einer guten Regierung*, 1759, and *Grundfeste der Macht und Glückseligkeit der Staaten oder Polizeiwissenschaft*, 1760-1761) put greater emphasis on the good of individuals.

8. J.H.G. von Justi, *Grundsätze der Policey-Wissenschaft* (Göttingen: Van den Hoecks, 1756) p. 4: "In weitläuftigem Verstande begreifet man unter der Policey alle Maaßregeln in innerlichen Landesangelegenheiten, wodurch das allgemeine Vermögen des Staats dauerhaftiger gegründet und vermehret, die Kräfte des Staats besser gebrauchet und überhaupt die

Glückseligkeit des gemeinen Wesens befördet werden kann; und in diesem Verstande sind die Commercien, Wissenschaft, die Stadt- und Landöconomie, die Verwaltung der Bergwerke, das Forstwesen und dergleichen mehr, in so fern die Regierung ihre Vorsorge darüber nach Maaßgebung des allgemeinen Zusammenhanges der Wohlfahrt Staats einrichtet, zu der Policey zu rechnen"; Partial French translation by Eidous, *Éléments généraux de police* (Paris: Rozet, 1769) introduction, § 2 (concerning police in the broad sense): "(...) under the name police we include the laws and regulations that concern the interior of a state, which endeavor to strengthen and increase its power, to make a good use of its forces, to procure the happiness of its subjects, in a word, the commerce, finances, agriculture, mining, woods, forests, etcetera, in view of the fact that the happiness of the state depends on the wisdom with which all these things are administered."

9. On the Congress of Vienna (September 1814 to June 1815), the final Act of which, 9 June 1815, brought together the different treaties signed by the great powers, see above, lecture 1 February 1978, note 9. The Holy Alliance, concluded in September 1815, was in the first place a pact of religious inspiration signed by the Tsar Alexander I, the Emperor of Austria Francis I, and the king of Prussia, Frederick William III, for the defense "of the precepts of justice, Christian charity, and peace" "in the name of the very Holy and indivisible Trinity." Metternich, who considered it "an empty and sonorous monument," was able to transform it into an instrument of the union of the allied powers against liberal and nationalist movements. It broke up in 1823, following the congress of Verona and the French expedition in Spain.

10. On the teaching of *Polizeiwissenschaft* in German universities in the eighteenth century, see above, lecture of 11 January 1978, note 25. See M. Stolleis, *Histoire du droit public en Allemagne, 1600-1800*, pp. 562-570.

11. On this bibliography, see M. Humpert, *Bibliographie des Kameralwissenschaften* (Cologne: K. Schröder, 1937), which goes back to the sixteenth century. The author lists more than 4000 titles, from 1520 to 1850, under the headings "science of police in the broad sense" and "science of police in the strict sense." See also, A.W. Small, *The Cameralists* (see above, lecture of 11 January 1978, note 25); H. Maier, *Die ältere deutsche Staats- und Verwaltungslehre* (Neuwied-Berlin: H. Luchterhand, 1966; considerably enlarged edition, Munich: DTV, 1986), and P. Schiera, *Il Cameralismo e l'assolutismo tedesco*.

12. Fénelon, François de Salignac de La Mothe (1651-1715), private tutor to the duc de Bourgogne from 1689 to 1694. Foucault is no doubt alluding to the *Examen de conscience sur les devoirs de la royauté* (first, posthumous edition published under the title *Direction pour la conscience d'un roi* [The Hague: Neaulme, 1747]) in *Œuvres de Fénelon* (Paris: Firmin Didot, 1838) vol. 3, pp. 335-347; English translation as, M. de Fenelon, *Proper Heads of Self-examination for a King* (London: 1747).

13. See above, p. 324.

14. Antoyne de Montchrétien (Montchrétien, 1575-1621), *Traité de l'œconomie politique* (1615) ed., Th. Funck-Brentano (Paris: E. Plon, 1889) Book 1, p. 25: "The northern peoples make better and more regular use of the police state (*l'estat de la police*) today than ourselves."

15. See above, this lecture, note 5.

16. Ibid.

17. See L. Turquet de Mayerne, *La Monarchie aristodémocratique*, Book IV, p. 207: "(...) in it [Police] is reduced all that could be thought or said concerning government: extending Police obviously through all the estates and conditions of persons, and in everything that they plan, do, maintain, and exercise."

18. Ibid. Book I, p. 14.

19. Ibid. p. 15.

20. Ibid. p. 20: "(...) to fill properly every office, in which it is necessary to employ educated people."

21. Ibid. pp. 19-20: "(...) veiller sur l'instruction de la jeunesse de tous estats, en ce que principalement le public requiert, & où il a droict & notoire interest, en toutes les familles; qui se reduict en trois chefs, sçavoir est Insitution aux lettres, en la pieté ou religion, & en la discipline militaire."

22. Ibid. p. 14: "That is, the Wealthy, with large incomes, the merchants and business men, the artisans, and for the last and lowest, laborers and work-hands."

23. Ibid. p. 22: "All those together who have reached the age of 25 will be required to appear before them [the Rectors of the Bureau of Police] in each district to declare the vocation they would like to follow and to register in one of the classes, according to their means, living, and industry, on pain of ignominy. For those who will not be entered in the registers of the Bureaux, must not hold the rank of citizen, but rather as dregs of the people, must be considered crooks and without honor; deprived of all privileges of good faith (. . .)"

24. Ibid. p. 23.

25. Ibid. pp. 24-25: "These public Rectors will also be concerned at every moment with publich health and, in times of contagion, will support the sick and remedy the accidents caused by such a disaster (. . .). Fires and major floods or deluges will also fall under their authority and concern since they are causes of impoverishment and bring about the indigence and poverty of the people."

26. Ibid. p. 24.

27. See, ibid. p. 25: "the Bureau of Markets."

28. Ibid. pp. 25-26.

29. Ibid. p. 14: "(. . .) the qualities of each class [= the five orders or classes making up the people] being purely private, the question is not one of Nobility or Commoner, but only of the means and ways that each must employ and observe in the Republic."

30. Ibid. p. 19.

31. Claude Fleury (1640-1723), priest and historian, assistant private tutor to the king's children alongside Fénelon—not to be confused with the cardinal de Fleury, who was also private tutor to Louis XV. He is the author of many works, of which the most famous is the *Institutions du droit français* (Paris, 1692), 2 volumes. See R.E. Wanner, *Claude Fleury (1640-1723) as an Educational Historiographer and Thinker* (The Hague: Martinus Nijhoff, 1975), and on his activity as publicist, G. Thuillier, "Économie et administration au Grand Siècle: l'abbé Claude Fleury," *La Revue administrative*, 10, 1957, pp. 348-573, and by the same author, "Comment les Francais voyaient l'administration au XVIIIe siècle: le Droit public de la France de l'abbé Fleury," ibid., 18, 1965, pp. 20-25.

32. We have been unable to find this and the previous quotation in the only edition of the *Avis au Duc de Bourgogne* known to us, in *Opuscules* (Nimes: P. Beaume, 1780) vol. 3, pp. 273-284. See, however, Fleury, *Pensées politiques*, ibid. p. 252: "It is the number of men and not the expanse of land that makes the strength of the state. It would be better to command one hundred men in a fertile island of two leagues than to be alone in an island of two hundred leagues: thus he who governs 100,000 men in a land of ten leagues will be stronger than he who has 200,000 scattered over one hundred leagues."

33. P.C.W. von Hohenthal, *Liber de politia*, ch. 1, I: "De copia civium" (§ VIII-IX) pp. 17-28.

34. C. Fleury, *Avis au Duc de Bourgogne*, p. 277: "Prince is father: feeding his children: seeking the means to provide the people with food, clothing, housing, heating. Foodstuffs: wheat and other grains, vegetables, fruit: promoting laborers, the most necessary of all subjects, hardworking, living on little, usually good people: the most honest means of earning is by Agriculture: the foodstuffs useful to life cannot be increased too much."

35. Ibid.: "Repopulating the villages and increasing the people of the countryside by reduction of the *Taille*, reduction of the Militia, &c."

36. See above, lecture of 18 January, pp. 31-33.

37. Mare-René de Voyer, marquis d'Argenson (1652-1721), father of the author of *Mémoires* (see, *Naissance de la biopolitique*, lecture of 10 January 1979, p. 22). He took over from La Reynie as general lieutenant of police in 1697, and then exercised the functions of president of the Council of finances and Guard of the Seals (1718). The phrase quoted is taken from a letter of 8 November 1699, quoted by M. de Boislisle, *Correspondence des Contrôleurs généraux*, vol. III, no. 38, and reproduced by E. Depitre in his introduction to Herbert, *Essai sur la police générale des grains*, 1753 edn., p. v [see above, lecture of 18 January 1978, note 7].

38. See C. Fleury, *Avis au Duc de Bourgogne*, p. 378: "Having care for the cleanness of towns for health, preventing popular diseases; good air and good water in abundance."

39. Jean Donat (jurist, Jansenist, king's lawyer at the Clermont bailiwick court, 1625-1696), *Le Droit public, suite des Loix civiles dans leur ordre naturel* (Paris: J.-B. Coignard, 1697, 2 volumes; 2nd edn., 1697, 5 volumes; republished Paris, 1829) reproduced in the "Bibliothèque de philosophie politique et juridique," Presses universitaires de Caen, 1989, Book I, heading

VIII: "Of Police for the use of seas, rivers, ports, bridges, roads, public squares, major routes and other public places: and what concerns the rivers and forests, hunting and fishing."

40. Ibid. 1697 2nd edn., vol. IV, pp. 224-225: "(...) it is for this use of this second kind of things [things produced by man, such us food, clothing, and housing] that, as they are necessary in society and man can only possess them and put them to use by routes that require different links and communications between them, not only from one place to another, but from every country to every other, and between the most distant nations. The facilitation of communications has been provided by God through nature and by man through police."

41. In the set of manuscript pages on police already referred to above (this lecture, note 2), Foucault quotes Delamare concerning this idea that "police is concerned with 'society' ": "Police encompasses in its object all the things that serve as foundation and rule for the societies that men have established amongst themselves." And he adds: "A set of individuals have relations of coexistence which mean that they live and dwell together. In short a population."

42. L. Turquet de Mayerne, *La Monarchie aristodémocratique*, Book 1, p. 4: "(...) without this communication the conveyance and maintenance of which is what is properly called Police, it is certain that we would be deprived of humanity and even more of piety, we would perish miserably through our failings, and would have neither love nor charity in the world."

43. N. Delamare, *Traité de la police*, 1705 edn., vol. 1, Preface without page numbers [second page].

44. See above, pp. 313-314. Full quotation in Latin is given above, in note 6 (this lecture).

45. P.C.W. Hohenthal, *Liber de politia*, p. 10.

46. See above, this lecture, note 8.

47. A. de Montchrétien, *Traité de l'œconomie politique*, p. 39.

48. Ibid. p. 40.

thirteen

5 April 1978

Police (continuation). ∿ *Delamare.* ∿ *The town as site for the development of police. Police and urban regulation. Urbanization of the territory. Relationship between police and the mercantilist problematic.* ∿ *Emergence of the market town.* ∿ *Methods of police. Difference between police and justice. An essentially regulatory type of power. Regulation and discipline.* ∿ *Return to the problem of grain.* ∿ *Criticism of the police state on the basis of the problem of scarcity. The theses of the* économistes *concerning the price of grain, population, and the role of the state.* ∿ *Birth of a new governmentality. Governmentality of the* politiques *and governmentality of the* économistes. ∿ *The transformations of* raison d'État: *(1) the naturalness of society; (2) new relationships between power and knowledge; (3) taking charge of the population (public hygiene, demography, etc.); (4) new forms of state intervention; (5) the status of liberty.* ∿ *Elements of the new art of government: economic practice, management of the population, law and respect for liberties, police with a repressive function.* ∿ *Different forms of counter-conduct relative to this governmentality.* ∿ *General conclusion.*

TODAY WE WILL END this slightly extended series of lectures. First of all a couple of words on what police was concretely—how the practice of police actually appeared in the texts. I think I gave you the general idea last week, but what concretely did a book devoted to police talk about? I think we should refer anyway to the text that was the fundamental compendium throughout the eighteenth century, the basic text of the practice of police, both in Germany and France moreover; although the compendium is in French, the German books always referred to it when it was a question of what was involved when talking about police. Delamare's compendium, a large, three volume collection of police ordinances appeared in, I no longer remember, 1711, 1708 . . . , anyway, it was republished several times in the eighteenth century.[1] Delamare's compendium, and those that followed it,[2] generally specify thirteen domains with which police must be concerned. These are religion, morals, health and subsistence, public peace, the care of buildings, squares, and highways, the sciences and the liberal arts, commerce, manufacture and the mechanical arts, servants and laborers, the theater and games, and finally the care and discipline of the poor, as a "considerable part of the public good."[3] Delamare regroups these thirteen rubrics[4] under more general headings, or rather more general functions, since if police is concerned with religion and morals, it is because it involves ensuring what he calls the "goodness of life."[5] If it is concerned with health and subsistence, it is because its function is the "preservation of life."[6] Goodness, preservation of life. Peace, the care of buildings, the sciences and liberal arts, commerce, manufacture and the mechanical arts, and domestic servants and laborers, all refer to the "convenience of life,"[7] and the theater and games refer to the "pleasures of life."[8] As for discipline and care of the poor, it is "a considerable part of the public good"[9] and involves the elimination, or at any rate control of the poor, the exclusion of those who cannot work, and the obligation of those that can work actually to do so. All of this constituted the general condition for life in society to be effectively preserved in terms of its goodness, convenience, and amenity. I think you can see that this confirms what I was saying to you last week, namely that police, in the general sense of the term in the seventeenth and eighteenth centuries, is concerned with living and more than just living, living and better than just living. As Montchrétien said, not only being is necessary, but also "well-being."[10] What is actually involved is the goodness, preservation, convenience, and pleasures of life.

When we look at the different objects thus defined as relevant to the practice, intervention, and also reflection of police, and on police, the first thing we can note is that they are all essentially what could be called urban objects. They are urban in the sense that some only exist in the town and because there is a town. These are roads, squares, buildings, the market, commerce, manufacture, the mechanical arts, and so on. Others are objects that are problems falling under police inasmuch as they are especially significant in towns. Health, for example, subsistence, the means for preventing scarcity, [the] presence of beggars, [the] circulation of vagrants—vagrants only become a problem in the countryside at the end of the eighteenth century. Let's say that all of these are therefore problems of the town. More generally they are problems of coexistence, and of dense coexistence.

The second thing we should note is that the problems with which police is concerned are also problems of the market, of buying and selling, of exchange, which are closely related to these problems of the town. It concerns the regulation of the way in which things can and must be put on sale, at what price, how, and when. It also concerns the regulation of manufactured objects, of the mechanical arts and, broadly speaking, craft industries. In short, it concerns the whole problem of the exchange, circulation, manufacture, and marketing of goods. Coexistence of men and circulation of goods: we should finish also by saying, the circulation of men and goods in relation to each other. It is the whole problem, precisely, of these vagrants, of people moving around. Let's say, in short, that police is essentially urban and market based, or to put things more brutally, it is an institution of the market, in the very broad sense.

So there is nothing surprising about certain facts. First, in the practices and real institutions of police, where do these ordinances collected in the big eighteenth century compendiums come from? Generally they are old, sometimes going back to the sixteenth, fifteenth, and fourteenth centuries, and they are essentially urban ordinances. That is to say, the practices and institutions of police often only take up these earlier urban regulations that developed in the Middle Ages and concerned forms of living together, the manufacture of goods, and the sale of foodstuffs. So seventeenth and eighteenth century police carries out a sort of extension of this urban regulation.

The other institution that is, as it were, a preliminary to police, is not urban regulation but the mounted constabulary, the *maréchaussée*, that is to say, the armed force that royal power was forced to deploy in the fifteenth century in order to avoid the consequences and disorders following war, and essentially the dissolution of armies at the end of wars. Freed soldiers, soldiers who had often not been paid, disbanded, made up a floating mass of individuals who were of course dedicated to every kind of illegality: violence, delinquency, crime, theft, and murder. The *maréchaussée* was responsible for controlling and repressing all these people on the road.

These are the institutions prior to police. The town and the road, the market, and the road network feeding the market. Hence the fact that in the seventeenth and eighteenth century police was thought essentially in terms of what could be called the urbanization of the territory. Basically, this involved making the kingdom, the entire territory, into a sort of big town; arranging things so that the territory is organized like a town, on the model of a town, and as perfectly as a town. We should recall that in his *Traité de droit public*,* which is very important for all these problems of the connection between police power and juridical sovereignty, Domat said that "it is by police that we create towns and places where men assemble and communicate with each other through the use of roads, public squares and (...) highways."[11] In Domat's mind, the link between police and town is so strong that he says it is only because there was police, that is to say, because we have regulated the way in which men, first, could and had to come together, and then, second, communicate with each other—in the broad sense of "communicate," that is to say, actually live together and exchange, live together and circulate, live together and speak, live together and buy and sell—it is because there was a police regulating this cohabitation, circulation, and exchange that towns were able to exist. Police, then, as a condition of existence of urban existence. Almost 150 years after Domat, in a general dictionary of police at the end of the eighteenth century, Fréminville gives the following, completely mythical explanation of the birth of police in France, saying that Paris became the first city of the world in the seventeenth century due to the exact perfection of its police.[12] Fréminville says that the rigorous police exercised in Paris made it such a perfect and marvelous

---

* Foucault adds: of the seventeenth century

model that Louis XIV "wanted all the judges of all the towns of his realm to create police along the lines of Paris."[13] There are towns because there is police, and it is because there are towns so perfectly policed that there was the idea of transferring police to the general scale of the kingdom. "To police," "to urbanize": I evoke these terms for you to see the connotations and echoes of these two words, along with the shifts and attenuations of meaning that occurred in the eighteenth century; but in the strong sense of these terms, to police and to urbanize is the same thing.

The other comment I want to make concerning this relationship between police and, let's say, urban existence, is that you can also see that police, the establishment of police, is absolutely inseparable from a governmental theory and practice that is generally labeled mercantilism, that is to say, a technique and calculation for strengthening the power of competing European states through the development of commerce and the new vigor given to commercial relations. Mercantilism is fully part of this context of European balance and intra-European competition I spoke about some weeks ago,[14] and it identifies commerce as the essential instrument and fundamental weapon in this intra-European competition that must take place in the form of equilibrium. That is to say, mercantilism requires, first, that every country try to have the largest possible population, second, that the entire population be put to work, third, that the wages given to the population be as low as possible so that, fourth, the cost price of goods is the lowest possible and one can thus sell the maximum amount abroad, which will bring about the import of gold, the transfer of gold into the royal treasury, or in any case, in this way the country will triumph commercially. In the first place gold will, of course, provide for the recruitment of soldiers and for the military force indispensable for the growth of the state and its game in the European equilibrium, and it will also provide for the stimulation of production, and hence new commercial progress. This strategy of commerce as a technique for the import of currency is one of the typical features of mercantilism. When *raison d'État* takes European equilibrium as its objective, with a military-diplomatic armature for its instrument, and when this same *raison d'État* takes the singular growth of each state power as its other objective with, at the same time, commerce as the instrument of this growth, you can see how and why police is inseparable from a politics of commercial competition within Europe.

Police and commerce, police and urban development, and police and the development of all the activities of the market in the broad sense, constitute an essential unity in the seventeenth century and until the beginning of the eighteenth century. Apparently, the development of the market economy, the multiplication and intensification of exchanges in the sixteenth century, and the activation of monetary circulation, all introduced human existence into the abstract and purely representative world of the commodity and exchange value.[15] Maybe, and maybe it should be deplored, in which case let's deplore it. However, I think something completely different emerges in the seventeenth century that is much more than this entry of human existence into the abstract world of the commodity. It is a cluster of intelligible and analyzable relations that allow a number of fundamental elements to be linked together like the faces of a single polyhedron: the formation of an art of government organized by reference to the principle of *raison d'État*; a policy of competition in the form of the European equilibrium; the search for a technique for the growth of the state's forces* by a police whose basic aim is the organization of relations between a population and the production of commodities; and finally, the emergence of the market town, with all the problems of cohabitation and circulation as problems falling under the vigilance of a good government according to principles of *raison d'État*. I don't mean that the market town was born at this time, but that the market town became the model of state intervention in men's lives. I think this is the fundamental fact of the seventeenth century, at any rate the fundamental fact characterizing the birth of police in the seventeenth century. There is a cycle, if you like, *raison d'État* and an urban privilege, a fundamental link between police and the primacy of the commodity, and it is insofar as there was this relationship between *raison d'État* and an urban privilege, between police and the primacy of the commodity, that the living and better than just living, the being and well-being of individuals really became relevant for government intervention, and for the first time, I think, in the history of Western

---

* Manuscript: "intra-state"

societies. If the governmentality of the state is interested, for the first time, in the fine materiality of human existence and coexistence, of exchange and circulation, if this being and well-being is taken into account for the first time by the governmentality of the state, through the town and through problems like health, roads, markets, grains, and highways, it is because at that time commerce is thought of as the main instrument of the state's power and thus as the privileged object of a police whose objective is the growth of the state's forces. This is the first thing I wanted to say concerning these objects of police, their urban model, and their organization around the problem of the market and commerce.

My second comment, still concerning the police I was talking about last week, is that police demonstrates the intervention of *raison d'État* and power in new domains. However, the methods used by police seem to me to be relatively, even entirely traditional. Of course, from the beginning of the seventeenth century the idea of a police power will be clearly distinguished from a different type of exercise of royal power, which is the power of justice, judicial power. Police is not justice. Whether written by those who support and justify the need for a police, or by jurists or parliamentarians who display a certain mistrust of police, all the texts agree on this: police is seen as not being justice.[16] Of course, like justice it derives from royal power, but it remains clearly separated from justice. At this time, police is in no way thought of as a sort of instrument in the hands of judicial power, as a sort of way of really applying regular justice. It is not an extension of justice, it is not the king acting through his apparatus of justice; it is the king acting directly on his subjects, but in a non-judicial form. A theorist like Bacquet says: "The right of police and the right of justice have nothing in common. (...) We cannot say that the right of police belongs to any-one other than the king."[17] Police consists therefore in the sovereign exercise of royal power over individuals who are subjects. In other words, police is the direct governmentality of the sovereign qua sovereign. Or again, let's say that police is the permanent *coup d'État*. It is the permanent *coup d'État* that is exercised and functions in the name of and in terms of the principles of its own rationality, without having to mold or model itself on the otherwise given rules of justice. So police, which is specific in its functioning and in its first principle, must also be specific in the modalities of its intervention. Still at the end, or in the middle of the eighteenth century, in the *Instructions* of Catherine II inspired by the French philosophers, and concerning her establishment of a code of police, she says: "Police regulations are of a completely different kind than other civil laws. The things of police are things of each moment, whereas the things of the law are definitive and permanent. Police is concerned with little things, whereas the laws are concerned with important things. Police is perpetually concerned with details," and finally it can only act promptly and immediately.[18] So there is a specificity of police compared with the general functioning of justice.

However, when we examine how this specificity actually took shape we see that police in fact knows, and in the seventeenth and eighteenth centuries knew, only one form, only one mode of action and intervention. Obviously, it does not operate through the judicial apparatus, but is a permanent *coup d'État* coming directly from the royal power, but what is the instrument of this permanent *coup d'État*? Well, it is the regulation, the ordinance, the interdiction, the instruction. Police intervenes in a regulatory manner. Again in the *Instructions* of Catherine II we read: "Police has more need of regulations than laws."[19] We are in a world of indefinite regulation, of permanent, continually renewed, and increasingly detailed regulation, but always regulation, always in that kind of form that, if not judicial, is nevertheless juridical: the form of the law, or at least of law as it functions in a mobile, permanent, and detailed way in the regulation.[20] Although it is completely different from the judicial institution, police employs instruments and modes of action that, morphologically if you like, are not radically different from those of justice. That police is an essentially regulatory world is so true that in the middle of the eighteenth century Guillauté, a theorist of police, wrote that police had to be essentially regulatory, but even so one had to avoid the kingdom becoming a convent.[21] We are in the world of the regulation, the world of discipline.* That is to say, the great proliferation of local and regional disciplines we have observed in workshops, schools

---

* Foucault adds in the manuscript: "And, in fact, the big practical treatises on police were collections of regulations."

and the army from the end of the sixteenth to the eighteenth century,[22] should be seen against the background of an attempt at a general disciplinarization, a general regulation of individuals and the territory of the realm in the form of a police based on an essentially urban model. Making the town into a sort of quasi-convent and the realm into a sort of quasi-town is the kind of great disciplinary dream behind police. Commerce, town, regulation, and discipline are, I think, the most characteristic elements of police practice as this was understood in the seventeenth century and the first half of the eighteenth century. This is what I would like to have said last week had I had the full time to describe this great project of police.

I would now like to return to what we started with right at the beginning. We will take the most precise of those texts that I tried to analyze, those that deal with what was called the police of grains and the problem of scarcity.[23] This puts us in the middle, or anyway at the end of the first third of the eighteenth century, and—because basically I have done nothing else for several months but try to provide you with a commentary on these texts on grains and scarcity, which, through some detours, was always the issue—I think now we can get a better understanding of the importance of the problem posed concerning the police of grains and scarcity, a better understanding of its importance and the fierceness of the discussions, as well as of the theoretical breakthrough and practical mutation that was being prepared on the basis of this problem and of these specific techniques and objects of police. It seems to me that through the problem of the marketing and circulation of grains, and through the problem of scarcity, we can see the concrete problem that was the basis for criticism of what could be called the police state, and for the direction taken by this criticism. The critique, dismantling, and break up of this police state to which so much thought had been given, and in which such hope had been invested at the start of the seventeenth century, can be observed in the first half of the eighteenth century through certain problems, and essentially those economic problems, and problems of the circulation of grains in particular, I have spoken about.

Let us take up again some of the themes and theses touched on at this time concerning the police of grains. The first thesis, you recall—I refer, broadly, to the physiocratic literature, but not exclusively, the problem being not so much the positive content of every thesis as what is at issue in each thesis, that of which one speaks and around which the problem is organized—the first thesis of this physiocratic literature, or more generally of the literature of the *économistes* is: If you want to avoid scarcity, that is to say, if you want an abundance of grain, first and foremost, it must be well paid for.[24] At the level of what it asserts, this thesis is opposed to the principle employed in all previous mercantilist policy, which said: There must be plenty of grain, and this grain must be cheap, because cheap grain will enable one to pay the lowest possible wages, and when wages are as low as possible the cost price of goods to be marketed will be low, and when this price is low one will be able to sell them abroad, and by selling abroad one will be able to import the greatest possible amount of gold. So, it was a policy of cheap grain for low workers' wages. Now, with the physiocrats' thesis I have just stated, by attaching fundamental importance to the link between the abundance of grain and its good price, that is to say, its relatively high price, you can see that the physiocrats, and more generally the eighteenth century *économistes*, not only oppose thesis to thesis, but above all [reintroduce]* agriculture itself, agricultural profit, the possibilities of agricultural investment, peasant well-being, the more than just living of the peasant population, into the analysis and objectives of political intervention. In other words, the schema that was entirely organized around the privilege of the town is thereby demolished. The implicit limits of the system of police, established by the urban privilege, break up and open onto the problem of the countryside and agriculture. The problematic of the *économistes* reintroduces agriculture as a fundamental element of rational governmentality. The land now appears alongside, and at least as much as and more than the town, as the privileged object of governmental intervention. It is a governmentality that takes the land into consideration. This governmentality not only takes the land into consideration, but it must no longer focus on the market, on the buying and selling of products, on their circulation, but first of all on production. Finally, third, this governmentality is no longer greatly interested in selling cheaply to others what has been produced at the lowest cost, but focuses on the

---

* M.F.: it reintroduces

problem of the return, that is to say, how the value of the product can be returned to its primary producer, namely the peasant or farmer. So it is no longer the town but the land, no longer circulation but production, no longer putting on sale or the profit from the sale, but the problem of the return that now appears as the essential object of governmentality. There is a dis-urbanization to the advantage of an agrocentrism, a substitution, or emergence anyway, of the problem of production as distinct from the problem of marketing, which is, I think, the first major breach in the system of police in the sense this was understood in the seventeenth century and at the start of the eighteenth century.

You recall that the second thesis was this: What will happen if the grain is well paid, that is to say, if one lets the price of grain rise as much as it wants, so to speak, as much as possible, according to supply and demand, according to its scarcity and consumers' desire? Well, the price of grain will not continue to rise indefinitely but will settle neither too high nor too low, it will settle simply at a level that is the just level. This is the thesis of the just price.[25] And why will the price of grain settle at this level, which is just? Well, in the first place because if the price of grain is sufficiently high, farmers will not hesitate to sow as much as possible precisely because the price is good and they will hope to profit greatly from this. If they sow a great deal there will be better harvests. When harvests are good there will clearly be less temptation to accumulate grain and wait for times of scarcity. Thus all the grain will be put on the market; and if the price is good, foreigners will of course try to send the greatest possible amount of corn in order to profit from this good price, so that the higher the price the more it will tend to settle and stabilize. Now you can see what is called into question by this second principle supported by the *économistes*. It is no longer the urban object, which was the privileged object of police, which is called into question. It is something else, namely regulation, the main means of the police system, which, as I was just saying, [in the form] of a generalized discipline, was the essential form in which one conceived of the possibility and necessity of police intervention. The postulate of police regulation was, of course, that things were indefinitely flexible and that the sovereign's will, or the rationality immanent to the *ratio*, to *raison d'État*, could obtain what it wanted from them. It is precisely this that the *économistes*' analysis calls into question. Things are not flexible for two reasons. The first is that not only is there a certain course of things that cannot be modified, but precisely by trying to modify it one makes things worse. This is why, the *économistes* explain, grain is dear when it is scarce. What will happen if one seeks to prevent the dearness of scarce grain by regulations that fix its price? Well, people will not want to sell their grain, and the more one tries to lower the price, the worse the scarcity will become, and prices will tend to rise, so that not only are things not flexible, but they are as it were recalcitrant and turn back against those who seek to modify them against their natural course. One gets a result that is the exact opposite of the one desired. So, there is a stubbornness of things. Not only will this regulation not go in the direction wished for, it is also quite simply pointless. Police regulation is pointless precisely because, as the analysis I have just been talking about shows, there is a spontaneous regulation of the course of things. Regulation is not only harmful, even worse it is pointless. So a regulation based upon and in accordance with the course of things themselves must replace a regulation by police authority. This is the second major breach opened up in the system of *Polizei*, of police.

The third thesis we find in the *économistes* is that the population is not a good in itself. Here again there is a fundamental break. In the system of police I referred to last week the only way in which the population was taken into consideration was primarily by seeing in it the factor of number: Is there sufficient population? And the answer was: There is never enough. Why is there never enough? Because one needs a large number of workers to work and manufacture many objects. One needs a large workforce to avoid wages rising too high and, as a result, to guarantee a minimal cost price of the things to be manufactured and put on the market. A large number of workers is necessary on condition, of course, that all these workers are working. Finally, a large workforce and workers in work is necessary on condition that they are docile and really apply the regulations imposed on them. Numbers, workers, and docility, or rather large numbers of docile workers, will ensure the, as it were, effective number one needs for a good police. The only natural datum introduced into the machine is the number. Things must be arranged so that people reproduce, and that they reproduce as much as possible.

Outside of this variable of number, individuals are no more than subjects: legal subjects and subjects of police, if you like, but anyway, subjects who have to apply regulations.

With the *économistes* we have a completely different way of conceptualizing the population. The population as an object of government will not be a particular number or the greatest number of individuals at work and applying regulations. The population will always be something else. In the first place this is because number is not in itself a value for the *économistes*. Certainly, the population must be of a sufficient size to produce a lot, and above all there must be a sufficient agricultural population. But it must not be too large, and it must not be too large precisely so that wages are not too low, that is to say, so that people have an interest in working and also so that they can bolster prices through their consumption. So population does not have an absolute value, but simply a relative value. There is an optimum number of people desirable in a given territory, and this desirable number varies according to resources, possible work, and the consumption necessary and sufficient to bolster prices and the economy generally. Second, this number, which is not an absolute value in itself, is not to be fixed in an authoritarian way. One is not to act like those utopians of the sixteenth century who said: Well, this is roughly the number of people that is necessary and sufficient to make happy cities. In fact, the number of people will adjust itself. It will adjust itself precisely according to the available resources. Population movements, possible birth control (I leave this problem aside here, it's not important), in any case, there will be a spontaneous regulation of the population that ensures—and all the *économistes* say this, Quesnay in particular stresses it[26]—[that] you will always have the number of people that is naturally determined by the situation in a given place. Within a certain time scale, the number of a population in a given place will adjust itself according to the situation without any need of intervention through regulations. Population is not therefore an indefinitely modifiable datum. This is the third thesis.

The fourth thesis of the *économistes* is this: Allow free trade between countries. Here again there is a fundamental difference with the system of police. You recall that the system of police involved ensuring that one sent the greatest possible amount of commodities to other countries, so

as to extract the greatest possible amount of gold and assure the return
or arrival of this gold into the country, and this was one of the fundamental elements of the police objective of increasing the state's forces.
Now, in these new techniques of governmentality evoked by the
économistes, there is no question of selling at any cost, so to speak, in order
to repatriate or import the greatest possible amount of gold, but instead
the question will be one of integrating foreign countries into mechanisms of regulation that function within each country. Profiting from
the high prices in foreign countries so as to send to them as much corn
as possible, and allowing the prices at home to rise so that foreign corn,
foreign grains will be attracted. One will therefore allow competition to
operate, but competition between what? This is not the competition-
rivalry I talked about last week, which was the system both of police and
of the balance of forces in the European space. Competition will be
allowed to operate between private individuals, and it is precisely this
game of the interest of competing private individuals who each seek
maximum advantage for themselves that will allow the state, or the
group, or the whole population to pocket the profits, as it were, from
this conduct of private individuals, that is to say, to have grains at the
just price and to have the most favorable economic situation. On what
will the happiness of the whole, of all and everyone, depend? It does not
depend, precisely, on that authoritarian intervention of the state in the
form of police, which controls the space, the territory, and the population. The good of all will be assured by the behavior of each when the
state, the government, allows private interest to operate, which, through
the phenomena of accumulation and regulation, will serve all. The state
is not therefore the source of the good of each. It is not a case, as it was
for police—as I was saying last week—of ensuring that the better than
just living is utilized by the state and then passed on as the happiness
or well-being of the totality. It is now a matter of ensuring that the state
only intervenes to regulate, or rather to allow the well-being, the interest of each to adjust itself in such a way that it can actually serve all. The
state is envisioned as the regulator of interests and no longer as the transcendent and synthetic principle of the transformation of the happiness
of each into the happiness of all. I think this is a crucial change that
brings us face to face with an essential element of the history of the

eighteenth, nineteenth, and also twentieth century, that is to say: What should the state's game be, what role should it play, what function should it perform in relation to that fundamental and natural game of private interests?

You can see how, through this discussion on grains, the police of grains, and the means for avoiding scarcity, a whole new form of governmentality is sketched out that is opposed almost term by term to the governmentality outlined in the idea of a police state. Of course, in the same period, in the eighteenth century, there are certainly many other signs of this transformation of governmental reason, of this birth of a new governmental reason. All the same, I think it is important to emphasize that, broadly speaking, this all really takes place by way of the problem of what is called, or will be called, the economy. At any rate, the first to criticize the police state in the eighteenth century were not the jurists. Certainly there was simmering discontent and outbursts among the jurists in the seventeenth century, and more than in the eighteenth century moreover, when, confronted with the police state and what it entailed with regard to the direct modalities of action of royal power and its administration, they were to some extent reticent, and sometimes critical with regard to its birth, but this was always by reference to a traditional conception of right and the privileges of individuals it recognized. For them it was only a question of limiting what they saw as an increasingly exorbitant royal power. Among the jurists, even among those who criticized the police state, there was never any attempt or effort to define a new art of government. On the other hand, it was the *économistes* who mounted a critique of the police state in terms of the eventual or possible birth of a new art of government. I think in some way we should compare these two great families that are separated by a century and in reality profoundly opposed. You recall that at the beginning of the seventeenth century there was* what was seen at the time as a veritable sect, as a sort of heresy: the *politiques*.[27] The *politiques* were those who defined a new art of government in terms that were no longer those of the great, how to put it? . . . conformity to the order of the world, to the wisdom of the world, to that sort of great cosmo-theology

---

* Foucault adds: what was present,

that served as the framework for the arts of government of the Middle Ages, and still of the sixteenth century. The *politiques* were those who said: Let's leave aside this problem of the world and nature; let's look for the reason intrinsic to the art of government; let's define a horizon that will make it possible to fix exactly what should be the rational principles and forms of calculation specific to an art of government. And they defined a new rationality by thus carving out the domain of the state in the great cosmo-theological world of medieval and Renaissance thought. The heresy of the *politiques* was a fundamental heresy. Well, almost a century later a new sect appeared, which was also seen as a sect moreover: the *économistes*.[28] With regard to what were the *économistes* heretical? They were not heretical with regard to the great cosmo-theological thought of sovereignty, but with regard to the thinking organized around *raison d'État*, with regard to the state, and with regard to the police state, and it was they who invented a new art of government, still in terms of reason, of course, but of a reason that was no longer *raison d'État*, or which was not only *raison d'État*, and which was, to put things more precisely, *raison d'État* modified by this new thing, by this new domain that was emerging: the economy. Economic reason does not replace *raison d'État*, but it gives it a new content and so gives new forms to state rationality. A new governmentality is born with the *économistes* more than a century after the appearance of that other governmentality in the seventeenth century. The governmentality of the *politiques* gives us police, and the governmentality of the *économistes* introduces us, I think, to some of the fundamental lines of modern and contemporary governmentality.

We should of course keep in mind that we are still in the realm of *raison d'État*. That is to say, in this new governmentality sketched by the *économistes* the objective will still be to increase the state's forces within an external equilibrium in the European space, and an internal equilibrium in the form of order. But this state rationality, this *raison d'État*, which continues in fact to dominate the *économistes'* thought, will be modified, and I would like to pick out some of these essential modifications.

First, you can see that in the kind of schematic analysis I sketched concerning the police of grains and the new economy in which this problem is thought out, there is reference to a whole domain of processes that we can call, up to a point, natural. Let's return for a moment to what I was saying some weeks ago.[29] I told you that in the medieval tradition, broadly speaking, or still in the Renaissance, a good government, a well-ordered kingdom, was part of a world order willed by God. As a consequence, good government was inscribed in this great cosmological-theological framework. With regard to this natural order, *raison d'État* carves out a new division, or even introduces a radical break, the state, which looms up and reveals a new reality with its own rationality. There is therefore a break with the old naturalness that framed medieval political thought. There is a non-naturalness, an absolute artificiality, if you like, at any rate a break with that old cosmo-theology, which brought the reproaches of atheism that I talked about.[30] So, there is an artificiality of the governmentality of police, of this *raison d'État*.

But now, naturalness re-appears with the *économistes*, but it is a different naturalness. It is the naturalness of those mechanisms that ensure that, when prices rise, if one allows this to happen, then they will stop rising by themselves. It is the naturalness that ensures that the population is attracted by high wages, until a certain point at which wages stabilize and as a result the population no longer increases. As you can see, this is not at all the same type of naturalness as that of the cosmos that framed and supported the governmental reason of the Middle Ages or of the sixteenth century. It is a naturalness that is opposed precisely to the artificiality of politics, of *raison d'État* and police. It is opposed to it, but in quite specific and particular ways. It is not the naturalness of processes of nature itself, as the nature of the world, but processes of a naturalness specific to relations between men, to what happens spontaneously when they cohabit, come together, exchange, work, and produce [...]. That is to say, it is a naturalness that basically did not exist until then and which, if not named as such, at least begins to be thought of and analyzed as the naturalness of society.

It is society as a naturalness specific to man's life in common that the *économistes* ultimately bring to light as a domain, a field of objects, as a possible domain of analysis, knowledge and intervention. Society as a specific field of naturalness peculiar to man, and which will be called civil society, emerges as the vis-à-vis of the state.[31] What is civil society if not, precisely, something that cannot be thought of as simply the product and result of the state? But neither is it something like man's natural existence. Civil society is what governmental thought, the new form of governmentality born in the eighteenth century, reveals as the necessary correlate of the state. With what must the state concern itself? For what must the state be responsible? What must it know? What must the state, if not control, at least regulate, or what kind of thing is it whose natural regulations it must respect? It is not a primitive nature, as it were, any more than it is a set of subjects indefinitely subject to a sovereign will and submissive to its requirements. The state has responsibility for a society, a civil society, and the state must see to the management of this civil society. This is of course a fundamental mutation with regard to a form of *raison d'État*, of police rationality that continued to deal only with a collection of subjects. This is the first point I would like to emphasize.

The second point is that in this new governmentality, and correlative to this horizon of social naturalness, you see the appearance of the theme of a form of knowledge that is—I was going to say, specific to government, but this would not be entirely exact. What are we actually dealing with in these natural phenomena the *économistes* were talking about? We are dealing with processes that can be known by methods of the same type as any scientific knowledge. The claim to scientific rationality, which was absolutely not advanced by the mercantilists, is assumed however by the eighteenth century *économistes*, who mean that the rule of evidence must be applied in these domains.[32] Consequently, these methods are not in any way the sorts of calculations of forces, or diplomatic calculations, that *raison d'État* called upon in the seventeenth century. The knowledge involved must be scientific in its procedures.* Second, this scientific knowledge is absolutely indispensable for good government. A government that did not take into account this kind of analysis, the knowledge of these processes, which did not respect the result of this

---

* The manuscript clarifies (sheet 21 of a lecture not paginated): "This knowledge is political economy, not as simple knowledge of ways of enriching the state, but as knowledge of processes that link together variations of wealth and variation of population on three axes: production, circulation, consumption. Birth, therefore, of political economy."

kind of knowledge, would be bound to fail. Indeed, we see this when, against all the rules of evidence and rationality, government controls the grain trade and fixes the maximum price: it acts blindly; it acts against its interest; it is literally mistaken, and mistaken in scientific terms. So, we have a scientific knowledge indispensable to government, but it is very important to note that this is not a knowledge of government itself, its knowledge, so to speak, a knowledge internal to government. That is to say, it is not at all knowledge internal to the art of government; it is no longer simply a calculation that should arise within the practice of those who govern. You have a science which is, as it were, tête-à-tête with the art of government, a science that is external to the art of government and that one may perfectly well found, establish, develop, and prove throughout, even though one is not governing or taking part in this art of government. But government cannot do without the consequences, the results, of this science. So, as you can see, a quite particular relationship of power and knowledge, of government and science appears. The kind of unity that still continued to operate, the kind of more or less confused magma, if you like, of an art of government that would be both knowledge and power, science and decision, begins to be clarified and separated out, and anyway two poles appear of a scientificity that, on the one hand, increasingly appeals to its theoretical purity and becomes economics, and, on the other, at the same time claims the right to be taken into consideration by a government that must model its decisions on it. This is the second important point, I think.

The third important point in this new governmentality is, of course, the sudden appearance of the problem of population in new forms. Previously, the question was basically not so much one of population as of populating or, on the contrary, of depopulation; it was number, work, and docility, all that I have already talked about. Now, however, population appears as a both specific and relative reality: it is relative to wages, to the possibilities of work, and to prices, but it is also specific in two senses. First, population has its own laws of transformation and movement, and it is just as much subject to natural processes as wealth itself. Wealth moves around, is transformed, increases or diminishes. Well, through processes that are not the same, but are of the same type, or at any rate just as natural, the population is transformed, grows, declines, and moves around. There is therefore a naturalness intrinsic to population. The other specific characteristic of population is that a series of interactions, circular effects, and effects of diffusion takes place between each individual and all the others that mean that there is a spontaneous bond between the individual and the others which is not constituted and willed by the state. Population will be characterized by the law of the mechanics of interests. In the naturalness of the population and the law of the composition of interests within the population you see the appearance of population as a reality that has a natural density and thickness that is different from the set of subjects who were subject to the sovereign and the intervention of police, even if it was a matter of police in the broad and full sense of the term employed in the seventeenth century. As a result, if population really is endowed with this naturalness, this thickness, with internal mechanisms of regulation, then this will be the reality that the state will have to be responsible for, rather than individuals who must be subjugated and subject to imposed rules and regulations. In the second half of the eighteenth century, taking responsibility for the population will involve the development of, if not sciences, then at least practices and types of intervention. These will include, for example, social medicine, or what at the time was called public hygiene, and it will involve problems of demography, in short, everything that brings to light the state's new function of responsibility for the population in its naturalness; the population as a collection of subjects is replaced by the population as a set of natural phenomena.

The fourth major modification of governmentality is this: What does it mean to say that the facts of population and economic processes are subject to natural processes? It means, of course, that not only will there be no justification, but also quite simply there will be no interest in trying to impose regulatory systems of injunctions, imperatives, and interdictions on these processes. The basic principle of the state's role, and so of the form of governmentality henceforth prescribed for it, will be to respect these natural processes, or at any rate to take them into account, get them to work, or to work with them. That is to say, on the one hand, intervention of state governmentality will have to be limited, but this limit will not be just a sort of negative boundary. An entire domain of possible and necessary interventions appears within the field thus delimited, but these interventions will not necessarily, or not as a general rule, and very often not at all take the form of rules and regulations. It will be necessary to arouse, to facilitate, and to *laisser faire*, in other words to manage and no longer to control through rules and regulations. The essential objective of this management will be not so much to prevent things as to ensure that the necessary and natural regulations work, or even to create regulations that enable natural regulations to work. Natural phenomena will have to be framed in such a way that they do not veer off course, or in such a way that clumsy, arbitrary, and blind intervention does not make them veer off course. That is to say, it will be necessary to set up mechanisms of security. The fundamental objective of governmentality will be mechanisms of security, or, let's say, it will be state intervention with the essential function of ensuring the security of the natural phenomena of economic processes or processes intrinsic to population.

This explains, finally, the insertion of freedom within governmentality, not only as the right of individuals legitimately opposed to the power, usurpations, and abuses of the sovereign or the government, but as an element that has become indispensable to governmentality itself. Henceforth, a condition of governing well is that freedom, or certain forms of freedom, are really respected. Failing to respect freedom is not only an abuse of rights with regard to the law, it is above all ignorance of how to govern properly. The integration of freedom, and the specific limits to this freedom within the field of governmental practice has now become an imperative.

You can see how that great over-regulatory police I have been talking about breaks up. The regulatory control of the territory and subjects that still characterized seventeenth century police must clearly be called into question, and there will now be a sort of double system. On the one hand will be a whole series of mechanisms that fall within the province of the economy and the management of the population with the function of increasing the forces of the state. Then, on the other hand, there will be an apparatus or instruments for ensuring the prevention or repression of disorder, irregularity, illegality, and delinquency. That is to say, the unitary project of police in the classical seventeenth and eighteenth century sense of the term—increasing the state's powers while respecting the general order—will now be dismantled, or rather it will be embodied in different institutions or mechanisms. On one side will be the great mechanisms of incentive-regulation: the economy, management of the population, etcetera. Then, with simply negative functions, there will be the institution of police in the modern sense of the term, which will simply be the instrument by which one prevents the occurrence of certain disorders. Growth within order and all positive functions will be assured by a whole series of institutions, apparatuses, mechanisms, and so on, and then the elimination of disorder will be the function of the police. As a result, the notion of police is entirely overturned, marginalized, and takes on the purely negative meaning familiar to us.

In brief, the new governmentality, which in the seventeenth century thought it could be entirely invested in an exhaustive and unitary project of police, now finds itself in a situation in which it has to refer to the economy as a domain of naturalness: it has to manage populations; it also has to organize a legal system of respect for freedoms; and finally it has to provide itself with an instrument of direct, but negative, intervention, which is the police. Economic practice, population management, a public law constructed on the respect of freedom and freedoms, and a police with a repressive function: you can see that the old police project, as it appeared in correlation with *raison d'État*, is dismantled, or rather broken up into four elements—economic practice, population management, law and respect for freedoms, police—which are added to the great diplomatic-military apparatus (*dispositif*) that has hardly changed since the eighteenth century.

So we have the economy, population management, law with the judicial apparatus, respect for freedoms, a police apparatus, a diplomatic apparatus, and a military apparatus. You can see that we can perfectly well construct a genealogy of the modern state and its apparatuses that is not based on, as they say, a circular ontology[33] of the state asserting itself and growing like a huge monster or automatic machine. We can construct the genealogy of the modern state and its different apparatuses on the basis of a history of governmental reason. Society, economy, population, security, and freedom are the elements of the new governmentality whose forms we can still recognize in its contemporary modifications.

If you give me two or three minutes, I would like to add this. I have tried to show how, as a project for conducting men, the pastorship and government of men, which was set up [and] developed with such intensity in the Middle Ages, provoked certain counter-conducts, or rather, I have tried to show how the art, project, and institutions for conducting men, and the counter-conducts that were opposed to this, developed in correlation with each other: there were all those kinds of movements of resistance or of the transformation of pastoral conduct that I listed. Well, I think we could say something similar, in short we could continue the analysis with regard to governmentality in its modern form. And basically I wonder whether we could not establish some, I don't say analogies exactly, but correspondences as it were. I tried to show you there were a series of exchanges, of reciprocal supports, between the pastoral art of conducting men and the counter-conducts that were absolutely contemporaneous with it, and that basically partly the same question was involved for both pastoral conduct and counter-conduct. I wonder whether we could analyze counter-conducts in the modern system of governmentality by saying that what is at stake in the counter-conducts that develop in correlation with modern governmentality are the same elements as for that governmentality, and that from the middle of the eighteenth century a whole series of counter-conducts have developed whose essential objective is precisely the rejection of *raison d'État* and its fundamental requirements, and which gets support from the very same thing that *raison d'État*, through the transformations I have indicated, ended up bringing to light, that is to say: elements of society opposed to the state; economic truth in comparison with error, incomprehension, and blindness; the interest of all as opposed to private interest; the absolute value of the population as a natural and living reality; security in contrast with insecurity and danger; and freedom in contrast with rules and regulations.

More schematically, and to summarize all that I have wanted to say, maybe we could say that *raison d'État* basically posited as the primary, implacable law of both modern governmentality and historical science that man henceforth has to live in an indefinite time. There will always be governments, the state will always be there, and there is no hope of having done with it. The new historicity of *raison d'État* excluded the

Empire of the last days; it excluded the kingdom of eschatology. Against this theme, which was formulated at the end of the sixteenth century and is still with us today, counter-conducts develop that make it a principle to assert the coming of a time when time will end, and to posit the possibility of an eschatology, of a final time, of a suspension or completion of historical and political time when, if you like, the indefinite governmentality of the state will be brought to an end and halted. By what? Well, by the emergence of something that will be society itself. The day when civil society can free itself of the constraints and controls of the state, when the power of the state can finally be reabsorbed into this civil society—into a civil society that I have tried to show was born within the form and analysis of governmental reason itself—time, the time if not of history then at least of politics, of the state, will come to an end as a result. This revolutionary eschatology constantly haunted the nineteenth and twentieth centuries. The first form of counter-conduct is the affirmation of an eschatology in which civil society will prevail over the state.

Second, I have tried to show you how the obedience of individuals was a fundamental principle for *raison d'État* and that henceforth the bonds of individual subjection no longer had to take the feudal form of their allegiance, but rather the form of a total and exhaustive obedience in their conduct to whatever the imperatives of the state may be. We now see the development of counter-conducts, of demands in the form of counter-conduct, whose meaning is: There must be a moment when, breaking all the bonds of obedience, the population will really have the right, not in juridical terms, but in terms of essential and fundamental rights, to break any bonds of obedience it has with the state and, rising up against it, to say: My law, the law of my own requirements, the law of my very nature as population, the law of my basic needs, must replace the rules of obedience. Consequently, there is an eschatology that will take the form of the absolute right to revolt, to insurrection, and to breaking all the bonds of obedience: the right to revolution itself. This is the second great form of counter-conduct.

Finally, I have tried to show you how *raison d'État* implied that the state, or those who represent it possess a truth concerning men, the population, and what takes place within the territory and the general mass made up of individuals. Against this theme of the state as the possessor of truth, counter-conducts will oppose the idea that at a given moment the nation itself, in its totality, must be able to possess exactly, at each of its points as in its mass, the truth of what it is, what it wants, and what it must do. This is the idea of a nation entitled to its own knowledge, or the idea of a society transparent to itself and possessor of its own truth, even if it is an element of the population, or an organization representative of the entire population, a party, which formulates this truth. In any case, the truth of society, the truth of the state, of *raison d'État*, is no longer to be possessed by the state itself; the whole nation is entitled to it. I think this is the third major form of counter-conduct, which you can see is opposed term for term to what characterized *raison d'État* in the sixteenth century, but which gets support from those different notions, those different elements that appeared in the transformations of *raison d'État*.

Whether one opposes civil society to the state, the population to the state, or the nation to the state, it was in any case these elements that were in fact put to work within this genesis of the state, and of the modern state. It is therefore these elements that will be at issue and serve as the stake for both the state and for what is opposed to it. To that extent, the history of *raison d'État*, the history of the governmental *ratio*, and the history of the counter-conducts opposed to it, are inseparable from each other.*

---

* Foucault leaves out here the two final pages of the manuscript in which, defining revolutionary movements as "counter-conducts, or rather types of counter-conducts that correspond to these forms of society in which the 'government of men' has become one of the attributes of society, if not even its essential function," he briefly examines the question of their "religious inheritance":

"The religious inheritance of the revolutionary movements of modern Europe is often invoked. It is not direct. Or at any rate, it is not a filiation, religious ideology-revolutionary ideology. The link is more complex and does not establish a connection between ideologies. To the state pastorate are opposed counter-conducts that have borrowed some of their themes from or modeled them on religious counter-conducts. The reason for the complexion of revolutionary movements should be looked for from the side of anti-pastoral tactics, schismatic or heretical breaks, and struggles around the power of the Church. In any case, there are phenomena of real filiation: utopian socialism [certainly?] had real roots, not in texts, books, or ideas, but in ascribable practices: communities, colonies, religious organizations, like the Quakers in America, in central Europe (...) and related [or] alternative phenomena: Methodism and the French Revolution. A case of religious ideology having [absorbed?] the revolutionary process? At least, in a country with a weak state structure, with a strong economic development, and with a multiple pastoral organization, the revolts of conduct were able to take more [paradoxically?] the 'archaic' form of a new pastoral."

❖

That's all I wanted to say. All I wanted to do this year was a little experiment of method in order to show how starting from the relatively local and microscopic analysis of those typical forms of power of the pastorate it was possible, without paradox or contradiction, to return to the general problems of the state, on condition precisely that we [do not make] the state [into] a transcendent reality whose history could be undertaken on the basis of itself. It must be possible to do the history of the state on the basis of men's actual practice, on the basis of what they do and how they think. Certainly, I do not think analyzing the state as a way of doing things is the only possible analysis when one wants to do the history of the state, but it is, I think, a sufficiently fruitful possibility, and to my mind its fruitfulness is linked to the fact that we can see that there is not a sort of break between the level of micro-power and the level of macro-power, and that talking about one [does not] exclude talking about the other. In actual fact, an analysis in terms of micro-powers comes back without any difficulty to the analysis of problems like those of government and the state.

1. Nicolas Delamare, *Traité de la police*. The work is made up of three volumes published in Paris by J. and P. Cot in 1705 (volume 1), then by P. Cot in 1710 (volume 2) and M. Brunet in 1719 (volume 3). A fourth volume, by A.-L. Lecler du Brillet, a student of Delamare, completed the set five years after the death of the author: *Continuation du Traité de la police*. *De la voirie, de tout ce qui en dépend ou qui y a quelque rapport* (Paris: J.-F. Hérissant, 1738). An enlarged edition of the first two volumes was published by M. Brunet in 1722. A fraudulent edition of the four volumes, a so-called second edition, appeared in Amsterdam, "at the cost of the Company," in 1729-1739 (see P.-M. Bondois, "Le Commissaire N. Delamare et le *Traité de la police*," p. 322, note 3). The first volume contains the first four books: 1. "Of Police in general, and its magistrates and officers"; 2. "Of religion"; 3. "Of morals (*mœurs*)"; 4. "Of health." The second volume contains the first 23 headings of Book 5, "Of provisions (*vivres*)." The third volume contains the rest of Book 5, and the fourth volume contains Book 6, "Of highways (*la voirie*)." The work remained unfinished, and only a part, scarcely one half of Delamare's program, was given definitive form. The books lacking are those that should have dealt with the safety of towns and highways, the sciences and liberal arts, commerce, manufacture, servants, domestics and laborers, and the poor.

2. See Edmé de La Poix de Fréminville, *Dictionnaire ou Traité de la police générale des villes, bourgs, paroisses et seigneuries de la campagne* (Paris: Gissey, 1758; reprinted Nîmes: Praxis, 1989), a compendium of police regulations presented under headings in alphabetical order; Du Chesne (lieutenant of police at Vitry-en-Champagne), *Code de la police, ou Analyse des règlemens de police* (Paris: Prault, 1757, 4th edn., 1768); J.-A. Sallé, *L'Esprit des ordonnances et des principaux édits déclarations de Louis XV, en matière civile, criminelle et beneficiale* (Paris: Bailly, 1771), Nicolas Des Essarts, *Dictionnaire universel de police* (Paris: Moutard, 1786-1791) in eight volumes, which, according to P.-M. Bondois, "Le Commissaire N. Delamare," p. 318, note 1, "completely plundered" the *Traité de la police*.

3. N. Delamare, *Traité de la police*, vol. 1, Book 1, heading 1, p. 4: "(...) since the birth of Christianity, the Emperors and our Kings have added to this ancient division the care and discipline of the poor, as a considerable part of the public good, of which they find no example in the Police of Athens, nor in that of pagan Rome."

4. Delamare himself only lists eleven. See ibid.: "Police, in our view, is thus entirely contained in these eleven parts that we will go through: Religion; the Discipline of morals; Health; Provisions; public Safety and Peace; Highways; the Sciences and Liberal Arts; Commerce, Manufacture, and the Mechanical Arts; Servants, Domestics, Laborers, and the Poor." The difference is due to the fact that Foucault presents the theater and games as a special heading, whereas it is included under the heading of morals, as Delamare explains, p. 4, (see below, note 8) and he distinguishes domains that Delamare combines. In his lecture "Omnes et singulatim," on the other hand, he speaks of "eleven things" that, according to Delamare, police must see to: *Essential Works*, 3, p. 320; *Dits et Écrits*, 4, p. 157.

5. *Traité de la police*: "(...) whereas the Greeks proposed the conservation of natural life as the first object of their Police, we have placed these cares after those that can make life good, and that we, like they, divide into two points: Religion and Morals." See ibid., p. 3: "The first legislators of the famous [Greek] republics, considering life to be the basis of every other good that is the object of police, and considering life itself, if not accompanied by a good and wise conduct, and by all the external aids necessary for it, to be only a very imperfect good, divided all of police into these three parts, the preservation, the goodness, and the pleasures of life."

6. Ibid.: "When we have taken up the preservation of life as the second object we have again followed in this respect the same subdivision, by applying the concerns of our police to these two important things: the health and subsistence of citizens."

7. Ibid.: "With regard to the convenience of life, which was the third object of the police of the ancients, we also subdivide it like them into six points: public Peace; the care of Buildings, Roads, and public Squares, and Highways; the Sciences and the liberal Arts; Commerce; Manufacture; the mechanical Arts; Domestics and Laborers."

8. Ibid.: "Finally, we have imitated those ancient Republics in the care they gave to that portion of Police that concerns the pleasures of life. Nevertheless, there is this difference between the ancients and ourselves, that as the games and spectacles were for them a considerable part of the worship of their gods, the only object of their Laws was to increase their number and magnificence: in our case rather, more in conformity with the purity of our Religion and

morals, their only object is to correct the abuses that excessive license may introduce into them, or to ensure their peacefulness. Hence instead of making them [games and spectacles] a separate heading in our Police, like the ancients, we place them under that which concerns the discipline of morals."

9. See above, note 3.

10. See previous lecture, 29 March 1978, p. 328.

11. J. Domat, *Le Droit public*, 1829 edn., Book 1, heading VIII, p. 150: "(. . .) it is by nature that one of the uses that God has given to the seas and rivers is that of opening up routes that communicate with every country in the world by navigation. And it is by police that we have made towns, public squares, and other places appropriate for this use, and that those of each town, province, and nation can communicate with all the other of every country by great highways."

12. E. de La Poix de Fréminville, *Dictionnaire ou Traité de la police générale des villes*, Preface, p. vi.

13. Ibid.

14. See lecture of 22 March 1978, p. 298 *sq*.

15. An allusion to the situationist critique of capitalism, which denounced the double reign of the fetishism of commodities and the society of the spectacle. Foucault returns to this in the following year's lectures. See *Naissance de la biopolitique*, lecture of 7 February 1979, p. 117.

16. See, for example, Charles Loyseau, *Traité des seigneuries* (Paris: L'Angelier, 1608, 4th enlarged edn., 1613), which, in the manuscript pages on police to which I have already referred (see above, lecture of 29 March 1978, note 2), Foucault cites on the basis of Delamare's *Traité de la police*, Book 1, section 1, p. 2: "It is a right, says this learned jurisconsult, without any application on the part of anyone, and in the sole interest of the public good, to enact regulations that commit and bind all the citizens of a town for their common good and utility. And I add that the power of the magistrate of police is close to and has much more of the nature of the power of the Prince than of the Judge, who is only entitled to pronounce between a Claimant and Defender."

The original text is the following: "(. . .) the right of police consists specifically in being able to make particular regulations for the citizens of his district and territory, which concern and bind all the people and which exceeds the power of a simple judge who can only pronounce between the claimant and defender, and cannot make regulations without the application of a claimant or hearing a defender. Thus this power is close to and has more of the nature of the power of the prince that of the judge, considering that these regulations are like laws and particular ordinances, which are also properly called edicts, as was said above in the third chapter," *Traité des seigneuries*, ch. IX, § 3, pp. 88-89.

17. Jean Bacquet (died c.1685), *Traicté des droits de justice* (Paris: L'Angelier, 1603) ch. 28, "If the rights of Police, of the Watch (*Guet*), and of the Highways Office (*Voirie*), belong to the high Justices, or to the king" p. 381: "That the right of Justice and of Police have nothing in common" (= the heading for section 3). "Also that the right of Justice does not contain in itself the right of Police, thus they are distinct and separate rights. So that a seigneur cannot claim the right of police under the shadow of his justice" (§ 3). "Moreover, it being certain that the exercise of Police contains in itself the preservation and maintenance of the inhabitants of a town, and of the public good of the latter, we cannot say that the right of Police belongs to anyone else but the King" (§ 4).

18. Catherine II, *Supplément à l'Instruction pour un nouveau code* (= *Instructions pour la commission chargée de dresser le projet du nouveau code de loix*), (Saint Petersburg: printed by the Academy of Sciences, 1769) § 535. See *Surveiller et Punir*, p. 215; *Discipline and Punish*, p. 213, where Foucault refers to the same passage. This text reproduces almost word for word a passage from Montesquieu's *Esprit des lois*, Book 26, ch. 24; *The Spirit of the Laws*, p. 517: "That the regulations of a police are of another order than the other civil laws": "Matters of police are things of every instant, which usually amount to but little; scarcely any formalities are needed. The actions of police are quick and the police is exerted over things that recur every day; therefore, major punishments are not proper to it. It is perpetually busy with details; therefore, great examples do not fit it."

19. Catherine II, *Supplément*; Montesquieu, *Esprit des lois*, p. 776; *The Spirit of the Laws*, p. 517: "It has regulations rather than laws."

20. See above, note 16.

21. M. Guillauté (officer of the *maréchaussée* of the Ile de France) *Mémoire sur la réformation de la police de France, soumis au roi en 1749* (Paris: Hermann, 1974) p. 19: "We do not have any regular towns except those that have been destroyed by fire, and it would seem that to have a police united in all its parts it would be necessary to burn what we have gathered of it; but this remedy is impractical, and it would seem we are for ever stuck with an old structure that we cannot demolish and that we must prop up in every part. (...) It is not a question of making society a religious house, which is not possible: we must reduce as much as we can certain inconveniences: but it may be dangerous to destroy them. It is necessary to take men to be what they are, and not as they should be. It is necessary to combine what the present state of society does or does not allow, and to work according to these principles."

22. See *Surveiller et Punir*, pp. 135-196; *Discipline and Punish*, pp. 135-228, Part Four, "Discipline."

23. See above, lecture of 18 January 1978, pp. 31-33.

24. On the "good price" of grains see, for example, F. Quesnay's article "Grains" (1757) in *F. Quesnay et la physiocratie*, vol. 2, pp. 507-509, and the article "Hommes" in ibid., pp. 528-530. See also, G. Weulersse, *Le Mouvement physiocratique*, Book 2, ch. 3: "Le 'bon prix' des grains," pp. 474-577; and *Les Physiocrates*, ch. 4: "Le programme commercial: le Bon prix des grains," pp. 129-171.

25. In the sense of good price or market price. See S.L. Kaplan, *Bread, Politics and Political Economy*, p. 59, n. 14: "Cf. Turgot's view in which the 'just price' was always supposed to be the true market price whether times were troubled or not. In his sense the just price was the natural price or what the *économistes* called the *bon prix*." On this latter notion, see the previous note. On the meaning of the concept of "just price" in the theological-moral tradition and the discourse of police up to the eighteenth century, see *Naissance de la biopolitique*, lecture of 17 January 1979, p. 49, note 2.

26. See above, lecture of 25 January 1978, notes 19 and 24.

27. See above, lecture of 8 March 1978, pp. 245-247.

28. See, for example, Grimm, who ridiculed all the failings of the sect, "its cult, its ceremonies, its jargon, and its mysteries" (quoted by G. Weulersse, *Les Physiocrates*, p. 25).

29. See above, lecture of 8 March 1978, pp. 235-236.

30. Ibid.

31. Foucault will examine this concept of civil society at great length in the last lecture, 4 April 1979, of *Naissance de la biopolitique*, p. 299 *sq*.

32. See the article "Évidence" of the *Encyclopédie* (vol. VI) written anonymously by Quesnay (included in *F. Quesnay et la physiocratie*, vol. 2, pp. 397-426).

33. This expression, which was already used at the end of the lecture of 8 March 1978 (see above, pp. 247-248: "I am well aware that there are those who say that in talking of power we do nothing else but develop an internal and circular ontology of power"), refers to criticisms certain people made of the analysis of power put to work by Foucault from the mid-1970s.

COURSE SUMMARY*

THE COURSE FOCUSED ON the genesis of a political knowledge that put the notion of population and the mechanisms for ensuring its regulation at the center of its concerns. A transition from a "territorial state" to a "population state"? No, because it did not involve a substitution but rather a shift of emphasis and the appearance of new objectives, and so of new problems and new techniques.

To follow this genesis, we took the notion of "government" as our guideline.

1. One would have to undertake a thorough investigation of the history of not only the notion but also the procedures and means employed to ensure the "government of men" in a given society. From an entirely preliminary approach it seems that for Greek and Roman societies the exercise of political power entailed neither the right nor the possibility of "government" understood as an activity that undertakes to conduct individuals throughout their lives by putting them under the authority of a guide who is responsible for what they do and for what happens to them. Following Paul Veyne's indications, it seems that the idea of a pastor (*pasteur*)-sovereign, or of a king or magistrate as shepherd (*berger*) of the human flock is only found in the archaic Greek texts or in a few authors of

* Published in the *Annuaire du Collège de France, 78ᵉ année. Histoire des systèmes de pensée, année 1977-1978, (1978)*, pp. 445-449, and in *Dits et écrits, 1954-1988*, eds., D. Defert and F. Ewald, with the collaboration of J. Lagrange (Paris: Gallimard, 1994) vol. 3, pp. 719-723. An earlier translation of this summary by Robert Hurley appears with the title "Security, Territory, and Population" in M. Foucault, *The Essential Works of Michel Foucault, 1954-1984, Vol. 1: Ethics: subjectivity and truth*, ed. Paul Rabinow, trans. Robert Hurley and others (New York: New Press, 1997) pp. 67-72 (see below, "Course Context," note 62).

the imperial epoch. On the other hand, the metaphor of the shepherd watching over his sheep is accepted when describing the activity of the teacher, the doctor, or the gymnastics master. Analysis of *The Statesman* would confirm this hypothesis.

The development of the theme of pastoral power took place in the East, and especially in Hebrew society. The theme is marked by a number of features: the shepherd's power is not exercised over a fixed territory so much as over a multitude moving towards an objective; its role is to provide the flock with its subsistence, to watch over it every day, and to ensure its salvation; finally, through an essential paradox, it is a power that individualizes by according as much value to a single sheep as to the whole flock. This type of power was introduced into the West by Christianity and was institutionalized in the ecclesiastical pastorate: the government of souls was formed in the Christian Church as a central and learned activity indispensable for the salvation of all and of each.

A general crisis of the pastorate opened up and developed in the fifteenth and sixteenth centuries. This occurred not only and not so much as a rejection of the pastoral institution, but in a much more complex form: the search for other (and not necessarily less strict) modes of spiritual direction and new types of relationships between pastor and flock; but also investigations of the way to "govern" children, a family, a domain, or a principality. At the end of feudalism, a general questioning of the way of governing and governing oneself, of conducting (*conduire*) and conducting oneself (*se conduire*), accompanies the birth of new forms of economic and social relations and the new political structures.

2. Next we analyzed some aspects of the formation of a political "governmentality," that is to say, the way in which the conduct (*conduite*) of a set of individuals became involved, in an increasingly pronounced way, in the exercise of sovereign power. This important transformation is indicated in the different "arts of government" written at the end of the sixteenth and in the first half of the seventeenth century. It is no doubt linked to the emergence of "*raison d'État.*" We pass from an art of governing whose principles were derived from the traditional virtues (wisdom, justice, liberality, respect for divine laws and human customs) or from common skills (prudence, reflected decisions, care in surrounding oneself with the best advisors), to an art of governing that finds the

principles of its rationality and the specific domain of its application in the state. "*Raison d'État*" is not the imperative in the name of which one can or must overturn all other rules; it is the new matrix of rationality according to which the prince must exercise his sovereignty in governing men. We are far from the virtue of the sovereign of justice, as too from that of Machiavelli's hero.

The development of *raison d'État* is correlative with the elimination of the imperial theme. Rome finally disappears. A new historical perception forms that is no longer focused on the end of time and the unification of all particular sovereignties in the empire of the last days. It opens onto an indefinite time in which states have to struggle against each other to ensure their own survival. More than the problems of the legitimacy of a sovereign's rights over a territory, what now appears important is the knowledge and development of a state's forces: in both a European and global space of competition between states, which is very different from the confrontation between dynasties, the major problem is that of a dynamic of forces and the rational techniques that enable one to affect it.

Thus, apart from the theories that formulated and justified it, *raison d'État* takes shape in two great assemblages of political knowledge and technology: a military-diplomatic technology that consists in securing and developing the state's forces through a system of alliances and the organization of an armed apparatus; the pursuit of a European equilibrium, one of the guiding principles of the treaties of Westphalia, was a consequence of this political technology. The other assemblage is that of "police," in the sense this word had at that time, that is to say, the set of means for bringing about the internal growth of the state's forces. At the point where these two great technologies meet we should place commerce and monetary circulation, their common instrument: it was expected that from enrichment through commerce one would have the possibility of increasing the population, manpower, production, and export, and of equipping oneself with strong and large armies. In the period of mercantilism and cameralism, the population-wealth couple was the privileged object of the new governmental reason.

3. The elaboration of this population-wealth problem (in its different concrete aspects of taxation, scarcity, depopulation, idleness-begging-vagrancy) is one of the conditions for the formation of political

economy. The latter develops when it is realized that the relationship between population and resources can no longer be managed through an exhaustive regulatory and coercive system that would strive to increase the population by increasing resources. The physiocrats are not anti-populationist in opposition to the mercantilists of the previous period; they pose the problem of population in a different way. For them, the population is not the simple sum of subjects who inhabit a territory, a sum resulting from the desire of individuals to have children or from legislation that encourages or discourages births. Population is a variable dependent on a number of factors, and these are by no means all natural (the tax system, the activity of circulation, and the distribution of profit are essential determinants of the population rate). However, this dependence can be rationally analyzed in such a way that the population appears as "naturally" dependent on multiple and artificially modifiable factors. Thus the political problem of population begins to emerge, splitting off from the technology of "police" and in correlation with the birth of economic reflection. The population is not conceived of as a collection of subjects of right, nor as a set of hands making up the workforce; it is analyzed as a set of elements that, on the one hand, form part of the general system of living beings (the population then falls under "the human species," which was a new notion at the time, to be distinguished from "mankind [*le genre humain*]") and, on the other hand, may provide a hold for concerted interventions (through laws, but also through changes in attitudes, ways of doing things, and ways of living that may be brought about by "campaigns").

THE SEMINAR

The seminar was devoted to what, in the eighteenth century, the Germans called *Polizeiwissenschaft*, that is to say, the theory and analysis of everything "that tends to affirm and increase the power of the state, to make good use of its forces, to procure the happiness of its subjects" and chiefly "the maintenance of order and discipline, the regulations that tend to make their life convenient and provide them with the things they need to live."

We tried to show what the problems were that this "police" had to address; the extent to which the role it was assigned was different from the role that is later given to the institution of the police; and what was expected of it in ensuring the state's growth in terms of two objectives: to enable it to stake out and improve its position in the game of rivalries and competition between European states, and to guarantee internal order through the "welfare" of individuals. Development of the state of (military-economic) competition, and development of the *Wohlfahrt* state (of wealth-tranquility-happiness): these are the two principles that "police" as a rational art of government must be able to coordinate. At this time "police" was conceived of as a sort "technology of state forces."

Among the main objects with which this technology had to be concerned was population, in which the mercantilists saw a source of enrichment and in which everyone recognized an essential component of the force of states. Amongst other things, management of this population required a health policy capable of reducing the infant mortality rate, preventing epidemics and lowering the rates of endemic diseases, intervening to modify and impose norms on living conditions (whether in the matter of diet, housing, or town planning), and adequate medical facilities. The development in the second half of the eighteenth century of what was called *medizinische Polizei*, public hygiene, and social medicine, should be re-inserted in the general framework of a "biopolitics"; the latter aims to treat the "population" as a set of coexisting living beings with particular biological and pathological features, and which as such falls under specific forms of knowledge and technique. This "biopolitics" must itself be understood on the basis of a theme developed since the seventeenth century: the management of state forces.

Papers were given on the notion of *Polizeiwissenschaft* (P. Pasquino), on anti-smallpox campaigns in the eighteenth century (A.-M. Moulin), on the 1832 cholera epidemic in Paris (F. Delaporte), and on the legislation concerning accidents at work and the development of insurance in the nineteenth century (F. Ewald).

COURSE CONTEXT

MICHEL SENELLART*

MICHEL FOUCAULT'S TWO COURSES, *Security, Territory, Population* (1978) and *The Birth of Biopolitics* (1979), which we publish at the same time,[†] form a diptych unified by the problematic of bio-power that was first introduced in 1976.[1] The first course begins by recalling this concept, which also, indicates the program of the second series of lectures in its title. So it would seem that the two courses do nothing else but retrace the genesis of this "power over life," in whose emergence in the eighteenth century Foucault saw a "major mutation, undoubtedly one of the most important in the history of human societies."[2] They would thus be in absolute continuity with the conclusions of the 1976 lectures. After a gap of one year—Foucault did not lecture in 1977—Foucault would take up from where he halted in order to give consistency, through historical analysis, to a hypothesis previously expressed in very general terms.

Carrying out this project, however, leads him to some detours that apparently take him away from his initial objective and reorient the lectures in a new direction. Actually it is as if the hypothesis of bio-power had to be placed in a broader framework in order to become really operational. The announced study of the mechanisms by which, in the eighteenth century, the human species entered into a general strategy of

---

* Michel Senellart is professor of political philosophy at the Lyon École normale supérieure des lettres et sciences humaines. He is the author of *Machiavélisme et Raison d'État* (Paris: PUF, 1989) and *Les Arts de gouverner* (Paris: Le Seuil, 1995). He is also the translator of M. Stolleis, *Histoire du droit public en Allemagne, 1600-1800. Théorie du droit public et science de la police* (Paris: PUF, 1998).
† In France the two courses were published at the same time, in 2004; G.B.

power, which is presented as the sketch of a "history of technologies of security,"[3] gives way, from the fourth lecture of 1978 to the project of a history of "governmentality" from the first centuries of the Christian era. Similarly, in the second course, the analysis of the conditions of formation of biopolitics is overshadowed by the analysis of liberal governmentality. What is actually involved in both cases is bringing to light the forms of experience and rationality on the basis of which power over life was organized in the West. But at the same time the effect of this research is to shift the center of gravity of the lectures from the question of bio-power to that of government, to such an extent that in the end the latter almost entirely eclipses the former. Consequently, in the light of Foucault's later work, it is tempting to see these lectures as the moment of a radical turning point at which the transition to the problematic of the "government of the self and others"[4] would begin. Breaking with the discourse of the "battle" employed from the start of the 1970s,[5] the concept of "government" would mark the first shift, becoming more pronounced from 1980, from the analytics of power to the ethics of the subject.

Although the genealogy of bio-power is approached obliquely, and as a result remains very allusive, it nonetheless continues to be the horizon of the two courses. In 1979, Foucault concludes the summary of the second course with these words:

> What should now be studied, therefore, is the way in which the specific problems of life and population were raised within a technology of government that, without always being liberal, far from it, has been constantly haunted by the question of liberalism since the end of the eighteenth century.[6]

So it is this project, to which the following year's course—"On the Government of the Living"[7]—still refers, that orientates Foucault's research through its many twists and turns. The question of bio-power, however, is inseparable from the work on the history of sexuality pursued concurrently with the courses. In 1976 he asserted that sexuality "exists at the point where body and population meet."[8] From 1978, and throughout the development that results in *The Use of Pleasure* and *The Care of the Self* in 1984, it will take on a new meaning, no longer representing only the point of articulation of disciplinary mechanisms and regulatory apparatuses (*dispositifs*), but the main theme of an ethical reflection focused on techniques of the self. A level of analysis is brought to light that was no doubt absent from the earlier works, but the contours of which are outlined from 1978 in the problematic of governmentality.

✤

We should recall first of all some of the elements of the historical, political, and intellectual context in which these lectures are inserted.[9]

Foucault's reflection on modern governmental rationality participates, first of all, in the rise of a way of thinking on the left—to which the "second left"[10] contributed—which had distanced itself from Marxism and was open to new questions (daily life, the situation of women, self-management, and so on[11]). In 1977 he attended the forum on "the left, experimentation, and social change" organized by *Faire* and *Le Nouvel Observateur*.[12] "I write and work for people who are there, these new people who raise new questions."[13] Foucault's refusal to take a position on the national elections of March 1978 is explained by this concern to participate in the renewal of left culture, aside from party strategies.[14] It is also within the framework of the debates provoked by the defeat of the left at this ballot and the perspective of the 1981 presidential election that we should understand the question raised the following year:

> Is there an adequate socialist governmentality? What governmentality is possible as a strictly, intrinsically, and autonomously socialist governmentality? In any case, (...) if there is a real socialist governmentality, it is not hidden within socialism and its texts. It cannot be deduced from them. It must be invented.[15]

This question, which gives the analysis of neo-liberal governmentality developed in the lectures all its depth, continues to occupy Foucault. It is the source of the project of the "white book" on socialist politics that he will propose in 1983: "Do the socialists have a problematic of government or do they only have a problematic of the state?"[16]

Another important phenomenon, the immense effect of which is reflected in some passages of the lectures, is the movement of Soviet dissidence, which then enjoyed increasingly wide support. In June 1977, Foucault, who had met Leonid Plioutch on his arrival in Paris in 1976, organized an evening with a number of dissidents at the Récamier theater to protest against Leonid Brezhnev's visit to France.[17] With reference to this movement, some months later he theorizes for the first time "the right of the governed, (. . .) more precise, more historically determinate than the rights of man," in the name of "legitimate defense with regard to governments."[18] The word "dissident" then entered into his vocabulary for a time. For example, at the end of 1977, in a preface to Mireille Debard's and Jean-Luc Hennig's book, *Les Juges kaki,*[19] he writes: "It is a matter of increasing the 'points of repulsion (*points de repulsion*)' in the political fabric and extending the surface of possible dissidences."[20] The trivialization of the term seems to have irritated him fairly quickly, however, since in the 1978 lectures he refuses to use to it with regard to revolts of conduct.[21]

However, from the point of view of Foucault's personal involvement, the main event is the Klaus Croissant affair at the end of 1977. A lawyer for the "Baader gang" (*Rote Armee Fraktion*), Klaus Croissant asked for the right to asylum in France, where he had found refuge in July 1977. On 18 October, three leaders of the RAF, who had been in prison in Stuttgart since 1972, were found dead in their cells. On 19 October members of the group retaliated with the assassination of the president of the employers, Hanns-Martin Schleyer, who had been abducted on 5 September. Incarcerated in the Santé on 24 October, Klaus Croissant was extradited on 16 November. Foucault, who participated in the demonstration before the Santé that day, had taken a firm position in favor of recognition of Croissant's right to asylum. The articles and interviews he published at that time are of particular interest with regard to the subsequent 1978 and 1979 lectures. Beyond the appeal, already referred to, to the "right of the governed,"[22] he introduces in fact the idea of the "pact of security" that henceforth links the state and the population:

What is taking place today then? The relationship of a state to the population is established essentially in the form of what could be called the "pact of security." Previously the state could say: "I will give you a territory" or "I will guarantee that you will be able to live in peace within your borders." This was the territorial pact, and guaranteeing borders was the major function of the state.[23]

The title of the 1978 lectures, *Security, Territory, Population*, is already contained in this phrase. But Foucault also stresses, and no doubt more clearly than in the lectures, the specific forms of struggle called forth by "societies of security." This is why, in his view, it is important not to reduce this new type of power to traditional categories of political thought, nor to attack it through the analytical grid of "fascism" or "totalitarianism." This criticism, repeated in the 1979 lectures,[24] was not only aimed at the leftist theses to which Foucault was quite close for a long time. It also explains his rejection of terrorism as a means of action that draws its legitimacy from the anti-fascist struggle.[25] His support for Croissant, in the name of the defense of the right to asylum, thus excluded any solidarity with terrorism. This position was no doubt at the origin of his breach with Gilles Deleuze, whom he no longer saw afterwards.[26]

The Croissant affair underscored the importance of the "German question" in Foucault's political reflection. Thus, one year later, he declared to *Der Spiegel*: "Purely and simply to ignore Germany was always a way for France to defuse the political or cultural problems that it posed."[27] The question arises at two levels: that of the division of Europe into antagonistic blocs (what are the effects of this for a Germany "cut in two"?[28]), and that of the construction of the European Community (what place will the Federal Republic occupy within it?). Hence the long expositions in the 1979 lectures devoted to the "German model," through the analysis of post-war Ordo-liberal thought:

[T]he German model (...) is not the model of the Bismarckian state becoming Hitlerian that is so often discredited, dismissed, held in contempt, and loathed. The German model that is spreading, (...) which is in question, (...) which is part of our actuality, structures it and picks it out according to its real contours, this German model is the possibility of a neo-liberal governmentality.[29]

For Foucault, the "German question," as it is posed acutely by the debate on terrorism, is therefore one of the essential keys to the political understanding of the present. His two journeys to Berlin to meet militants of the alternative left, in December 1977 and March 1978, are also linked to this concern.[30]

In April 1978, having finished his lectures, Foucault traveled to Japan for three weeks. He gave lectures there in which he summarized his analysis of pastoral power[31] and situated it in the perspective of the *History of Sexuality*,[32] the second volume of which he was then drafting.[33] Furthermore, he set out his conception of the philosopher's role as the "moderator of power," in the great tradition of the anti-despotic philosopher going back to Solon, but running counter to its classical forms:[34]

> Maybe philosophy can still play a role on the side of counter-power, on condition that, in facing power, this role no longer consists in laying down the law of philosophy, on condition that philosophy stops thinking of itself as prophecy, pedagogy, or legislation, and that it gives itself the task of analyzing, elucidating, making visible, and thereby intensifying the struggles that take place around power, the strategies of adversaries within relations of power, the tactics employed, and the sources of resistance, on condition, in short, that philosophy stops posing the question of power in terms of good and evil, but poses it in terms of existence.[35]

It is in the same spirit that on his return from Japan Foucault reinterprets the Kantian question, "What is *Aufklärung?*"[36] to which he will constantly return.[37] In a vocabulary that is quite new in comparison with his writings of previous years, he explains in this way the critical project within which he inserts his analysis of governmentality.

In parallel with this theoretical work, Foucault conceives the program of "reporting ideas," bringing together intellectuals and journalists in detailed investigations on the ground.

> We must be present at the birth of ideas and the explosion of their force, and not in the books that state them, but in the events in

which they manifest their force, in the struggles that are waged for or against ideas.[38]

The first of these reports, which appeared in *Corriere della sera*, was carried out by Foucault in Iran from 16 to 24 September 1978,[39] some days after "black Friday,"[40] and then from 9 to 15 November 1978, during the big riots and demonstrations against the Shah.[41] At this time he met in particular the liberal ayatollah Chariat Madari, the second religious dignitary of the country, who was hostile to the exercise of political power by the Shiite clergy,[42] and in the extension of the lecture given some months earlier,[43] Foucault was interested in the idea of "good government" set out by the ayatollah.[44] "Islamic government," Foucault writes, would not designate "a political regime in which the clergy would play a role of direction or supervision,"[45] but a double movement of the politicization of traditional structures of society in response to present problems, and the opening up of a "spiritual dimension"[46] in political life. On this occasion Foucault pays warm tribute to the action and teaching of Ali Chariati,[47] who died in 1977, and whose "shadow (...) haunts all of Iran's political and religious life today."[48] In the light of these great doctrinal, "liberal" and socialist, figures, Foucault's famous phrase about "political spirituality," which has been the source of so many misunderstandings, is understandable:

> What is the meaning, for the [Iranians], of seeking, even at the cost their life, that thing the possibility of which we others have forgotten since the Renaissance and the great crises of Christianity: a *political spirituality*. I can already hear some French people laughing, but I know they are wrong.[49]

In an interview given at the same time (the end of 1978), recalling the student strikes of March 1968 in Tunisia, where he was then teaching, Foucault again links "spirituality" to the possibility of sacrificing oneself:

> In today's world, what can prompt in an individual the desire, the ability, and the possibility for absolute sacrifice, without there

being any reason to suspect in their action the least ambition or desire for power and profit? That was what I saw in Tunisia, the evidence of the necessity of myth, of a spirituality, the unbearable quality of certain situations produced by capitalism, colonialism, and neocolonialism.[50]

The Shah relinquished power on 16 January 1979. On 1 February, Khomeini, in exile since 1964, made a triumphant return to Iran. The execution of opponents of the new regime by Islamic paramilitary groups began shortly after. Foucault then became the object of severe criticism, from both the left and the right, for his support for the revolution.[51] Without wanting to enter into the polemic,[52] he chose to respond with an article-manifesto in *Le Monde* of 11-12 May, "*Inutile de se soulever?*"[53] Asserting the transcendence of the uprising in relation to any form of historical causality—"the man who rebels is ultimately inexplicable"[54]—he contrasts "the spirituality that those going to their deaths called upon" and the "bloody government of a fundamentalist clergy."[55] The uprising is that "wrenching-away that interrupts the flow of history" and introduces "subjectivity" into it.[56] Spirituality, a generator of insurrectional force,[57] is therefore inseparable from the ethical and political subjectivation on which Foucault is then reflecting.[58] The "subject" no longer designates simply the subjected individual, but the singularity affirmed in resistance to power—the "revolts of conduct" or "counter-conducts" considered in the 1978 lectures.[59] It is this necessary resistance ("the power that one man exerts over another is always perilous"[60]) that also justifies the invocation of "inviolable laws and unrestricted rights." Foucault thus opposes his "theoretical morality" to the calculations of strategists:

(...) the strategist being the man who says, "What does a particular death, a particular cry, a particular revolt matter when compared to the great necessity of the whole, and, on the other hand, what does a general principle matter in the particular situation in which we are living?", well, it is immaterial to me whether the strategist is a politician, a historian, a revolutionary, a follower of the shah or of the ayatollah; my theoretical morality is opposite to theirs. It is "antistrategic": to be respectful when a singularity revolts, intransigent when power violates the universal.[61]

The problematic of "governmentality" is set out between the political refusal of terrorism and this praise of revolt in the name of an "antistrategic morality."

STRUCTURE AND STAKE OF THE LECTURES

Security, Territory, Population[62]

The 1978 lectures mark the opening of a new cycle in Michel Foucault's teaching at the Collège de France.

Although the lectures appear to bear on a set of objects that are completely different from those of the years 1970-1975, the 1976 lectures are in fact inserted within the continuity of the same research program. As Foucault announced the previous year, he had to "bring this cycle to an end."[63] His project was to study "the mechanisms with which, since the end of the nineteenth century, we sought to 'defend society,'" extending his previous work on "the slow formation of a knowledge and power of normalization based on traditional juridical procedures of punishment."[64] This involved analyzing the theory of social defense, which appeared in Belgium around 1880, for decriminalizing and medicalizing young delinquents.[65] In reality the lectures present a very different content, since they no longer deal with social defense but with war in historical discourse. However, social defense does not entirely disappear, but is resituated in a more general genealogical perspective that allows us to take account of the "great retreat from the historical to the biological" in the "idea of social war."[66] Thus, defense of society is tied up with war by the fact that at the end of the nineteenth century it is thought of in terms of "an internal war"[67] against the dangers arising from the social body itself.

This is when Foucault puts forward the concept of bio-power or biopolitics for the first time, and taken up in *La Volonté de savoir* the same year,[68] introduces the notion of population—"a global mass that is affected by overall characteristics specific to life (. . .) like birth, death, production, illness, and so on"[69]—and rectifies his earlier hypothesis of a "generalized disciplinary society"[70] by showing how the techniques of discipline are linked up to regulatory apparatuses (*dispositifs*).

> After the anatomo-politics of the human body established in the course of the eighteenth century, we have, at the end of that century, the emergence of something that is no longer an anatomo-politics of the human body, but what I would call a "biopolitics" of the human species.[71]

Starting from the conclusions of the 1976 lectures, the 1978 lectures propose to extend and deepen this theoretical shift. After the study of the discipline of the body, that of the regulation of populations: thus a new cycle opens up that some years later will lead Foucault towards horizons that his auditors at that time could not suspect.

The title of the lectures, *Security, Territory, Population*, exactly describes the problem raised. The problem is, in fact, what is involved in this new technology of power that appeared in the eighteenth century, which has the population as its object, and which "aims to establish a sort of homeostasis (...) by achieving an overall equilibrium: the security of the whole with regard to its internal dangers."[72] Foucault contrasts this technology of security with the mechanisms by which the sovereign, until the Classical Age, strove to ensure the safety of his territory.[73] "Territory" and "population" thus function as the antithetical poles between which research will be set out. How have we passed from sovereignty over the territory to the regulation of populations? What were the effects of this mutation at the level of governmental practices? What new rationality henceforth governs them? The stake of the lectures is now clearly defined: seeing whether, through the history of technologies of security, "we can (...) speak of a society of security."[74] This is as much a political as a historical stake, since it concerns the diagnosis of the present: "can we say that the general economy of power in our societies is becoming a domain of security?"[75]

Foucault follows this program, up to the lecture of 1 February, on the basis of three examples taken from the seventeenth and eighteenth centuries: the spaces of security, with the problem of the town, which leads him to emphasize the relations between a population and its "milieu"; the treatment of the aleatory, with the problem of dearth and the circulation of grain, which enables him to link the question of "population" to liberal political economy; and finally, the form of normalization peculiar to security, with the problem of smallpox and inoculation, which leads him to distinguish disciplinary "normation" (*normation*) from normalization in the strict sense. At the end of this route, which follows quite closely the plan outlined in 1976,[76] Foucault arrives at what, according to him, was "the correlation between the technique of security and the population."[77] The emergence of the latter, as idea and reality, is not only important at the political level. It also has a decisive meaning on the epistemological plane, as is clear from the way in which, in the light of population, Foucault reformulates the archeology of the human sciences set out in *The Order of Things*:

> (...) the theme of man, and the human sciences that analyze him as a living being, working individual, and speaking subject, should be understood on the basis of the emergence of population as the correlate of power and the object of knowledge. (...) [M]an (...) (...) is nothing other than a figure of population.[78]

The analysis of apparatuses of security relative to the population progressively led Foucault to accentuate the concept of "government." While the term is employed first of all in its traditional sense of public authority or the exercise of sovereignty, gradually, thanks to the physiocratic concept of "economic government," it acquires a discriminating value, designating the techniques specific to the management of populations. "Government," in this context, then takes on the strict sense of the "art of exercising power in the form of the economy,"[79] which allows Foucault to define economic liberalism as an art of government.

Thus, the problematic triangle—security-territory-population—that served as the initial framework of research, is replaced by the systematic series, security-population-government. This is why Foucault chose to devote the lecture of 1 February to the third term. This lecture, which is presented as a logical extension of the previous lectures, in actual fact marks a profound turning point in the general orientation of the lectures. Foucault introduces here, in fact, the concept of "governmental-ity," by which he suddenly shifts the stake of his work in a sort of dra-matic theoretical turn. After having separated the problem of government, as it arises in the sixteenth century, from the stratagems of the clever prince described by Machiavelli, and having shown how "population" allowed the art of government to be unblocked in relation to the double, juridical and domestic model that had prevented it from finding its own dimension, Foucault returns to the title of the lectures, which no longer seems to him to be suitable for his project:

(...) if I had wanted to give this year's lectures a more exact title, I certainly would not have chosen "security, territory, population." What I would really like to undertake is something that I would call a history of "governmentality."[80]

Is this turn a simple deepening of the initial hypotheses, or is it part of that crawfish approach by which Foucault humorously describes his mode of advance ("I am like the crawfish, I move sideways"[81])? The question is no doubt beside the point. The invention of the concept of "governmen-tality" arises both from the development of a pre-established plan (which corresponds, as we have seen, to the first four lectures), and from a thought in movement that decides, on the basis of what it discovers, to re-invest certain earlier analyses (concerning the art of government and the pastoral of souls[82]) in a broader theoretical perspective. Maybe more than any other moment in Foucault's teaching, this illustrates his taste for the labyrinth "into which I can venture, in which I can move my discourse, opening up underground passages, forcing it to go far from itself, finding overhangs that reduce and deform its itinerary."[83]

A new field of research opens up with this concept—no longer the history of technologies of security, which provisionally recedes into the background, but the genealogy of the modern state—the theoretical and methodological presuppositions of which are clarified in the next lecture. It involves applying to the state the "point of view" he had adopted previously in the study of the disciplines, separating out relations of power from any institutionalist or functionalist approach.[84]

This is why Foucault redefines what is at stake in the lectures:

> Is it possible to place the modern state in a general technology of
> power that would have assured its mutations, its development, and
> its functioning? Can we talk of something like a "governmentality"
> that would be to the state what techniques of segregation were to
> psychiatry, what techniques of discipline were to the penal system,
> and what biopolitics was to medical institutions?[85]

The problematic of "governmentality" therefore marks the entry of
the question of the state into the field of analysis of micro-powers. It is
worth making some comments on this:

1. This problematic answers the frequently made objection that
Foucault ignores the state in his analysis of power. This analysis, he
explains, no more excludes the state than it is subordinate to it. It is neither a question of denying the state nor of installing it in an overarching
position, but of showing that the analysis of micro-powers, far from
being limited to a precise domain defined by a sector of the scale, should
be considered "as a point of view, a method of decipherment valid for
the whole scale, whatever its size."[86]

2. Foucault's new interest in the state, however, is not restricted to
these methodological considerations. It also derives from the expansion
of the field of analysis carried out at the end of the 1976 lectures. The
management of "biosociological processes of human masses," unlike the
disciplines deployed in the framework of limited institutions (school,
hospital, barracks, workshop, and so on), involve in fact the state apparatus (*appareil*). The "complex organs of coordination and centralization" required for this end are found at the level of the state. Biopolitics
therefore can only be conceived of as "bioregulation by the state."[87]

3. In Foucault, taking the question of the state into account is
inseparable from criticism of its current representations: the state
as timeless abstraction,[88] as pole of transcendence,[89] instrument of class
domination,[90] or cold monster,[91]—in his eyes, all are forms of an "overvaluation of the problem of the state"[92] to which he opposes the thesis

that the "composite reality"[93] of the state is no more than "the mobile effect of a regime of multiple governmentalities."[94] In 1979 the same approach allows him to link the question of the state to that of "phobia of the state,"[95] whose "inflationist" effects he stresses.[96]

The analytical perspective of "governmentality" is not therefore a break in Foucault's work with regard to his earlier analysis of power, but is inserted within the space opened up by the problem of bio-power.[97] So it would not be accurate to claim that from this time the concept of "government" replaces that of "power," as if the latter now belonged to an outmoded problematic. The shift from "power" to "government" carried out in the 1978 lectures does not result from the methodological framework being called into question, but from its extension to a new object, the state, which did not have a place in the analysis of the disciplines.

The stages of this "governmentalization of the state" are the object of the nine last lectures, through the analysis of the Christian pastorate (lectures 5 to 8, of 8, 15 and 22 February, and 1 March 1978), the transition from the pastorate to political government (lecture 9, of 8 March), to the art of government according to *raison d'État*[98] (end of lecture 9 to lecture 11, from 8 to 22 March), and of the two technological systems by which it is characterized: the diplomatic-military system organized in terms of the maintenance of European equilibrium (lecture 11), and police, in the classical sense of "the set of means necessary to bring about the growth, from within, of the forces of the state"[99] (lectures 12 and 13, of 29 March and 5 April).[100] The final lecture ends with the return to the problem of population, whose site of emergence Foucault can now define better, "branching off from the technology of 'police' and in correlation with the birth of economic reflection."[101] It is because the problem of population is at the heart of criticism of the police state by political economy that liberalism appears as the form of rationality specific to the apparatuses (*dispositifs*) of biopolitical regulation.

This is precisely the thesis that the 1979 lectures propose to develop.

The birth of biopolitics

From the first week, these lectures appear as the direct continuation of the previous year's lectures. Stating his intention to continue what he had started to say the previous year, Foucault first of all clarifies the choice of method that will govern his analysis[102] and then summarizes the final lectures devoted to the government of *raison d'État* and criticism of this in terms of the problem of grain. In the eighteenth century, the principle of the external limitation of *raison d'État* by right is replaced by a principle of internal limitation in the form of the economy.[103] Political economy, in fact, contains within itself the requirement of a self-limitation of governmental reason founded on knowledge of the natural course of things. It therefore marks the irruption of a new rationality in the art of government: governing less, out of concern for maximum effectiveness, in accordance with the naturalness of the phenomena one is dealing with. Foucault calls this government, which is linked to the question of truth in its permanent effort of self-limitation, "liberalism." The object of the lectures is to show how this liberalism constitutes the condition of intelligibility of biopolitics:

> With the emergence of political economy, with the introduction of the limitative principle into governmental practice itself, an important substitution is carried out, or rather a doubling, since the subjects of right over whom political sovereignty is exercised appear themselves as a *population* that a government must manage.
>
> The line of organization of a "biopolitics" finds its point of departure here. But who does not see that this is only part of something much larger, which [is] this new governmental reason?
>
> To study liberalism as the general framework of biopolitics.[104]

The following plan is announced: to study liberalism first of all in its original formulation and its contemporary, German and American, versions, and then come to the problem of the politics of life.[105] In actual fact, only the first part of this program is realized, Foucault being led to develop his analysis of German neo-liberalism at greater length than he envisaged.[106] This interest in the social market economy is due not only to the paradigmatic character of the German experience. It is also explained by reasons of "critical morality," faced with "that kind of laxity" that, in his eyes, constitutes an "inflationist critique of the state" that is quick to denounce fascism in the functioning of Western democratic states.[107] The "German question" is thus placed at the heart of the methodological, historical, and political questions that form the framework of the course.

The second and third lectures (17 and 24 January) are devoted to the specific features of the liberal art of government as outlined in the eighteenth century. In the first place, in these lectures Foucault explains the link between truth and liberal governmentality through an analysis of the market as a site of veridiction, and he specifies the modalities of internal limitation that derive from this. Thus he reveals two ways of limiting public power corresponding to two heterogeneous conceptions of liberty: the revolutionary, axiological way, which founds sovereign power on the rights of man, and the radical, utilitarian way, which starts from governmental practice in order to define the limit of governmental competence and the sphere of individual autonomy in terms of utility. These two ways are distinct, but they are not mutually exclusive; the history of European liberalism since the nineteenth century should be studied in the light of their strategic interaction. It is also this interaction that clarifies, or puts in perspective, the way in which, from 1977, Foucault problematizes the "rights of the governed," in comparison with the more vague and abstract invocation of "human rights."[108]

After having examined the question of Europe and of its relations with the rest of the world according to the new governmental reason, in the third lecture Foucault returns to his choice of calling "liberalism" what in the eighteenth century appears rather as a naturalism. The word liberalism is justified by the role liberty plays in the liberal art of government: a liberty no doubt guaranteed, but also produced by this art of government, which, in order to achieve its ends, needs continually to create, maintain, and frame it. Liberalism can thus be defined as the calculation of risk—the free play of individual interests—compatible with the interest of each and all. That is why the incitement to "live dangerously" entails the establishment of multiple mechanisms of security. Liberty and security: it is the procedures of control and forms of state intervention required by this double exigency that constitute the paradox of liberalism and are at the origin of the "crises of governmentality"[109] that it has experienced for two centuries.

The question now then is whether that crisis of governmentality characterizes the present world and to what revisions of the liberal art of government it has given rise. Starting from the fourth lecture (31 January 1979), the study of the two great neo-liberal schools, German ordoliberalism[110] and American anarcho-liberalism,[111] correspond to this diagnostic task and is Foucault's sole incursion into the field of contemporary history throughout his teaching at the Collège de France. These two schools do not just participate in an identical project of the radical reform of liberalism. They also represent two distinct forms of the "critique of the irrationality peculiar to excessive government,"[112] one stressing the logic of pure competition on the economic terrain, while framing the market through a set of state interventions (theory of the "politics of society"), and the other seeking to extend the rationality of the market to domains hitherto considered to be non-economic (theory of "human capital").

The final two lectures deal with the birth in eighteenth century thought of the idea of *homo œconomicus* as a subject of interest distinct from the subject of right, and of the notion of "civil society" as correlative of the liberal technology of government. Whereas in its most classical version liberal thought opposed society to the state, as nature to artifice or spontaneity to constraint, Foucault highlights the paradox that constitutes their relation. Society, in fact, represents the principle in the name of which liberal government tends to limit itself. It obliges it to ask itself constantly whether it is not governing too much and, in this respect, plays a critical role with regard to all excessive government. But it also forms the target of a permanent governmental intervention, not in order to restrict formal liberties on the level of practical reality, but in order to produce, multiply, and guarantee those liberties that the liberal system needs.[113] Society thus represents at once "the set of conditions of least liberal government" and the "surface of transfer of governmental activity."[114]

ESSENTIAL CONCEPTS

We will end this presentation with some comments on the two fundamental concepts—"government" and "governmentality"—around which the lectures are organized.

Government

The problematic of the art of government is outlined for the first time in the 1975 lectures, *Abnormal*. Contrasting the model of the exclusion of lepers with that of the inclusion of plague victims,[115] Foucault then credited the Classical Age with the invention of positive technologies of power applicable at different levels (state apparatus, institutions, the family):

> The Classical Age developed therefore what could be called an "art of government," in the sense in which "government" was then understood as precisely the "government" of children, the "government" of the mad, the "government" of the poor, and before long, the "government" of workers.[116]

Foucault specified three things that should be understood by "government": the new idea of a power founded on the transfer, alienation, or representation of individual wills; the state apparatus (*appareil d'État*) set up in the eighteenth century; and finally, a "general technique of the government of men" that was "the other side of the juridical and political structures of representation and the condition of the functioning and effectiveness of these apparatuses."[117] This is a technique, the "typical apparatus (*dispositif*)" of which consisted in the disciplinary organization described the previous year.[118]

The analysis of "government" in this course was not limited to the disciplines, but extended to the techniques of the government of souls forged by the Church around the rite of penance.[119] Discipline of bodies and government of souls thus appear as the two complementary faces of a single process of normalization:

> At a time when states were posing the technical problem of the power to be exercised on bodies (...), the Church was elaborating a technique for the government of souls, the pastoral, which was defined by the Council of Trent and later taken up and developed by Carlo Borromeo.[120]

The art of government and the pastoral are two threads pursued once again by the 1978 lectures, but with some significant differences. First of all, there is a considerable extension of the chronological framework: the pastoral is no longer constituted in the sixteenth century, in reaction to the Reformation, but from the first centuries of Christianity, the government of souls being defined by the Fathers as "the art of arts" or the "science of sciences."[121] Foucault therefore re-inserts the Tridentine pastoral in the long life of the Christian pastorate. Next, there is a refocusing of the art of government on the actual functioning of the state: government, in its political sense, no longer designates the techniques by which power is connected to individuals, but the actual exercise of political sovereignty[122]—we have seen above the methodological stake to which this new "point of view" corresponded.[123] Finally, there is a shift from the analysis of the effective mechanisms of power to "self consciousness of government."[124] This move, however, does not break with the "microphysical" approach of previous works. As he explains in the introduction to the 1979 seminar, for Foucault it is not so much a question of studying the practices as the programmatic structure inherent in them, in order to give an account of the ensuing "procedures of objectivation":

> All governmentality can only be strategic and programmatic. It never works. But it is in relation to a program that we can say that it never works.
>
> Anyway, it is not the effects of social organization that I want to analyze, but the effects of objectivation and veridiction. And this in the human sciences → madness, the penal system, and in relation to itself, insofar as it is reflected → governmentality (state/civil society).
>
> It is a matter of asking what type of practice governmentality is, inasmuch as it has effects of objectivation and veridiction regarding men themselves by constituting them as subjects.[125]

Governmentality

(a) Formulated for the first time in the fourth lecture of 1978 (1 February 1978), the concept of "governmentality"[126] progressively shifts from a precise, historically determinate sense, to a more general and abstract meaning. In fact, in this lecture it serves as the name for the regime of power deployed in the eighteenth century, which "has the population as its target, political economy as its major form of knowledge, and apparatuses of security as its essential technical instrument,"[127] as well as the process that has led to "the pre-eminence over all other types of power—sovereignty, discipline, and so on—of the type of power that we can call 'government.'"[128] It thus designates a set of elements whose genesis and articulation are specific to Western history.

To governmentality's character as event, in its historical and singular dimension, are added the limits of its field of application. It does not define just any relation of power, but the techniques of government that underpin the formation of the modern state. In fact, governmentality is to the state

(...) what techniques of segregation [are] to psychiatry, (...) techniques of discipline (...) to the penal system, and biopolitics to medical institutions.[129]

At this stage of Foucault's reflection, "governmentality" is therefore the concept that allows a specific domain of power relations to be cut out, in connection with the problem of the state. This double, *événementiel* and regional character of the notion will tend to disappear over the following years. From 1979, the word no longer only designates the governmental practices constitutive of a particular regime of power (police state or liberal minimum government), but "the way in which one conducts people's conduct," thus serving as an "analytical perspective for relations of power" in general.[130] If this perspective, then, is always put to work within the framework of the problem of the state, the following year it is detached from it in order to become coextensive with the semantic field of "government,"

(...) this notion being understood in the broad sense of procedures for directing human conduct. Government of children, government of souls and consciences, government of a household, of a state, or of oneself.[131]

"Governmentality" seeming from then on to merge with "government,"[132] Foucault strives to distinguish the two notions, "governmentality" defining "a strategic field of power relations in their mobility, transformability, and reversibility,"[133] within which the types of conduct, or "conduct of conduct," that characterize "government" are established. More exactly—for the strategic field is no more than the actual interplay of the power relations—he shows how they are reciprocally implicated, governmentality not constituting a structure, that is to say "a relational invariant between (...) variables," but rather a "singular generality,"[134] the variables of which, in their aleatory interactions, correspond to conjunctures.

Governmentality is thus the rationality immanent to the micro-powers, whatever the level of analysis being considered (parent-child relation, individual-public power, population-medicine, and so on). If it is "an event,"[135] this is no longer so much as a determinate historical sequence, as in the 1978 lectures, but inasmuch as every power relation is a matter for a strategic analysis:

A singular generality: its only reality is that of the event (*événementielle*) and its intelligibility can only make use of a strategic logic.[136]

It remains to ask, what link joins together these types of *événementialité* in Foucault's thought: that which is inscribed in a particular historical process peculiar to Western societies, and that which is theoretically anchored in a general definition of power in terms of "government."[137]

(b) For Foucault, the analysis of types of governmentality is inseparable from analysis of corresponding forms of resistance, or "counter-conducts." Thus, in the eighth lecture of 1978 (1 March) he establishes the inventory of the main forms of counter-conduct developed in the Middle Ages in relation to the pastorate (asceticism, communities, mysticism, Scripture, and eschatological beliefs). Similarly, the analysis of modern governmentality, organized in terms of *raison d'État*, leads him, at the end of the course, to highlight different sources of specific counter-conducts, in the name of civil society, the population, or the nation. Being the symptom, in every epoch, of a "crisis of governmentality,"[138] it is important to ask what forms these counter-conducts take in the current crisis in order to define new modalities of struggle or resistance. The reading of liberalism that Foucault proposes can only be understood on the basis of this questioning.

In this regard it seems to us to be interesting to quote the following passage from the manuscript in which Foucault defined governmentality as a "singular generality." We see here, in fact, how for Foucault politics is always conceived from the point of view of forms of resistance to power[139] (this is, moreover, the only text, to our knowledge, in which he refers to Carl Schmitt):

The analysis of governmentality as singular generality implies that "everything is political." This expression is traditionally given two meanings:

—Politics is defined by the whole sphere of state intervention, (...). To say that everything is political amounts to saying that, directly or indirectly, the state is everywhere.

—Politics is defined by the omnipresence of a struggle between two adversaries (...). This other definition is that of K. (sic) Schmitt.

The theory of the comrade.

(...)

In short, two formulations: everything is political by the nature of things; everything is political by the existence of adversaries.

It is a question of saying rather: nothing is political, everything can be politicized, everything may become political. Politics is no more or less than that which is born with resistance to governmentality, the first uprising, the first confrontation.[140]

(c) If the 1978 and 1979 lectures have remained unpublished until now, with the exception of the fourth lecture (1 February) of 1978,[141] and some extracts from the 1979 lectures,[142] the problematic of governmentality, based notably on the summary given by Foucault in his 1979 Stanford lectures,[143] has given birth to a vast field of research for a number of years in Anglo-Saxon countries and, more recently in Germany[144]—"governmentality studies." The latter have even found a place in sociology and political science departments of some universities. The point of departure of this movement was the publication in 1991 of *The Foucault Effect: Studies in governmentality*, edited by G. Burchell, C. Gordon, and P. Miller,[145] which contained, in addition to Foucault's lecture on the subject, a long introduction by Colin Gordon providing a detailed synthesis of the 1978 and 1979 lectures, and a set of studies focused, in particular, on the notion of risk (the conception of social risk, modalities of risk prevention, the development of insurance techniques, the philosophy of risk, and so on).[146] A considerable literature in the field of the social sciences, political economy, and political theory has developed from this that it is clearly not possible to list within the framework of this presentation. For an overview one can refer to Mitchell Dean's *Governmentality: Power and rule in modern society*,[147] and the article by Thomas Lemke, "Neoliberalismus, Staat und Selbsttechnologien. Ein kritischer Überblick über die *governmentality studies*."[148] The recent application of the concept of governmentality to domains as distant from Foucault's central interests as human resource management,[149] or organization theory,[150] testifies to the malleability of this analytical scheme and its capacity to circulate in the most varied spaces.

I would like to thank Daniel Defert for the generosity with which he made Michel Foucault's manuscripts and dossiers available to me, and my wife, Chantal, for her precious assistance in the work of transcribing the lectures.

1. See, *"Il faut défendre la société."* Cours au Collège de France, 1975-1976, eds., M. Bertani and A. Fontana (Paris: Gallimard-Le Seuil, "Hautes Études," 1997), lecture of 17 March 1976, pp. 216-226; English translation by David Macey, *"Society Must Be Defended." Lectures at the Collège de France*, English series ed., Arnold I. Davidson (New York: Picador, 2003) pp. 242-254; and *La Volonté de savoir* (Paris: Gallimard, "Bibliothèque des histoires," 1976) pp. 181-191; English translation by Robert Hurley, *The History of Sexuality. Volume 1: An Introduction* (New York: Pantheon, 1978) pp. 138-145.

2. "Les mailles du pouvoir" (1976) *Dits et Écrits*, 4, p. 194.

3. See above, lecture of 11 January 1978, p. 11.

4. This is the title of the final two courses of 1983 and 1984. It is also the title of a book announced by Foucault in 1983 for the collection "Des travaux" that he created with Paul Veyne and François Wahl. See the course summary for 1981, "Subjectivité et verité" in *Dits et Écrits, 1954-1988*, eds. D. Defert and F. Ewald, with the collaboration of J. Lagrange (Paris: Gallimard, 1994) in 4 volumes, vol. 4, p. 214, where Foucault states his project of taking up the question of governmentality in a new aspect: "the government of the self by the self in its connections with relations to others." English translation by Robert Hurley, "Subjectivity and Truth" in *Essential Works of Foucault 1954-1984. Vol. 1: Ethics: Subjectivity and Truth*, ed. Paul Rabinow (New York: New Press, 1997) p. 88.

5. "La Société punitive," unpublished lecture of 28 March 1973: "Power is won and lost like a battle. At the heart of power is a warlike relation and not a relation of appropriation." See also, *Surveiller et Punir* (Paris: Gallimard, "Bibliothèque des histoires," 1975) p. 31; English translation by A. Sheridan, *Discipline and Punish. Birth of the Prison* (London: Allen Lane, and New York: Pantheon, 1977) p. 26. The aim of the 1976 course *"Il faut défendre la société"; "Society Must Be Defended,"* was, if not to dismiss this conception, then at least to question the historical presuppositions and consequences of recourse to the model of war as analyzer of power relations.

6. *Naissance de la biopolitique. Cours au Collège de France, 1978-1979*, ed., M. Senellart (Paris: Gallimard-Le Seuil, "Hautes Études," 2004), "Résume du cours," p. 329.

7. This course in fact deals with the government of souls, through the problem of the examination of conscience and confession (*l'aveu*).

8. *"Il faut défendre la société,"* p. 224; *"Society Must Be Defended,"* pp. 251-252.

9. We only refer here to the events to which Foucault was linked and which found a direct or indirect echo in the lectures.

10. At the Nantes congress of the Socialist Party in June 1977, "Michel Rocard developed his conception of two political cultures of the left: one, Jacobin and statist, accepting alliance with the communists, the other, decentralizing and regionalist, which rejects it, and soon called the 'second left.'" D. Defert, "Chronologie," *Dits et Écrits*, 1, p. 51.

11. For a retrospective view of this period, see his interview with G. Raulet in the Spring of 1983, "Structuralisme et poststructuralisme," *Dits et Écrits*, 4, pp. 453-454; (Amended) English translation by Jeremy Harding, "Stucturalism and Post-structuralism," *Essential Works of Foucault 1954-1984. Vol. 2: Aesthetics, Method, and Epistemology*, ed. James D. Faubion (New York: New Press, and London: Allen Lane, 1998) p. 454: "New problems, new thinking—these have been crucial. I think that one day, when we look back at this episode in French history [from the first years of Gaullism], we will see in it the growth of a new kind of Left thought that—in multiple and nonunified forms (perhaps one of its positive aspects)—has completely transformed the horizon of contemporary Left movements."

12. For more details about this forum, see the introduction to the interview with Foucault, "Une mobilisation culturelle," *Le Nouvel Observateur*, 12-18 September 1977; *Dits et Écrits*, 3, pp. 329-330. Foucault was in the "médecine de quartier" workshop. See also the special supplement, *Forum*, "Les hommes du vrai changement," in the same issue of *Le Nouvel Observateur*, pp. 47-62.

13. "Une mobilisation culturelle," p. 330.

14. See, "La grille politique traditionelle," *Politique-Hebdo*, 6-12 March 1978; *Dits et Écrits*, 3, p. 506.

15. *Naissance de la biopolitique*, lecture of 31 January 1979, p. 95.

16. Quoted by D. Defert, *"Chronologie,"* p. 62.

17. Ibid. p. 51. See D. Macey, *The Lives of Michel Foucault* (New York: Pantheon Books, 1993) pp. 379-381.
18. "Va-t-on extrader Klaus Croissant?" *Le Nouvel Observateur*, 14 November 1977; *Dits et Écrits*, 3, p. 362 and p. 364: "The traditional conception [of the right to asylum] put 'politics' on the side of the struggle against the governors and their adversaries; the current conception, born from the existence of totalitarian regimes, is focused on a figure who is not so much the 'future governor,' but the 'perpetual dissident'—I mean someone who is in overall disagreement with the system in which he lives, who expresses this disagreement with the means available to him, and who is hounded as a result of this."
19. Mireille Debard and Jean-Luc Hennig, *Les Juges kaki* (Paris: A. Moreau, 1977).
20. "Préface," *Dits et Écrits*, 3, p. 140. This text appeared in advance sheets in *Le Monde*, 1-2 December 1977.
21. See lecture of 1 March 1978, p. 201: "And after all, who today does not have his theory of dissidence?"
22. See above, note 18.
23. "Michel Foucault: la sécurité et l'État," *Tribune socialiste*, 24-30 November 1977; *Dits et Écrits*, 3, p. 385. See also, "Lettre à quelques leaders de la gauche," *Le Nouvel Observateur*, 28 November-4 December 1977; *Dits et Écrits*, 3, p. 390; English translation by Robert Hurley, "Letter to Certain Leaders of the Left," *Essential Works of Foucault, Vol. 3: Power*, ed. James D. Faubion (New York: New Press, 2000, and London: Allen Lane, 2001) p. 427.
24. See *Naissance de la biopolitique*, lecture of 7 March 1979, p. 191 *sq*. See p. 197: "(...) I think that what we should not do is imagine that we are describing a real, present process concerning ourselves when we denounce statization, or fascization, the imposition of state violence, etcetera."
25. On the opposition of this type of terrorism of small political groups to a terrorism anchored in a national movement and, thereby, "morally justified (...) even if one may be very hostile to this or that type of action," see "Michel Foucault: la sécurité et l'État," pp. 383-384 (a position very close to that maintained by R. Badinter, "Terrorisme et liberté," *Le Monde*, 14 October 1977). See also, "Le savoir comme crime," *Jyôkyô*, April 1976; *Dits et Écrits*, 3, p. 83, on the counter-productive nature of terrorism in the West, which can only obtain the opposite of what it aims for: "(...) terror only brings about blind obedience. To use terror for the revolution is in itself a totally contradictory idea."
26. See Didier Eribon, *Michel Foucault* (Paris: Flammarion, 1989) p. 276, which in support of this explanation cites a passage from Claude Mauriac's diary, dated March 1984, *Le Temps immobile* (Paris: Grasset) vol. 9, p. 388. With Guattari, Deleuze had published an article on Klaus Croissant and the Baader group in *Le Monde*, 2 November 1977, "Le pire moyen de faire l'Europe," in which, presenting the German Federal Republic as a country "in condition to export its judicial, political, and 'informative' model, and to become the skilled organizer of repression and brainwashing in other states," he expressed his fear of "the whole of Europe coming under the type of control called for by Germany," and gave backing to terrorist action: "(...) since the last century the question of violence, and even of terrorism, as a response to imperialist violence in very diverse forms, has constantly troubled the revolutionary and workers' movement. The same questions are raised today with regard to the people of the Third World, whom Baader and his group claim to represent, considering Germany to be an essential agent of their oppression" (republished in G. Deleuze, *Deux Régimes de fous, et autres textes* [Paris: Minuit, "Paradoxe," 2003] pp. 137-138). See also, D. Macey, *The Lives of Michel Foucault*, p. 394: "Foucault had refused to lend his name to a petition being circulated by Félix Guattari. It too opposed the extradition of Croissant, but it referred to West Germany as 'fascist'." This is the context for the text by Jean Genet quoted by Foucault in *Security, Territory, Population*, lecture of 15 March 1978, above p. 264.
27. "Une énorme surprise," *Der Spiegel*, 30 October 1978; *Dits et Écrits*, 3, pp. 699-700.
28. Adopting the words of an East German writer, Heiner Müller, in 1979 Foucault says: "Rather than invoke the old demons with regard to Germany, we should look at the actual situation: Germany cut in two (...). We cannot understand the multiplication of security measures in Federal Germany without taking account of a very real fear that comes from the East" ("Michel Foucault: 'Désormais, la sécurité est au-dessus des lois'," *Le Matin*,

18 November 1977; *Dits et Écrits*, 3, p. 367). It is important to place these statements in the climate of Germanophobia that was then very widespread in France and to which Günther Grass, for example, reacted in the following way: "When I ask myself where in Europe today there is the danger of a movement of the aggressive right—I avoid saying 'fascism,' which comes too easily to the mouth—then I observe Italy or England, and I see the emergence of problems there that frighten me (. . .). But I would not think of saying: England is on the road to fascism" (Debate with Alfred Grosser published in *Die Ziet*, 23 September 1977 and republished by *Le Monde*, 2-3 October 1977).

29. *Naissance de la biopolitique*, lecture of 7 March 1979, p. 198.

30. See D. Defert, "Chronologie," p. 52 and p. 53.

31. See *Security, Territory, Population*, lectures of 8, 15, 22 February and 1 March.

32. See "La philosophie analytique du pouvoir" (27 April 1978); *Dits et Écrits*, 3, pp. 548-550, and "Sexualité et pouvoir" (20 April 1978), ibid. pp. 560-565.

33. This was the volume on the reformed pastoral, *The Flesh and the Body* (*La Chair et le Corps*), announced in *The History of Sexuality*, *Vol. 1*, p. 21, note 4, the manuscript of which was totally destroyed.

34. "La philosophie analytique du pouvoir," p. 537.

35. Ibid. p. 540.

36. "Qu'est-ce que la critique?" (lecture to the Société française de philosophie, 27 May 1978), *Bulletin de la Société française de philosophie*, 2, April-June 1990 (Paris: Armand Colin) pp. 35-63. This text is not included in *Dits et Écrits*.

37. See " 'Omnes et singulatim': Toward a Critique of Political Reason" (the two Tanner lectures delivered at Stanford University, 10 and 16 October 1979), *Essential Works of Foucault*, 3, pp. 298-299: "(. . .) since Kant, the role of philosophy has been to prevent reason going beyond the limits of what is given in experience; but from the same moment, (. . .) the role of philosophy has also been to keep watch over the excessive powers of political rationality (. . .)" (French translation by P.E. Dauzat, " 'Omnes et singulatim': vers une critique de la raison politique," *Dits et Écrits*, 4, p. 135); "Qu'est-ce que les Lumières?" (1984), *Dits et Écrits*, 4, pp. 562-578; English translation by Catherine Porter (amended), "What is Enlightenment?" in *Essential Works of Foucault*, 1, pp. 303-319; "Qu'est-ce que les Lumières?" (extract from the first lecture of the 1983 lectures, "Le Gouvernement de soi et des autres"), *Dits et Écrits*, 4, pp. 679-688; English translation by Colin Gordon, "Kant on Enlightenment and revolution" in Mike Gane and Terry Johnson, eds. *Foucault's New Domains* (London: Routledge, 1993), originally published in *Economy and Society*, vol. 15, no. 1, February 1986.

38. "Les 'reportages' d'idées" (*Corriere della sera*, 12 November 1978), *Dits et Écrits*, 3. Of the reports envisaged, on Vietnam, the USA, Hungary, Spanish democratization, the collective suicide of the sect led by Jones in Guyana, the only ones to appear were those of Foucault on Iran, A. Finkielkraut on the America of Jimmy Carter, and André Glucksmann on the "boat people." Finkielkraut's report, introduced by Foucault's text that we quote here, notably contained a chapter on the Chicago neo-liberal school, "Il capitalismo come utopia," to which Foucault will devote two lectures in the following year's course, *Naissance de la biopolitique*, lectures of 14 and 21 March 1979. See, A. Finkielkraut, *La Rivincita e l'Utopia* (Milan: Rizzoli, 1980) pp. 33-44.

39. In Iran Foucault met Pierre Blanchet and Claire Brière, journalist of *Libération*, who in April 1979 will publish *Iran: la révolution au nom de Dieu* (Paris: Le Seuil, "L'Histoire immédiate"), followed by an interview with Foucault, "L'esprit d'un monde sans esprit," *Dits et Écrits*, 3, pp. 743-756; English translation by Alan Sheridan, "Iran: The Spirit of a World Without Spirit" in M. Foucault, *Politics, philosophy, culture.* ed., Lawrence D. Kritzman (New York and London: Routledge, 1988) pp. 211-224. The interview is preceded by these few lines: "At a time when the classical schemas of armed struggle are called into question, the event questions us. What could the strength of this people be who have overthrown the Shah without firing a single shot? Is it the strength of a spirituality rediscovered through a religion, Shiite Islam? What can the future be of this revolution that has no equivalent in the world?" p. 227. The text on the back cover of the book, extending this question, noted: "Is not this irruption of spirituality in politics also fraught with a new intolerance?"

40. On 8 September, the army fired on the crowd massed in Jaleh Square, causing thousands of deaths. See, "L'armée, quand la terre tremble," *Corriere della sera*, 28 September, *Dits et Écrits*, 3, p. 665.

41. See the box "Chronologie des événements d'Iran" (from 8 January 1978, date of the first demonstrations at Qom, repressed by the army, until 31 March 1979 and the adoption by referendum of the Islamic Republic), *Dits et Écrits*, 3, p. 663. On the precise circumstances of Foucault's visits and his relationships with members of the Iranian opposition in exile, see D. Defert, "Chronologie," p. 55; D. Eribon, *Michel Foucault*, pp. 298-309; and D. Macey, *The Lives of Michel Foucault*, pp. 407-411. For a commentary on Foucault's articles, see H. Malagola, "Foucault en Iran" in A. Brossat, ed. *Michel Foucault. Les jeux de la vérité et du pouvoir* (Presses universitaires de Nancy, 1994) pp. 151-162.

42. When he received Foucault, Chariat Madari "was surrounded by several human rights activists" ("À quoi rêvent les Iraniens?" *Le Nouvel Observateur*, 16-22 October 1978, *Dits et Écrits*, 3, p. 691). See P. Blanchet and C. Brière, *Iran: la révolution*, p. 169. See also G. Kepel, *Jihad. Expansion et déclin de l'islamisme* (Paris: Gallimard, 2000) p. 157: "The majority of the clergy was not ranked behind the revolutionary conceptions of Khomeini, who wanted to replace the Pahlavi empire with a theocracy (*velayat-e faqih*) in which supreme power would be held by a *faqih*—that religious figure specialized in Islamic law behind which Khomeini himself could be seen. Most of the clergy, behind the great ayatollah Shari'at Madari, were opposed to this. They were content to call for the greatest possible autonomy, and control of their schools, of their social work, and of their financial resources that faced encroachments of the state, but they had no ambition to control a power that theologically was considered to be impure—until the return of the hidden Imam, the messiah who will fill the shadows and iniquity of the world with light and justice." After coming into conflict with Khomeini, in February 1979, for having encouraged the creation of the Popular Republican Party, Chariat Madari ended his days under house arrest.

43. See in particular, *Security, Territory, Population*, lecture of 15 February 1978, above pp. 154-156, concerning the relations between the pastoral power of the Church and political power.

44. "We are waiting for the Mahdi [the twelfth Imam, or hidden Imam], but every day we fight for a good government" quoted by Foucault in "Téhéran: la foi contre le chah," *Corriere de la sera*, 8 October 1978, *Dits et Écrits*, 3, p. 686; the same quotation appears in "À quoi rêvent les Iraniens?" p. 691.

45. "À quoi rêvent les Iraniens?" p. 691.

46. This expression appears twice, ibid. pp. 693-694.

47. Professor of sociology at the University of Mashhad, Ali Chariati (1933-1977) was linked with a number of intellectuals in Paris, notably Louis Massignon, of whom he was the follower, and Frantz Fanon, whose *Les Damnés de la terre* (*The Wretched of the Earth*) he translated. Excluded from the University, he pursued his teaching in a religious institution in the north of Teheran. His audience was such that the regime blocked the building. Imprisoned for 18 months, he then chose exile in London where he died of a heart attack. On his thought see, D. Shayegan, *Qu'est-ce que révolution religieuse?* (Paris: Presses d'aujourd'hui, 1982; republished Albin Michel, 1991) pp. 222-237. In an interview with P. Blanchet and C. Brière, "Comment peut-on être persan?" *Le Nouvel Observateur*, 25 September 1982, D. Shayegan situates Chariati in the line of those who, like Frantz Fanon and Ben Bella, "thought it was possible to harmonize the profane and the sacred, Marx and Mohammed." See also, P. Blanchet and C. Brière, *Iran: la révolution*, pp. 178-179, and G. Kepel, *Jihad*, pp. 53-54 *et passim*, which stresses the influence of Chariati (Shari'ati) on the Islamic-revolutionary movement of the people's Mujaheddin (p. 56 and p. 154; see note 14, pp. 555-556, on this movement). The standard work on Chariati is now the great biography by Ali Rahnema, *An Islamic Utopia: A political biography of Ali Shari'ati* (London: Tauris, 1998).

48. "À quoi rêvent les Iraniens?" p. 693.

49. Ibid. p. 694. On the polemics aroused by this analysis of "Islamic government," see D. Eribon, *Michel Foucault*, p. 305, and the "Répons de Michel Foucault à une lectrice iranienne," *Le Nouvel Observateur*, 13-19 November 1978, *Dits et Écrits*, 3, p. 708. One is astounded that, more than twenty years after the publication of these articles, a fashionable editorialist can still present Foucault as the "advocate of Iranian Khomeinism in 1979 and

therefore theoretically in support of its violent actions," A. Minc, "Le terrorisme de l'esprit," *Le Monde*, 7 November 2001.

50. "Entretien avec Michel Foucault" (end of 1978), *Dits et Écrits*, 4, p. 79; English translation by Robert Hurley, "Interview with Michel Foucault," *Essential Works of Foucault*, 3, p. 280.

51. Increasingly critical support, as is shown by his "Lettre ouverte à Mehdi Bazargan," *Le Nouvel Observateur*, 14-20 April 1979, *Dits et Écrits*, 3, pp. 780-782; English translation by Robert Hurley, "Open Letter to Mehdi Bazargan," *Essential Works of Foucault*, 3, pp. 439-442.

52. See "Michel Foucault et l'Iran," *Le Matin*, 26 March 1979, *Dits et Écrits*, 3, p. 762.

53. "Inutile de se soulever?" *Le Monde*, 11-12 May 1979, *Dits et Écrits*, 3, pp. 790-794; English translation by Robert Hurley, "Useless to Revolt?" *Essential Works of Foucault*, 3, pp. 449-453.

54. Ibid. p. 791; ibid. p. 449.

55. Ibid. p. 793; ibid. p. 451 (translation amended; G.B.).

56. Ibid.; ibid. p. 452: "People do revolt; that is a fact. And that is how subjectivity (not that of great men, but that of anyone) is brought into history, breathing life into it."

57. On this analysis of religion in terms of force, see "Téhéran: la foi contre le chah," *Dits et Écrits*, 3, p. 688: "The Shiite religion (...) is today what it has been several times in the past: the form taken by political struggle when this mobilizes the popular strata. From thousands of discontents, hatreds, and miseries it fashions a force. (...)"

58. The word appears twice in *Security, Territory, Population*, at the end of the 7th lecture (22 February 1978) pp. 184-185 in the framework of the "history of the subject" opened up by the analysis of the Christian pastorate.

59. See the lecture of 1 March 1978. It is interesting in this regard to bring together one of Foucault's examples and the analysis of Shiite spirituality put forward by Henry Corbin in his monumental work, *En Islam iranien* (Paris: Gallimard, "Bibliothèque des idées," 1978). The latter, in fact, recapitulating the principal aspects of Shiite eschatology, at the center of which is the person of the 12th Imam, sees in this the core of a "spiritual chivalry" insepara-ble from the concept of the "Friends of God," of which the "Green Island" of the *Gottesfreunde*, founded by Rulman Merswin at Strasbourg in the fourteenth century, will be one of the historical recurrences in the West (vol. 4, pp. 390-404). See the lecture of 1 March 1978, p. 211 on Rulman Merswin and the Oberland Friend of God. At the time Foucault was giving his lectures he could not have known this text, which appeared in April 1978. We know, however, that he read Corbin before going to Iran (see the editor's note in *Dits et Écrits*, 3, p. 662). The words he uses with regard to Chariati, "whose death (...) has given him the privileged place in Shiism of the invisible Present, the Absent always there" ("À quoi rêvent les Iraniens?" p. 693) seems like the trace of Corbin's on the 12th Imam "hidden to the senses but present in the heart of his faithful" (p. xviii).

60. "Inutile de se soulever?" p. 794; "Useless to revolt?" p. 452.

61. Ibid.; ibid. p. 453 (translation amended).

62. The lectures were announced in the *Annuaire du Collège de France, 77ᵉ année* with the title "Security, territory and population." However, Foucault refers to the title twice during the lectures—first to explain it (1st lecture) and then to correct it (4th lecture)—in the form "Security, territory, population," and this is the title we have chosen.

63. *Les Anormaux. Cours au Collège de France, année 1974-1975*, eds., V. Marchetti and A. Salomoni (Paris: Gallimard-Le Seuil, "Hautes Études," 1999), "Résumé du cours" p. 311; English translation by Graham Burchell, *Abnormal. Lectures at the Collège de France 1974-1975*, English series editor, Arnold I. Davidson (New York: Picador, 2003), "Course Summary" pp. 329-329.

64. Ibid.; ibid.

65. Clarification provided by D. Defert in J.-Cl. Zancarini, ed., *Lectures de Michel Foucault* (ENS Éditions, 2000) p. 62. "In Belgium, in 1981, Foucault" Defert adds "had moreover given a seminar on this subject, which interested him." This was the set of lectures entitled "Mal faire, dire vrai. Fonctions de l'aveu," that Foucault gave in Louvain, in Spring 1981, in the framework of the Franqui chair. On this seminar, see F. Tulkens, "Généalogie de la défence sociale en Belgique (1880-1914)," *Actes*, 54, Summer 1986, special issue: *Foucault hors les murs*, pp. 38-41.

66. *"Il faut défendre la société"* lecture of 10 March 1976, p. 194; *"Society Must Be Defended"* p. 216.

67. Ibid.; ibid.
68. *La Volonté de savoir*, p. 184; *The History of Sexuality. Vol 1: An Introduction*, p. 140.
69. *"Il faut défendre la société"* lecture of 17 March 1976, p. 216; *"Society Must Be Defended"* pp. 242-243 (translation amended).
70. Ibid. p. 225; ibid. p. 253. This is, he adds, "no more than a first and inadequate interpretation of the idea of a normalizing society" (translation modified). The notion of "disciplinary society" appeared for the first time in *Le Pouvoir psychiatrique. Cours au Collège de France, année 1973-1974*, ed. J. Lagrange (Paris: Gallimard-Le Seuil, "Hautes Études," 2003) lecture of 28 November 1973, p. 68; English translation by Graham Burchell, *Psychiatric Power. Lectures at the Collège de France 1973-1974*, English Series editor Arnold I. Davidson (New York and Basingstoke: Palgrave Macmillan, 2006) p. 66. It is then taken up in *Surveiller et Punir*, p. 217; *Discipline and Punish*, p. 216.
71. Ibid. p. 216; ibid. p. 243 (translation slightly modified). See also *La Volonté de savoir*, p. 183; *The History of Sexuality, vol. 1*, p. 139: "(. . .) starting in the seventeenth century, this power over life developed in two main forms; these forms were not antithetical however; they constituted rather two poles of development linked together by a whole intermediary cluster of relations. One of these poles—the first to be formed, it seems—focused on the body as machine: its training (*dressage*), the optimization of its capabilities, the extortion of its forces (etcetera ...), all this was ensured by the procedures of power that characterized the *disciplines: an anatomo-politics of the human body*. The second, formed somewhat later, around the middle of the eighteenth century, focused on the species-body, the body (. . .) serving as the basis of biological processes: propagation, births and mortality, the level of health, life expectancy and longevity (. . .). Their supervision was effected through an entire series of interventions and *regulatory controls: a biopolitics of the population*. The disciplines of the body and the regulations of the population constituted the two poles around which the organization of power over life was deployed."
72. Ibid. p. 222; ibid. p. 249 (translation slightly modified).
73. On the constant correlation of the notions of "territory" and "sovereignty" in the lectures, see in particular the lecture of 25 January 1978, pp. 64-65: "(. . .) the traditional problem of sovereignty, and consequently of political power linked to the form of sovereignty, had always been either that of conquering new territories or, alternatively, holding on to territory conquered. (. . .) In other words, it involved something that we could call precisely the safety (*sûreté*) of the territory or the safety of the sovereign who rules over the territory."
74. Lecture of 11 January 1978, p. 11.
75. Ibid.
76. Foucault then distinguished three major domains of biopolitical intervention at the end of the eighteenth and the beginning of the nineteenth century: (1) the processes of birth rates and mortality, inducing a new approach to the problem of morbidity; (2) the phenomena of old age, accidents, and disabilities, etcetera, which alter the capacities of individuals; and (3) the relationships between people, as living beings, and their milieu, basically through the problem of the town (*"Il faut défendre la société"* lecture of 17 March 1976, pp. 216-218; *"Society Must Be Defended"* pp. 243-245). The major difference between this description and the examples chosen in 1978 lies, of course, in the absence of the problem of grain. In other words, it is the question of liberalism as a new governmental rationality that is unformulated in the 1976 lectures.
77. Lecture of 11 January 1978, p. 11.
78. Lecture of 25 January 1978 p. 79.
79. Lecture of 1 February 1978, p. 95.
80. Ibid. p. 108.
81. *Naissance de la biopolitique*, lecture of 31 January 1979, p. 80.
82. Both, as we recall later, were already the object of Foucault's attention in *Les Anormaux*; *Abnormal* (see below, pp. 386-387.
83. *L'Archéologie du savoir* (Paris: Gallimard, "Bibliothèque des sciences humaines," 1969) p. 28; English translation by A. Sheridan, *The Archeology of Knowledge* (London: Tavistock and New York: Pantheon, 1972) p. 17.
84. In the manuscript of the lectures, Foucault clarifies the political effects of this methodological choice. See the lecture of 8 February 1978, footnote * pp. 119-120.

85. Ibid. p. 120.
86. *Naissance de la biopolitique*, lecture of 7 March 1979, p. 192.
87. *"Il faut défendre la société"* lecture of 17 March 1976, p. 223; *"Society Must Be Defended"* p. 250.
88. See *Naissance de la biopolitique*, lecture of 10 January 1979, p. 4, concerning universals to which Foucault chose to oppose the point of view of a methodological nominalism, and also the lecture of 31 January 1979, pp. 78-79.
89. See, *Security, Territory, Population*, lecture of 5 April 1978, p. 358.
90. See lecture of 1 February 1978, p. 109.
91. Ibid. and *Naissance de la biopolitique*, lecture of 10 January 1979, p. 7.
92. Lecture of 1 February 1978, p. 109.
93. Ibid.
94. *Naissance de la biopolitique*, lecture of 31 January 1979, p. 79. This is how we should understand the initially somewhat obscure expression of a "governmentalization of the state" that Foucault uses at the end of the fourth of the *Security, Territory, Population* lectures (1 February 1978, p. 109).
95. *Naissance de la biopolitique*, lecture of 31 January 1979, p. 79.
96. Ibid. lecture of 7 March 1979, pp. 192-196. This criticism of the "phobia of the state" is echoed, in an opposite fashion, by the questions Foucault then raised (but did not express in the lectures) about the "desire for the state" in the classical period. See, "Méthodologie pour la connaissance du monde: comment se débarrasser du marxisme," interview with R. Yoshimoto (25 April 1978), *Dits et Écrits*, 3, pp. 617-618: "This year I am giving a course on the formation of the state and I analyze, let's say, the bases of the means of state realization over a period going from the sixteenth to the seventeenth century in the West, or rather the processes in the course of which what is called *raison d'État* is formed. But I have come up against an enigmatic part that can no longer be resolved by the simple analysis of economic, institutional, or cultural relations. There is in these processes a sort of gigantic and irrepressible thirst requiring recourse to the state. We could talk of desire for the state."
97. It is in fact in view of tackling "the problem of the state and population" that Foucault justifies the development of this analytical perspective. See the lecture of 8 February 1978, p. 115.
98. Foucault's main source in these lectures is E. Thuau's *Raison d'État et Pensée politique à l'époque de Richelieu* (Paris: Armand Colin, 1966; republished, Paris: Albin Michel, "Bibliothèque de l'évolution de l'humanité," 2000). He does not seem to have read, at this time, F. Meinecke's classic work, *Die Idee der Staatsräson in der neueren Geschichte* (Munich-Berlin: Oldenburg, 1924); French translation by M. Chevallier, *L'Idée de la raison d'État dans l'histoire des Temps modernes* (Geneva: Droz, 1973); English translation by Douglas Scott, *Machiavellism. The Doctrine of Raison d'État and its Place in Modern History* (Boulder and London: Westview Press, 1984) that he mentions in October 1979 in his "Omnes et singulatim" p. 150; p. 314. Generally speaking, Foucault does not take into account the many German and Italian works that have appeared on the subject since the 1920s. For a complete bibliography, before and after 1978, see G. Borrelli, *Ragion di stato e Leviatano* (Bologna: Il Mulino, 1993) pp. 312-360, and the regular instalments of the *Archivio della Ragion di Stato* (Naples) since 1993.
99. See "Course Summary" above, p. 365.
100. On this series of lectures, see ibid., pp. 365-366.
101. Ibid. p. 366. See the lecture of 5 April 1978, pp. 351-353.
102. See above, note 84.
103. In the manuscript on "government," which served as the introduction to the 1979 seminar, Foucault describes this transition as "the great shift from juridical veridiction to epistemic veridiction."
104. Manuscript for the first lecture. See *Naissance de la biopolitique*, lecture of 10 January 1979, footnote * p. 24.
105. See *Naissance de la biopolitique*, lecture of 10 January, p. 23 *sq*. The plan outlined here is made more specific (and, thereby, retrospectively clarified) later on. See the lecture of 31 January 1979, p. 80 *sq*.

106. See, ibid. beginning of the lecture of 7 March 1979, p. 191: "(. . .) I really intended, at the start, to speak to you about biopolitics and then, things being what they are, I have spoken to you at length, and maybe for too long, about neo-liberalism, and even neo-liberalism in its German form." See also the "Résumé du cours," ibid. p. 323: "In the end, the course this year was devoted entirely to what should have been only its introduction."
107. Ibid. lecture of 7 March 1979, pp. 194-196.
108. Obviously, this is not a matter of reducing the problematic of the "rights of the governed," inseparable from the phenomenon of dissidence (see "Va-t-on extrader Klaus Croissant?" p. 364), to that of the independence of the governed according to the utilitarian calculus, but of stressing a proximity, which is no doubt not foreign to Foucault's interest in liberalism at this time.
109. *Naissance de la biopolitique*, lecture of 24 January 1979, p. 70.
110. The French bibliography on the subject being extremely limited, apart from the thesis of F. Bilger, *La Pensée économique libérale de l'Allemagne contemporaine* (Paris: Librairie générale de Droit, 1964) that Foucault made use of, we note the recent appearance of the colloquium, P. Commun, ed., *L'Ordolibéralism allemand. Aux sources de l'économie sociale de marché* (Université de Cergy-Pontoise, CIRAC/CICC, 2003).
111. See *Naissance de la biopolitique*, "Résumé du cours," pp. 327-329.
112. Ibid. p. 327.
113. See the final lecture of *Security, Territory, Population* (5 April 1978) pp. 352-354 to which Foucault explicitly refers in *Naissance de la biopolitique*, p. 300, when he speaks of "an omnipresent government" which, while respecting "the specificity of the economy" must "manage society (. . .) manage the social."
114. 1981 manuscript on "Liberalism as art of government" in which Foucault, referring to the seminar of the previous year, recapitulates his analysis of liberalism. This analysis notably connects up with the analysis put forward by P. Rosanvallon, *Le Capitalisme utopique. Critique de l'idéologie économique* (Paris: Le Seuil, "Sociologie politique," 1979) pp. 68-69 (republished with the title *Le Libéralisme économique. Histoire de l'idée de marché* [Paris: Le Seuil, "Points Essais," 1989]) with which it sometimes seems to enter into dialogue (see Foucault's reference to this book in *Naissance de la biopolitique*, "Résumé du cours," p. 326).
115. Models that, in 1978, he places in the framework of his analysis of technologies of security (see the lecture of 11 January 1978, pp. 8-10).
116. *Les Anormaux*, lecture of 15 January 1975, p. 45; *Abnormal*, pp. 48-49.
117. Ibid.; ibid. (translation amended).
118. See *Le Pouvoir psychiatrique*; *Psychiatric Power*, lectures of 21 and 28 November and 5 December 1973.
119. *Les Anormaux*, lecture of 19 February 1975, pp. 158-180; *Abnormal*, pp. 167-199.
120. Ibid. p. 165; ibid. pp. 177-178.
121. See *Security, Territory, Population*, lecture of 15 February, pp. 150-151.
122. *Naissance de la biopolitique*, lecture of 10 January 1979, p. 4, where Foucault explains that by "art of government" he understands "the rationalization of governmental practice in the exercise of political sovereignty."
123. See above, notes 84 and 85.
124. *Naissance de la biopolitique*, lecture of 10 January 1979, pp. 3-4: "I have not studied, I do not want to study real governmental practice as it developed in determining the situation one is dealing with here and there, the problems raised, the tactics chosen, the instruments utilized, forged, or reshaped, etcetera. I wanted to study the art of government, that is to say the reflected way of governing well and also and at the same time the reflection on the best possible way of governing. That is to say I have tried to grasp the level of reflection in the practice of government and on the practice of government."
125. Manuscript of the introduction to the 1979 seminar.
126. Contrary to the interpretation put forward by some German commentators—see, for example, U. Bröckling, S. Krasmann, and T. Lemke, eds. *Gouvernementalität der Gegenwart. Studien zur Ökonomisierung des Sozialen* (Frankfurt/Main: Suhrkamp, 2000) p. 8—the word "governmentality" could not result from the contraction of "government" and "mentality," "governmentality" deriving from "governmental" like "musicality" from "musical" or "spatiality" from "spatial," and designating, according to the circumstances,

the strategic field of relations of power or the specific characteristics of the activity of government. The translation of the word by *"Regierungsmentalität,"* which appears in the text presenting the colloquium "Governmentality Studies" in Vienna on 23-24 March 2001, is therefore a mistranslation.

127. Lecture of 1 February 1978, p. 108.
128. Ibid. A process summed up in the sequence: pastoral power—military-diplomatic apparatus—police (pp. 108-109).
129. Lecture of 8 February 1978, p. 120. See above, p. 388.
130. *Naissance de la biopolitique,* lecture of 7 March 1979, p. 192.
131. Course summary, "Du gouvernement des vivants" (1980), *Dits et Écrits,* 4, p. 125; English translation by Robert Hurley, "On the Government of the Living" in *The Essential Works of Foucault 1954-1984. Volume 1: Ethics: Subjectivity and Truth,* ed., Paul Rabinow (New York: New Press, 1997) p. 81 (translation slightly modified).
132. On government as a practice consisting in the "conduct of conducts," see also "The Subject and Power" in *The Essential Works of Foucault 1954-1984. Volume 3: Power,* ed. James D. Faubion (New York: New Press, 2000) p. 341. This essay was originally published as an appendix to Paul Rabinow and Hubert Dreyfus, *Beyond Structuralism and Hermeneutics* (Chicago: University of Chicago Press, 1982); French translation by F. Durand-Bogaert, "Deux essais sur le suject et le pouvoir" in H. Dreyfus and P. Rabinow, *Michel Foucault. Un parcours philosophique* (Paris: Gallimard, "Bibliothèque des sciences humaines," 1984) p. 314.
133. *L'Herméneutique du sujet. Cours au Collège de France, année 1981-1982,* ed., F. Gros (Gallimard-Le Seuil, "Hautes Études," 2001) p. 241; English translation by Graham Burchell, *The Hermeneutics of the Subject. Lectures at the Collège de France 1981-1982,* English Series Editor Arnold I. Davidson (New York and Basingstoke: Palgrave Macmillan, 2005) p. 252. See also the Course Summary for 1981, "Subjectivité et vérité," *Dits et Écrits,* 4, p. 214; English translation by Robert Hurley, "Subjectivity and Truth" in *Essential Works of Foucault,* 1, p. 88: one of the objectives of the study of "governmentality," beyond the criticism of current conceptions of "power," was the analysis of the latter "as a domain of strategic relations between individuals or groups in which what is at stake is the conduct of the other or others (...)" (translation modified).
134. Manuscript on governmentality (untitled, bundle of eleven sheets numbered 22 to 24 and then not paginated) inserted between the lectures of 21 February and 7 March 1979 of *Naissance de la biopolitique.*
135. Ibid.
136. See above, note 134.
137. See "Deux essais sur le sujet et le pouvoir" p. 314; "The Subject and Power" p. 341: "The relationship proper to power would therefore be sought not on the side of violence or of struggle, nor on that of voluntary contracts (all of which can, at best, only be the instruments of power) but, rather, in the area of that singular mode of action, neither warlike nor juridical, which is government."
138. *Naissance de la biopolitique,* lecture of 24 January 1979, p. 70.
139. See again, "Deux essais sur le sujet et le pouvoir" p. 300; "The Subject and Power" p. 329 in which Foucault suggests a new way of investigating power relations that would take "the forms of resistance against different forms of power as a starting point."
140. Manuscript on governmentality cited above, note 134. Foucault's writing being difficult to decipher in several places, we have not quoted the passages where our transcription contained too many gaps or uncertainties.
141. This lecture appeared in Italian in *Aut-Aut,* no. 167-168, 1978, then in French in *Actes,* 54, Summer 1986. This is the text, perceptibly different from the one we publish here, that is reprinted in *Dits et Écrits,* 3, pp. 635-657. An English translation of the Italian version of this lecture appeared in the English journal *Ideology and Consciousness,* 6, 1979.
142. Extract from *Naissance de la biopolitique,* lecture of 31 January 1979, with the title "La phobie d'État," *Libération,* 967, 20 June-1 July, 1984 (translated into German in U. Bröckling, S. Krasmann, and T. Lemke, eds., *Gouvernementalität der Gegenwart,* pp. 68-71), and from the lecture of 24 January 1979, with the title "Michel Foucault et la question du libéralisme," *Le Monde,* supplement to the issue of 7 May 1999. We should recall, furthermore, that the first lectures of both courses were published in the form of cassette recordings with the title *De la gouvernementalité* (Paris: Le Seuil, 1989).

143. *"Omnes et singulatim"* pp. 134-161 (French); pp. 298-325 (English).

144. Apart from the work already cited (above, notes 126 and 142), see the many articles by T. Lemke, which follow on from his remarkable work, *Eine Kritik der politischen Vernunft. Foucaults Analyse der modernen Gouvernementalität* (Berlin and Hamburg: Argument Verlag, 1997).

145. Graham Burchell, Colin Gordon, and Peter Miller, *The Foucault Effect. Studies in Governmentality* (London: Harvester Wheatsheaf, 1991).

146. See the articles by J. Donzelot, "The mobilisation of society" (pp. 169-179), F. Ewald, "Insurance and risk" (pp. 197-210), D. Defert, " 'Popular life' and insurance technology" (pp. 211-233), and R. Castel, "From dangerousness to risk" (pp. 281-298). Daniel Defert's text is a general introduction to the work of the research group "on the formation of the insurance apparatus, considered as a schema of social rationality and social management" (p. 211) established in 1977 with Jacques Donzelot, François Ewald and other researchers that gave rise to a number of papers: "Socialisation du risque et pouvoir dans l'entreprise" (Typescript, Ministry of Work, 1977) and "Assurance-Prévoyance-Sécurité: Formation historique des techniques de gestion dans les sociétés industrielles" (Typescript, Ministry of Work, 1979). For a discussion of this set of works, see P. O'Malley, "Risk and responsibility" in A. Barry, T. Osborne, and N. Rose, *Foucault and Political Reason: Liberalism, Neo-Liberalism and rationalities of government* (London: University College, 1996) pp. 189-207.

147. Mitchell Dean, *Governmentality: Power and rule in modern society* (London: Thousand Oaks, and New Delhi: Sage Publications, 1999).

148. *Politische Vierteljahresschrift*, 41 (1), 2000, pp. 31-47.

149. See especially, B. Townley, *Reframing Human Resource Management: Power, ethics and the subject at work* (London: Thousand Oaks, and New Delhi: Sage Publications, 1994); E. Barratt, "Foucault, HRM and the ethos of the critical management scholar," *Journal of Management Studies*, 40 (5), July 2003, pp. 1069-1087.

150. See A. McKinlay and K. Starkey, eds., *Foucault: Management and organization theory, from Panopticon to technologies of the Self* (London: Thousand Oaks, and New Delhi: Sage Publications, 1998), and the colloquium "Organiser après Foucault," held at the École des Mines, Paris, on 12-13 December 2002.

NAME INDEX

Abeille, L.-P., 35-36, 37, 38, 39, 40, 41, 43-44, 50n.1, 52nn.17, 19, 20, 23
Acarie, B. (née Avrillot), 197, 219n.18
Achenwall, G., 283n.61
Adam, C., 249n.4
Albert le Grand, 225n.66
Albertini R. von, 281n.25
Alembert, J. Le Rond d', 27n.37, 81n.8
Alexander I, Tsar, 330n.9
Amalrik, A., 221n.27
Amaury de Bène, 211, 220n.20
Ambrose, Saint, of Milan, 154, 160n.62, 166, 180, 186n.3, 189n.38
Ammirato, S., 280n.20
Ancelet-Hustache, J., 223n.53, 225n.67
Anne of Austria, 281n.30
Aquinas. see Thomas, Saint
Archytas de Tarente, 137, 157n.4
Argenson, M.-R. de Voyer d', 324, 331n.37
Argenson, R.-L. de Voyer d', 51n.15, 53n.26
Ariès, P., 250n.6
Aristotle, 84n.34, 113n.25, 192, 217n.2
Armelle, Nicolas, 197, 219n.16
Arnauld, A., 86n.48
Aron, R., 131n.9, 251n.22
Arumaeus, D., 251n.24
Augustine, Saint, of Hippo, 189n.36
Avenel, D.L.M., 307n.11

Baader, A., 281n.28, 372, 393n.26
Bacon, F., 81-82n.13, 267-72, 277, 282nn.38-41, 45, 288
Bacquet, J., 339, 360n.17
Bailly, P., 224n.55
Barucq, A., 133n.26
Basil, Saint, 223n.45
Bataillon, M., 219n.15
Battista, A.M., 281n.24
Bayard, canon, 159n.51, 188n.27
Ben Bella, A., 395n.47
Benedict, Saint, 153, 160n.54, 166, 169, 170,

172, 178, 186nn.8, 11, 187nn.14, 15, 18, 188n.23, 189n.35, 223n.45
Bentham, J., 25n.11, 83n.26, 117, 131n.8
Bernoulli, D., 81n.8
Bertani, M., 24n.1, 392n.1
Bertelli, S., 111nn.3, 4
Bérulle, P. de, 219n.18
Besançon, A., 155, 161n.63
Bilger, F., 399n.110
Bizet, J.-A., 223n.52
Blanchet, P., 394n.39, 395nn.42, 47
Bloch, E., 249n.1
Bodin, J., 283n.63
Boisguilbert, P. Le Pesant de, 50n.9
Boislisle, M. de, 331n.37
Bondois, P.-M., 53n.26, 359nn.1, 2
Bonneau, A., 250n.6
Borrelli, G., 398n.98
Bossuet, J.-B., 246-47, 253n.44, 264
Botero, G., 237-38, 239, 250nn.19, 20, 280n.20, 288-89
Botkine, L., 157n.3
Boulier, J., 220n.21
Boullée, E.-L., 17-18, 26n.33
Bremond, H., 219nn.16, 17, 18
Brezhnev, L., 161n.64, 372
Brian, E., 283n.64
Brière, C., 394n.39, 395nn.42, 47
Brocard, L., 82n.20
Brossat, A., 395n.41
Brown, P., 222-23n.44, 283n.60
Buchon, J.A.C., 253n.41
Buffon, G.L. Leclerc de, 27n.37, 85n.34
Bukovsky, V., 221n.27
Burlamaqui, J.-J., 303, 310n.31
Busch, J., 222n.43
Butler, K.T., 253n.42

Calvin, J., 160n.56
Campenhausen, H.F. von, 161n.62
Canguilhem, G., 27nn.36, 37, 38, 80n.1

Cantillon, R., 51n.15, 83n.20
Capelle, G.-C., 220n.20
Cassian, J., 166, 176, 186nn.5, 6, 188n.31, 189n.33, 223nn.45, 50
Castel, R., 117, 131n.3, 401n.146
Catherine II, Empress, 329n.2, 340, 360nn.18, 19
Césaire de Heisterbach, 220n.20
Chaignet, A.E., 157n.4
Chappuys, G., 250n.19
Chariati [Sharicati], A., 375, 395n.47, 396n.59
Charlemagne, Emperor, 264, 289, 304
Charles-Daubert, F., 252n.40
Charron, P., 263, 281nn.24, 26
Chartier, R., 250n.6
Chaunu, P., 219n.18, 222n.43
Chemnitz, B.P. von [Hippolithus a Lapidel], 240, 241, 251n.24, 257, 258, 261, 264, 277, 279n.11, 280n.22, 281n.27, 288
Chenonceaux, C. Dupin de, 50n.9, 310n.31
Child, J., 131n.5
Chiquot, A., 225n.68
Chollet, A., 220n.20
Choublier-Myskowski, N., 112n.19
Chrysostom, Saint John, 154, 160n.61, 166, 168, 186n.9
Cicero, 113n.25, 133n.35
Clapmar, A. [Clapmarius], 283n.63
Clark, J.M., 225n.67
Clausewitz, K. von, 90, 305-6, 309n.23
Clément VI, Pierre Roger, Pope, 224n.55
Clément, C., 242, 252n.31
Cliquot-Blervache, S., 51n.15
Cohn, N., 218nn.10, 11, 13, 219n.14, 220nn.20, 21, 25, 222nn.39, 41, 42, 224nn.55, 64, 225n.70, 226n.72
Commun, P., 399n.110
Compère, M.-M., 250n.6
Condé, Prince L.J. de Bourbon, 281n.31
Condillac, E. Bonnot de, 73-74, 83n.26
Conring, H., 283n.61
Contzen, A., 244, 252n.38
Copernicus, N., 234
Corbin, H., 225n.68, 396n.59
Corneille, P., 265, 282n.36
Cristiani, L., 159n.44, 218n.9
Croissant, K., 372-73, 393nn.18, 26
Crucé, E. [Emery La Croix], 303, 309nn.26, 30
Cuvier, G., 77-78, 86nn.45, 46
Cyprian, Saint, 152-53, 159nn.51, 52, 166, 170, 174, 186n.2, 187nn.16, 19, 188n.27

Dabenton, J. see Jeanne Dabenton
Daguillon, J., 225n.66
Daire, E., 83n.22

Damilaville, E.N., 83n.22
Daniel, Y., 221n.27
Darwin, C., 78
Daumas, F., 133n.26
De Mattei, R., 252n.29
De May, L., 252n.40
De Vooght, P., 220n.21
Debard, M., 372, 393n.19
Debongnie, P., 222n.43
Decius, Roman Emperor, 187n.16
Defert, D., 24n.2, 161n.64, 190n.43, 223n.51, 251n.22, 392nn.4, 10, 16, 394n.30, 395n.41, 396n.65, 401n.146
Delamare [de La Mare], N., 45, 50nn.3, 4, 53n.26, 327, 329n.1, 332nn.41, 43, 334, 359nn.1, 3, 4
Delaruelle, E., 222n.43
Delatte, A., 138, 140, 157nn.5, 6, 7, 8
Delattre, L., 27n.35
Deleuze, G., 373, 393n.26
Delumeau, J., 224n.56
Demosthenes, 138
Denifle, H., 225n.68
Denis, E., 222n.39
Depitre, E., 50nn.7, 8, 51n.16, 52n.17, 331n.37
Des Essarts, N., 359n.2
Descartes, R., 230, 249nn.3, 4, 5, 286
Destutt de Tracy, A.L.C., 83n.26
Dexter, G., 112n.15
Diderot, D., 27n.37, 83n.22
Diès, A., 158n.10
Dolhagaray, B., 160nn.55, 56, 59
Domat, J., 336, 360n.11
Donnadieu, L., 307n.12, 308n.18, 309nn.20, 21, 310nn.31, 32
Doretheus of Gaza, 189n.37
Dostoevsky, F., 252n.37
Draguet, R., 188n.30
du Chastelet, P. Hay, 246, 253n.43, 258, 280nn.12, 19
Du Chesne, 359n.2
Duby, G., 159n.40, 301, 309n.22
Dupin. see Chenonceaux
Dupont de Nemours [Du Pont de Nemours], P.S., 51n.14, 52nn.17, 19, 53n.28, 113n.23
Durkheim, E., 84n.33
Duroselle, J.-B., 221n.31
Dürr, L., 133n.24
Duvillard, E.E., 61, 81n.10

Ebeling, H., 157n.1
Eckhart, Master J, 223n.52
Ehrard, J., 53n.27
Elias, N., 250n.6
Elkan, A., 111n.6
Elyot, T., 90, 112n.13

Engels, F., 85n.41
Engemann, J., 133n.36, 157n.1
Erasmus, D., 250n.6
Eribon, D., 281n.28, 393n.26, 395nn.41, 49
Esquirol, J.-E. D., 131n.4
Estienne, H., 132n.18
Eudes, Saint Jean, 219n.17
Evagrius of Pontius, 188n.30, 189n.37
Ewald, F., 24n.2, 392n.4, 401n.146

Fanon, F., 395n.47
Felsing, F., 283n.61
Fénelon, F. de Salignac de La Mothe, 318, 330n.12
Fichte, J.G., 15, 26n.26
Finkielkraut, A., 394n.38
Firpo, L., 111n.10, 250n.19
Fleischauer, C., 113n.26
Fleury, C., 323-24, 331nn.31, 32, 34, 38
Fliche, A., 221n.30, 222n.43
Fontana, A., 24n.1, 392n.1
Forbonnais, F. Véron-Duverger de, 52n.17
Formey, S., 251n.24
Fouquet, N., 265, 281n.32
Frachetta, G., 252n.29
Francis I, (1494-1547) King of France, 247
Francis I, (1768-1835) Austrian Emperor, 330n.9
Frederick II, the Great (1712-1786), 90, 97, 112n.12, 113n.26
Frederick William I, (1668-1740) King of Prussia, 25-26n.25
Frederick William II (1744-1797), 330n.9
Fréminville, E. de La Poix de, 336-37, 359n.1, 360n.12
Friend of God, Oberland, 209, 211, 225nn.67, 68, 396n.59
Froissart, J., 121, 132nn.12, 15, 16

Galiani, abbot F., 52nn.16, 19
Galileo, G., 234, 241, 286
Gaston d'Orléans, 281n.30
Genet, J., 264, 281n.28, 393n.26
Gentillet, I., 90, 111-12n.11, 244
Gilson, E., 225n.66
Ginzberg, L., 133n.36
Ginzburg, A., 221n.27
Glucksmann, A., 394n.38
Godefroy, F., 132n.11-20
Gogol, N., 155, 161n.64
Gonnard, R., 27n.39
Goudart, A., 83n.20
Gournay, V. de, 35, 51nn.10, 15
Gradowicz-Pancer, N., 222n.44, 223n.45
Graunt, J., 74, 84nn.28-33
Gregory Nazianzen, 150-51, 159n.46, 188n.28, 192, 193, 217n.1

Gregory the Great, Saint, 153, 159nn.47, 53, 168-69, 172, 174, 180, 181, 186nn.10, 13, 187n.22, 188nn.24-26, 28, 189n.39-42
Grelot, P., 133n.28
Grimm, F.-M. de, 361n.28
Gros, F., 186n.5, 218n.6, 400n.133
Grosser, A., 394n.28
Gruppe, O.F., 137, 157n.6
Guarnieri, R., 219n.14
Guattari, F., 393n.26
Guéroult, M., 308n.14
Guerry, A.-M., 24n.7
Guicciardini, F., 297, 308n.16
Guilhem, C., 219n.15
Guillaume le Breton, 220n.20
Guillauté, M., 340, 361n.21
Guy, J.-Cl., 189n.32
Guyénot, E., 84n.34

Habermas, J., 85n.35
Hadewijch d'Anvers, 218n.12, 219n.14, 222n.42
Hadot, I., 190n.44
Hadot, P., 111n.1, 189n.37, 249n.2
Hajek, J., 221n.27
Hamp, V., 133n.28
Harnack, A. von, 217n.6
Hautersierck, F. Richard de, 81n.9
Havel, V., 221n.27
Heisterbach, C. de. *see* Césaire de Heisterbach
Hennig, J.-L., 372, 393n.19
Henry III, King of France, 268, 282n.44, 283n.55
Henry IV, 298, 308n.18
Herbert, Cl.-J, 50nn.7, 9
Hobbes, T., 73, 103, 245
Hohenthal, P.C.W. von, 313, 324, 327, 329nn.4, 6, 331n.33, 332n.45
Hoke, R., 251n.24
d'Holbach, P.H., 85n.34
Hull, C.H., 84n.28, 283n.60
Hume, D., 81n.30
Humpert, M., 330n.11
Huss, J., 197, 204, 208-9, 220n.21, 221n.32, 224nn.56, 57
Hyma, A., 222n.43

Innocent III [Lothaire Conti] Pope, 217n.4, 220n.20
Innocenti, P., 111nn.3, 4
Isabel de la Cruz, 197, 219n.15
Isocrates, 138, 157n.9

J.-B. P. (Frère), 218n.12, 219n.14, 222n.42
Jacob, F., 85n.34, 86n.45, 196

Jarry, E., 221n.31
Jaubert, A.P., 71, 83n.21
Jeanne Dabenton, 197, 211, 219n.13, 225n.70
Jeanne de la Nativité, 219n.16
Jenner, E., 80n.4
Jeremias, J., 133nn.28, 30, 31
Jerome, Saint, 166, 170, 186n.7, 187n.20, 189n.36
Joachim of Fiore, 214, 225n.72
Johannet, J., 161n.64
John the Visionary, Abba John, 188n.32
John, V., 114n.31, 283n.61
Jones, H., 218n.6
Jost, W., 133nn.28, 30, 31, 36, 157n.1
Judge, E.A., 223n.44
Julia, D., 250n.6
Jundt, A., 224n.63, 225nn.67, 68, 69
Jurin, J., 81n.8
Justi, J.H.G. von, 314, 327, 329n.7, 329-30n.8
Justin, Marcus Junianus Justinus, 133n.36

Kant, I., 307n.1
Kaplan, S.L., 50n.4, 51nn.12, 13, 52n.19, 53n.26, 361n.25
Kellermann, 90
Kelsen, H., 56, 80n.1
Kempf, Th.H., 133n.28
Kepel, G., 395nn.42, 47
Kepler, J., 234, 286
Khomeini, R., 376, 395n.42
King, J., 329n.3
Kraeger, P., 84n.28

La Coste, P., 80n.6
La Mothe Le Vayer, F., 93-94, 112nn.19, 20
La Perrière, G. de, 90-91, 92-93, 96, 97, 99, 100, 102, 112nn.15, 18, 113nn.24, 28-30
La Reynie, G.N. de, 53n.26, 331n.37
Labande, E.-R., 222n.43
Lagrange, J., 24n.2, 83n.26, 363, 392n.4, 397n.70
Lamarck, J.-B. Monet de, 20, 27n.36, 78, 86nn.44, 45
Lancelot, C., 86n.48
Landry, A., 82n.18, 85n.40
Larrère, C., 85n.40
Launay, M. de, 85n.35
Lazersfeld, P., 84n.28
Lazzeri, C., 281n.24, 307n.11
Le Bras, H., 81n.8, 82n.13, 84n.28, 221n.31
Le Bret, P. Cardin, 263, 281n.25
Le Brun, L.S.D., 81n.9
Le Droumaguet, R., 80n.4
Le Goff, J., 221n.36
Le Maître, A., 13-14, 15, 16, 17, 25n.12

Le Mée, R., 27n.39
Le Trosne [Letrosne] G.-F., 51nn.12, 14, 53n.28
Leclercq, Dom J., 220n.20
Ledoux, C.-N., 18, 27n.34
Leff, G., 224n.64
Leibniz, G.W., 296, 308n.14
Lelièvre, P., 17, 26nn.31, 32, 27n.35
Lemercier, J., 26n.29
Leo, H., 90, 111n.4
Léonard, E.G., 220n.25, 249n.1
Lerner, R.E., 224n.64
Letaconnoux, J., 51n.9
Libera, A. de, 225n.66
Linneaus, C. von, 84n.34
Lisieux, I., 250n.6
Livet, G., 308n.17, 309nn.24, 25
Longhurst, J.E., 219n.15
Louis XIII, 15, 261, 281n.30
Louis XIV, 15, 246, 247, 265, 305, 337
Louis, P., 113n.25, 132n.22, 157n.1
Loyseau, C., 360n.16
Lucas, L.-P., 309n.26
Lupus, Marius, 153, 160n.59
Luther, M., 196, 221n.32

Macek, J., 222n.39
Macey, D., 24n.1, 392n.1, 393nn.17, 26, 395n.41
Machault d'Arnouville, J.-B., 51n.10
Machiavelli, N., 31, 50n.2, 65, 89, 90, 91, 92, 93, 96, 98, 100, 111nn.4, 5, 10, 112n.12, 113n.26, 242-43, 244, 245, 252nn.26, 39, 253n.42, 259, 271, 272, 280n.17, 380
Machon, L., 245, 252-53n.41, 253n.42
Maier, H., 251n.24, 330n.11
Malagola, H., 395n.41
Malthus, T.R., 77
Mani, 217n.3
Marc, C.C.H., 131n.4
Marchetti, V., 25n.8, 396n.63
Marguerite Porete, 197, 219n.14
Marie de Médicis, 281n.30
Marie des Vallées, 197, 219n.17
Marin, L., 252n.40
Markus, R.A., 223n.45
Martin V [Ottone Colonna] Pope, 224n.56
Marx, K., 77, 85n.41, 243
Massignon, L., 395n.47
Mauriac, C., 281n.28, 393n.26
Mazarin, J., 241, 252n.40
McFarlane, K.B., 159n.44

Mehdi Bazargan, 396n.51
Meine, H., 281n.28
Meinecke, F., 111n.5, 307n.11, 398n.98
Meinhof, U., 281n.28
Merswin, R. *see* Rulman Merswin
Metternich[-Winneburg] C.W.L. de, 330n.9
Meysonnier, S., 51n.15
Michel, A., 53n.27, 84n.34, 219n.14, 221nn.34, 36, 224nn.60, 61, 251-52n.25, 283n.64, 398n.98
Milcent, P., 219n.17
Miller, G., 80n.2
Minc, A., 396n.49
Mirabeau, V. Riquettti de, 71, 82n.20
Moheau, J.-B., 22, 23, 27nn.39-42
Montaigne, M. de, 193, 217n.3
Montaigu, Lady [Eléonore Beaulieu], 80n.6
Montesquieu, C. de Secondat de la Brède de, 81n.13, 360n.18
Montrchétien [Montchrétien] A. de, 318, 322, 328, 330n.14, 332n.47, 334
Moreau de Séchelles, J., 51n.10
Morellet, A., 51n.15
Moser, J.J., 329n.6
Moulin, A.-M., 25n.10, 80nn.2, 4, 81nn.4-6, 367
Mousnier, R., 329n.3
Müller, H., 393n.28
Münzer, T., 249n.1
Murphy, A., 51n.15

Naudé, G., 245, 252n.40, 261, 263, 266, 280nn.20, 21, 24, 282n.37
Naves, R., 113n.26
Naz, R., 160n.55
Necker, J., 52n.17
Nekrasov, V., 221n.27
Newton, I., 20, 26n.33, 27n.37
Nicolas de Bâle, 225n.68
Nietzsche, F., 114n.39
Novatian [Novatianus], 187n.16

Ourliac, P., 222n.43

Pachomius, Saint, 222n.44
Pajot, H., 309n.26
Palazzo, A., 255-56, 257, 258, 259, 274, 279n.2, 280n.15, 287-89, 307n.3
Palladius, 188n.30
Parker, G., 26n.30, 307n.9
Paruta, P., 90, 112n.14
Pasquino, P., 114n.33, 367
Pasteur, L., 58
Patermutus, 189n.33
Patočka, J., 221n.27
Patullo, H., 83n.22

Paul, Saint, 181, 189n.42
Paulin of Milan [Paulinus Tyrius], 160n.62
Peil, D., 133nn.28, 36
Perrot, J.-Cl., 13, 25n.11, 27n.39, 82n.18, 83n.22
Perrot, M., 25n.11
Petty, W., 84n.28, 283n.60
Pfister, C., 308n.18
Philip V, King of Spain, 307n.12
Philo of Alexandria, 133n.36
Philolaüs, 157n.4
Pianzola, M., 249n.1
Pichery, E., 186n.5, 223n.45
Pignarre, R., 132n.22
Pius V, Pope, 241, 252n.29
Plato, 113n.25, 123, 129, 138, 139, 141, 142, 143, 144, 145, 146, 147, 155, 158nn.11, 12, 13, 14, 164, 167, 168, 289
Plioutch, L., 221n.27, 372
Plumart de Dangeul, L.J., 50n.9
Politi, L. [Ambrogio Catarino], 90, 111n.10
Post, G.E., 133n.28
Prat, F., 221n.33
Procacci, G., 111n.4, 253n.41
Pseudo-Archytas, 137
Puech, H.-C., 218n.6
Pufendorf, S. von, 98, 113n.27, 133n.25
Pütter, J.S., 329n.6
Pythagoras, 137-38, 140, 147, 157n.4

Quérard, J.-M., 52n.17
Quesnay, F., 50n.5, 52n.19, 71, 72, 77, 82n.19, 83n.22, 85n.40, 95, 113n.23, 345, 361nn.24, 32

Rabbow, P., 190n.44
Racine, J., 265, 282nn.33,36
Rahnema, A., 395n.47
Ranke, L. von, 90, 111n.5, 305
Rapp, F., 225n.67
Rath, W., 225n.68
Rathé, C.E., 112n.11
Ray, J., 84n.34, 234
Razzell, P.E., 80n.2
Regnault, L., 223n.47
Rehberg, A.W., 90, 111n.3
Repgen, K., 308n.17
Reynié, D., 281n.24
Ricardo, D., 85-86n.42
Richelieu, A.J. du Plessis de, 26nn.29, 32, 114n.32, 241, 242, 245, 252n.40, 253n.41, 264, 272, 281nn.25, 30, 283n.59, 289, 307n.11
Ridolfi, A., 90, 111n.7
Robinet, A., 308n.14
Rohan, H. de, 307n.11

Rousseau, J.-J., 17, 53n.24, 73, 85n.34, 95, 106, 107, 112n.21, 113n.22, 114n.36
Rousseau, M., 26n.32
Rufin [Tyrannius Rufinus], 159n.47
Rulman Merswin, 211, 225nn.67, 68, 396n.59

Saint-Martin, R. de, 242, 252n.33
Sakharov, A., 221n.27
Sallé, J.-A., 359n.2
Salleron, L., 83n.22
Salomoni, A., 25n.8, 396n.63
Schelle, G., 51n.15
Schiera, P., 114n.33, 330n.11
Schmidt, C., 225n.68
Schmitt, R., 136, 157nn.2, 3
Schnur, R., 251n.24
Sciacca, E., 112n.15
Seibert, I., 133nn.25, 27
Seneca, 189n.36
Senellart, M., 24n.6, 25n.25, 369, 392n.6
Shakespeare, W., 265, 282n.36
Sharicat Madari, 395n.42
Shayegan, D., 395n.47
Sigismond of Luxembourg, King of Hungary, 221n.39
Simon, M., 217n.6
Sinyavsky [Siniavski], A. [Abram Tertz], 155, 161n.64
Sirmond, J., 261, 280n.19
Small, A.W., 26n.25, 330n.11
Socrates, 140, 158n.39
Solzhenitsyn, A.I., 201, 221nn.27, 29
Sophocles, 113n.25, 132n.22
Spengler, J.J., 82n.18, 19
Spinka, M., 220n.21
Starobinski, J., 26n.33
Stegmann von Pritzwald, K., 157n.1
Stobaeus, 137, 157n.4
Stolleis, M., 25n.25, 251n.24, 307n.9, 330n.10, 369
Strauch, P., 225n.67
Struensee, J.F., 26n.26
Sully, le bienheureux Heinrich Seuse [Henri], 289, 298, 299, 307n.8, 308nn.18, 19

Tacitus, 240, 252n.26, 283n.63
Talleyrand [C.M. de Talleyrand-Périgord], 309n.21
Tannery, P., 249n.4
Testard, M., 186n.3
Thiers, L.-A., 85n.36, 305
Thomas à Kempis, 222n.43
Thomas Münzer. see Münzer, T.
Thomas, Saint, Aquinas, 113n.25, 250n.7, 258, 328
Thrasymachus, 139, 140

Thuau, E., 242, 251n.25, 252n.26, 253n.41, 280n.19, 281nn.24, 25, 29, 282n.37, 283n.59, 308n.18, 309n.20, 398n.98
Thuillier, G., 81n.10, 331n.31
Trudaine de Montigny, J.C.P., 51n.14
Turgot de l'Eaulne, A.R.G., 51nn.14, 15, 361n.25
Turquet de Mayerne, L., 313, 319, 321, 322, 326, 329nn.3, 5, 330n.17, 332n.42

Ulrich Engelbert de Strasbourg, 211, 224n.66

Valdès, P. see Waldo, P.
Valentinian I [Flavius Valentianus], Roman emperor, 154, 161n.62
Vallières, A. de, 279n.2
Vandenbroucke, Dom F., 220n.20, 222n.41, 223n.52, 225n.68, 226n.72
Vattel, E. de, 310n.31
Vauban, S. Le Prestre de, 253n.43
Vernet, F., 220n.20
Véron de Forbonnais, F. see Forbonnais, F. Véron-Duverger de
Veyne, P., 131n.9, 148, 158-59n.40, 239, 251nn.21, 22, 363, 392n.4
Vigny, Vigné de, 18, 19, 27n.35
Villari, P., 111n.5
Vilquin, E., 27n.39, 82n.15, 84n.28
Virgil, 22, 27n.41
Voisé, W., 308n.14
Voltaire [Arouet, F.M.], 85n.34, 112n.12
Voöbus, A., 223n.44

Wahl, F., 392n.4
Wakefield, G.S., 159n.45
Waldo, P., 218n.9
Wallhausen, J.J. von, 26n.30
Walter, L.G., 249n.1
Wanner, R.E., 331n.31
Ward, B., 223n.47
Weber, M., 250n.6
Wenceslas IV, King of Bohemia, 218n.11, 220n.21
Weulersse, G., 51nn.11, 14, 52nn.17, 18, 53n.28, 82nn.18, 19, 361nn.24, 28
Wolff, C. von, 299, 309n.21
Workman, H.B., 159n.44
Wyclif [Wycliffe], J., 149, 153, 159n.44, 160n.56, 197, 204, 208, 209, 219n.19, 220n.21, 221nn.32, 37, 224n.56

Xenophon, 158n.10

Zeiller, J., 221n.30
Zeller, G., 309n.20
Zinoviev, A., 221n.27

Subject Index

Abundance, 37, 144
of citizens, *copia civium*, 324, *see also* Hohenthal
excess of and collapse of prices, 32, 33, 34
of harvests, products, 38, 68, 342
of men, 323
monetary, 103
sources of, according to Quesnay, 85n.40
of wages, 82n.19, *see also* Weulersse
Abundance/scarcity (fluctuations), 36-37, 59, 68
A-governmentality of nature, 239
Anabaptism, anabaptists, 200, 209, 220n.25, 249n.1
Anti-Machiavelli (literature), 90-91, 92, *see also* Elyot, Frederick II, Gentillet, La Perrière, Paruta
Anti-pastoral, 150, 204, 208, 215
Apatheia, 178, 179, 189nn.36, 37, 206
Apparatus (*dispositif*), 62, 107-108, 247, *see also* Security
of discipline, 218n.7, 371, 378, 386
of European equilibrium, 316
military-diplomatic, 296, 303, 305, 354
permanent military, 305
political, of police, 296, 306, 382
of power, 6, 148, 386
of relations between states, permanent, 303
of security, 6, 11, 21, 30, 34, 37, 45, 46-47, 48-49, 59-60, 64, 379, 388
and disciplinary mechanisms, 44, 46, 371
of sovereignty, 218n.7
Art of government, 79, 92-93, 94-95, 100-105, 107, 237, 242-44, 252n.39, 253n.43, 259-60, 278, 286, 287, 289, 311-12, 319, 347-48, 351, 379, 384, 386-87, 399nn.122, 124, *see also* Governmentality, *Raison d'État*

Artificiality, 15, 17, 19, 47, 52n.19, 59, *see also* *Économistes*, Society
of politics, 263, 280-81n.24, 349
versus naturalness, 22, 61, 73, 366
Ascesis, 205, 223n.46
Asceticism, 149, 195, 204-208, 211, 224n.63, 249n.3, 266-67
excess peculiar to, 205, 208
Auxiliary arts of politics, 145-46

"Balance", 19, 184, 260, 270, 297, 298-300, 302, 310n.32, *see also* Equilibrium, European
Better than just living, more than just living, 326-27, 334, 338, 346, *see also* Police, Well-being; Delamare, Montchétien
Biopolitics, 24n.1, 120, 367, 370, 377, 378, 381, 382-84, 397n.76, 399n.106, *see also* Human species; Lamarck
Bio-power, 1, 24n.1, 369, 370, 377, 382, *see also* Biopolitics, Human species, Milieu, Naturalness

Cameralism, Cameralists, 15, 25-26n.25, 68, 69-70, 101, 114n.33, 329n.7, 365, *see also* Mercantilism; Justi, Stolleis
Cameralistics (*Cameralwissenschaft*), 25-26n.25, 330n.11
Capital city. *see* Town; Le Maitre
Capitalizing (a territory, state, province), 15, 17, 20
Cheapness, 36, 37, 342, *see also* Abundance
Christianity, 153, 164-65, 167, 169, 170, 173, 174, 178, 183, 186n.5, 194, 205, 207, 214-15, 217n.6, 297, 364, *see also* *Apatheia*, Church, Pastorate
beginning of, 150, 359n.3, 387
Eastern, 154, 155, 166, 196, 206
medieval, 202, 260, 308n.15
and Scripture, 159n.44, 176, 213, 218n.11, 225n.72, 246, 247

Christianity - *continued*
  Western, 129-30, 147-48, 149, 154,
    190n.43, 191, 193, 196, 231
Church, 155, 166, 169, 204, 208, 291, 300,
    386
  Catholic, 88, 120, 149-50, 153, 202, 215,
    229, 241-42, 318
  Christian, 129-30, 148, 149, 152, 364
  doctrine of, 88, 180, 209
  feudalization of, 203
  as institutionalization of a religion, 148
  Protestant, 88, 149, 153, 215, 229, 241
  universalist functions, 316
  Western, 154, 205
Circulation, 16-17, 26n.32, 49, 51n.10, 64,
    70, 76, 267-68
  beyond borders, 325-26
  commercial and political freedom of, 14-15,
    33-34
  field, space of, 13, 325, 326
  fine materiality of exchange and, 339
  good and bad (metaphor of blood), 18, 65
  of grains and freedom of, 33-34, 40, 49,
    50nn.7, 8, 9, 51nn.10, 13, *see also*
    Herbert
  inter-state monetary, 315
  monetary, 270, 291, 338, 365, *see also*
    Market town
  urban, 13, 20, 21, 29, 336, 338, *see also*
    Vigny
  of wealth, 70, 76, *see also* Gournay
Circulation of men, 325, 335
Circulation of merits and faults, 179
  technique of, 184, *see also* Pastorate
Circulation of the truths of teaching, 212
City (city-state), 129, 145, 167-68, 173, 242,
    252n.31, 313, 319, 329n.5
  forms of organization of, 147
  functions of, 18-19, 139, 140, 143
Code of Canon law, 160n.59
Code of police, 340, 359n.2, *see also*
    Catherine II, Du Chesne
Cohabitation of men, 336, 338, 349
Commerce, 15, 25n.20, 51n.15, 70, 283n.60,
    316, 323, 330n.8, 334, 337-38, 339, 365
  circular process of exchange, 122, 335
  external flow of, 76, 270
  extra-urban, 338-39, *see also* Capital city;
    Le Maître
  factor of European competition, 337
  freedom of, 33, 309n.26, *see also*
    Circulation, *Économistes*, Liberalism
  of grains, 33-35, 50n.1, 50-51n.9, 51nn.12,
    14, 52n.17, *see also* Abeille, Gournay
  intra-urban, 18-19
  main instrument of state's strength, 339
  technique for import of currency, 337

Common good, 232, 233, 360n.16
  and family economy, 95
  the end of sovereignty (according to
    jurists) and "suitable end"
    (according to économistes), 98, 99,
    113n.21
Communication, object of police, 326,
    332nn.40, 42, 360n.11
Communities, 147, 154, 160n.59, 166-67,
    168, 175, 203, 208, 273, *see also*
    Counter-conduct(s)
Conduct, 14, 43, 71, 121, 174, 193, 195, 197,
    198, 199, 201, 207, 388, *see also*
    Government, Counter-conduct(s)
  of conduct, 389, 400n.132
  conflicts of, 197, 198
  daily, 180-81
  economic, 250n.6
  governmental, 67, 197
  of individuals, 74, 88, 94, 154, 207, 230,
    346, 363, 364
  insurrections of, 228, 238, *see also*
    Anabaptists, Communities, the
    People; Bacon
  integral, 181
  medical, 200
  of men, 139, 194, 230
  moral, 71, 112n.19, 121, 198
  pastoral, 195, 204, 355
  political, 198
  of souls (*oikonomia psuchôn, regimen
    animarum*), 151, 159n.47, 192-93, 231,
    see also Economy, Pastorate
Contagion, urban, 63, 64
Contract
  notion of, 107
  social, 44, 53n.24, 107
  theory of, 103, 245, *see also* Art of
    government, Sovereignty
Controls
  collective and individual, 16
  regulatory, 24n.5, 39, 353
Cosmos, 250n.17, 257, 266, 276, 349
  de-governmentalization of, 236, *see also*
    Naturalness
Counter-conduct(s), 196, 201-2, 389-90, *see
    also* Insubordination, Insurrection,
    Revolt
  asceticism as form of, 204-8, 214
  community as form of, 208-12, 214, 215
  eschatological belief as form of, 214-16, 356
  history of, 217n.5, 357
  mysticism as form of, 212-13, 214, 215
  pastoral, 202, 204, 207, 208, 212, 229,
    231, 355
  return to Scripture as form of,
    213, 214

Coup d'État
  permanent (police), 339-40
  and *raison d'État*, 261-67, 277
  theories of, 261, 280nn.19, 20, *see also*
    Naudé, Sirmond
Criminality, urban, 4-5, *see also* Repression,
  Statistics
Crisis, crises, 5, 153, 220n.21, 375
  as circular sudden bolting, 61
  of governmentality, 30, 384-85, 389
  of pastorate, 193, 202, 215, 231, 364, *see*
    also Chaunu
  of subsistence, 50n.4, 101

Dangerousness, 7, 18, 61, 202, 270, *see also*
  Disciplinary mechanism, Security
Dearth. *see* Scarcity
Delinquency, 118, 202, 336, 353, 377
  and breach of social contract, 44
  cost of, 9, *see also* Repression, Statistics
Demographic expansion, 103
Depopulation. *see* Population
Direction, 3, 75, 125, 137, 144, 160nn.57, 61,
  180, 195, 233
  of everyday conduct, 154
  pastoral, of souls, 227, 228, *see also*
    Conduct
  spiritual, 72, 147, 171, 181-82, 190nn.43,
    44, 197, 364
Disciplinarization of the army, 16, 119,
  340-41
Disciplinary
  corpus, 7
  mechanisms, 5-6, 7, 8, 44, 46, 55, 62,
    69, 119
    and apparatus (*dispositif*) of security, 6,
      371
  techniques, 7, 8, 9, 48, 57
  treatment of multiplicities in space, 17
Discipline (cellular, military, worker, penal,
  religious, school, generalized), 8, 17, 21,
  25n.25, 26n.30, 45-47, 55-57, 117-18,
  131n.7, 198, 222n.41, 223n.45, 328,
  330n.21, 340-41, 343, 359n.3, 378
  history of, 107
  instrument of penance, 386, *see also*
    Apparatus (*dispositif*)
  mode of individualization of
    multiplicities, 12
  of poor, and care, 334
  and space, 19, 20, 29, 44-45, *see also*
    Spatial distribution
Disciplines, the, 63, 74, 397n.71
  point of view of, 118
  "practical disciplines" (Hay du
    Chastelet), 253n.43
Disobedience, 71, 160n.54, 188n.23, 200

Disorder, 46, 196, 280n.16, 336
  elimination of (police), 354
Dissidence, 89, 161n.64, 198, 200-202,
  220-21n.27, 221n.29, 372, *see also*
  Counter-conduct(s)

Economic analysis
  behavior, 41
  government, 33-34, 50n.5, 76
  thought, 33, 35, 51n.15, *see also* Physiocrats
Économistes (of eighteenth century), 51n.15,
  99, 348, 349, 350, 361n.25
  birth of, 272
  literature, 342
  on population, 345
  theses, 342-47
Economy, 33, 48, 93, 94-95, 103,
  106, 201, 272, 305, 347, 348, 354,
  399n.113
  German national, 15
  management of, 31, 32, 106-107
  market, 41, 338, 383
  of merits and faults, 173, 183
  of obedience, 14, 71, 75, 98, 99, 277
  of pastoral power, 235
  as physics, 47, 53n.28
  of power, 10-11, 67, 83-84n.27, 95, 195,
    378, 379, *see also* Population,
    Sovereignty
  of salvation, 235
  as science of government, 104, 131n.1
  of souls, 192-93, 227
  theorists of, 34, 37, *see also* Political
    economy
  of truth, 355
Education, 138, 146, 158n.34, 321, 329n.7
  of children, 117, 143, 229-30, 231
  of the Prince, 94, *see also* La Mothe
    Le Vayer
  problematic of in sixteenth century,
    88, 231
Empire, 130, 132n.23, 155, 156, 187n.16,
  217n.4, 229, 240, 247, 290, 292, 297,
  304, 307n.9, 309n.30
  end of Roman (peace of Westphalia), 291
  universal, 260
Endemic diseases, urban epidemics,
  endemic-epidemic, 10, 57-58, 62, 63,
  64, 65, 67, 81n.8, 367, *see also*
  Inoculation
Equilibrium, European, 299, 300, 312,
  314-16, 337, 365, 382
Eschatology, 214, 300, 356
Event, treatment of, 33, 41-42

Family, instrumentality of, 105, *see also*
  Government

Famine. *see* Scarcity (dearth)
Felicity, 144, 327
  of the state (Chemnitz), 257, 258, 277,
    280n.13, *see also* Happiness; Thomas
    Aquinas, Delamare, Hohenthal
Freedom, ideological and technique of
  government, 48

Genealogical analysis, 117
Genealogy
  of the state, 119, 276, 354, 380
  of technologies of power, 36
Genetic analysis, 117
"Good government" of the state, 95, 232,
  319, 349, 375, *see also* Police
"Good price" and "Just price", economic
  theses of, 33, 341-47, 361n.24
Government, 88-89, 93-94, 96-99, 107, 272,
  363-66, 375, 382, 386-87
  analogies of, 232-34
  economic, 33-34, 50n.5, 53n.28, 77,
    85n.40, 95, 113n.23, 116, 379, *see also*
    Physiocrats; Quesnay
  ethical-juridical conception of, 73
  of men, 123-28
    and management of population, 48-49,
      73, 104-105, 354
    versus administration of things, 49
  pastoral, 151, 163, 217n.1, 235-36
    in comparison with ruling, 174
  of the people, 267
  political, 89, 93-94, 112n.19, 287, *see also*
    La Mothe Le Vayer, Machiavelli
  of population, 66-67, 74, 76, 105-106
  practices of (of oneself, souls, conduct,
    states), 88, 93, 121, 151, 159n.47, 177,
    230-31, 364, 370, 386
  science of, 104, 106, 131n.1
  of sovereignty, 23, 71, 73, 76, 102, *see also*
    Mercantilism
  techniques of, 31-32, 34, 48, 83n.25, 106,
    109, 345-46, 388, *see also*
    Apparatuses of security,
    Governmentality
  territorial, 20, 97, *see also* Sovereignty
  three types of, moral, economic, and
    political (La Mothe Le Vayer), 93-94
Governmentality, 108-109, 115-16, 339,
  342-43, 347-54, 355, 371, 373, 377,
  381-82, 384, 387-91
  history of, 24n.3, 108-109, 122, 370, 380
  and modernity, 109, 312, *see also*
    Liberalism, Police, *Raison d'État*
  negation of, 217n.5, 244, 390
  and pastorate, 135, 165, 184-85, 202,
    217n.5, 239, *see also* Apparatuses of
    discipline, Security, Pastorate

and "perpetual peace", 260
  political, and birth of modern state, 120,
    165, 354, 380, 381, 388
  and the political party, 199, 220n.24
  state, an episode of, 248
Governmentalization
  of the *res publica*, 236, 258, 267
  of the state, 109, 110, 122, 382
Growth of state, of forces of the state, 314,
  316, 338, 339, 365

Happiness, 144, 258, 260, 327, *see also*
  Felicity; Delamare, Thomas Aquinas,
  Turquet de Mayerne
Heresy, heresies
  medical, 199
  of the Middle Ages, Cathar dualist, 194,
    see also Counter-conduct(s),
    Pastorate
  of obedience (J. Huss), 209
  of the *politiques*, 245-46, 347, 348

Ideology, 215-16
  of Condillac, the *Idéologues*, 73, 83n.26
  of freedom, modern forms of the economy
    and liberal politics, 48, *see also*
    Freedom, Ideological
Illegalities, 336, *see also* Repression
Individualization in Christian pastorate
  (analytical identification, subjection,
  subjectivation), 175, 184, 223n.51, 231
Inoculation, anti-smallpox, 58, 80n.6,
  81n.8, 367
Institution
  of market, 335
  of police, 326, 335-36
  of the police (in modern sense),
    329n.1, 354
  psychiatric, 117
"Institution-centric", 116
Insubordination, 194, 200
  desertion-insubordination, 198

Jurists, 73, 98, 102-103, 299, 347

Law. *see* Legal code, Norm
Legal, juridico-legal code, 5, 7
  and negative thought, 44-46
Liberal (the word), 37, 384
Liberalism, 383, 384
  ideology and politics of, 48
  principle of, 48
Liberality, private for public benefit, 251n.22

Market, 39, 40, 41-42, 45, 52n.20, 320, 335,
  336, 338, 341, 343, 344, 361n.25, *see also*
  "Good price" and "Just price",

Market - *continued*
economic theses of, Space, Institution,
Police, Market town
Market town, 63-64, 338
Mechanisms
of encouragement-regulation, 325
juridical-legal, 5
market, 40, *see also* Physiocrats
of regulation, 346, 352, 354
of transfer, 173
Mercantilism, mercantilists, 32, 68, 69-70,
101, 102, 104, 116, 272, 277, 337, 367
Milieu, 22-23, 27n.36
of jurisdiction, the republic, 256-57
notion of associated with circulation and
causality, 21
notion of in biology and physics, 20,
27n.37, 78
and population, 77-78, 378-79
and territory, 29, 30, *see also* Apparatuses
of security
Misfortune (cosmological-political
concept of), 31
Multiplicity, 61, 129, 148, 238, 298
of dissidence, 120
human, 26n.30
of individuals, 21
on the move, and pastoral power,
125-26
of a people, 11
of practices of government, 88, 93
of subjects, 11
Myth, of *The Statesman*, 144

Naturalness
of cosmos, 349
of human species, 21-22
medieval conception of, 349
of population(s), of their desire, 70-74,
352
social, 349-50, *see also* the Économistes
Norm (law and), 56, *see also* Kelsen
Normal/abnormal, 57, 63
Normality, differential (normal curves of
distribution), 63, *see also* Statistics
Normalization, 63
disciplinary, 56, 57
procedures and techniques of, 56
security and, 11, 49, 379, *see also*
Apparatuses of security
Normation, 57, 80n.1, 379, *see also*
Disciplinary techniques

Obedience, 176, 178, 189n.35, 205, 207,
208, 356, 235
different aims in ancient Greece and
Christian pastorate, 177

generalized, of party, 179, 201
pastoral rule of, 208
population/sovereign, 68, 71
state of, in Christian pastorate, 177, 183,
see also Apatheia, Economy,
Eschatology; Joachim de Fiore
subjects/sovereign, wills/sovereign, 65, 71,
75, 99
territory/sovereign, 14
unitary type of conduct, 174
Obedience/disobedience, 71, 200
of the people, 267, 277, *see also*
Insubordination, the People, Revolts;
Bacon
reciprocity of, and distribution of in
communities, 211
reversal of in asceticism, 207-208
Opinion, 167, 268-69, 272
public, 51n.9, 275

Panopticon, 25n.11, 66, 83n.26, 131n.8, *see
also* Bentham
Pastoral, 148, 154
Catholic or Protestant, 88
Christian and governmentality, 165, 197
Christian and Hebrew theme of shepherd,
differences, 165
Christian and modern state, 165
and government of men, 123-29, 227, 355,
see also Art of government, Conduct
and law, 167, 179, 183, 208
obedience and resistance, 201, *see also*
Dissidence; Solzhenitsyn
and *Raison d'État*, 261
and the Reformation, 149
reorganization of, 150
of souls, 227, *see also* Government
teaching, 180-81, 183, 213
techniques, 150-51, 192, 193, *see also*
Gregory Nazianzen
Pastorate, 125-28, 166-67, 168, 169-72,
180-81, 184, 192, 193, 199
autonomy of, 152
Christian, and Hebrew theme of the flock,
128, *see also* Shepherd (*berger*)
Christian, as art of governing men, 147-50
and art of government, governmentality,
150-51, 165
crisis of, 193, 231, 364
history of, 147-50, 184
institutionalization of, 164, 178, 202, 203
and government of souls, 364
origins of, 123-26
and principle of analytical responsibility,
169-70
and principle of sacrificial reversal, 170-71,
see also Asceticism

Pastorate - *continued*
  and principle of the exhaustive and
    instantaneous transfer, 170, *see also*
    Economy
  and principle of the integral and
    paradoxical distribution of power,
    169
  and relation to truth, 167
  in relationship between God and men,
    124, 151-52
  and return to Scripture, 213, *see also*
    Individualization, Revolts,
    Sovereignty
  spread of, in small communities, 147
People, the, 37, 122, 270, 271-72
  versus population, 43-44, *see also* Abeille,
    Bacon
Philosophy, 230
  politics of truth, 3
  Pythagorean, 140, *see also* Delatte
  utilitarian, 73, 74
Physiocracy, 53n.28
Physiocrats, 34, 35, 36, 37, 44, 47, 51n.14,
    52nn.17, 18, 19, 59, 65, 69, 70, 71, 73,
    82n.19, 99, 106, 323, 342, 366
  doctrine, 33
  literature, 341-42
  principle of "economic government", 33,
    116, 379
Police, 94, 317, 322-26, 330n.17, 331-32n.39,
    332nn.40, 41, 340-41, 345-46, 359nn.4,
    7, 361n.21
  apparatus (*dispositif*), element of
    governmental rationality - the good
    use and orderly growth of the state's
    forces, 296, *see also* Growth of state
  the condition of existence of urban life,
    334-35, 339
  and civil society, 349-50
  definition in eighteenth century, 110,
    312, 314
  definition in sixteenth and seventeenth
    century, 110, 312-14
  disciplinary, of grains, 45, 53n.26, 341, 347,
    348-49, *see also* Delamare
  and economy, 94
  and European equilibrium, despite growth
    of forces of the state, 314-16, 338, 365
  and governmentalization of the state, 110,
    348-49
  growth of state's forces and European
    equilibrium, 314-16, 338, 365
  the market, 335
  medical, 58-59
  and order, over-regulation, and
    elimination of disorder (eighteenth
    century), 343-44, 353-54

permanent *coup dÉtat* - direct
    governmentality of the sovereign, the
    right of police independent of the
    right of justice, 339-40, 360nn.16, 17
political apparatus of (mechanism of
    security), 278, 306
  and population, 325, *see also* Population
  role in seventeenth century, 314
  science of, *Polizeiwissenschaft*, 318, 330n.11,
    366
  state, *Polizeistaat* - birth and criticism of,
    318, 319, 347
  theory of (Fénelon, Fleury), 318
  universal (Crucé), 303, 309n.27
Political economy, 53n.28, 76-77, 85n.42, 95,
    106-107, 108, 112-13n.21, 328, 383
  birth of, 106
  conditions of formation, 365-66
Politics, 3, 33, 93-94, 145, 246-47, 263, 265,
    286, 287, 289, 293, 295
  of bodies (the *Idéologues*), 83-84n.27
  "born with resistance to governmentality",
    217n.5, 390
  of circulation, 14-15, 34, 64-65, *see also*
    Capital city
  essence of, 139, 144, 146, *see also* Art of
    government, Police
  general strategy of power, 1
  of health, of the urban space, 325
  localization of sovereignty, 23
  and model of the sheep-fold, 130
  modern political societies, 47, *see also*
    Physiocrats
  and order of nature, 47
  and strategy (Clausewitz), 90, 305-306,
    309n.23
  theory and technique of security, 11, 379
Population, 10, 11, 21, 27nn.39, 40, 30, 38,
    42-43, 67, 68, 69, 70-74, 75, 76, 77, 78,
    79, 81nn.10, 13, 82nn.19, 20, 85nn.37,
    40, 104-106, 110, 116, 141, 158n.38, 194,
    218n.11, 224n.55, 270, 277, 324, 325,
    328, 337, 345, 351-52, 366, 367, 377, 378
Power, 66, 69, 95, 102, 108, 116,
    126, 203, 209, 247-48, 294, 327,
    382, 388-89
  Christian pastoral, 128, 165-66, 169,
    183-84, *see also* Individualization
  general economy of (and technology of
    security), 10-11, 30, 117, 120
  mechanisms of, 1-3, 64, 75, 79, 387
  paradoxically distributive character of
    pastoral, 169
  pastoral, 123, 126-30, 148-50, 153-55,
    160n.58, 164-66, 180, 184, 202, 204,
    208, 210, 212, 215-16, 235, 364, *see
    also* Multiplicity

Power - *continued*
  pastoral and political, 154-55, 247
  political, 11, 64, 140, 150, 154-55, 164,
    165-66, 363
  technologies of, 34, 36, 48, 117-18, 119,
    128, 378, 386
  territorial, of sovereignty, 23, 64, 65, 75,
    94, 96, 98, 102, 232
  theory of, 2
Prevailing disease, 60
Prince
  according to Bacon, 268-72, *see also* the
    People
  according to Le Maître, 13-17
  according to Loyseau, 360n.16,
    see also Police
  according to Machiavelli, 65, 89-93, 96,
    98, 242-45, 271-72, 380, *see also* Anti-
    Machiavelli, Principality
  according to Palazzo, 255-59, 287-89, *see*
    also Raison d'État
  from rivalry between to competition of
    states, 293-95
Principality (relationship of prince to),
  91-92, 98-99, 243, 244
Public good, 98

Raison d'État (ratio status), 111n.5, 174,
  239-48, 251-52n.25, 252nn.26, 30, 255,
  257-67, 273, 275, 277-78, 279n.11,
  280nn.13, 19, 20, 22, 290, 292-93,
  348-50, 356-57, 389
  and apparatus of police, 306, *see also*
    Police
  and death of Empire, 247
  "domination over peoples" (Botero),
    237-38
  emergence of, 259, 364
  and essence-knowledge relation, 257
  and European "balance", European
    equilibrium, 314-15, 316, 337-38, 365,
    382
  "expansion of state", 289
  and "interests of state", 307n.11
  maintenance of state's integrity, 287
  mechanism of state's functioning, 287
  and naturalness of society, 349, *see also*
    Counter-conduct(s)
  political principle of intelligibility,
    governmental reason, 286-87
  and urban privilege, 338
  versus economic reason, 348, *see also*
    Économistes
Repression, cost of, 5, 9
Resistance, Revolt, Resistance of conduct,
  159n.41, 194-200, 217n.5, 218n.7, 228,
  270, 372, 376

to medical conduct, 200
  and military desertion, 198
  to pastoral conduct, 195, 200, 228, 355
  political, 196, *see also* Abeille, Bacon
Right(s), 37, 61, 64, 69, 70, 79, 173, 302,
  347, 351, 356, *see also* Kelsen, Pufendorf,
  Rousseau
  common (Naudé), 280n.20
  of the governed, 372, 384
  individual freedom as, 353, *see also*
    Liberalism
  of justice and of police, 339,
    360n.17
  of man, 372, 384
  of nations, *jus gentium*, 303
  natural, theorists of, 73
  private, universe and world of,
    300-301
  public (Domat), 96, 336
  seigniorial, 321
  war of, 301

Salvation, 148, 173
  of all, aim of sovereignty, 98, *see also*
    Common good
  of the nation, 198
  and notion of election, 235
  of one's country, subsistence, 126
  in pastorate, 229, 231
    of the flock, 126, 128, 172
    of individual, and of all and each,
      166-67, 168
    of souls, 192
  and *Raison d'État*, 126, 260, 261, 262-63,
    267, 277, 290
  relation to law and truth in Christian
    pastorate, 167, 183
  and sacramental power, 203
  and sacrifice of shepherd in Hebrew
    theme and in West, 128, 130
  in sixteenth century, 89, 184, 229, 230,
    231, 364
  and theological-political continuum,
    233-34
Scarcity (dearth), 30, 31, 36, 50n.4, 52n.19,
  59, 335, 341, 379
  anti-scarcity system, 32-33, *see also*
    Mercantilism
  as "chimera" (Abeille) chimerical fear of,
    38, 40, 41, 42-43
  problem of scarcity (dearth)-scourge, 34,
    41, 42, 43, 45, 50nn.3, 9, 52n.19,
    53n.26, 59, 63, 64, 341
Security, 19, 46, 48, 60, 108, 297, 300
  and "laisser faire", 45, 353
  mechanisms, 7-8, 9, 10, 20, 23, 47, 49, 59,
    64, 296, 306, 353

Security - *continued*
    and of security-population-government,
        76, 88
    society of (twentieth century), 11, 373, 378
    technique of, 11, 34, 379, *see also* Endemic
        diseases
    technologies of, 8, 59, 64, *see also*
        Apparatuses of security, Disciplinary
        mechanisms
    and history of, 10-11, 369-70, 378, 380
Shepherd *(berger)*, 125, 127-29, 144-47, 152,
    163-64, 168, 285
    functionary, 139
    human, 143, 363-64
    magistrate-shepherd, Pythagorean theme
        of, 137-38, 140, 147
    of men, 123-24, 141, 158n.16, 164-65
    metaphor, 124, 137, 138-39, 140
    paradox of, 128-29, 169
    of people, 136-37
    singleness of, 143, *see also* Multiplicity,
        Pastorate
Shepherd-flock relationship, 124, 136, 151,
    157n.8, 214, 237, 363, *see also* Pastoral
    power, Pastorate
Sovereign-subject relationship, 21, 25n.20,
    29-30, 65-66, 71, 96, 136, 236, 339, *see*
    also Common good, Contract,
    Obedience, Population, Principality
Sovereignty, 64-65, 98-99, 102-104,
    106-108, 195, 234, 236-37
    historical-religious, 229, *see also* Analogies
        of government
    imperial, 155
    juridical, 22, 94, 96, 104, 107, 336
    and multiplicities, 11, 12
    and naturalness of population, 72, 74, 352
    political and Christlike *(christique)* theme,
        155, 156
    and political reason, 23, 246
    principle of, and art of government, 107,
        243-44
    and spatial distribution, spatial hierarchy
        - disciplined space, 14, 29, *see also*
        Bentham, Le Maître
    and urban functions - political circulation,
        commerce, 14-15, 25n.20, 29
    territorial implantation of, 11, 12, 14, 15,
        16, 20, 29, 65
Sovereignty-discipline-governmental reason,
    107, *see also* Governmentality,
    Obedience, Pastorate
Space (territorial, of circulation), 21, 30,
    109, 291-92, 314, 325, 326
    disciplinary, disciplined, 12, 17, 19,
        22, 29, 47
    of market, 45

of security, 11, 20, 378-79
Spatial distribution (criterion of distinction
    between discipline and security), 14, 56
Species, human, 1, 21-23, 75, 369-70, *see also*
    Naturalness
State(s), 13, 30, 68-69, 93-95, 118-19, 165,
    237-38, 247-48, 256-60, 262-64,
    266-67, 274, 286, 314-19, 323, 327, 346,
    350, 380, 388
    administrative, 12, 108-109, 110
    birth of, 109
    European, and competition between, 293,
        294-95, 305, 314, 365, 367
    "expansion" of, 289, 292, *see also* Growth;
        Chemnitz
    of government, 110
    hereditary, 308n.19
    of justice, 108-109, 109-10, 322
    overvaluation of the problem of, 109, 381-82
    police, 318, 319, 322, 341, 347, 382
    of population, 69, 116, 146, 158n.38, 325
    preservation, force, power, wealth of, 101,
        238, 242-43, 288, 289, 295, 296, 367,
        see also Church, Empire, Government,
        Governmentality, Growth of state,
        Police, *Raison d'État*
    purpose of, 277
    territorial, 15, 89, 363, *see also* Sovereignty
    and truth, 276, 356-57
    welfare, *Wohlfahrt*, 367
Statistics, 8, 10, 24n.7, 81nn.8, 10, 104, 274,
    283n.61
    common instrument between police and
        European equilibrium, 315
    science of state, 100-101
    secrets of power, 275
Subject, 42-43, 66, 70, 78, 92, 156, 165,
    235-36, 260, 350, 352, 376
    history of, 184
    legal, 21, 345
    of police, 327, 345
Subjection *(assujettissement)*, 184, *see also*
    Individualization
Subjectivation, 184, 231

Techniques, history of, 8, 150
Technologies, history of, 8, 10-11, 369-70,
    378, 380
Territory, 11, 13-14, 20, 23, 29, 64-65, 68, 70,
    92, 96, 100, 110, 125, 129, 257, 264,
    302, 303, 304, 317, 323-24, 336, 345,
    353, 360n.16, 365, 378
    foundation of principality or sovereignty,
        96
Town(s), 12, 14, 15-21, 25n.16, 257, 303, 335,
    336-37
    capital, 15, *see also* Le Maître

Town(s) - *continued*
 disciplinary, 19
  and in form of Roman camp -
   Kristiania, Gothenburg,
   Richelieu, 15, 16
 insecurity of, 18
 market, 63-64, 338
 people of, 32, 33, 125
 planning in eighteenth century, 29, *see also*
  Vigny
 spatial opening up of, 13

Truth, relation to - Antiquity and Christian
  pastorate, 181, 183

Uncertainty (*l'aléatoire*)
 elements of, in state, 20, *see also* Leibniz
 treatment of, 11

"Well-being" of individuals, 328, 334,
  338, *see also* Better than just living;
  Montchrétien
"Wisdom" of prince, 100, 273